MW00583247

RADICAL SACRIFICE

CIVIL WAR AMERICA

*Peter S. Carmichael, Caroline E. Janney,
and Aaron Sheehan-Dean, editors*

This landmark series interprets broadly the history and culture
of the Civil War era through the long nineteenth century and
beyond. Drawing on diverse approaches and methods, the
series publishes historical works that explore all aspects of
the war, biographies of leading commanders, and tactical and
campaign studies, along with select editions of primary sources.
Together, these books shed new light on an era that remains
central to our understanding of American and world history.

RADICAL SACRIFICE

THE RISE AND RUIN OF
FITZ JOHN PORTER

WILLIAM MARVEL

THE UNIVERSITY OF NORTH CAROLINA PRESS

Chapel Hill

© 2021 The University of North Carolina Press

All rights reserved

Designed by Jamison Cockerham
Set in Arno, Scala Sans, Brothers, and Cutright
by Tseng Information Systems, Inc.

Cover photographs: (top) Major General Fitz John Porter;
(bottom) President Lincoln with General George McClellan
and a group of officers; both courtesy Library of Congress.

Manufactured in the United States of America

The University of North Carolina Press has been a member
of the Green Press Initiative since 2003.

LIBRARY OF CONGRESS CATALOGING-IN-PUBLICATION DATA
Names: Marvel, William, author.
Title: Radical sacrifice : the rise and ruin of Fitz John Porter / William Marvel.
Other titles: Civil War America (Series)
Description: Chapel Hill : The University of North Carolina Press, [2021] |
Series: Civil War America | Includes bibliographical references and index.
Identifiers: LCCN 2020037027 | ISBN 9781469661858 (cloth) | ISBN 9781469661865 (ebook)
Subjects: LCSH: Porter, Fitz-John, 1822–1901. | United States—Armed
Forces—Officers—Biography. | United States—History—1849–1877.
Classification: LCC E467.1.P8 M37 2021 | DDC 973.7/3092 [B]—dc23
LC record available at https://lccn.loc.gov/2020037027

For my father,

REUBEN J. MARVEL JR.,

1909–1998

U.S. Navy, 1932–1954

The last living witness to the only enemy attack

on American soil during World War I

at Orleans, Massachusetts

July 21, 1918

CONTENTS

ILLUSTRATIONS

A section of illustrations begins on page 141

PREFACE

One of the questions still asked by amateur enthusiasts of Civil War history is whether Fitz John Porter was really guilty of the accusations that led to his dismissal from the army. For serious scholars, his technical innocence has long since been established, and the only lingering doubt is whether he deserved his fate for reasons unrelated to his actions on the battlefield or the charges against him. Opinions on that vary, and are sometimes influenced by an interpretive prejudice reminiscent of the political partisanship that defined the debate in the nineteenth century. *was he a scapegoat L*

In his original court-martial, Porter became a scapegoat for John Pope and Irvin McDowell. They had both performed poorly at Second Bull Run, but their self-interested hostility would not have led to Porter's professional destruction had it not been for his proximity to George McClellan. By the summer of 1862 *Mc Dowell* McClellan personified resistance to turning the war into an abolition crusade, making him anathema to Radical Republicans, and as his most trusted comrade and confidant Porter supplied an excellent surrogate sacrifice. The Radical-dominated Committee on the Conduct of the War searched for misconduct, and Senator Zachariah Chandler flung malicious accusations with a false air of authority as a committee member, but no heinous crimes could be found. In the end it was the Radicals in Lincoln's cabinet who had to strike the blow. Secretary of War Edwin Stanton secured a new judge advocate general he could rely on to "get" Porter, and Stanton's fingerprints are evident in the selection of a court heavily weighted with officers likely to vote for conviction. In the days before the trial, Stanton and his cabinet collaborator, Treasury Secretary Salmon P. Chase, personally cultivated bias against Porter among some of those court members, and Porter was convicted before the trial began.

Fixing the blame for Second Bull Run on Porter also promised to absolve the president from responsibility for elevating Pope, authorizing his disastrous campaign, and giving him tens of thousands of men McClellan had counted on. Whether Lincoln tried to goad Pope into filing charges by acquainting him with Porter's insulting communications about him is beyond determining, but the president's political interests gave him no incentive to question a conviction. Just as the trial began, Lincoln admitted that he considered Porter guilty of disobedience of orders, and that "his failure to go to Pope's aid in the battle of Friday had occasioned our defeat, and deprived us of a victory that would have terminated the war."[1] Fifty-three days later he accepted a verdict that confirmed his prejudgment, and approved the sentence on the strength of a conspicuously jaundiced summary of the case written by the prosecutor himself. As an experienced lawyer, Lincoln could hardly have failed to notice either the relentless one-sidedness of that summary or the prosecution's prominent emphasis on absurd claims of clairvoyance by a key witness. Any curiosity kindled in the president's mind by such blatantly prejudicial signals must have been smothered by the political benefits he would realize from the decision.

Sixteen years later, a board of highly regarded officers reviewed the case. They concluded that Porter had been entirely innocent and had not contributed to the defeat at Second Bull Run at all, deliberately or otherwise. Only Congress could offer legal redress, however, and there Porter again faced stubbornly partisan political obstruction. Most Republicans—including the vindictive Chandler, a perfectly unethical James A. Garfield, and the bombastic John A. Logan—denied Porter justice at every turn. When their factual claims were disproven and their procedural objections failed, they simply resorted to bloody-shirt sentimentality. *16 years later*

In the middle of the twentieth century, Otto Eisenschiml became Porter's best-known historical champion, which may have done the wronged general's reputation more harm than good. Eisenschiml, a chemist and industrial executive who pursued history as an avocation, had earned a merited reputation as something of a crackpot with his absurd theory that Stanton orchestrated Lincoln's murder. His hyperbolic prose diminished his persuasiveness generally, and his accusations against Stanton in regard to the assassination discredited his more justifiable suspicions about Stanton's malicious involvement in the Porter case. The principal modern judgment against Porter came from another amateur historian, mathematician Kenneth P. Williams, whose sole work in Civil War history suffered from inadequate research and betrayed glaring disdain for McClellan and his associates.

Since then, the scope of study into Second Bull Run has expanded enormously, and Porter's innocence of the specific charges levied against him seems still more obvious. John Hennessy's intensely detailed report on troop movements only marked the beginning of his research into that battle, which culminated in *Return to Bull Run*, and that book is unlikely ever to be surpassed unless Hennessy revises it himself. While he subjected Porter to some evenhanded criticism, he unequivocally acquitted him of any wrongdoing.

Historians nevertheless still tend to fault Porter for his justifiable lack of confidence in his commanding officer at that battle, or for the political differences that transformed his doubts into contempt. In 1960 Allan Nevins charged that Porter's "spirit was viciously bad" and that he was "violently hostile to all who wished to fight 'an abolition war.'" Two years later he alleged that Porter "wished to see Pope fail," inaccurately adding that the "evidence is clear" on that point. Nevins considered that exaggerated indictment enough to merit Porter's removal, even if "dismissal in disgrace was too severe a penalty." Stephen Sears concurred somewhat more gently in 1999, citing the reaction to Porter's conviction by McClellan's former staff officer, Charles Russell Lowell, who wrote a friend that Porter's "frame of mind was un-officer-like and dangerous." Yet Lowell had no way of knowing Porter's frame of mind; he also sympathized greatly with Porter, whom he supposed had been "demoralized" by Pope, and he considered Porter "no worse than twenty thousand others." Lowell admitted, too, that both he and the recipient of his letter might have felt the same as Porter under similar circumstances.[2]

Lowell was correct in supposing that much of the army was highly disgruntled with both the administration's political leadership and the army commanders chosen to replace McClellan. Nine days after Lowell put those words to paper, his Harvard classmate Charles Francis Adams Jr. expressed his own dissatisfaction to his father—who was President Lincoln's ambassador to the Court of St. James's. "You have no idea of the disgust felt here towards the Government," Captain Adams began, one week after Burnside's ill-fated Mud March. "Unable to run the army themselves, they take away McClellan, and when that leads to terrible disaster, they cashier Fitz John Porter, one of the best officers we have." Adams also suggested that the army might rebel against such leadership and march on Washington—echoing a similar warning of Porter's that Nevins evidently mistook for serious, seditious sentiments rendering him unfit for service.[3]

Widespread as such discontent was in the Army of the Potomac, especially among officers of a conservative turn, it caused no particular dereliction of duty. Those "demoralized" by the Emancipation Proclamation resigned—or tried to, until the War Department began punishing such politically embarrassing expressions of opposition with dishonorable dismissals. Most of those who were not allowed to resign continued to plug along conscientiously, if not cheerfully. The example made of Porter neither soothed nor subdued their disgust with the course of events: officers such as Captain Adams, Colonel Charles Wainwright, Major Henry Abbott, and Major General William Franklin served resolutely until the end of the war or the end of their lives. Their dislike of administration policy was no more virulent, and was often less overt, than that of Radical officers who had opposed Lincoln's more conservative position on slavery earlier in the war. Antislavery generals who publicly offended the president through their actions during his conservative phase were merely relieved of duty and reassigned; those who displeased Radical Republicans, if only by the opinions they were presumed to hold, might be court-martialed, imprisoned without trial, dismissed, shelved, or hounded and harassed until they resigned. That disparity illustrates the partisan prejudice to which perfectly loyal, conservative officers were subjected by their government, and they are often held to the more demanding side of a double historical standard today.

The supreme irony of Porter's dismissal for disloyalty to his commanding officer is that he was so consistently dogged in his loyalties. Regardless of consequences, he clung to his friends through adversity as devotedly as he did in prosperity. He regretted Albert Sidney Johnston's decision to cast his lot with the Confederacy, but persistently maintained the memory of Johnston's antebellum patriotism. He defended his next army commander, Robert Patterson, against a tidal wave of criticism for his last campaign, always contending that Patterson's failure in the Shenandoah Valley was predetermined by decisions made in Washington. Porter's legendary loyalty to McClellan was deemed the cause of his purported disloyalty to Pope, yet Porter served Pope conscientiously on the battlefield, offering honest advice and attempting to obey his ambiguous and misguided orders. That he did so while harboring deep and justifiable contempt for Pope's abilities illustrates that Porter's sense of duty prevailed over his personal opinions.

His admitted disdain for Pope also confirms that his close attachments to other commanding officers originated in sincere regard. Porter's punctiliously subordinate correspondence with McClellan could easily be interpreted as sycophantic flattery had he not remained so faithful to his former commander when that association became a distinct liability. So close were they for sixteen crucial months that their stories were essentially one, and Porter's steadfast allegiance to his flawed friend betokened his own foremost virtue.

Porter's military career coincided precisely with the events that provoked the final struggle over the soul of the nation, and he participated in every scene of that drama. He fought valiantly in Mexico, trained hundreds of West Point cadets who would command troops in the Civil War, and took part in the hunt for John Brown in Kansas. He figured prominently in the Utah War, and his inspection of U.S. forts in Charleston Harbor led to the assignment of Major Robert Anderson there. Porter brought troops out of Texas after David Twiggs surrendered them, and at the outbreak of hostilities he organized some of the first militia and Regulars to go to the defense of Washington. Porter was bringing troops down from Harrisburg to subdue rebellious Baltimore when the secretary of war ordered them back. After telegraphic communication with Washington was cut off, Porter took the responsibility of issuing orders in Winfield Scott's name to assure that Union forces retained control in volatile St. Louis.

The man later castigated as a traitor to the Union cause did more to preserve that Union than any of those officers who later judged him unworthy to remain among them. They had no occasion to assess Porter's past service in determining whether he deserved expulsion and infamy, and many of them so desired his downfall that they would have wished to avoid considering it.

So unfairly was Porter treated that a biographer runs the risk of affording him more sympathy than he deserves. He left sufficient evidence of his own share of personal and professional failings, but none egregious enough to warrant what was done to him. His career was extinguished too soon to determine whether his star would have shone brighter or flickered out under other commanders, or in independent command. Despite showing great administrative energy, along with unquestionable courage and talent on the battlefield, his principal legacy was his dismissal—even after it began to carry the asterisk denoting exoneration. For that reason, no doubt, Porter still lacked a biography nearly two centuries after his birth. Becoming the victim of inequity does not necessarily justify an examination of one's life, but the neglect of Porter has been particularly unfortunate. Illuminating his story inevitably sheds a harsher light on those who, through active malice or passive assent, abetted the injustice he suffered. They include the primary actors in the entire epoch: without adequate revelation of their roles in such a dark saga, the history of that era remains incomplete.

RADICAL SACRIFICE

1

REDEMPTION

FJC Father

Even among his family, little was known of Fitz John Porter's father, and some of what was known was left unsaid. The same may have been true of his grandfather, David Porter, a mariner who successively commanded two privateers in the American Revolution and surrendered the larger of them to a British frigate.[1]

David Porter was serving as first mate on a revenue cutter in Baltimore when President Washington considered him for promotion to command of the cutter. Inquiries among New Englanders revealed that David Porter had kept "a Public house of Ill fame" in Boston, and that some unsavory questions may have attended his surrender of the *Aurora*, but after nine years in Baltimore he seemed more or less reformed. Merchants there thought him "sober & industrious though an unfortunate man," and noted that he had several small children dependent on his government earnings. Considering official dissatisfaction with the commander of the cutter, and Porter's evident popularity among the Baltimore merchant class, Washington commissioned him a sailing master.[2]

"Captain" Porter, as he was known, was still only a sailing master sixteen years later. He died on duty at the New Orleans station on June 22, 1808, leaving two sons who were both already in the naval service. The elder son, also named David Porter, held the line rank of master commandant when his father died, and at the age of thirty-two he donned the epaulettes of a captain. That was then the navy's highest rank, but as commander of a squadron he later earned the unofficial title of commodore. He arranged to have his father's body brought back for interment in Baltimore, perhaps during the same voyage that introduced him to a motherless boy—later famous as David Farragut—whom he took in, and for whom he obtained a midshipman's appointment well before the boy entered his teens. Commodore Porter had already done the same for his own younger brother, John Porter, who had entered the navy as a midshipman in 1806, while in his early teens.[3]

Commodore Porter was eighth in rank on the navy list in 1826, when he resigned from the service to protest a temporary suspension he considered unjust. The first two admirals in the U.S. Navy grew up in his household, but his younger brother, John Porter, did not fare so well. John was serving as a junior officer aboard the U.S.S. *Congress* late in 1813, when it put into the Portsmouth Navy Yard for repairs that took more than a year. During that interlude he met Eliza Chauncy Clark, the only child of the customs agent in nearby York, Maine. Porter's first independent command came with the new fourteen-gun brig *Boxer*, which he sailed to the Mediterranean in the summer of 1815. Just before leaving on that cruise (or just after returning from it) he married Miss Clark, who was fifteen years old and pregnant by the time he departed. At the end of the year he came back from the Mediterranean, took another leave, and sailed the *Boxer* from New York for the Gulf of Mexico on February 27, 1816. He was gone for nearly two more years.[4]

The *Boxer* cruised mainly between Havana and New Orleans, hunting slave ships and pirates and encountering some of each. This early cruise inspired correspondence in which he betrayed a complaining disposition that aroused the ire of his immediate superior, who was also a close friend of Commodore Porter. When the *Boxer* left port in October of 1816, Lieutenant Porter accused Captain Daniel Patteson of having forced the ship to sail without adequate supplies, leading Patteson to file an objection with the secretary of the navy. In June of 1817 Porter complained that his charts depicted the depth of the water inaccurately, which may have brought his first command to an abrupt and ignominious end. Four months later the *Boxer* was wrecked trying to negotiate the South Pass of the Mississippi River.[5]

Losing his first ship did not end Lieutenant Porter's career, but the navy appeared hesitant to trust him with another vessel. He spent the next couple of years at the Washington Navy Yard, and from there he was sent back to Portsmouth. A promotion to master commandant came to him through a combination of seniority and attrition, and with it he could afford to lodge his growing family in a large house alongside South Mill Pond, near the yard, where Eliza's uncle had recently lived. When they moved in, the Porters had a four-year-old daughter, Lucia, and a newborn encumbered with the ponderous name of William Charles Bolton Smith Porter. By the close of 1821 Eliza was pregnant again, and on August 31, 1822, the day after Bolton's second birthday, she bore another son whom they called Fitz John Porter, "Fitz" meaning "son of" John Porter.[6]

A few months later John Porter left home for a relatively brief cruise, joining the West Indies Squadron then commanded by his brother David, whose influence may have been what got him back to sea. It was John's first chance to stride a quarterdeck in more than five years, but it was not an auspicious assignment. Despite holding enough rank to command a corvette, he was given a three-gun tub called the *Greyhound*—a moldering schooner bought on the cheap to fill out the commodore's "Mosquito Fleet." The commodore's little brother set out with a reckless contempt for his vessel.[7]

Midshipman David Farragut, Commodore Porter's foster son, served under John on the *Greyhound*, and Farragut had the deck the afternoon they sailed south, in February of 1823. Years later he remembered the skipper sitting at the stern bundled in his cape as a gale kicked up, and when Farragut suggested shortening sail Porter ordered him to desist. The *Greyhound* raced far ahead of the rest of the convoy, bounding dangerously over rising swells, but Porter insisted on keeping her under full canvas. "If she can't carry the sail," he sneered, "let her drag it," and Farragut feared the masts would indeed snap. When Porter went below for the night, leaving him in command, Farragut immediately ordered all but the foresail furled.[8]

John Porter's bravado, which his brother's biographer attributed to drunkenness, continued after they reached the West Indies. The *Greyhound* was sailing alone when three British warships hove into view, including a frigate and a twenty-gun brig. The brig came out to bring the *Greyhound* to with a shot across the bow, and Porter brazenly responded with a shot of his own. But for British restraint, the brig might have riddled the schooner with a broadside.[9]

No sooner did the *Greyhound* reach the fleet than the ship and its commander became embroiled in a serious incident with Spanish authorities in Puerto Rico, presaging the controversy that would end Commodore David Porter's career. Alcohol or some other equally destructive habit may well have aggravated John Porter's defiant and pugnacious nature, for a few years later the commodore recorded specific regret that his younger brother did not "mend his ways." That regret may have triggered official orders that prematurely ended John Porter's second and last seagoing command. By midsummer the *Greyhound* and its surly commander were already on their way home, on the excuses that yellow fever had broken out and the schooner needed extensive repairs. It said something about the department's poor regard for John Porter's talents that he was returned to his vague subordinate position at the Portsmouth Navy Yard.[10]

He rejoined his family in the house on South Mill Pond by the end of September. On August 9, 1824, the fourth Porter child came into the world. In honor of John's father or his brother, or both, the boy was called David, but like several of his cousins of the same name he was distinguished by a middle name. Both David St. Leon Porter and Fitz John Porter, who was then more than two years old, were baptized on January 21, 1825, at St. John's Episcopal Church, overlooking the harbor and the navy yard.[11]

Fitz John Porter later claimed that his father "died soon after the birth of my brother David," but John Porter lived more than seven years after that event. For reasons that can only be surmised, he took a long leave of absence late in 1825, remaining without occupation for nearly three years. In the last days of 1828 he returned to his father's native Boston, on a humiliating assignment as commander of the dismasted hulk used as a receiving ship for recruits at the Charlestown Navy Yard.[12] Captain Charles Morris, who had been his commanding officer at Portsmouth and knew him well, suspended him from duty on February 2, 1829, having learned from the surgeon that Porter had just tried to kill himself by swallowing laudanum. Morris ordered him to Watertown, four miles away, to "a private establishment for insane persons." Porter remained in that hospital, officially on leave of absence, until September 2, 1831, when he died.[13]

According to Fitz John Porter's late-life recollection, his family left the Portsmouth house two years after his father's death, going to Alexandria, which was then still part of the District of Columbia. That chronology seems distorted by confusion over when his father died. John Porter's children likely never saw him after his breakdown, early in 1829, and he may also have been absent during his long leave, starting in 1825. Fitz John had just turned nine when his father finally died, but he might have remembered it as about six years earlier if prolonged absence had preceded the event. Adjusting for that mistake, the move to Alexandria would have been undertaken around 1827, which is not at all unlikely if Eliza gave up on her husband's ability to provide for her and the children. The family left the Portsmouth house early enough that Fitz John retained only two dim memories from playing in the yard, involving a tumble into the millpond and an unpleasant encounter with a big snake.[14]

Although she was descended from a Maine family, Eliza Porter always gave her birthplace as Virginia, and her middle son claimed that old friends in Alexandria helped her start a boarding school in that city. Census information corroborates both that occupation and the earlier move, showing that Eliza had already established herself there at least by 1830, while her husband was still alive. Besides her children, her household that year included a score of young ladies between the ages of fifteen and twenty, with three young slaves to serve them.[15]

Eliza arranged for Fitz John's formal education at the Alexandria Boarding School, founded a few years previously by a Quaker teacher from Pennsylvania named Benjamin Hallowell. The Porter household shrank abruptly in the summer of 1835: Bolton secured a warrant as a navy midshipman on July 29, doubtless through his uncle's intercession; on August 25, Lucia married a Louisiana planter named John Waddell. Then, early in October, Fitz John made the trek back to New Hampshire to start college preparation at Phillips Academy, in Exeter.[16]

Fitz John Porter often gave an age inconsistent with the year of his birth, as though he were unable to remember it. For much of the 1860s he indicated that he was as much as three years younger than he really was. When he reported at

Exeter on October 12, 1835, he said he was fourteen, but he had celebrated his thirteenth birthday only six weeks previously.[17]

His class consisted of about two dozen scholars, most of whom had arrived a month before. To start so late required the permission of his instructors, who examined him for his basic preparation, but they found him ready and gave him a room in the home of Mary Rindge, an elderly woman who boarded students. The school offered one course in college preparation, heavily studded with Greek and Latin, and maintained a more practical program in what was characterized as the English Department. Each was three years long, with a fourth year for an advanced class in the classics for those who wished to stay on. Young Porter started with the classical curriculum, spending his first year with Alexander Adam's Latin grammar and Liber Primus—reading Horace, Virgil, and Caesar's Commentaries while studying both ancient and modern geography and basic arithmetic.[18]

He performed remarkably well that first year. In recitation he stood with the best in his class, earning an average weekly mark of 7 more than three-quarters of the time, and never falling below 6. Only one student was awarded an 8 during the entire year—and only for one week—while many slipped to a grade of 5 and a few were marked at 4. Fitz John's deportment was considered "good," as was his application to his studies, but the instructors seemed most impressed with his improvement, which they considered "highly commendable."[19]

Although he passed his examination in the summer of 1836, Porter did not continue in the college preparatory program, shifting instead into the English Department. The change probably reflected his mother's plan to secure a free education for him at the U.S. Military Academy, where the English program's concentration on science and math would have been more useful. Because of the different material in that curriculum, he may have had to be examined anew to advance to the second class: besides English grammar, the first year involved algebra and an 1830 text called *The Political Class Book*, which was intended to instruct older students in the "origin, nature, and use of political power." The second year entailed geometry, trigonometry, ancient history, logic, and rhetoric, along with more English grammar and composition. The third year offered even more varied practical studies, from surveying, navigation, and astronomy to chemistry, natural philosophy (essentially physics), and "moral, political, and intellectual philosophy." Instruction was also offered in French for those who were interested. As that era's international language of military science, French was required at West Point, and it was obvious by 1838 that Porter's family hoped to send him there, so an introductory French course would also have been useful.[20]

Fitz John left Exeter in August of 1838, a few days before he turned sixteen.

In the school register that was closed out in 1840 he was the only member of his class for whom the notes on his further education remained blank, but that reflected no lack of effort. The month he finished at Phillips, his mother sought help obtaining a cadet appointment for him from her brother-in-law, Commodore Porter, who was then chargé d'affaires at the American consulate in Istanbul. She also enlisted the aid of Fitz John's older cousin, Robert Henry Eddy, a civil engineer in Boston. Military careers provided a standard solution for the sons of the financially embarrassed. The commodore himself, whose fortunes had diminished significantly, had gotten his son Theodoric into West Point in 1835.[21]

No West Point appointment came that year, but Fitz John had already gone directly from Phillips to another private school. Stephen Weld, a Harvard alumnus, ran a preparatory school in Jamaica Plain, just outside Boston, and Eliza Porter installed her middle son there. Commodore Porter was promoted to minister resident at Istanbul in 1839, but he had not yet presented his papers when, in January of 1840, he joined his sister-in-law in another plea on his nephew's behalf. They sought an appointment at large as a special case, on the grounds that Fitz John was the son of a deceased officer in the navy, for the War Department gave preference to the sons of officers who died on active duty. Eliza provided a recommendation from George Evans, a Whig congressman from Maine who knew her family, but it was an election year and President Martin Van Buren was fighting for his political life against another Whig, William Henry Harrison. Van Buren may have felt compelled to confine such patronage to applicants backed by powerful Democrats, and again the application failed.[22]

A year later Ambassador Porter had officially taken his post, and in January of 1841 eighteen-year-old Fitz John Porter used his uncle's added prestige in a third, all-or-nothing application. His recommendations were all supplied by prominent Whigs. George Evans renewed his support, and Congressman Joseph Tillinghast of Rhode Island offered his, but the key endorsement came from Senator Daniel Webster—who, like the applicant, was a New Hampshire native. Webster was about to resign his Senate seat to serve as President Harrison's secretary of state, and his name may have been intended to sway the new president, but that wasn't necessary. Two weeks before the statutory close of his political career, with no further reason to focus on the political persuasion of those who sponsored academy applicants, Van Buren himself selected Fitz John Porter. Like all other appointees, Porter was instructed to report by July 1, 1841.[23]

Most aspiring cadets of that era arrived in June, undergoing a physical and taking a brief examination before the academic board in some basic math, reading, and writing, to confirm that they were prepared to begin the course. Professor Albert Church conducted the examination in mathematics, quizzing the applicants on decimals and fractions. For some, the test for literacy included nothing more than reading a few lines aloud and writing out a sentence or two to demonstrate the legibility of their handwriting and their competence in composition. Some who had not yet doffed their civilian dress nevertheless failed and were declared "found" (that is, "found deficient") and sent home. In all, 123 young men ranging from barely sixteen years old to not-quite twenty-one emerged as admitted cadets in what would become the class of 1845 — including Porter, who for once gave his correct age of eighteen years and ten months.[24]

For the entering fourth-classmen, or plebes, July 1 began the summer encampment in which they would learn the basics of military discipline, drill, and practices. All cadets participated in the encampment save those who had just finished their second year, and had gone home for the only furlough of their four-year course. The rest bivouacked in tents pitched on the plain high above the Hudson River, forming an impromptu battalion with temporary corporals, sergeants, and officers chosen from among the upperclassmen.[25]

One of the first traditions the plebes learned, aside from their fate as the objects of deviltry among upperclassmen, was the system of demerits used to measure the severity of offenses against orders and army regulations. Seven different degrees of "criminality" could earn anywhere from one to ten demerits, and any cadet who accumulated two hundred demerits in a single year (or one hundred in six months) would be recommended for dismissal. Cadet Porter did not complete three weeks of the encampment without incurring his first demerits. The infraction consisted of failing to position his left foot at quite the right angle while standing at attention on parade. That was deemed an offense of the second grade, worth two demerits, although citing him so harshly for so minor a fault hinted at a desire to make an example of him, and demonstrate that even the most conscientious plebe could err. More than ten more weeks passed, and the academic year was well begun, before he incurred another demerit, this time for arriving late for the breakfast roll call.[26]

The habit of time management came with the regimented schedule. The morning gun sounded at 5:00 in summer, and 6:00 in winter. Drums then thundered for several minutes, during which all cadets spilled out of bed, dressed, and fell in for roll call. In the summer encampment, two hours of close-order drill preceded breakfast and filled most of the day between meals, broken only by dancing lessons — for which it does not appear that ladies were often present to serve as partners. Outside of summer, cadets had half an hour after reveille to ready their rooms and themselves for inspection. At 7:00 they marched to breakfast in silence, and usually in perfect step: Porter accumulated two more demerits early in October for not stepping off in precise cadence. After breakfast they marched back to their barracks for a few minutes of hypothetical recreation, but the morning's recitations began at 8:00 and lasted three hours. Drums beat them back to their rooms at 11:00 for two hours of study, with the "dinner" roll call held at 1:00, recitations resuming at 2:00, and drill taking up the afternoon from 4:00 until 5:30. Then came more ostensible leisure, which the most attentive cadets devoted to study or preparing for the daily dress parade at 7:00 P.M., which was immediately followed by "supper." After the evening meal another period of recreation lasted until 8:00, when the drums again called the corps to quarters to study, or to clean and maintain equipment. The fluttering rhythm of tattoo brought silence to the barracks at 9:30, and at 10:00 the last lights flickered out. Periodic guard duty further encumbered a cadet's day, robbing him of sleep.[27]

Captain Charles F. Smith, a tall, striking man whose dignity Cadet Ulysses Grant particularly remembered, was serving his last year as the commandant of cadets when Porter arrived; if Superintendent Richard Delafield was ill or absent, Smith commanded the post. Smith had held a commission in the 2nd Artillery since he graduated from West Point himself, sixteen years before, but he was charged with teaching infantry tactics. For assistants he had one lieutenant for each of the four cadet companies. Plebes trained only as infantry, practicing close-order drill in platoon and company formations every afternoon through the autumn and in the spring.[28]

In his plebe year, Porter's academic requirements were limited to mathematics and French, with ninety-minute recitations of French each day, and an hour of math. In September he began with algebra, which he had first studied at Exeter six years before. In the spring he progressed to geometry, trigonometry, and mensuration, all of which he had also encountered previously. His instructors in that discipline were all academy graduates of a few years' standing, acting as assistants to Mr. Church, the lone professor of mathematics, who had graduated first in the class of 1828.[29]

Three men of French heritage taught that language. Claudius Berard, who had fled Napoleon's empire a generation previously to avoid compulsory service in the army, headed the department. He was assisted by a first-generation American named Hyacinthe Agnel and by Lieutenant Théophile Marie d'Oremieulx, a young Parisian of recent immigration whose broken English hampered his ability to convey French. Berard was regarded as one of the more engaging members of the faculty. "As for the other teachers in French," remembered Orlando Willcox, "the less said the better."[30]

Porter fared slightly better in French than in mathematics. By the end of his first year at West Point, academic and disciplinary attrition had reduced his class from 123 to 76, among whom he ranked eighth in French and ninth in mathematics. Diligent self-discipline accounted for a paltry thirteen demerits, placing him twenty-fifth in conduct in the entire corps of 217 cadets, and that elevated him to sixth place in his class overall. He just missed having his name published in the next *Army Register*, which listed the five most distinguished cadets in each class. As he had at least since he was thirteen, the middle son of Widow Porter showed his appreciation for the opportunity he had been given through restrained behavior and intense devotion to his duties and his studies.[31]

As a cadet Porter crossed paths with dozens of men who would serve with or against him when they were all general officers. A first-classman named John Pope may have joined in deviling Porter and his fellow plebes in the summer of 1841, and sometime during his four years at the academy Porter must have met the post adjutant, Lieutenant Irvin McDowell. George Brinton McClellan, a stocky lad from Philadelphia who arrived in the summer of 1842, would become his closest friend, and that association would have the greatest impact on Porter's life. At five months short of sixteen, McClellan was the youngest of all who reported with the class of 1846, yet he may also have been the best educated, having already completed two years of preparatory school and two at the University of Pennsylvania. Cadet Willcox, another future general, thought McClellan was "the most popular, if not most prominent, cadet in the corps" during all their years together at the academy. Willcox praised McClellan for his "charming address and manners" and for being "void of pretension, and a steadfast friend."[32]

McClellan and Porter may have begun their friendship as cadets, but their chances for interaction would have been limited until they both became upperclassmen. During the summer encampments they would have belonged to different companies, to which cadets were assigned by their height: at nearly twenty years of age, Porter had probably reached his adult height of five feet, eleven inches, and would have been a head taller than the fifteen-year-old McClellan. The stratified curriculum, meanwhile, always kept them in different classrooms during the academic year.[33]

Third-classmen continued to attend recitations in French during both fall and spring, but only every other day. In the fall they devoted the same hour on the alternate days to English grammar, composition, and rhetoric, and in the spring to geography, all of which fell within the Department of Ethics. Mathematics remained the primary academic focus, with more advanced geometry for an hour and a half every day and calculus and surveying added in the spring. In their second year Porter and his classmates also started to learn drawing under Robert Weir, an artist of considerable accomplishment, who taught them topography in the fall and added the human figure in the spring. They also started to drill with artillery as part of their tactical schedule.[34]

Porter had slipped slightly in academic standing by June of 1843. Another seventeen cadets had resigned or been dismissed from his class, and ten more had been turned back to repeat the year with another class. Of the remaining forty-nine he ranked tenth in English, eleventh in math, sixteenth in French, and twenty-first in drawing. In overall standing he placed ninth, just below Charles P. Stone of Massachusetts; Stone was another disciplined and punctilious soldier, and Porter dogged his heels on the class list until they graduated. The youngest of the eighty-three plebes, McClellan, numbered third in his class.[35]

A deficiency in conduct accounted as much for Porter's slide in class rank as his difficulty with drawing, or his apparent inattention to French. The demerit system included a provision for increased accountability as a cadet advanced through the program: the total demerit count for third-classmen was increased by one-sixth, for second-classmen by one-third, and first-classmen by one-half. Porter accrued sixteen demerits between June 16, 1842, and June 15, 1843, so two were added as his one-sixth premium. That placed him forty-sixth in the corps for conduct. Stone, who earned only a single demerit all year, ranked fourth.[36]

It was not that Porter had suddenly cast all caution to the wind. As in his plebe year, his demerit total represented only nine separate infractions, but in that first year they had all consisted of inadvertent omissions or minor instances of tardiness: in January of his plebe year he had been charged two demerits for not answering loudly enough to his name at roll call. By the beginning of his second year he appeared to be growing somewhat comfortable with the demands of the academy, and perhaps he harbored less fear of dismissal. For the first time, and also for the second time, he was cited for transgressions of a social nature. He earned two demerits on Sunday, September 18, 1842, for making noise in his room at noon, and one month later a charge of "visiting" added five demerits to his record. Holding conversation with cadets at unauthorized times or places accounted for the preponderance of his demerits the rest of his days at the academy, but on Christmas Eve of 1842 he was penalized for remaining in bed after reveille. He was caught in a similar violation on a Monday morning three weeks later.[37]

While the rest of the corps moved into tents for the summer encampment of 1843, the survivors of the class of 1845 went on furlough. Porter left no record of his activities between his appointment and his graduation, but his lifelong devotion to his mother and his lack of alternatives imply that he went to visit her in Alexandria, where she returned after Lucia died, in 1839. Eliza's youngest son, David, was approaching his twentieth birthday and may still have been at home, but Bolton was on duty in the navy. Lucia's widowed husband entrusted their one sickly child, Lucian, to the care of his grandmother, and the support he sent replaced the income Eliza lost when she closed her boarding school. Only Bolton was yet earning enough to send her anything, but with that and her little navy widow's pension she managed to survive.[38]

In the fall Porter reported back to the academy to study chemistry, landscape drawing, and natural philosophy, which included mechanics, electricity and magnetism, acoustics, optics, and astronomy. He performed best that year in natural philosophy, and improved in drawing, but chemistry proved trying enough that he finished only a few places above the middle of the class. He and Stone both dropped a couple of places in class standing, to tenth and eleventh, respectively, but Porter fell again in conduct, landing exactly one-third of the way down the corps in seventieth place. Only seven times had demerits been counted against him, but three of them were for "visiting" when he should have been in his quarters, and in one instance, only five minutes before "lights out." That cost him eight demerits—the most he ever received for a single offense— and one Sunday a couple of months later he drew another five for talking with the "inmates" of another barrack. He must have begun sampling the nicotine habit that spring, for his last five demerits in his third year came when, for the first of several times, he was caught smoking during a recreation period.[39]

After the summer of 1843, even some of the more restrained cadets faced social temptation from the presence of Ambrose E. Burnside, a tall, burly plebe from Indiana. Willcox, who also came to West Point that year, thought Burnside "the soul of 'fun, frolic and friendship,'" and declared that he was "the idol of the class, our leader in everything but studies." Burnside tallied innumerable demerits for visiting and talking at inopportune moments, and once for "playing" in the sickroom. Willcox noted that Burnside's charm often allowed him to escape the consequences of his garrulous, jovial character, but by the end of his first year he stood within two demerits of the fatal two hundred. That put him fourth from last in conduct in the cadet corps, and no one below him continued. McClellan, who was equally well liked, knew Burnside well at West Point. Evidently so did Porter, for in an 1880 letter to Burnside he referred to their "old" friendship, and before 1861 they could have fallen in together only at the academy.[40]

In their fourth year the cadets finally met the legendary Dennis Hart Mahan, in whose class they spent as much as three hours every day learning civil and military engineering, more drawing, and the science of war. As department head, Mahan was assisted by Lieutenants John Newton and Gustavus W. Smith, both of whom had been first-classmen when Porter was a plebe. Mahan's students regarded him as the sternest member of the faculty, and his demanding attitude emanated from the conviction that the material he taught was the most important of their military education. Under him they learned to design and build fieldworks, permanent fortifications, and just about anything else. Mahan had printed his own handouts on those military subjects and on architecture in general, and he familiarized his students with construction machinery and such specific tasks as stonecutting. His instruction in military theory included the composition of armies, varieties of attack and defense, and a discussion of "mines and other accessories," which he presented as legitimate weapons of war—contrary to the opinion of some of his students, against whom mines were later used. Mahan's influence on the military course of the Civil War has been emphasized to the point of exaggeration, and his real legacy may have lain with the feats of civil engineering his training made possible. Fitz John Porter and his classmate Charles Stone would benefit more from Mahan's instruction after they shed their uniforms than while they wore them.[41]

Two decades later Porter and Stone profited particularly from their study of mineralogy and geology that year. In each of those subjects they had the use of relatively recent texts, while the Ethics Department assigned an eighteenth-century treatise on rhetoric. The post chaplain taught a class in what was then called "moral science," and offered an introduction to logic, but he probably left the section on constitutional law to the lieutenant serving as his assistant.[42]

In their senior year cadets were bombarded with new subjects, and professors like Mahan wanted to add more, leading to administrative discussion of expanding the course to five years. The schedule in 1844–45 included advanced principles of infantry tactics and all aspects of artillery, with a French text on tactical theory and instruction in the properties and performance of different types of gunpowder, guns, and projectiles. Captain Erasmus Keyes, whose later promotions to colonel and brigadier general would date simultaneously with Porter's, was his instructor in artillery. Keyes was also the nominal instructor of cavalry, but the curriculum did not yet offer a course in cavalry tactics, and the graduating class learned equitation under a civilian. Virtually every army officer except those of company grade in the infantry had to know how to ride, and in the academy stable they practiced riding, jumping, and such mysterious mounted saber exercises as "cutting Turk's head." Porter took naturally to the saddle, and officers who knew him later all recalled him as an accomplished horseman with a "fine seat."[43]

Major General Winfield Scott convened the annual inspectors of cadets at West Point on June 2, 1845, to evaluate their performance and determine the order of their placement. William H. C. Whiting stood first in the class and first in all five academic departments. Right behind Whiting in infantry tactics came Fitz John Porter, who placed tenth in engineering, tenth in mineralogy and geology, and twelfth in the artillery course. His worst performance came with nineteenth place in ethics, which included such new and complicated subjects as law and logic, but the inspectors gave less weight to that department in determining class rank. The original 123 entrants in the class had been whittled down to 34, but with those who had been turned back from earlier classes a total of 41 young men graduated with the class of 1845. Porter's conduct had improved slightly, with only four instances of smoking and visiting and a single uniform violation, putting him sixty-second in conduct among all cadets. That was a very respectable showing for a first-classman whose demerits were subject to 50 percent inflation, and with his good grades in engineering, science, and tactics he finally ranked eighth in his class. Stone came in just ahead of him again.[44]

The same academic board that had initially examined the appointees in 1841, consisting of the heads of the various departments, met again on the morning of June 19, 1845, to decide which cadets would be offered places in the higher branches of the service. Mahan, who usually had his way in such matters, recommended only the five top scholars as qualified for all five branches, including the corps of engineers. Going down the academic order of the class, he restricted the next nine graduates — including Stone and Porter — to ordnance, artillery, infantry, and the dragoons, or mounted infantry. Failing a commission in the engineers, the ordnance was considered honorable enough that Stone requested that assignment, but the field regiments offered a better chance for a reputation, if not advancement. Porter, the good horseman, selected the dragoons and indicated no alternative, but choices were dependent on vacancies.[45]

Graduation in late June afforded every cadet an appointment as a brevet second lieutenant. A "brevet," from the French word for an honorific title, was usually awarded to commissioned officers as an unofficial promotion for distinguished service, in lieu of decorations. For cadets, a brevet second-lieutenancy amounted to something of a probationary warrant, pending full commission. Delays in matching requests with vacancies inevitably forestalled even the brevet commission until mid-July or later, although it was always antedated to the first of the month.

A three-month furlough also customarily followed graduation. Young men who had only been home once in four years eagerly anticipated that interlude, especially as they faced the prospect of long postings in isolated locations. Fitz John Porter had to postpone that pleasure, but for reasons he could hardly regret. His strong performance in tactical studies, and especially in infantry, probably lay behind orders for him to remain at the academy under the commandant of cadets, to drill the new cadets through the summer encampment. At the end of June, no longer a cadet but not yet an officer, he herded scores of nervous plebes into their first formation atop the bluff overlooking the Hudson, guiding them into the positions and movements he had learned four summers before. Some of those novices would know him later as their commanding officer or colleague, but they would probably never again regard him with greater awe than they did that summer day of 1845 on the plain at West Point.[46]

2

THE GATEWAY

Within seventy-two hours of Fitz John Porter's graduation from West Point, Texas agreed to annexation by the United States, thereby launching a course of events that would determine Porter's entire military career. In New England, where the acquisition was presciently viewed as a source of trouble, Texas was cynically regarded as having annexed the United States. Mexico did not recognize the independence of Texas in the first place, and U.S. troops aggravated that dispute by camping below what the Mexican government recognized as the southern boundary of its own fractious province. Provocative clashes required only the passage of time.[1]

Those troops were just approaching the coast of Texas toward the end of July, when Porter accepted his commission as brevet second lieutenant. He did so with a touch of disappointment, for the U.S. Army fielded only two regiments of the dragoons he had favored, and there had not been enough vacancies among the officers to honor his preference. The best the War Department could offer was a spot in the 4th Artillery, and Porter accepted it. His summer on the West Point cadre came to an end with the beginning of the academic year, and he proceeded to his mother's home in Alexandria on the postponed furlough, to await orders for a specific assignment.[2]

That assignment took him down the Potomac River and Chesapeake Bay to Fort Monroe, overlooking Hampton Roads from Virginia's Old Point Comfort. Several companies of the 4th Artillery comprised the garrison there under Colonel John Walbach, who had entered the army while George Washington still lived. Porter arrived at the fort in the autumn of 1845.[3]

Artillery regiments of that era usually trained as infantry, with only a portion of the complement detailed to fieldpieces or the big guns in the forts. Fort Monroe afforded pleasant surroundings and comfortable quarters, and as much as Porter had wished for mounted service he reconciled himself to his posting. The following spring, when tensions escalated on the Mexican frontier, Congress authorized recruiting for a regiment of mounted rifles, preliminary to transforming the two dragoon regiments into light cavalry. With Porter's preference still on file, the adjutant general offered him a transfer to the new regiment, which was all the buzz among promotion-conscious officers. Porter, who had evidently heard of some dubious appointments to that unit, declined on the grounds that he did not want "to be placed under the command of those of my own class, who were declared deficient at the Military Academy."[4]

Four companies of the 4th Artillery left Fort Monroe late in 1845 for Texas, where Brevet Brigadier General Zachary Taylor commanded the troops that so annoyed the unstable Mexican government. Porter's company and one other remained at Fort Monroe through the winter, with Major John L. Gardner in command. Meanwhile, President James Polk sent an emissary to Mexico to resolve the Texas dispute, but antagonism over the annexation and military encroachment left the Mexican president reluctant to accept that envoy. Then a coup toppled the government and elevated a general to the presidency, at which Polk's man asked for his passport and went home.[5]

In the spring Taylor moved his command deeper into contested territory. Texas claimed the Rio Grande as its border with Mexico, and U.S. forces took position at the mouth of that river, establishing a supply base at Point Isabel. Twenty miles upriver, Taylor's men began work on a fort opposite the Mexican town of Matamoros. Pedro de Ampudia, the new commander of a Mexican army gathering at Matamoros, demanded that Taylor retire north of the Nueces. That demand had just been rejected when Taylor's chief quartermaster disappeared on a ride outside camp, and a detachment of the 4th Infantry went looking for him under Lieutenant Theodoric Porter — Fitz John Porter's first cousin. This Lieutenant Porter's company surprised and dispersed a party of Mexican "guerrillas," but Theodoric Porter himself was killed hours later in a retaliatory ambush. The U.S. Army counted Fitz John Porter's cousin as the first of its officers to die in battle in the war with Mexico.[6]

On April 24 the Mexican commander apprised Taylor that he considered hostilities begun, and his troops attacked a company of Taylor's dragoons as they scouted the river crossings, killing nearly a score of them and capturing the rest. Taylor called on the governor of Texas for volunteers to reinforce his three thousand Regular Army troops against a Mexican force he estimated at twice that size. He retreated to Point Isabel, leaving a small garrison in the new fort opposite Matamoros. Early in May, while President Polk prepared a request for a declaration of war, Taylor returned to relieve the besieged fort, attacking the Mexican army and hurling it back across the river.[7]

That brought the rest of the 4th Artillery from Fort Monroe, and Fitz John Porter came with it. Those last two companies arrived at Point Isabel early in the summer of 1846, and Porter eagerly anticipated joining the rest of his regiment at the front. Like many a young, ambitious soldier, he craved battlefield experience for the professional advantages it might bring — as he confessed to his Boston cousin, Robert Henry Eddy. Instead, the latecomers joined the garrison of Fort Polk, at Point Isabel, around which camped upwards of eight thousand Regular Army troops and twelve-month volunteers.

"Here we are out of reach of danger and honor," Porter complained at the end of August, lamenting that he had "no prospect of joining the army until too late." Fifty leagues deep in Mexico, Taylor was maneuvering his brigades to fight the principal Mexican army at Monterey. Wagon trains up to two miles long rumbled away from Point Isabel with his supplies, but the garrison heard little from the front except through sick men trickling back to recuperate or exhausted short-term volunteers on their way home. Vast expanses of glimmering campfires sparkled romantically around the port and the outlying islands at night, but with dawn such picturesque images evaporated, and the rising sun revealed a cemetery growing larger daily, half a mile from the fort. Flies pestered the sleeping troops, forcing them awake before the sun rose. Sand flew into the eyes and food with every breeze, Porter told his cousin Robert, and the water tasted ominously brackish. "Glory such as I see around me daily I court not," he wrote, having only recently arisen from a sickbed himself. "The hospital is teeming with it."[8]

Taylor captured Monterey in late September. That ended the fighting for a time, to the disgust of brevet second lieutenants who had not been able to participate in the battle. As winter began, Fitz John Porter's company finally marched away from Point Isabel to join Brevet Brigadier General William Worth's division at Saltillo, nearly three hundred miles to the west. They hastened through Camargo, where adobe hovels stood amid rich agricultural surroundings and measles was taking a heavy toll on volunteers — and the undisciplined volunteers were abusing the inhabitants, to the disgust of Regulars. The principal feature of the northern provinces seemed to be a conspicuous absence of attractive women: "They are nearly all exceedingly ugly," one officer reported to his wife, assuring her that he had not seen a pretty girl since crossing into Mexico. Here Porter ran out the year in what promised to be another disappointingly quiet assignment.[9]

January of 1847 at last brought some cheering news for Porter in the form of a commission that erased the "brevet" from his rank. Within five more years, West Pointers would collect immediate appointments as full second lieutenants on the day they graduated, but it had taken Porter a year and a half to make that leap; his classmate Charles Stone waited nearly two years. Porter's commission had been issued on Christmas Eve, and although it was dated back to June he may have fretted that so long a wait would delay his next promotion, especially if fortune confined him to backwater posts.[10]

The new year also improved his luck in that regard. Taylor's vanguard at Victoria lay nearly five hundred circuitous miles above Mexico City, and the

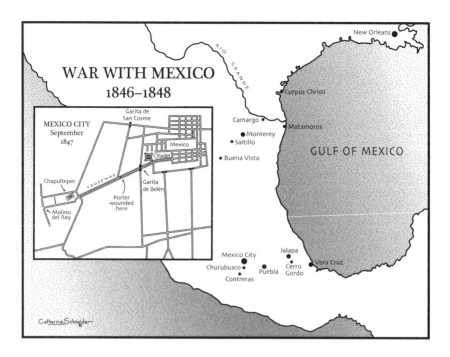

same distance back to Point Isabel. Winfield Scott had devised a plan for landing a new army at Vera Cruz, on the Gulf of Mexico, and marching the two hundred fifty miles to Mexico City from there. Early in January Scott arrived on
the Rio Grande to collect that new army, much of which he intended to draw
from General Taylor's troops in the interior. With Lieutenant Porter trundling
along, Worth's division turned back to Point Isabel and boarded transports for
Lobos Island, north of Vera Cruz, where dozens of troopships lay anchored by
late February.[11]

Before beginning his campaign, Scott reorganized the Regular Army regiments and the volunteers who were already arriving from New Orleans. He
placed all the volunteers in three brigades under Major General Robert Patterson, and divided the Regulars into two large brigades commanded respectively
by Worth and Brigadier General David Twiggs. John Gardner's battalion of the
4th Artillery went with Twiggs.[12]

The predictable onset of yellow fever around Vera Cruz demanded a speedy
capture. That mosquito-borne disease beset the coast from about the middle of
April until the middle of November, and Scott's soldiers lacked the immunity
of the natives, so it was essential the army advance into the highlands before
the annual epidemic struck. Surfboats shuttled Lieutenant Porter and most of
Scott's army ashore on March 9, leaving perhaps five weeks in which to force the
surrender of the port and proceed inland. Scott knew that a dispatch to Taylor
explaining the Vera Cruz operation had been intercepted, and he anticipated

a warm welcome from Antonio López de Santa Anna—the quondam general, president, and dictator who had resumed power. Santa Anna had marched north to try crushing Taylor's depleted army before facing Scott, but Taylor had dealt him a bloody repulse at Buena Vista, near Saltillo. The Vera Cruz landing therefore encountered no resistance, but bad weather delayed the landing of heavy artillery, so March had almost expired before the city surrendered.[13]

Scott spent the first days of April reorganizing his two Regular Army brigades into divisions of two brigades each. General Twiggs assigned Brigadier General Persifor Smith to command his first brigade, while Colonel Bennet Riley took his second brigade—including the 4th Artillery, with Lieutenant Porter. Twiggs led the march out of Vera Cruz on April 8, headed for the city of Jalapa, sixty-five miles to the northwest and more than four thousand feet higher in elevation. Mountains topped with snow stood within sight as the column left the coastal camp.[14]

Three days later Twiggs encountered his first opposition, forty-five miles up the National Road from Vera Cruz, just as he reached the cordillera. Santa Anna had replenished and reorganized his army after the disaster at Buena Vista. He arrayed artillery and infantry on high ground overlooking some two miles of the road Scott's army would have to travel, from just above the village of Plan del Rio to a ranch known as Cerro Gordo. Sheer heights cut by the Rio del Plan protected the right and rear of the Mexican position, to the southwest, while steep, rugged, trackless hills lay on Santa Anna's left, to the northeast. He had chosen formidable ground, and his troops outnumbered Scott's entire army, so Twiggs awaited the arrival of Robert Patterson's volunteer brigades, following a day behind him. Patterson had come down sick, so Twiggs took command of the combined forces, and one of his staff officers detected a weak spot in the Mexican lines that could be flanked by a long detour over difficult terrain. Twiggs planned an attack, but even as a major general of militia Patterson outranked him, and Patterson sent orders ahead to wait for Scott before taking aggressive action.[15]

Scott brought most of the rest of the army up a few days later. Lieutenant Pierre G. T. Beauregard, of the engineers, found the enemy's extreme left anchored on two tall, round hills—one known locally as Cerro Gordo, or El Telegrafo, and the other as La Atalaya. Santa Anna's main camp at Cerro Gordo ranch lay directly below those hills. The next day Captain Robert E. Lee reconnoitered even farther into that precipitous landscape, marking out a route through the chaparral and briars for a flank movement around Santa Anna's left that would cut off his retreat to Jalapa.[16]

On April 17 Scott started Twiggs's division over Lee's trail, intending to put him in position for an attack on the morrow. Persifor Smith was sick, too, and Colonel William Harney of the 2nd U.S. Dragoons took command of Smith's brigade. His task was to secure the crest of La Atalaya for an artillery position while Bennet Riley's brigade continued toward the National Road to block the Mexicans' retreat. Riley's brigade consisted that day of only the 2nd U.S. Infantry and the 4th U.S. Artillery, but Scott had reinforced him with a brigade of volunteers under Brigadier General James Shields. After several hours of arduous scrambling, Harney's men attracted the attention of Mexican pickets, and when the Americans tried to ascend La Atalaya they met enemy forces sweeping down from El Telegrafo. In an unintended battle, Harney drove the counterattack back into the valley and started up El Telegrafo toward the key position. A rain of musketry and artillery fire stopped Harney's men on the steep slope, from which they did not retire until after dark.[17]

Music and cheering echoed from the Mexican camps, where many thought they had put the Americanos to flight. Instead of retreating, Scott's soldiers were preparing for the next day's assault. John Gardner's 4th Artillery spent most of the night wrestling big fieldpieces and howitzers over Lee's rude track from the National Road and up the side of La Atalaya. A captain, the regimental adjutant, and three lieutenants of the 4th Artillery—Calvin Benjamin, Samuel Gill, and Fitz John Porter—supervised the lifting of the guns in the darkness, by rope, to the summit. By dawn the battery was in position.[18]

The battle began with a diversionary attack on the Mexican right, at the lower end of Santa Anna's position, by volunteers under Gideon Pillow. Pillow, who lacked any military experience, had been appointed a brigadier general by his former law partner, President Polk, and in the private opinion of professional soldiers he was worse than useless. The only step he took toward fulfilling his instructions that morning was to attract enemy fire prematurely with his own indiscreet shouting.[19]

At the other end of the line, the freshly posted artillery atop La Atalaya opened a brisk fire on the Mexican battery on El Telegrafo. Riley's brigade and Shields's volunteers struck for the National Road, led by Captain Lee and Lieutenant Benjamin's company of the 4th Artillery, which accompanied Lee as a personal escort. Riley veered off to the left, toward Cerro Gordo, while Shields continued straight ahead, and Colonel Harney's brigade swept down from La Atalaya and surged up El Telegrafo again. With the artillery to cover their ascent, Harney's men fared much better than they had the previous afternoon, and the sharp incline seemed to pose a worse impediment than the red flame of hostile fire blazing down from the crest. The cloud of blue uniforms burst over the top of the hill and engaged the defenders with the bayonet while some of the 2nd Infantry from Riley's brigade, under Lieutenant Nathaniel Lyon, came up the other side and helped drive the enemy from the hill. At the behest of General Twiggs, much of the 4th Artillery followed Lyon, fighting as infantry. From there Riley's brigade swarmed down to attack the Mexican camp at the base of the hill. Shields reached the National Road on the back side of that camp and veered toward Cerro Gordo, trapping nearly half of Santa Anna's army while the rest fled in every direction. As word of the rout spread along the Mexicans' line, white flags sprang up as far down as Pillow's command, and the fighting was over well before noon.[20]

Santa Anna left behind a large part of his army and much booty, including gold coin, cannon, and what was assumed to be his own artificial leg. Regulars started after him, but by then most of the fugitives had too much of a lead. Scott paroled the prisoners on their pledge not to fight until they were exchanged for American prisoners, and he destroyed the captured ordnance. The next day Twiggs and his division led the pursuit, plodding through torrential downpours toward the city of Jalapa, seemingly in the shadow of snowcapped Pico de Orizaba, 18,500 feet high.[21]

The stone-paved road wended steadily uphill between blooming bushes into a cooler climate. The vanguard reached Jalapa just before noon on April 19, and the soldiers found it vastly different from northern Mexico. Lieutenant George B. McClellan pronounced Jalapa "the most beautiful place I ever beheld." The women of the town "were generally pretty," he added—nor was he the only American to note that sudden and welcome change. Lieutenant Raphael Semmes, on a mission for the U.S. Navy, alluded to "the fleeting beauties of the fair Jalapeñas," and even as the rain still drizzled over the emerald hills he found the city "picturesque in the extreme."[22]

Part of the army pressed on past Jalapa under Worth, but General Scott lingered there, keeping Twiggs and his division with him. When supply trains reached Jalapa, weeks later, Scott proceeded over the Sierra Madre Oriental a hundred miles to Puebla, entering that city on May 28. Twiggs followed the commanding general the next day, with the 4th Artillery in tow. Second Lieutenant Porter did not yet know that his promotion to first lieutenant became effective that day, but a shortage of officers fit for duty gave him his first executive experience as commander of Company F.[23]

The division of Regulars under Twiggs moved into barracks-like buildings, an abandoned nunnery, and the unfinished wings of an ancient church, all of which Worth's men vacated for them. Mexico City lay only eighty miles away, but for the next ten weeks Scott's army rested at Puebla, seven thousand feet above sea level, while the general and a State Department emissary conducted hopeless negotiations with Santa Anna. The Mexican leader used the lull to raise a new army, while Scott's outnumbered troops enjoyed the unusual comfort of sleeping out of the weather. With garrisons at Vera Cruz and Jalapa, and a thousand or more on the sick list, Scott could depend on barely six thousand men ready for duty, officers included. Puebla's population approached eighty thousand, but the residents had much to lose and seemed happy to leave the fighting to the armies. The wealth of the place amazed the Americans: Lieutenant

John Sedgwick thought the seventeenth-century Spanish cathedral might be "the most splendid building on the continent."[24]

On July 17, Porter's entire regiment made a pleasure excursion to the pyramid of Cholula. The Aztec temple, already thought to be two millennia old, stood eight miles west of Puebla. With a base more than a quarter of a mile square, it was the largest pyramid in the world. Those who climbed the heavily vegetated sides to the chapel on the summit had a grand view of the snow-covered, volcanic peaks on the range to the west: if no treaty were agreed upon, they would have to cross over those mountains.[25]

After it became clear that Santa Anna would accept no peace without taking a more painful drubbing, Scott awaited only reinforcements and resupply from the coast before calling in his garrisons and marching on Mexico City. Congress had recently authorized eight new regiments for the Regular Army—the so-called 1847 Regiments, composed of raw recruits—and they began joining Scott at Puebla in July. George Cadwalader, a brigadier of Pennsylvania militia, commanded three of those regiments, including the 14th U.S. Infantry. Fitz John Porter's brother, twenty-two-year-old David St. Leon Porter, had landed at Vera Cruz with that regiment as a brand-new second lieutenant, but there would be no fraternal reunion at Puebla. The 14th Infantry did not march for the interior soon enough, and on June 30 the younger Porter died of yellow fever.[26]

Three more of those new regiments arrived in Puebla on August 6 under Brigadier General Franklin Pierce, a former U.S. senator from New Hampshire. The next day Scott reorganized his army, giving Cadwalader's and Pierce's brigades to Pillow, whom President Polk had promoted to major general, but Twiggs led the march out of Pueblo with the "real" Regulars once again in the lead. That division ascended the road leading into the mountains that isolated Puebla from Mexico City, cresting the pass at an elevation between ten and eleven thousand feet, where rarefied air left them panting and queasy. The entire valley of Mexico opened before them on the descent in a memorable spectacle, and five days later the leading regiments fell out at Ayotla, less than twenty miles from the capital.[27]

Extensive lakes narrowed the approaches to Mexico City. The direct road from Ayotla ran across a narrow causeway through marshland, and that causeway lay under the muzzles of artillery and within range of considerable infantry on a height called El Peñón. The southern route, below the lakes, led to the village of San Agustín, just below the Pedregal—a presumably impassible barrier of rugged volcanic rock, several miles wide and devoid of vegetation. That road bent north toward the capital, running between the Pedregal and Lake Xochimilco to the village of San Antonio and, farther on, to a well-fortified bridge that blocked any crossing of the Churubusco River. There, near the convent of San Mateo, heavy guns and thousands of infantry awaited any advance. After several days of reconnoitering, Scott decided to turn south, below Lake Chalco, and strike by way of San Agustín.[28]

Worth's all-Regular division led that roundabout march on August 15, followed by Pillow's. Later that day General John Quitman started off with a makeshift division of three volunteer regiments, a battalion of U.S. Marines, and a company each of artillery and dragoons. To keep Santa Anna guessing, Twiggs remained at Ayotla another day with the same division of old-army Regulars he had commanded from Vera Cruz.[29]

Twiggs had his men up by 3:30 A.M. on August 16, and under way by 6:00. His route to San Antonio covered at least twenty-five miles, but only three miles into it Twiggs spotted Mexican cavalry and infantry on his flank who appeared to number two or three times the size of his entire division. He sent out three regiments to confront them, including the 4th Artillery, but the enemy showed no more audacity than most of Santa Anna's fresh conscripts: both horse and foot fled before a thousand or so American muskets after a few volleys from the field battery that accompanied them. The delay nonetheless held up the day's march, and the twinkling of their comrades' distant campfires provided the only contact between Twiggs's column and the rest of the army that night.[30]

On August 18, Worth's division finally chased the enemy out of San Agustín, only nine miles below Mexico City, taking possession and moving on within sight of the next Mexican defenses at San Antonio. Twiggs lagged six miles or more behind him, but when the 4th Artillery camped that afternoon one of Lieutenant Porter's comrades climbed a hill for his first glimpse of the capital, and Twiggs reached San Agustín on the morning of the nineteenth. By then Worth had found the road to San Antonio too heavily fortified to take by direct assault, and engineer officers were scouting the Pedregal for a route that flanked those works. Escorted by the 4th Artillery, Captain Lee was laying out such a road from San Agustín, trying to connect with an existing route that would circle the Pedregal to the west and north, taking the Churubusco bridge in the flank, well behind San Antonio. As the workmen following Lee neared the agricultural hamlet of Padierna, on the western fringe of the Pedregal, they came within sight and range of several thousand Mexican soldiers dug in on a hilltop directly opposite Padierna. From that height General Gabriel Valencia commanded a daunting array of heavy artillery, and he was well supported with cavalry.[31]

Pillow's division trailed behind Twiggs, supplying the fatigue crews. When Valencia spotted their progress, his artillery opened fire. Pillow waived his superior rank to Twiggs, who deployed Pillow's field battery and mountain howitzers to confront the heavy guns of the enemy. The American gunners suffered dearly, but the noise and smoke did distract the enemy enough for Bennet Riley to lead his brigade farther up the Pedregal and emerge near San Geronimo, north of Valencia's position. Neither Twiggs nor Pillow followed — Twiggs being detained by a lame foot on a path too precarious for horses — but eventually Pillow sent Cadwalader's brigade trailing after Riley.[32]

The 4th Artillery still had the lead of this flanking force, with Company G thrown out as skirmishers under Captain Simon Drum — a classmate of Captain Lee's. Drum had the assistance of Lieutenant Porter, who had turned over command of Company F to Lieutenant George W. Getty when the division left Puebla. As they burst out into the road, Drum's skirmishers ran into Mexican lancers and dropped a few of them out of their saddles, putting the rest to flight. A force of several thousand infantry reinforcements for Valencia appeared on the far side of San Geronimo, preceded by more lancers, but Company G scattered those horsemen as well, and the rest came no farther.[33]

Cadwalader joined Riley that afternoon, and later still came Persifor Smith, with his brigade. By virtue of his brevet as a brigadier, Smith took command. Caught between two superior forces of the enemy, Smith wanted to attack Valencia from behind but dared not turn his back on those reinforcements above San Geronimo. After dark he decided to make a morning attack on the rear of Valencia's bastion. In the middle of the night Scott sent him two regiments from Quitman's division under James Shields, and Smith posted Shields as a rear guard while he started the three other brigades toward the back of Valencia's hilltop. Captain Lee volunteered to traverse the treacherous Pedregal in the darkness to apprise Scott and arrange a diversionary attack from Valencia's front: just as Lee started a cold rain set in, drenching the troops but guiding Lee's way with occasional bolts of lightning.[34]

Smith hoped to approach in silence under cover of the darkness and take the works by the bayonet. So black was the night that each man had to stumble along holding the equipment straps of the man in front of him lest anyone get lost, yet whole companies did lose their way. Dawn had already come before Smith had his men in position, and Pierce's brigade had begun to feign the frontal attack. The rain had ceased when Colonel Gardner's 4th Artillery led the right wing of Riley's brigade up the hill; part of the 2nd Infantry advanced at the head of the left wing. Several companies of Valencia's foot soldiers spilled over the crest to meet this unexpected attack, followed by gunners who wheeled a brace of light fieldpieces into position by hand. Gunpowder on both sides remained dry enough to ignite, but the Mexican infantry fired wildly, then broke and ran after a volley from the 4th Artillery. The two guns, meanwhile, kept belching grape and canister. Their aim was little better, although one blast tore the tassels off the flag of Gardner's regiment and another killed the color bearer. At the call to charge, the 4th Artillery leveled bayonets and broke into a run, with Captain Drum lurching ahead of his company and placing a hand on one of the guns as though to claim it. He, Lieutenant Porter, and the entire regiment swept over the crest and down the other side, followed by the rest of Riley's brigade. The enemy infantry and cavalry scattered everywhere.[35]

Shields swung his little brigade to block their retreat to the north, and Smith's troops fired into the retreating masses from above while Pierce's infantry riddled them from the front. The fusillade killed and wounded hundreds of the thronging fugitives. More than eight hundred surrendered, including four generals, and all twenty-two guns in Valencia's redoubt fell into Smith's hands. The two brass six-pounders that had been brought to bear against the assault, including the one Captain Drum had claimed with a touch, turned out to be guns lost by another company of the 4th Artillery at Buena Vista, six months earlier. General Scott, who was on hand when the recovered guns came down, declared that they would belong to the 4th Artillery thenceforth and that they should be inscribed to document their recapture in a battle he misnamed "Contreras." In honor of Drum's conspicuous part in seizing the cannon they were assigned to his company, along with a couple of other guns from the day's booty. Horses, harness, and other equipment he drew from the ordnance train, and Drum's company turned in its muskets to become an actual artillery battery.[36]

The Mexican reinforcements above San Geronimo turned back to bolster the defenses at the Churubusco bridge. Twiggs, Pillow, and Shields sped after them to attack that stronghold from the west while Worth slipped around the San Antonio defenders and assaulted Churubusco head-on. The 4th Artillery alone remained to corral the prisoners and collect the captured ordnance, but from the fortified hilltop they could see the battle at the bridge. Before the day ended the span was taken and the Mexicans were pouring back toward their capital, but the price had been heavy. Smith's casualties at Padierna came to fewer than sixty men killed or disabled, but at Churubusco Scott lost a thousand from an army not ten times that large.[37]

Despite the cost of the American victory, the panicked retreat of Mexican forces from their seemingly impregnable positions elicited another appeal for negotiation from Santa Anna. Hoping the defenders had seen enough battlefield defeat to accept terms, General Scott consented to a short truce to test the depth of that sentiment, while his army made camp five miles south of the city. By September 6, Scott understood that Santa Anna was merely stalling again, and ended the cease-fire.[38]

Santa Anna was suspected of using the truce to cast cannon in an old foundry half a mile from the castle of Chapultepec, which loomed on a hilltop a couple of hundred feet over the city. On September 7 Scott issued orders for a frontal assault on the foundry, as a first step in capturing the capital. Captain Ephraim Kirby Smith, whose brother Edmund would surrender the last Confederate army eighteen years later, received his instructions that evening; before retiring he wrote to his wife, deploring the time and momentum lost in useless peace talks. Hundreds more sick men had fallen out of the ranks since the double victory of August 20, he estimated, and provisions were growing short, yet they had to begin their fighting once again from a dead stop. "Tomorrow will be a day of slaughter," he warned his wife.[39]

The objective was Molino del Rey, a long, rectangular stone and stucco complex that had long since fallen out of use — as a foundry or anything else. Half of it had been a flour mill, and the other half a gunpowder mill. It faced an improvised fort in another stone structure half a mile away called Casa Mata, which had once been the magazine where the gunpowder was stored. A brigade of Mexican infantry defended each of the structures, while a third brigade and a large battery occupied a ditch before and between the two; a division of cavalry waited on the other side of a ravine, should any American troops try to flank the position in that direction. Long-range guns at Chapultepec bore on much of the ground the attacking forces would have to cover.[40]

Scott assigned William Worth's division the task of capturing the impromptu bastion, strengthening him with Cadwalader's brigade and nine pieces of artillery. A pair of twenty-four-pounders stood on the hillside descending toward the mill, to batter down the walls, while four field guns gave more direct support to the infantry on Worth's left. Three guns of Captain Drum's new battery came into play: Lieutenant Calvin Benjamin took an eight-pounder out on the main road to Mexico City, to discourage any reinforcements, while Captain Drum himself and Lieutenant Porter swung the two Buena Vista guns into position on the far right of Worth's deployment, beside John Garland's infantry. Drum prodded his men awake at three o'clock in the morning, and just at dawn he placed his two guns a little over a thousand feet from Molino del Rey, behind some shrubbery that veiled them from Chapultepec.[41]

Worth gave the artillery but little time to batter at the masonry of the mill before he hurled a storming party of several hundred infantry toward the western end of the Molino, trying to cut the Mexican line in half. The storming party had not been furnished ladders to scale the walls, and the Mexican artillery lacerated them with rapid-fire blasts of canister. Then a counterattack by Mexican infantry drove the stunned survivors back the way they had come. To fill that void Worth sent in a light battalion under Captain Smith, who had predicted a slaughter and soon fell victim to it. Next, Worth launched an attack from his left against Casa Mata, and that brigade trotted toward a similar fate; the brigadier went down with two wounds, and after a long, withering exchange with the enemy his men shrank back to their supporting artillery.[42]

While artillery took over the fight on the left, Garland's brigade started forward, and after firing a round apiece the two Buena Vista guns moved with it. Horses in both gun's teams had already been wounded, and Captain Drum chose to advance the pieces by hand, he and Porter each taking command of one of the six-pounders. A gradual downhill slope allowed them to keep up with Garland's men as the fitful assault periodically recoiled in the face of blistering volleys, and then resumed under the hectoring encouragement of the officers — Porter included. Worth threw most of Cadwalader's brigade in, and the fight grew close. With Captain Robert Anderson of the 3rd Artillery lending a hand, the two fieldpieces reached the nearest corner of the mill and started raking the ditch with canister until the defenders spilled out of their works and began falling back into or beyond the mill. At one point a white flag fluttered up on the wall in front of Drum's section, but just as Drum ordered his men to stop firing a handful of Mexicans near the white flag shot one of his gunners dead, so the battle resumed. American foot soldiers smashed through gates at either end of the mill complex, driving out or capturing the last of the garrison. Fugitives scampered through the woods toward Chapultepec, from which reinforcements tried to recapture the lost ground, but Drum and Porter drove them back with canister.[43]

The worst of the fighting was over within a couple of hours, and the last counterattack receded later in the morning. Most of the Americans were returning to their camps by midday, with the sun sitting high and hot. The cost had again been far greater than the gain, with nearly eight hundred casualties representing a full quarter of the men Worth had on the field. Mexican observers insisted that Santa Anna never fielded as many troops as Scott and his subordinates estimated, and the reported odds did seem eternally flattering to the victors, but the American soldiers believed at the time that they were extensively outnumbered. Captain Anderson supposed that Santa Anna was happy to lose one battle after another with his overwhelming forces, allowing him to whittle Scott's army down to negligible size and finally annihilate it. One of Scott's own staff officers conceded that the army could survive few more such victories, and a lieutenant on Twiggs's staff admitted that the heavy casualties cast a gloom over the camps. Some of Scott's troops thought their army in so desperate a situation that they deserted into the countryside.[44]

There remained the thorny matter of capturing the city itself. The choices lay between an assault on the *garitas*, or gates, directly below the city, or an attack on Chapultepec, west of the city. From that castle, where the cadets of Mexico's military academy were quartered, an aqueduct and elevated causeway led straight across the broad marshes that surrounded the capital, entering the city through the Belén Gate; a similar causeway veered north before turning sharply east, toward the San Cosme Gate. On September 11 Scott decided to go by way of Chapultepec.[45]

To hold Santa Anna's attention on the southern gates, Scott left Twiggs with Riley's brigade and a couple of batteries to feign an attack there, meanwhile swinging the balance of the army toward Chapultepec. On the night of September 11 American artillery started creeping into position to bombard the castle, in preparation for an infantry assault. Captain Drum brought up three heavy guns—all captured Mexican pieces—and unlimbered them half a mile south of Chapultepec, beside the main road from the village of Tacubaya. Lieutenants Benjamin and Porter each took command of a gun, and at dawn of the twelfth they moved into place behind protective earthworks. Several other batteries occupied works to their left, including one constructed by Lieutenant McClellan and an enormous mortar operated by Porter's West Point rival, Lieutenant Stone. At seven o'clock, not long after the sound of beating drums drifted down from Chapultepec, all those guns opened on the castle and the woods below it, where Mexican reinforcements huddled.[46]

All day they kept up the fire with two sixteen-pounders and an eight-inch howitzer, occasionally sending a charge of canister down the road when enemy infantry threatened to advance. Not until evening did Drum's officers and men retire for some sleep while others took their places. Scott issued orders for the infantry assault in the morning. He called for volunteers for storming parties, equipping them with tools and ladders, and issued final orders late that night. General Worth feared they would be beaten, and even General Scott admitted some doubts.[47]

At daylight of September 13 the bombardment resumed. Drum's eight-inch howitzer burst after the second round, and Lieutenant Benjamin went looking for a replacement from the captured ordnance. A solid shot from Chapultepec killed one gunner, wounded a corporal, and broke the wheel of one of the sixteen-pounders, but that gun returned to action with a new wheel within minutes. After another two hours Scott called for the bombardment to pause, signaling the assault, and Drum had his crew wrestle their gun into the road and roll it toward the castle, to support the attack. Benjamin soon followed him with a nine-pounder he had requisitioned. Porter had sent for another eight-inch howitzer, and it arrived just in time for him to throw three more shells at the infantry and batteries at the base of Chapultepec before he ceased fire, fearful of hitting his own men.[48]

Persifor Smith's Regular brigade assailed a battery planted where the Tacubaya road met the Chapultepec causeway, east of the citadel, with James Shields coming up behind at the head of his New York and South Carolina volunteers and U.S. Marines. Captain Silas Casey led a storming party from Riley's brigade, including many volunteers from the 4th Artillery, but Casey started for the rear early, wounded, leaving his column to Captains Gabriel Paul and Benjamin Roberts. Shields and the two volunteer regiments left the road and bolted cross-country for the castle, finding a break in the stone wall that surrounded it. From the vicinity of Molino del Rey, Pillow sent two regiments down the road that passed just north of Chapultepec while the rest of his division and another storming party swarmed through the grove west of Chapultepec, aiming for the opposite slope.[49]

Blue uniforms surged up the slope of Chapultepec, engulfing a battery on the way, and scaling ladders soon clattered against the ramparts of the fortress. Santa Anna had reduced the garrison to avoid casualties from the American artillery, which had kept up such an intense fire with an abundance of captured ordnance and ammunition that Mexican reinforcements had not been able to run the gantlet when the time came. Remarkably few of Scott's men fell in the assault, and within an hour the Mexican flag came down and Old Glory fluttered up in its place.[50]

After the castle had been secured, the fight swung back to the causeways as Santa Anna defended the gates into the city. Scott wanted Quitman to demonstrate against the heavily defended Belén Gate from the Chapultepec causeway while Worth's troops made the main attack on the San Cosme Gate, where he expected less resistance. Enthusiasm or ego dissuaded Quitman from such restraint, and his half of the fight grew especially bloody. From the captured battery at the intersection of the Tacubaya and Chapultepec roads Quitman himself led a mélange of his and other troops toward the city. The Mounted Rifles—the regiment Lieutenant Porter had declined to join—took the van, fighting on foot; the South Carolinians Shields called his Palmettos went with them. Captain Drum abandoned his big gun at the brink of a deep ditch at the captured barricade, commandeering a light Mexican fieldpiece on the far side. Lieutenant Benjamin followed with the nine-pounder.[51]

Other troops from Smith's brigade filled in the ditch, and eventually Porter was able to wheel the eight-inch howitzer over it. Drum and Benjamin had to advance their fieldpieces on the causeway, which consisted of a wide roadway divided by a massive aqueduct, while the foot soldiers fought from one arch of the aqueduct to the next. They had progressed about a mile by late morning when, at a building General Smith called Casa Colorada, they encountered another barricade augmented by an artillery redan shielding two guns. The marsh prevented anyone from leaving the causeway to flank the position, and the Americans suffered heavily there, as Scott had anticipated. The delay allowed Porter and his howitzer to catch up, but before he could bring the gun into battery a spent canister round or grapeshot struck him in the shoulder with enough force to knock him unconscious. Soldiers carried him to the protection of one of the aqueduct arches, and Captain Drum took Porter's heavier howitzer in place of his puny four-pounder fieldpiece. When the infantry finally overran the redan, Benjamin's crew seized a sixteen-pounder the Mexicans left behind and started rolling it toward the Garita de Belén, another mile away.[52]

Three guns and a well-garrisoned fort known as the Ciudadela protected the gate itself, which lay at the intersection of the Chapultepec causeway and the causeway from the village of Piedad, to the south. The battle raged there at length, and Porter, who staggered up to report to Drum, was sent back twice for more ammunition. Both the howitzer and the sixteen-pounder were running low when Drum dispatched him a third time, but as he was bringing up another wagonload a round shot broke the axle. With both guns out of ammunition, Drum retrieved Benjamin's nine-pounder and had it wheeled completely through the gate to punish the defenders from their vulnerable side. He was killed at the gun, and with many of their men dead or wounded Benjamin took over loading and firing it with the help of the first sergeant, but both were fatally injured by the same projectile. As Porter raced to the gate he encountered men carrying Drum, Benjamin, and the sergeant to the rear. Thus did he learn that through attrition he had become commander of the battery, in which only a handful of privates and one corporal remained standing. "There has been no greater slaughter in any one company during the whole war," wrote Lieutenant Daniel Harvey Hill, of the same regiment, who noted that more than two-thirds of Company G had been killed or disabled.[53]

By then it was a couple of hours past noon, and U.S. forces held control of the Garita de Belén the rest of the afternoon, with some troops advancing into the city, but Mexicans maintained a heavy fire against them and still held the Ciudadela. Worth's men had crossed the San Cosme causeway and fought their way house to house toward that gate, which they approached toward dusk. Scott ordered Worth and Quitman to settle in where they were and be prepared to combine against the Ciudadela in the morning.[54]

Before dawn a deputation of city leaders awakened Scott to say that the Mexican army was gone, and he sent Quitman ahead to the Grand Plaza in the center of the city to raise the United States flag over the National Palace. Guerrillas and bandits continued sniping at the victors through September 14, killing and wounding scores in Scott's depleted army, which he thought now numbered fewer than six thousand. Troops roamed the streets and raided houses throughout the city, killing every armed man they found. D. H. Hill, who had complained that Major John Gardner seemed too timid in command of the 4th Artillery on September 13, blamed Gardner for the regiment taking a marginal role in eradicating the guerrillas. By the next day those irregular fighters were driven out, or underground. Assassins continued to target American soldiers who prowled the city alone at night, but for the conquerors and inhabitants of Mexico City the fighting was essentially over.[55]

3

THE MAJOR

Along with the other officers in General Twiggs's division, Porter took quarters in the National Palace. Mexico City proved disappointingly small, but in their newfound moments of leisure the officers toured the churches, museum, and government buildings. Wealthy dons who shunned Scott's forces in public entertained the officers in their homes. The impoverished *lépero* class glared sullenly, and the priests, whom the soldiers thought influenced the léperos, seemed even more hostile. Most of the officers returned the sentiment in full, considering the clerics lecherous and corrupt.[1]

Two weeks into the occupation, the 4th Artillery marched to Chapultepec to escort the bodies of Captain Drum and Lieutenant Benjamin back to the city, where they were sealed in lead coffins and buried in the gardens at the National Palace. There the pair would lie until the remains could be taken home. The regiment had suffered so heavily in officers and men that a first lieutenant sometimes had to assume command.[2]

Some of Scott's officers met in a building near the Grand Plaza in October and established a fraternal order they called the Aztec Club. General Quitman accepted the presidency, and a membership fee of twenty dollars afforded members access to a comfortable clubhouse in a private home. Over the next few weeks 160 of the officers quartered in and around the capital were welcomed to membership, including Lieutenant Porter. Most were Regulars who shared similar professional training, generally conservative views, and a conciliatory attitude toward populations they had conquered.[3]

When Major Gardner resumed command of the 4th Artillery he applied to have the regiment transferred to Vera Cruz — "to be out of harm's way," suspected Lieutenant D. H. Hill, who doubted the old major's courage; "I believe that he would make a good village Postmaster," Hill supposed. Gardner's officers hated the idea of such garrison duty — some because it would shelve them, and some because Vera Cruz would be a deadly post if the war lasted into another season of *vomito*, as the Mexicans called yellow fever.[4] The transfer to Vera Cruz never came to pass, but on the first of November a long wagon train started for Vera Cruz under an escort that included Company G, 4th Artillery, commanded by Lieutenant Porter. Porter soon relinquished command to Lieutenant Mansfield Lovell, who exchanged the battery's captured heavy artillery for light fieldpieces at Vera Cruz and led it back to Mexico City in December.[5]

In another reorganization of the army, Scott gave Company G of the 4th Artillery to General Patterson's division. As the executive officer of one of Patterson's two artillery batteries, and one of the most experienced officers in his division, Lieutenant Porter must have become acquainted with the general during the two months they occupied the same camp. They would also have encountered each other at the Aztec Club, and their association would have some influence on Porter's future.[6]

Early in February, Porter and his company turned away from the comforts of the city, marching more than fifty miles south to support a brigade sent to collect district assessments in the city of Cuernavaca. The battery arrived on February 5 and remained until near the end of May, when brigade, battery, and all marched back to the capital in preparation for the long journey home.[7]

In June, with a treaty ratified, the army of occupation started packing up and marching for the coast, where the season for yellow fever was already well under way. Battery G went into camp at Jalapa on June 10, and within a fortnight the other scattered companies of the 4th Artillery reunited there. After several days' rest the regiment started making its way toward the coast in small detachments and by short marches, lingering in the healthier highlands as long as possible while transports carried the rest of the army away from the coast. On June 30 the leading company reached the campsite where Twiggs had camped the night before the battle of Cerro Gordo — "a low, dirty, unhealthy place," complained Lieutenant Francis Collins, in Company C. It was, he said, "the limit of the vomito." For that reason the pace of the march accelerated, and on July 3 the leading company caught sight of the Gulf of Mexico, bedding down that night in steaming Vera Cruz. For lack of transports those first arrivals endured ten days in their miasmic camp while their surgeons howled — wanting the men to march back into the mountains until the ships arrived — but by the middle of July the entire regiment had sailed.[8]

Company G stopped at New Orleans just long enough to unload the battery horses before continuing around Florida and up the coast to the old post at Fort Monroe. The ships carrying various fragments of the 4th Artillery dropped anchor in Hampton Roads in the middle of August. Colonel Walbach greeted them at the fort, and that night Lieutenant Porter and his surviving comrades slept in their old quarters for the first time in more than two years — "as though we had not been absent," remarked Lieutenant Collins.[9]

Company G remained at Fort Monroe for ten weeks, recruiting. The muster roll tallied only three dozen men, present and absent, but the general depot supplied eleven more through September and October. In September Porter acknowledged a brevet promotion to captain for his services at Contreras, and he commanded the company that fall while Lieutenant Lovell sailed for New York on a convalescent furlough. Porter was still in command on November 6, when his company and six others of the 4th Artillery took ship for Florida under Major Gardner—now a brevet colonel. Eleven days later, after another trip around the tip of Florida, they clambered into boats in Pensacola Bay and scattered toward three different forts guarding the harbor. Gardner and three companies, including Porter's, landed at Fort Pickens.[10]

In March came another brevet promotion for Porter, to major, in recognition of the accolades he earned for his part in the capture of Mexico City. John Sedgwick, whose commission as captain in the line was announced in the same order, discounted the worth of brevet promotions. "The staff and the particular friends of the General are all sure to get one," Sedgwick explained to his father, "and then if there are any left, others that happen to be in Washington get them." Captain Drum had helped Porter to win his brevet, first by praising him for Molino del Rey and then by getting killed, which ended any chance of Drum reaping the reward. Porter did deserve the acclaim, and unlike Sedgwick he relished it. For the next dozen years he would be known as "Major" Porter, and he had earned the title less than four years after his graduation from West Point. To him and those below him, it seemed a meteoric rise.[11]

Porter performed well in the increasingly scientific artillery service, the intellectual demands of which ranked second only to the engineering department in the middle of the nineteenth century. He always preferred the cavalry, and it galled him over the years that his request for that branch was never gratified, but he found himself in demand for duties that required technical expertise. The U.S. Coast Survey was mapping the shore of northwest Florida when he arrived there, and officers connected with the survey apparently recommended him to the superintendent for duty with their team. Porter was one of several in his regiment "who are qualified by turn of mind for said service," wrote the superintendent, but it went to someone else. Then, only three months into his stay at Fort Pickens, he received orders to report to West Point as assistant professor of natural and experimental philosophy.[12]

He arrived early in March of 1849 for six and a half years that may have been the most pleasant portion of his army career. The former classmates and comrades then on the faculty included William B. Franklin, who had graduated first in the class of 1843 and who taught the same subject as Porter. With the post engineer company he also found George McClellan, the second-ranking graduate of 1846, who had followed him and Simon Drum onto the Pedregal on that blazing August day in 1847. In his months of teaching that era's version of physics, Porter mingled mainly with the second-classmen, but he would have come to recognize those who graduated in June — at least three of whom he would face across different battlefields, thirteen years hence.[13]

At the end of summer Porter assumed new responsibilities as assistant instructor in artillery. On the first day of classes, 221 cadets spilled out of the barracks for morning roll call, and all but 30 of them would eventually graduate, but a few, such as Cadet Philip H. Sheridan of Ohio, were forced to repeat a year. That September morning the assembled corps included 45 young men who would become full generals in the U.S. service or in the Confederate army; a handful of others would earn a star by brevet. Some of them would later command troops under Porter — or, like John Bell Hood, lead those who fought him. A few would grow very close to Porter. High in the first class stood nineteen-year-old Gouverneur Kemble Warren, from nearby Cold Spring, New York; Elisha G. Marshall, from central New York, lagged much lower in the same class, in his fifth year at the academy. Robert E. Patterson, son of General Patterson, had already been turned back from the class of 1850, and was repeating his third year.[14]

It became obvious early on that Porter would be a strict disciplinarian and a demanding instructor. Those were the qualities remembered most often by former cadets after Porter's death, sometimes with ameliorating reflections on his fairness, impartiality, courtesy, and dignity.[15] One vivid recollection from early in Porter's tenure on the faculty dated from that first autumn, in 1849, during artillery drill. Clouds gathered quickly and burst into a drenching downpour, and while the infantry battalion ran for cover Porter sat calmly on his horse, continuing to exercise the crews throughout the torrent.[16]

Projecting the voice was as crucial to the commander of troops on parade as it was to an actor on the stage, and Porter's was more penetrating than most. Caleb Huse, who graduated in 1851 and later joined Porter on the faculty, remembered that few of the infantry instructors could even make themselves heard by everyone in their own formations as they marched at one end of the plain. Meanwhile, as Porter ordered the gun crews "Forward into battery, left oblique, trot, *march!*" not only the gunners but the entire infantry battalion at the far end of the same field could hear what Huse called his "clear tenor."[17]

Judging at least by the old-age memories of his former students, Porter was held in high esteem by a cadet corps that could be incisive in its mimicry and ridicule. There were few lieutenants with brevets as major, Huse noted, adding that the cadets "looked up to him as quite superior to the other lieutenants on duty as instructors." Although George Ruggles was stripped of a cadet office three months before graduation when Porter caught him returning from an illicit frolic, he remained an admirer of the "major." Ruggles portrayed his old instructor as "of most soldierly appearance and carriage, rather cold than magnetic, but eminently just and always an example for our emulation." Porter was on the staff from the day Ruggles arrived at West Point until he graduated, and half a century later Ruggles could not recall a single complaint or criticism about him. "He won and always commanded our highest respect and admiration," Ruggles insisted.[18]

Andrew Evans corroborated Ruggles in describing Porter as proud and "perhaps haughty," but he considered that becoming in someone of Porter's "great dignity." Competence and confidence afforded him a reassuring presence. During the dangerous mounting of huge siege guns, Porter managed to convey his own composure to the students when nerves and knowledge made the difference between gratifying achievement and grievous accident; he could maneuver the light battery or work the guns with impressive speed and precision. The most convincing evidence of the cadets' regard for Porter may have been Evans's observation that he was one instructor for whom they concocted no nickname.[19]

Cyrus Comstock, who attended West Point during Porter's last four years on the faculty, shared that esteem until his final year at the academy. After receiving an admittedly gentle and merited correction from Porter, Comstock started referring to him with mild disrespect as "Fitz John," and his professed fondness withered under increasingly rigorous criticism and discipline. He had observed as early as his second year that Porter never hesitated to report misbehavior, and that poor drill performances "disgusted" him, while disappointment in or disapproval of cadets provoked him to sharply sarcastic commentary.[20]

After two years of hardship in Mexico and isolation in coastal forts, the long sojourn along the Hudson offered inviting social opportunities for Porter as part of the academy faculty. In June each year wealthy New Yorkers flocked to West Point, summering at Cozzens's Hotel. At the annual examinations those visitors enjoyed the parades, the riding and fencing exhibitions, and the shooting, taking great amusement in the target practice of Porter's students with siege guns, field artillery, and mortars. They rusticated on the Hudson well into autumn, attending special exhibitions now and then, and they often invited post officers to dine. Alone or with fellow officers, Porter's reserve sometimes melted at the tables of refined sojourners such as Gramercy Park lawyer George Templeton Strong, whose family the major impressed with his volubility each summer.[21]

In his early months on the staff, Porter lived in humbler post housing with several bachelor officers. Three other members of the regular faculty took rooms there by the summer of 1850, as did McClellan and one other engineer officer. McClellan, who had been on duty at West Point for months when Porter arrived, may have suggested that he lodge with them. It was probably in that house that the most momentous and influential friendship of Porter's life began to flourish.[22]

Late that summer another brevet major who had graduated in the class after Porter's arrived on a tour of court-martial duty. Thomas J. Jackson, a quirky Virginian, declined Porter's offer to share his room and ended up taking his meals at the poorly heated hotel. Jackson ate mainly rice, as Porter later remembered, and with none available at the hotel he nearly starved. "He fancied all other food went into his leg & kept his system unequally balanced," Porter later told a younger officer, "and he would not go to the mess lest he should be tempted with the flesh pots." Jackson was "silent & morose," Porter said, and he was a hypochondriac. He took daily walks, in which he periodically threw his cane from his left hand to his right, and then back again, fearing that "one side of his body should get more exercise than the other."[23]

Porter made the most of the relative wilderness of Orange County, particularly in his first year or two. He, McClellan, and Dabney Maury, a lieutenant from Virginia, fished for perch in the Hudson and its tributaries and hunted in the mountains upriver from the academy. Before the railroad came, isolation gave West Point an epic grandeur, moving an editor to compare the river vistas favorably to anything on the Rhine. Maury, Porter, and a couple of other regular companions enjoyed hunting expeditions over the mountain to the farm of Micah Dickerson, on the Newburgh Turnpike, who offered rooms for the stage traffic. One major appeal of the spot was evidently Dickerson's "handsome and cultivated daughter," Mary, who cooked, polished their boots, and provided their evening music. Porter and Maury also befriended a wealthy iron manufacturer, Peter Townsend, and would ride to his estate for the evening, sleeping there and riding back in time for duty in the morning.[24]

Late in November of 1850, Porter took a week's leave for a trip to Washington. The packet boat was likely still running to New York that late in the year, otherwise the only way out of West Point was by stagecoach over the mountains to the Erie Railroad. He arrived in the capital November 26, took a room at Willard's Hotel on Pennsylvania Avenue at Fourteenth Street, and collected his mother from Alexandria. After another night at Willard's, he brought her up to Orange County to live with him in Cornwall. Eliza's older son, Bolton, had been at sea almost continually since his promotion to lieutenant in the spring of 1849; her grandson, Lucian, had gone back to his father's plantation in Louisiana, and with no income but her pension she had to depend on her two remaining children for housing. She and Porter soon moved into more spacious quarters, sharing one of West Point's bigger stone houses with the family of Porter's old French professor, Hyacinthe Agnel. Soon after they arrived at West Point, Porter applied for 160 acres of bounty land authorized for Mexican War veterans by recent legislation, intending to hold it for the benefit of his mother should anything happen to him.[25]

While he was nominally the assistant instructor of artillery, Porter tended to attract additional duties as his superiors recognized his broad competence and his eagerness to serve. During any vacancy he was likely to be asked to shoulder temporary responsibilities, such as at the end of 1850 and early in 1851, when he assumed the jobs of recruiting and administrative reporting for the dragoon detachment at West Point. George H. Thomas, another first lieutenant and brevet major, relieved him after a few months, taking over as chief instructor of cavalry and artillery early in 1851.[26]

All who saw Porter noticed his soldierly appearance. He always wore the double-breasted coat of a field officer, as his brevet rank allowed. He stood ramrod straight, and taller than most of his contemporaries at five feet, eleven inches. His horsemanship drew admiring notice, and in the 1850s he wore a close-trimmed version of the muttonchops known as English side-whiskers then favored by such highly regarded officers as Captain Robert E. Lee. Lee, the most prominent if not the most senior of the engineers in Scott's Mexico City campaign, took charge of West Point as superintendent in the summer of 1852, under his brevet rank of colonel.[27]

A couple of weeks before Lee's arrival, a court of inquiry convened to look into numerous cases, including a scandal among some upperclassmen who had been deviling newly appointed cadets during their entrance examinations. John M. Schofield, who had just completed his third year, had been instructing a few aspiring cadets in mathematics the previous June when some of his classmates wandered into the room to haze his pupils. Schofield was offering practical problems, such as how long it would take a frog to jump out of a well of a certain depth if it could leap eight feet high but fell back four feet each time. In vulgar echo of that question, Oliver D. Greene of the first class braced one of the novices, asking him "if a man farted on the first round of a ladder, how high would he get before he shit?" Another upperclassman ordered Plebe Dabney Herndon to draw an "inverted woman." Testimony put Schofield out of the room at the time, but the court tried him for disorderly conduct, neglect of duty, and disobedience of orders for "failing to exercise proper vigilance and discipline." Porter was appointed to the court-martial, along with George Thomas, Lieutenant Colonel Philip St. George Cooke of the 1st Dragoons, and ten other officers, with Major John Lee as judge advocate.[28]

One of the court members had been reinstated to the army himself only a year and a half before, after being sentenced to dismissal for a host of serious violations. Brevet Lieutenant Colonel Benjamin S. Roberts, an 1835 West Point graduate, had resigned under duress in 1839, after $3,000 in government funds disappeared from his custody. In 1846 he secured reappointment to the new regiment of mounted rifles, but three years later he had been convicted at Fort Laramie of gross and habitual neglect of duty, falsifying his accounts and official returns, and conduct unbecoming an officer—for repeatedly lying to different officers to cover his malfeasance. One former comrade characterized Roberts as a "barefaced swindler," perhaps in humorous explanation of the initials in his signature. Some highly respected career officers considered Roberts's word worthless even under oath, but early in 1851 he persuaded the secretary of war to disapprove the worst of his convictions, allowing him to return to duty. Now he sat in judgment on Cadet Schofield.[29]

The court determined that Schofield had been present for at least a portion of the hazing, and while he had tried to dissuade the other upperclassmen from it, he had not reported them to the staff. For that he was found guilty of the charges, and his general conduct came under scrutiny in order to determine an appropriate sentence. Schofield had finished his third year sixth in his class, and several professors praised his deportment. Two cadets confirmed that Schofield was universally "considered as a gentleman," and the court seemed content to suspend him for a year, allowing him to return in the summer of 1853.[30]

Someone on the staff must have immediately complained. During the court of inquiry Lieutenant John M. Jones, an assistant instructor of infantry tactics, had described Schofield as "very inferior" in character, adding that he had opposed Schofield's appointment as a cadet officer in the first class. The commandant of cadets thought Schofield conducted himself well enough, but he deferred to the commander of his company, adding that Lieutenant Jones had opposed Schofield's promotion. The court that had dealt relatively leniently with Schofield on Tuesday reconvened on Wednesday, September 29, and without explanation converted his sentence to outright dismissal. Five members of the court, with Roberts among them, endorsed a petition recommending executive clemency, which would have instantly restored him in his original class, but Porter and Thomas were among those who did not sign.[31]

Dismissal constituted an unduly harsh punishment in Schofield's case, and clemency seemed perfectly reasonable. The same court issued similar petitions for cadets guilty of far more deliberate and serious infractions, including outright insubordination, with as many as eleven members voting for reprieve, including Thomas and Porter. The record of Schofield's trial offers nothing to justify such severity, and the court may have resorted to technical dismissal and immediate reinstatement to sustain discipline in principle without doing him any harm. Only seven of the thirteen officers assigned to the court had to be present to conduct business, and Schofield was restored immediately, as though the signatures of five members represented a majority of the court on that day. Schofield saw the record sixteen years later, and may have been misled by the jumble of loose clemency petitions in the same file with his, but he came away convinced that only Thomas and Porter had declined to sign. It evidently pained him to think that those two had denied him leniency, because he admired them both and later treated both quite generously. He could not fathom why they "could not find it in their hearts to recommend clemency to an erring youth." [32]

Disciplinarian though he certainly was, Porter hardly seemed so unyielding. A couple of years later, when confronted with another opportunity to show sympathy for a faltering cadet, Porter responded magnanimously enough. William Woods Averell had accumulated 108 demerits between July and December of his final year, for which he was facing suspension. Colonel Lee advised him to consider whether any of his infractions involved extenuating circumstances that might persuade the reporting officers to forgive them, and Averell went to both Porter and Delos B. Sacket, who had cited him for a total of seven. "After a few kind words of admonition," as Averell put it, they both agreed to recommend removal of the seven demerits. Lee expunged one himself, reducing Averell to the maximum allowable for a half-year, and seven years later Averell was commanding cavalry under Porter — leading it against their former superintendent. [33]

By the time of the Schofield court-martial, Colonel Lee had installed Porter as the riding instructor. Apparently he began by standing in for the regular assistant instructor of cavalry, Sacket — an enormous dragoon officer weighing nearly 250 pounds. After a couple of lessons with Porter, Cadet Comstock remarked that he liked him as well as he had Sacket, and in the spring of his third year he still enjoyed Porter's artillery classes. Comstock bristled the next August, when Porter first corrected him in directing the artillery battery, and by December he seemed delighted to avoid Porter for his next artillery course. As graduation approached, with the studious Comstock and a much-younger Godfrey Weitzel vying for first place, Porter and some of his better friends on the faculty appeared to work hard at "hiving" them, or catching them in compromising behavior. Porter rebuked them in "his inimitable drawl," wrote Comstock, and held them to demerits that drew extra duty or confinement to quarters, but at the last minute he withdrew the most consequential charges. Six weeks before graduation, when he assigned Comstock as chief of caissons for the first time, Porter "got sarcastic as usual" and told the cadets their drill was worse than that of raw volunteers. Still, he ranked Comstock first in his class in artillery drill. [34]

When George Thomas returned to his regiment in the spring of 1854, Porter became the chief instructor of both artillery and cavalry tactics. The addition of riding instruction and cavalry tactics to his duties encouraged Porter to hope that he might eventually see a reassignment to the cavalry, where he had always wanted to serve. In addition to his classes, Porter also spent much of 1854 acting as post adjutant to Colonel Lee, replacing Seth Williams. Early that summer he went to New York City on the adjutant's annual junket to supervise the printing of the cadet register. On that errand he may have visited with some of the New Yorkers who were then flitting back and forth between the city and West Point.[35]

In the last week of October that year, New York City's leisure class enjoyed a display of Major William Hardee's new drill manual for light infantry, demonstrated on the West Point plain by the corps of cadets. The exhibition drew militia bigwigs from Pennsylvania, Massachusetts, and New York, including socialite Captain Daniel Butterfield of the 71st New York Militia. Stubborn traditionalists scorned the new system as the Shanghai Drill, in evident allusion to the double-quick movements it required, and after the exercises Colonel Lee entertained the questions of the civilians. He and some of the professors explained the differences between Hardee's forthcoming manual and General Scott's slower-paced 1835 version. Tactical instructors added some commentary of their own, including Hardee himself and Porter, who admitted that he was growing pretty rusty in infantry drill after seven years of artillery and cavalry duty.[36]

Such an event may have been the occasion of Porter's first encounter with Harriet Pierson Cook, the niece of Nancy Holbrook. Mrs. Holbrook and her late husband, a wealthy New York merchant, had raised Harriet in their home. They lived at 66 Union Place, a comfortable house on a half-acre lot dominating the northeast corner of Fourth Avenue and East Eighteenth Street, just above Union Square. Mrs. Holbrook and Miss Cook belonged to Trinity Church and attended services at Trinity Chapel, as did Porter's Gramercy Park friend and sometime host, George Templeton Strong. Strong knew Mrs. Holbrook's nearest neighbors, and was still in direct touch with Porter as late as mid-September of 1855, making him a likely medium of introduction.[37]

This was Porter's last year of teaching cadets. He enjoyed a longer stint than usual among active-duty officers assigned as academy faculty, most of whom served between two and four years. As he approached the age of thirty-three he had become one of the army's senior first lieutenants, and he grew restless for a position that would allow him to advance further. In March of 1855 Congress authorized the organization of two regiments of cavalry, and officers who had gone so long without promotion submitted a flurry of applications for commissions. Porter sought one for himself, still craving duty in a mounted arm, and several of his colleagues from the West Point staff were favored with promotions: Delos Sacket was made a captain in the 1st Cavalry. George Thomas jumped to major in the 2nd Cavalry, and the superintendent, Robert E. Lee, rose to the full rank of lieutenant colonel in the same regiment.[38]

Porter would be left out. No promotion in the line came to him, and he was passed over for a position in the Adjutant General's Department, which he also applied for when the new regiments began creating vacancies. The adjutant general's slot carried only the rank and pay of brevet captain, but it would have averted the impending likelihood of reassignment to his regiment in some obscure fort. That appointment went to a lieutenant even more senior than Porter, while Porter's application for promotion in the line, with a preference for the cavalry, went awry. Late in the fall, after he had been transferred to a remote wilderness post, he learned from his mother how his promotion had been foiled by misunderstanding. Eliza had gone to see Secretary of War Jefferson Davis herself early in November, asking why her son was overlooked, and she was told he had declined a promotion to captain in the infantry. Porter immediately wrote to Davis, explaining that had he known of any such offer he would have accepted it, notwithstanding his preference for the cavalry, but by then Davis had no further promotions to offer.[39]

Thus, instead of riding the plains with the cavalry that autumn or taking command of his own infantry company, Porter reported to Fort Brady, at Sault Ste. Marie, on Michigan's Upper Peninsula. Compared to the prestige of West Point and the social opportunities of the lower Hudson Valley, the tiny outpost on the Canadian border must have seemed desolate. The closest he came to civilization in ten months was a jaunt by water down to Detroit the next spring, to buy supplies for the fort, but in the summer of 1856 his earlier exchange with Secretary Davis saved him from his woodland exile. In apparent compensation for his disappointment over the promotion, Davis offered him the next opening in the adjutant general's office. Porter made haste to accept, even agreeing to waive any chance of promotion in his old regiment for this opportunity to move closer to the heart of army operations.[40]

With the new assignment Porter left Fort Brady on August 6, bound for Fort Leavenworth, Kansas, where the army was trying to keep the peace between proslavery and Free State settlers. On its way up the Missouri River, Porter's steamboat echoed with talk of the Kansas troubles. "Every man was armed with his revolver and knife," Porter remembered later, "and flooded with Dutch courage." Persifor Smith, now a brevet major general, commanded the Department of the West from Leavenworth, and Porter became his assistant adjutant general. Marauding the previous spring by proslave Missourians, and retaliatory raids by abolition factions under John Brown, James Lane, and others, had initiated widespread violence that was aggravated by opportunistic brigands. Detachments of a few hundred soldiers, mostly mounted, ventured west and north from Leavenworth in search of armed bands of any political persuasion. Porter arrived at the end of August, just as competing rumors of invasions by "border ruffians" and a "Northern army" of abolitionists electrified the population. A couple of days after his appearance at Fort Leavenworth, citizens of the nearby community drove all the suspected Free State sympathizers out of town.[41]

For two months it was Porter's task to coordinate the movements of detachments Smith had sent out to keep the peace. One of the first letters he wrote began with a vicarious reprimand to the commander of the troops in the field. On behalf of the general, Porter chastised Lieutenant Colonel Cooke—he of the West Point court-martial, who had entered West Point when Porter was an infant—for not reporting his whereabouts often enough. He also lectured Cooke for crediting the peaceful pretensions of large, armed bands. That letter set a sour tone that persisted between Porter and Cooke for the next thirty years.[42]

Cooke had been patrolling near Lecompton when Governor John Geary warned that hundreds of men under Lane were coming that way from Nebraska City—where Porter's Mexican War bounty land lay. With a squadron of dragoons, some infantry, and Porter's old Company G, 4th Artillery, Cooke turned north. On October 3 he combined forces with a detachment of the 1st Cavalry under Joseph E. Johnston, a Virginian whom Porter had befriended in Mexico.[43]

Free State fighters were indeed abundant in the vicinity of Nebraska City at that time, but most of them were traveling north, on a roundabout route back to the East through Iowa. John Brown was then on his way out of Kansas with a fair-sized wagon train, and Cooke hoped to arrest him for murdering five unarmed men on Pottawatomie Creek in May. On the night of October 5 Cooke diverted a mounted company to a house where Brown was reported to be resting, but he had departed that afternoon. Hastening on to the Nemaha River, south of Nebraska City, Cooke and Johnston missed their prey again when Brown's party risked getting lost on the unmarked prairie to skirt the cavalry that was blocking the only road. Cooke and Johnston stopped the rest of the train, consisting of well over two hundred heavily armed men and five women carrying no furniture or farm implements, and arrested them all.[44]

Cooke and Johnston came that close to stopping the man who, three years later, would put a match to the powder keg American politics had become. Cooke returned to Kansas, leaving Johnston behind to keep watch and report back through Porter—whom Johnston affectionately called "Master Fitz"—but after the Kansas election of October 6 tensions momentarily subsided. On November 11 General Smith assured the adjutant general "that I consider tranquility and order entirely restored in Kansas." On that news, Major Porter applied for his first leave of absence in eleven years. By the end of November he was back in New York City, boarding in the home of his cousin, Lieutenant David Dixon Porter of the U.S. Navy.[45]

He clearly started his leave in New York to indulge his interest in Harriet Cook, but in late December he took the train to Baltimore and thence to the College of St. James, located between Hagerstown and Williamsport, Maryland. There his mother was again living with her grandchild, Lucian Waddell, who had taken a position as tutor at the college. On New Year's Eve, Porter reported in Washington for temporary duty as overseer of publication for the 1857 edition of the U.S. Army regulations, which took him back to New York. The manuscript arrived late in January at his room in the St. Denis Hotel, and after negotiations with New York publishing houses he settled on Harper Brothers. Early in March he expressed the first unbound copies to Washington, delivering the balance of the run to a quartermaster in New York by March 12.[46]

One week later, the thirty-four-year-old Major Porter and Miss Cook, who was not quite twenty-four, appeared in Trinity Chapel to be married by their young Episcopal priest, Morgan Dix. The bride's parents, John and Julia Cook, may have been present; Julia's sister Nancy Holbrook, who had raised Harriet, would certainly have attended. Porter's brother and his cousin had both gone back to sea, and no close comrades or friends were then in the city to act as best man, so the priest's father, former U.S. senator John A. Dix, stood in as a witness.[47]

Porter and his bride moved into Mrs. Holbrook's house at 66 Union Place, which would remain his home of record for the next decade. He was awaiting imminent instructions from the adjutant general about another publication project—a report by his friend and classmate McClellan of his observations among European armies in the Crimean War. No more than a week after his wedding, Porter returned to Washington for that manuscript, perhaps taking Harriet along for a honeymoon, but in a few days he was back in New York. He spent another seven weeks there, attending to the editing and printing preparations. Early in May he paid an official visit to General Scott, who had moved army headquarters to West Point, where they discussed his next assignment.[48]

That conversation would lead to the longest overland journey of Porter's life. The federal government was then facing a challenge from Brigham Young, the Mormon leader who had been serving as territorial governor of Utah. Soon after assuming the presidency, James Buchanan assigned a non-Mormon successor, Alfred Cumming, but it looked as though a military presence might be necessary to seat him over Young's opposition. General Scott had ordered William Harney to Fort Leavenworth from duty in Florida, and as Harney made his way up the Mississippi and Missouri Rivers newspaper speculation already had him bound for Utah with several thousand men. Meanwhile, Porter saw General Scott on subjects that may have included Utah, after which Porter began heading his letters "Head Quarters Department of the West, New York City," as though he, too, were bound for Leavenworth. Instead, he remained in New York four more months, floating between his publishing project in the city and court-martial duty at West Point.[49]

General Smith labored under the ailment that would kill him ere many months: he was commanding the Department of the West from a sickbed in the East. Harney, as a brevet brigadier, was the next most senior man fit for a campaign. General Scott harbored reservations about Harney, whom he resented for the habit of communicating directly with his civilian superiors, but by the middle of June Scott gave him to understand that he would probably command the Utah expedition. At the end of June, Harney had specific orders to proceed with his command, which would act as a posse comitatus in case the Mormons resisted Cumming's installation as governor.[50]

Rumors circulated that Harney was reluctant to undertake the campaign — as were many of the officers and enlisted men, who respectively began submitting their resignations or deserting from the post. Harney warned that he had encountered heavy snow in the Rockies as early as the beginning of October, and he seemed to suggest that the campaign should have gotten under way sooner. He started the better part of two infantry regiments and a battery westward in July, as ordered, but three weeks later he reported pessimistically on nearly half the two-thousand-head herd of cattle for the Utah forces being stolen by raiding Cheyenne. Smith's illness and a plea by the governor of Kansas to keep Harney at Leavenworth inspired Scott to make Harney acting commander of the Department of the West and replace him at the head of the Utah army with Colonel Albert Sidney Johnston. Johnston — a Kentuckian, and no relation to Porter's friend Joe Johnston — would need an adjutant general: Smith's disability freed Porter, and late in August he finally did draw orders to return to Fort Leavenworth, but with an assignment to the Army of Utah, rather than the Department of the West.[51]

Leaving McClellan's manuscript at 66 Union Place, he bid good-bye to Harriet, who was four months' pregnant. On September 1 he started from New York City on what he knew would be a long and potentially dangerous assignment. His mother met him in Baltimore when he changed trains there, but they had only a few hours before she started back to the College of St. James, and he dared not reveal the specifics of his mission. "I thought it would break her heart," he told Harriet.[52]

It was a four-day train trip to the Mississippi from Baltimore, during which Porter slept in his seat, fully clothed, when he slept at all. He arrived in steaming St. Louis on September 7, and there met Colonel Johnston himself, who had occupied another car on the same train all the way from Indianapolis. They were unacquainted, but perhaps Johnston wore his uniform, which would have distinguished him. If not, he was still an imposing figure at fifty-four years of age: he stood an inch over six feet — two inches taller than Porter, whose contemporaries considered him tall — and had added little if anything to the 180 pounds he carried in his prime. The next day the two started up the Missouri by steamboat, sharing a stateroom. They arrived at Fort Leavenworth on September 11, 1857. That very day, twelve hundred miles to the west at a place called Mountain Meadows, Mormon militiamen intent on keeping "gentiles" out of

Utah slaughtered well over a hundred men, women, and children bound from Arkansas to California.[53]

Johnston, whose rightful command consisted of the 2nd U.S. Cavalry, had left his regiment back in Texas under Lieutenant Colonel Lee. Hearing of Johnston's new assignment, Lee addressed the colonel at Fort Leavenworth and congratulated him on having secured Fitz John Porter as his adjutant general.

"I am glad you have him with you," Lee wrote. "He is an able aid in the field, & valuable everywhere."[54]

4

DESERET

William Harney's adjutant general, Captain Alfred Pleasonton, turned the funds for the Utah army over to Porter. Harney's misgivings about the expedition should have left him and Pleasonton content to be relieved from that assignment, but their relations with their successors appear to have been less than harmonious. Porter had probably not seen Pleasonton since their cadet days, but Pleasonton—a noticeably mendacious self-promoter—showed marked antagonism when they next met, five years later. In official communications Johnston commended Harney's preparations and cooperation, but Harney waited to acknowledge Johnston's orders superseding him until he received direct confirmation from Scott. Porter, meanwhile, betrayed some disdain for Harney, and shared that poor opinion with those in higher station. That censorious nature would become more apparent over the years, if not more pronounced.[1]

Porter had no sooner reached Fort Leavenworth than he entertained Harriet with an old story about Harney preparing for an Indian campaign, and curtly refusing a junior officer's request to carry along some books. "We're going out to fight Indians," Harney purportedly said; "we're not going to read books." Yet seconds later Harney's commissary officer asked for authorization to transport two barrels of whiskey. "Anything in reason, Major," Harney is supposed to have replied; "anything in reason."[2]

Through officers at Leavenworth whom he knew from earlier days, Porter also heard of Harney's dissatisfaction with either the expedition itself or its tardy start. He described a "spirit of discontent" permeating the post, but claimed that it dissipated as soon as he and Johnston arrived, ascribing that instantaneous transformation to Johnston's "firmness, energy and kindness." Porter eventually relayed tales of Harney's demoralizing lack of enthusiasm to General Scott's adjutant general, Major Irvin McDowell, with whom Porter had grown friendly during his long stint in New York. As Porter surely anticipated, McDowell passed those criticisms on to Scott.[3]

Colonel Cooke led the advance on September 17 with six companies of the

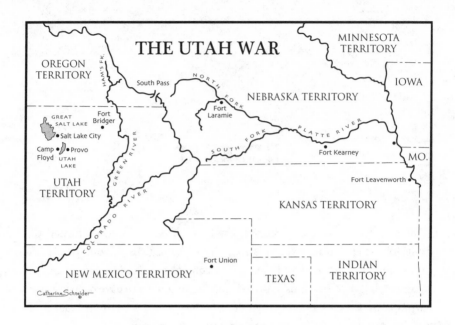

THE UTAH WAR

2nd Dragoons, escorting the wagon train and Governor Cumming, his wife, and a number of federal appointees. That morning Johnston dispatched a smaller train of twenty-one wagons guarded by five dozen troopers, and that afternoon he and Porter saddled up to canter away after them. They caught up with the smaller train and then overtook Cooke's column fifteen miles from Fort Leavenworth, just in time to camp for the night. The next day, taking the sixty cavalrymen and the twenty-one wagons, Johnston and Porter trotted ahead of Cooke. They covered more than thirty miles of a rolling plain, passing a wayfarer fresh from Utah who reported Indian depredations in the mountains and thousands of Mormons under arms, preparing to confront the U.S. Army.[4]

For ten hours every day, Johnston and Porter rode side by side. At night they shared a tent. Adjutants often grew close to the officers they served, but during their weeks on the trail Porter and Johnston developed a powerful bond.[5]

By the seventh day they traversed a harsher, more invariable environment, and early that morning they encountered a detachment of the 1st Cavalry on its way back to Leavenworth from Fort Kearney. In what he considered a "sea of barrenness," Porter rejoiced to find one company of that column commanded by his burly old friend Delos Sacket, to whom he entrusted a letter for Harriet.[6]

Fort Kearney itself appeared on the horizon on September 24 — "as miserable a hole as Uncle Sam ever built for his servants," Porter informed Harriet, with many of its structures made of stacked sod. In an official letter to Washington he described it as "a collection of miserable hovels that no white man should be forced to occupy." A few frame houses had been built on that bare landscape, but wind whistled through the walls, and Porter wondered how habitable they would be when the mercury plunged below zero. He showed no regret at leaving there the following morning.[7]

They had not gained many miles on the fort the next morning when they spotted their first buffalo—a monstrous, solitary bull that loomed into sight as they crested an undulation in the trail. Great herds of bison grazed nearby, and as the human caravan hove into view those beasts spooked and ebbed away in a dark tide. Pronghorn, too, bounded gracefully away at their approach. The leading horses flushed prairie chickens from tall grass alongside the well-worn trail, and an occasional wolf lurked in the distance. As September waned the column crossed the South Platte River and hugged the right bank of the North Platte, approaching what would become the border of Wyoming. In that vicinity they met Captain Stewart Van Vliet, a quartermaster whom Harney had sent ahead during the summer to divine whether the Mormons would accept the presence of federal troops. Three weeks out from Salt Lake City, Van Vliet told Johnston that the Mormons intended to resist him by preying on his herds and supplies and laying waste to the countryside, and if that failed to stop him they meant to fight him "to the death." Equally distressing was his report that snow fell at Fort Bridger on the night of September 15, covering the grass their animals would need for grazing. Fort Bridger lay four hundred miles ahead, and barely a hundred from Salt Lake City.[8]

The roads remained firm until the first of October, when the vanguard ran into deep sand. Then a two-day deluge slowed the march. By October 2 they had only made Scott's Bluff, and were already later than expected when they rode into Fort Laramie, near dusk on October 4. Johnston had hoped to reach Salt Lake City by October 20, leaving Cooke's slower convoy no more than a month behind, but an early winter would confound even that schedule.[9]

The infantry and artillery sent out by Harney in July had crossed the nebulous boundary between Nebraska and Oregon Territories a week before. Colonel Edmund B. Alexander commanded that contingent, with his own 10th Infantry, much of the 5th Infantry, a battery of the 4th Artillery, and a makeshift battery under Lieutenant Jesse Reno. Faced with a virtual declaration of war from Brigham Young, Alexander was turning those troops north, up Ham's Fork of the Green River, by which he considered taking a roundabout route to Salt Lake City. On October 4—the day Johnston arrived at Fort Laramie—the 5th Infantry and Reno's battery left the crossing of the Green River on the way to join Alexander at Ham's Fork. That evening a Mormon raiding party attacked three unguarded supply trains lagging behind at the Green River, burning scores of wagons. With them were lost nearly fifty tons of ham and bacon, a hundred tons of flour, bread, soap, and coffee, tens of thousands of rations of dried vegetables and fruit, vinegar, molasses, beans, sugar, and camp supplies. The raiders set fire to the grass as well, to starve the army's teams and mounts.[10]

Dawn of October 5 found the Utah army spread across nearly seven hundred miles of mountains and prairie, with Colonel Alexander's wing on Ham's Fork, Johnston's party at Fort Laramie, and Colonel Cooke's big detachment at Fort Kearney. Johnston did not hear about the burning of the supplies until October 12. To catch up with Alexander, he and Porter had gone ahead with only a squad of dragoons, leaving most of the escort at Fort Laramie. At the Three Crossings of the Sweetwater River, just short of South Pass, a pair of express messengers hired by Alexander to carry letters to Fort Laramie apprised Johnston of the raid. They also mentioned Alexander's decision to march north, up Ham's Fork, which alarmed Johnston because that route could trap the command for the winter without supplies. He doubted that any orders from him could reach Alexander because of Mormon parties roving between them, and the only other troops within a day's march were fifty infantrymen under Lieutenant Colonel Charles F. Smith. The messengers left Johnston carrying his order to hurry the rest of his escort, more of Colonel Smith's infantry, and two mounted companies under another Smith—Lieutenant William D. Smith, of the 2nd Dragoons.[11]

Johnston and Porter hastened ahead to South Pass, overtaking Colonel Smith and persuading sixty civilian workmen on the South Pass wagon road to enlist for a short term as volunteer militia. They were all waiting near South Pass to be reinforced by Lieutenant Smith's little battalion when a snowstorm struck on October 17, and that night some of their mules died in the cold. The next day, with the temperature just above freezing, the snow began to melt enough that the draft animals could graze, but winter was evidently on them. Writing to General Scott, Johnston apprised him that "our most potent enemy at present is the snow."[12]

Communications between the divided elements of Johnston's army took days to deliver, and letters to the East were weeks on the road. The dispatch Johnston intercepted from Alexander was already four days old when he read it, and McDowell did not receive Johnston's messages of October 13 and 15 until November 16. Newspapers located as far west as the Mississippi River published no tidings of the Mormon depredations until six weeks after the raid on the supply train.[13]

Despite the army's vulnerable position, Porter showed stubborn optimism in his letters home, even when he began to see that it was too late to press on to Salt Lake City before winter. "In a few days we will be on the Pacific side of the Rocky Mts," he wrote, "& then hurrah! for Utah! We will have a large force here in the spring & before the summer ends the troubles will cease, & when I have done my duty I will return home rejoicing."[14]

No one with that expedition would be going home soon. October had nearly run out before Lieutenant Smith and his hybrid command reached South Pass, bringing more provisions, and the following day Johnston led the procession through that gap in the Continental Divide. Lieutenant Smith's wagon train, added to Colonel Smith's, constituted the main food supply for the entire Utah army. With the volunteer militiamen, perhaps three hundred men walked or rode alongside to defend those stores. More snow fell on October 25, and thereafter even the daytime temperatures plunged. Covering ten to fourteen miles a day under the guidance of Jim Bridger, the aging mountain man who had built the fortified trading post that carried his name, Johnston and Porter reached the mouth of the Big Sandy River on October 30. Colonel Smith led the head of the train on past Ham's Fork, camping on Black's Fork. Four days later Johnston and his adjutant caught up with him, finding the 10th Infantry camped nearby and the balance of Alexander's command within reach.[15]

The material losses were not quite so devastating as Johnston had feared. After a quick inspection, a commissary officer informed Porter there might be enough supplies left to keep two thousand men alive for seven months, so Johnston asked army headquarters for another shipment no later than June 1. He had already concluded that it was too late to cross the Wasatch Mountains into the Great Basin; the best he could do was march on Fort Bridger, chase away the Mormon rebels reportedly in possession of it, and go into winter quarters there.[16]

A blizzard of heavy, wet snow set in during the march of November 6, alternating with rain. The next day it turned too cold for more rain, and after weeks without grain or corn and too little grass the horses and mules started dropping. So long was the train that portions did not start until afternoon, making camp near midnight. Well after daylight on November 8 a captain in the 10th Infantry set out a thermometer that recorded only three degrees above zero, and he discovered that several of his mules had died during the night. The next day he found the roadsides littered with horses and mules that were dead, dying, or too exhausted to continue. "Hundreds of animals die every twenty-four hours," he informed his wife, comparing their march with Napoleon's ill-fated Russian campaign.[17]

The blizzard seemed not to dampen Porter's spirits. Perhaps for the sake of his "Hattie," he characterized the entire army as "in good cheer" over having concentrated their forces, and he welcomed the snowfall for having wet the grass enough to foil the Mormons from burning it ahead of them. Fifty of their draft animals died every mile, he admitted, and the bitter nights depleted their cattle herds "like a pestilence." He described the full fury of the storms in his official reports as he argued Johnston's case for having decided to hibernate at Fort Bridger, but even those missives conveyed resilient morale. Only in retrospect, months later, did he admit having had some apprehension that the snows and the Mormons might combine to kill them all.[18]

So depleted and weakened were the teams, and so ferocious was the weather, that the army's march to Fort Bridger crept along at an average of two miles per day, with each day's march followed by several of rest. Porter recounted that they were four days traversing the last six miles.[19] Colonel Cooke's column suffered even worse from the elements. On the stormy night of November 10 his thermometers burst, indicating that the mercury must have fallen to twenty-five degrees below zero. Three-quarters of his mules perished in one night, and even after the weather moderated nearly half his horses died, presumably from starvation. He cached or abandoned wagons for want of teams, and distributed equipment rather than leave it: all his men, mounted or afoot, arrived near Fort Bridger on November 19 armed with new Sharps carbines.[20]

A generation later, Cooke claimed that Colonel Johnston, whom he called "an intimate friend of mine," seemed uncharacteristically timid when they were reunited at Fort Bridger. According to Cooke, he urged Johnston in vain to continue the march over the next range of mountains to Salt Lake City, and even offered to make the trek alone with his dragoons, for whom he then had fewer than 150 malnourished horses. Cooke's confidence in the endurance of his command improved remarkably in the three decades that intervened between his arrival at Fort Bridger and his telling of the story, and his animosities had sharpened as well. As a Virginian who remained loyal to the Union when his sons did not, Cooke made no effort to conceal his disapproval of Johnston's later allegiance to the Confederacy—or his contempt for Johnston's adjutant general, against whom he bore more than one grudge. It was the first time he detected such "weakness" in Johnston, Cooke wrote: capitalizing on a presumed fault popularly attributed to Porter by his enemies after the Civil War, Cooke insinuated that Johnston had grown overcautious "because he was associated with one F.J.P."[21]

Johnston moved the main body of his little army two miles up Black's Fork from Fort Bridger, establishing a camp there that he called Camp Scott. Like most of the officers, Johnston and Porter set up housekeeping and office quarters in wall tents eight feet wide and sixteen feet long, and tall enough to stand upright in the middle. They stacked their trunks in the rear, with low iron cots on either side, while toward the front stood a sheet-iron stove and a writing table piled with books and papers. To save candles, they propped the canvas door open during the daylight. The enlisted men arrayed their bedding around the circular floors of conical, teepee-like tents recently invented by Henry Sibley, a bibulous brevet major serving in Cooke's 2nd Dragoons. Sibley's tents saw their first field trial at Camp Scott, while Sibley faced his own trials—literally as well as figuratively—with the contentious Colonel Cooke.[22]

Once the camp was established, Captain Randolph B. Marcy led a detachment southward on a grueling and perilous expedition to New Mexico for more cavalry mounts and draft animals. He was to bring them back in the spring, when grazing improved and more grain and corn had been stockpiled. The commissary captain who had predicted a seven-month supply of rations reconsidered after overhauling the trains, suggesting that the daily ration should be trimmed a little to stave off a shortfall. Salt was scarce as well, and on November 26 Porter recorded, "We have not a pint of salt in the whole army." Word of that shortage made its way to Brigham Young, who sent eight hundred pounds on pack mules in halfhearted diplomacy, but Johnston would take no gifts from an enemy of his government. Only if Young pledged his loyalty anew could they resume polite relations, insisted Johnston — who would withdraw his own loyalty to the United States a little over three years later.[23]

Young confidently implied that he expected the soldiers to retreat in the spring. Johnston assured Young that he would advance, attacking anyone who stood in his way, and with deep distrust of the Mormons he kept strong guards over the remaining supplies and surviving animals. His adjutant general fully shared his contempt for the sect. Porter heard firsthand from gentile Utah refugees of widespread murders by the Mormons, and he was probably present when the Shoshone chief Washakie revealed that Young had sought his help in exterminating the soldiers. Porter wrote McDowell that Mormons were "cowards, like all assassins and bullies," mocking their religious devotion and their morals generally. They would "steal, rob, lie, murder, assassinate, brag, intimidate, deny their faith, crouch, be as humble as Uriah Heap — anything to gain a point, to milk a gentile, or deceive one, or to serve their prophet. Anything except suffer martyrdom, which they would like to do if it did not hurt and [they] could come back to this world again safe and sound." Time and events would only reinforce his abysmal opinion of the denomination.[24]

Porter's correspondence simultaneously betrayed an admiration for Johnston. Hints of high regard were to be expected of a loyal adjutant, especially in official or potentially public communications. It would have elicited no surprise that Porter commended Johnston to the adjutant general's office for his efforts to insure the safety, supplies, health, and comfort of his men; neither did it seem unusual for Porter to offer lengthy, detailed descriptions of their travails in the snow to justify the decision to winter over. Porter's letter to General Scott's adjutant, which may have been intended for the newspaper circulation it ultimately received, further credited Johnston with having earned "the unbounded confidence of the army" for his judgment and sacrifice. "We have all endured alike," Porter assured McDowell, "and the fact that Colonel Johnston has on the march 'footed it,' as did the men; suffered the same exposure; and will not permit the officer to receive more than the soldier, has endeared him to all."[25]

Such complimentary remarks might have been interpreted as mere flattery from an ambitious subordinate, but Porter waxed at least as laudatory in the long daily descriptions he compiled for his letters home. Aside from the longing for his expectant "Hattie," he apprised her that he was personally and professionally content, and he credited that in no small measure to his "commander & intimate associate." Johnston, he assured her, was "the kindest purest & most honest gentleman it has been my good fortune to be associated with."[26]

Their encampment enjoyed milder weather than the surrounding ranges, with occasional snows that revived the grass for their herds when it melted off. Springlike temperatures settled in after Washington's Birthday, followed by heavy snows toward spring, but in a few days it was all gone. During seven months at Camp Scott, Porter occupied himself from nine in the morning until three in the afternoon each day, filing reports and keeping up with correspondence. At the end of those office hours he and Johnston sat down to their second and last meal of the day, after which they always took exercise together, walking anywhere from four to seven miles. Porter's workday occasionally began earlier once the army settled into a relatively normal routine, and often lasted until eight or nine in the evening, after they returned from their constitutional. Between the monotony and press of paperwork, the daily notes he made for Hattie dwindled to weekly summaries that went to Fort Laramie with the army's monthly express couriers. The regular mail came haphazardly, and often contained few private letters or none, aggravating the isolation with anxiety about home.[27]

In March a mounted traveler rode into Camp Scott from the direction of Salt Lake City wearing what Porter called "a very self satisfied air." This was Thomas L. Kane, who had come to Salt Lake City by the California route as a pretended emissary of President Buchanan, and he informed Colonel Johnston that he was "a bearer of dispatches to you and to Gov. Cumming." Johnston had him led to the governor "like an ass," wrote Porter, who judged him to be precisely that, but Kane lingered nearby, cultivating an acquaintance with Cumming.[28]

By then the soldiers were growing restive. Social calls helped to alleviate the boredom, and on their afternoon rambles Johnston and Porter would stop in at the tents of the regimental officers; sometimes one would host a party. Johnston invited a few guests now and then, often including Jim Bridger and Lieutenant John Newton of the engineers, and Porter would wait on the table, serving the portions on tinware as though it were a silver service. President Buchanan's appointee as federal judge had erected a large tent as his territorial court, where he was preparing treason indictments against Mormon leaders, and in that canvas tribunal he held a levée on April 2. Porter had evidently abandoned at least one of his early vices, and the tobacco smoke from that gathering drove him out of the tent early; he disapproved of the drinking, too.[29]

Dwindling herds of undernourished stock and shrinking stores of staples forced some painful dietary restraint as spring progressed. The wives of a few officers and enlisted men endured the hardships of the camp, affording a welcome touch of civilization and — in the case of some common soldiers' wives — very popular cooks for what food there was. The last Porter knew about his own wife, she should have been having her baby before spring, but April came without word from her. Childbirth still presented abundant danger in 1858, and as the days passed he grew fretful about it. On April 13 he finally learned that she had borne him a son on the last day of February. They named him Holbrook Fitz John Porter, "Holbrook" honoring the aunt and uncle who had taken Harriet in and given her the education her parents could not afford.[30]

April proved a pivotal month in the war. Passing between the lines once more, Kane persuaded Governor Cumming that he would be welcomed by Young, who was beginning to think better of defying an army that would soon be stirring. On the same day that Cumming left for Salt Lake City, President Buchanan succumbed to his own reservations about the wisdom of having dispatched the army to Utah. A financial panic in the autumn of 1857 had wrought acute economic distress, and more trouble loomed in Kansas. The president also faced congressional resistance to his plan for expanding the army he needed to quell the Mormon uprising. In what he meant as an olive branch backed by a sword, Buchanan offered all Mormons a full pardon for any crimes they had committed during the uprising so long as they would submit to federal authority. Two official emissaries from the president delivered that proclamation to Camp Scott on May 29, and a few days later they headed for Salt Lake City with an escort.[31]

One week later, Captain Marcy returned from New Mexico with fresh cavalry mounts and mules, accompanied by Colonel William Loring, who had come up from Fort Union with a battalion to foil any Mormon attempt to steal or scatter the herd. With that reinforcement of men and animals, Johnston headed into Utah. He had no idea where negotiations sat when he started his army away from Camp Scott on June 13; he and Porter rode out the next day, and a rear guard trailed after them on June 15, leaving behind bare chimneys and tent frames.[32]

The army ascended the Wasatch Mountains on June 20, filing through Echo Canyon, where Young had planned to ambush them. Rumors had filtered back that the Saints had accepted Buchanan's terms, but Johnston proceeded cautiously. On June 25 the column crested Big Mountain — twice as high as Mount Washington, reflected a New Hampshire officer. Below lay the Great Basin, and a glimpse of the Great Salt Lake. The next day took them over Little Mountain, through a narrow defile called Emigration Canyon, and into the outskirts of Salt Lake City.[33]

There the regiments stopped, unfurled their colors, and began to march in cadence for the benefit of any onlookers, of which there were few: Young, fearing the troops' vengeance, had ordered everyone out of Salt Lake City. The band of the 10th Infantry began tooting marching tunes to keep everyone in step. Green vegetation in the expansive yards of the adobe-brick houses gladdened the hearts of Easterners tired of sand and sagebrush, but there was not a person or an animal to be seen outside the marching column. Every window had been boarded up, and an eerie quiet prevailed except for the music, the creaking of wheels, and the shuffling of feet. One magnificent mansion with an unusual number of gables arose before them, behind an adobe wall, and someone recognized it as Brigham Young's home: each gable marked an apartment for one of his many wives. On learning this, the regimental adjutant cantered up to the bandmaster to make a private request of him, whereupon the horns struck up "One-Eyed Riley"—perhaps the bawdiest song of that era. Most of the men knew at least a few verses of that ballad about a houseguest's licentious antics with tavernkeeper Riley's daughter, and they began to smile and hum in two-four time.[34]

The eight-mile-long column kept moving straight through town to the south, in search of a more isolated camp. For two weeks the troops sojourned near the Jordan River and Utah Lake as caravans of Mormon families returned from their hiding places—Young having agreed to at least nominal submission in return for amnesty. Johnston eventually moved his army to a spot in Cedar Valley, calling it Camp Floyd.[35]

Then began a mad scramble to build shelters for the whole command before winter set in again. The only timber stood miles away in the hills, but it served for sills, plates, and rafters while hundreds of hired Mormons made adobe bricks from the surrounding soil, stacking them dry. Slowly, a small city grew in a grid. Johnston and Porter enjoyed a substantial office and private quarters with a kitchen, parlor, and bedrooms fifteen feet square. As much as the Mormons seemed to hate the soldiers, they welcomed them as customers for kitchenware, cloth, and furniture, charging as much as ten times what Porter would have expected to pay in shops on Broadway.[36]

Early in their occupation of Cedar Valley, Colonel Johnston—by then a brevet brigadier general—asked to be relieved. The prospect allowed Porter to dream briefly of returning to the East with him, but Johnston's request was denied. Porter still held out hope for an assignment to Oregon, where some of the Utah troops were wanted, but that fell through, too. He assured Harriet that if he could get leave he would come home to her and the new child, but he was not the only officer with a child born since his departure: it was a common misfortune among those who chose the profession of arms. Others with that army had been away from home much longer than he had.[37]

"I know the permission would not be granted," Porter told his wife. "If I were able I would be sorely pressed to throw up my commission & join them. That is an impossibility as I have no other means of support & I am resolved to give to my son the inheritance of a fair name among his companions & friends. I brought nothing into the world. I can take nothing more out, but I will go out with an unblemished reputation."[38]

In part, perhaps, Porter and his chief were condemned to remain in Utah by the esteem in which they were held at headquarters, where they may have been considered irreplaceable in so delicate a department. Commenting on a letter of Porter's, General Scott remarked that he had the utmost confidence in "the judgment, patriotism and the truth of Bvt. Brig. General Johnston and the chief of his staff—Major Porter."[39]

Some officers did secure leave, and Porter said good-bye to some valued associates, including Randolph Marcy, but he congratulated them on getting away. Like many in that army, he harbored deep contempt for the Utah theocracy and all its adherents. He considered Salt Lake City "a miserable place," admitting he would do almost anything to get away from the Mormons, whom he dismissed as "robbers and assassins."[40]

As he and other officers had in Mexico, Porter wrote bitterly of the grip the church had on the resident population. He seemed most offended by polygamy, and when he heard that Governor Cumming's wife defended it, he wondered what she would think if her husband embraced the practice. Captain Jesse Gove, of the 10th Infantry, pitied the condition of Mormon women, suspecting that they were "under the most positive bondage," and from their dejected appearance he supposed they would escape if they could. They seemed terrified of holding perfectly innocent conversation with any men but their husbands. The soldiers generally believed that apostate Mormons risked murder by that sect's "destroying angels," and when an officer's dog carried home the severed head of what appeared to be a woman at least one captain assumed she had been killed for infidelity to her husband, or to the church.[41]

Tensions resurfaced often enough with the Mormons that the atmosphere at Camp Floyd alternated between tedium and fury. The presence of the army served as a perpetual reminder of federal authority, which Young's followers still resented. Soldiers were not safe in Salt Lake City alone. Mormon police in the city struck Porter as corrupt enforcers of Mormon hostility toward nonbelievers; he maintained that when any dispute arose between citizens and soldiers "a hundred Mormons will be ready to swear to the statement of one." Late in November of 1858 several army officers ran afoul of Mormon assailants who shot a surgeon in the arm and beat a dragoon lieutenant with a cudgel. Camp Floyd momentarily seethed with frenzy, but no one was ever held accountable.[42]

The embers burst back into flame in March of 1859. The federal judge at Provo attempted to indict certain Mormons for an assortment of crimes, including the Mountain Meadows massacre and other murders, and the appearance of armed Mormons in Provo prompted his appeal for guards from Camp Floyd. Johnston complied, sending Captain Henry Heth with his company of the 10th Infantry. Mormon leaders complained to Governor Cumming, who seemed to have fallen under the thrall of the charismatic Young, and Cumming protested that only he had the power to order Johnston's troops out. Johnston disagreed, arguing that the judge also held authority to ask for the services of a posse comitatus to administer the law. He implied, too, that if Cumming tried to overrule the judge he would be interfering with "a coordinate branch of the Territorial government." Cumming countered with a direct appeal to President Buchanan, who emasculated the judicial system of the territory by prohibiting Johnston from using troops except on the "written application" of the governor. That hamstrung most prosecutions, and soured relations between Johnston and Cumming.[43]

Mormons may have feared a repetition of the persecution they had endured years before, in their enclave on the Mississippi River, but enmity flowed both ways. Porter harbored deep bias against the Saints, speculating on the army's power to sweep Mormonism from the face of the earth and expressing a willingness to take part in that task.[44]

During the court proceedings at Provo, General Johnston evicted some Mormon ranchers who were grazing their stock a few miles west of Camp Floyd. He claimed the land for the army (and most Utah land did lack a secure title from legitimate government authority), but soldiers were also reportedly buying contraband liquor from Mormons there. A squad from the 10th Infantry went out to drive the herdsmen off, but a young man named Howard Spencer refused to leave when ordered away by Sergeant Ralph Pike. Spencer suddenly seized a pitchfork, and Pike quickly reversed his weapon, bringing the butt down hard on Spencer's head. The blow fractured Spencer's skull, but a surgeon removed bone fragments from the injury and after a few months Spencer recovered. Mormon witnesses insisted that Spencer had merely used the pitchfork to fend off Pike's clubbed musket, and that summer Pike was called to Salt Lake City to answer an indictment for assault with intent to kill.[45]

The grand jury was composed of Mormons, as the petit jury would be, and conviction seemed inevitable. Johnston assigned Porter to accompany the defendant and see that he had counsel. Pike was a popular soldier, and Porter may have had a personal attachment to him, because he and Pike had both been born and bred in New Hampshire, and Pike had had a brother killed at the Garita de Belén the day Porter was wounded there. Some of Pike's squad went along as witnesses, and a lieutenant and ten men served as a "posse." Pike carried his own revolver in a buttoned-down holster. At noon on August 12, Porter and his party left the courtroom to go to lunch, and as they approached the Salt Lake

House they had to push through a crowd that included Howard Spencer, who surprised Pike and shot him in the abdomen. As Spencer fled, a cluster of other men closed ranks and impeded his pursuit, allowing Spencer to escape on a horse tethered nearby. Porter had Pike carried to his hotel room, and fetched the judge to come take his sworn statement.[46]

Pike lingered for a couple of days before peritonitis carried him off, and only by intense vigilance was Johnston able to restrain his troops. Porter's complaint about a Mormon tendency to conspiratorial perjury seemed borne out by the inability of any witnesses to identify the well-known Spencer, who was only tried for the crime thirty years later, and acquitted by a Mormon jury.[47]

Murder was not the only crime that seemed to follow the Mormon migration. Charges of counterfeiting had arisen along the way, and Mormons close to Young concocted one such scheme while Johnston's army lay at Camp Floyd. Major Porter figured prominently in their discovery and prosecution.[48]

As Porter related it decades later, in the winter of 1859 Myron Brewer, a Mormon suspected of being one of Young's spies at Camp Floyd, approached Johnston about a government fraud Young was planning. Johnston told Porter of it, wondering if it was a trick meant to embarrass the army, and asked him to interview the man and determine whether there was anything in it. Porter quizzed Brewer about it, and he revealed a plan to forge the checks of the post quartermaster, which were drawn on the U.S. Treasury. He said that David McKenzie, an engraver in Young's tithing office, was preparing plates for printing the counterfeit checks, and had all the blanks and ink for printing them. Young was fully aware of the project, Brewer added, offering to let Porter know when the first fakes were to be passed.[49]

A little later, Brewer told Porter that Young had "discovered" the plot and had forbidden McKenzie to carry it out, in what Brewer considered a charade meant to allow Young plausible deniability. Then a counterfeit turned up, and Brewer was arrested with much theatrics, to mask his treachery: he offered a confession, as though under duress. Porter collected affidavits, after which he awakened Captain Heth in the middle of the night and started with him to Salt Lake City, where they roused the chief justice of the territorial courts. Presenting the affidavits, Porter asked for a warrant to search McKenzie's home and Young's tithing shop, which sat within the walls of his personal compound. The plates, checks, and ink were all found. Ultimately McKenzie was convicted of forgery and sentenced to a term in the tiny territorial prison, but he was the only one punished. Young managed to evade prosecution, partly because McKenzie testified that he had carried out the fraud despite Young's warning to desist.[50]

The limited conviction in the forgery case, along with the assassination of Brewer a few months afterward, suggested that, in Utah, Brigham Young was still stronger than the federal government. That obvious imbalance made it all the more agreeable for General Johnston and Major Porter when, in February of 1860, orders came to Camp Floyd for them to leave the department. On the first of March they appeared at a parade of the entire garrison; a battery fired a brigadier's salute, and Johnston said his good-byes in a stentorian tone one captain interpreted as evidence the general was celebrating his departure with both spirit and spirits. With a flourish of his cap he galloped off toward the south, followed by Porter and sixty or so soldiers who were nearing discharge. After four weeks in the saddle and a few nervous encounters with desert tribes, they arrived in Los Angeles March 29. That same day the Overland Mail coach stopped on its way north, and Porter bid farewell to his chief, climbing aboard for San Francisco and the weekly steamer to Panama.[51]

5

SECESSION

The California steamers dropped passengers on the Pacific side of the isthmus, and the Panama Railroad carried them fifty miles to the Caribbean port of Aspinwall. At Panama, Porter had the opportunity for a rare visit with his remaining brother, Bolton, who was the senior lieutenant aboard the U.S.S. *Levant*. That eighteen-gun sailing sloop reached Panama in mid-April and remained until May 10. If Porter saw a U.S. warship there he would have inquired for his brother, and through family letters he may even have known which ship Bolton was serving on, but the chances of such an encounter were less than even. Porter probably hastened through to Aspinwall without so fortuitous a reunion. On April 28 he rejoined Harriet at 66 Union Place — where, after greeting his two-year-old son for the first time, he went straight to bed, sick.[1]

Whatever the ailment was, it hung on for weeks, and on June 7 he asked for three months' leave. He had taken none for three years, and it was granted readily enough, but while he was able to remain in New York and acquaint himself with his new family he was still expected to sit on courts-martial at West Point. He turned that into a vacation for Harriet and Holbrook, taking rooms at Cozzens's Hotel through much of July and August. After a month's extension on his leave he reported for duty in Washington on October 1 but was sent straight back home to 66 Union Place. His only assignments for the next month consisted of inspecting troops, but on November 4 he was called to the War Department, in Washington.[2]

Taking the earliest train Monday, November 5, Porter reached the capital that night and reported at the War Department the next morning — election day. He had no chance to vote, but like many professional soldiers he may never have voted. Close association with Southern officers had probably given his view of the volatile slave controversy a conservative tinge, but that may not yet have guided him to sympathy with the Democratic Party. His regard for order and aversion to radical politics reflected the reserve of old-line Whigs, and his West Point applications suggested Whig family connections in the recommendations and advocates he sought. His conversion to Democratic identity could have begun as late as his interlude as the chief subordinate of George McClellan, whose early influences also leaned heavily Whig.[3]

With two Democrats and a slaveholding ex-Whig splitting the conservative vote in 1860, the election of Abraham Lincoln seemed probable, and discussion ran rife in the Deep South about secession if he won. The most strident disunion talk came from South Carolina, where hostility to federal authority had been building for decades, and that hostility occasioned Porter's next mission. His orders directed him to leave immediately for Charleston, to examine the condition of the forts and forces in and around the harbor. He boarded the first train south and spent the next thirty-six hours riding the complicated rail network through Virginia and the Carolinas. On the evening of November 7 his train pulled into Charleston, where trouble had already erupted between U.S. soldiers and local citizens.[4]

Government troops there were posted at Fort Moultrie on Sullivan's Island, along the northern fringe of the harbor. They consisted of two companies of the 1st U.S. Artillery and the regimental band, all under command of Brevet Lieutenant Colonel John L. Gardner—Porter's battalion commander in Mexico, whom D. H. Hill had considered too timid for any job more dangerous than village postmaster. Only that morning Gardner had sent a detail into Charleston by boat, to collect all the small-arms ammunition at the U.S. Arsenal. With the election of Lincoln seemingly imminent, that action aroused suspicion. The owner of the Charleston wharf refused to let the first cartloads be loaded in the boat, and a crowd congregated to back him up, forcing the soldiers to return everything to the arsenal. Bitterly resenting civilian interference in army operations with all the nationalism of an old Regular, Porter saw this as an ominous transgression, and reported with implied censure on how lightly Colonel Gardner seemed to take the affront.[5]

Lieutenant Theodore Talbot considered Gardner "utterly incompetent to command a post under the most favorable circumstances," and "peculiarly unfit" for the explosive situation in Charleston. Besides Gardner, the garrison consisted of a surgeon, an engineer, six line officers, and seventy-eight enlisted artillerymen, of whom one-fifth were confined for some form of misbehavior. Lieutenant Talbot showed signs of a heart ailment that would kill him in a year and a half, and Porter detected occasional negligence in one or two of the other officers. He turned more critical of the enlisted men, whose lethargy he interpreted as the result of lax discipline. His diagnosis seemed borne out by the large number of men under punishment.[6]

Moultrie lay unguarded and vulnerable to a sudden attack from the landward side. A single ordnance sergeant occupied Castle Pinckney, a masonry battery on an island near the city, while pentagonal Fort Sumter stood unfinished in the center of the harbor, full of civilian workers supervised by army engineers.

Porter saw significant defensive advantages at Sumter, but he advised against reinforcing either it or Castle Pinckney in the current political excitement. He suggested, instead, that "a proper commander" could discreetly pursue other defensive precautions. Noting that those measures might have been undertaken "several weeks since, when the danger was foreseen," he implied that Gardner was not that "proper commander."[7]

Porter remained in Charleston only two days, returning to Washington by November 11 to file his report. The War Department responded promptly, replacing Gardner with Major Robert Anderson, a more energetic Kentuckian whose Southern roots might ease sectional fears and whose loyalty might inspire imitation. By November 16 the Sumter garrison knew that Gardner had been relieved, and welcomed the news.[8]

From Washington, Porter returned to New York to inspect more recruits. Shortly before Christmas he saw Albert Sidney Johnston, who had just been given command of the Department of the Pacific. He and Porter had kept in close touch since they parted in California, and Johnston had asked for Porter as his adjutant again, but Porter had declined another faraway assignment that might last for years. The two nevertheless arranged to meet in New York City when Johnston arrived there to take ship for the isthmus and San Francisco, and their conversation naturally drifted to South Carolina's secession convention. Like Major Anderson, his fellow Kentuckian, Johnston seemed to regard disunion fanatics with the dread and aversion then common in the Border States. Certainly he sympathized with slaveholders' complaints of hostile Northern activism, but he hoped the Union would stand. Porter remembered him alluding to fear of a separatist conspiracy on the West Coast, and asserting that he would have nothing to do with it. Johnston assured him that he would utter no word and take no action favorable to secession "while he was an officer of the army," although that qualifying phrase carried portentous implications. Porter remained optimistic, assuring Johnston that all would be well if the president stood firm and acted energetically. That meeting was the last time Porter ever saw his old chief.[9]

No sooner had Porter said good-bye to General Johnston than the Deep South slave states started edging inexorably toward secession. South Carolina went out first, on December 20, and in January South Carolina forces fired on the chartered steamer *Star of the West* as it tried to bring supplies and reinforcements to Fort Sumter. War seemed imminent for days thereafter, but tempers cooled. Meanwhile, Porter remained close to army headquarters in New York City. Infrequently he traveled farther afield to sit on a court-martial case, but through most of December, January, and part of February he awaited orders for other special assignments.[10]

During that winter he and his mother had occasion for some concern about his brother, Bolton. The *Levant* had sailed from Panama to Hawaii in thirty-eight days the previous May and June, lingering there until September 18 before starting back to Panama. The ship had not been seen since, and after eleven weeks newspapers began paying ominous attention. The *Baltimore Exchange* reasoned that the *Levant* should have reached Panama by December. On January 8 Lieutenant Matthew Fontaine Maury apprised the *National Intelligencer* that other sailing ships had taken longer to make shorter trips when they were becalmed, and he thought there was still some hope. A few weeks after that an Alexandria paper relayed a secondhand tale that the sloop had hailed a whaler, and reported making a digression into the South Seas, but that appears to have been a hoax. The next reliable news involved logbook reminders of violent storms that had pounded the latitudes the *Levant* would have had to traverse, shortly after it left Hawaii.[11]

Two weeks after Texas declared itself out of the Union, Porter received orders involving some sea travel for him. Old David Twiggs, the department commander in San Antonio, had been pleading with Washington since late December for instructions in case of secession. All his requests reached the War Department after Joseph Holt succeeded John B. Floyd as secretary of war, but Holt had responded to none of them. Twiggs, who admitted that he would follow his native Georgia if it left the Union, wanted the government to either tell him how to proceed or relieve him of his command as soon as possible. The latter request was granted at the end of January, but he had no word of it before Texas voted to secede.[12]

Holt probably hesitated to issue orders because of executive equivocation. He meant to pull all troops out of Texas, salvaging what supplies and equipment they could bring with them but abandoning the rest, and army headquarters had started looking for steamers as early as January 30. Adjutant General Samuel Cooper—who would cast his lot with the secessionists himself in another month, ordered Porter to go to Texas and bring as many of the troops home as he could. Porter remembered great confusion surrounding the mission. He had to write his own orders, but Holt revised them to omit Porter's contingency plans in the event of secession, refusing to even dignify secession with the acknowledgment that it was possible.[13]

Once back in New York, Porter inspected the musty, long-disused sidewheel steamer *Daniel Webster*. Leaving Harriet heavy with child again, he boarded the ship on February 15. In his stateroom he carried $40,000 in cash for chartering ships, and in steerage he found berths for ninety-two recruits for Florida forts.[14]

A thousand armed Texans entered San Antonio while Twiggs was negotiating with Texas commissioners over the withdrawal of U.S. troops and ordnance from the state. Heavily outnumbered and uncertain what was expected of him, Twiggs reasoned that his uncommunicative superiors in Washington wanted no civil war, so he agreed to march his troops away with their small arms and artillery. That seemed to be the best possible outcome in the face of executive passivity, but the general's acknowledged Southern sympathies made him a convenient scapegoat for presidential inaction: citing Twiggs's "treachery," Buchanan peremptorily dismissed him from the service in which he had spent half a century.[15]

Eight days out of New York, the *Daniel Webster* docked at Key West. Sixty-two of the recruits went ashore with Porter the next day, February 23, and he left some cash and supplies for the commander at Fort Taylor. That afternoon he did the same at Fort Jefferson, on Dry Tortugas, eighty miles into the Gulf of Mexico, but he kept the rest of the recruits with him to protect the ship and the money. He directed the captain of the steamer to Indianola, on the Texas coast nearest to San Antonio, but once there he learned the state had seceded and that Twiggs had surrendered the department. Continuing south to Brazos Santiago, where he had served nearly fifteen years before, Porter encountered Texas troops and one of the Texas commissioners, who offered to ride with him to Fort Brown. From there he sent orders in the name of General Scott to commanders of posts farther up the Rio Grande to hurry down their men and guns. Rather than risk a collision with Texans at Brazos Santiago, he brought the *Daniel Webster* down to the mouth of the river, six miles away, and by March 8 artillery batteries were rolling in to take ship.[16]

So many troops, guns, and teams appeared that the *Webster* could barely accommodate half of them. Porter considered finding passage for the surplus troops from Tampico, in Mexico, until he heard of another ship at Brazos Santiago. Riding over, he found the *General Rusk* getting up steam for Galveston with secessionist volunteers who were going home, and for $12,000 the captain agreed to return from that trip and pick up the rest of Porter's men. While the *Rusk* made its way to Galveston and back, Porter found a schooner that could pass the bar and load the *Webster*, and it tracked back and forth all day March 19. Late that night the *Webster* started across the Gulf while the *Rusk* docked nearby to board everyone else. Three days out they crossed paths with the *Star of the West*, bound for Brazos Santiago to pick up the next contingent of troops, but no more U.S. soldiers would leave the Department of Texas except as paroled prisoners of war.[17]

The *Webster* stopped at Dry Tortugas, leaving two companies of artillerymen to strengthen the Fort Jefferson garrison. The *Rusk* delivered two more companies to Fort Taylor and returned to Texas while Porter and the *Webster* proceeded to New York with the three remaining companies. They arrived in New York Harbor on March 30, and Porter went home to find Harriet holding a newborn daughter, whom they named Lucia Chauncey Porter in memory of his older sister.[18]

The seven little republics from South Carolina to Texas had formally united as the Confederate States of America, with Jefferson Davis as president. Tension over the federal garrisons along the Southern coast had worsened during Porter's absence, and after some early equivocation President Lincoln was showing the firmness Porter had wished to see in Buchanan. A week after Porter's return, Lincoln decided to send a vessel to Fort Sumter filled with provisions, and to warn the South Carolinians that if this ship was fired upon it would be followed by reinforcements. The reinforcements would consist of two hundred recruits from Fort Columbus, and on the afternoon of April 8 Porter inspected them. Afterward he watched them board the *Baltic* for Charleston, where Brigadier General Pierre G. T. Beauregard commanded Confederate forces. When the last recruit had climbed the gangplank, Porter turned to inspect a smaller detachment destined for Florida, to help defend Fort Pickens against more Confederates under Braxton Bragg.[19]

On Porter's return from Texas he had found a letter from Sidney Johnston at 66 Union Place that described the Washington's Birthday celebration in San Francisco. "Would that [the] pure patriotism so predominant here prevailed all over our country," Johnston remarked of the spirit he sensed that day. Assuming that the general would stick to the army and the Union, Porter hoped that his influence as a soldier and Southerner would inspire others, and squelch disloyalty in Kentucky. Years later Porter recalled urging Secretary of War Simon Cameron to have confidence in Johnston, and Cameron gave him permission to write the general via Pony Express with an offer of a high command. Porter wrote that letter on April 8, the day he inspected the recruits for the *Baltic*, but the next day Johnston wrote his resignation and asked to be relieved, choosing to follow his adopted state of Texas. The War Department had already surreptitiously sent Colonel Edwin Sumner to replace him, but Johnston followed orders from Washington to the last, handing the department over in what Sumner called "good order." On the chance that Johnston followed Porter's advice to sail for New York, General Scott ordered his arrest on arrival there, but Johnston traveled overland into the Confederacy.[20]

Thanks to diplomatic meddling by Secretary of State William Seward, Lincoln's announcement of the relief expedition to Fort Sumter led the Confederates in Charleston into the trap of firing the first shot. Early on April 12, before the supplies and reinforcements could enter the harbor, Confederate guns opened on the fort, which surrendered the next day. Amid another nationalistic frenzy like the one that had followed the firing on the *Star of the West*, President Lincoln called on the states for seventy-five thousand militia. Six Border State governors refused outright, and those from Maryland and Delaware hesitated. The president's proclamation sent Virginia tumbling into secession, and Maryland appeared to be leaning that way, which would have left the national capital surrounded by hostile territory. Fear of an attack on Washington, or an uprising within it, had haunted capital-city loyalists for weeks, and the onset of hostilities brought that apprehension to the fore.

Porter wrote to George McClellan on the day of the militia call, encouraging him to offer his services. "Such men as you and Cump Sherman and Burnside are required to counterbalance the influence of Davis, Bragg & Bea[u]regard," he urged his old friend, who was living in Cincinnati and serving as president of a railroad. McClellan opened that letter on April 18. He had already been offered the post of chief engineer for Robert Patterson, under whom he and Porter had served in Mexico, and he had also been asked to lead Ohio's troops. The position McClellan wanted most was Patterson's own, in command of the forces from his native Pennsylvania, and he asked Porter to lobby General Scott about it: if Scott dropped a word with Governor Andrew Curtin, the Pennsylvania command might be his. Broken telegraph lines delayed Porter's response, and McClellan accepted the Ohio command, asking for Porter as adjutant general of the Ohio troops — essentially as his own chief of staff. Scott had already given Porter other work in the East.[21]

Reliable officers were in great demand for special duties. On the evening of April 16, Porter walked into Willard's Hotel with Irvin McDowell and a third officer. In the lobby they spotted Lieutenant William Averell, who was still recovering from a badly broken leg, and they took him aside to ask if he could travel to Fort Arbuckle, deep in Indian Territory. They needed Averell to collect all the troops in the territory and bring them back to Fort Leavenworth, as Porter had done in Texas. Averell readily agreed and left the next day, bearing orders in Porter's handwriting.[22]

Porter himself embarked on another special mission on April 18. McDowell collared him at the War Department, telling him Secretary Cameron wanted him to go to Harrisburg right away to oversee the mustering and transportation of Pennsylvania's volunteers. Before leaving, Porter dropped in on General Scott, who had moved his headquarters back to Washington. Scott anticipated Rebel efforts to cut Washington's rail connection with the North, to starve the city into submission. Waiving written instructions for lack of time, he told Porter to act on his own discretion and, if necessary, to enforce his orders in Scott's name. With nothing more than that and perhaps a satchel of extra clothing, Porter made for the train station. He stayed that night in Baltimore, continuing to Harrisburg the next morning on the Northern Central Railroad, through Cockeysville and York. That was the same road the Pennsylvania troops would have to travel, on their way to Washington.[23]

There were plenty of troops to muster. Porter wired the commanders of arsenals in Philadelphia, Pittsburgh, and Springfield, Massachusetts, to send rifles, ammunition, and equipment, remarking that the shortages of those items "could not have been worse had it been premeditated." Hours after he arrived in Harrisburg, a heckling crowd confronted the 6th Massachusetts as it passed through Baltimore, and the throwing of stones led to the firing of shots. Four soldiers and a dozen citizens died, including men, women, and children. The mayor begged federal officials to send no more troops through his city, and that night Maryland militia rode out to prevent their passage by burning the railroad bridges above Baltimore. The next day the mayor went to Washington personally, obtaining the president's promise to divert troops around the city, by way of Havre de Grace and Annapolis.[24]

Intelligence of the riot and the cutting of communications bemused state officials at Harrisburg. In a recollection of dubious accuracy, Alexander McClure later described Curtin and General Patterson (who would then have been in Philadelphia) as paralyzed by uncertainty. They and their aides advised caution, McClure claimed, but Porter said that he would "march the troops through Baltimore or over its ashes to the defence of the capital of the nation." Whatever Porter actually said, he did order up four companies of the 2nd Cavalry from Carlisle Barracks under the command of his former faculty colleague George Thomas. While quartermasters scrambled to arm and equip those Regulars, Porter started militia brigadier George Wynkoop down the Northern Central with three thousand Pennsylvania militia to guard that line. Porter went with them as far as Ashland, Maryland, less than fifteen miles from Baltimore, where two old Regular Army officers happened along and helped him to settle the militia into camp and establish adequate guards. The president of the Northern Central—Simon Cameron's son, James—had organized working parties to rebuild the bridges, but neither they nor Thomas had arrived by the afternoon of April 21, and Porter went back to Harrisburg looking for them.[25]

The telegraph lines to Washington had been severed, and messages had to be carried by hand on a roundabout route, so Porter knew nothing of Lincoln's pledge to keep troops out of Baltimore. He was in Governor Curtin's Harrisburg office when a telegram arrived from St. Louis, complaining that General Harney was standing in the way of organizing volunteers there. The message was signed by Frank Blair, the brother of Lincoln's postmaster general, who wanted it relayed to Washington. Blair suspected that secessionists would seize the St. Louis arsenal, with its tens of thousands of rifles, and he recommended that Harney be replaced. Scott and Cameron had both given Porter license to invoke their authority in forwarding troops and protecting the railroad, and to save a two-day delay he risked exercising it in far-off Missouri. Relieving Harney was a decision for others, but Porter wired Blair in Cameron's name (and Harney in Scott's) to let Captain Nathaniel Lyon muster the troops, arm them, and use them to protect public property.[26]

Giving Lyon such power may have thrown fuel on the smoldering fire in St.

Louis. Lyon, a radical abolitionist with an authoritarian manner, undermined the wavering unionism of Missouri's state-rights advocates while the Southerner Harney might have appealed to them. The uncompromising Lyon quickly became the darling of unconditional unionists, who regarded the violent reaction to his intransigence as proof that he was the man for the hour. Years later, after Porter had been smeared as disloyal, he pointed justifiably to the risk he took in appointing Lyon as evidence of his deep devotion to the Union. Lyon did prove inflammatory, but Porter's course bespoke determined opposition to secession.

Accompanied by Major Thomas and the cavalry, and followed by the construction gangs, Porter left Harrisburg that night and started back toward Ashland. His train stopped at York on the news that another locomotive was approaching from the south. Further advice revealed that the engine carried a courier with vague messages to withdraw Wynkoop's militia from the railroad line and send them back to Harrisburg. Suspecting a trick, Porter hesitated to comply. He remonstrated all night with Wynkoop and the quartermaster at Ashland, who had brought the orders from Cameron and Scott. Even after Porter saw the orders, on the evening of April 22, he pointed to a last-minute amendment to them requiring that "the railroad be kept open at all hazards," and he tried in vain to persuade Wynkoop to stay where he was. In a recollection sustained by contemporary correspondence, Simon Cameron later claimed he gave the quartermaster a verbal message for Porter to bring the troops on to Washington, too—also "at all hazards"—but the quartermaster forgot to deliver it. The militia consequently returned to Harrisburg, and soon thereafter the bridges north of Ashland were also burned, effectively cutting that line. For the immediate future, Pennsylvania troops had to go by way of Philadelphia and the ferry landing at Havre de Grace.[27]

"All my work is undone," Porter grumbled to Harriet (who, two days before, might have looked from the windows of 66 Union Place on the periphery of an enormous patriotic rally at Union Square). "I am about to bring back the troops which I had placed so as to overawe Baltimore, conquer it if necessary, secure communications with Washington and throw in a large supply of provisions."[28]

He made a hasty trip to Philadelphia on April 23 to consult with General Patterson, whom Scott had named to command the Department of Washington, encompassing Maryland, Delaware, and Pennsylvania. The order had been delayed by the interruption of the telegraph lines, but everyone knew about it by April 21, and Porter wanted to acquaint Patterson with all the developments along the rail corridor. He returned to Harrisburg the same night. All day April 24 he pressed officials in Philadelphia and New York to send men, provisions, and horses and equipment for Thomas's cavalry, several more companies of which were arriving from Texas. Two decades later James Cameron remembered that Porter "never seemed to eat or sleep, but was eternally on the alert," encouraging the soldiers and their officers and showing the civil authorities "how to bring order out of chaos." On the morning of April 25, with the mustering and transportation of troops under way, he considered his work finished and started back to Washington. He rode the cars as far as Hagerstown, Maryland, where he hired a carriage for the rest of the trip.[29]

Porter called at General Scott's headquarters to offer him and Secretary Cameron a verbal report on the events of the previous week, and the general ordered him to Philadelphia, to serve as Patterson's assistant adjutant general. In an era when militia commissions were considered equivalent to those of Regular Army officers, Major General Patterson stood second in rank only to Scott, and he required an important command. The general-in-chief evidently thought Patterson also needed an especially efficient chief of staff.[30]

On April 27 Porter traveled to Philadelphia via Annapolis, stopping there to deliver instructions to Benjamin Butler, the militia brigadier whose troops held that city. Scott wished Butler to stay there, Porter said, and "stud" the railroad to Relay House with guards, to keep the way to Washington open. Porter remembered Butler, the epitome of a political general, gruffly replying that, "damn it," he knew what to do.[31]

Washington held so little in the way of arms and equipment that, while Scott badly needed men to defend the capital, he asked Patterson to send none who were not fully equipped. Armories in the North suffered equally from shortages of arms and accoutrements, having emptied their storehouses to satisfy Porter's initial demands. The only abundant resource seemed to be volunteers, so Patterson collected them in camps of instruction until they could be supplied, but Scott had outlined a plan to seize Baltimore with columns from Washington, Annapolis, York, and Havre de Grace, He needed many of Patterson's troops, and wanted to move by early May, but Patterson complained of quartermaster and ordnance deficiencies, arguing that his new regiments could take the field only by carrying ammunition in their pockets. He proposed occupying Havre de Grace from Philadelphia on May 7, but George Cadwalader, his division commander there, protested that many regiments lacked uniforms, serviceable weapons, tents, cookware, or anything to protect their ammunition from the weather. To hamper his movements further, Patterson found that the horses he had bought for his wagon train had been called for in Washington, and additional purchases had been suspended.[32]

Porter wrote to Colonel Edward Townsend, Scott's principal adjutant, to "beg and implore" for delay in the advance on Baltimore. He confirmed Cadwalader's assessment of his men's weapons, calling them "horrible," and rain was falling as he wrote, which he expected to ruin what ammunition the men carried. The regimental officers had made it clear that they would resign rather than lead their men into action unarmed, he added. Porter said he had called two Ohio regiments to Philadelphia in hopes of "stirring up Pennsylvania pride," and he promised to try the Baltimore movement with troops "not so squirmish" as Cadwalader's if it could be done. Porter closed with a plea that Patterson be allowed discretion at his end about the timing of the advance, and that the ordnance officer at the arsenal be ordered to supply his needs. As late as May 11 Patterson was still reporting that the arsenal would require two more weeks to equip the men who had already been mustered.[33]

They need not have worried about arms or ammunition. Baltimore's mayor, considering the crisis over, had asked the commander of the militia to disband his battalions, and Patterson could have secured the rail and telegraph lines with one regiment. Ben Butler, who must have learned of the demobilization from informants who made their way to Annapolis, saw a chance for a personal coup by taking the city alone. Citing "verbal directions" from a purported War Department envoy whose name no one recognized, Butler loaded two infantry battalions and a brace of fieldpieces on rail cars early on May 12, riding into Baltimore unchallenged.[34]

General Scott raged at Butler for exceeding his orders so audaciously and taking such grave risks without a word to his superiors or adjoining commanders; nor did it soothe Scott's temper that Butler had stolen the glory for himself. The return of Baltimore to federal control freed Patterson's army for operations farther afield, however, and allowed contractors to catch up with quartermaster and ordnance requisitions. The quartermaster general of Pennsylvania offered some four thousand complete sets of infantry equipment if they could be replaced by other sets produced later at federal arsenals. The Philadelphia arsenal expected only eight hundred sets per week from its contractors, but Cameron balked at the militia offer until Patterson noted that some regiments might be discharged before they were equipped. With only one week left in May, General Scott assigned a senior ordnance officer to arm Patterson's troops, whom he then ordered into western Maryland, to confront a Confederate army gathering at Harper's Ferry.[35]

That Rebel army had just come under the command of its "other" General Johnston—Joe Johnston, who knew Porter from Mexico and the Kansas troubles. He arrived at Harper's Ferry to find some five thousand men in camp. They were fairly well armed, but their ammunition supply amounted to barely two dozen cartridges apiece, with only enough percussion caps to discharge about half of them.[36]

On May 28 Porter started shuttling thousands of Pennsylvania and New York volunteers toward Chambersburg, where Patterson had already established a camp. That day Porter heard from George McClellan, whose army of Ohio, Indiana, and loyal Virginia volunteers had crossed the Ohio River the day before and was moving due east. McClellan said that his men were in posses-sion of "Parkersburg" (meaning Clarksburg) and within thirty miles of Grafton, where he would strike the Baltimore & Ohio Railroad. He had not yet set foot over the river himself, but already he called rather peremptorily on Patterson to dispatch a force "at once" to Cumberland, nearly a hundred miles east of Grafton, to cooperate with him as he advanced; he sent a less demanding appeal to Governor Curtin. Porter gently reminded McClellan that the only enemy threat to Cumberland lay at Harper's Ferry, another eighty miles east, assuring both him and Curtin that Patterson would help as much as he could when the time was right.[37]

Porter and Patterson moved their headquarters to Chambersburg on June 2. The capacity of the Cumberland Valley Railroad limited them to bringing six regiments a day from Harrisburg, and it was even slower going from Chambers-burg to Hagerstown, where the railroad ended. They also faced a shortage of wagons and teams, which local citizens seemed reluctant to hire out to the army. Porter imposed relatively spartan limitations on officers' baggage as transporta-tion became their most troublesome problem. The delay did no real harm, be-cause spring rains had swollen the Potomac beyond fording, and Patterson still expected to have most of his troops in Hagerstown by June 10. Porter told Colonel Townsend that they were "working like bees," but it was the evening of June 15 before he and Patterson proceeded to Hagerstown to launch their invasion.[38]

Patterson made his headquarters in the Hagerstown Female Seminary, just north of town. Less than ten miles to the south lay the College of St. James, where Porter's mother and nephew lived. The road from the seminary to the army's advance division, at Williamsport, passed within three miles of the col-lege, and one of Patterson's brigades lay camped there, so Porter probably found an excuse to turn that way for a brief visit.[39]

Porter had kept spies ranging ahead, gathering intelligence that included Johnston's daily issue of thirteen thousand rations. His informants also told him of an oversized regiment of Kentucky Rebels holding Maryland Heights, oppo-site Harper's Ferry, with heavy guns mounted there. Rather than attacking such defenses with green troops, Patterson opted for flanking Johnston out. He ar-ranged his nineteen regiments into five brigades, giving the three largest ones to Cadwalader, including all his Regulars and Colonel Ambrose Burnside's well-drilled Rhode Island regiment and battery. The other two brigades, with only six regiments between them, went to William Keim, a major general of Pennsylva-nia militia. Cadwalader was only a major general by brevet, but that brevet had been won on the battlefield in Mexico, whereas Keim had never served in the field. Cadwalader would lead the army over the Potomac.[40]

Patterson had finally detached an Indiana regiment to hold Cumberland

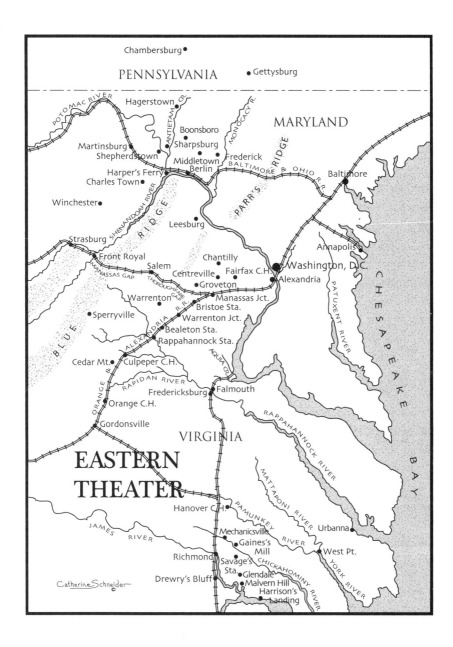

as McClellan moved closer, but the Indiana colonel bellowed for reinforcements to face the rumored approach of several thousand Rebels. At midnight of June 15 Porter rode down to Williamsport to select those reinforcements from George Thomas's brigade of Cadwalader's division. He chose Burnside's Rhode Islanders, two guns of his battery, and a couple of companies of Thomas's 2nd Cavalry. It took almost all the wagons the army had left to carry that relief expedition's supplies.[41]

Cadwalader forded the river the next day, seizing a loop of Virginia real estate as far down as Falling Waters. He had crossed the river upstream from Harper's Ferry, intending to flank the Confederates out of that position and perhaps swing behind them to cut off their retreat, but it was too late for that. Johnston had burned the bridges there and at Shepherdstown before withdrawing to Winchester, where he called out Virginia militia and started digging earthworks. He had posted an advance brigade of Virginia infantry at Martinsburg under Thomas J. Jackson — the hypochondriac of the rice diet. Johnston had also sent three battalions toward Romney, which was what had so panicked the Indiana colonel at Cumberland. J. E. B. Stuart patrolled the roads from Martinsburg to Williamsport with his Virginia cavalry, sending Johnston fairly accurate estimates of Cadwalader's strength.[42]

Cadwalader had stood on the Virginia side only a few hours when General Scott directed Patterson to send all the Regular infantry and cavalry back to Washington, as well as Burnside's Rhode Islanders. Patterson recalled Burnside as ordered, but asked to keep the Regulars, who were the spine of his amateur army. A concentration of Confederate forces outside Washington made Scott anxious to have the reinforcements, and he insisted on having the Regulars. Porter immediately ordered back all Thomas's cavalry, the only two battalions of Regular infantry, some companies of artillery, and Burnside's regiment, with his battery. He warned them to keep their destination secret, but within two days Johnston had a report of that movement from a minister who overestimated its size by a factor of two: the men in the column had volunteered to the reverend that they were going to Washington.[43]

That left Patterson with no artillery and only one company of cavalry consisting of Pennsylvania militia. Digging in on the Virginia shore, Cadwalader suffered an alarm of his own by misinterpreting news of Jackson's advance to Martinsburg as the beginning of an attack on his riverside perimeter. Like the information Johnston was receiving, the report also seriously inflated Jackson's numbers, indicating that Cadwalader would be outnumbered two to one. Without enough cavalry for reconnaissance and little hope that Cadwalader could defend his bridgehead without artillery, Patterson called him back to the Maryland shore.[44]

The greatest disappointment was the loss of the Regulars, and especially their officers. A pair of them commanded two of Patterson's five brigades, and the newest recruits among the Regulars were better trained than any of the militia or volunteers. Their presence inspired the novices with a confidence that evaporated as soon as the professionals marched away. Senator John Sherman of Ohio, serving as a volunteer aide with Patterson, told the secretary of war how suddenly reverting to the defensive had demoralized all the troops on the upper Potomac. Their enlistments would "melt away" before they could accomplish anything, Sherman anticipated, and that disappointment would probably discourage them from reenlisting for the three-year term the government had begun to require.[45]

The impending dissolution of Patterson's army posed a serious concern. With the president's proclamation for ninety-day troops more than two months old, Patterson reminded Scott that his militia would soon be entitled to muster out, and he expected nearly all of them to demand it. In his entire remaining force, only one regiment had signed up for more than three months.[46]

That problem loomed less ominously in the army gathering at Washington, where Irvin McDowell had been catapulted to brigadier general and given command of those forces. He organized a five-division field army of forty-seven infantry regiments, eight light batteries, and a squadron of cavalry: the infantry included many three-month regiments, but most had enlisted for two or three years. Scott would have preferred taking time to raise and train a bigger army, but political pressure demanded action before the three-month troops went home, and that sand was fast running out. The largest Confederate army held Manassas Junction, a railroad intersection twenty-five miles from Washington, with detachments ranging even closer, and Scott hoped McDowell could overwhelm it while Patterson held Johnston at bay. A resounding defeat so early in the life of the Confederacy might well have been expected to bring an end to the experiment in rebellion.[47]

In a private letter to Colonel Townsend, Porter conveyed his own doubt that more than a couple of hundred Confederates lay opposite Williamsport. He thought Cumberland safe, too, suspecting that Johnston had gone south and east — closer to Manassas Junction, and within better supporting distance of that other Confederate force. Porter posed a strategic suggestion when he mentioned to Townsend that he hoped Scott would order their army to Leesburg — or to Martinsburg, and thence to Charles Town. At either place they could obtain supplies by rail, and while Leesburg would take them out of the Shenandoah Valley it would bring them closer to Manassas, if Johnston got away from them. Porter's wish for a direct order may have reflected Patterson's exasperation with Scott's vague instructions.[48]

With Johnston at Winchester and Beauregard now commanding the bigger Rebel force at Manassas, sixty miles and two mountain ranges separated the main Confederate contingents. For Jackson, at Martinsburg, the distance was even greater, while the westernmost outpost at Romney and the easternmost at Fairfax Court House lay a hundred miles apart. The Manassas Gap Railroad partially compensated for the distance, and Johnston's troops could ride more than halfway if he chose to join Beauregard, but his position would have been compromised if Patterson moved to Leesburg — smack between the two Rebel armies, and theoretically near enough to help McDowell defeat Beauregard before Johnston could come to his rescue. Patterson appeared to follow

Porter's advice when he suggested to Scott that he abandon the Hagerstown-Williamsport-Martinsburg line, shift his supply base to Frederick, and position his army at Leesburg.[49]

With the persistent shortage of wagons, crossing at Williamsport again to march on Martinsburg would create a long, slow, vulnerable line of communications, although veering back to Charles Town would shorten it. Supplies could be had more easily there from Harper's Ferry, coming by rail from Baltimore or by canal boat from Washington. With enough warning, there might even be a slim chance of winning a race with Johnston to Manassas: a march of twenty-four miles from Charles Town would bring infantry to the railhead at Leesburg, although the rail route from Leesburg to Manassas was twenty miles longer than Johnston's would be. Advantages of supply, mobility, mutual support, and relative position to enemy forces would all have been improved by moving directly to Leesburg.

At such a distance Scott seemed averse to issuing a direct order. Instead, he gave Patterson vague instructions for restrained aggression, holding his position in front of Johnston and offering battle if not outnumbered, but without pursuing Johnston if he retreated toward Winchester. That final prohibition was superfluous, for a lack of transportation forced Patterson to stop for supplies every couple of days, but Porter supposed that Scott feared pressing Johnston because it would drive him to join Beauregard and attack McDowell.[50]

Before moving into Virginia again Patterson waited for his chief engineer, Captain John Newton, to conduct an extensive examination of the enemy's strength. Newton, a loyal Virginian who had served as chief engineer of the Utah army, returned to Hagerstown at midnight on June 27. He reported that Johnston held Bunker Hill, between Martinsburg and Winchester, with about 5,500 men, and that Jackson had 4,500 more on the Potomac at Shepherdstown. Another 5,000 Confederate infantry and "nearly" a thousand cavalry guarded the river crossings to Jackson's left and right, he estimated, and the Rebels had between twenty and twenty-four guns. His tallies only slightly exceeded the observations of David Hunter Strother, a local Union man who had watched Johnston's main body march through Charles Town on June 15: Strother counted twenty-three guns, 600 cavalry, and somewhere between 10,000 and 12,000 infantry.[51]

That would have left Johnston nearly equal to Patterson in infantry, more than equal in cavalry, and far superior in artillery. Scott had finally allowed Patterson to keep George Thomas and two companies of the 2nd Cavalry, as well as a battery of the 4th Artillery that was crippled by unbroken horses and a dearth of harness. Patterson's infantry amounted to fewer than fourteen thousand men. Nearly even numbers did not bode well for an attacking force, since the defender held a natural advantage, but Scott promised reinforcements, and on June 30 Patterson announced he would ford the Potomac at daylight the next morning.[52]

He did not cross until the morning of July 2, taking about eleven thousand men, and the army had not gone far when the first blood was drawn. Near Falling Waters a few Virginia companies from Jackson's brigade and a single gun contested Patterson's advance, opening fire and forcing the two leading Union brigades to deploy. Their line overlapped the little Confederate battalion, and after a few volleys it fell back on Jackson's main line. Stuart's cavalry harried Patterson's flank, trapping dozens of Pennsylvanians and shooting a few, but Jackson and Stuart both withdrew toward Martinsburg once they were satisfied that Patterson's entire army was coming.[53]

Patterson pushed his way into Martinsburg, forcing Jackson back near Bunker Hill, where Johnston took up a strong defensive position with his whole force. Patterson knew by then that Scott planned to launch an operation against Manassas "early next week," which would have been the week of July 8; he hoped to deploy some 35,000 men against Beauregard, who did not have two-thirds that many. Engineer Captain James Simpson then guessed Patterson had 10,000 men at Martinsburg, and Captain Newton had recently put Johnston's force at 15,000, but Patterson still seemed confident. He wanted to strike at Winchester immediately—despite Porter's ardent advice against it, which was seconded by all the Regular Army officers. One of Patterson's aides said the Regulars thought the fight at Falling Waters had "got his Irish blood up," but Porter told the aide he had done his duty by offering his opinion, and thereafter he said no more against it. Patterson assured Scott on July 4 that he would linger at Martinsburg only to collect provisions for another march: once supplied with enough for two or three days, he would "advance to Winchester to drive the enemy from that place, if any remain." After that, Patterson hoped Scott would allow him to continue to Charles Town and Leesburg, to combine forces with a brigade in that vicinity commanded by Porter's classmate Charles Stone.[54]

The next day, Patterson succumbed to false rumors of Johnston receiving heavy reinforcements from Manassas, and asked Stone to join him at Martinsburg as soon as possible. By July 6 Patterson feared Johnston might have accumulated as many as twenty-six thousand men, and he called in the Indiana regiment at Cumberland. Strother, a native of the region, rode into Patterson's camp and relayed his June 15 estimates of Johnston's forces to Porter and Captain Newton, but years later he claimed they seemed skeptical. They may have trusted Strother's count, given Newton's June 27 estimates, but they probably considered his information stale after three weeks.[55]

Scott promised to bolster Patterson with two new Wisconsin regiments, but they would be more than a couple of weeks coming and would not be fully equipped. In addition, the general-in-chief sent four New York regiments, along with Charles Sandford, an old major general of New York militia. Patterson postponed further movement until some of those troops arrived, and on July 7 Johnston left Bunker Hill for a position closer to Winchester, expecting that Patterson would not attack. That same day Colonel Townsend wrote Patterson that McDowell's army was having its own troubles getting ready to move: a shortage of horses would require a delay until at least the end of the week.[56]

Stone reached Martinsburg with his brigade on July 8. Two of the New York regiments came in that day, as well, with Sandford and the other two regiments following a day or two later. Patterson wrote Scott on July 9 for clarification of his orders and to coordinate his movements with McDowell's. Alluding to a letter that Scott said Sandford was bringing, Patterson told Scott, "I hope it will inform me when you will put your column in motion against Manassas and when you wish me to strike." Johnston had not yet established his reputation for conducting Fabian retreats, but Patterson showed justifiable concern about extending his line of communications much farther, predicting it would be cut. Echoing Scott's earlier advice, he said he would not pursue if Johnston retired. "I am very desirous to know when the General-in-Chief wishes me to approach Winchester," he concluded, suggesting that Scott inform him of the day in a cryptic telegram beginning, "Let me hear of you on . . . ."[57]

Now that he believed Johnston had been heavily reinforced, Patterson's aggressive promise to "advance to Winchester to drive the enemy from that place" had withered into an expectation that he would simply "approach Winchester." That softening of spirit may have reflected the advice and opinions of the professional soldiers around him, who considered his strategic position "false" and his undisciplined, dissatisfied troops unreliable. The unanimous opinion of those men finally led Patterson to call a council of war on July 9, consisting of Cadwalader, Keim, three brigade commanders (including George Thomas), Captains Simpson and Newton, and his commissary and quartermaster. Porter did not join the council, which came to the consensus that it would be foolhardy to attack Johnston from Martinsburg. Explicitly or implicitly, all advised moving directly to Charles Town and making their advance from there.[58]

The council based its opposition on logistics and on the effectiveness of the strategic threat their army posed to Johnston — and the threat they faced from him. Comparative strength played no part in their opposition to the attack, although an inflated impression of enemy numbers seemed as common in Patterson's army as it was in Johnston's, where Patterson was also credited with about twenty-six thousand. Johnston misunderstood that Patterson was "greatly superior" in artillery before he was reinforced, and he learned that more artillery was coming with the reinforcements. His Martinsburg information network believed Patterson had 32,000 men. "We overrated each other's strength greatly," Johnston later conceded.[59]

Some commanders also overrated the strength of their own forces, at least in retrospect. Officers who joined Patterson late in the campaign, and especially those opposed to his Democratic politics, offered personal estimates and hearsay that their reinforcements gave him as many as 25,000 men. Patterson's own aides cited official returns, which put his maximum troop level somewhere between 18,000 and 19,000, of whom only 15,000 to 16,000 were "fighting men."[60]

Many of Patterson's troops had to be detailed as laborers or guards for the supply train, the five hundred wagons of which provided barely half the capacity needed to carry subsistence and ammunition. The army's animals consumed twenty-six tons of forage per day, and rations had to come twenty miles from the railhead at Hagerstown. Vehicles not laden with ammunition were in perpetual motion, and the demand for food left little or no room for more durable supplies, such as shoes and clothing. Nearly as many of the soldiers in Patterson's camps wore gray uniforms as blue, and both colors were growing threadbare and frayed, with some regiments looking downright ragged. Worse yet, shoes were wearing out throughout the army, seriously impeding mobility.[61]

The best hope of holding Johnston in the Shenandoah Valley during the attack on Beauregard died when General Scott failed to act on Patterson's formal June 21 proposal to transfer his operations to Leesburg. Porter had encouraged that change of base privately through Colonel Townsend, and may have initially suggested it to Patterson because of the logistical and strategic advantages that could have deprived Beauregard of crucial reinforcements. Martinsburg posed no such advantages, as all the professional soldiers save Winfield Scott seemed to understand. Patterson may have comprehended the superiority of the Leesburg route himself, but he at least echoed the reasoning of his staff advisers when he assured Scott that the reasons for preferring Leesburg would be obvious to him. As Patterson's engineers pointed out, Johnston could cut off their supply line at any time if they advanced from Martinsburg, or bring 12,000 of Beauregard's men by rail in a single day to crush them. He could also hold them where they were until it was too late, and beat them to Manassas with the same 12,000 men to defeat McDowell, while there was nothing Patterson's army could do about it from Martinsburg. If Beauregard were attacked, Johnston would go to his aid, and Patterson's staff knew it. Porter testified the next winter that it was equally apparent "that it was an utter impossibility for us to hold him."[62]

Nonetheless, they made the attempt. On July 12 Scott answered Patterson's communication of three days before with a telegram urging him to "let me hear from you on Tuesday." By their prearranged code, this meant that McDowell would begin his movement against Manassas on July 16. Scott also instructed Patterson to move in the direction he had proposed on July 9 — that is, change his base to Charles Town. If Johnston decamped to join Beauregard and it was "too hazardous to follow him," Patterson was to head for Manassas by way of Leesburg.[63]

Marching immediately to Charles Town might have been interpreted by Johnston as an intention to cooperate with McDowell against Beauregard, and that could have spoiled Scott's plans by sending Johnston racing to Manassas. Patterson waited three days at Martinsburg, hoping that his presence might detain Johnston, while an aggressive advance would probably drive him to Beauregard. During those three days Patterson accumulated wagons and teams enough to transfer his supplies to Charles Town, and he began worrying about the morale of his troops. The three-month terms of the men who composed his army were almost up, and at Martinsburg he learned that most of them had no intention of remaining beyond their time. Porter had circulated an order on the night of July 8 for a march beginning the next day, but numerous officers descended on him to "beg" for the order to be rescinded. One of them described his men as "very much demoralized," and said they would refuse to advance any farther. On July 13 the officers of the 6th Pennsylvania went so far as to present Patterson with a letter diplomatically suggesting that their men expected to be in Harrisburg by July 22.[64]

With his reluctant and poorly shod army, Patterson began a threatening movement toward Winchester on July 15, to coordinate with McDowell's anticipated attack at Manassas. The leading brigades passed the spot Johnston had intended to defend in early July and went into camp that evening at Bunker Hill, about halfway to Winchester. The next day Colonel David Birney led six companies of his 23rd Pennsylvania, two companies of cavalry, and four pieces of artillery down the Valley Pike toward Winchester, following instructions to make it seem that the whole army was behind him. Birney supposed he had covered more than half the remaining distance to Winchester when Stuart's cavalry confronted him. After exchanging a few rounds the Rebel horsemen fell back, and Birney continued. Johnston, who had finally begun receiving reinforcements, had put the militia to work building breastworks of fence rails and earth; he blockaded the roads by felling trees into them, and called some of Jackson's infantry into line on Stuart's warning of the enemy's approach. When Birney reached the obstructed roadway he concluded that he had frightened the enemy enough and retired to Bunker Hill. While Birney's men went back into camp, Patterson reminded Scott that many of his three-month men seemed ready to throw down their arms when their terms ended, in a few days' time.[65]

Holding the position at Bunker Hill veiled the transfer of quartermaster and commissary stores from Martinsburg to Charles Town. Patterson had hoped to remain at Bunker Hill another day, but he thought he had satisfied Scott's desire for a July 16 diversion. Through the negligence of regimental officers or his inspector general, many of Patterson's troops had not brought three days' rations as ordered, and by the morning of July 17 some in the ranks had not eaten in over a day; others were already a meal or two behind. Rather than see hunger aggravate the troops' demoralization, Patterson turned for Charles Town. Marching into the Jefferson County seat that afternoon, his army presented what one chaplain considered "a woe-begone appearance," with trousers "out at the knees and out at the seat, flaunting their shoddy fragments in the breeze." Whole regiments had no coats or shoes.[66]

George Thomas promptly led what Porter called "quite a heavy reconnaissance" back toward Winchester, to keep pressure on Johnston and show him they were not going to join McDowell. Porter wrote orders for the whole army to follow, expecting now that the supply train could travel with them, but officers of the three-month regiments came into headquarters to object. Their men thought they were entitled to be home by the time their enlistments expired, which meant that most of them should already be leaving, and they thought Patterson needed to make a public appeal to them.[67]

The ninety-day men crowded the streets around the courthouse where John Brown had been tried, and Patterson resorted to his renowned oratorical talents. Regiment by regiment, he asked them to reenlist for the three-year term, or at least stay on a week or ten days, through the most crucial period of their service. The first regiment replied with complaints about their ragged pants and disintegrating shoes. Patterson's own son commanded the 17th Pennsylvania, and everyone expected those Philadelphians to comply, but even they balked. Of the Pennsylvania regiments alone, eighteen were due for discharge within a week, beginning the next day. Porter, who did not attend Patterson's speech, recalled that a few regiments agreed to stay, including the Indianans who had come from Cumberland, but most of the willing could not have marched for lack of shoes. Patterson reported at the time that only three regiments volunteered for another ten days of duty, and seven years later the chaplain of the 11th Pennsylvania corroborated him.[68]

That appeal forced those ninety-day men to declare, publicly, whether they would sacrifice a few days at the moment of danger after having flocked to the colors at the height of patriotic hysteria. Their refusal sent them home in more shame than glory, and most of them began excusing themselves at Patterson's expense. They insisted he had been timid and dithering, which discouraged them from continuing to serve under him. That was the line taken by officers of a Radical Republican stripe, such as Colonel Birney, who scorned the limited war espoused by conservative generals, and it was the tale told by most historians of the reluctant regiments Patterson had addressed. Later, some of them blamed Patterson's chief of staff, excusing their own refusal to extend their terms with irrelevant allusions to the false accusations subsequently levied against Porter.

One even fantasized that Porter—who was not present when Patterson addressed the troops—had made an uninspiring speech of his own. A generation later, that same imaginative memoirist insisted that the soldiers had been "unanimous and enthusiastic that they would not ask for their discharge while the emergency for their service continued."[69]

Patterson telegraphed Scott to warn that he could rely on none of the men to extend their time, adding that some had sworn they would not stay one additional hour. Still believing Johnston "greatly superior" in numbers, Patterson also obviously deemed the Confederate troops more reliable man for man. Throwing the responsibility on Scott, he asked at 1:30 A.M. on July 18 if he should attack under those circumstances. Annoyed by the communications lag (which Patterson had cited as one reason against the Martinsburg line), Scott emphasized the more aggressive side of his equivocal earlier directives, declaring that he expected Patterson to attack the enemy, and beat him. At the least he should detain the Rebel forces with "threats and demonstrations"—which Porter and even some of Patterson's worst critics considered utterly impossible. Scott wondered if Johnston had not already "stolen a march" on Patterson, and reinforced Beauregard at Manassas, where the oft-postponed attack by McDowell had still not begun.[70]

Scott's telegram was Patterson's first inkling that McDowell had been further delayed, and he indignantly replied that Johnston had stolen no march on him. That may still have been true when he sent the wire, but it would not be for much longer. An hour after midnight on July 18 Johnston learned that McDowell was moving on Manassas, and with that news he received orders to go to Beauregard's aid "if practicable." Noting that Charles Town was twenty-three miles east of Winchester, as though comparing the relative speed with which he and Patterson could reach Manassas, Johnston decided it was more than practicable. By early afternoon his Confederate troops were tramping eastward, with Jackson's brigade in the lead.[71]

Since Patterson's last crossing of the Potomac, Scott's nebulous orders to him had indicated that if Johnston withdrew, Patterson should follow him—or, if that was "too hazardous," make for Manassas by way of Leesburg and Alexandria. Still uncertain whether Johnston had left the valley, Scott refrained from ordering Patterson to the attack, instead apprising him that his ninety-day men were bound to federal service until their respective mustering-out dates—and then he dropped a broad hint that a week was "enough to win victories," alluding to the week during which most of Patterson's army was due to go home. By that comment Scott seemed to ignore the widespread demoralization Patterson had described, and that his little army would be shedding regiments every day of that week. Then, in apparent contradiction of that aggressive sentiment, Scott advised Patterson to dig in and wait for help "when abandoned by the short-term volunteers."[72]

Even if Patterson had known that Johnston was going to join Beauregard, the number of barefoot troops at Charles Town would have precluded sending more than a small portion of his command to the Leesburg railhead. With so few regiments willing to fight, apparently he did not press George Thomas to test Confederate strength at Winchester, so he learned of Johnston's departure only on July 20. By then Johnston and most of his troops had already reached Manassas, and the rest were well on their way. The short-term men were abandoning Patterson in droves by then, so he fell back on Scott's orders for that contingency and retired to Harper's Ferry on July 21. He asked if he should send all the three-month men home, evacuate Harper's Ferry, and hurry to Alexandria with the recently arrived three-year regiments. Two days later, after McDowell had been trounced at Bull Run and the fugitive fragments of his army had fled back to Washington, Scott dismissively replied that Patterson's dwindling army was "not wanted" in the capital. Apparently Scott did not want Patterson in Washington, either, or anywhere else, and the order for mustering him out had already been issued.[73]

That implied rebuke closed Patterson's forty-nine-year military career, and he spent much of his remaining two decades trying to justify his course. Republican newspapers in particular started casting him as the architect of defeat — inflating the number of his troops, exaggerating their readiness, and vastly underestimating how quickly he might have reached the Bull Run battlefield. Once discharged from service, he could not ask for a court of inquiry. The only investigation that ever touched on his campaign on the upper Potomac was conducted by the Joint Congressional Committee on the Conduct of the War — a body dominated by Radical Republicans, whose questions and conclusions reflected their agenda. That agenda was inimical to the conservative attitudes shared by Patterson, Porter, and most of the Regular Army establishment. By emphasizing the refutable testimony of hostile witnesses and rejecting harder evidence in Patterson's favor, the committee saddled him with the ultimate responsibility for McDowell's defeat at Bull Run.[74]

McDowell had indeed worried beforehand about Johnston getting loose, but by his own overestimate of enemy strength he had originally expected to fight 35,000 Confederates. That was more than he faced even after Johnston's arrival, yet in the wake of his humiliating defeat McDowell identified Johnston's reinforcements as the deciding factor. McDowell had then become popular in Radical circles, and the committee embraced his conclusion as its own. It would not be the last time McDowell foisted blame for a defeat at Bull Run on someone else.[75]

General Scott faulted Patterson mostly for not holding Johnston at Winchester with threatening demonstrations.[76] The one reconnaissance from Bunker Hill had not constituted much of a threat, or diversion, but it did keep Johnston in place until the day after Patterson understood McDowell was going to make his attack. Had the professional soldiers at Patterson's headquarters known that McDowell would not even reach the Bull Run battlefield until July 18, they might have advised remaining at Bunker Hill despite the hunger and restiveness of the men. Combined with the slow and circuitous line of communications between Washington and Martinsburg, the repeated postponements in McDowell's offensive played as great a role in Johnston getting away as did Patterson's caution: Scott wanted frequent reports from Patterson, and Patterson needed clear instructions based on his reports, but the communications lag thwarted them both. The tentative tone and vacillating spirit of Patterson's dispatches to Washington suggested that he was at least as anxious about misconstruing Scott's instructions as he was about confronting an enemy he considered stronger.

Had Scott been present to observe the problems of supply, transportation, and discipline that Patterson faced, he might have been more understanding, especially since Scott himself was responsible for Patterson's unfortunate location. Porter did see those impediments clearly, and while he did not agree with all of Patterson's decisions he always defended Patterson's management of the campaign. That might have been mistaken for evidence of Porter's perennial loyalty toward those he served so closely had it not required him to assign much blame to General Scott, whom he had also served and admired.

Patterson departed on July 25. Major General Nathaniel Banks replaced him that day, bringing his own assistant adjutant general. That left Porter unemployed, but Banks made him his inspector general, assigning him to organize, train, and equip the three-year regiments that were dribbling into Harper's Ferry daily. Without another opportunity to distinguish himself, Porter expected to be tainted with "the odium which has been thrown unjustly upon Patterson," and in a letter to McClellan he hinted at wanting more "satisfactory" service. By then, McClellan was in a position to help.[77]

6

THE GENERAL

Like his friend Charles Stone, Porter had been promoted to colonel in the Regular Army in May, with command of a new regiment that existed only on paper. Rather than leave the field to begin recruiting that regiment, he had remained on duty with Patterson, who tried to have his son appointed to raise the men so Porter could stay with him. Porter craved something more prominent than leading a regiment, but on August 7 he formally accepted command of the 15th U.S. Infantry, declaring himself ready for any service the War Department might assign.[1]

By the time he accepted his promotion, he knew that his only remaining sibling was probably dead. In June a mast thought to be from the *Levant* had washed ashore in the Hawaiian Islands. Months later a morbid prankster set a bottle adrift in the Atlantic with a macabre message purporting to be from the last three members of the crew, and speculation about their survival persisted for decades. Because the discovery of the mast indicated the ship had broken up, rather than sunk, the idea that the crew could have been shipwrecked on a deserted island lingered in seagoing lore. As late as 1904 a U.S. warship scoured much of the *Levant*'s presumed route for "doubtful" islands, reasoning that if any crewmen had reached a habitable shore they might still be alive, but most people abandoned hope in the summer of 1861. On June 30 naval authorities decided that the *Levant* had gone down with all hands, declaring Lieutenant William C. B. S. Porter dead as of September 18, 1860 — the day the ship left Hilo. The day after the rout at Bull Run, President Lincoln signed a bill awarding a pension to Lieutenant Porter's widow.[2]

As the last survivor of his parents' children, Porter must have taken an additional measure of satisfaction in the president appointing him a brigadier general of volunteers, right on the heels of his promotion to colonel. The deaths of two sons in their country's service had expunged any stain his father had left on the family name, the honor of which seemed fully restored by the elevation of the third son to the second-highest rank the army then offered. He accepted on August 9.[3]

The disaster at Bull Run had illuminated the glaring need for better training and discipline in the army, and for organizational genius. That had brought McClellan to Washington to take command of the defeated army, and he had recommended Porter for a star even before receiving Porter's letter hoping for a better assignment. McClellan initiated a flurry of fledgling brigadiers, including several other friends of his and Porter's from the old army, including Stone, William B. Franklin, and William F. Smith (known as "Baldy" in Porter's class).[4]

Such promotions in McClellan's coterie infuriated aging career officers who had spent decades in backwater posts, one of whom fumed that many of them, including Franklin, Stone, and Porter, deserved no promotion at all. The elevation of men who had been lowerclassmen when he graduated from West Point particularly rankled an ambitious captain of engineers, John Pope, who had asked the president for a direct commission as brigadier general. Lincoln, who was a friend of Pope's father, explained that he had not jumped anyone so many grades at once, but Pope countered that both McDowell and the new quartermaster general, Montgomery Meigs, had been mere captains, with McDowell (like Porter) a major only by brevet. Pope went on to complain that Porter, Stone, and Franklin had all been junior to him in Regular Army rank, and as an Illinois resident he enlisted political supporters who wielded great influence with the president. Several of them "demanded" that Lincoln give Pope a permanent Regular Army appointment as a brigadier, rather than a temporary volunteer commission like the others. Lincoln yielded enough to grant Pope a star, but only as a volunteer, and with the same May 17 date of rank—although he placed him senior to Porter, Stone, and Franklin.[5]

Porter remained at Sandy Hook, Maryland, opposite Harper's Ferry, late into August, preparing new troops for Banks and consulting with Stone and McClellan about affairs on the upper Potomac. On August 24 Colonel Townsend assigned him to McClellan's department, at McClellan's request. At first Porter took charge of all the new regiments in Washington, but on August 28 McClellan gave him his own field command. Adding two regiments to a big brigade that had recently belonged to General William T. Sherman, McClellan divided it into two brigades and called it a division—Porter's division, as its veterans would proudly remember.[6]

Porter's new command lay camped around Fort Corcoran, on the heights across the Potomac from Georgetown, overlooking the Aqueduct Bridge. The fort stood at the northeast corner of a broad plateau, with twenty-four-pounder guns covering the aqueduct and the Georgetown Ferry. A mile to the south, the Doric-columned mansion that had been Robert E. Lee's home faced Washington City from the wooded crest of Arlington Hill. Behind it, on the western side of that hill, a series of redoubts studded a line of earthworks that ran south for three miles before veering abruptly east at Four Mile Run and following that stream to the Potomac. That shallow perimeter marked the Federals' foothold in Virginia as September opened, most of it lying within the old boundary of the District of Columbia.[7]

Sherman had had some trouble in three of his regiments, in which many of the men thought they had enlisted for the ninety-day emergency but had been mustered for two years. The colonel of the 13th New York had resigned, along with some of his officers, at the first sign that the regiment would be held to a two-year term. Discipline deteriorated in all three units, whose men had refused to do any more duty after the last of the militia went home. Sherman had trotted out his detachment of Regular cavalry and wheeled in an artillery battery, unlimbering the guns with the muzzles aimed at the disaffected camps. Guard details went into two of the regiments and clapped irons on a hundred of the most stubborn mutineers, taking them away between bayonets. Sherman feared he would have to order the gunners to fire, but the rest of the mutineers sullenly submitted.[8]

Such was the recent experience of one-third of the men over whom Porter assumed command, ten days later. The Bull Run veterans of the 13th New York remained the most blatantly bitter over the extension of their enlistments, and equipment shortages deepened their resentment. Their ragged coats and pants had just been replaced, but no headgear, shoes, or stockings had come with them. Neither did they have serviceable blankets or guard tents, so their picket details had to sleep uncovered in those thick Potomac mists. Since the mutiny, they had also seen much drudgery, chopping trees or digging latrines and entrenchments instead of drilling. Desertions, dismissals, and discharges, not to mention arrest and confinement, had reduced the regiment to barely a third of its complement.[9]

Porter learned of the trouble in the 13th New York the day after he took command. He called the companies out on parade, bringing the officers to the front. The new colonel, John Pickell, had graduated from West Point before Porter was born, and had served in the army through four presidential administrations. Porter, whom one hostile volunteer officer called "the extreme West Pointer," lectured the sixty-two-year-old Pickell and his subordinates on how easily control was lost. In a private memoir Porter claimed he made a simple appeal to their "good sense and patriotism," bidding them to condition their men to strict submission and teach them the need for it. Nothing more was necessary, he remembered, adding that thereafter the 13th New York took to the traces and pulled with a will.[10]

Porter's recollection notwithstanding, his imposition of a series of courts-martial likely exerted a more direct effect on discipline. He ordered several dozen officers and men into arrest from the 13th, 14th, and 41st New York and the 9th Massachusetts, for offenses ranging from minor insubordination to mutiny and assault with a deadly weapon. Over the next ten weeks different courts cashiered officers and sentenced men to drumming out of camp, tattooing on the hip, or hard labor with ball and chain for anywhere from two months to a year.[11]

Two days after Porter assumed command, John Martindale arrived in camp with a three-week-old commission as brigadier general and orders to take command of one of Porter's brigades. Five days after that, George W. Morell followed him to Porter's headquarters with a similar commission, taking over the other brigade. Martindale and Morell were both forty-six-year-old New Yorkers, and both had graduated in the West Point class of 1835, with Morell ranking first and Martindale third. Both had also resigned from the army early: Martindale never served on active duty, and Morell spent two years in the engineers. Lieutenant George Meade, another 1835 graduate of the academy, had grumbled to a comrade in 1856 about the obscurity endured by those classmates who had left the army. "Morell is a poor lawyer in NY," Meade lamented, adding that the same was true of Martindale. Morell would prove as dependable a friend to Porter as Martindale would be a personal foe.[12]

All Porter's regiments desperately needed instruction on the drill field, including the oldest of them. He imposed a rigorous training schedule, alternating drill with fatigue duty, and as the senior surviving veteran of the 4th Artillery's bayonet charge at Padierna he emphasized bayonet practice. He roused the men at all hours to respond to real or imagined alarms, which hardened them to the rigors and uncertainty of soldiering. One such alarm came on September 7, on the intelligence that the Confederates were striking tents and loading wagons in their main camp at Manassas. Whether that portended a withdrawal or an advance McClellan did not know, but he seemed to bet on the former when he warned all his division commanders to have their troops ready to move on short notice with two days' cooked rations. No movement followed, and the information from Manassas proved false, but on September 13 McClellan reported that the enemy had amassed as many as 170,000 men in front of the Arlington lines, and was about to spring.[13]

From his earliest days in Washington, McClellan had credited absurd estimates of Confederate strength supplied by deserters, refugees, or incompetent operatives, and his closest subordinates shared that credence, including Porter. In fact, barely 35,000 Confederates stood present for duty within striking distance of Washington, and Rebel leaders optimistically supposed they would need 60,000 to launch an offensive. Instead of preparing for an assault on the seat of federal power, the Rebels were about to retire from their most advanced positions, from the heights of which they could look down on their foes in the Potomac basin.[14]

Porter took a keen interest in a novel means of detecting threatening enemy movements. Another native of New Hampshire, Thaddeus S. C. Lowe, offered his services to the government as an aeronaut and brought his hydrogen balloon to the front, making his first ascent from Fort Corcoran within hours of Porter's arrival there. He took General McDowell aloft, and on the sultry afternoon of September 4 Porter went up over the fort with them. From an elevation of eight hundred feet they could see Confederates digging earthworks on Upton's and Munson's Hills, a few miles in advance of the constricted Union perimeter.[15]

Over the next week Porter asked Lowe to conduct an aerial observation nearly every clear day. He arranged for the balloon to go aloft where McClellan and other prominent officers could see it in action, adding that he had recommended the funding of two more balloons and telling Lowe to "strike while the iron is hot." The demonstration went well, and Porter assured Lowe that he was "of value now," urging him to submit estimates for what he would need to expand his operations. Lowe guessed at the price of two new balloons and suggested a portable inflation apparatus, to relieve him of nightly trips to Washington for hydrogen. Porter forwarded those estimates and enthusiastically recommended more balloons, pointing out that such reconnaissance would prevent any significant number of the enemy from approaching within eight or ten miles without being seen. "It costs several lives now to obtain a portion of the information which may be derived by means of the balloon," he concluded.[16]

September 25 saw the first aerial observation for active operations when Baldy Smith, whose division lay on Porter's right, launched a foraging expedition to the village of Lewinsville. Porter sent Lowe up to watch for enemy interference. Late in the morning Lowe caught the glint of bayonets to the northwest as Smith sent five thousand men forward, but the Confederates seemed preoccupied with parading their troops for spectators who crowded the slope of Munson's Hill. Lowe came down at noon, buffeted by stiff winds. He felt sure the enemy intended no "great movement," but a small force did venture out from Falls Church and fire on Smith after he had filled his quartermaster wagons with forage. The sound of the guns and his own ground reconnaissance left Porter worried that Smith might be cut off. He begged Lowe to risk the wind for another look, but Smith had enough infantry and artillery to drive the Rebels away, and he returned in triumph.[17]

Taking the forage served partly to disguise that the expedition amounted to a reconnaissance-in-force. From an advanced position at Ball's Cross Roads, three miles from the banks of the Potomac, "Professor" Lowe had been surveying the length of the Confederates' first line from the air, suggesting that McClellan might be contemplating a movement. He coveted the two fortified hills in the middle of that line, to the left of Porter's position, and the Rebels seemed to suspect as much. On the morning of September 28 Union pickets in front of Munson's Hill detected that their Confederate counterparts had slipped away during the night, and all day only a handful of Rebel cavalry remained about the earthworks at the crest. The brigadier whose men faced Munson's Hill apprised McClellan, who sent orders to ease forward cautiously. That evening a Michigan regiment swept up the hill and seized the abandoned works, from which the enemy had enjoyed an excellent view of Washington City—while Washingtonians could discern their Confederate flag with telescopes. The position had served the Rebels mainly as an observation post: the earthworks consisted of simple trenches, and the "artillery" consisted of painted logs and pasteboard tubes.[18]

As other troops occupied Munson's and Upton's Hills, Porter moved one brigade three miles forward from Fort Corcoran and seized two taller crests in the western corner of the old district boundary. He bivouacked most of the brigade on Hall's Hill, where he and his staff slept under a tree the night they occupied the place. His pickets also occupied Minor's Hill, a couple of miles away, which offered the highest vantage point within the old district line (officially Arlington County, since 1846); from its crest Porter could look down on Falls Church, where Rebels had left rumors behind to discourage pursuit. Inhabitants of purported loyalty told Porter that Confederate leaders dining in the town recently had discussed plans to pull back to a stronger position and lure McClellan into pursuit, hoping to pounce on him with 175,000 men. McClellan evidently fell for the ruse, and his troops dug in at their new positions instead of chasing the outnumbered Rebels, as McDowell and at least one other division commander thought they should have done.[19]

Porter had called Alexandria home for some years. He probably credited the local inhabitants with greater fidelity than the times warranted, and his credence in them may have influenced McClellan. Porter had shown similar faith in reports from friendly Virginians on the upper Potomac, which had led him to accept estimates of Confederate strength that had been exaggerated for the enemy's benefit. He tried to cultivate spies and informants wherever he served, but some of his operatives proved useless, or worse. He hired one man for service on the Arlington line whom he later arrested for theft, concluding that he was "a gasbag and a humbug."[20]

Three members of the Orléans family, claimants to the throne of France, saw the movement to Munson's Hill from McClellan's headquarters. François d'Orléans, the somewhat deaf Prince de Joinville, rode along as a civilian observer and deemed himself an unofficial consultant to McClellan; his young nephews, Philippe d'Orléans (nominally the Comte de Paris) and Robert d'Orléans (the Duc de Chartres), held volunteer commissions as captains with appointments as aides-de-camp to McClellan. These nomadic noblemen found the Confederate hills still abundantly wooded behind those rudimentary entrenchments, mostly with oak, chestnut, and cedar thickets. The new occupants quickly cleared a field of fire and dropped a tangle of abatis to slow any attempt to recover the heights by assault. Philippe, who kept a dense journal of his adventure, marveled at the speed of the deforestation. "It's destruction on a grand scale," he wrote.[21]

Professor Lowe started taking observations from Upton's Hill almost immediately, taunting the Rebels with the portrait of General McClellan painted on his balloon, the *Intrepid*. On the last day of September the colonel of one of McDowell's regiments treated Lowe to lunch before joining him in an ascent: training his glass several miles to the west, he spotted Rebel cavalry galloping somewhere between the Union pickets outside Falls Church and Beauregard's headquarters at Fairfax Court House. Near sunset of the same day, Philippe d'Orléans went up to a thousand feet with Lowe and McDowell, gasping in delight at the spectacular glow cast over the landscape. He discovered that he could read the terrain as easily as if it were a relief map, and was surprised to learn that the Rebels lacked tents, which might have revealed the extent of their presence in the distance. The smoke from their campfires served the same purpose, purling up through the canopy of the forests in which the pickets lurked.[22]

Into early autumn Porter used Sherman's former headquarters for his own — a spacious home with a wraparound porch and carefully groomed grounds on the bluff overlooking the Potomac from near Fort Corcoran. That luxury ended on October 10, when he moved his staff and most of the rest of his division to Hall's Hill. His tent and those of his brigadiers occupied a pine grove not far from a large but apparently empty home that some of the staff officers coveted for more comfortable quarters. His division had just been augmented by a third brigade commanded by Daniel Butterfield, son of the founder of the Butterfield Overland Mail Company and an antebellum officer of gentlemen militia. Porter had met him at Martinsburg in July, as colonel of the 12th New York. Judging Butterfield a strict disciplinarian and an effective drillmaster, Porter had suggested him to McClellan, who sometimes asked for Porter's recommendation on prospective general officers.[23]

Over the next several months Porter devoted most of his attention to drilling the troops and acquainting himself with the officers of the dozen infantry regiments in his division. McClellan had given him two regiments of Pennsylvania volunteer cavalry, with experienced officers from the West Point class of 1855 commanding both, and Porter's artillery consisted of two Regular Army batteries. The volunteer infantry brought the greatest trouble in the way of undesirable officers. In Martindale's brigade the 13th New York continued to flounder, and Porter court-martialed numerous officers, forcing others to resign — or rejecting resignations submitted on frivolous excuses.[24]

Porter commended Colonel Pickell for prompt action when the worst company in the 13th New York showed more signs of mutiny, but Pickell was an abolitionist who eventually caused a controversy himself. When a cavalry officer from Washington brought his own slave to the camp at Hall's Hill as his servant, Pickell lured the lad away and hid him in his own quarters. Porter ordered Pickell to turn the slave out, and the old man surreptitiously raised a stink over it.[25]

About a month later Porter called for a board of officers to examine Pickell's fitness for service, and especially his hearing, his memory, and his ability to mount a horse, but Pickell's worst deficiency seemed to be administration. His regiment had dwindled so from desertion and recruiting lethargy that to replenish its ranks Porter had personally intervened with New York's governor and superintendent of recruiting. Pickell's muster rolls were a shambles, carrying enlisted men as officers while vacant commissions went unreported; the man acting as adjutant of the regiment turned out to be a private. Pickell had recently solicited an appointment as brigadier general, but while Porter complimented Pickell's efforts with the 13th New York he gently suggested that the old man was already expending "as much energy as his age and bodily strength will permit." The board that finally examined Pickell showed less tact, and found him pathetically deficient. Colonel Jesse Gove, a Regular officer who had served with Porter in Utah, recorded that Pickell was "the merest child in his profession: he could not answer the simplest questions." Despite Pickell's plea for McClellan to do him "justice," the old colonel was summarily discharged. Porter's confirmation as brigadier general came under attack by Radical Republican senators soon thereafter, and Porter supposed the old man had carried them an exaggerated tale about the runaway slave.[26]

Pickell's immediate successor in command wrought no miracles with the regiment. Most of that hard-luck unit garrisoned Fort Corcoran, under Lieutenant Colonel Carl Stephan (who would report himself sick during the worst fighting of the first campaign, and resign soon afterward). An inspection report on Fort Corcoran enumerated numerous serious deficiencies, and Porter found it disturbing enough to have a separate copy transcribed for Stephan's edification.[27]

The 25th New York posed an even greater challenge. Insubordination was the rule in that regiment, which averaged three desertions a week over two years, including the major, quartermaster, and other officers. A Pennsylvania soldier in a nearby camp dismissed the regiment as a collection of "New York roughs, Bowery boys, 'Dead Rabbits,' etc." Colonel James E. Kerrigan, a Tammany Democrat freshly elected to Congress, apparently set the example for misbehavior. He finagled commissions for three of his brothers, managing the regiment more as if it were a gang than a military organization, and he made no effort to instruct the men or instill the slightest discipline. General Martindale, whose brigade included this problem regiment as well, inspected the 25th New York in mid-October and reported it in abominable condition: officers and men were drinking, arguing, and fighting, and when called into formation many of those in the ranks stood half-dressed and barefoot. In defiance of Martindale's direct order, Colonel Kerrigan refused to undergo inspection with them, and the general ordered him into arrest.[28]

Kerrigan could not be trusted to remain in quarters under arrest. He enjoyed the loyalty of his most obstreperous men, who might be expected to resist any effort to confine him. To avoid such a confrontation, on the morning of October 18 Porter called the 25th New York into line and brought all his nearby regiments out under arms while a guard detail took charge of Kerrigan and escorted him to Washington. Porter cautioned that Kerrigan, who showed undue sympathy with the Confederate cause, might be communicating with the enemy, and advised that his movements and contacts be closely watched: Kerrigan sometimes left camp in civilian clothes and remained absent overnight, while one of his lieutenants had given himself up to the enemy and gone to Richmond, from which he was writing to the colonel. Most of the officers of the 25th signed a testimonial to their leader's virtue. Porter asked headquarters to keep Kerrigan in close confinement, preventing him from crossing the river to visit the regiment. "His influence here will be most pernicious," Porter warned, "and will probably be productive of disastrous effects."[29]

While the colonel awaited trial, Porter supported Martindale's efforts to weed incompetents out of the regiment and promote promising officers. Two of Kerrigan's brothers resigned immediately after his arrest, and the third was fatally wounded—whether by an antagonistic comrade or a Confederate marksman was never established. Over the next few weeks more than a dozen officers of the 25th were pressured into resigning or dropped from the rolls as deserters, including a surgeon who had been filching from the hospital fund. One captain who had spent months at home on recruiting duty without enlisting a man was ordered back to camp, but resigned instead; private soldiers who still refused to go on duty were given the choice of compliance or Dry Tortugas, and most submitted. Another man took temporary command, and his strict discipline momentarily accelerated the desertion rate, but the erstwhile mob started looking like a regiment.[30]

Just as Porter relied on regimental and brigade commanders of firmness and competence to mold their men into trustworthy components of his division, so McClellan needed generals of similar talents to lead his divisions. Of about thirty generals under McClellan's direct command, Porter was hardly the most senior, but many thought him the best of the lot, and some already suspected that he was the commanding general's favorite. Porter's calm and seemingly judicious nature made him a valuable confidant and counselor. His talent for training raw recruits and reconciling them to strict discipline gave McClellan an excellent opportunity to showcase the development of his army—and Mc-

Clellan needed such a display by late October, after a disastrous little battle at Ball's Bluff, near Leesburg, where Charles Stone's division had taken a pounding to no evident purpose.

To test the results of eight weeks' work with his command, Porter proposed a review for Saturday, October 26, with a division drill and sham battle. That forenoon he formed his three brigades, batteries, and cavalry in a twenty-five-acre field, with McClellan and his staff in attendance. Porter led the various brigades through the evolutions of drill, maneuvering them by regiment, battalion, company, and file, and finally formed them in double ranks, three brigades deep. From there they wheeled out by companies and marched before the assembled visitors, then resumed their formation. McClellan and his guests trotted between the ranks, and as they approached each regiment its band would erupt in brass and percussion, falling silent as the next band began its own selection. For the finale Porter deployed the division in line of battle, bringing each company into line by regiment at the double-quick, as in the "Shanghai Drill" demonstrated at West Point seven years before. Each rank loosed a blank volley before retiring behind another rank to load, while the new front rank fired in turn. The sound of the exercise carried into the streets of Washington, where the unexpected echo of gunfire roused apprehension. With the sulfurous smoke wafting over the field and their ears still ringing, the men marched back to their quarters toward four o'clock, anxious for their first food since dawn.[31]

The troops moved with admirable speed, thought Philippe d'Orléans, but he found fault with many of the junior officers. Of the brigadiers, he deemed Martindale "the true soldier, glaring always and swearing without cease, but briskly leading his brigade." The prince considered Butterfield "the beau of New York transformed into a general." He saw nothing noteworthy about Morell, but he thought Porter might be the most distinguished man in the army, "slim and delicate in appearance, with a black beard and a small and lively eye." Porter evinced a reserved but determined air, according to the Comte de Paris, and he maneuvered his troops "perfectly."[32]

That review of Porter's division came just as McClellan expected to assume command of the entire U.S. Army, in place of General Scott. McClellan had begun to antagonize Scott early in his tenure with vast overestimates of Confederate strength and alarmist warnings that implied Scott was neglecting Washington's safety. He had come to ignore General Scott in official communications, dealing directly with the secretary of war or the president. Scott intended to retire once an acceptable replacement appeared, and he hoped it would be Henry Wager Halleck, an intellectually inclined former army officer who was then still in California. McClellan maneuvered for the top command himself before Halleck reached the East.[33]

The night before he reviewed Porter's division, McClellan sat until well after midnight with three Republican senators. He led them to believe that General Scott was impeding his efforts to move against the enemy, and the following evening those senators waited on the president, urging him to shelve the old general. Having learned that Scott intended to retire immediately, McClellan spent most of the last day of October composing a report for Secretary Cameron designed to persuade the president to name him general-in-chief. He wrote it at the home of Edwin M. Stanton, who had briefly served in Buchanan's cabinet. Stanton habitually cultivated the friendship of powerful figures, and had begun ingratiating himself to McClellan soon after the general reached Washington. He drafted the opening part of McClellan's report, which ended with the suggestion that Cameron show it to the president.[34]

Once back at his headquarters, McClellan asked one of the French princes to have their horses saddled, and in the evening they slipped away together to Hall's Hill—"to seek refuge in Fitz Porter's camp," as McClellan told his wife. The three of them sat around the campfire late into the night while the two generals digested the news and discussed the possibilities. The next day Scott formally retired, and Lincoln appointed McClellan "to command the whole Army."[35]

Porter never recorded his thoughts about the retirement of Scott, whom he had seemed to hold in high esteem until the old general blamed Patterson for failing to hold Johnston at Winchester. That may have weakened his admiration for Scott, and he had begun finding fault with Scott's tactical and administrative wisdom in letters to Manton Marble, influential editor of the New York World.[36] McClellan's personal annoyance with Scott did not improve Porter's image of the old hero, and he may have been prodding Marble to editorial criticism for McClellan's benefit. Porter gave McClellan the same loyalty he usually accorded his superiors, but his personal affection and his faith in Little Mac's ability enhanced the intensity of that professional obligation. McClellan reciprocated both Porter's friendship and his confidence, regarding him privately as his chief subordinate and causing them both trouble by betraying that view through word and deed.

On his fourth morning as general-in-chief, McClellan met the division commanders of the Army of the Potomac at the brick house he was renting at the corner of H Street and Madison Place—the house where Dolley Madison had lived out her last years. Mathew Brady came to photograph all the generals with the Young Napoleon, as friendly newspapers were calling him. The weather was clear and unseasonably warm, so they sauntered outside, using the rear wall of the house for a backdrop. Baldy Smith, Franklin, Samuel P. Heintzelman, Andrew Porter, and McDowell lined up on McClellan's right, with George McCall, Don Carlos Buell, Louis Blenker, Silas Casey, and Fitz John Porter on his left. The two most senior, McDowell and McCall, took position at McClellan's elbows while Smith and Porter stood at either end, but their positioning implied more deference to seniority than headquarters usually observed.[37]

Philippe d'Orléans saw great virtue in McDowell, whom he applauded for gracefully accepting his demotion to division command after Bull Run. McDowell appeared to do all he could to support McClellan, believed the prince, who commented that it took a rare disinterest for McDowell to regard his successor as a friend instead of a rival. "He is a big man," the prince noted, "a little clumsy in appearance, of chubby figure, with simple, frank, and affable manners. He speaks French perfectly." McDowell's attention to detail had made him valuable to Scott in the old days of the Regular Army, but his fellow generals recognized that he lacked any talent for inspiring his troops.[38]

McCall elicited less enthusiasm from the Comte de Paris. He was nearly sixty, which his dyed hair failed to disguise, and the prince attributed the poor discipline in McCall's division to his diminished energy. The prince described white-haired Silas Casey as "an old man with a head like a bald parrot, who mounts a horse like a sick monkey," adding that he was given the regiments no one else wanted. The prince heard it said that Buell and Porter were the best generals with the army at Washington; he failed to make it clear whether that comparison encompassed McClellan himself, but he left no doubt that Porter had surpassed everyone else in training his troops. Porter had the best-looking division in the army, in the opinion of the prince, and McClellan took enormous pride in it.[39]

McClellan held a review of Buell's division under bright autumn skies on November 8. The Prince de Joinville and his nephews rode along, but they found the event a little slow and dull; evidently so did McClellan's horse, which fell asleep. It was Porter's division that elicited the grandest compliments from the house of Orléans, the next day. The troops had formed on the field by 11:00 A.M. as usual, and soon afterward there began a drizzle that gradually intensified into a full-fledged storm. As he had on the parade ground at West Point, Porter ignored the weather: his men followed the same choreography they had performed two Saturdays previously, including the sham battle, while the mud deepened beneath their feet. From lines of battle they swung into hollow squares, and once again the hillsides echoed with the dull, damp reverberations of musketry and cannon. The men marched back to camp at midafternoon drenched to the skin, but a week later McClellan issued a general order praising their proficiency in drill, calling Porter's division "a model for the Army." Such a comment would have been intended to initiate competition among other commands, but it probably also aroused jealousy among some of the older division commanders.[40]

Wednesday, November 20, provided the premier military spectacle thus far in the war. Official Washington took a holiday, and all morning carriages crowded across the Long Bridge and down the Columbia Turnpike to Bailey's Cross Roads, at the junction of the Leesburg Pike. There, on a broad and relatively level plain below Munson's Hill, seven divisions—over sixty thousand men—formed ranks under the direction of General McDowell as a thick morning fog reluctantly disintegrated. The president and his family came to participate, along with most of the cabinet and department functionaries galore. Thousands of spectators ringed the field, taking the highest ground they could find. Riding from Washington at the head of a brigade of cavalry, McClellan burst onto the field waving his cap, giving the crowd (and the dignitaries) a hint of his popularity as forty acres of massed troops cheered their commander. Batteries fired salutes, raising clouds of acrid smoke. After a barrage of anthems and accolades, McClellan, the president, and a long gaggle of officers and hangers-on mounted horses and threaded their way at a gallop through the long, deep ranks.[41]

A few unique uniforms stood out, such as two regiments in Butterfield's brigade wearing jaunty new Zouave uniforms, trimmed in red, but for the civilians clinging nervously to their saddles the inspection passed in a long blue blur. Lincoln rode with his elbows tucked into his sides, wrote the Comte de Paris, holding his hat out before the faces of the troops like a blind man begging. The tour consumed as much as an hour and a half, after which the riders returned to a rise at the front of the massive formation and gathered to watch as the army peeled off, one regiment or battery at a time, and marched past on its way to camp. When the last man had passed, one of the president's private secretaries realized that it must have been the largest military parade the continent had ever seen.[42]

Four days later, the fine autumn weather gave way to signs of winter. Late on the afternoon of November 24, McClellan and his staff galloped from Washington to Porter's headquarters, which consisted of a tent village in the remaining pines on the slope of Hall's Hill. They all retired to Butterfield's nearby camp for an "excellent soup," but as the headquarters entourage prepared to leave snow began falling in fat flakes, filling their eyes and noses as they rode back in the dark. Several wet days followed, and then came the freezing nights and daytime thaws, to soften the roads enough for wheeled vehicles and marching men to churn them into deep mud.[43]

The great review of November 20 had demonstrated a comforting degree of competence in the army, but that caused important persons to wonder why it was not put to use. The month had hardly run out when the president prepared a few questions for McClellan about a hypothetical movement against Joe Johnston, who had assumed overall command of Confederate troops in northern Virginia. The collective effect of Lincoln's inquiries was to ask why McClellan's vast and well-trained army could not begin doing something.[44]

Lincoln's anxiety for military action could only have intensified with the reconvening of Congress, which created a joint committee to investigate the conduct of the war. Republicans filled all but two of the seats, and the committee came to be dominated by Ben Wade and Zachariah Chandler — the most visible and vocal of the Radical Republicans who sought to bend the war to the goal of abolition. The prominence of those two did nothing to endear the generally high-minded Radicals to conservatives in or out of the army. Wade, though honest and principled, was crusty and belligerent. Chandler struck Navy Secretary Gideon Welles as "vulgar and reckless," and he was frequently drunk, even in the Senate, which only amplified his arrogance. Welles thought Wade tainted by his association with Chandler.[45]

Chandler made his motion to form the joint committee on December 8, the same day he received a letter from William Doubleday, whose cousin Abner had been at Fort Sumter and with Patterson in the Shenandoah Valley. The Doubledays were thoroughgoing abolitionists, and like most fervent followers of a cause they suspected anyone who failed to share equal enthusiasm of harboring the opposite viewpoint. From such a biased perspective did William offer his cousin as witness to what he called the "proslavery" attitudes of McClellan, Porter, and dozens of other generals whose appointments would be coming to the Senate for confirmation. Chandler took the hint, especially in regard to McClellan and Porter.[46]

The president's questions to McClellan involved how quickly he could start his troops in motion if he decided to move without further reinforcement or training. The earliest McClellan thought possible was December 15, and the latest Christmas Day. Gossip from either the White House or McClellan's headquarters carried that reply to the streets, and Confederate operatives in Washington warned of an imminent movement just before Christmas. A banker in the city attributed the tidbit to "General Porter," who reportedly let it slip in front of one of the banker's friends, but very likely he was talking about Provost Marshal Andrew Porter — if there was even any truth to his claim. McClellan offered no outward hint of any such intention, although the Comte de Paris claimed he knew the general had a campaign planned and meant to launch it soon. A Union division meandering near Dranesville ran into Rebels on December 20, engaging in gunfire that Porter reported hearing from Minor's Hill, fifteen miles away, but the clash signaled no offensive. Rather than preparing for a campaign, Porter was allowing his men to build winter huts when McClellan asked him to exercise his division again on December 21.[47]

Ellen McClellan had come to Washington, and attended the review. Many of the officers in Porter's division brought their wives down, boarding them in the city or nearer camp. Generals starved for feminine society invited the women to dinner parties, along with their husbands if they were not on duty. Hattie Porter stayed in New York, so Porter hoped to dash home for a few days at Christmas, but after the review he provided a banquet for McClellan, his wife, and their staffs, serving roast beef, turkey, oysters, and of course champagne.[48]

While Porter's division paraded for the McClellans, Ben Wade sent the commanding general a request to come before the joint committee as its introductory witness. McClellan responded the next day, offering to appear a little after 10:00 A.M. on Monday, December 23, but he awoke that morning too sick to leave his quarters. His chief of staff (and father-in-law), Randolph Marcy, came down with something equally virulent. It was soon understood that both of them were suffering from typhoid fever, which they may have contracted during Porter's feast after the December 21 review: in mid-December surgeons had specifically investigated that disease in Porter's division, and it had since surfaced in the ranks of Porter's sharpshooter regiment. Headquarters tried for some time to pass McClellan's illness off as a severe cold, but he grew worse for a week and could hardly leave his bed for over two weeks. With both the general-in-chief and his chief of staff confined, there was no one to tell the president what should be happening to prepare the army for the field, or where it should go when it did move.[49]

During McClellan's illness, the Radicals of the joint committee began their own campaign. They started interrogating his troop commanders on Christmas Eve and kept at it until he could leave his sickbed. Porter appeared before Wade, Chandler, and three of the other members of the committee late on the morning of December 28. They wanted to know whether the army could move against the enemy immediately, and if not why: could an active campaign be conducted in the winter, and would remaining in their present camps until spring demoralize his men? Porter sometimes declined to answer, noting that as the commander of one division he knew too little about the army as a whole. He inadvertently revealed one factor curbing McClellan's aggressiveness when he estimated Confederate strength in northern Virginia at 160,000 men, but the congressmen had no means of knowing how badly exaggerated that number was.[50]

Wade broached the subject of grouping the divisions into corps, which was becoming a popular theme among Radicals, and he wondered who would be in charge if the army were attacked in McClellan's absence. That led Porter to replies that would have echoed with intense irony a year later. He said the commanders of adjoining divisions would inevitably go to the aid of those under attack, at which Wade asked if he would go to the assistance of a comrade's beleaguered troops because he was "compelled to."

"If I did not do it," Porter replied, "I should deserve to be hung." Wade then inquired if a general had the right to refuse an appeal for assistance, or to disobey such a call from the senior officer on the field if he thought it imprudent. Porter said the general had to judge that for himself. "If he disobeys that order he does it on his own responsibility," he added.

"And he always has a discretion over it?" Wade asked.

"He must have," said Porter, "but he exercises it at his own peril." Exactly a year after Porter uttered those last few comments, the members of a hostile court-martial would have relished a transcript of them.

After releasing Porter, the committee put many of the same questions to General Morell. More than once Wade asked Morell, a brigade commander, what he would do if he were the general-in-chief. As Porter had evidently deduced, at least some of the congressmen — and Wade in particular — seemed to be looking for contradictory testimony, or for material they might use to corner McClellan.[51]

The two generals described the ground as finally frozen solid in those last days of 1861. That made it easy to move artillery, Porter admitted, but Morell told Wade that Virginia's red soil "cuts up more quickly than any I ever saw before," so a little rain or warm weather would render most of the roads impassable. That winter tended to bring a lot of precipitation, too, sending complaints of torrential rain and deep mud filtering homeward from Porter's division.

"When it rains here it makes a business of it," wrote a Massachusetts soldier, early in November. "We are still on Hall's Hill, up to our knees in mud and water," he reported in mid-January, and two weeks later he said he hadn't seen the sun for three weeks; it was raining, snowing, or hailing constantly, and mud was a foot deep. The colonel of his regiment confirmed his observations, and on February 18 General William T. H. Brooks, who was camped nearby, wrote his father that "I never saw or heard of as much mud — mud everywhere — tis nothing but mud." That winter a private in Porter's 18th Massachusetts claimed that eight weeks passed without sunshine and corroborated the depth of the mud, cursing the fog and mist that prevailed when it wasn't raining. Many attributed rampant sickness and mortality to the cold, wet weather, which grew worse as spring approached. "Sunday morning was clear and warm," a Pennsylvanian wrote from Butterfield's brigade early in March, "at noon it rained, before night we had five inches of snow, during the night it rained and in the morning it was all slush, before noon the snow was all gone and last night it rained in torrents, washing great gullies in the streets."[52]

Such letters contradicted Porter's belief that staying in camp all winter would not harm morale, but his assertion that the army would profit from more preparation rang true — and especially in his division. By the end of the year Porter's distant but dignified manner, stern discipline, and attention to training had won the admiration and even the affection of men in some of his most rebellious regiments. Two days after Christmas the adjutant of the 13th New

York—he who had really only been a private—assured his little brother that Porter commanded "the best 13,000 soldiers in the world," and he described "Fitz John" as something of a father figure.

"A handsome man he is, slender but erect. A few gray hairs among his raven locks, a full black beard kept neatly trimmed, an eye like a diamond, slow and deliberate in his speech, with a low, clear, distinct utterance, prompt and decisive in his actions. Cold, heartless, unimpassioned, and a *terrible, terrible, terrible* disciplinarian. . . . But such a splendid soldier. . . . Ed, I honor, admire, revere, and could almost devote my life for that man."[53] Porter evidently had the magic touch.

Lincoln's intense concern over McClellan's condition blinded him to such progress in building the army, especially after a grilling by Wade's committee on the evening of January 6. The congressmen learned that the president knew nothing about the commanding general's plans, and one of them remembered that Lincoln seemed to doubt that he had a right to know, since he was not a military man.[54]

McClellan's health was actually already improving, but he told the president nothing of it, perhaps to avoid pressure to testify to the joint committee in a weakened condition. Porter was called back about the Patterson campaign, and the president urged McClellan on January 9 to see the committee that day, if he could. He did not, yet the day before he had asked Porter to come in and see him from Hall's Hill. Porter made more trips into Washington during the worst of McClellan's illness than he usually did, and sometimes he remained overnight.[55]

In the absence of an official second-in-command, or any communication from McClellan's staff, Lincoln convened Generals McDowell and Franklin and some cabinet officers in the White House on January 10 to ask how the army might be used. Porter was not called in, suggesting that Lincoln was not yet aware of him as McClellan's special confidant. McDowell outlined the requirements for moving against Johnston's lines at Manassas, and Franklin suggested sending part of the army down the Chesapeake Bay to strike Richmond from below. The next evening the two generals returned to the White House, having agreed to recommend the movement on Manassas. Postmaster General Montgomery Blair, who was also a West Point graduate, preferred sending the army to Fort Monroe, to march up the York River peninsula toward Richmond or to capture Norfolk.[56]

On the morning of January 13, a wan and wary George McClellan appeared at the next White House gathering of the generals and department heads. Oblivious to the anxiety his long silence had aroused, McClellan clearly resented the conference as an intrusion. He said he had his own plans, with their own schedule, and he stubbornly declined to reveal them before so many people, lest they filter into the newspapers. Franklin tipped McClellan's hand by admitting that he had mentioned the peninsula route because he knew it was part of the commanding general's plan. That prompted McDowell to say he had been "completely in the dark" about that, thereby implying that Franklin must be another of McClellan's intimate confreres. Franklin and Porter had both testified before the joint committee about their private consultations with the general-in-chief, and that information was circulating in Radical channels through the increasingly hostile Wade and Chandler.[57]

Secretary of War Simon Cameron did not attend that meeting, having been squeezed out of the cabinet by January 13. Lincoln replaced him with Edwin Stanton, who spent a few busy days that week pretending to be the best friend of both McClellan and the Republicans he needed to confirm him as head of the War Department. McClellan initially greeted the appointment as a stroke of luck, but Stanton ended his first day in office by meeting secretly with the general's worst enemies among the Radicals, with whom he promptly allied himself.[58]

Porter may have seen Stanton for the first time the next day, when McClellan brought all his generals to the War Department to meet the new secretary.[59] A year later, both McClellan and Porter would regret ever having heard his name, and it was only days before Stanton's first blunder threatened trouble in Porter's division. As a contract attorney for the War Department, Stanton had successfully contested a petition by three-month soldiers seeking release from a three-year regiment; as secretary of war, he disapproved the desertion conviction of another man who had left a two-year regiment under the same circumstances. According to Stanton, the defendant had been illegally held beyond his time — yet his case was identical to the one Stanton had prosecuted, and to that of many in the 2nd Maine and several two-year New York regiments that had mutinied over it. With several such regiments in his division, Porter wrote to McDowell, who also had a few of them, pointing out the adverse implications of the decision. Both Porter and McDowell appealed to headquarters, Porter predicting that if the decision were not reversed, "I shall lose the greater portion of four of my best regiments."[60]

Two days later, Stanton hinted his commitment to the Radicals by ordering the arrest of Charles Stone. Radicals resented Stone for returning runaway slaves to loyal Maryland owners, as the Fugitive Slave Act still required. Stone's efforts to impose discipline in his division had also made him some enemies, and numerous officers in a particularly refractory regiment began impugning his loyalty. With no better excuse than falsehood and malicious innuendo, Stanton ordered McClellan to relieve Stone from duty and hold him under guard. McClellan hesitated for ten days, until pickets caught a suspicious fellow whose answers to leading questions vaguely corroborated the accusations of disloyalty. Stone was sent to Fort Lafayette in New York Harbor early in February, essentially to punish him for obeying a law Congress did not repeal until mid-March. He remained imprisoned over six months, without charges.[61]

The arrest cast a sudden pall over Porter's demeanor. A staff lieutenant misunderstood that Porter feared some of the accusations might be true, but Porter was instead probably ruminating about Stanton, whom he and McClellan were already learning to mistrust. Even Stone's successor as division commander considered Stone perfectly innocent, and Porter suspected that Stone was being persecuted for his conservatism and his failure to adopt Radical doctrine.[62]

News of Stone's confinement came soon after Porter returned to camp from a few days' absence. He probably learned of Stanton's order for Stone's arrest on the day it was issued, January 28, because he came into Washington that afternoon to spend the night at McClellan's house, and both of them were old friends of Stone. Porter came back into the city on the evening of January 31, attending a party that drew half the diplomatic corps and a host of Washington beauties to Secretary of State Seward's home on Jackson Square; then he disappeared from camp and capital for six days to visit his family. He returned to Hall's Hill on February 6, riding back to camp on roads that had become quagmires.[63]

Such mud provided a good argument against any direct attack on the Rebel position at Manassas. Soon after recovering from his illness, McClellan had begun developing a plan to shift his army to Urbanna, on the Rappahannock River, to strike at Richmond so far below Manassas that Johnston could not retire in time to defend it. On February 3 he presented that plan to the president, through Stanton. He had shared the idea with Porter by late January, and early in February Porter expected an imminent movement. Stephen M. Weld Jr., the son of Porter's preparatory school teacher, joined his staff just then, and the general refused him lumber for a floor in his tent on the grounds that they would soon be leaving Hall's Hill.[64]

Another month would pass before that happened, during which Union armies in the West and on the North Carolina coast made great strides against the enemy — all by traveling on the water. Ulysses Grant, now a brigadier general, led an army up the Tennessee River, and his naval escort blasted Fort Henry into submission on the same day Porter navigated those bottomless Virginia roads on his return from leave. Ambrose Burnside seized control of North Carolina's Albemarle Sound when he captured Roanoke Island in another amphibious operation. Then Grant's army captured Fort Donelson on the Cumberland River, taking many thousands of prisoners and forcing Porter's erstwhile chief, Sidney Johnston, out of his Kentucky line and all the way to Mississippi.

Those and other successes prompted widespread hope that a similar triumph in Virginia would crush all support for the rebellion — unless the abolition aims of the "ultras," or Radical Republicans, motivated the South to hold out to the bitter end: George Meade, commanding a brigade in McCall's division, presciently feared that such a change in the character of the war could prolong the conflict for years. He also worried that the victories of waterborne armies elsewhere would lead McClellan's critics to demand the same success from him in mud-bound Virginia.[65]

Edwin Stanton implied such a demand with an absurd letter to the *New York Tribune*, rebuking McClellan and the Regular establishment for concentrating on "military combinations and organizing victory." The recent battles were won by troops simply rushing into battle, he postulated, dismissing military science in favor of "pursuing and striking the foe" with the spirit of Old Testament warriors. His letter publicly rejected everything McClellan and Porter stood for.[66]

It could only have been Porter who, after Fort Donelson, told Lieutenant Weld of Grant's deadly personal failing. For all Grant's energy and industry, his friends from the old army knew that he was "just as likely to be drunk in the gutter as to be sober," and with his passion for self-control, Porter recoiled from such weaknesses. He ascribed the events in Tennessee to General Buell, whom McClellan had sent to direct operations below the Ohio River.[67]

Weld was relieved to find Porter especially ascetic in his appetites, for he had heard that the high living of the generals cost their staff officers dearly. Still, the division did not lack for social entertainment. There was a party every weekend at George Morell's brigade camp, over on Minor's Hill, with the headquarters house decked in flags, the 4th Michigan band blaring, and occasional salutes from Charles Griffin's six-gun battery; guests might include one or two of the French princes and some of the British legation, or the commanders of neighboring divisions and their wives. One afternoon in the middle of February, Porter and his staff received a former Whig governor of Massachusetts and his wife at Hall's Hill with an elegant luncheon. Two nights later General Butterfield, whose salary amounted to nothing against his personal fortune, hosted a dinner party for Porter and his other brigadiers, along with the ambassadors from France and Russia. Then Martindale's staff invited Porter's staff to share "a handsome bill of fare" at their headquarters—ten yards from Porter's—with toasts and singing and drinking until midnight. On March 1 Porter welcomed a visit from J. Howard Foote, a New York importer of musical instruments who was married to Hattie Porter's younger sister, Eliza, and for several days Foote accompanied the general and his staff on their rambles.[68]

Such festivities in the bleak, muddy, deforested landscape of Arlington County sustained officers' morale while they waited for the roads to dry. A different effect may have been wrung from the enlisted men confined to the musty darkness of their stockaded tents, who smelled the filet mignon and heard the raucous singing. The officers' parties also gave ammunition to critics of McClellan. Prominent among those critics by then—and surreptitiously so from the moment he rose to power — was Edwin Stanton, who conspicuously denied a newspaper report that he had credited McClellan with the recent victories. That removed the last doubt at army headquarters that Stanton had "sold out" to the Radicals. Indeed, in currying favor with the Radical editor of the *Tribune*, Stanton had specifically promised to end "the champagne and oysters on the Potomac."[69]

7

THE PENINSULA

Impatience for activity in the East prompted President Lincoln to issue an executive order demanding a general advance by Washington's Birthday. McClellan complied by mounting an expedition up the Potomac to Harper's Ferry, where he intended to cross his forces and seize Winchester. Men, artillery, and supplies headed upriver, and a flotilla of canal boats followed via the Chesapeake & Ohio Canal, for use as massive pontoons in a bridge he expected to span the river. The president also authorized the next phase of operations—transferring much of the army somewhere down the Potomac—and the War Department began rounding up transportation. Orders to Porter, Baldy Smith, and McCall portended imminent, rapid movement, sending ripples of excitement through the camps: Porter transferred his sick to Washington, and the troops sat in idle anticipation throughout a day and night, in a torrential downpour, but it all ended in anticlimax. The only lock leading into the Potomac measured a few inches narrower than all the rest, and the canal boats would not fit. That stopped the grand movement cold.[1]

Stanton put that irksome impediment in the worst possible light, provoking the president to level a furious tirade at General Marcy. When McClellan returned to Washington he meant to go to Lincoln to explain, and the president wished to speak to him, too, but Stanton dissuaded McClellan from it by disingenuously assuring him that everything had been smoothed over. The embarrassment may have impelled McClellan to greater energy, and he bade his chief engineer to develop a plan to eliminate Confederate batteries on the lower Potomac that had long been blocking river traffic from the capital.[2]

The resulting plan led to a conference on March 3 in which all the division commanders met at army headquarters, opposite the southeast corner of Jackson Square. Porter rode in with Butterfield and Lieutenant Weld, taking it at a gallop most of the way from Hall's Hill. The generals argued options and details all through the afternoon and into the evening, poring over maps scattered across a dining table as heavy rain and sleet fell outside. McClellan had not appeared before Porter finally dismissed Weld, telling him the meeting would last until midnight.[3]

Porter stayed overnight in Washington, and when he returned in the morning he initiated surveys of the road from Falls Church to Fairfax Court House, in obvious preparation for an advance directly on Manassas. "The roads today are as bad as I have seen them," he reported to McClellan on March 6: the soil was so saturated that the main turnpike was impassible for artillery or wagons, and horses sank beyond their fetlocks nearly everywhere. Three bridges were out, and the entire road would have to be corduroyed. It would take six hundred men an entire day to cut the logs and lay them in the roadbed, he estimated.[4]

On Friday, March 7, Porter received another summons to army headquarters, where he again met the other division commanders. Under pressure from Lincoln, McClellan asked them to act as a council of war, deciding between two plans of general campaign: should the army advance against Manassas, with a flanking column along the Occoquan River (which McDowell and the president favored), or should it follow McClellan's plan of moving down to Urbanna? The chief engineer, along with McDowell, Edwin Sumner, and Samuel Heintzelman, voted for the former, but the other eight division commanders all supported McClellan's idea.[5]

With that they went to the White House, without McClellan, where Lincoln and Stanton asked them individually when the troops should begin moving. Most preferred late March — Porter specifically named March 25, Franklin March 22, and Smith said not before the third week of March. Then Stanton asked if the army should be organized into corps, which they all favored, but he failed to ask when it should be done. They surely all understood McClellan's reluctance to appoint corps commanders until he had seen his generals perform in the field, but at least within McClellan's staff it was known that he wanted Porter and Franklin especially.[6]

The president regretted their decision about the campaign but accepted it, and he welcomed their opinions on corps organization. The next day he issued an order creating four corps, naming the four senior generals to command them: McDowell, Edwin Sumner, Heintzelman, and Erasmus Keyes. The president also insisted that McClellan rid the Potomac of those Rebel batteries before he took more than two corps downriver, and afterward he was to leave what his corps commanders thought were enough troops to defend the capital. Finally, he had to start active operations within ten days — by March 18.[7]

That same day, Porter sent out one of his cavalry squadrons, which found the enemy picket line noticeably reinforced. This aroused Porter's suspicion, and he asked to borrow Lowe's balloon for an observation, but it was in Washington. The next morning, March 9, the president showed much alarm (and Stanton fell into sheer panic) at reports that the Confederate ironclad *Virginia* had shattered the Union fleet at Hampton Roads, sinking two frigates and grounding two others. Later that same day McClellan rode out to Hall's Hill to look into those extra Rebel pickets. Porter was still unable to get the balloon, but one of Morell's regiments entered Vienna, and by evening Porter and McClellan were certain the Rebels had withdrawn from Fairfax Court House. They had also fallen back from their positions upriver and had abandoned the batteries on the Potomac.[8]

Planning to lunge at Manassas the next morning, McClellan asked to suspend the corps organization temporarily, so he could take the scattered divisions forward directly from the camps they occupied. Stanton balked at first, but an hour after midnight McClellan telegraphed from Porter's headquarters to say that he would have to countermand the army's marching orders if he first had to organize the divisions into corps. Near 3:00 A.M., Stanton yielded. After a couple of hours' sleep, Porter and his staff ate breakfast before first light on March 11 and the division started toward Fairfax Court House in pouring rain, leaving all the huts standing empty at Hall's Hill and Minor's Hill.[9]

Porter's division took the lead through desolated country. Not a fence or a haystack stood, and most of the houses had been stripped of windows and often their siding, besides being sacked of their contents. Franklin marched behind Porter and McDowell followed Franklin, slogging over sodden roads that exhausted the troops. The Comte de Paris assumed that McClellan kept Porter and Franklin in front to let them win some laurels against any Confederates they encountered, so they could earn the corps commands denied by their lack of seniority. One of Porter's cavalry regiments led the advance under William Averell, and by late morning had cleared the way as far as the dilapidated town of Fairfax Court House. From the weathered look of the predominately wooden buildings, a corporal in the 13th New York judged that no new houses or barns had been raised there in a century.[10]

Porter arrived there at noon, commandeering the empty home of Dr. William Gunnell for quarters and headquarters. McClellan and his staff lodged nearby, in Beauregard's old headquarters at the home of Thomas Love. Staff servants kindled roaring fires in every room of both houses while the cavalry ventured ahead again. A couple of hours later Averell sent back word that he was just entering the works at Centreville, where a resident told him the Confederates had been gone more than thirty hours. Manassas was also reportedly abandoned, and Averell's informant had seen heavy smoke from that direction the day before.[11]

McDowell's division pushed on to Centreville the next day while Porter's rested. McDowell joined McClellan and his staff in a ride through the abandoned camps and charred supply depots, offering a guided tour of the battlefield of July 21 from the hilltop where the tide had turned. In the midst of his explanation he began weeping in frustration at the memory, eliciting genuine sympathy from McClellan and his aides, including even those who disliked the smug and portly general.[12]

Johnston had decamped via turnpike and railroad, burning the bridges in his wake. A lagging squad of Louisiana Tigers picked up by Porter's men bragged that Johnston took ninety thousand men with him, but by their winter huts Colonel Gove doubted that more than twenty-five thousand had wintered there. With such soupy roads it made no sense to give chase, and Johnston would have been too close to Richmond for any force to overtake him from Urbanna, either.[13]

While McClellan contemplated those factors, he learned that the president had deposed him as general-in-chief, on the grounds that on an active campaign he would be busy enough with the Army of the Potomac. This was the second executive order in three days tending to isolate McClellan, for the corps organization had thrust a theoretical barrier between him and his closest advisers, forcing him to communicate with Porter, Franklin, and Smith through intermediate commanders. McClellan may have been trying to lift his own spirits from those serial blows when he called for an impromptu review of his favorite troops toward dusk on March 12, parading Porter's division in the fields near Fairfax Court House. The billowing banners, the rhythmic pulsing of regimental bands, and the frenzied cheering of troops who loved him soothed the romantic spirit of the beleaguered Young Napoleon as a scarlet sunset faded into moonlight.[14]

In a whirlwind of activity McClellan mapped out a new campaign. He would transport his army down the Potomac all the way to Fort Monroe, and from there proceed up the right bank of the York River to Richmond. During two rainy days after the moonlight parade he organized the logistics sufficiently to order the troops toward Alexandria, where they would board steamers. When Porter's division formed ranks well before dawn on March 15 the rain was coming down "in sheets," and it continued to pour until the command fell out, after dark, a few miles short of Alexandria. Most of the men had left their shelter tents as roofing on their huts, to which they had expected to return. Many had brought only their woolen blankets, and some of those had been sodden since the first night's rain. One of Morell's staff officers conceded that by the time they camped "every one was pretty well drenched"—including himself, despite his India rubber poncho.[15]

"I have seen some bad weather and some suffering," admitted a Regular Army captain from McClellan's class at West Point, "but last night and yesterday evening beat it all." All night his men stood in "cold pelting rain," unable to coax a fire to life. With most of their camp equipment still at Hall's and Minor's

Hills, not three hours' march away, the troops huddled there for several days, waiting for a fleet of transports to carry them downriver.[16]

Porter must have found a house to use, for as he waited he wrote to Manton Marble. His introduction to Marble may have come through McClellan's friend Samuel L. M. Barlow, who was part owner of the *World*, but he also knew one of Marble's reporters, Edmund Stedman. Porter had just received a letter from Stedman, advising him to prod McClellan to action to appease rising public impatience and forestall the growing popularity of abolitionist generals. At a recent speech given by antislavery activist Wendell Phillips, Stedman had heard the crowd hiss every time Phillips mentioned McClellan, and cheer wildly whenever he alluded to Major General John C. Frémont, the Republicans' 1856 presidential candidate.[17]

Porter addressed that concern in the letter to Marble. He had been urging Marble for months to see General Patterson's side of the dispute with Scott, and pleading for editorial patience about McClellan's deliberation in moving against the enemy. "It will come upon you quickly," he had promised of McClellan's offensive, in late November, and he had predicted that the war would be over by the first of May. Now the enemy had slipped away from McClellan's army after seven sedentary months, and Porter felt compelled to defend his chief still more vigorously. He knew that Radicals wished to replace McClellan with Frémont, who had been relieved of command in Missouri for such sins as declaring slaves free on his own authority. The Frémont faction smelled blood with McClellan's removal as general-in-chief, especially because the order removing him had restored Frémont to duty — albeit in a geographically awkward new department designed for political expedience rather than strategic sense. Radicals showed such fervor for Frémont that Porter credited "the abolition element" with alerting Confederates to the Urbanna plan, so as to allow them a timely escape from Manassas and embarrass McClellan.[18]

Frémont would demoralize the army, Porter assured Marble, and officers would resign in droves. Asserting that only McClellan had the confidence of the men necessary to beat the enemy, Porter asked Marble to take McClellan's part against those who would see him replaced. The president responded to press opinion, he pointed out, and all would be well if Lincoln could be made to stand firm against the Radicals. Not only was McClellan the better general, but his campaign by way of the lower Chesapeake was certain to succeed. "Our army is ample to whip anybody in Rebeldom," he concluded, "and we would march to victory."[19]

Porter gave no public hint of aversion to administration policy. Shunning active politics as most Regulars did, he reserved his partisan impulses for private communications, but a citizen's right to a private opinion no longer enjoyed the sanctity of old — especially for officers of a conservative stripe. Radicals would have regarded Porter's letter to Marble as an egregious partisan offense, but his partisanship was only incidental, whereas theirs was fundamental: they tried to manipulate military affairs for the sake of political goals, while Porter resented their political agenda mainly for the impediment it would pose to military success.[20]

Porter had his own reason to mistrust "the abolition element." The Senate had confirmed him as a brigadier general in executive session on March 7, but on March 13 Senator Chandler persuaded his colleagues to recall it. As Charles Stone's persecution attested, Radicals such as Chandler already frowned on officers who showed insufficient sympathy for their program. After six weeks Chandler finally made a motion to reconsider the confirmation, but he lost the vote and Porter kept his commission for the present. Porter heard about it weeks afterward, and suspected that Colonel Pickell's tale-telling lay behind it.[21]

The division assignments to the various corps caused some complaints. The teetotaler McDowell saw reasons why the division of Joseph Hooker should not form part of his corps, and officially those reasons may not have included Hooker's well-known appetite for the bottle. McDowell asked for one of the divisions that had been assigned to Erasmus Keyes of the Fourth Corps, and McClellan obliged him by shifting Hooker to the Third Corps, commanded by Samuel Heintzelman. As the transports began gathering off the Alexandria wharf McClellan also reassigned Porter from Keyes to the grizzled, crabby, and critical Heintzelman. The third division in Heintzelman's corps was commanded by Charles S. Hamilton, a West Point classmate of Ulysses Grant's and a well-connected, calculating backbiter. Heintzelman valued punctuality, which he did not detect in his own staff officers, in McClellan, or in the senior officers in his corps, save Porter. At 10:00 A.M. on March 20, Heintzelman appeared in Alexandria to meet McClellan and his division commanders to resolve some complications about embarking their troops, and he noted petulantly that "no one was prompt but Porter."[22]

Hamilton's division boarded the transports first, beginning Monday, March 17. Heintzelman soon found that the contractors had overestimated the capacity of the vessels. More steamers had to be engaged, but the first of Hamilton's division started off on Tuesday and the last of it went ashore at Fort Monroe by Thursday evening. It was not until Friday morning, March 21, that Porter's division started over three miles of muddy road toward the Alexandria waterfront. The gangplanks of two dozen vessels groaned beneath his men's feet all afternoon and into the night, with a regiment or so climbing aboard each ship. One of General Morell's more fastidious staff officers cringed at having to share accommodations with the largely Irish 9th Massachusetts, which he characterized as "a pretty dirty lot." Thinned out as it was by resignations, desertions, prison sentences, and the wholesale discharge of undesirables and minors, the

13th New York fit aboard the little steamer *Hero*. Jesse Gove's 22nd Massachu- setts required the big oceangoing side-wheeler *Daniel Webster*, on which Porter had sailed back from Texas, one year before.[23]

Porter chose that commodious, familiar ship for himself and his staff, and early on Saturday morning the *Webster* came back to the wharf to pick up the general and his horse. He complained of a quartermaster having failed to load grain and hay for the animals, and several more hours were lost in that task. The 12th New York, recently assigned to Butterfield's brigade, was still taking ship late that morning when most of Porter's flotilla weighed anchor and started downriver.[24]

As the unfinished dome of the Capitol drifted into the distance, one of Por- ter's aides remarked to a comrade that it might be a long while before any of them returned. He left unasked the more pressing question of who among them would never lay eyes on it again. Late that night, Colonel Gove—one of those who would look no more upon Washington City—stood mesmerized on deck by the romantic glimmer of lights from the fleet as it drifted down the broad, dark river beneath a third-quarter moon.[25]

Heintzelman arrived at Fort Monroe first, about ten o'clock Sunday morn- ing, and was greeted by seventy-eight-year-old Major General John Wool, the post commander. Porter's ship hove into view off Old Point Comfort four hours later. The ironclad *Monitor* lay nearby, dented but unimpaired two weeks after its contest with the C.S.S. *Virginia*. Porter went to the fort for orders, taking a room at the Hotel Hygeia while the transports disgorged his troops. Several regiments had already assembled on the wharf by nightfall and disappeared into the darkness, down a muddy road leading to the ruins of Hampton, three miles away.[26]

The next morning, March 24, Heintzelman sent Porter ahead to find a good campground. His and Hamilton's divisions were but the vanguard of the host that would follow, but they already needed more room and fresh water than any forces that had yet passed that way. Riding out from the hotel, Porter settled on Hampton itself, burned nearly to the last building the year before when it was evacuated by the same John Magruder who still commanded the Confederate troops that lay ahead. With a blaze kindled in the fireplace of a gutted house, the staff extemporized seats in the remains and sipped coffee while servants pitched the headquarters tents on a grassy common amid the rubble.[27]

Hampton occupied the concave extremity of the geographical feature Union soldiers soon capitalized as the Peninsula, as though there were no other. Some twenty circuitous miles away lay the Revolutionary earthworks encircling the village of Yorktown, where General Magruder's army waited. The York River ran only half a mile wide there, with Gloucester Point projecting from the left bank, and big Confederate guns frowned over the water from either side, discouraging the U.S. Navy from guarding that flank, as McClellan had expected. The Peninsula stretched no more than ten miles wide there as the crow flies, but nothing ran so straight in this oldest settled portion of Virginia. The Warwick River, rising from marsh a mile and a half south of Yorktown, wound toward the James in three great bends, and Magruder put it to use as his principal line of defense. Depending for flank protection on the swamps that bordered both sides of the main road, he maintained pickets as far toward Hampton as a place called Big Bethel, where the war's first real battle had ended in Union defeat the previous June. With Yankees advancing again, Magruder sent artillery ahead to fill the redans that had stopped them once before.[28]

Big Bethel, named for a church in that location, sat on the north branch of the Back River about eight miles above Hampton. Porter moved his headquarters three miles closer to Big Bethel on March 25, camping at New Market Bridge. His division again formed the advance of the army, and after sending two regiments on a scout to Big Bethel on March 26 he sent word back to Heintzelman that he could seize that spot if the general so wished. Evidently Heintzelman did so wish, and that evening Porter extracted more information about the Confederate defenses from a pair of ragged fugitives from the slave-labor force that had been working on Magruder's Warwick River line. Hungry and exhausted, the pair of "contrabands" stood before a blazing fire in the headquarters circle amid staff officers and servants as Porter questioned them. When he had gleaned all he thought he could, he ordered someone to find food for them and began planning for the next morning's work.[29]

At 6:00 A.M. Porter led two brigades toward Big Bethel, sending a skirmishing party from the 1st U.S. Sharpshooters ranging ahead of them, distinctively clad in forest green uniforms. Part of Baldy Smith's newly arrived division trailed behind Porter, and Heintzelman tagged along at the rear, in nominal supervision. The sharpshooters had been temporarily (and unhappily) armed with Colt revolving rifles instead of the Sharps breech-loading rifles they had expected, but they found little use for them that day. A couple of soldiers had slipped beyond Porter's pickets that morning, prowling for plunder, and they had been scooped up by a Rebel patrol that pumped them for the intelligence of Porter's approach. The unsupported Rebel artillery at Big Bethel had therefore already flown when the sharpshooters pounced, at noon. Two or three dozen Rebel videttes still waited near the empty earthworks, but at sight of the enemy they galloped back to their main squadron farther up the road, and when the Union skirmishers reached them the horsemen all fell back.[30]

With Morell's brigade in the lead, Porter sent his troops up the direct road to Yorktown while Smith veered left toward Warwick Court House, near the mouth of the Warwick River. Porter ventured as far as Howard's Bridge over the Poquoson River, about eight miles from Yorktown, where his skirmishers encountered a battery supported by infantry; the sharpshooters loosed a volley at them, without response. Magruder had garrisoned another advanced outpost at Young's Mills, below Warwick Court House, but Smith stopped far short of that. Questioning inhabitants black and white, Porter accurately guessed Confederate strength at a maximum of fifteen thousand men, and he confirmed General Wool's information that Magruder was building breastworks all the way across the Peninsula.[31]

Heintzelman went back to his headquarters. Smith's troops bivouacked in the woods, but Porter led his division back to New Market Bridge by evening, and before going to bed he chastised the colonel of the 4th Michigan for letting his men wander off to pillage isolated cabins. Like most career officers, Porter loathed depredations against civilians for humanitarian and political reasons, but he feared the corrosive effect on discipline even more. Stragglers had betrayed his reconnaissance, and he had already formally complained about marauders from Hamilton's division. To deter it, he ordered his pickets to shoot anyone outside the lines who refused to come in, regardless of what uniform they wore.[32]

Sometime after breakfast, Porter gave Heintzelman his conclusions on the enemy position. The old general relayed Porter's information and opinions to McClellan, at Alexandria, padding Porter's estimate of Magruder's forces by a third, in apparent echo of a report General Wool had made two weeks before. Porter emphasized his lower calculation the next day, skirting the chain of command to telegraph McClellan personally. The Rebels' heavy guns all pointed toward the river, he added, showing that they expected the main assault to come from the navy, as McClellan had hoped. His message revealed that the personal connection between Porter and McClellan had survived the interposition of a corps commander.[33]

In that telegram, Porter also alluded to supply problems. The blame seemed to lie with the army's chief quartermaster, Stewart Van Vliet—whom Porter and Sidney Johnston had met on the North Platte in 1857. On the evening of April 2, after McClellan's steamer docked at Fort Monroe, Heintzelman, Porter, and Smith went aboard to plan a general advance, which made the shortages of tools, transportation, and supplies stand out. Van Vliet had not yet arrived, and inadequate facilities for unloading men and materials had caused trouble from the outset. Porter, who tended to be critical of colleagues in the presence of sympathetic superiors, was surely among those Heintzelman described as speaking "freely" of Van Vliet's incompetence, and suggesting his removal. The exchange soured McClellan on Van Vliet, whom he described a few hours later as "ever late when most needed."[34]

Lingering in McClellan's stateroom aboard the *Commodore* until two o'clock in the morning of April 3, the generals concluded to attack Yorktown early on April 4 despite the shortcomings in supply. Porter had promised Manton Marble a lightning campaign once it began, and it made sense to strike while Magruder remained so weak. By then parts of three Union corps had already reached the Peninsula, and McClellan issued orders for five divisions—totaling well over fifty thousand men—to move against the Yorktown line. Porter would lead on the right, toward Yorktown, followed by Hamilton's division and that of John Sedgwick—the first division from Edwin Sumner's Second Corps. On the left, Keyes would move on Young's Mills and Warwick Court House with Smith's division in front and another division, under Darius Couch, trailing behind Smith. All were instructed to camp for the night before the Confederate outposts at Howard's Bridge and Young's Mills.[35]

Porter led off with William Averell's 3rd Pennsylvania Cavalry, immediately followed by the 1st U.S. Sharpshooters. Some of the sharpshooters had not yet been armed at all, and Porter supplied them with what axes he had, using them as a pioneer corps to rebuild burned bridges and clear felled trees from the roadway. Big Bethel posed no real obstacle, and it was not until the column reached Howard's Bridge that any impediment appeared that the pioneers could not handle. At the bridge redoubt a couple of brass fieldpieces opened on the Yankees, who stood back and waited for the 5th Massachusetts Battery to wheel up and unlimber. Shot and shell from their three-inch ordnance rifles drove the two Rebel guns away, and Porter's men settled in for the night, with Morell's brigade camped at the head of the division in the village of Cockletown, six miles from Yorktown.[36]

On March 30 Porter had described Magruder's works extending west from Yorktown, toward Williamsburg. It came as a surprise to General Keyes six days later when, after easily chasing the Rebels from Young's Mills, he spied a line of works on the far side of the Warwick River. He had expected to cross there without much opposition and turn toward the Williamsburg Road, cutting off Magruder's retreat, but in torrential downpours that afternoon he suddenly regarded the dammed and swollen Warwick as an impenetrable barrier. In his front he saw no point he could assault "without an enormous waste of life."[37]

The rain turned the roads to soup—or molasses, thought a lieutenant in Couch's division. On the right, Porter pushed on from Cockletown until his skirmishers reached the intersection of the Warwick Road, a couple of miles south of Yorktown and near the headwaters of the Warwick River. Magruder kept the plurality of his command at that geographically vulnerable spot, but Heintzelman's column would have outnumbered that portion by a factor of six. A pontoon bridge would have been useful then, but McClellan may have been hobbled less by the lack of a bridge train than by a telegram handed to him as the soggy, dreary day of April 5 drew to a close. The message announced that the president had decided to withhold McDowell's corps from him—the largest corps by far in his army. With that reduction in his ultimate strength, McClellan's burst of aggression evaporated and he began to see the odds mounting against him.[38]

"Deserters say they are being re-enforced daily from Richmond and from Norfolk," he wrote that evening, beseeching the president not to make him fight the entire Rebel army "with diminished numbers." Heintzelman and Keyes sympathized with him, Heintzelman deeming it "a great outrage" while Keyes wrote to Senator Ira Harris, of New York, seeking support for McClellan's original four-corps campaign. Franklin informed McClellan of McDowell's assertion that he regretted the change, lest McClellan think he had been angling for a separate command. McDowell had also interpreted the orders as a "blow" at McClellan, who suspected—not without reason—that it had come from Stanton's efforts to find a rival for him. Porter adopted that interpretation, and it spread contagiously to his staff.[39]

Edwin Stanton had, perhaps, orchestrated the decision as much to hamper McClellan as to protect Washington, but it created as much of a psychological handicap as a strategic hardship for the general. The day after McClellan learned the bad news, he began accepting inflated estimates of Confederate reinforcements that essentially doubled Magruder's force. Three days afterward, writing to Flag Officer Louis Goldsborough, the naval squadron commander at Hampton Roads, he remarked, "I am probably weaker than they now are or soon will be."[40]

Stanton inflicted far more damage on the manpower of every Union army by ordering an end to all recruiting. A few weeks would illustrate the sheer stupidity of that decision, and professional soldiers recognized immediately that the armies would dwindle rapidly from attrition unrelated to battle. At that same juncture, the Confederacy had begun augmenting its own forces through comprehensive conscription. Stanton's behavior suggested either foolishness or faithlessness, and conservatives everywhere began to suspect him of a deliberate attempt to hinder the war effort—and McClellan—in accordance with a Radical program.[41]

Seething over what he saw as another hurdle set by the meddling amateurs to whom he answered, McClellan decided to halt his fledgling offensive and bring up siege guns he had intended for use at Richmond. He kept in touch with the naval commander, still hoping the gunboats would brave the York River batteries to flank Magruder out of Yorktown. He positioned Porter's division on the extreme right of the line, against the York River and amid a growing network of forts and entrenchments, and Porter started looking for gun positions that might enfilade those river batteries.[42]

The only dry-land passage to Yorktown lay in Porter's sector, and as early as the evening of April 5 Magruder threw infantry out to challenge Porter's pickets.

The clash led Colonel Gove to complain of unfair reporting by a correspondent of the *New York Tribune* serving in the 1st U.S. Sharpshooters, who described one company of Gove's 22nd Massachusetts retreating at a "double-quick run." Gove scrawled off an angry correction to the newspaper, and when it went through channels for approval Porter advised caution, although he did so in unusually candid language for an official communication. Porter assured Gove that he, McClellan, and Gove's brigade commander, Butterfield, all knew the aspersion to be false; he failed to name Heintzelman, having perhaps not discussed the point with him. "The remarks of newspaper correspondents I consider beneath notice," Porter added, "especially those which appear in the New York Tribune, which is the exponent of a party which seems to be anxious to slacken the character of all that is good and pure and to detract from the good conduct of meritorious officers and men."[43]

Professor Lowe's balloon traveled with Porter's division. On April 6, Porter took it up to a thousand feet for nearly two hours, sketching what he saw through his glass. When he came down he presented a report in an informal council of war. That evening he went up again with the Duc de Chartres, and then Butterfield took a turn aloft. McClellan took all they found as confirmation that the enemy had been heavily reinforced and that his own weight of numbers no longer told. The river batteries at Gloucester Point and Yorktown had also been substantially augmented. In passing that information on to Washington, McClellan pointedly lamented the absence of McDowell's corps, asking the president if he might at least have the division commanded by his other close confidant, William Franklin.[44]

The next afternoon turned cold and rainy, and the storm lasted for more than three days with fluctuating intensity, complicating the supply difficulties as the bottom fell out of the roads. The skies did not clear until the morning of April 11, and Porter sent early for the balloon, anxious to make an observation. Some of Lowe's employees brought it and inflated it before dawn, and Porter showed up alone with his telescope, pencil, and pad of paper; he wore his overcoat against the morning chill and the colder air above. James Allen, the assistant in charge of the balloon, was not yet on hand, so Porter jumped into the basket alone and cast the anchors off. Two or three ropes usually tethered the craft, but only one was attached that morning. He had hardly begun his ascent when he felt a sharp tug, after which the basket started skyward at such a clip that he knew the line had broken. Before rising out of earshot he shouted down to ask what he should do, and a chorus of replies directed him to the valve.[45]

A pair of cords operated the valve at the neck of the balloon, but they had been gathered and secured to the netting there, at the base of the balloon, ten feet or more above him. His only recourse was to shinny up one of the ropes, clamber over the collar that cinched them together between the basket and the balloon, and continue upward — and outward, beyond the periphery of the basket. With one hand he freed the cords, clenched them between his teeth, and began lowering himself back to the collar. From there he would have to drop into the basket, but he could not feel it as he kicked with his feet. Looking directly downward from such a height made him dizzy, but with no alternative he did look, and when he saw the basket swing beneath him he let go, falling into it.[46]

At lower altitude a light wind had carried him to the southeast, toward Fort Monroe, but during his climb he had risen so high that the air current had shifted the other way. By the time he dropped into the basket he had drifted across the Warwick River and well behind Magruder's line. With a pull on the valve lines he could feel and hear the gas as it blew straight toward him, and the balloon began to descend slightly. That quelled his alarm, and he started drawing the terrain and works behind enemy lines as the glow of the rising sun began to spread across the Peninsula. He had attained a greater height than in any of the controlled observations he had made. Wagon trains looked like caravans of ants, and he could not distinguish men except in groups, by using his glass, yet by some acoustical aberration he could hear the echo of voices. He made out the pentagonal outline of Fort Monroe, and Norfolk across the water. As sunlight burned its way westward he detected the coveted spires of Richmond. Releasing more gas in small increments, he descended low enough to regain the breeze toward Fort Monroe, and as he passed back over the Warwick River he tugged more ambitiously on the valve.[47]

When he could distinguish the Stars and Stripes, he began looking for a place to land, trying to avoid treetops and the long rows of stacked arms with their gleaming bayonets threatening to impale him. A hundred feet from the ground he saw his chance, and pulled hard on the valve lanyard. As the last of the hydrogen escaped he began to plummet. His descent was slowed only slightly by the fluttering fabric of the deflated balloon, and his fall was finally broken by the ridgepole of an empty wall tent belonging to officers of the 72nd Pennsylvania. The soldiers who gathered around him mistook him for Professor Lowe, and in such an undignified position he let them think it. Drawing his overcoat closed to disguise his general's uniform, he asked them to fold up the balloon and inquired for their brigadier, who turned out to be his acquaintance, William Burns. The news of his predicament had already alarmed army headquarters, and General McClellan was near distraction when Porter sauntered in "just as cool as usual" to report what he had seen.[48]

Years later, Porter learned the tether rope had been weakened with acid in one spot by laborers from the balloon team who were not happy with Mr. Allen, and had sabotaged it in the expectation he would be the first to go up. At the time, Porter blamed the accident on Allen, and he insisted that the professor send a new man.[49]

That evening McClellan wrote Secretary Stanton to assure him that he was doing all he could "to attack with least possible delay," but he had already sat before Yorktown for an entire week, conducting reconnaissance. Besides picketing the open ground near the town, Porter's division spent the next two weeks engaged in bundling fascines and gabions to reinforce the earthworks they were raising, or bridging streams and corduroying the saturated roads in anticipation of bringing the heavy siege guns up from Fort Monroe. The 1st U.S. Sharpshooters kept the Rebel gunners' heads down during the day, but Porter's staff especially feared a big pivot gun that could swivel its muzzle away from the river and reach their camp. Porter — like Hamilton, on his left — supplied heavy drafts of fatigue crews at night. As the month waned, Porter's and Hamilton's work details turned to building batteries for the siege artillery, and Hamilton maintained that his division was regularly called on for an undue share of the labor while Porter's men relaxed.[50]

Hamilton was a querulous man, but he was not the only one who complained about Porter, and especially after McClellan essentially elevated him above the corps commanders by naming him "director of the siege" on April 27. That order required Porter to report to McClellan at least twice each day, and it gave him effective command of the front-line trenches. He was to supervise the construction of the heavy batteries, determine which troops and how many would man the works, and when (or whether) the guns would open fire. The generals delegated daily to command the trenches and each division's field officer of the day had to report to Porter thereafter, and take orders from him.[51]

That reinstated Porter as McClellan's right-hand man at least for the duration of the siege. The order formalized a position Porter had assumed gradually, as McClellan delegated a succession of additional responsibilities to him without consulting Heintzelman. Porter had written to Marble as early as April 18 as though he were the driving force behind the siege operation, predicting that the big guns would open fire by April 22. On April 26 he was still promising that the "overwhelming batteries" would open fire, but without naming a date.[52]

President Lincoln had granted McClellan's plea for Franklin's division, which came by steamer to a landing three miles behind Porter's position on Wormley Creek. McClellan's own headquarters sat alongside Porter's division, and jealousy over the commanding general's favoritism had begun to infect the upper echelons of the Army of the Potomac by the time Franklin's troops arrived. Joe Hooker, who already envied Porter's prominence, had then just arrested one of his own brigadiers, Henry Naglee, and Heintzelman observed suspiciously that both Porter and McClellan interceded on Naglee's behalf.

Naglee, a West Pointer who had graduated with Martindale and Morell, may have benefited from their recommendations, but he also shared McClellan's conservative politics, and they had common friends in high places. McClellan had him released from arrest and reassigned him to Silas Casey's division, on the left of the line. When he arrived there, Naglee sent McClellan a personal note expressing his regret at having to be so far from him, signing off with "love to Marcy & Porter."[53]

Within two days of Porter's assignment as director of the siege, Heintzelman heard grumbling from at least three generals in his corps who were displeased with McClellan, and especially about his affinity for Porter. One of them suggested that the only way he could win any recognition would be to change his name to Porter. That was probably Hamilton, whom McClellan relieved from duty and sent home the next day. One of the others may have been Martindale, who reported critically on the commanders of guard details and working parties failing to report to him when he acted as general of the trenches, and he seemed to blame it on interference by Porter. Charging that the complaint was unjustified and hypocritical, Porter threw the blame at least partly back on Martindale. A similar exchange in early April, when Martindale found fault with Porter for assigning his brigade surgeon to serve as division medical director, had ended more amicably: Porter had assured Martindale of his friendship, and told him that "no act of mine & properly understood will ever lead to any difficulty." April ended less harmoniously for them.[54]

The batteries were finally supposed to be nearing completion by May 1, but McClellan's request to have some of the largest siege pieces sent from Washington betokened further delays that strained executive impatience. Fearing "indefinite procrastination," Lincoln wired McClellan to ask if he intended to do anything, but the general was waiting for precisely the right moment: Porter kept the siege batteries silent lest they prematurely reveal their positions. Rebel batteries were burning most of the gunpowder along the lines, and they seemed to step up their fire on May 2. Despite having been down sick early on May 3, Porter spent the rest of the day applying the finishing touches. He even had a bombproof shelter completed for his observation post, expecting to telegraph reports from there to McClellan during the bombardment—which he and McClellan decided to open on May 5.[55]

Porter also made an ascent with Professor Lowe on May 3, attracting artillery fire that burst all around the balloon, and one round passed between the ropes securing the basket. A few shells landed in the encampments below—one nearly striking McClellan and his staff, inspiring them all to throw themselves face-first into the dirt. Porter ordered Lowe to have the balloon taken down, and with wild gesticulation the aeronaut signaled the ground crew to reel them in.[56]

The Rebel guns thundered long into the night without doing much damage, but the sun rose to an eerie stillness. Pickets reported the enemy works empty on the Union right, with explosions echoing and fires burning somewhere in Yorktown. At McClellan's behest Porter threw out a regiment to investigate. Heintzelman went up in the balloon, from which he could see neither a gun nor a man in the Rebel camps, where the tents stood abandoned, and he watched Porter's infantry enter the works. Porter wired back to McClellan that the U.S. flag was flying over Yorktown.[57]

McClellan sent his available cavalry after Johnston's retreating army, with Hooker's division and Baldy Smith's on the march behind the cavalry. Hooker claimed he was held back by Butterfield, who neglected to release Hooker's portion of the trench guards. Porter's division occupied Yorktown, and McClellan paused in that frenzied hour to name him military governor of the place. It was a tiny realm, described by a Sanitary Commission nurse as a single street facing the river with "perhaps a dozen, good old houses, and the ruins of a few others." Heintzelman sent a note approving of Porter's appointment, but hoping he would not be detached for long, admitting, "I do not like to lose the services of so valuable an officer."[58]

Hooker and Smith caught up with Johnston's rear guard on May 5 at Williamsburg, a dozen miles away over roads in deplorable condition. McClellan remained behind, sending Franklin's brigades up the York River on their transports to West Point to intercept the Confederate retreat. Cannonading from the direction of Williamsburg announced the collision between the pursuit and the Rebel rear guard, but they echoed for two hours before McClellan took to the saddle. He only turned for the sound of the guns when Rhode Island governor William Sprague, who had ridden with the advance, came pelting back from the fight to urge McClellan onward. Sprague caught him with Porter and Franklin — which did not surprise Sprague, who had tattled to Stanton two days previously that McClellan effectively subordinated his corps commanders to those two and Baldy Smith. McClellan galloped away, reaching the engagement just as it came to a disappointing conclusion. As would happen repeatedly during the campaign, the commanding general was not present on the field during most of the fighting, and this time he had little good to say about how it had been managed by those who were.[59]

The Confederate army sped away as rapidly as the roads allowed. During the night of May 6 steamers unloaded Franklin's division at West Point, forty miles from Richmond, where the Mattaponi River joined the Pamunkey to form the York River. Franklin established a landing on the right bank of the Pamunkey River, just upstream from West Point. Confederate cavalry and infantry attacked him there the next morning with surprising fury, and he sat back to wait for more troops. By May 9 Johnston had put his whole command between Richmond and McClellan's army.[60]

Porter began loading his men and guns on transports on May 7 for the trek upriver to West Point. He and his staff went aboard the *State of Maine* with the 1st U.S. Sharpshooters, which had discarded its Colt revolving rifles for new Sharps breechloaders. The first of his men landed at West Point the next evening under bright moonlight. Colonel Gove seemed dismayed, or disgusted, that Martindale devoted all his attention to bringing his horses ashore, ignoring his brigade. Sailors lightered the last of the division to the dock the next morning. A volunteer nurse on a nearby hospital ship saw the steamers "black with men," describing for a friend how "the little boats foam over with them (like your ale) on the way to shore."[61]

Using the battle at Williamsburg as his excuse, McClellan asked Stanton if he could break up the corps organizations, or remove the commanders he had found wanting. Stanton deferred to the president, who gave his assent but accompanied it with some political advice. Noting that General Hamilton had agitated a swarm of powerful politicians when he was deposed, Lincoln warned McClellan that it had cost him some valuable support in Congress. After that, he wondered whether McClellan felt strong enough to remove all his corps commanders at once. The president added that some observers saw McClellan's wish to abolish the corps organization as "an effort to pamper one or two pets," and eliminate their rivals. Lincoln said he was "constantly told" that McClellan never consulted with his aging corps commanders, instead communing with no one but Porter, "and perhaps General Franklin."[62]

Considering that Lincoln and Stanton had been the only officials he had consulted about dissolving the corps, McClellan had cause to identify the secretary of war as the chief observer the president alluded to. If such a motive had occurred to Stanton, he might also have originally favored the formation of corps at least partly because of the distance it would insinuate between McClellan and "his pets." Yet the president was correct, and some senior officers thoroughly resented Porter. Keyes's chief of staff had begun commenting captiously about him in private, and the jealousy toward Porter had grown so pervasive that staff officers at the brigade level in his division sensed it. "McClellan's pets, they call us," confessed George Morell's assistant adjutant general, who deduced when they landed at West Point that McClellan was looking for a way to "patch up a corps for Porter."[63]

A few days later, McClellan did just that. George Sykes had brought a small division of Regular Army troops, and McClellan added these to Porter's division to create the Fifth Provisional Corps. Taking Baldy Smith's division from Keyes, he did the same for Franklin, cobbling together what he designated as the Sixth Corps. With Porter in corps command, Morell took over his old division, and Colonel Gove detected that Martindale was *"mad"* at being passed over. Only a day before, Gove had recorded Martindale's "sneaking conduct" in appropriating the regimental wagons of the 22nd Massachusetts for his personal use, and when Martindale missed the promotion, Gove predicted there would be the "Devil to play."[64]

8

MAIDEN BATTLE

From West Point the York River Railroad ran more or less straight to Richmond, crossing the Pamunkey at White House — a substantial plantation owned by Robert E. Lee's middle son, "Rooney." The modest house sat on the spot where George Washington had courted the widow Martha Custis a century before. Marching from the landing near West Point under a broiling sun on May 13, Porter's two divisions rested at Cumberland Landing the next day, where clouds of dust filled everyone's eyes, noses, ears, and mouths. Resuming the road in a cold rain on May 15, the new corps joined much of the rest of the army at White House on the evening of May 16, camping just over twenty-five miles from the Confederate White House.[1]

For the next few days the army edged toward Richmond, one town or railroad station at a time. On May 18 Keyes and the Fourth Corps held the advance at Baltimore Cross Roads, and Heintzelman's Third Corps lay at New Kent Court House, while Sumner's Second Corps lingered on the bank of the Pamunkey at Cumberland. Franklin had advanced to Tunstall's Station on the York River Railroad, and Porter lagged in the rear at White House, near McClellan's headquarters; Porter ventured out himself to scout the roads for McClellan, riding with the cavalry in one of those soaking Peninsula downpours. The next day Keyes slogged his divisions over sodden roads for Bottom's Bridge on the Chickahominy, sixteen miles from Richmond, while other troops marched up to take his place. Porter advanced to Tunstall's Station, with McClellan in tow.[2]

By now the C.S.S. *Virginia* had been scuttled and the U.S. Navy controlled the James River almost as far as Richmond: Confederate batteries stopped the gunboats at Drewry's Bluff on May 15, barely ten miles downriver. McClellan might have enjoyed a much safer and more convenient supply line had he shifted his army to the James, but he stuck to the York River Railroad at least in part because the president had finally agreed to let McDowell join him. McClellan wanted him to come by water, which would be more secure and might also put McDowell more obviously under his command. Lincoln insisted that

McDowell march down from Fredericksburg, keeping his forty thousand men between the Rebel army and Washington; he also prohibited McClellan from detaching any troops from McDowell, or ordering him away from the Washington corridor. McClellan argued that the enemy's strategic route to Washington lay miles west of Fredericksburg, through Gordonsville and Manassas, and that on the road from Fredericksburg McDowell offered no protection to the capital. He was correct, too, as Robert E. Lee would demonstrate three months later, but Lincoln was not to be dissuaded.[3]

The president's exercise of what would later be called micromanagement showed a lack of faith in McClellan, who in turn mistrusted the administration, if not Lincoln himself. Like McClellan, Porter believed that the interference originated with Stanton, whom he suspected of manipulating military operations to favor politically palatable generals, and to diminish McClellan. Stanton, Lincoln, and Treasury Secretary Salmon P. Chase had accompanied General Wool when he seized Norfolk, and Porter accused Stanton of denying McClellan the credit of having drawn Norfolk's garrison away to defend Richmond. McClellan appeared convinced that McDowell was intriguing to be left behind, and Porter thought Stanton was at least colluding with McDowell, so he could swoop down on Richmond just in time to become the hero of the hour.[4]

McClellan's army ranged along sixteen miles of the Chickahominy River by May 23. His right stretched upriver to Mechanicsville, a village with a score of deserted homes, where a sign declared that Richmond lay five miles to the south. His left was anchored on Bottom's Bridge, below the railroad. Porter and Franklin held the upper reaches, where telescopic observations from the balloons revealed people walking and riding on the streets of the capital. Keyes and Heintzelman secured the left of the line downstream, with Sumner positioned between the two extremities. The next morning a brigade from Smith's division seized Mechanicsville while the 4th Michigan, from Porter's old division, cleared a crossing three miles downriver, at New Bridge. Under fire from Rebel skirmishers, some of the Michiganders forded the Chickahominy above the bridge in water up to their armpits, holding their rifles and cartridge boxes above their heads. Then, sweeping down the far bank, they drove the bridge guards away with considerable loss, hauling back dozens of prisoners and claiming to have killed dozens more.[5]

About the same time, Keyes sent a brigade reconnoitering from Bottom's Bridge toward Seven Pines, an intersection on the Williamsburg Road eight miles east of Richmond. Two months after Porter established his first camp at Hampton, the trap seemed to be closing on Richmond. Porter exploited the progress to try wringing a little appreciation from one of his worst enemies back in Washington, sending Zachariah Chandler a telegram complimenting the 4th Michigan on its successful first operation. As he reminded the obstinately unfriendly senator, the previous winter Porter had told him there was "no better or more gallant regiment in the service" than that one, from Chandler's home state.[6]

Seizing Richmond so early seemed likely to end the war promptly. That made the promising strategy of the junction with McDowell particularly crucial to conservatives such as Porter and McClellan, who dreaded the revolutionary designs of Radicals like Chandler. McDowell faced a Rebel division under Joseph Anderson, and Lincoln asked McClellan if he could sever Anderson's supply line. McClellan had already taken steps in that direction, sending Porter reconnoitering toward Hanover Court House, where the railroad to Fredericksburg crossed the Pamunkey River. Porter dispatched two regiments of infantry and another of cavalry under Robert O. Tyler, colonel of the 1st Connecticut Heavy Artillery, who destroyed all the known bridges and ferries on the Pamunkey. Tyler's scouts found that General Lee's wife and daughters were staying at a nearby home as refugees, and when the Lees' host saw the Union cavalry he hurried to Hanover Court House to alert a Rebel detachment there. Tyler was aware that he had done so, but he had been told of the Confederates by local slaves, so he called for reinforcements to continue his mission. Colonel Gouverneur K. Warren of the 5th New York brought the men of his own Zouave regiment, in their baggy red trousers, and took command of the expedition. Porter directed him to eliminate all the river crossings as far north as he could, to prevent Anderson from surprising them from behind.[7]

With the president's anxiety for the safety of Washington aggravated by Stanton's cultivation of that sentiment among Radical Republicans, a good opportunity to seize Richmond was lost: McDowell should have been able to roll over the remnant of the Confederates in his front through late April and early May, while McClellan had most of the Confederates transfixed on the lower Peninsula. Lincoln again interfered in the last week of May, thwarting yet another promising chance to gobble up Richmond. Thomas J. Jackson, known as "Stonewall" since Bull Run, had led a small army down the Shenandoah Valley, soundly thrashing Nathaniel Banks, who scampered from Winchester all the way back across the Potomac. That threw the government into another fright. A terror-stricken Stanton called on the governors for troops, illegally authorizing another levy of useless three-month militia, and the president held up McDowell's march on Richmond to send him chasing after Jackson. By the afternoon of May 25 Lincoln was unnerved enough to add that if McClellan did not attack Richmond soon it might be time to "give up the job and come to the defence of Washington." Later that evening he indicated that McDowell not only would be delayed now, but would not be coming at all, and he asked McClellan to "do the best you can with the forces you have."[8]

That executive trepidation frustrated and discouraged the professional soldiers. Even McDowell told the president that canceling his march was "a crush-ing blow to us." For all McClellan's suspicion that McDowell had sought the detachment of his corps in a bid for independent command, McDowell begged the president to let him go to McClellan, arguing that he could never overtake Jackson in time. A few weeks later McDowell was still grieving to his wife and to a wealthy friend in New York over the lost opportunity, essentially accusing the president of stupidity in breaking up and exhausting his powerful corps for a wild goose chase.[9]

Before receiving Lincoln's warning about withholding McDowell, McClel-lan heard an exaggerated secondhand report that seventeen thousand Con-federates were headed for Hanover Court House. Two days previously the lancers of the 6th Pennsylvania Cavalry had informed Porter that Confeder-ates were "very strong at Hanover Court-House," and this suggested that they were being heavily reinforced. Seventeen thousand only slightly exceeded the generous estimate of troops credited to Anderson, who had slipped away from McDowell's front, reaching Hanover Junction the night of May 25. That left him one long day's march from McClellan's right flank, and much closer by train. Fearing Anderson would be cut off from Richmond when the Yankees took Mechanicsville, Johnston had called him back to his main body via a more roundabout rail route. McClellan mistook Anderson's retreat as an attack on his extended right flank, and sent Porter to Hanover's shire town to confront the threat.[10]

Porter seemed unconvinced that any worrisome number of Rebels lurked in that vicinity, and he told Warren "not to be disturbed by reports of large forces." Union intelligence conflated Anderson, whose three brigades camped at Han-over Junction the night of May 25, with one brigade under a political general from North Carolina named Lawrence O'Bryan Branch, who was posted near the courthouse. Porter correctly guessed that Branch had been sent there to guard the Virginia Central Railroad, rather than to attack him. On Monday eve-ning, May 26, the commander of the 1st U.S. Cavalry tested Branch's pickets, interpreting their encampment for the rumored Rebel strike force, although he guessed it at no more than "5,000 to 6,000." In fact it was smaller still, but just as Porter started toward Hanover Court House, Branch was moving a couple of miles below that place, by a route far enough west to be missed.[11]

Porter led Morell's division from his headquarters on the plantation of Dr. William F. Gaines at four o'clock on the morning of May 27. Two regiments of cavalry and a battery of horse artillery preceded them. Rubber ponchos would have been necessary to keep all the additional ammunition dry, because rain had been falling in torrents all night and continued all morning; the downpour doused most campfires, leaving the division to march all day without coffee. Warren, whose impromptu brigade still lay at Old Church, five miles closer to the Pamunkey, started two hours later. Porter planned to ferret the Confederates out with the cavalry, engaging them from the front with Morell's division and surprising them with Warren storming in on their left flank.[12]

Warren's camp lay closer to the objective, but those marching with Porter had to cover about eighteen miles over roads he called "horrible." A Massachusetts sergeant remembered marching through mud a foot deep, "of the adhesive variety." His colonel, Gove, who made the trip on horseback, thought they only covered ten miles. The lieutenant colonel of the 9th Massachusetts judged the distance at twice that far, and a Pennsylvanian stretched it to twenty-four miles, but all seemed to agree on the depth and consistency of the road. A battery of artillery rolled with each brigade, and the guns and caissons churned the highway into a gelatin that frequently held them fast until infantrymen put their hands and backs to the wheels. Most of the troops marched without knapsacks, burdened mainly by two days' rations and pockets filled with extra ammunition, but even under light loads they and their officers collapsed by the score along the road. When the rain finally subsided the sun burned through and beat unmercifully upon the sopping-wet soldiers.[13]

Late that morning and nine miles below Hanover Court House, the cavalry started driving in Rebel pickets, running down a few and capturing them — "big strapping fellows," remarked a Massachusetts corporal. Two hours later, two miles or more south of the courthouse village, the vanguard passed the Ashcake Road, leading to the left toward Richmond. Just beyond there, at the next intersection, the cavalry spotted the harbingers of the 28th North Carolina, an unusually large regiment that Branch had sent looking for the rumored Yankee advance. After exchanging a few shots, Porter's cavalry pulled aside while he brought up his perennial skirmishers, the 1st U.S. Sharpshooters, and ordered Martindale to augment them with the 25th New York. The New York regiment moved to the front, numbering about four hundred of all ranks; it was somewhat improved from Colonel Kerrigan's days, with a host of new officers chosen from among sergeants of the 13th New York.[14]

Six companies of the 25th New York swept forward down the road under Colonel Charles Johnson — two on one side and four on the other, with four companies in reserve. James Lane, the colonel of the 28th North Carolina, engaged the New Yorkers only with his skirmishers, wheeling most of his regiment in an arc that allowed him to enfilade the Federals' flank. A devastating fusillade crumbled the right of the Yankee line, throwing it back on the reserve companies, and that wing of the New York regiment scattered into nearby woods. Johnson moved the companies on his left up to a house at the intersection, but the Rebels across the road loosed another volley into them and charged, driving them off to the west, toward the railroad and the rest of Branch's brigade. The New Yorkers left behind a heavy sprinkling of officers and men dead on the ground; two companies of the 25th disappeared from the field altogether, most of them having thrown down their arms and surrendered. Once across the road the Carolinians formed a line of battle in the open, only to find an entire Union brigade arrayed before them.[15]

That brigade was Butterfield's. Martindale had brought only three of his five regiments to the field. As the 25th New York moved against Lane's regiment, Porter sent Martindale and his last two regiments to the left, down the Ashcake Road, to destroy the railroad and cut the telegraph lines. Martindale turned that way with the 22nd Massachusetts and the depleted 2nd Maine, fielding fewer than twelve hundred men combined, while Butterfield spread his four regiments out in a front two regiments wide. Under covering fire from a battery of Regular artillery, Butterfield advanced on Lane's regiment, passing clustered fragments of the 25th New York and the strangely sedentary 1st Sharpshooters — not one of whom was killed that day. Lane dispatched a man to Branch, seeking reinforcements, but the pair of regiments Branch sent ran into Martindale's two on the Ashcake Road. Lane was outnumbered about three to one and had no choice but to make a fighting withdrawal. He backed toward Hanover Court House, ordering a courier to hasten there in search of potential support; if he found no friendly troops there, he was to ride to Hanover Junction, more than a dozen miles away, where some of Anderson's men may still have lingered.[16]

In what was doubtless a deliberate ruse, one of Lane's North Carolinians fell into Butterfield's hands as the opposing lines neared Hanover Court House, telling him that eight Confederate regiments had slipped around the Union right. That alarming disinformation exerted the desired effect, and Butterfield stopped in his tracks, throwing skirmishers out on his flanks. He relayed the claim to Porter, who soon rode up with Morell, the two cavalry regiments, and the artillery that had been supporting Butterfield. Porter decided to move Martindale from the Ashcake Road out to the right, to watch for the purported flanking column, which he supposed had come from the larger force thought to be at Hanover Court House. Supposing that Lane had served as the advance guard of that main body, he ordered Butterfield to keep going. Lane retreated through the village, where no additional Rebel forces joined him, and Union cavalry took over the pursuit while Butterfield stopped.[17]

Martindale claimed that he was already in trouble when the order arrived to march away, and had already asked Porter for help. Colonel Gove thought his regiment and the 2nd Maine were fighting five Rebel regiments, although Branch indicated only two actively engaged at that point. Martindale pulled Gove's men out of line and directed them as Porter wished, leaving the little 2nd Maine to contend with both Rebel regiments, but he maintained that he warned Porter the enemy was on the left, rather than the right. Porter wanted to "let them go" and leave them for the cavalry to deal with, Martindale recounted, so he reined toward Porter to remonstrate with him in person, but encountered Morell first.[18]

Porter mentioned no message from Martindale, and none has ever surfaced. Gove wondered whether Martindale had informed Porter, suspecting a breakdown in communications, and Porter remembered a signal officer apprising him that the enemy was behind them—but only after Branch's troops emerged from the woods to chase Martindale. Yet Porter had to approve the report in which Martindale alluded to Porter's response to his warning. Porter's orders also reveal that he misunderstood Confederate dispositions, as Martindale asserted, and discounted any appreciable force of Rebels on his left—where most of them were. Until hearing from the signal officer, Porter had expected to find the enemy mainly in front, at the county seat, except perhaps for the putative flanking force on his right.[19]

Thinking perhaps that the report of an enemy attack on his rear announced the appearance of those eight phantom regiments, Porter sent all his infantry back toward the Ashcake Road. Butterfield faced his brigade about and put everyone into a double-quick, with two regiments dashing cross-country to cut off an arc in the road. Warren had reached Hanover Court House by then, and Porter ordered him off with the cavalry portion of his command to destroy more of the Pamunkey bridges. Meanwhile, he took the 5th and 13th New York from Warren and trotted them back to Martindale's aid. Morell's former brigade, under Colonel James McQuade, had just passed by on its way to the village when Porter himself rode up, turned it around, and sent it to the rescue at the double-quick.[20]

Martindale had already snagged a tardy element of Butterfield's brigade—the 44th New York—to confront Branch's aggressive thrust from the Ashcake Road. That regiment lined up with the 2nd Maine and the even smaller remnant of the 25th New York. Those three regiments were taking a beating from three larger North Carolina regiments, and had lost three guns of the battery that stood with them, when McQuade's brigade and Warren's demi-brigade trotted up. Morell personally positioned McQuade's 14th New York to relieve the 2nd Maine and 25th New York, which were nearly out of ammunition and had been whittled down to fewer than five hundred men between them. With the 13th New York alongside, the 14th leveled its fire on Branch from the front while three other regiments moved in on his left flank. The combination drove the Rebels back "in the most indescribable disorder," wrote the lieutenant colonel of the 9th Massachusetts. A semiliterate private in the 14th New York corroborated the impact of their fire, telling his sister that "wen wea give them the vollie wea sent them a Kiteing."[21]

Elisha G. Marshall, the latest colonel of the 13th New York and one of the plebes Porter had drilled at West Point in 1845, thought General Martindale acted rather strange that day. A few months after the battle, Marshall wrote that he was marching his regiment toward the fighting when Martindale rode up in a state of intense agitation: his face contorted in fear, Martindale tore off his hat and shouted, "Here is the old Thirteenth, follow me." Marshall saw no need for that melodramatic display, adding that it caused "confusion" in his regiment. Contributors to Martindale's hometown newspapers ascribed a more flattering tone to the general's behavior: one claimed that he led the 44th New York into action personally, getting wounded in the foot for his pains; another described the 13th New York raising a spontaneous cheer to Martindale's frenzied greeting.[22]

That evening Porter dispatched a note to McClellan describing the results of his first battle. "We whipped them and have driven them from the ground," he wrote, "killing a large number and taking a great many prisoners." His first dispatch from the battlefield conveyed intelligence that Branch had commanded 13,000 men, and a little later he revised that to 10,000 on the field and 10,000 more "ready to come," which may have alluded to Anderson's division. Six weeks later, he reduced that estimate, but still credited Branch's enhanced brigade with "8,000 or 9,000," or double its numbers. He also guessed that about 200 Rebel dead lay on the ground, and he counted 730 prisoners already sent in; he spoke of one Confederate found beneath his horse who was assumed by the stars and trim on his uniform to have been a colonel. Branch reported only 66 killed, not counting Lane's losses. Neither of them named any field officers killed, but except for the wounded Branch left behind he said nothing of prisoners, either, although he lost so many that Porter called for additional cavalry to escort them to the rear. One of the prisoners complained bitterly that they had been told the Yankees would not fight.[23]

On their way to support Porter, the Regular Army regiments under George Sykes passed hundreds of those prisoners. "They generally wore dirty grey," observed Captain John Ames of the 11th Infantry, who seemed to have forgotten how dirty everyone in his own army was. They all said they had been conscripted under the new law, which accounted for the size of some of Branch's regiments, and many of them said they were happy to have been captured. Some were barefoot, Ames added, "and all looked aguish and rather hungry."[24]

The day after the fight, some of the victors buried the dead while others pillaged a trainload of supplies and mail left on a siding. The loot included clothing, footgear, bedding, knapsacks, personal trunks, and small arms, including pistols and Bowie knives, as well as large quantities of sugar and tobacco. A New York officer appropriated fresh underwear, socks, a pair of boots, and some blankets. One Pennsylvanian took a Bowie knife that he soon threw away, rather than carry. Rebel love letters provided wry entertainment that afternoon.[25]

That morning Porter sent Colonel Gove with his regiment and a company of cavalry to scout the road to Richmond as far as he dared. At the same time he ordered Major Lawrence Williams, commanding the 6th U.S. Cavalry, to ride north and destroy the Virginia Central bridge over the South Anna River, between the county seat and Hanover Junction. Williams accomplished his mission—despite being "more or less drunk," in the judgment of one of his captains. Gove, who seemed to be as much a favorite of Porter as Porter was of McClellan, reported directly to Porter on his return that afternoon, bypassing his brigade and division commanders. He found McClellan there with him, relishing "a glorious victory." Gove told him the enemy was still thick at Ashland, seven miles away on the Richmond, Fredericksburg & Potomac Railroad. Slaves in that vicinity seemed unanimous in the belief that legions of Confederate soldiers lay somewhere between the rail line to Fredericksburg and the Virginia Central Railroad that served Hanover Court House. Porter selected another of his preferred professionals, Warren, to take a closer look toward Ashland and burn a few more bridges on his way.[26]

The battle of May 27, and perhaps the soaking rain of that morning, had cost Porter much of his ammunition, and his dispatches betrayed some concern over that, with so many Rebels reputedly lurking nearby. He suggested that McClellan send out another division or two, and appealed for ammunition for both small arms and artillery—sending twice for rifle cartridges. Before noon on May 28 his concern abated when a neighborhood resident assured him that Anderson's Confederates were making haste for the safety of Richmond. The same informant also heard a rumor that McDowell was on the way south from Fredericksburg, after all.[27]

With his objective accomplished, Porter started his infantry and artillery back toward the Chickahominy on May 29, leaving some cavalry to watch for any developing threat to the flank. That morning part of the 6th Cavalry sped back to the South Anna River, well beyond the charred remnants of the Virginia Central bridge, to burn the trestle on the Fredericksburg line. They met no enemy, and neither did Warren until he had reconnoitered five or six miles back toward Ashland, when he ran into some pickets. That evening the cavalry also turned for home.[28]

Compared to earlier actions in the campaign, the results of the battle had been quite satisfactory, and Porter made them more so by heavily overestimating enemy numbers and inflating Confederate casualties. In fact, a force less than half the size of his own had given him some trouble, albeit more through luck than tactics. By driving straight for Hanover Court House on the strength of obsolete intelligence, Porter had allowed a sizable force to strike him from behind. That was a mistake his cautious commander would never have made, but by taking the risk Porter had won a battle, if not as handily as he believed.

McClellan gushed over the triumph, exaggerating it as a "glorious victory over superior numbers" and copiously praising Porter. "The old rascal has done all I could ask," he told Ellen. He chastised Lincoln and Stanton for belittling Porter's accomplishment, for on McClellan's grandiloquent announcement of the results the president merely complained that the second South Anna rail-road bridge had not yet been destroyed. Porter's staff heard that Stanton, in one of his frequent moments of spite, had suppressed a dispatch from a reporter who had portrayed the battle in McClellan's glowing terms. Porter's battle was "one of the handsomest things of the war," McClellan insisted, and newspapers of a Democratic stripe started to see it that way. A week later the *New York Herald* suggested as much in a bold headline predicting that Hanover Court House was "The Last Great Battle." As it happened, it was neither the last nor the great-est battle, even in that waning month of May.[29]

The rumor of McDowell's march was mistaken. Half his corps was still stum-bling around the Shenandoah Valley looking for Stonewall Jackson, but one of his division commanders had ordered cavalry to scout below Fredericksburg, spawning the rumor. Those horsemen rode within twenty-five miles of Han-over Court House, but returned to camp near Fredericksburg the same night.[30]

Thinking that this foray screened McDowell's approach, Joe Johnston made hasty plans to stop him by attacking Porter and collapsing McClellan's right. Johnston relaxed a little when the Yankee cavalry returned to Fredericksburg, and he called off the assault, but he expected McDowell eventually. That be-hooved him to cripple McClellan beforehand, and an opportunity presented itself when the skies opened up again on the evening of May 30. A thunderstorm struck at 4:30 in the afternoon and raged until well after dark with deafening thunder, crashing bolts of lightning, and a deluge that lifted the Chickahominy out of its banks. Several men were struck by lightning, which the fixed bayonets of stacked arms seemed to invite; one bolt killed a quartermaster sergeant in Porter's old division. Some of the reconstructed bridges washed away, and the swollen river divided McClellan's army. The morning of May 31 opened cloudy and damp, with the corps under Keyes and Heintzelman, amounting to about thirty-four thousand men, effectively isolated south of the river. On short notice Johnston was able to mobilize some fifty thousand Confederates against them in a surprise attack that ought to have been devastating, and nearly was.[31]

Johnston intended James Longstreet to throw six brigades against Couch's division, encamped around Fair Oaks Station on the York River Railroad. Mean-while, Daniel Harvey Hill would attack Silas Casey's division at Seven Pines, a mile to the south on the Williamsburg Road. Longstreet missed his cue, but just before noon Hill struck, sending Casey's division flying in disarray. Phil Kearny came to Casey's aid from Heintzelman's corps, but fell back when flanked. Part of Couch's division sidled over to help, but Rebels swept around behind them and they ran, too.[32]

As the sound of the battle drifted up the river, Professor Lowe launched his balloon from Gaines's farm. He saw "large bodies" of the enemy directly across the river, where Johnston had posted the remainder of his army as a bluff. Lowe sent down a telegram describing the Chickahominy as a "lake," reporting a column of blue attempting to cross it in the vicinity of the fighting, downstream. That was Sumner's corps, easing across on two precarious bridges that still spanned the torrent — one of which was carried away soon after the troops crossed. With the remnants of Couch's division, Sumner confronted Longstreet's tardy attack at Fair Oaks, allowing Keyes and Heintzelman to deal with Hill's assault at Seven Pines, and by nightfall the offensive had been contained. A counterattack in the morning recovered all the lost ground, but it had been a ferocious contest and the regained acreage was littered with hundreds of dead from both armies. Porter had reported losing only 355 men at Hanover Court House, but the three Union corps engaged in Johnston's attack tallied five thousand casualties. The Confederates had suffered even worse, and Johnston himself had been wounded.[33]

One of the French princes thought that was the time to hammer the Rebels on the other end of their line, where it should be thin. Heintzelman and Keyes could hold their own, he supposed, while Porter and Franklin could "put the river behind them" and strike a heavy blow. McClellan, who had been sick and still was, planned a less ambitious maneuver, consisting of an attack by two or three divisions to test enemy strength on the heights opposite New Bridge. Lowe had gone up in his balloon again that morning from Porter's camp at Gaines's farm, spotting heavy columns of Confederates on the road to New Bridge; later in the day he reported them "much stronger" than in the morning. Those reports, which Porter would have had directly from the balloon, may have worried him and Franklin that they were being lured into a trap. Back with McClellan, the Comte de Paris was waiting to carry the order for the New Bridge attack when a telegram arrived explaining that Franklin and Porter considered the passage of the river "impracticable." In a rare display of impatience with his closest subordinates, McClellan crumpled the unfinished order in his hands, squeezing it into a tight ball in his right fist.[34]

In his initial report to the War Department that day, McClellan blamed the near disaster on Casey, whose division had given way "unaccountably and discreditably." A week later he relieved Casey of one of his three brigades, and hinted that the old man ought to be transferred to a training role in the rear. Finally, McClellan relieved him of division command altogether, assigning him to the depot at White House. Casey complained all the way to the president about the injustice of it all, and eventually he would enjoy some vicarious revenge.[35]

Twice now had the president withheld McDowell's corps from McClellan, both times in support of unnecessary field operations conducted by incompetent generals to whom he had given armies for purely political reasons. Finally recognizing the damage his fragmentation of military departments had caused, Lincoln took preliminary steps to consolidate them, and particularly in Virginia. He added Fort Monroe and its garrison to McClellan's command on the first of June, and a week later he instructed Secretary Stanton again to let McDowell go to Richmond. In token of his readiness to join the fray, McDowell telegraphed that he was sending George McCall's division of Pennsylvania Reserves immediately by water, adding that he would bring the rest of his corps overland, arriving within ten days. Mistaking that it was McDowell's decision to bring most of his troops by land, McClellan took that message as the fawning insincerity of a schemer whose intrigue had been foiled. Absorbing their chief's misinterpretation, McClellan's staff unfairly suspected McDowell of maneuvering to retain an independent command.[36]

Addressing Stanton, McClellan pointed out that the bridges Porter had burned would prevent the Fredericksburg force from taking supplies by railroad, while those missing bridges and any bad weather would make road travel extremely difficult. Illustrating how much faster troops could be ferried by steamer, he added that he was then sending back the transports that had already delivered McCall's division. He also warned that he would have to extend his right dangerously thin to hold the way open for McDowell by land. What he did not say, although he later claimed to have been considering it, was that he could bring his right wing over to the south bank of the Chickahominy with the rest of the army if McDowell came by water. That would give him a more secure tactical position and allow for a shorter, safer supply line to the James River.[37]

McClellan vacillated almost daily in assessing the president's attitude toward him, believing Lincoln his best friend one day and his determined foe the next. A letter from a Washington functionary on that very subject may therefore have meant more to the general at the time than it was really worth. Joseph C. G. Kennedy, a name-dropping gossip who headed the Census Bureau, had ingratiated himself to innumerable bigwigs over the autumn and winter, and a letter from him arrived at headquarters in the middle of June. Kennedy claimed that the president invited him for a stroll on the White House grounds on Sunday, June 8, during which Lincoln talked of McClellan "in very kind terms" and said he had "never wavered" in his good opinion of him. Kennedy delighted in showing off his correspondence from prominent figures, but he disavowed any desire for a reply from the busy general.[38]

The account of Lincoln's expressed regard comported with a letter McClellan received from the president a few days later, but already Lincoln's latest promise of reinforcement from McDowell seemed to be in jeopardy. McDowell himself warned McClellan that lethargy in relieving his divisions in the Shenandoah Valley would prevent him from meeting McClellan by his implied arrival date of June 18. The president hinted that one of those divisions was too worn out to go at all.[39]

At that juncture Robert E. Lee, who took command of the Army of Northern Virginia when Johnston was wounded, conspicuously reinforced Jackson's Shenandoah Valley army with three brigades of infantry and some artillery. Perhaps to create a false impression of great secrecy, Lee asked his secretary of war to persuade the Richmond papers to publish nothing about the transfer of troops, but he made no effort to disguise the movement itself. News of it leaked quickly to Union scouts through several sources, serving Lee's initial purpose of sufficiently alarming officials in Washington that they would again postpone McDowell's march and refrain from detaching any more of his corps. McCall's division of Pennsylvania Reserves would be the last troops McClellan would get from McDowell, and McClellan put them under Porter's command although McDowell considered them on loan. That addition to his corps elevated Porter's status again: while the army remained on the Chickahominy, Porter would command the army's right wing.[40]

By adding to Jackson's force, Lee also meant to build a powerful flanking column that could crush McClellan's right wing and preclude any junction with McDowell. In preparation for that, he ordered J. E. B. Stuart to take some cavalry behind Porter's corps for a look at the roads and impediments such a column might face. Stuart, always on the lookout for a chance to perform a spectacular stunt, rode out of Richmond on June 12 with several squadrons of mostly Virginia cavalry and a pair of guns. He put them into camp that night at Hanover Station on the Virginia Central, near the battlefield of May 27, and early the next morning they all rode southeast, close to the Pamunkey River. He flushed a hundred men of the 5th U.S. Cavalry who, having no carbines, fell back after emptying their revolvers. Another couple of companies of the 5th Cavalry joined them and engaged the Rebels near Old Church. The heavily outnumbered Yankees charged the head of Stuart's column but were driven off, leaving behind a wounded captain and some prisoners.[41]

Lieutenant Richard Byrnes, an Irishman who had worked his way up through the ranks of the 1st Cavalry before the war, effectively doomed any pursuit of Stuart when he reported having seen five or six regiments of infantry with Stuart's cavalry. Because of that erroneous report, Philip St. George Cooke, the old dragoon officer who commanded the cavalry behind Porter, hesitated to gallop after the raiders without infantry support. George Sykes gave him Warren's little Zouave brigade, composed of the 5th and 10th New York Volunteers. Cooke, who happened to be General Stuart's father-in-law, slowed his pace to that of the foot soldiers. Lieutenant Weld, of Porter's staff, had gone toward Old Church to replenish the larder for his mess, and he recognized Stuart's men for the enemy just in time to miss being taken by them. Peering from behind a fence as they filed past, he saw that some had gray uniforms and some bluish-gray, while others wore white shirts, or red, "and in fact all the colors of the rainbow were there." They amounted to no more than a single large regiment, he judged—all cavalry, and moving at a fair clip.[42]

McClellan was finally getting over another bout of fever, and had just dismantled his headquarters beside the home of Dr. Henry Curtis—who then lay on his deathbed in the house. Moving south of the Chickahominy, McClellan raised his tents in the yard of another physician, Dr. Peterfield Trent, leaving Franklin and Porter to manage things on the left bank. As the unofficial wing commander, Porter monitored Stuart's progress, forwarded reports, and directed the pursuit on that side of the river.[43]

From Old Church, Stuart decided to ride completely around McClellan's army, rather than turn back and face those who would be chasing him. He rode into the night, burning schooners on the Pamunkey and a supply caravan from White House. A detachment stopped at Tunstall's Station and tried to halt a passing train, shooting a couple of the crew in the process. Leaving the flaming glow of wagons and a railroad car behind them, the Rebels kept to the saddle most of the night, finding their way by a moon just past full. Porter had McCall send a brigade of his Pennsylvania Reserves after them under John F. Reynolds, who reached Tunstall's Station about midnight. Five miles ahead, Stuart's horsemen were mounting up just then to start for Forge Bridge, far down the Chickahominy, where they arrived at daylight. It had rained steadily on June 9 and 10, as it had for most of early June, and the river was running high, but it fell two feet during the course of the raid. Using the wreckage of the old bridge, a team of Virginia cavalrymen improvised a footbridge, while others swam the horses to the other bank. The last man had reached safety before Cooke left Tunstall's Station, twelve hours behind. From there, Stuart had only to veer far enough toward the James to avoid McClellan's outposts.[44]

A few Union and Confederate horsemen had been killed, along with some teamsters and railroad hands, and Stuart's men brought back a gaggle of prisoners and a herd of captured horses and mules. Other than providing the intelligence Lee wanted, the operation had accomplished little of real military value save boosting the morale of those who made the raid and embarrassing the Army of the Potomac. Porter, Warren, and a number of others in the Fifth Corps considered Stuart's success a family affair, and held Cooke responsible for having allowed his daughter's husband to escape. Warren had very much doubted the presence of Rebel infantry, and had vainly urged Cooke to run Stuart down with the cavalry while Warren positioned his own infantry to shut off the raiders' escape. Major Henry Clitz, the West Point classmate whom Porter asked to investigate the raid, found that a gap had been left between the cavalry pickets, but he did not think the enemy had come through in that particular spot. Clitz did imply that Cooke had been extremely slow in responding to the first warning of the raid, taking nearly eight hours to reach the scene with cavalry; infantry had beaten him there by half an hour.[45]

Porter waxed sarcastic in his official report. "General Cooke seems to have regarded his force as a reserve for the day of battle," he charged, "and not therefore expected to perform any picket duty." He found fault with both Cooke and one of his subordinates for not joining their commands to lead the chase earlier, and expressed surprise "that when Cooke did pursue he should have tied his legs with the infantry command." In the following days he kept a close eye on Cooke, posting the cavalry himself and closely monitoring picket details, and he turned increasingly critical of Cooke whenever he mentioned him. He asked his old friend Delos Sacket to inspect Cooke's cavalry, and Sacket suggested reorganizing all the cavalry under one man, to improve efficiency and consolidate responsibility.[46]

Before lunch on June 18, McClellan notified the War Department that several deserters had brought in stories of reinforcements going to Stonewall Jackson from Richmond. Those were the three brigades Lee had sent, but McClellan could not confirm the story. Lincoln replied within hours that a French citizen passing through Fredericksburg had also reported seeing thousands of Confederates who were ostensibly on their way to Jackson, and he suggested this as an opportunity: estimating that between ten and fifteen thousand men were involved, he told McClellan it amounted to the same thing as a reinforcement of a similar number to him, and asked when he was going to attack. With McCall's division and the garrison at Fort Monroe he thought McClellan had all the men he needed, but he still implied that more of McDowell's troops would be coming eventually. The next day Lincoln questioned all those independent reports of Jackson's reinforcements, suspecting a ruse, but he equivocated again on June 20 and decided to err on the side of Washington's safety, retaining McDowell's remnants still longer.[47]

Lincoln's latest refusal to send McDowell's corps carried quickly from McClellan's eye to Porter's ear, and then to Manton Marble's desk at the *World*. Porter scrawled his thanks to Marble for his editorial appeals to reinforce McClellan, and then reported the failure of that effort. Only days before, Porter himself had taken command of the most recent contribution from McDowell's corps, yet he accused the administration of having "persistently turned a deaf ear" to McClellan's repeated pleas for more troops. He asserted that Lincoln was dominated by the "incompetent" Stanton, who hoped to postpone any triumph over the Rebels until emancipation could be made the price of peace. Stanton had engineered the withholding of McDowell's corps for that purpose, Porter insinuated, and wished to install McDowell as commander of the army.

Porter reasoned that when McClellan captured Richmond he would use that cachet to insist on a rapid restoration of the status quo antebellum, while McDowell would make no such demand.[48]

Porter enjoyed special insight into McClellan's thinking, and they both foresaw that military success would initiate a struggle over the extent of demands on the seceded states. They suspected Radical Republicans of trying to prolong the war long enough to extinguish slavery by force or fiat; Radicals, meanwhile, thought that they and other conservative generals were trying to delay victory until war weariness necessitated a negotiated peace that might preserve slavery.

Porter was correct that McDowell would not have imposed political demands on his civilian superiors, but more in subordinate deference to them than because he was pandering to Radical doctrine. McDowell's identification with that faction emanated more from his friendship with Salmon P. Chase than from any demonstration of Radical sympathy; he, like McClellan and Porter, seemed inclined to conciliation. He was not well regarded for tactical talent at Stanton's War Department, either. Joseph Holt, a former secretary of war under Buchanan who was still hanging around the department, learned that lesser officials there thought McDowell had "few if any qualifications for the high command he holds." Similar sources contradicted Porter's suspicions about the president's perfidy, informing Holt sometime after the middle of June that Lincoln was McClellan's last friend in the administration.[49]

By then the rest of the Army of the Potomac had gravitated below the Chickahominy, leaving Porter alone on the north side. With the divisions of Morell and Sykes, McCall's Pennsylvania Reserves, the 8th Illinois Cavalry, and control of a preponderance of the army's artillery reserve, Porter fielded nearly thirty thousand men. Most of Cooke's new cavalry reserve also reported to him, adding a couple of thousand more men. His was the largest corps in the army, but his front covered nearly fifteen miles, from the Chickahominy River above New Bridge to Mechanicsville, and then northeastward to Hanover Court House and the Pamunkey River. Cavalry performed much of his picket duty and reconnaissance, including a regiment borrowed from General Franklin. Videttes kept within sight of each other to detect raids and give warning of any assault, but heavy rain on primitive roads impeded infantry from responding rapidly to any threat. Anxiety over his vulnerable position and the widespread belief that the Confederates had the bigger army lay behind Porter's insistence that he needed still more troops. As June wound down, McClellan's chief broker of intelligence reported the Confederates numbering "over 180,000 men," and McClellan thought that estimate conservative. Lee actually had barely half that many present for duty, against McClellan's 110,000.[50]

Through most of June, Porter's headquarters tents stood in a field by Dr. Gaines's manor house, about five miles away by roundabout roads from Mc-

Clellan's camp at Dr. Trent's, across the river. Baldy Smith had occupied Gaines's home, but now he was south of the river, too. Early in the staff's residence there, Lieutenant Weld had gushed over the splendor and order of the place — an inadvertent tribute to the forty-three slaves who had lived there. The towering, symmetrical oaks that shaded the yard particularly pleased Weld's sense of order. "There is an air of neatness about the place which resembles New England," he told his father. At first they enjoyed edible treats from neighbors who were either friendly or wished to appear so, but accumulated annoyances eroded their comfort. Lieutenant Weld gagged at the ferrous flavor of the water. Driving, nightlong thundershowers forced him to protect his tent with a trench that turned into a moat. He found the ticks "decidedly disagreeable." Headquarters wagons rutted Dr. Gaines's pastoral grounds, and the teams crowded his barnyard, while the officers stabled their horses in his barn. Soldiers' graves dotted the estate (and the doctor swore that when the Yankees left he would dig up the bodies and feed them to his hogs). The hayloft had been commandeered for the sick. To remind them of the danger, they could look down on Rebel troops across the river.[51]

McClellan still planned a siege, for all that he talked of a great battle for Richmond. Four weeks after the fight at Hanover Court House, Porter was just starting to mount heavy artillery on the length of the Chickahominy within his bailiwick. Five 4.5-inch ordnance rifles arrived on June 23, and he arrayed them in front of Walker Hogan's house, just above New Bridge. He contemplated an assortment of heavy ordnance on the hill by Dr. Gaines's house, including a thirty-pounder Parrott rifle with which to answer Rebel guns planted near the homes of widow Mary Price and her neighbor, Dr. John Garnett.[52]

Something unusual seemed to be afoot that afternoon. McCall's pickets, near Mechanicsville, heard the Confederates beating the long roll in their camps across the river, and it had initiated a lot of activity. Farther upstream, at Meadow Bridge, other pickets heard railroad cars running in and out of Richmond all afternoon, and Rebel guards bantering with them from across the river had warned ominously that they had better get away from there. Contrabands slipping into Porter's lines also carried vague but ominous snippets of information, hinting first that Richmond was being evacuated and later that an attack was coming. On Smith's front, just downriver from Porter on the other side, the Confederate picket line around Dr. Garnett's property had been reduced and pulled back. The same appeared to be true at Mrs. Price's, in front of Porter, who by late evening thought it best to prepare against an assault. He decided to receive the attack on the ridge east of Mechanicsville, behind Beaver Dam Creek, which fed a gristmill owned by Dr. John Ellerson — another local doctor whose wealth depended as much on agriculture as on medicine. Reynolds pulled back from Mechanicsville with his own brigade and most of another from the Pennsylvania Reserves, settling in on the bank of the creek.[53]

Another persistent thunderstorm soaked the soldiers who lay waiting for the enemy, but the night passed quietly and in the morning Reynolds moved back to his advanced position. The Chickahominy had risen ten inches overnight, however, and it was still rising. That caused Porter some concern, especially when Cooke reported a slave having brought word of "an almighty lot" of Rebels about ten miles above Hanover Court House, but nothing came of it. A deserter assured Porter the Rebels were not considering an attack, and by nightfall the gossip relayed through the slave network had reverted to speculation about a Confederate evacuation.[54]

While McClellan and Porter attended to such worries, President Lincoln made a flying visit to West Point to consult with the retired Winfield Scott on the strategic impotence in northern Virginia. Frustrated by the consequences of his own haphazard creation of military departments for political generals, the president asked the country's strategist emeritus what he should do. Scott told him essentially what McClellan had been saying for three months: Frémont and Banks had plenty of men to defend Washington, especially if one of McDowell's divisions were left at Manassas, while the troops at Fredericksburg were useless there and incapable of moving anywhere else in time to be of use. Most of McDowell's corps could be sent to McClellan, Scott added, and the surest and fastest route would be by steamer, up the York River. With that, he predicted, McClellan should be able to seize Richmond, which Scott supposed would crush the rebellion even that late in the game.[55]

Lincoln took virtually none of that advice. He had evidently already decided on his course, and when he returned to Washington he found a general waiting there whom he had sent for before leaving for West Point. Brash and beefy John Pope, now a major general, had captured one of the most hapless Confederate armies in the West, and Lincoln gave him command of the combined armies of Banks, Frémont, and McDowell. They all outranked him, but he was a protégé of Halleck and had won a small victory, which was more than any of them could say. His new command would be called the Army of Virginia, and rather than protecting Washington and reinforcing McClellan it would go after Stonewall Jackson.[56]

McClellan still thought McDowell was on his way, because Porter had heard through someone in McDowell's corps that it was about to march, with the expectation of reaching McClellan by June 26. The president left McClellan wondering, and that may have inspired the general's frustrated telegram to Stanton, announcing the highest estimate yet of Confederate strength and predicting, accurately, that he was about to be attacked. Lincoln replied on June 26, but still he said nothing about McDowell, whom he had already decided to assign permanently to Pope's army. Stanton only helped to worsen McClellan's uncertainty by asking "to what point you desire any other force to be sent."[57]

Perhaps McClellan had an inkling about the new Army of Virginia. Lincoln's order creating it was not a day old when McClellan urged Stanton to put "some one general" in command of all the troops in northern Virginia. He offered that advice as though it were a last request, for by then the attack he anticipated had come.[58]

The house where Fitz John Porter was born in Portsmouth, N.H., stands a few rods from its original location, and his equestrian statue was erected where the house sat at the time of his birth.
Author's photo.

The commanding officer's quarters at Camp Floyd, Utah, in January of 1859. The officer to the left of the doorway may be Porter, who lived in the building with the post commander, General Johnston.
National Archives.

McClellan and his division commanders outside his quarters in Washington, November 4, 1861. From left to right stand William F. Smith, William B. Franklin, Samuel P. Heintzelman, Andrew Porter, Irvin McDowell, McClellan, Erasmus D. Keyes, Don Carlos Buell, Louis Blenker, Silas Casey, and Porter.
Library of Congress.

The camp of Porter's division at Hall's Hill, December of 1861,
with the 2nd Maine Volunteers in formation in front of its tents.
National Archives.

Thaddeus S. C. Lowe's balloon being inflated at Porter's camp
on Gaines's farm, north of the Chickahominy, June 1, 1862.
Library of Congress.

Porter and his staff in the headquarters camp behind Westover plantation, mid-August of 1862. Porter sits in the camp chair, with his aide George Monteith behind his right shoulder. His adjutant, Fred Locke, stands to the left of Monteith, with his hand on his sword. The servant standing at right, identified as "Mrs. Fairfax," was present in most of the camp photographs, always wearing a different dress.
Library of Congress.

Porter's daughter Evelina Porter Doggett examining the battlefield of Bull Run in company with the superintendent of the national battlefield there, June 20, 1947. She stands on the gravel Gainesville Road just above Dawkin's Branch, which runs under the bridge behind her. *Joseph Mills Hanson photo, Otto Eisenschiml Collection, Abraham Lincoln Presidential Library and Museum.*

President Lincoln with McClellan at Porter's camp outside Sharpsburg on October 3, 1862. Left to right are Delos B. Sacket, George Monteith, Nelson B. Sweitzer, George W. Morell, Alexander S. Webb, McClellan, an army scout named Adams, Dr. Jonathan Letterman, an unidentified soldier, Lincoln, Henry J. Hunt, Porter, Joseph C. G. Kennedy, Frederick T. Locke, Andrew A. Humphreys, and George A. Custer. *Library of Congress. Porter sent his aide Stephen M. Weld Jr. a copy of this photo in which Adams is identified as Custer, Kennedy as Porter's aide John F. McQuade, and Custer as "Colonel Batchelder."*

Porter's court-martial, as depicted in *Harper's Weekly*,
January 3, 1863. David Hunter sits at the left end of the table, and John
Pope at the right end. Porter stands with his arms folded.

OPPOSITE Thomas Church Haskell Smith, who served as John Pope's military aide
and star witness in Porter's court-martial, whose purported clairvoyance earned
unusual credence from those with an interest in seeing Porter convicted.
Library of Congress.

Black Hawk, Colorado, as Porter found it when he arrived there in 1864.
George Wakely photo X-2001, Western History Collection, Denver Public Library.

Theodore Fitz Randolph, Porter's friend from Morristown, N.J.
Library of Congress.

The Aztec Club annual reunion at Robert Patterson's home in Philadelphia, September 16, 1873. Front, left to right, are Porter, Henry Coppee, Patterson, President Ulysses S. Grant, George A. H. Blake, John G. Barnard, O. L. Shepard, and William H. French. In the rear,, from left to right, Milledge L. Bonham, Charles I. Biddle, John J. Abercrombie, Zebulon B. Tower, John M. Cuyler, T. L. Alexander, Robert E. Patterson, Frederick D. Grant, Orville E. Babcock, E. L. F. Hardcastle, William F. Barry, and Cadmus M. Wilcox. *HSP photograph collection [V59]. Historical Society of Pennsylvania.*

The New Jersey State Asylum for the Insane at Morris Plains, then boasting the largest continuous footprint of any building in the United States, the construction of which Porter superintended.
Library of Congress.

Porter's last home, where he lived from 1897 and where he died on May 21, 1901.
Author's photo.

Porter's statue in Hazen Park, Portsmouth, on the spot where he was born.
Library of Congress.

9

THE SEVEN DAYS

McClellan had finally offered a little aggression of his own on June 25, push-ing "Fighting Joe" Hooker's division beyond Seven Pines on the Williamsburg Road to seize a spot called Oak Grove. A letter from a New Hampshire sergeant who went into the fight on the skirmish line was already on its way to his mother that morning, conveying his belief that "the Rebels will skedaddle as they did at Yorktown." Instead, the Rebels threw themselves at the Yankees and drove them back where they came from, leaving that sergeant and many of his comrades dead on the field. McClellan rode out from the Trent house and watched from an earthwork while his men tried again, in the afternoon. Eventually Hooker and Phil Kearny retook the new ground, but at considerable cost.[1]

On his return to the Trent house, McClellan found the runaway servant of an officer in the 22nd North Carolina, from Ambrose Powell Hill's division, which was then moving toward Meadow Bridge on the Chickahominy, above Mechanicsville. The young man had found his way to the river and bolted into Porter's lines. He accurately described the troops that had been sent to Jack-son, and from the chatter of Confederate officers he had deduced that Jackson would attack Porter's position the next day, swooping down from above, while Lee struck from below. His most troubling claim was that Lee's force would be augmented by Beauregard's army, from the West: he said he had seen it arrive with his own eyes. With Jackson and Beauregard, Porter estimated there might be two hundred thousand Rebels to contend with. Confederate records later made such apprehensions seem absurd, but they were widely credited at the time, and the readiness to stand and meet such odds revealed a degree of sang-froid unappreciated in the light of later information.[2]

McClellan had his horse saddled again and raced to Porter's headquarters at the Gaines house. The Comte de Paris accompanied McClellan, noting that some of Porter's young aides-de-camp showed more alarm than he thought becoming. McClellan remained well into the night while Porter reprised his dispositions of the previous evening, leaving heavy guards at Meadow Bridge and the bridge on the Mechanicsville Turnpike. Porter trusted John Reynolds to hold his main line along Beaver Dam Creek with his brigade of Pennsylvania Reserves, well supported.[3]

After midnight on June 26, McClellan and the Comte de Paris rode back from Gaines's plantation to the Trent place through dense forests glittering with fireflies. A few months later, writing from his British manse, the erstwhile aide and last royal prince of France described the general revealing on that ride what he meant to do. Lee evidently hoped to force him to fall back above the river to defend his supply line to White House, but McClellan feared that such a retreat would demoralize his troops. If he could not maintain his position north of the river he would abandon that line completely and strike for a new base on the James River. If Jackson was bearing down on Porter's flank, McDowell would not likely be coming that way, which obviated the need for Porter extending his line so far to the north. The only reason Porter would have to fight at all would be to buy time to bring enough supplies south of the river for the withdrawal. Long trains were constantly creeping over the bad roads from White House, and Porter had complained about how that burdensome task monopolized his transportation.[4]

If Philippe d'Orléans correctly recalled the time of their conversation, it lends support to McClellan's later assertion that he was not forced to change his base by defeat north of the Chickahominy. He was obviously considering giving up the north bank, for the next day he suggested that Porter collect his wagons and send them across the river if Jackson proved too strong for him. That would have required abandoning the base at White House, but such apparent readiness to retreat could have disguised a more aggressive purpose. Porter was having no trouble handling the enemy the next afternoon, when McClellan revealed a determination to let Lee cut off his communications "to ensure success." That odd comment, with later statements from Porter and others, may betoken a vague plan for Porter to lure most of Lee's army north of the river, freeing McClellan to attack Richmond with the greater part of his own. That would have been as intrepid a strategy as Lee ever pursued, and the logic of it occurred even to civilians inside the beleaguered capital.[5]

Lee himself entertained a little anxiety over that possibility, especially after the sharp fight at Oak Grove. Still, he decided to take the risk inherent in his bold plan of flanking the Union position and driving for McClellan's supply line. Success depended on Jackson, who was coming down from Ashland and was lagging behind schedule already. Longstreet's Division and that of D. H. Hill were secluded in woods along the Mechanicsville Turnpike, and A. P. Hill's so-called Light Division lay near Meadow Bridge. General Branch's North Carolina brigade waited a few miles above Meadow Bridge. When Jackson began his march that morning, he was to notify Branch, who would cross the river and turn downstream, clearing Meadow Bridge for A. P. Hill to cross. They

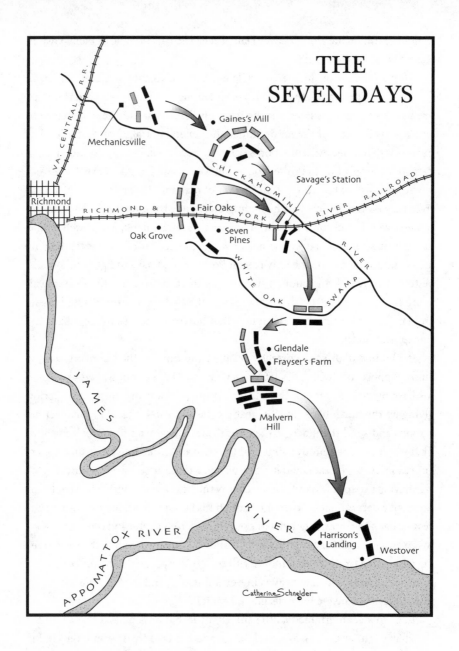

THE
SEVEN DAYS

Gaines's Mill

Mechanicsville

VA. CENTRAL R.R.

CHICKAHOMINY

Savage's Station

Richmond

RICHMOND & YORK

Fair Oaks

RIVER RAILROAD

RIVER

Oak Grove

Seven
Pines

WHITE

OAK

SWAMP

JAMES

Glendale

Frayser's Farm

Malvern
Hill

RIVER

APPOMATTOX RIVER

Harrison's
Landing

Westover

Catherine Schneider

would all continue down to the turnpike and drive Porter's pickets from that
bridge, allowing Longstreet and D. H. Hill to come over and extend their lines
of battle parallel to Beaver Dam Creek, in echelon. That broad, staggered formation would have reached beyond Porter's right flank, but by then Jackson was
also supposed to show up, even farther beyond that flank—and behind it, Lee
hoped. Had all gone as Lee intended, Porter would have felt compelled to fall
back fast, before Jackson closed off his retreat.[6]

All did not go as intended. Jackson arrived late, and he never gave the signal

Branch expected, so his brigade remained where it was. Worse still, Lee's directions were based on a faulty map that left Jackson several miles from Porter's flank. When Jackson had fulfilled all the literal meaning of Lee's instructions, he simply stopped.[7]

After taking a second look at Reynolds's position in the morning light, Porter returned to the Gaines house and the telegraph. Just before noon he had the operator inform General Marcy that his cavalry videttes had been driven in by Confederate horse and foot: Stuart had swung wide to the west with a brigade to meet Jackson on his road from Ashland to Pole Green Church. At 12:45 McClellan ordered Heintzelman and Keyes to have all the troops they could spare ready to move on short notice in whatever direction they might be ordered, but no further orders came. One hour later, Porter passed on a message from George Stoneman, whose cavalry had also caught sight of a Rebel column on the road to the Pamunkey River, below Hanover Court House. Contrabands said other Confederates were headed down the far side of the Pamunkey, too, and an expressman added that cavalry from that column had swum their horses over the river and cut off some of Stoneman's command. Supposing this was an attempt to sever the supply line from White House, Stoneman had ordered the 8th Illinois to report to Porter, and Cooke was going to do the same with most of his cavalry, reserving five squadrons to protect the baggage train. At three o'clock even Martindale, whose brigade Porter had sent out to the extreme right of Reynolds's line at the creek, reported the enemy advancing "in every direction." Porter had Reynolds pull in all his pickets, including those in Mechanicsville.[8]

As though alarmed, McClellan ordered Porter to top off all his ammunition, supply his men with two days' rations, and send his wagons to Savage's Station, south of the river. Gunfire echoed from the distance just as the distribution of ammunition and food began.[9]

That gunfire signaled the beginning of fighting at Beaver Dam Creek. Unable to bear the suspense, A. P. Hill had finally pushed across at Meadow Bridge and launched the attack without Jackson's cooperation. To negotiate the ravine cut by the creek, Hill's men first had to struggle through the tangled tops of trees McCall had felled for impromptu abatis. After wading the creek and the marshy ground on either side of it, they had to climb the other bank, all under concentrated fire from Pennsylvanians protected by rifle pits. At 4:40 in the afternoon Porter heard heavy cannon fire from the Richardson farm on the road to Pole Green Church, to the northwest. That was the road Jackson was using, but what Porter heard was a brigade of Hill's Georgians trying to turn McCall's right flank, whom McCall met with a battery. A single regiment of Pennsylvania Reserves behind those guns "mowed down" the Georgians, who retreated to the western bank and retired out of sight. Hill's artillery hurled fusillades of shells at McCall's right wing, and McClellan asked if Porter needed help, but Porter thought he could manage until dark.[10]

Porter did worry about his cavalry. No word had come from Stoneman since early afternoon, and two infantry regiments sent for his use had not been heard from. Porter tartly informed headquarters that Cooke gave him no information from the vicinity of Old Church, as instructed, and seemed to content himself with looking after the trains. Fearing that Stoneman himself might be cornered, Porter sent him orders to retire toward White House, and join the resistance there.[11]

McCall's third brigade, under George Meade, moved up behind the breastworks at Beaver Dam Creek, and later Porter had Morell lend him two more brigades. Longstreet and D. H. Hill moved into position as Lee had intended, but by then the daylight was fading. A. P. Hill's premature initiation of the fight had robbed Lee's plan of momentum, but he had made enough noise to unsettle the Union commander. Showing more apprehension than his official communications yet revealed, McClellan came over to Porter's headquarters around seven o'clock that evening. He wanted the 4.5-inch battery Porter had just emplaced at Hogan's removed to the south side, but Porter had no spare teams for that. McClellan left some of his staff officers at the Gaines house to solve that problem while he and Porter rode to the creek for a look at the fight. Within eighty minutes McClellan sent the secretary of war three separate dispatches, praising Porter's men for fighting "superbly" and "splendidly," but predicting that they could not long resist the overwhelming numbers he said they faced. He warned that his communications might be cut at any moment and that he could not prevent it.[12]

As the firing died out in the darkness, the two generals had telegraphers tap off reassuring messages to their wives. McClellan revealed that they misunderstood the day's attack to have come from Jackson himself, telling Ellen they had "again whipped secesh badly." Overestimating the number of troops he had faced, Porter informed Harriet that the day had ended in victory "against great odds," comforting her with the news that he and "all your friends" were safe.[13]

Porter's tent had been struck. By the light of his last campfire at Gaines's he and McClellan talked over plans for the morrow. McClellan contemplated drawing back to a new defensive line: his chief engineer, John Barnard, had found a likely spot to the east, beyond Dr. Gaines's grain mill, and would stay behind to lead Porter there if McClellan decided on it. Porter composed one account, probably in the early 1880s, explaining that McClellan wanted him to cover the army's withdrawal south of the river, in preparation for the shift to the James; Porter said he argued against it, suggesting either bringing the entire army north of the river for a fight to the finish or giving him reinforcements enough to hold Lee off while McClellan attacked Richmond. McClellan promised to send him Henry Slocum's division of Franklin's corps, which seemed consistent with the latter option, but as Porter told it they parted that night without determining a specific plan. He was left unaware which position he was to defend — or exactly why he was to defend it, and how desperately.[14]

Nearly three decades later, Porter's medical director recollected lying nearby and overhearing McClellan emphasize "the absolute necessity" of Porter holding his ground, telling him, "Whichever of the two positions you take, *hold* it." The doctor said Porter assured McClellan, "I shall hold it to the last extremity." With only a couple of hundred wounded to be cared for that night, the corps medical director could have been lounging around headquarters, but his precise recollection of the generals' dialogue after a generation awakens some doubt.[15]

In 1895, a few years after the doctor first told this story to a Boston audience, Porter gave a subtly different understanding of his orders to historian John Ropes, who had heard the doctor's account. In that recollection, McClellan was going to decide whether to reinforce him after determining whether to leave him at Beaver Dam Creek or pull him back beyond Gaines's Mill. If he were reinforced, it would be to cover preparations for the change of base; if he were not, it would mean McClellan needed all his remaining troops to capture Richmond, and Porter would hold Lee back whatever the cost. Those alternatives involved crucially different levels of sacrifice for his command. Leaving the nonappearance of reinforcements as Porter's only signal for a fight to the last man would have vastly increased the chances of miscommunication, yet they exchanged no written word about it.[16]

McClellan's version of his plan, composed during the year after the event, included no hint of an attack on Richmond. Instead, he described Porter's fight on June 27 as a delaying action allowing for the withdrawal of the trains and heavy guns and time to arrange the change of base. Porter was essentially covering a retreat. McClellan maintained as much in his official report, and near the end of his life he insisted that "every energy of the army was bent" toward that goal from the evening of June 26. Writing twelve days after their evening conference, Porter corroborated that assertion in his own report. He alluded to the possibility of the army converging below the river to attack Richmond if they beat Lee on the north side, but said that plan was scuttled by Jackson outflanking him on the right.[17]

Decades afterward, in an article on Gaines's Mill for the *Century*, Porter offered another vague explanation of their plan. He wrote that he was "determined to hold my position at least long enough to make the army secure," which suggests the protective action of a rear guard during the accumulation of supplies. Then he added that, with some reinforcements from McClellan, he hoped to "so cripple our opponents as to make the capture of Richmond by the main body of the army, under McClellan, the result of any sacrifice or suffering on the part of my troops or myself." Unraveling that awkward sentence fails to relieve it of ambiguity. Read one way, it implies that he hoped to do enough damage to Lee that his army could no longer defend its capital. Another interpretation evoked the valiant image of Porter detaining Lee north of the river, perhaps holding him back at any cost, while McClellan tried to force his way into Richmond with his other four corps. In his magazine article, Porter only hinted at what he suggested more directly in private correspondence and his manuscript memoir: when he and McClellan parted that night, he expected to make a desperate stand in favor of an advance on the city.[18]

In a private memoir that Baldy Smith left unpublished during his lifetime, he maintained that he and Franklin hailed McClellan as he returned from his conference with Porter. Despite the skepticism warranted by some of the more unconvincing interactions described in Smith's memoir, the Comte de Paris confirmed their stop with Smith, but he recorded none of their conversation. Smith alleged that he and Franklin proposed bringing Porter's troops back to the south bank of the Chickahominy, to hold the riverbank and prevent Lee from crossing while the rest of the army threw itself on Richmond. He neglected to mention any reply from McClellan, who ultimately chose no variation of that tactic, and squandered what those other generals regarded as a glaring opportunity. By the time Porter wrote his own account of this epoch for public consumption, it was well known how few Confederates remained south of the river, which threw McClellan's timid behavior in a bad light. Porter's nebulous latter-day portrayal of his assigned role on June 27 may reflect reluctance to emphasize that his friend had frittered away a gift for which Porter's troops paid a heavy price.[19]

What Porter may not have understood, either that night or years later, was that McClellan had already abandoned any serious intention of an imminent advance on Richmond. In the twenty-four hours since he had told the Comte de Paris of his contingency plan for establishing a new base, he had adopted that alternative. He would abandon White House altogether and bring the entire army south of the river, but without the aggressive intent Smith and Franklin may have proposed—and which Porter mentioned as a possibility in his subsequent report. Bedeviled by visions of superior forces on both flanks and by anxiety over supply logistics if he did strike at Richmond, McClellan would elect to retreat across twenty miles of relatively unfamiliar countryside to the James River. There he could create a secure depot under the protection of navy gunboats, and resume the campaign from that point. Cavalry patrols had been that far; he thought he could make it with a little head start if he could collect eight days' rations in his wagons and in the men's knapsacks and haversacks. Whatever options Porter thought they had left open, McClellan had satisfied himself that a retreat was perfectly feasible "if one became necessary," and he already deemed it necessary.[20]

There yet remained the question of whether Porter should hold Beaver Dam Creek or be withdrawn. Back at his own headquarters, McClellan concluded that the position at Beaver Dam Creek had been flanked, and decided to pull Porter back. Barnard had chosen the hills to the southeast of Dr. Gaines's house and mill, east of a place called New Cold Harbor and south of an earlier tavern at Old Cold Harbor. The Chickahominy ran right behind those hills, and by spreading his troops in a broad arc Porter could anchor both flanks on the marshy bottoms of that river's tributaries. Boatswain's Creek (known as Boatswain's Swamp, in that locality) conveniently protected much of the front of that arc. In the wee hours of June 27 Porter instructed Butterfield to detail a regiment to haul the 4.5-inch guns away by hand, as no spare teams had ever been located. Porter also fretted about his sick and wounded, for whom he had requested ambulances, but so far none had shown up.[21]

Butterfield parked the heavy guns near the farm of Pitman Watt and his mother. Joseph and Catherine Adams's farmhouse sat half a mile southeast of the Watt house, and half a mile northeast of them stood the home of John McGhee. The plateau within that triangle was known locally as Turkey Hill. McGhee, who was a miller as well as a farmer, probably operated Dr. Gaines's mill, a mile and a half northwest of the Watt place. Standing alongside the main road from Cold Harbor to Mechanicsville, Gaines's Mill was powered by the headwaters of Powhite Creek. Boatswain's Swamp, at the foot of Turkey Hill, ran roughly parallel to Powhite Creek half a mile away, creating a broad, irregular, and soggy ravine.[22]

At daylight of June 27, as Porter began withdrawing from Beaver Dam Creek, he wrote McClellan that he hoped to do without any help from the rest of the army, but he did ask that potential reinforcements be kept handy. He and Barnard gauged the defensive potential of Turkey Hill, choosing a perimeter between Boatswain's Swamp, on the left, and Elder Swamp, on the right. It seemed too long a line for three divisions, so Porter asked Barnard to appeal to McClellan for more troops, and for enough axes to hew the trees along the banks of Boatswain's Swamp into abatis and breastworks, which had proven so effective at Beaver Dam Creek. Barnard, who was quite deaf, returned to McClellan's headquarters to report, and presumably to convey Porter's requests, if he had heard them. The commanding general had finally retired to get some sleep, and Barnard declined to disturb him. He never delivered either of Porter's messages.[23]

Asking for more troops risked confusing any prearranged signal McClellan and Porter may have concocted involving the arrival of reinforcements, but it was a perfectly reasonable request. Porter had accepted McClellan's inflation of Confederate numbers since at least the beginning of the year, but on the north side of the Chickahominy he really was outnumbered. Even after losing four men to Porter's one on June 26, Lee still fielded nearly twice as many men as Porter, who feared even worse odds. On the authority of deserters and citizens, Porter credited Jackson's command alone with fifty thousand men. Officers in the Pennsylvania Reserves thought they had faced seventy thousand men at Mechanicsville — quadruple the force A. P. Hill had deployed. A brigadier in the Reserves estimated the enemy at eighty thousand the next day, and Heintzelman credited the Rebels with fully that many on the north side of the river.[24]

Morell's division started for the new position early, passing the old camps by the Gaines house, marching down the ravine, and forming ranks on the military crest of Turkey Hill. Sykes's Regulars spread out to Morell's right. McCall, whose men had slept little in their rifle pits during the night, did not get the word to move until an hour or so before first light, which came around 4:30 that morning. Implicitly criticizing the tardy decision to move, McCall complained of having to withdraw in the face of the enemy in daylight, but he kept up a sporadic fire until the last gun rolled away. The Rebels began to follow a couple of hours after sunrise. By 9:00 A.M. McCall had passed Gaines's Mill, uncovering the partially destroyed New Bridge as he disappeared down the marshy defile cut by Boatswain's Swamp.[25]

Charles Griffin, a Regular Army artillery captain newly promoted to brigadier, brought up the rear of Porter's corps with Morell's old brigade. As his column dropped into the ravine, Griffin left Colonel Thomas Cass and his 9th Massachusetts to watch the road at the crest, alongside Gaines's Mill. When the harbingers of A. P. Hill's command came into view, Cass's regiment of Boston Irishmen threw out a heavy line of skirmishers and opened fire. Eventually a South Carolina brigade trotted across and charged, and the Massachusetts men scampered off to join their comrades on Turkey Hill, a mile away. Their skirmish near Gaines's Mill gave the impending battle its name.[26]

At an early hour Henry Slocum's division started over the bridges to Porter, as McClellan had promised, but for reasons Porter could not fathom that column turned around and marched back. In his 1895 letter to John Ropes, Porter wrote that when he saw Slocum coming he thought McClellan had decided to reinforce him, evidently to cover the withdrawal rather than attack Richmond. When Slocum turned back, Porter said, he thought McClellan had changed his mind and would attack Richmond after all. That heavily corrected missive, written when Porter was old and sick, conflicts directly with his earlier manuscript memoir. In that account, he alluded to asking for reinforcements specifically to hold Lee off while McClellan turned on Richmond, and McClellan promised to send Slocum. In the Ropes letter Porter also seemed to forget that he had asked Barnard to appeal for reinforcements.[27]

If he and McClellan did leave two possible options open, as Porter purportedly understood, McClellan might have been expected to apprise him of his final decision sometime during that bloody day. That Porter would be left to guess whether he should fight to his "destruction" seems unlikely, and the absence of any further notification hints that they had come to a tentative plan, either for a withdrawal or for a determined stand to cover the storming of Richmond. Like the ambiguous characterization of his role in his *Century* account of the battle, Porter's letter to Ropes emits an air of disingenuous evasion that seems especially puzzling because Porter himself had nothing to hide. Until the final minutes of June 27, he waged a courageous and creditable defense against superior forces led by the most renowned generals in the Confederate army. Unless his contradictions resulted from failing health and memory, his most logical purpose, again, would have been to shield his old friend's name from reproach for not taking advantage of a sacrificial fight they had agreed on.

Only one interpretation can reconcile the contention that they reached no final tactical decision before the battle with the absence of further communication on the subject. If they determined to let the Confederates exhaust their infantry against formidable defenses, as they had at Beaver Dam Creek, they may well have expected it to take more than one day. There would then have been no need to discuss the details of an attack on Richmond until the enemy had worn himself out in fruitless frontal assaults: further consultation could have waited at least until the night of June 27. If that was McClellan's plan, he sharply reduced the odds of success by failing to reinforce Porter at the outset or to supply him with tools to fortify his position. McClellan's nap, or perhaps Barnard's hearing loss, could be said to have cost Porter the battle.

A few axes borrowed from battery wagons allowed some of Porter's men to cut logs for breastworks. Some regimental commanders also had their men pile Mrs. Watt's fence rails for a little cover, but most of Porter's men stood unprotected. A second requisition for axes went unanswered until the battle neared a crisis.[28]

Anticipating that Porter would entrench on the next ridge from Beaver Dam Creek, near Dr. Gaines's house and Powhite Creek, Lee waited for Jackson to appear behind the Union right flank. Jackson had to backtrack for several miles after a wrong turn, and that left him late once again. D. H. Hill, whose division was to support Jackson, reached Old Cold Harbor first, and turned south toward Turkey Hill. Had Porter retired only as far as Powhite Creek, Hill would have come in behind him, but as Hill's skirmishers moved toward McGhee's house, just after noon, they ran head-on into Sykes's Regulars and opened on them with artillery. Sykes replied with two batteries, which jousted with Hill's guns and "badly crippled" some of them. The only significant loss Sykes suffered was Major Delozier Davidson, who ended a twenty-four-year army career by ducking into the woods. Hill retired after a couple of hours, leaving the right of Porter's line quiet for a time, but Sykes noted that this was "only the lull that precedes the storm."[29]

Next came A. P. Hill, straight from Gaines's Mill and New Cold Harbor. He threw a brigade at the middle of Porter's line, but Warren's two-regiment New York brigade and part of Griffin's brigade drove it back while Union artillery belched rapid volleys of shot and shell, some of which exploded among Warren's infantry. Hill sent one brigade after another against Sykes's left and Morell's right, but Porter's lines still held as the musketry and artillery fire intensified. Once or twice, after breaking a Confederate charge, some of Porter's men impetuously chased the Rebels back into the swamp.[30]

At midafternoon Longstreet moved in to support A. P. Hill's renewed assault, aiming for the Union left. He struck Butterfield's brigade, on Porter's extreme left, and Martindale, on Butterfield's right. Both Union brigades were stacked two regiments deep, and Butterfield, who was having an easier time of it, sidled a regiment over to help Martindale. The open fields on the far side of the creek and the swampy banks ran wider in their front, offering more time to punish the Confederates with musketry and artillery before they came close enough to cross bayonets. Union artillery across the Chickahominy raked the right flank of Longstreet's lines as they rolled toward Turkey Hill. Furious firing by Butterfield's and Martindale's front-rank regiments repelled two of Longstreet's brigades as they made successive attempts, but the repeated assaults began to tell. Porter started pulling McCall's exhausted troops from his reserve, throwing them into line here and there, and at 2:15 he called on McClellan for help. Admitting that he was "hard pressed" at some points, he added that his bridge to McClellan's headquarters was threatened. He asked for one brigade immediately from the division he had been promised, and for the rest of it "tonight, for work tomorrow." He still remained confident of holding his position, and his intention of doing so into the next day supports the idea that they planned on wearing the enemy out as much as possible before launching that attack on Richmond. During most of the day, Porter inflicted at least twice as many casualties as he suffered, and such lopsided losses might have continued with decisive effect had he been able to build extensive breastworks.[31]

Martindale, who submitted his report nine months later, had developed a deep personal grudge against Porter by then, and he insinuated that Porter had deliberately sabotaged the defense. He criticized Porter's location of the firing line and posting of the artillery, complaining that those factors prevented any pursuit of the Rebels — as though chasing after a stronger foe were prudent. "The design of battle seemed to contemplate that we should simply hold our position," Martindale remarked, accusatively. That was true, as would have been apparent had McClellan used Porter's fight to mount a determined drive against Richmond. Ever protective of McClellan, Porter later maintained that the commanding general "undertook to advance upon Richmond" but was discouraged from it by the opposition of Sumner, Heintzelman, and Keyes, who feared that they were about to be attacked.[32]

If McClellan ever entertained a thought of throwing the rest of his army at the Confederate capital that day, he abandoned the idea after hearing from his corps commanders below the Chickahominy. From his balloon above Dr. Trent's house, Professor Lowe reported as early as 8:15 A.M. that the enemy was "in large force" — in fact, "very large" — in their entrenchments south of the river. Half an hour later, while McClellan would still have been sleeping, Smith saw "six or eight" regiments moving from the Confederate left toward Sumner's front. At 9:20, noticing a Rebel balloon in the air near Richmond, Lowe offered his amateur opinion that "the enemy might make an attack on our left at any moment." McClellan awoke from his nap to a sheaf of these alarming communications, and collectively they appear to have relieved him of any transient pugnacity. When Franklin informed him that several Rebel regiments were moving back toward Smith's division (likely the same ones that had sidled the other way), McClellan failed to detect the ruse. The Confederate commander on that front, John Magruder, was making "demonstrations" to simulate imminent action, disguising weakness with bravado. He was the chief guardian of Richmond, but was outmanned more than two to one. A thousand men would die under Porter's command that day to buy McClellan that numerical advantage.[33]

In response to Porter's appeal, Slocum's division lumbered up Turkey Hill, shouldering through parades of walking wounded and trains of ambulances. Even after the last of that division reached the field, Porter had only twelve brigades to withstand the twenty-six he faced, and his line was growing tattered. Men who had emptied their cartridge boxes had started rifling those of the dead and wounded. Because the reinforcements had not been handy, Porter had to deploy Slocum's troops as they arrived, plugging holes and relieving those who had run out of ammunition. He directed them himself, distributing them by regiments — much to the annoyance of the testy Slocum.[34]

The Union line still held as the afternoon waned, each regiment dressing ranks after every separate rush. Jackson had shown up from the north — later than expected again, but with nine more brigades to wield against the tired Yankees. Some of them stormed across the ground A. P. Hill had contested, aiming for the nexus of Morell's and Sykes's divisions, while others drove straight toward Sykes's Regular regiments on the right of Porter's line. One of Slocum's brigades leaped in with the Regulars, including the 16th New York, which was wearing broad-brimmed straw hats bought for the regiment by the colonel's wife. A St. Lawrence Valley farm boy among those New Yorkers thought that their distinctive headgear made them special targets: they seemed to draw especially heavy fire, all of it aimed high, and most of his wounded comrades were shot in the upper extremities.[35]

Late in the day a quartermaster wagon finally brought two hundred axes, but they were brand-new, with loose heads and handles. Porter still hoped to hold his ground until dark, as McClellan urged, and spend the night building breastworks, so he detailed two hundred men from the Pennsylvania Reserves to helve the axes. While they whittled at the handles, the rest of their brigade went into action.[36]

Soon after 5:00 P.M. things began to look a little grim on Porter's front, and he sent more urgent appeals across the river. "Hold your own," McClellan adjured him in melodramatic reply, promising more reinforcements. "You must beat them if I move the whole army to do it & sacrifice all on this side." With his umbilical to White House effectively lost, sacrificing everything on the right bank would have doomed his army, but McClellan intended to lose nothing on the south side. Hyperbole notwithstanding, he dispatched only two of Sumner's brigades to the beleaguered Porter while Longstreet, Jackson, and the Hills pounded relentlessly at the weakening blue crescent behind Boatswain's Swamp.[37]

The blazing sun dropped below the horizon, and Porter thought he had won the day, although the pressure on Sykes was bending his line back on the right. Then, on his left, John Bell Hood's fresh brigade of mostly Texans plunged across the swamp and up the hill with fixed bayonets. Unlike their predecessors, they never stopped to fire. They struck the part of Porter's line he considered strongest, where he had arrayed his heaviest concentration of guns and his infantry had been able to fashion scant breastworks. The brunt of the charge fell on Griffin's and Martindale's men, who had beaten back numerous assaults that long, broiling day, but the speed of Hood's approach surprised them, and some regiments were nearly out of ammunition. Rebels burst through the two smallest regiments, the 2nd Maine and 13th New York, and hurtled on into the 22nd Massachusetts, killing Colonel Gove and scattering some of the Pennsylvania Reserves. Porter galloped over to the breach and tried to rally men to fill it, but he had no more reserves. Martindale's line disintegrated, and whole regiments of Yankees either surrendered or ran for their lives. Martindale outstripped many of his men, ignoring a staff officer who chased after him, shouting his name; he headed straight for the bridges, crossing the river ahead of his command—and ahead of nearly everyone, noted the commander of a cavalry squadron.[38]

With that the entire front began to collapse, and a growing wave of Rebels rolled up the hill in the gloaming, flushing fugitives ahead of them. One enemy phalanx came unrecognized within eighty feet of the 12th U.S. Infantry, loosing a volley that leveled scores of Regulars. The color bearer of the 11th Infantry fell riddled with bullets, and the survivors fired only once before bounding to the rear. Confederates swept around the Watt house, where surgeons operated on the wounded as bullets bored through the walls. A few brave souls formed briefly around Morell, who stood by a flag he had driven into the dirt, but that line quickly crumbled. Most of Griffin's brigade had fled, and Porter put that old artilleryman in charge of all the guns, but with infantry pouring past them the gunners would not stay. Some units marched off the field in relatively good order, but others scattered to the rear. Confederates swarmed around the artillery that had repulsed the earlier assaults, shooting the horses to trap the guns and caissons. From his post near the Chickahominy, on Porter's extreme left, General Cooke flung the 5th U.S. Cavalry headlong into the Texans, whose first volley sent horsemen and riderless horses bolting through the batteries. That wrought utter panic in the encroaching darkness, and a wide-eyed mob abandoned all the guns.[39]

Guided by Captain George A. Custer of McClellan's staff, the two brigades from Sumner crossed to Porter's aid over the Grapevine Bridge, forcing their way through a dense throng of stragglers. A lieutenant in the leading regiment called it a disorganized mob of random infantry, dismounted cavalry, and artillerymen without guns or caissons, steadily pressing to the rear as ambulance drivers tried to work their way through with wounded men. "We moved steadily down the hill," he noted soon afterward, "parting the crowd from right to left as water is parted by the bows of a ship." Thomas Francis Meagher, commanding the Irish Brigade, threw out a company of the 69th New York with fixed bayonets to clear a path. His Irishmen came up over the rear slope of Turkey Hill at a double-quick, in two lines of battle, with the gold harp on their emerald flag glittering in the fading light. Porter saw them as they neared the Adams house, where his surgeons were still operating on the wounded, and there he halted them. Sykes and some of the Regulars yet held fast on the right, and the fresh brigades lined up on their left to cover the retreat of the rest. Darkness brought an end to the fighting, and the Confederates busied themselves with their booty, collecting more than a score of cannon and over three thousand prisoners, including the worst wounded. In their haste to escape, the Yankees had left behind knapsacks by the thousands.[40]

Designating locations closer to the river for each of his divisions to reform, Porter left aides shouting like circus barkers to divert men from the fugitive column to the appropriate spots. When enough troops had been reorganized to man a defensive line against a night attack, Porter headed for McClellan's headquarters, where Franklin, Heintzelman, and Sumner repaired for an impromptu council of war. This camp had also been dismantled, and the generals did their talking on their feet, amid the redolent resin of the evergreen arbors that had shaded the tents of general and staff. McClellan made one tardy and half-hearted suggestion for taking advantage of the situation. The Comte de Paris heard later that he proposed striking a desperate blow at Richmond while so much of the Rebel army remained north of the Chickahominy, but Heintzelman easily dissuaded him from it. Heintzelman himself described the commanding general making a very different proposal, to abandon all the works, wagons, provisions, and ammunition they had accumulated south of the river and march back to the north side for a grand battle there. In the end another battle was not deemed wise with a third of the army badly beaten and the supply line lost, or about to be. They would turn in haste for the James River.[41]

Porter insisted on having commissary stores first. "My men *must* have provisions," he warned headquarters. "A large portion of the command have none, and they must have them to-night." He needed ammunition, too.[42]

By dawn the last of Porter's troops had crossed to the right bank of the river, destroying the bridges behind them. General Barnard reported somewhat inaccurately that all the wagon bridges below Mechanicsville and above the York River Railroad had been destroyed "as far as practicable." Slocum's division and Sumner's brigades went back to their own corps. Stoneman's cavalry and the two infantry regiments Porter had lent to him had been cut off, and had retreated to White House to escape in the general evacuation of that place.[43] Porter had Morell's and Sykes's divisions with him, and McCall's Pennsylvania Reserves lay nearby, but he doubted any of them would be of much use that morning. "I cannot depend on anything here today," he confessed to General Marcy. "Am collecting regiments and reforming commands but will not have much reliable for hours." He asked for a couple of Sumner's regiments just to guard the river crossings, where the water ran low enough that his own men had been able to wade it.[44]

Porter had lost nearly one-fifth of the men in his three infantry divisions, with particularly heavy casualties among his regimental commanders. Four of the officers leading his thirty-seven infantry regiments had been killed outright, including Porter's old Utah comrade Jesse Gove; his West Point classmate Major Henry Clitz fell grievously wounded at the head of the 12th U.S. Infantry and was captured. The colonels of the 1st and 4th Michigan were wounded, as was the major commanding the 25th New York, who was also captured. The colonel of the 16th Michigan fell into enemy hands, as well. And then there was Major Davidson, in command of the 4th U.S. Infantry, who deserted the field and was also scooped up by the enemy. One of Porter's best brigadiers, John Reynolds, was cut off when the lines broke, and Rebels snared him in the woods the next morning. Many of those men's successors in command had become casualties before the battle ended.[45]

Miraculously, neither Porter nor any of his staff had been wounded seriously enough to mention. Stephen Weld, Porter's aide and the son of his preparatory tutor, had been captured early in the day.[46]

The sheer ferocity of the Confederate attacks shocked the Yankees as much as the bloodshed had dismayed them. "They fight like tigers," remarked a New Jersey officer. Some who had faced the Rebels thought they had fortified themselves for battle with whiskey left behind by Union quartermasters.[47]

The major obstacle on the way to the James was another of those marsh-bordered creeks known as White Oak Swamp. Because of his position on the extreme left, Keyes led the retreat, sending his first two brigades across freshly constructed bridges as soon as they were finished. Keyes detached one brigade to destroy the downstream bridges over the Chickahominy and headed generally south with the rest, toward the intersection of the Charles City Road, where they might anticipate the first threat from Richmond. Porter's bloodied divisions followed that afternoon. Morell struck off at 2:00 P.M., and Sykes followed at 6:00 in the evening. McCall, who was traveling with thirteen batteries of the reserve artillery, fell far behind the first night, and lost touch with Porter.[48]

The Comte de Paris watched Morell's division pass Savage's Station that afternoon, where enormous piles of ammunition, supplies, and personal property stood waiting for the torch. He noted how shrunken the regiments were, but the upright demeanor of the remaining men surprised him. Their carriage gave no hint of demoralization, and they seemed to be on the mend already.[49]

Frightened teamsters had blocked the road ahead with a tangle of disorganized caravans. "At last General Fitz John Porter rode up," reported an exasperated brigade quartermaster, "and with the genius of a true general produced order out of chaos." Morell crossed the swamp that night and camped. Sykes marched until two in the morning, bivouacking in the rain. On Sunday morning, June 29, Morell was just preparing to move when McClellan and his staff rode up and stopped for breakfast with him. Porter followed soon after, and directed Morell to Glendale, where the Long Bridge, Charles City, and Quaker Roads met in a tangled intersection, and there Morell formed a line of battle to secure that crossroads. Sykes joined him there, while McClellan ordered Keyes to push ahead to the banks of the James River. Sykes, Morell, and much of the reserve artillery trailed after Keyes early on June 30, another steaming day in a region where drinking water remained scarce. Keyes and Porter moved with little interference, but the other three corps fought a series of rear-guard actions every day and marched every night, with little sleep and short rations. After Morell and Sykes departed the intersection, Heintzelman and Sumner held off fierce attacks on either side of Glendale during the afternoon and evening, while Franklin stood guard at the tail of the army.[50]

McCall's Pennsylvanians had caught up during the night, but an incompetent guide soon led them astray. Porter, whom McClellan had ordered ahead with the rest of his corps, lost track of the Reserves, and after spending the night finding the right road they ran into the swirling battle at Glendale the next day. The fighting went on into the darkness, and McCall himself was captured before the contestants parted. Without much help from McClellan, who had gone ahead again, the army slipped past the crossroads at Glendale during the night, but the dead and all except the walking wounded had to be abandoned.[51]

The next road junctions where the Confederates might interdict the retreat lay on (and on the far side of) a broad, open plateau known as Malvern Hill. High at the southern end of the hill stood the Malvern house, a seventeenth-century manor overlooking the James River, Carter's Mill, and two precipitous roads leading to the new base of operations McClellan had chosen at Harrison's Landing. Keyes marched up the hill, past the Malvern manse, and down to the bottomland to guard the river road from Richmond. Porter halted his corps short of the crest, where another route crossed their road to the landing. At 2:00 A.M. Heintzelman reached Porter's headquarters at the Malvern house, described by one of Morell's aides as "an old picturesque brick house, surrounded by splendid white oak trees, on a terrace as fine as Hyde Park." McClellan was there with Porter, discussing the next day's agenda. McClellan instructed Heintzelman to consult with Barnard and with his erstwhile subordinate, Porter, about where to post his men. Once again the commanding general departed without giving notice to Sumner, the next general in rank; apparently he meant to retain technical command himself while effectively putting Porter in charge. The chief of topographical engineers stayed behind as McClellan's proxy, lending a semblance of legitimacy to Porter's authority.[52]

This would be the third occasion within six days in which McClellan chose Porter to command the field in the face of imminent attack. McClellan's personal courage never came into question, for he had endured plenty of danger during the Mexican War, but the confidence he exuded in the training camps and on the parade field seemed to flag in battle. That weakness became increasingly obvious as success grew more elusive, and his communications with Washington had borne a frantic note after Porter's line broke at Gaines's Mill. At such junctures he appeared to lean heavily on Porter, whose morale showed no signs of wavering under adversity, danger, or the grave responsibility that seemed to hobble McClellan.

Dawn of July 1 revealed a landscape so easy to defend that it lifted the spirits of many a tired Yankee. A Massachusetts man estimated two thousand acres of open land spreading before him. A lieutenant from Michigan marveled at the beauty of the terrain, with "slopes gradual & free from abruptness." That gentle slope and the lack of cover posed a daunting challenge to advancing infantry, and Porter bestrewed the hillside with artillery to take full advantage of it. Heintzelman feared that the line was too long to defend, but it was stacked four corps deep. Heintzelman also worried about their right flank, although a stream called Western Run gave better protection there than Turkey Run did, at the bottom of a bluff on the Union left.[53]

The road to the Malvern house ran a mile due south up the hill. Among other names, this was called the Quaker Road, after numerous Quaker families in the vicinity, including the Crews and the Binfords. Less than halfway up the hill, a byroad to Richmond left the Quaker Road at ninety degrees to the west, across Turkey Run, and just beyond that intersection the Carter's Mill Road angled away from the Quaker Road to the east, toward the mill and Harrison's Landing. Porter had formed Morell's division west of the Quaker Road and perpendicular to it, with Griffin in front, beside the Crew house. He also put Griffin in charge of the wide phalanx of artillery that Colonel Henry Hunt, commander of the artillery reserve, had unlimbered in front of Griffin's brigade. Martindale's brigade lay behind Griffin, and Butterfield took position right in back of him. Sykes hung just behind Butterfield with his two brigades of Regulars and Warren's two regiments. At Griffin's right, just across the Quaker Road, stood the West house; from there, Darius Couch's division of Keyes's corps extended Griffin's line eastward as far as James Binford's house, on the bank of Western Run, with Heintzelman and Sumner backed up behind him.[54]

Militarily their position felt fairly secure, but food was running short again and no one knew when or where some might be had. Much of Porter's corps, at least, had been out of rations for the better part of a day, and some for longer.[55]

Some of the hungriest men under his command were those of the 1st U.S. Sharpshooters, whom Porter had spread in a skirmish line out in front of everyone, low on the narrow neck where the ground started its climb. The man who had recruited them, Colonel Hiram Berdan, left his regiment in that advanced position with "some incoherent orders" on the excuse that he had to go look for ammunition for their Sharps rifles. They saw him no more that day.[56]

Lee intended more frontal assaults like those that had won the day at Gaines's Mill, but without the added impact of a threat to the Union rear. Most soldiers on both sides, including McClellan, saw this stop at Malvern Hill as nothing but another rear-guard action in a harried retreat, but the defensive possibilities of the site suggested a potential alternative. In the age of the rifle, assaults from longer distances had grown extremely dangerous, and innovative generals had begun to understand that defending forces enjoyed a significant advantage, especially when protected by breastworks. Porter especially understood this (hence his wish for axes at Gaines's Mill), and he relished a chance to punish the enemy from such a position. Beaver Dam Creek had taught him much. On the slope of Malvern Hill he had only been able to dig rudimentary breastworks, again for lack of sufficient tools, but the ground itself presented an inviting opportunity. Lee recognized the "great natural strength" of the position, and he saw the earthworks, but he gauged the mood of the Army of the Potomac as desperate, and supposed that a concerted drive by enough infantry would again pierce its line. Had he been able to coordinate the attacks of the different commands he might have achieved that end, but bad maps and obscure road names again thwarted him.[57]

To Lee's frustration, the rest of the morning passed uneventfully while he awaited his freshest divisions. Near midday he finally sent a stray Virginia brigade groping toward Porter's left front, along the bluff west of Malvern Hill. The Rebels spilled out of the woods "like bees," and the green-clad U.S. Sharpshooters scrambled back to the foot of Malvern Hill after firing a few quick and careful shots apiece. The Union batteries leveled furious volleys at the Virginians, who took refuge in a ravine northwest of the Crew house, where they huddled through several hours of that unpleasantly sultry day.[58]

"I thought the fight was over," admitted one of the sharpshooters as that first tentative approach fizzled. Porter knew better, and described the lull as an eerie silence like the deceptive calm Sykes had noted at Gaines's Mill. Lee had just about decided that he would wait until the next day to make his main attack when, late in the afternoon, miscommunication led John Magruder to initiate the first of several fragmented attacks. On the strength of two long-delayed, obsolete orders from Lee, Magruder supported those pinned-down Virginians near the Crew house with a couple of brigades on each side before flinging them toward Griffin's brigade. Griffin's infantry kept still while his artillery tore unmercifully at the dun-colored lines. After taking fearful casualties, most of Magruder's survivors sought what cover there was, waiting for reinforcements or artillery support.[59]

Union artillery drew the most blood. Limber crews raced ammunition to the gunners, who loaded and fired feverishly, switching from shell and case shot to canister as the tattered Rebel ranks came into range. One battery fired 1,392 rounds during the late afternoon and evening. Witnesses on either side again used the metaphor of men falling like grass before the reaper. Empty caissons bounded for the rear to replenish their contents, and fresh batteries wheeled into line. Porter had ordered Colonel Henry Hunt to bring his reserve artillery into close support, and Hunt pulled batteries from it to replace each one that had fired its last rounds.[60]

D. H. Hill also misunderstood a signal, and tried the Union right, held by Darius Couch. Porter had borrowed a brigade from Sumner's corps for ready reserves, and he rushed it down the hill just then to help Couch. Hill complained that his division fought the Union army "without assistance from a single Confederate soldier," but he managed to cause some serious trouble for

Couch, whose infantry surged out in front of its own artillery to repel him. That neutralized the firepower of the gunners, who feared firing into the backs of their friends, and Confederate brigades advanced one after the other. The two lines blazed away at each other long enough that ammunition also began running short in some of Couch's regiments. Porter rode up then, leading a brigade drawn from Heintzelman, which he waved into place on Couch's right.[61]

As at Gaines's Mill, Porter began to worry as the sun sank low. Hill claimed that he broke the Federals' line and sent them into retreat twice, but he must have misinterpreted the withdrawal of batteries that had been relieved. Couch looked as though he still needed help, and the enemy was also throwing more weight into Magruder's attack on Griffin's left and front. Porter had asked Sumner for another brigade to meet that assault, but long, anxious minutes passed before the emerald flag of Meagher's Irish Brigade again caught his eye. Remembering the same banner coming to his rescue four nights previously, Porter turned to gallop up the hill and guide the Irishmen into line. His horse stumbled and threw him headlong, but despite being bruised and shaken he regained his feet to the cheers of those who had seen him fall, and had supposed him wounded. His horse had not been injured, either, and he remounted to lead the reinforcements into line, but the situation seemed sufficiently dire that as he rode along he shredded his diary and dispatch book, lest he fall into enemy hands.[62]

"At 6:30 things looked very black," wrote Morell's assistant adjutant general. "Then up came Porter, who took command in person, with Meagher's Irish brigade." As Meagher's regiments deployed, Porter revealed the degree of his concern when he called for a battery of thirty-two-pounder howitzers with yawning muzzles that could belch canister by the half-gallon.[63]

He need not have worried, for the tide had turned despite fierce ardor in the fresh Confederate regiments. Hill's attack was losing a stream of stragglers to the rear and finally he retired, claiming that he had faced ten-to-one odds. Magruder threw more infantry at Porter's left, and Griffin's batteries belched canister into the charging ranks. Still they came, at a run, and as they neared the muzzles of the guns three of Griffin's regiments stepped out to meet them in another fierce, close-range contest in the twilight. The colonel of the 4th Michigan, wounded at Gaines's Mill, fell dead here. A bullet shattered the jaw of Colonel Cass of the 9th Massachusetts, who died more slowly. That left Griffin with only one surviving colonel, whose regiment had faced to the left, resisting efforts to turn that flank. Muzzle flashes marked the positions of the two sides as the dusk faded to darkness, and at last they ceased to sparkle. Some of the nearest of the jumbled Confederate regiments hugged the ground where they were, but most had fallen back, shattered to no effect. "We drove them back handsomely," Heintzelman observed, "and pushed them a mile and a half." Porter's field guns inflicted still more carnage on the fleeing Rebels, who prepared for the counterattack they expected after such a beating.[64]

There would be no counterattack. At 9:30 that night Porter went back to the Malvern house to dash off a report for McClellan, informing him that the enemy had been driven "beyond the battlefield." With some food, ammunition, and reinforcements, he thought he would have no difficulty maintaining his position, and that he could even advance. "Without these," he added, "we must retire." Commending all who had helped win the day, he hinted at his preference for an advance by adding, "If they cannot reap the full fruits of their labors, they can only regret the necessity which will compel us to with draw." Colonel Hunt and a staff officer took that message to McClellan, whose headquarters at that moment lay near or aboard the gunboat *Galena* at Haxall's Landing, two miles away. McClellan might have been sufficiently discouraged by Porter's stated wants to opt for retreat had he not already determined on it anyway, once he heard the firing subside. As Porter's note left the Malvern house, orders for the withdrawal were already on their way there, with instructions to demolish the carriages and spike the tubes of the heavy guns that had aided the victory, if they could not be moved. Instead of sending those desperate-sounding orders to Sumner, his most senior subordinate, McClellan addressed them to Porter, his de facto chief deputy.[65]

10

MANASSAS REVISITED

As the crescent moon set and darkness enveloped Malvern Hill, Porter took the road to Harrison's Landing leading his own corps, Couch's division, and the artillery reserve, which had been traveling under his command. In the final decade of his life Porter reportedly implied, in private, that he had advised McClellan to hold Malvern Hill, or even advance. Perhaps it was true, too, or possibly others amplified his claim in crafting a collective narrative attributing the retreat of the Army of the Potomac to McClellan's paranoia. In August of 1885 McClellan was still alive, and in an article about the battle published that month Porter sought to protect his old friend's reputation by ascribing his own optimism on the night of July 1 to his narrow field of observation. "From my standpoint I thought we could maintain our position," he wrote, "and perhaps in a few days could improve it by advancing. But I knew only the circumstances before me, and these were limited by controlling influences." As always, he left the impression that McClellan, with his wider sources of information, knew what was best.[1]

At least three former Union generals, including two of Porter's wartime friends, recalled him characterizing his communication with McClellan as active advice to make an advance. In a memoir written after he had become disenchanted with McClellan, Baldy Smith remembered Porter saying on the morning of July 2 that he had spent the night urging McClellan to go into Richmond. Thomas W. Hyde wrote in 1894 that Porter had recently told him how, as the fighting closed, Porter had "sent an urgent message to General McClellan advising an advance on Richmond." McClellan critic Alexander Webb, a Porter admirer and former chief of his staff, allegedly confided in a 1905 interview that Porter "went to McClellan on the gunboat and begged him to advance, but he would not." Porter's daughter heard the same story, decades later, but apparently not from her father.[2]

In public, at least, Porter never described such stubborn lobbying, and the chronology left little time for it. McClellan's instructions for the withdrawal reached Porter within half an hour after he sent his own more aggressive message, and in his article on the battle Porter asserted that he promptly disseminated them. An officer at Morell's headquarters admitted that the order was met with surprise there, but contemporary sources reveal none of the dismay and outrage it was later said to have kindled. Soldiers of all ranks naturally regretted leaving their dead and wounded for the third time in five days, and stumbling through another night retreat, but most of them obeyed the order with a mixture of resignation and relief.[3]

Florid tales of furious denunciations of the order by indignant generals materialized only decades later, after the real strength and condition of the Confederate army became clear. Such information began leaking back to Union generals in a few weeks, when John Reynolds returned from captivity in Richmond, where he talked with Confederate acquaintances from the old army. Joe Hooker would have been privy to such gossip, for some of his surgeons had been captured with the wounded at Glendale, and later told him that the Confederates who fell back from Malvern Hill were "totally demoralized." Such subsequent intelligence explains Hooker's boastful assertion to the Joint Committee on the Conduct of the War that McClellan could have gone right into Richmond on July 2. No such sentiment actually flourished the night of July 1, and it took years to cultivate the impression that it had.[4]

John Martindale, the brigadier in Morell's bloodied division who had fled the field at Gaines's Mill, was one who did want to remain. After the withdrawal began, Martindale encountered Dan Butterfield and George Morell. Calling them and the colonel of the 2nd Maine together, Martindale questioned the order to retreat and suggested that they use the leverage of their successful stand to negotiate their way out of a predicament he considered hopeless. "I propose that we stay here and give ourselves up," he said, suggesting that they might be able to ask for terms. Morell immediately spurned the notion, and said they would proceed as ordered. At that Martindale fell silent and joined the retreat, again leaving his brigade to fend for itself. An hour or so later, Porter doubled back from near the head of the column in response to a call to McClellan's headquarters. On the way he spotted Martindale riding alone, and wondered why the brigadier was not with his brigade, but in his rush to respond to McClellan's summons he let Martindale go unchallenged.[5]

Before turning back to see McClellan, Porter left instructions with Fred Locke, his chief of staff, to guide the column to the landing. Most of the troops followed a single road for eight miles to Berkeley, the magnificent Harrison family estate on the James, but the glut of traffic slowed the march painfully. The leading elements still struggled along a few miles from the goal at 5:00 A.M., when the rising sun began to lighten a murky sky and the clouds opened with merciless ferocity. A man in the Second Corps told his uncle that he had never seen it rain so hard in his life. One officer called the roads "mortar beds," and another described thousands of soaked brogans churning the mud knee-deep.

General Couch, who traveled with Porter's vanguard, recalled a few years later that the march soon turned so disorderly that he considered it "a perfect rout," despite the lack of pursuit. The darkness bred confusion and a mixture of the different commands, he said, and the deepening mud transformed the army into "a mob." The road was filled with stragglers asking for their regiments, or for the James River. Morell's assistant adjutant general called the retreat "a regular stampede."[6]

A few reinforcements from northern Virginia and some supplies awaited them at Berkeley. The two infantry regiments Porter had lent to Stoneman were there, having escaped in the evacuation of White House Landing. One of them belonged to Martindale, and he camped with it when he arrived, so by the end of the retreat he was again technically present with part of his command.[7]

The site McClellan had chosen ranged from Kimmage's Creek, near Berkeley Plantation, to Westover, the ancestral estate of the Byrd family, a mile downriver. Swamp-bordered Herring Creek ran parallel to the river for most of that distance, about a mile inland, before veering abruptly toward the river just below Westover. That initially defined McClellan's encampment, where his army lay all through the downpour of July 2, sleeping cold and wet on spongy ground. The next day J. E. B. Stuart circled around Herring Creek, cresting a ridge on the left bank from which his horse artillery lobbed a few shells into the camp before a Federal brigade chased him off. Eventually McClellan posted several divisions over there, keeping the entire army under cover of the Union gunboats. Within ten days a staff officer described "a most profound state of quiet" in Porter's camps.[8]

That quiet was hardly disturbed by a brief visit from the president, who came down by steamer to have a look at the army himself. He reviewed the troops rather languidly. Some who missed him thought it a "small loss," but Lincoln was pleased to find the troops more numerous and less disorganized than he had feared. He interviewed McClellan and his generals individually, asking about the number and condition of their commands, whether the army was safe, and whether it should be removed from the Peninsula. McClellan was particularly sensitive about leaving the Peninsula because of the failure that such a withdrawal would imply. Porter was even more adamant, calling it "impossible." The only place Lincoln would move the army was back to northern Virginia, to join Pope, and Porter predicted it would "ruin the country." Sumner and Heintzelman agreed. Only Keyes thought it might be done "safely," and Franklin actively recommended it, suggesting they take the line of the Rappahannock River.[9]

The manor houses of Berkeley and Westover stood as the bookends of the cantonment. McClellan established army headquarters on the grounds of Berkeley, at the western extremity, and Porter raised his tents at the other end, behind Westover. The Georgian residences on the two abutting plantations lay a mile apart by the river, but the road between them followed a horseshoe course nearly three miles long. McClellan still anticipated an attack from legions of Confederates, and he revealed how much he valued Porter's moral support in battle when he announced that he would relocate his headquarters beside Porter's if that attack came.[10]

McClellan also submitted Porter's name to the War Department as the hero of the campaign for his "energy, ability, gallantry and good conduct." He asked brevets for Porter to brigadier and major general in the Regular Army for Hanover Court House and Gaines's Mill. Had another grade of brevet existed, he said he would have asked it for Malvern Hill, which he deemed the premier victory of the Seven Days. Even a brevet as major general of volunteers would have elevated Porter over all the other corps commanders, McClellan thought, but Stanton had already promoted all the corps commanders to major general in the volunteers. He kept Sumner on top with an additional brevet as major general in the Regulars.[11]

The commanding general's obvious favor for Porter aggravated the most senior generals in the army, some of whom had been complaining of it to exalted army visitors for two months already. Grizzled old Heintzelman, who relished the idea of a promotion over the even-older Sumner, grew especially catty about his younger rival. McClellan issued a congratulatory Fourth of July order to the army, but when Porter did something similar for his corps Heintzelman saw something perniciously presumptuous in it. He credited gossip about Porter's "want of generalship" at Gaines's Mill—which was precisely the phrase used in regard to Porter's fight there by Heintzelman's caustic division commander, Phil Kearny. Stanton, perhaps hoping to stir discontent for the army commander within his own officer corps, let it be known among the generals that McClellan had recommended only Porter for promotion. When Heintzelman learned of it, he sat down and wrote directly to Stanton, submitting a copy of his report of the campaign.[12]

Porter spent the lull weeding his command of unwanted officers. The collapse of his brave stand at Gaines's Mill remained a sore point even after the victory at Malvern Hill, and General Cooke offered a potential source of blame. The stampede initiated by the repulse of Cooke's reckless charge "caused the loss of this action and the abandonment of eight pieces of artillery," Porter contended, asking McClellan to remove Cooke from command of the cavalry. McClellan complied with Porter's appeal the next day, and Cooke went back to Washington as their lifelong enemy. Porter may also have found fault with Barnard, the chief engineer, whose failure to deliver crucial messages on June 27 Porter always recited as a factor contributing to his defeat, and McClellan asked for Barnard to be reassigned.[13]

Silas Casey's position as commander of the White House supply base had become obsolete when it was evacuated, and McClellan had evidently been pressured into giving him the division of Pennsylvania Reserves. Porter understood that Stanton had personally ordered Casey to that command, and he recoiled in horror at the prospect of having Casey in his corps. During the captivity of McCall and Reynolds, the Reserves had fallen to Truman Seymour, a West Point contemporary of Porter's, and Porter wanted him to stay. He pleaded with McClellan to find something else for Casey. "Seymour has earned the command and is equal to it in every emergency," Porter insisted, in a confidential note, "He will make something of them; Casey never will. They will respect him; Casey never. Seymour has now got them in better shape than they have been in since the fight." In desperation he asked if the order couldn't be suspended. McClellan accommodated Porter immediately, earning the two of them another bitter foe. Casey went to the president, presenting himself as "aggrieved," and in the autumn Lincoln consulted with Stanton on what they might give him to do. Soon thereafter Stanton determined some mutually gratifying assignments.[14]

General Martindale came next. No sooner had the army reached Harrison's Landing than he applied for a leave of absence, claiming typhoid fever, and he went straight to Washington to recuperate among the politicians. On August 3, Porter asked McClellan to relieve Martindale from duty with the Fifth Corps for proposing the surrender of the army and for absenting himself from his command. Porter said those actions "have destroyed whatever of confidence, as a general and as a disciplinarian, I have had in him for the past two months, and I have reason to believe that of the brigade." He wanted Martindale apprised of the reason for his removal, as he apparently was, yet Martindale waited nearly ten weeks to request a court of inquiry, taking a vacation in the meantime. His friend Secretary Seward asked Stanton to give Martindale a furlough, contending that he had "distinguished" himself on the Peninsula and needed rest because of exertion and illness.[15]

During the retreat from the Chickahominy, Martindale must also have waxed critical of Porter's generalship, because George Meade suspected that Porter's accusations came in retaliation for those comments. Meade, who had witnessed the confusion in the retreat from Gaines's Mill—and whom Porter had recommended for brevets—had his own doubts about Porter's generalship.[16]

Martindale did show the white feather at Gaines's Mill, and charges on that score would have seemed reasonable. Clearly he was also deeply discouraged after Malvern Hill, despite the bloody repulse of the Rebels, but complaining of that without mentioning his flight from the battlefield at Gaines's Mill made no sense. Perhaps that was the only misconduct for which Porter could find witnesses, but by early August he may also have felt a need to illustrate that in McClellan's army there was no tolerance for the notion of giving up. General Marcy had gone to Washington after the Seven Days, and in trying to explain to Stanton the intense difficulties and dangers McClellan had faced he had used the word "capitulation." Stanton may well have distorted the context when he told the president that McClellan's father-in-law and chief of staff was talking surrender, and Lincoln called Marcy on the carpet to reprimand him for even using the word. McClellan would have heard about this when Marcy returned, on July 24, and nine days later McClellan demonstrated his aversion to defeatist talk by passing on Porter's objection to Martindale's.[17]

Mail went home by boatloads in the first week or two of respite on the James. No one in the Army of the Potomac had found time to write since Gaines's Mill, and most of Porter's men had lost their knapsacks, with all their stationery. Sutlers, who materialized magically wherever needy soldiers congregated in relative safety, showed up at Harrison's Landing hawking pens and paper among their wares.[18]

Porter participated more enthusiastically than prudently in that epistolary excess. Certainly he wrote to Harriet, and the loss of those letters casts frustrating shadows. He told his old tutor, Stephen Weld, of the money he had sent by flag of truce to his captured son, and digressed to acquaint him with the Potomac army's lack of confidence in John Pope and his campaign. Porter asked a cousin who worked in the Navy Department in Washington to have one of his uniform coats altered for a major general, and could not refrain from disparaging Zachariah Chandler for telling lies about McClellan on the Senate floor.[19]

To his ultimate regret, he maintained communication with civilians whose influence he valued and whose discretion he overestimated. The most fateful letter he wrote from Westover went to Joseph Kennedy, the census chief, who prodded him to invective about John Pope by enclosing a copy of Pope's insulting official allusions to the Army of the Potomac. In preparing to take the field with the Army of Virginia, Pope had published an address to his new troops in which he ridiculed McClellan's renowned caution and implicitly insulted his audience. "I come to you from the West," he announced, "where we have always seen the backs of our enemies." Introducing himself as the man chosen to reverse their record of defeats, he scoffed at the concern for "lines of retreat" and "bases of supply" so common in McClellan's dispatches. "Let us study the probable lines of retreat of our opponents," he proposed, "and leave our own to take care of themselves." Within weeks his disdain for such vital military precautions would yield stunning failure, leaving his boasts echoing with eternal irony, and after Edwin Stanton's death Pope blamed him for the contents of the address. That was not true, but either of those men was capable of the arrogance the document betrayed, and both harbored the antagonism toward Mc-

Clellan that it implied. As a dinner guest at the home of Secretary Chase, Pope admitted having urged the president to remove McClellan from command, and promptly.[20]

Pope was the great Radical hope, ready to wage hard war against all Confederates, armed or not. He had already issued a general order declaring private property fair game for Union armies in enemy territory—which, in Radical parlance, implied the confiscation of slaves as well as livestock and provisions. Such open license for marauding troubled officers who knew how quickly it would erode discipline, and the implied hostility to slavery worried generals who feared that it would only intensify enemy resistance. During Lincoln's tour of Harrison's Landing, McClellan had presumptuously handed the president a letter advising against just such a course, and Porter concurred with McClellan on that point.[21]

Supposing that Kennedy shared his disapproval, Porter let fly injudiciously at Pope, whom he may have met during his first year and Pope's last year at West Point. "I regret to see that Genl. Pope has not improved since his youth," Porter began, "and has now written himself down what the military world has long known, an ass." Pope's address to his troops made him look "ridiculous," Porter went on, and it reflected badly on the president who had selected him, who already lacked the confidence of the army.[22]

Porter's response would have taken two or three days to reach Washington, but it should have been in Kennedy's hands by Sunday, July 20. On Tuesday, Kennedy folded Porter's reply into a letter to Secretary Seward—another celebrity whose acquaintance he had cultivated—hinting that Seward should overlook the indiscreet language of Porter's letter and imbibe the "reliable information" in it. The only information it contained consisted of Porter's scorn for Pope and his mistrust of Lincoln. Rather than returning the letter after he read it, as Kennedy had asked, Seward showed it to Lincoln. Pope was still in Washington, and he saw it as well.[23]

Seward would have carried Kennedy's letter into the White House on July 23. That was the day Henry Halleck reported there to accept the vacant post of general-in-chief. Halleck, who had arrived during the previous night and lodged at Willard's Hotel, had been offered the post at least partly on the recommendation of his former subordinate, Pope. Navy Secretary Gideon Welles read the interactions of Stanton, Chase, and Pope as a conspiracy to replace McClellan altogether by installing Halleck as general-in-chief and giving Pope both major armies in Virginia. Welles probably also sensed the palpable dissatisfaction with McClellan at the White House, where Lincoln's personal secretary was deprecating the "wretched conclusion" of McClellan's own "boasting addresses and orders."[24]

Lincoln had invited Ambrose Burnside in to meet Halleck when he arrived.

Early in July, Burnside had brought his Ninth Corps from North Carolina to Newport News, on the tip of the Peninsula, and since then he had been awaiting orders to join McClellan with that command. Because of his success in North Carolina, Burnside was an unwitting candidate to replace McClellan, with whom he remained a close friend: he seemed to consider himself Little Mac's advocate in Washington. The president authorized Halleck to make his own visit to Harrison's Landing, to determine McClellan's strategic preferences, and Halleck requested that Burnside accompany him. They departed together at two o'clock the next afternoon, July 24, and Quartermaster General Montgomery Meigs went with them to offer advice on supply.[25]

The president warned Halleck before he left that McClellan would not fight. They could send him a hundred thousand troops and he would offer gushing thanks, promising to seize Richmond on the morrow; then he would cite new reports that the enemy had four hundred thousand men, and plead for more reinforcements.[26]

Halleck's party arrived at Berkeley Plantation on the afternoon of July 25, not long after Porter finished a review of his corps. Halleck promptly asked what McClellan planned to do, now that his army had taken three weeks for rest and refitting. McClellan proposed seizing the vulnerable rail center at Petersburg, on the far side of the James — a blow that would have almost completely isolated Richmond and Lee's army — but Halleck summarily vetoed the idea. McClellan then said he would make another attempt at Richmond, if he could have thirty thousand more men. Stanton's closure of recruiting stations the previous April still hobbled Union recruiting, and Halleck countered with an offer of twenty thousand — the most Lincoln had authorized. If they were not enough, the army would have to return to a point where it could join forces with Pope. McClellan recoiled internally at that, fearing that Pope would be placed over him as he had been over other more senior generals, but he worried more openly about the impact of another retreat on army morale. Halleck finally asked him to consult with his officers about which course to follow and to have a decision for him in the morning.[27]

While Halleck talked with McClellan, Meigs sat outside the tent, jabbing with a stick at the coals of a campfire alongside other senior officers. McClellan's bristling resentment of Halleck and the Washington bigwigs he represented had filtered into the upper echelons of the officer corps, and it simmered around that fire. A quarter of a century later Meigs recalled hearing someone propose that the army march on Washington instead of Richmond, to "clear out those fellows." Just then a pair of bushy muttonchops drifted into view on the far side of the circle, and Meigs heard Burnside say, "I don't know what you fellows call this talk, but I call it flat treason, by God!" According to Meigs, that broke up the circle.[28]

Then Halleck headed for bed, and McClellan summoned his corps commanders and Burnside for a lengthy conference. Heintzelman came late, and Keyes retired early. Franklin, who was not well, came and went. John Newton, still just a brigadier in Slocum's division but a respected engineer of old, also took part. They were almost evenly divided. Keyes, Franklin, and Newton all thought the army should abandon the James. Sumner, Heintzelman, and Burnside all favored making another attempt at Richmond from Harrison's Landing. Burnside, who was the only one to name all the participants and cite their opinions, could not remember Porter firmly specifying an opinion for either alternative. Heintzelman, who may have come in after adverse opinions were voiced, instead thought that everyone agreed with his preference for an immediate advance. Inevitably Porter did offer his thoughts at least to McClellan, and in the morning McClellan told Halleck he would take the twenty thousand reinforcements and move against Richmond.[29]

The steamer carrying Halleck, Burnside, and Meigs had not docked in Washington when McClellan telegraphed that returned prisoners reported thousands of Rebel reinforcements coming into Richmond from the Carolinas. They also raised the old specter of Beauregard's army on the way from Mississippi, which McClellan had fretted over since before Mechanicsville.

"Can you not *possibly* draw 15,000 or 20,000 men from the West to reinforce me temporarily?" he asked, urging that the rest of the troops in North and South Carolina also be sent to him, along with any others Halleck could scrape up. When Halleck reached army headquarters on July 27, that telegram awaited him, fully corroborating Lincoln's pessimistic prediction. Halleck informed Lincoln that McClellan had done as expected. Lincoln's response was to call Burnside into his office and ask him if he would take command of the Army of the Potomac. Burnside blanched at the prospect, insisting that McClellan was the only man for that job.[30]

McClellan learned of that exchange through Burnside himself, and was not surprised. He had already assured his wife that Halleck "would relieve me tomorrow if he dared do so," and admitted drawing into his "shell." In his dejection he turned to his two perennial sources of inspiration—his devoted enlisted men and Porter. Visiting wounded men in the hospital lifted his spirits, but the only major general he fully trusted was "Fitz Porter," who "stuck through it all most nobly." Porter, he assured Ellen, was "all that I thought him & more. Nothing has depressed him; he is always cheerful, active & ready, & is much more efficient than all put together."[31]

Affairs hung in limbo until July 30, when McClellan asked for more cavalry and again emphasized the increasing strength of the enemy. Halleck's response was to order him to send his sick away and prepare for a movement "in any direction," giving no hint of where because he did not know himself. Late that night Pope reported rumors of the Rebels evacuating Richmond, and while Halleck suspected it might be a trap he suggested that McClellan push a force toward the city to test the accuracy of Pope's sources.[32]

Two more days passed before McClellan received that message, and he waited another day to make the desired reconnaissance, which went astray on its first attempt. "Give me Burnside," he promised Halleck, as though he did not have plenty of troops for a reconnaissance, "and I will stir these people up," but Halleck refused. Not until August 5 did McClellan manage to recapture Malvern Hill with two divisions, and send cavalry out to test the approaches to Richmond, but by then Halleck had decided on his course. He had already ordered Burnside to the mouth of Aquia Creek, the Potomac River landing nearest Fredericksburg, and on the evening of August 3 he directed McClellan to follow with his whole army.[33]

Burnside inadvertently emphasized McClellan's worst flaw by replying to Halleck's order as soon as he received it, reporting that his troops were already embarking and would arrive at Aquia Landing the next day. After three days, Halleck had to remind McClellan of his orders to remove the sick and reconnoiter toward Richmond, and a week after directing the withdrawal of the army from Harrison's Landing he added a minatory warning against any further delay.[34]

McClellan may have hoped to stall long enough to excite public opinion against the withdrawal and persuade Halleck to rescind the order. Toward that end, Porter dashed off a six-page letter to Manton Marble, at the World, outlining the advantages of the James River line and the disadvantages of an attack from Pope's direction. The river provided secure supply as far as Harrison's Landing, he argued, and a much shorter line to defend from there to Richmond than Pope's hundred-mile umbilical. He advised putting no faith in Pope or anything he said, noting his reputation for prevarication in the old army, where "he was never known to tell the truth when he could gain his object by a falsehood." He predicted that "within three weeks you will see Pope's waning fortunes" (erring by only four days), but if McClellan were given fifty thousand men he thought Richmond would fall within those same three weeks. A month earlier Lincoln himself had made a similar claim to the nation's governors: "If I had 50,000 additional troops here *now*," the president wrote on July 3, "I believe I could substantially close the war in two weeks." Yet on July 2 Lincoln had called McClellan's recent request for fifty thousand men "simply absurd." Indeed, thanks to Stanton's April recruiting blunder, it would have been impossible to satisfy.[35]

Porter seemed confident of bringing enough pressure to prevent the withdrawal, assuring Hattie in her retreat at Cozzens's Hotel that prospects were "bright" for the success of McClellan's army. Still, no public furor arose. On

August 10 Halleck insisted on immediate action, demanding an explanation for McClellan's procrastination. That same day, Porter wrote to Marble again to belittle the plan of reinforcing Pope with the Army of the Potomac, meanwhile enumerating the deficiencies of all the generals who favored that movement. Pope was "a fool," he wrote, and McDowell "a rascal" — Porter's old friendliness toward McDowell having been soured by McClellan's suspicion that he was angling to regain army command. Halleck had "brains," Porter admitted, but he lacked independence. The collective strategic mistakes of those three "deserve defeat," Porter insisted, particularly noting the danger in Burnside's isolated position. "God spare us from our friends," Porter remarked, concluding with a hyperbolic lament that echoed the treasonous grumbling General Meigs claimed he heard around the campfire. "Would that this army was in Washington to rid us of incumbents ruining our country." As had become his habit in his more rancorous letters to Marble, he failed to append his signature.[36]

Pope had just suffered one "deserved" defeat. Satisfied that McClellan would remain idle, Lee had sent Stonewall Jackson north with more than a third of his surviving army, and Pope had pushed Nathaniel Banks beyond the Rappahannock River, nearly to the Rapidan. On August 9, Jackson caught Banks at Cedar Mountain, giving him a savage pounding.

Rumors of immediate movement raced around Harrison's Landing, but several days still passed before the first organized body of troops left camp for Fort Monroe, on foot. The senior generals, who would have much work to do once the order came, seethed with curiosity. In his diary, Heintzelman grumbled that only McClellan's father-in-law, Randolph Marcy, knew when they would go; then he added, "I suppose, however, that General Porter knows," again betraying irritation with his former subordinate. "There is great dissatisfaction about Porter," he noted, and much of what he heard probably emanated from the carping of McClellan detractor Phil Kearny, who considered Porter "good in nature, but weak as water."[37]

McClellan made one last appeal late on August 12, forwarding an accurate report that the Rebels had sent much of their army against Pope and had left Richmond thinly defended. He asked Halleck if an attack just then wouldn't draw the enemy off Pope, even if Richmond were not captured. McClellan's advice was sound, but Halleck would have none of it and repeated the order to start his troops. Burnside came down to the Peninsula again to prod his old friend, probably at Halleck's request, but by the time he arrived the movement had begun. Porter's corps marched first, following the river road through Charles City Court House and aiming for a two-thousand-foot pontoon bridge spanning the broad mouth of the Chickahominy at Barrett's Ferry. The vanguard of Heintzelman's corps turned northward, toward Jones's Bridge, to avoid crowding the road.[38]

Porter seemed to supervise the withdrawal as he had the siege and much of the fighting, reporting back to McClellan on the progress of his own corps as well as Heintzelman's and Franklin's. On August 16, the third evening from Westover, his corps passed through Williamsburg by the light of a waning moon, and there some slaves were arrested with letters for their owners in Richmond. The letters revealed that most of the Confederate army had departed the city to pounce on Pope. Porter sent a dispatch back to McClellan about it, but he had lost telegraphic contact in that direction, so he also forwarded the news to Halleck by way of Fort Monroe. For all his mutinous invective about Pope deserving defeat, Porter moved quickly to go to his aid. Disobeying McClellan's instructions to stay within supporting distance of the next corps, he threw his column into a forced march to Fort Monroe, wiring ahead to have transports ready.[39]

Before McClellan received the note about the intercepted intelligence he learned that Porter had sped away, and sent him unusually curt orders to stop where he was, but it was too late. Driving his men under a blazing sun, Porter passed through Yorktown the next day and pressed on: a private in the 44th New York estimated that his regiment covered twenty-five miles. Captain John Ames of the 11th U.S. Infantry noticed that clouds of fine road dust caked the hair, beards, and clothing of his men, transforming them "from blue federals to grey-white Rebels." By the afternoon of August 18 Porter's command camped right where he had begun the campaign, five months before.[40]

John Tucker, the assistant secretary of war, had gone to Old Point Comfort to facilitate the embarkation of McClellan's troops. Porter appealed to him for transportation, and Tucker found it; later he remembered Porter as "zealous and energetic" about boarding his men. The Pennsylvania Reserves embarked on the morning of the nineteenth. McCall and Reynolds had been exchanged only the day before, traded for two generals Grant had captured in the West, but McCall was heading home, sick, and Reynolds took command. The Reserves had to sit out a storm overnight, but they cast off on August 20 and reached Aquia that night. Trains took them to Falmouth, from which Burnside sent them legging it up the Rappahannock the next afternoon, and Reynolds reported to Pope at Rappahannock Station, where McDowell had his headquarters. Pope reattached him to McDowell's corps, so Porter's command shrank back to two divisions for the remainder of this new campaign.[41]

Morell's division left next, arriving at Falmouth right behind Reynolds, and some of Sykes's Regulars came with them. So did Porter, who was suffering from dysentery. Burnside greeted him at his headquarters — a sprawling Georgian manse on the heights overlooking Fredericksburg. The headquarters tents stood close against the building on the side facing the Rappahannock, in the shade of some catalpa trees. Porter retained command of his troops, but he directed their movements from a cot in Burnside's tent, sending Morell after Reynolds on the night of August 22 and starting Sykes the next morning.[42]

Pope had fallen back behind the Rappahannock, dividing his army on either side of Rappahannock Station, astraddle the Orange & Alexandria Railroad that was his lifeline. Pope's sudden concern about his communications amused officers in the Army of the Potomac. George Meade, leading one of Reynolds's brigades, chuckled at the irony that "Pope has been obliged to show his *back* to the enemy and to select a *line of retreat*." The day after Meade made that observation, J. E. B. Stuart slipped around Pope's right flank, passed through Warrenton, and struck Catlett's Station, more than a dozen miles behind Pope's rear at Rappahannock Station. Torrents of rain fell that evening, foiling Stuart's main goal of burning the rail bridge over Cedar Run, but he cut the telegraph and captured Pope's quartermaster and several hundred prisoners and horses. The booty included Pope's personal baggage, with his dress uniform, but it also yielded Pope's headquarters paperwork, which helped Lee to determine the next phase of his campaign.[43]

The downpour raised the Rappahannock too high for crossing at the usual fords, preventing a similar flank movement by Confederate infantry, and Meade noted that they were protected more by Providence than by "Mr. Pope's genius." Meade clearly concurred in the low opinion of Pope held by McClellan and Porter, and if that was not the consensus among old Regulars it was the majority opinion. Burnside deduced as much from conversations with generals passing through Falmouth, many of whom found the notoriously mendacious Pope personally objectionable, and most doubted he could handle a large army.[44]

Similar doubts plagued generals under Pope's direct command. One of his brigadiers, John P. Hatch, confessed that he had no confidence in the blustering Pope, and that he would be "astonished" if he accomplished anything. Brigadier General Jesse Reno, leading the portion of the Ninth Corps with the Army of Virginia, betrayed his own scorn for Pope and reported that Banks harbored "a great deal of hard feelings" against Pope for sacrificing him at Cedar Mountain. Marsena Patrick, a brigade commander in McDowell's corps, considered Pope's introductory address "very windy & somewhat insolent," and it worried him to see that Pope's staff was filled with "politicians & rowdies" who were "anything but soldiers." In the opinion of Alpheus Williams, who commanded a division under Pope, "more insolence, superciliousness, ignorance, and pretentiousness were never combined in one man." Those well-informed opinions trickled down through the grades. The lieutenant colonel of the 6th Wisconsin, in McDowell's corps, considered Pope "a braggart and a villainous perverter of facts." Lieutenant Weld, just back from captivity, quickly absorbed Porter's opinion that Pope was "a complete failure." Although Weld had never met the man, he relied on the widespread opinion of others who did know him when he assured his father that Pope "can handle 10,000 men, but no more."[45]

A brigade commissary in Banks's corps recoiled at the brigandage to which Pope's order had given license, and his disgust was broadly shared. The lack of discipline in the Army of Virginia shocked and angered senior officers from the Army of the Potomac, who attributed it to Pope's recklessness in authorizing the appropriation of private property. Half a dozen "rounding soldiers" from a command Pope had left to guard Manassas Junction raided a nearby farm owned by a loyal New Yorker on August 25. Colonel Orlando Poe, who led a brigade from McClellan's army to Warrenton Junction on August 25, raged over the murder of an old man that day by one of Pope's cavalrymen: less than a mile from Poe's tent, the trooper had pushed his way into a house and shot the unarmed homeowner in the head, in front of his family, for resisting the intrusion. "The discipline of this army bears no comparison with that of the Army of the Potomac," Poe fumed, "and unless the authorities are very careful the army will degenerate into a band of thieves and robbers." Pope's orders and the example set by his men soon infected some portions of the Fifth Corps, and until Porter rejoined his men some of them began satisfying their appetites from farmers' fields, orchards, and barnyards.[46]

Pope reciprocated the mistrust and antipathy of McClellan's officers, and soon enough he would show it. Porter had not even reached the Army of Virginia from Fredericksburg when Pope — probably nettled by Porter's letter to Joseph Kennedy — asked his chief of staff if he did not think Porter would fail him. His chief of staff was Colonel George Ruggles, who had known Porter as his instructor at West Point, and Ruggles later admitted that the idea of Porter failing anyone struck him "like a thunderclap." Ruggles was also a good friend of Alexander Webb, who had just been assigned as Porter's inspector general. Some days later, with his hostility to McClellan fully fixed, Pope made a point of treating Webb boorishly when he stopped at Army of Virginia headquarters on his way to join Porter. Ruggles invited Webb to breakfast with the staff, but Pope came in and called Ruggles aside, scolding him in muffled tones. Ruggles told Webb that Pope "says he won't have any of General McClellan's staff at his table," so Webb took up his hat and departed.[47]

By the morning of August 25 Porter had recovered sufficiently to mount a horse and chase after Morell and Sykes. Reynolds had been covering Kelly's Ford, but Pope had taken him away the day before, drawing up to Warrenton with him and leaving the ford guarded only by a handful of cavalry, without a word to Porter. That alarmed Porter, for the water had already dropped low enough by then at most of the upriver fords for even infantry to cross. Morell was raising telegraph poles and lines as he moved, hoping to keep in touch with

Burnside, but the uncovered fords left that line vulnerable. Porter posted a brigade at each. He sent at least four telegrams to Falmouth on the twenty-fifth, hinting at his reservations about Pope's judgment and openly doubting the "uncertain data" Halleck provided, the latest of which he found to be stale by at least three days. Porter's last dispatch that evening, received by Burnside well after midnight, included the claim of a deserter that the Confederates were moving to Pope's right, around Warrenton.[48]

That deserter was talking about Stonewall Jackson, who had started north that morning on a wide detour around Warrenton, beyond the confluence of rivers that created the Rappahannock, and behind the Bull Run Mountains. For a week Lee had sashayed up the Rappahannock in search of unguarded fords, fighting little battles daily, but Pope's intercepted correspondence confirmed that McClellan's army was on its way from Falmouth. Desperate to defeat the Union forces in detail, he divided his army to cut Pope's supply line and force him to retire. Jackson was aiming for Manassas Junction, some fifty miles by his roundabout route, and twenty miles behind Warrenton: when he cut the railroad there, Pope would have to fall back fast, moving away from the reinforcements coming his way from Falmouth—just as he was already moving away from Porter.[49]

Screened by cavalry, Jackson passed unnoticed through Thoroughfare Gap in the Bull Run Mountains on August 26, crossed the Warrenton Turnpike, and hit the railroad at Bristoe Station, five miles below Manassas. He arrived at sunset, captured two trains as they arrived, and sent J. E. B. Stuart with a mixed command of horse and foot to seize the massive supply depot at Manassas Junction. The next day Jackson left Richard Ewell's division at Bristoe as the other two divisions moved up to Manassas to rifle the captured provisions. While most of his men filled their haversacks he diverted some of them to disperse several small bodies of Union soldiers who challenged him like terriers snapping at a lion.[50]

Pope, thinking he had Jackson trapped, turned his own army around and headed for Manassas, as hopeful of destroying the Confederacy's most legendary soldier as he was of restoring his line of communications. Captain William Paine of Pope's staff (who disliked his chief, as several of the staff did) found the general intensely excited. So was McDowell—who, in his glee at the idea of regaining his reputation on the same field where he had lost it, repeatedly muttered in French that they would have a great battle on the morrow.[51]

One brigade that confronted Jackson came from McClellan, whose army was bypassing Aquia and landing at Alexandria. Heintzelman's two divisions, under Joe Hooker and Phil Kearny, had already come down from that direction and joined Pope near Warrenton. Hooker, who was in the rear, faced about and led the way to Bristoe, where he ran into Ewell as he was falling back up the tracks toward Manassas. By dark Jackson's men had satisfied their wants from the cornucopia there, and they set the remainder afire before disappearing into the night.[52]

With the telegraph lines to Pope's army cut as well as the railroad, Porter became Washington's only source of timely information, via the operator at Falmouth. Porter knew that soon enough, but his dispatches to Burnside carried the colloquial tone he would have assumed with an old friend and fellow McClellan admirer: they oozed with disgust for Pope's arrogance and injudicious strategy. On the afternoon of August 27 he forwarded Pope's order spinning the army around and rushing it back to Manassas, commenting that it "indicates the future as well as the present." From Warrenton Junction, Porter misread the Manassas affair as another of Stuart's raids, scoffing at the alarm and the sight of all their wagon trains "rolling along rapidly to the rear, as if a mighty power was propelling them." The enemy evinced utter disrespect for Pope, he noticed, and he hoped to be ordered away—back to a reunited Army of the Potomac. He cautioned Burnside that he considered most of his dispatch private, but authorized him to use it if it would help rescue him from Pope. "I find I am to take care of myself in every respect," he complained again, later that evening. "Our line of communications has taken care of itself, in compliance with orders." As a result, the army lacked enough provisions for three days. He noted wryly (and with some exaggeration) that the enemy had even captured Pope's and McDowell's wardrobes and liquor.[53]

Had Porter known Burnside was sending those dispatches to Washington unedited, he might not have included such overtly critical comments on Pope's generalship. His hint about the personal nature of his telegrams escaped Burnside, whose naive nature allowed him to agree with staff officers who thought he should not deprive the president of any information. Porter was able to forgive Burnside despite the great trouble it caused him, but their mutual friend Franklin ultimately considered Burnside a fool for not culling the personal content.[54]

Porter had reported to Pope in person the morning of August 27, finding him in the telegraph shanty at Warrenton Junction with Colonel Ruggles. Later Porter recalled Pope's manner toward him as "irritating" from that first encounter, and Ruggles described Pope as "reticent and uncommunicative" when Porter asked about Pope's plans. Supposing that his own presence might be an embarrassment, Ruggles left the office. A certain reserve on Pope's part would have been natural, since he was already aware of Porter's low opinion of him through the Kennedy letter, but in fact Pope had no coherent plan. When Porter came out of the telegraph office he asked Ruggles about it, and Ruggles said if there was a plan he knew nothing about it. That information left Porter looking "dejected," Ruggles thought.[55]

At 6:30 P.M. on the twenty-seventh Pope wrote Porter an order from Bristoe Station, where Hooker's men had just closed a fierce fight and were running low on ammunition. The order arrived at Porter's headquarters at Warrenton Junction three hours later by the hand of Captain Joseph Rodman Drake DeKay, of New York City. Like Porter, DeKay was the son of a naval officer who died young, leaving a family in financial straits but with political connections. De-Kay's pecuniary embarrassment appeared to end when he snared an army commission a month into the war — and he would subsist thereafter on government appointments from the State Department and the state of New York. He spent the first half of the war as an aide to a succession of generals who were favorites of the Radical Republicans. That did not necessarily mark him as an abolitionist, but he did have a reformer's impulse, and his intense temperance activism would one day excite the *New York Tribune* to unflattering commentary.[56]

DeKay remained in the tent while Porter discussed the order with Morell, Sykes, and Butterfield. Pope wanted his corps on the road at 1:00 A.M. in order to be at Bristoe by daylight. "It is necessary on all accounts that you should be here by daylight," insisted Pope, who still expected to catch Jackson there in the morning. Porter handed it to one of his three generals, who read it and passed it along. DeKay later claimed that as Porter sent the order around he said, "Gentlemen, there is something for you to sleep upon," and that he gave the distinct impression he was not going to obey it. Porter may have said something in the same ironic tone he had been using with Burnside, because if the order were obeyed to the letter none of them or their troops would enjoy much sleep that night. The other three generals heard Porter say nothing to suggest the order would not be obeyed, but they all objected vociferously that their men had covered great distances that day: Sykes had marched his brigades twelve to fourteen miles, and Porter had hurried Morell's men from Kelly's and Barnett's Fords, which Morell estimated as respectively seventeen and nineteen miles. The division behind them had gone into bivouac at night while the road was still filled with "thousands" of what its commander thought were Porter's exhausted stragglers.[57]

Had McClellan posed such a demand, Porter would surely have made a strenuous effort to comply, and not merely because they were friends. Porter knew that McClellan cared deeply about the welfare of the common soldiers, and that a request for such extreme exertion would have emanated from dire need. The doubts Porter entertained about Pope's judgment, however justified, probably played a greater part in his ultimate decision about the desired movement than even he realized. That decision would ultimately head a list of accusations that Porter had been disobedient, and it was the only one with even a semblance of merit.

There existed numerous impediments to consider in determining how best to satisfy the spirit of the order. DeKay himself, though mounted and alone, had taken three hours to deliver the message from Bristoe. He conceded that the road was clogged with the wagons that had been passing all day, but he had passed the last of them at Catlett's Station, and expected they would soon be out of the way. DeKay suggested they might march on the railroad tracks, and the generals refrained from laughing at the image of so many men stumbling through the darkness over piled rails and ties and the burned bridges and culverts — not to mention the artillery and wagons that would have to follow. Although DeKay later denied it, Butterfield recalled him describing the night as "very dark," and nearly everyone concurred. Sykes thought it "unusually dark." Porter's chief of staff, Colonel Locke, said it was "extremely dark," and in groping his way through the camp on an errand for Porter he stumbled over a stump and injured himself badly. General Heintzelman, whose camp lay a few miles away, confirmed that it was a "very dark" night. Warrenton Junction was barely two days past the new moon, and that sliver had not risen in the latitude of Warrenton Junction when DeKay arrived.[58]

Pope, who had reason to minimize the distance between Warrenton Junction and Bristoe Station, remembered them as "about 9 miles" apart, but it was more like a dozen miles by the roads of 1862. Sykes, whose men were exhausted from a grueling march that broiling day, doubted they could cover so much ground in four hours with such impediments. He argued that they would move faster if the men slept longer and marched in daylight. Porter noted that the order required them to be at Bristoe at daylight, remarking that it "must be obeyed." For the past year he had served under a commander who trusted him, under whom he dared to exercise the broad discretion that was crucial to a corps commander operating far afield. He sent a couple of aides to look into the congestion on the road, but then the generals all stepped outside and saw how dark it was, whereupon Porter told them to have their men all in line, ready to march, by 3:00 A.M. With that he wrote Pope a note explaining the situation, and what he had decided.[59]

11

DAWKIN'S BRANCH

Reveille sounded in Sykes's camp between two and two-thirty in the morning on August 28. An aide he sent out to lead the column came back to say it was so dark that neither he nor the squad of soldiers he took with him could find the road. As soon as he could distinguish the road, Sykes sounded the advance, but they had not made two miles before they ran into the tail of the tangled wagon train, right where DeKay had last seen it. Every teamster moved as he pleased, and Sykes finally had to call up his cavalry escort and deploy them with drawn sabers to keep the wagons off to one side. Four months later he told Porter's court-martial, "I do not think that in my military life I ever had so much trouble with a train as I had that day."[1]

Stephen Weld preceded Porter, finding the road "completely blocked" by wagons. They were parked beside the road and in the road, often with their teams unhitched or unharnessed, and tethered to the wheels or poles. The road itself twisted through dense woods that crowded it narrower than ten feet in places. Once Porter and his staff worked their way up to the front they lit into the teamsters themselves, forcing them aside to let the troops pass. Porter, whom Weld always found perfectly calm under the most trying circumstances, seemed unusually annoyed at the drivers and wagon masters. Leaping into the congestion as he had at Savage's Station, he "spoke pretty sharply" to some of the teamsters, clearing a path for the fighting men. The head of the corps took six full hours getting to Bristoe Station, where Porter reined up ahead of the infantry. As soon as he arrived he sent Colonel Locke and a couple of aides looking for the ammunition train.[2]

Several years later David Hunter Strother, one of Pope's aides, claimed that Porter's ten-o'clock arrival elicited "much indignant comment among the staff officers on this dangerous delay," yet no danger attended the delay. Porter was not the only tardy corps commander, either: Franz Sigel started several hours later than ordered. For all the haste Pope had demanded of Porter, he showed no real need for him. After running down the ammunition train, Lieutenant Monteith encountered Pope and asked if he had orders for the Fifth Corps, but he had none; nor did he know where the enemy was. Sykes and Morell moved their divisions from the smoldering embers of the Bristoe railroad depot to a watering station east of there and made camp, remaining there all day and into the next morning.[3]

Porter's usual courtesy disguised his poor opinion of Pope when they met at Bristoe, and Pope showed no rancor toward him. Weld discerned no word or air of censure or complaint from Pope over the failure to arrive at daybreak, remarking that the encounter between the two generals "was pleasant enough, so far as I could see." They dismounted and sat on the grass together, talking for quite some time.[4]

Late in the afternoon Lieutenant Colonel Thomas C. H. Smith, an aide of Pope's, called at Porter's tent about the ammunition he had requested. Locke had found the train by then, at Manassas, and had stopped it beside the road, but Porter had not yet been notified. Porter may have waxed a little critical over the misdirection of those wagons, for the colonel responded defensively. Smith, who later acted as Pope's partner in prevarication, described Porter's manner as "sneering" — presumably in regard to Pope. Crediting his own clairvoyance, Smith claimed months later that he instantly deduced from their brief conversation that Porter was not disposed to support Pope and that he would "fail" him. He could cite no word or action of Porter's as evidence, offering only his own intuition to substantiate an absurd assertion that he left the tent "certain that Fitz John Porter was a traitor." Porter ate dinner with the staff shortly after Smith left, and Lieutenant Monteith found the general "vexed" by his visitor's insolent manner.[5]

Seven miles northwest of Porter's camp, McDowell was having trouble of his own with a wagon train as he approached Gainesville on the Warrenton Turnpike. Franz Sigel's corps still lay ahead of McDowell, blocking his way. As the assigned commander of that column, McDowell ordered Sigel's train culled of everything but ammunition wagons, even shunting aside Sigel's private mess wagon.[6]

With his army spread five miles wide between Porter on the railroad and McDowell on the Warrenton Turnpike, Pope expected to sweep up Jackson, but the elusive Stonewall had vanished. A flurry of contradictory orders soon highlighted Pope's confusion, moving Porter to still more sarcasm about the management of that army, and it overflowed in a dispatch he sent back by mounted messenger a few hours after his corps arrived at Bristoe. "All that talk of bagging Jackson, &c., was bosh," he informed Burnside: Pope had neglected to plug Thoroughfare Gap, and Jackson had presumably slipped back through. "The enemy have destroyed all our bridges, burned trains, &c., and made this army rush back to look after its line of communications and find our base of subsistence. . . . There is a report that Jackson is at Centreville, which you can believe or not." Mocking Pope's assurances that McDowell would prevent Longstreet from taking them in the flank, Porter said he next expected to hear that Longstreet was following them up through Warrenton, to strike them from behind.[7]

Porter's conception of the tactical situation was as mistaken as Pope's, whose marching orders for the day showed that he still thought Jackson lingered at Manassas Junction. Jackson was no longer there — or at Centreville, where witnesses had seen his columns marching the previous night — but neither had he escaped back through the gap. While Porter wrote to Burnside, Jackson's divisions were gathering in the woods five miles to Porter's left, just north of a tiny settlement called Groveton, four miles down the Warrenton Turnpike from Gainesville and right in McDowell's path. Longstreet, meanwhile, did threaten the Union left flank, and McDowell was moving in a direction that would soon have put those Rebels in the rear of Pope's army. Longstreet's half of Lee's force was circling around by the route Jackson had taken, and was just then approaching Thoroughfare Gap. Hampered by Pope's orders to hurry all his troops forward, McDowell dared not stop to hold the gap in force, but he did send cavalry to watch it, leaving James Ricketts behind with his lone division to resist Longstreet if he showed up. Before long a cavalryman came racing back to say that Longstreet was on his way through — as Porter had predicted. Ricketts moved to confront him, outnumbered about five to one.[8]

McDowell alerted Pope to Longstreet's appearance, but heard nothing in reply until late that afternoon. Pope had long since learned that no Confederates remained at Manassas Junction, but at first he imagined that Jackson had withdrawn to Gum Spring, fifteen miles to the north, and ordered McDowell that way to head him off. Only minutes afterward, McDowell's warning about Longstreet reached Pope and he all but forgot about Jackson, promising McDowell reinforcements that would have given him nine divisions to Longstreet's five. This sudden new determination to crush Longstreet evaporated as quickly as it had arisen when new reports placed "the enemy" (meaning Jackson) on the Washington side of Bull Run, and Pope again reversed all the troops then in motion — including McDowell, whom he turned back toward Centreville.[9]

McDowell dutifully redirected his troops, but after three contradictory orders within an hour he decided it was time to pay Pope a visit. He and a portion of his staff started for Manassas Junction, taking the road past the crumbling remains of a brick chapel called Bethlehem Church. They reached the junction at sunset, but learned that Pope had moved on to Centreville. Distant sounds of musketry and artillery carried their way from the direction whence they had come, and on the correct assumption that his own troops were under attack McDowell led everyone cross-country toward the gunfire. His command was engaged on two fronts, as it happened, with Ricketts retiring from Thoroughfare Gap before Longstreet while Rufus King's division was fighting Jackson above the Warrenton Turnpike. McDowell led his party into swampy ground around the headwaters of Flat Run, and had to turn back. By the time they found a road, darkness had ended the fighting, and the silence left them disoriented. They wandered around lost until stumbling onto the road to Bethlehem Church. Following that, they turned off on the Sudley Road, toward New Market, dismounting among some of Sigel's troops well after midnight to sleep on the ground near the battlefield of the previous year.[10]

Pope had seen the flashes of King's battle from a vantage point several miles to the east, where he had last gone chasing Jackson. He immediately assumed that King's division was blocking Jackson's retreat on the turnpike, and later said he sent King several orders to hold his position, but no such order was ever found and King never mentioned receiving one.[11]

Jackson had no intention of retreating. Instead, he had attacked Brigadier General John Gibbon's brigade of King's division as it passed up the Warrenton Turnpike. The little battle produced intense musketry and heavy casualties for the numbers engaged, subsiding only when darkness enveloped the field and the combatants fell back where they had stood when it began.

At three o'clock on the morning of August 29, Pope wrote Porter that McDowell had "intercepted the retreat of Jackson," directing Porter to leave Bristoe with his entire command "at the first dawn of day" and march for Centreville. At that moment Pope evidently believed that McDowell, with Sigel in support, still held the turnpike west of Jackson, facing him head-on. He seemed intent on gathering Heintzelman, Porter, and Reno's little Ninth Corps east of Jackson, to attack him from behind. Pope's final and most crucial misunderstanding about the location of his troops was his belief that Ricketts remained behind at Thoroughfare Gap, blocking Longstreet.[12]

Pope's ignorance emanated partly from McDowell's absence, which removed a relay in communications. No one knew where McDowell had gone, and King's division stood alone before Jackson. Following his last instructions, Reynolds had taken the Pennsylvania Reserves down the Gainesville Road toward Manassas, then turned up the Sudley Road to the battlefield of First Bull Run, where his division spent the night. Sigel's corps had followed a similar route and bivouacked nearby, on and around Henry Hill, where the tide had turned in the 1861 battle. Ricketts had confronted Longstreet's advance at Thoroughfare Gap through the afternoon, but had been outflanked and had fallen back to Gainesville after dark. King had just suffered at least his second epileptic seizure within a week, and with no corps commander to consult he grew anxious about his precarious position. An hour or two after midnight, he started his division toward Manassas Junction, arriving there early in the morning of August 29. He warned Ricketts where he was going, and Ricketts retreated by way of Bristoe Station to avoid Jackson, remaining out of communication until the sun rose high the following day. At 3:00 A.M., as Pope wrote Porter's orders, he imagined that five Union divisions stood before Jackson to the west, but the last of those divisions—Ricketts's—was already beginning its retreat. Longstreet's road to Jackson lay wide open.[13]

Captain Strother, the aide Pope chose to deliver his message to Porter, described "broad daylight" in the camp of the Fifth Corps when he rode in, yet he also claimed that Porter asked him to light a candle so he could read the order. Strother ostensibly glanced at the general's watch as he struck the match, finding the time to be "5:20 exactly," but that would have been a quarter-hour before sunrise if the watch was adjusted to local time. According to Strother's patently imprecise memory, he found Porter asleep on his cot. Porter invited him to breakfast, sitting at an improvised table with his staff and writing dispatches and the orders for Sykes and Morell to ready their men for the road.[14] At 6:00 A.M. he started a note to Burnside, to whom he relayed the inaccurate troop dispositions Strother had carried from Pope's headquarters—flavoring it with his usual measure of skepticism about the information, and about Pope.

"McDowell near Gainesville; Heintzelman and Reno at Centreville, where they marched yesterday, and Pope went to Centreville with the last two as a body guard, at the time not knowing where was the enemy and when Sigel [i.e., King] was fighting within 8 miles of him and in sight. Comment is unnecessary. The enormous trains are still rolling on, many animals not having been watered for fifty hours. I shall be out of provisions to-morrow night. Your train of 40 wagons cannot be found. I hope Mac is at work, and we will soon get ordered out of this. It would seem from proper statements of the enemy that he is wandering around loose; but I expect they know what the[y] are doing, which is more than anyone here or anywhere knows."[15]

In the first version of Strother's journal, published five years later, he maintained that Porter stopped writing at one point to ask him how to spell "chaos." In a still-later version, Strother added that the question allowed him to deduce what the general was thinking and writing about, yet none of Porter's dispatches to Burnside or anyone else during the campaign included that word. Strother maintained his consistently negative depiction of Porter in his published journal, depicting episodes such as the inaccurate breakfast vignette that carry a distinct air of after-the-fact revisions.[16]

Near Manassas, John Gibbon awoke in a quandary. His corps commander, McDowell, was still missing, and King, his division commander, had not yet recovered from his latest seizure, so Gibbon ventured up to Centreville to familiarize Pope with the situation and seek orders. By then Pope finally knew that King had abandoned his position on the other side of Jackson; he also knew that neither Sigel nor Reynolds was there, and that Ricketts had probably withdrawn as well. Once aware that King was at Manassas, Pope decided to divert Porter from his northeasterly path to Centreville and direct him west-northwest on the road to Gainesville, taking King's division with him to reoccupy the abandoned position. He evidently meant to alert McDowell to that plan, wherever he was. Giving the instructions to his aide-de-camp, Captain John Piatt, Pope sent him back toward Manassas over the Centreville Road looking for McDowell. Then he wrote the same order out for Porter and gave it to Gibbon, who would return to his brigade by the Sudley Road. "Be expeditious," Pope urged Porter, "or we will lose much."[17]

Pope obviously intended those three divisions to reestablish the anvil against which he could hammer Jackson with all the other troops he could find. Pope's logic in that first hour of daylight presumed not only that Jackson was in retreat but also that Porter could outmarch him to Gainesville via the longer road, and that Longstreet lurked nowhere nearby. He was mistaken in all three suppositions.[18]

Sykes had his division on the road by 7:00 A.M., as soon as breakfast had been cooked and swallowed. Morell followed right behind him. By then the sound of artillery echoed from the north, where Sigel had engaged Jackson a mile above the Warrenton Turnpike. Still guided by the orders to go to Centreville, seven miles to the northeast, Porter wondered why he would be needed there when the battle appeared to be brewing above the turnpike, seven miles to the northwest. His column nevertheless kept moving east at a good stride, coming upon the wreckage of Jackson's raid at Manassas Junction four miles later. Captain John Ames of the Regulars guessed the damage at two million dollars in burned cars and stores. (A Confederate witness had hopefully estimated the destruction as "several millions.") The sight moved Porter's men to inventive expression of their own poor opinions of John Pope, especially when they considered that their shrunken haversacks might have accommodated the provisions Jackson had destroyed. "We swore furiously at Mr. General Pope, the bombastic," Ames conceded.[19]

As his two divisions marched through Manassas toward Centreville they passed the elegant brick home of William Weir, just beyond the junction. McDowell stood in the yard, wearing the hot-weather headgear one of his staff officers called "an immense Japanese wash-bowl" — probably a pith helmet. He had awakened before dawn to seek the scattered divisions of his own corps and had located Reynolds, leaving him near the turnpike to support Sigel. Coming back to Manassas looking for Pope, he had found King stretched out on the floor of a room in the Weir house, exhausted from his seizures and lack of sleep. McDowell learned that Ricketts's division was still somewhere beyond Bristoe Station, in retreat, and when he saw flags of the Fifth Corps passing by he sent for Porter, telling him what he knew about the dearth of Union troops to the west of Jackson. That made it even more odd that the Fifth Corps should be ordered to

Centreville, but those were Porter's most recent orders and he rode away with his column, the head of which was already well on the way to Mitchell's Ford, over Bull Run.[20]

Porter's leading regiment had not yet reached the run when, around nine o'clock, Captain Piatt came riding along in the opposite direction, asking whose troops they were. Soldiers pointed out Porter, and Piatt told him Pope wanted him to take his own corps and King's division and make for Gainesville. Seeing no written dispatch, Porter assumed the order was only oral, and meant for him, but Piatt continued on to give the written version to McDowell, the intended recipient. Those orders made more sense to Porter, even if he didn't have them on paper, so he immediately stopped the troops. He sent Locke and at least one of his couriers back to Manassas to face the column about and put it on the right road while he wrote a message for Pope. Hoping Pope might still be "near Bull Run," where the 3:00 A.M. orders had been headed, Porter asked his new medical director, Robert Abbott, to find him and deliver the message. The dispatch he gave Dr. Abbott repeated the gist of Piatt's verbal order, including what news he had from McDowell, and he asked that Pope send any subsequent orders in writing: Piatt was a perfect stranger to him, and the potential for error or deception troubled him. While Abbott headed across Bull Run with the note, Porter turned back toward Manassas Junction.[21]

At the junction Sykes spotted the ammunition train, reminding Locke of it, and Locke stopped the two divisions to distribute additional cartridges. That took as much as three-quarters of an hour, during which Gibbon returned with the written copy of the same order Piatt had recited. Porter soon rode up, read it, and doubled back to the Weir house to see if McDowell knew more about Pope's plans, or could tell him about the terrain he would be traversing. McDowell lent him a map showing the terrain toward Gainesville. He suggested, too, that Pope would eventually fall back behind Bull Run and form a new line with reinforcements from McClellan. Through Piatt, McDowell had learned of Pope assigning King to Porter, and bridled enough at the idea to dispatch a messenger to ask Pope to rescind that part of Porter's orders. He said nothing to Porter about that, but did ask him to place King on his right when they moved up the road, so the division would remain near enough to Reynolds that McDowell could easily resume command of it.[22] King had finally reported himself too sick to continue in command, so his division would move under John Hatch, the senior brigadier.[23]

With Morell in the lead this time, marching by the flank, the Fifth Corps wound back through the smoldering ruins at the junction. Crossing the tracks of the Manassas Gap Railroad, the column turned to the right, toward Gainesville and Sudley Springs. After two and a half miles the Sudley Road broke off to the north and the Gainesville Road bent to the northwest, passing what was left of Bethlehem Church half a mile farther on, where Rebel videttes bolted away without firing a shot. This was the route, running roughly parallel to the Manassas Gap line, that McDowell and King's division had followed in the opposite direction the night before. A mile and a half short of the turnpike, where the main road bent to the left in an arc that struck the pike near Gainesville, the colonial-era Warrenton and Alexandria Road veered off to the right.[24]

More of J. E. B. Stuart's cavalry was staking out the intersection of the old highway and the Gainesville Road then, just beyond the infantry Longstreet had deployed to guard his right. From different vantage points Rebel scouts saw the head of Porter's corps coming from Manassas, followed by King, and some wider-ranging horsemen detected Ricketts moving toward Manassas from Bristoe. Alarmed at the size of those columns, Stuart detailed a few squads of troopers to trot back and forth on the Gainesville Road, dragging brush to create the impression of approaching Confederate reinforcements. He emphasized the impact of that ploy six months later, after learning that the Yankees had stopped short at sight of dust clouds, but most of that dust was raised by Longstreet's infantry as he positioned it between there and the turnpike.[25]

Charles Griffin's brigade led Porter's corps up the Gainesville Road, setting a vigorous pace that Morell estimated as "nearer three than two" miles an hour. They passed King's division, still resting alongside the road about a mile from the junction, and King's men started falling in to follow when the last of Sykes's division had passed. Beyond the remnants of the church a Union cavalryman pulled up alongside Griffin and warned him that another trooper had been captured by Rebels a short distance ahead. Griffin cast a few companies of Pennsylvanians out as skirmishers half a mile in front of his column, and posted some flankers on the sides. Another mile out, Morell met a second horseman just from Gainesville who warned him that a Rebel skirmish line was already passing through when he left.[26]

Dawkin's Branch crossed the Gainesville Road a mile and a quarter before the Washington and Alexandria Road, and five miles from Manassas Junction. The stream itself posed no obstruction to infantry, running about eight feet wide and nearly dry on that scorching day. It might have risen knee-deep in a good rain, but in 1862 no Virginian would have thought it called for a bridge, and a man who forded it that day said there was not much water in it. Making its way to Broad Run over the millennia, the stream had carved a wide swale out of a plateau, leaving a pair of opposing ridges that were now covered in thickets and timber of pine and oak. Open ground spread half a mile beyond the ridges before more heavy timber occluded everything beyond, and there lay the Confederates, masked by the foliage; the clearing around a nearby house offered an excellent position for artillery, thought Stuart. As Griffin's skirmishers crossed the branch and started up the other slope, Rebel videttes fired on them and Morell

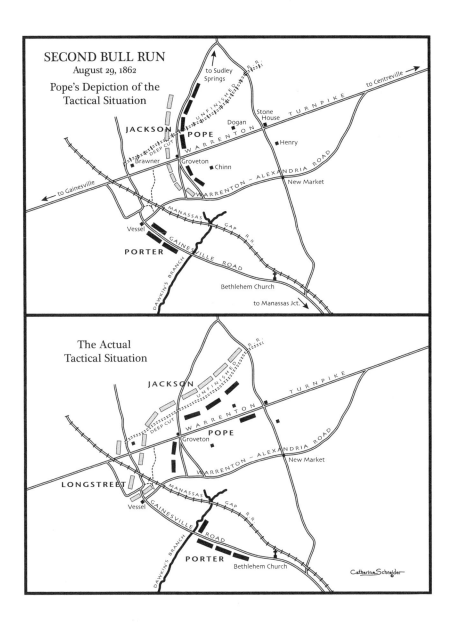

SECOND BULL RUN
August 29, 1862

Pope's Depiction of the
Tactical Situation

to Sudley
Springs

to Centreville →

R. R.

UNFINISHED

Stone
House

TURNPIKE

Dogan

JACKSON

POPE

WARRENTON

Henry

DEEP CUT

Brawner

Groveton

Chinn

WARRENTON – ALEXANDRIA ROAD

New Market

← to Gainesville

MANASSAS

GAP

R R

Vessel

GAINESVILLE ROAD

PORTER

DAWKIN'S BRANCH

Bethlehem Church

to Manassas Jct.

The Actual
Tactical Situation

R. R.

JACKSON

UNFINISHED

TURNPIKE

WARRENTON

DEEP CUT

POPE

Groveton

WARRENTON – ALEXANDRIA ROAD

New Market

LONGSTREET

MANASSAS

GAP

R R

Vessel

GAINESVILLE ROAD

DAWKIN'S BRANCH

PORTER

Bethlehem Church

Catherine Schneider

brought the column to a halt. His watch was broken, but a few months later he remembered hearing the first shots at Dawkin's Branch "about 11 o'clock in the morning," which he later revised to "about eleven or twelve o'clock." Morell's column had covered about nine miles since shortly after 7:00 A.M., marching at a pace that might have brought it there by 11:30, considering the stop for ammunition.[27]

Porter came up fifteen or twenty minutes after those first shots. The skirmishers sent back two or three prisoners in butternut suits whom Porter questioned at length, and one of them admitted that he belonged to Longstreet's corps. Nearly three hours earlier, John Buford's Union cavalry brigade had spotted what had to be one of Longstreet's leading divisions marching into Gainesville, barely four miles beyond Porter's skirmishers. A courier was taking a roundabout route to Manassas with General Buford's warning, but Longstreet's troops had covered several miles in the meantime. Porter's column had not trudged past Bethlehem Church, in fact, when Confederate infantry seized the turnpike junction two miles beyond Gainesville. Some of that infantry had turned immediately down the Gainesville Road, and it was waiting just beyond the intersection with the Warrenton and Alexandria Road when Porter came into view.[28]

Porter called for Dan Butterfield, directing his attention to a white house about a mile beyond the branch, on the other side of the Manassas Gap Railroad. That was the spot Stuart had thought advantageous for artillery, and Porter ordered Butterfield up there to see what was in the woods beyond. There was no cavalry with Porter's column, so Butterfield moved out in advance with his staff to reconnoiter, leaving the senior colonel to deploy his brigade behind him.[29]

Butterfield's regiments were sliding into line of battle and moving ahead when Surgeon Abbott rode up, bringing Porter the latest instructions from Pope. Responding to both McDowell's appeal for King's division and Porter's request for written orders, Pope had supplied the two of them with a vague and rambling program for the day's work. He instructed them to continue toward Gainesville with their "joint commands" — which forever identified the document as the "joint order." Pope misunderstood that Heintzelman, Sigel, and Reno were already approaching Gainesville on the turnpike, and once Porter and McDowell met those other corps Pope wanted them to halt. Longstreet was at that moment blocking the turnpike and funneling men down the Gainesville Road, but Pope was under the delusion that Longstreet would not reach the field until the next day, or even the day after.[30]

It was not clear what Porter and McDowell should do when they stopped, for Pope also reminded them that they would probably have to retire behind Bull Run for provisions during the night. Like Lee's orders to Stonewall Jackson at Beaver Dam Creek, Pope's joint order bore no instructions for engaging the enemy.

McDowell came galloping to Porter's front with his own copy of the order — "quite excited," according to Locke's courier. In the presence of several of Porter's officers he remarked in a commanding tone, "Porter, you are out too far." Some bystanders heard him add, "This is no place to fight a battle."[31] He was evidently referring to the mile-wide gap between Porter's right flank and the left of Reynolds, who was spreading the Pennsylvania Reserves out below Groveton to confront Longstreet's advance units as they arrived.

McDowell nonchalantly produced the warning from John Buford, which had failed to impress him enough to forward it to Pope, but it corroborated Porter's mounting suspicion of Longstreet's arrival. McDowell's memory proved very porous a few months later, but one detail he remembered was Porter waving his hand at the clouds of dust in the distance and saying, "We cannot go in there anywhere without getting into a fight." McDowell also recalled making the heroic reply that a fight was "what we came here for," but that rejoinder hardly comported with his obvious lack of enthusiasm for the isolated attack Porter was contemplating.[32]

Even without the joint order, McDowell's seniority gave him command authority over Porter once they came together by virtue of the Sixty-Second Article of War. Porter took the criticism of his deployment as an order to desist, and he recalled Butterfield's brigade. Butterfield and his staff had pushed too far ahead to hear the orders, and had just run into Rebel skirmishers when Butterfield saw his own troops disappearing back over the branch. That brought him cantering in, too.[33]

Followed by a few of their staff officers, McDowell and Porter reined off into the timber to the north, to see if troops could move that way toward Reynolds. It was farther to Groveton that way than they had supposed, and the terrain looked hopelessly difficult; a man raised in that vicinity called it "almost a jungle." Their horses had some difficulty scrambling over the railroad embankment, but the two generals ranged fairly deep into the woods without finding a path where artillery could move. A stream purled around the foot of a hill, and with so little water in that vicinity they let their horses drink while they talked. Porter suggested holding fast where he was while McDowell took King's division around the Sudley Road to fill the gap on the left of Reynolds. At that moment McDowell suddenly spurred off back toward the Gainesville Road, without a word. Porter called after him, asking what he should do, but McDowell was already out of earshot, disappearing down the road toward Bethlehem Church.[34]

So abrupt was McDowell's departure that he left behind his cavalry escort and his chief of staff, Edmund Schriver. Glancing at the troopers behind Schriver, Porter said he had no cavalry and asked if he might borrow some of his, as couriers. Schriver left behind half of them when he turned back to follow McDowell.[35]

Returning to the ridge behind Dawkin's Branch, Porter ordered Morell to start moving some troops to the right, in hopes of making a connection with Reynolds himself. Morell sent Griffin out, but faulty maps and thick vegetation had obscured the distances and difficulties between Dawkin's Branch and Groveton. Griffin started off to the right, but had barely crossed the Manassas Gap Railroad, a quarter of a mile away, when he ran into ravines too steep for the artillery he needed to take with him.[36]

Porter did not know that McDowell meant to take back control of King's division, for the joint order failed to specify as much and McDowell did not reveal that he had asked Pope to give King back to him: the last McDowell had said on the subject was to ask Porter to keep King on his right. Supposing that he still had the use of that division, Porter sent Locke to the rear with a message for King to stand ready, intending to bring him up in support of his battle line. Neither Locke nor his courier had ever met King, but they found his division still resting near Bethlehem Church, and spotted McDowell standing near a fence with another officer. Locke dismounted and approached them, asking the other man if he were King. On what he perceived as an affirmative reply, Locke delivered the message, but the man gestured toward McDowell. Evidently having decided to adopt Porter's last suggestion, McDowell said he was going to move to the right, taking King's division with him, and that Porter could stay where he was: if he had to fall back, he could align on McDowell's left. With that, King's division started away.[37]

The officer with McDowell may have misunderstood Locke when he asked who he was, because King later testified that he did not know Locke and did not remember meeting him that day. King said he had reported himself unfit for duty by then (and one of his brigade commanders thought that was correct), but King also indicated that he was in the vicinity of Bethlehem Church about the time Locke indicated. King also conceded that he was very sick from what is generally recognized to have been multiple epileptic seizures, which can affect memory when or after they occur. This encounter with Locke was another episode of August 29 that escaped McDowell's memory, and no one was ever able to deduce who else the man might have been. Locke's unwavering certainty that the officer was King would damage his credibility at a critical moment for Porter.[38]

When Locke came back and related his exchange with McDowell, Porter felt sure, finally, that McDowell had decided to adopt the suggestion he made while they were reconnoitering across the railroad: by taking King's division to the right, McDowell implied that he intended to fill the void between Porter's corps and Reynolds, which would more safely comply with the joint order. Regarding McDowell's remark about staying where he was as an order from the senior officer of the "joint command," Porter waited only for King to come in on his right. The interpretation of McDowell's comment as an order quickly filtered down through the senior officers of the corps, and Colonel Warren heard about it from Locke later that same day. A week later, Warren told his brother that they should have attacked right then, "but McDowell would not let us." Staff officers with McDowell also understood that he had given Porter orders "as senior officer."[39]

Despite McDowell's poor memory of what transpired on August 29, he did insist that before bolting away he told Porter to "put your force in here." He later tried to characterize that as an order to attack, but he also argued that his authority over Porter ended when he rode away. That equivocation effectively relieved him of any responsibility for whatever Porter did thereafter — or did not do.[40]

General Stuart might claim that his brush-dragging discouraged Porter from making an attack, but the real credit belonged to Pope's joint order. That ambiguous message brought the chronically uncommunicative McDowell to Dawkin's Branch, allowing him to interrupt Porter's preparations for an attack and take King's division away. It also gave Porter the impression that McDowell was his immediate superior for the day, leading him to send his reports to McDowell instead of directly to Pope, who might at least have been more responsive.

McDowell later said that in abandoning Porter he was taking advantage of the second paragraph of Pope's joint order, which allowed him or Porter to vary from it "if any considerable advantages are to be gained." He never explained what advantage it gained, and his failure to follow through on his nebulous plan with Porter wrought ample damage. He cut the strength of Porter's command nearly in half, sharply reducing his capacity for offensive movement in his isolated position, and he took King and Ricketts out of action for all but the last few minutes of fighting that day — besides immobilizing Porter for hours, waiting for the execution of a plan McDowell had abandoned. Worst of all, he left Porter with the impression that theirs was still a joint command, with McDowell in charge. Fitz John Porter, John Pope, and the Union cause would all have benefited had a Rebel sharpshooter been able to knock McDowell out of the saddle when he arrived at Dawkin's Branch, leaving Porter in unquestionable control.[41]

While he waited for McDowell to come in on his right, Porter tried to discern the position and strength of the enemy before him, sending out the 13th New York to augment his skirmish line. That once-mutinous little regiment had been groomed to remarkable efficiency by its latest colonel, Elisha Marshall, who had drilled as a West Point plebe under the newly graduated Porter. As the senior officer, Marshall took command of the skirmishers while Morell deployed his infantry and artillery on the ridge behind Dawkin's Branch.[42]

Porter asked Colonel Marshall to cross the open ground ahead of them and delve into the timber beyond. Marshall eased his regiment over the ridge into the open, down the ravine, and up into the woods on the other side, where cavalry pickets fired a few rounds at his men and retired. More Confederates came up to challenge the New Yorkers, and eventually Marshall heard infantry commands and the creaking of artillery deeper in the woods. He held his ground the rest of the day, sending frequent runners to Morell with verbal observations.[43]

When Marshall reported a pair of Rebel regiments and two batteries taking position a mile ahead of Dawkin's Branch, Morell sent that information to Porter, predicting that they might find it a little hot ahead. The ground the Confederates held bore such similarities to Porter's enviable position on Malvern Hill that he directed Morell to move everyone under cover behind the crest, to invite an attack rather than make one. "We must hold that place and make it too hot for them," he wrote, telling Morell to conceal his main line in the thick pine scrub beside the road. "I would get everything, if possible, in ambuscade."[44]

Marching up the railroad just then came Abraham Piatt's brigade of barely eight hundred men, thrown together from garrison fragments in Washington. They marched under a superfluous division commander, Brigadier General Samuel Sturgis, and had been temporarily attached to Porter's corps. When Sturgis reported, Porter told him to leave his men where they stopped, on his extreme right near Griffin. There they sat the rest of the day, perfectly idle. Time would show that it would have been better for Porter if they had never come.[45]

The fighting above the Warrenton Turnpike subsided to artillery duels and heavy skirmishing for most of the afternoon. When it picked up again, around four o'clock, it seemed to Marshall that things were going badly for Sigel, Heintzelman, and Reno. Those ominous dust clouds still hovered beyond the woods held by Longstreet's skirmishers, and the sound of battle had migrated eastward, as though Pope were being driven back, which might compromise Porter's line of retreat. Enemy cheering, which Marshall described as "a continual yelling" distinguishable from the concerted hurrahs of Union troops, indicated by their drift and exhilaration that the Rebel forces were gaining ground. Porter sent two worried messages to McDowell, asking what he meant to do and what he knew.[46]

Four hours after McDowell sped away from Dawkin's Branch, he had still not brought King's division in on the left of Reynolds. Instead, on Pope's order McDowell sent a brigade across the turnpike to support artillery in action against Jackson, but he kept most of King's division standing along the Sudley Road, near Henry Hill.[47]

The two messages from Porter did reach McDowell, but he never forwarded them to Pope or responded to them, leaving Pope uninformed and Porter anxious. Apparently McDowell forgot about those dispatches altogether, for they spent many years lost among his papers. Because of McDowell's silence, Porter feared that nothing he had sent overland to Groveton had made it through. Some of his couriers came back saying they had run into Rebels, and he feared that others had been captured. His men were completely out of food and running low on water, and—as Pope's joint order had anticipated—he would have to retire to get any. He moved his headquarters from near Dawkin's Branch back to Bethlehem Church, to shorten his circuitous line of communications with McDowell, but still he could raise no word from that sphinx. At the church Porter dismounted to lie down, as he had done at every opportunity that day, trying to conserve his strength against the intestinal fever that still weakened him.[48]

Confederate troops had been maneuvering in front of Colonel Marshall all afternoon. At one point a Virginia brigade threw skirmishers out to meet him, pushing his regiment back into the woods. Marshall later detected a brigade-sized force sidling around his left, and saw other troops moving into positions to the right of the road. When he reported that apparent aggression, in addition to the sinister shift of the gunfire at Groveton, Porter suspected he was being cut off and was about to be attacked. Morell suggested by dispatch that they should retire, and Porter momentarily agreed, concluding that he should fall back on Manassas. He sent Lieutenant Weld to find McDowell, or King, and warn them of his plans, but he waited for a reply before retiring because it would uncover McDowell's left flank. Sending Morell orders to hold on and post his men to resist any attack, Porter finally decided to ride up and assess the situation himself.[49]

Before mounting up, he directed Piatt's motley little brigade to fall back on Manassas, probably reasoning that it would be best to get it out of the way. Beyond Bethlehem Church, Piatt's men encountered James Ricketts's division, finally marching from the junction to join McDowell.[50]

In response to Porter's instructions to push a party over and see what was threatening Marshall's left, Morell sent out the 22nd Massachusetts. J. E. B. Stuart may have seen that movement, and he probably spotted the dust of Ricketts's division, so he warned Longstreet of "heavy columns" moving against his right. It was then "a late hour in the day," by Longstreet's recollection, and "toward evening," according to the major of the 13th New York. As a precaution, Longstreet sidled Cadmus Wilcox's three brigades over to brace his right. Writing his report on the battle amid the earlier sunsets of October, Wilcox underestimated the time of his movement as 4:30 or 5:00 P.M.[51]

From the ridge by Dawkin's Branch, Porter determined that he faced little risk of an immediate assault. Longstreet was holding back for a more propitious opportunity to strike a devastating blow without such a threat as Porter hanging on his right flank. Nor had the battle lines around Groveton swung in the ominous direction Marshall had thought: the point of assault had simply changed, carrying the din with it. Porter sent a messenger to recall Piatt, but the dispatch announcing his intention to retreat was on its way to Pope, who would always thereafter cite Piatt's aborted movement as evidence that Porter did retreat when ordered to attack.[52]

Pope, who had been confused about the location of the enemy for days, still badly mistook Confederate dispositions, and he would cling persistently to that misunderstanding in the face of all contradictory evidence. Months later he testified that on the afternoon of August 29 Jackson's divisions "occupied a line perpendicular to the Warrenton turnpike, and at or near the town of Groveton." Yet Jackson did not have a man anywhere near the turnpike: his line began half a mile north of the Groveton intersection and curved away to the northeast behind the cut of an unfinished railroad to Sudley Ford, nearly two miles above the pike. The Confederate troops perpendicular to the turnpike beyond Groveton consisted of Longstreet's wing of Lee's army, the presence of which Pope stubbornly refused to acknowledge. He also remained adamant that Jackson was in retreat, and trying to stave off the attacks of his pursuers.[53]

Under that self-deception, late in the afternoon Pope ordered Porter to "push forward into action at once on the enemy's flank, and, if possible, on his rear, keeping your right in communication with General Reynolds." Porter had already tried to stretch Griffin's line toward Reynolds, finding it impossible. "Keep heavy reserves," Pope added, unaware that McDowell had marched away with nearly half the troops under Porter's command; like McDowell, Pope advised Porter to fall back to his right and rear if forced to retreat, as though to maintain that impossible connection with Reynolds. George Ruggles composed the order, heading it at 4:30 P.M., and he must have taken a few minutes to write it and make the routine copies. Pope chose his own nephew, Captain Douglass Pope, to deliver Porter's copy.[54]

Even from Bethlehem Church, messages to McDowell or Pope still took nearly an hour to deliver. Late that afternoon Porter handed Lieutenant Weld a copy of his dispatch to McDowell and King, indicating his intention to retreat to Manassas. Weld rode up the Sudley Road to the 1861 battlefield, where he found King's division under General Hatch, to whom he showed the dispatch. Hatch told him they were driving the enemy. Weld sent his courier back to Porter with that information before taking the message to McDowell, who had gone to Pope's headquarters, on the hill where the opening volleys of First Bull Run had been fired. McDowell was heading for his horse as Weld arrived, and after looking at the dispatch he pointed to Pope as the man who should have it. Weld read Pope the message aloud and gave him the written version, asking if there were any reply. Pope must not have been listening very well, for as he tucked Porter's note in his vest pocket he only told Weld to say, "We are having a hard fight." Weld later estimated this exchange as "at least" 5:00 P.M., but the sun hung low enough to blind him when he glanced toward artillery firing in the distance. Pope showed no disappointment at Porter's warning that he was about to retreat, despite having ordered him to the attack.[55]

Years later, crafting a history of the battle more flattering to Pope, Colonel Smith depicted McDowell handing that dispatch to Pope, who instantly flew into a rage over Porter's impending retreat, swearing he would have him arrested. Perpetuating Pope's private myth that Porter actually had retreated,

Smith claimed that McDowell came to Porter's defense. Porter was not as good a soldier as his reputation implied, McDowell supposedly explained, and he had probably withdrawn only because of a "military mistake," which momentarily mollified Pope. This unconvincing little drama was never mentioned by either of the other men and was never published while they lived.[56]

Pope's 4:30 order was nearly two hours on the way, assuming that Ruggles's watch reflected local mean time — and soldiers' watches tended to vary widely, in that era before standard time. Before it arrived, Lieutenant Weld's courier brought Porter the overly optimistic tidings from Hatch. With less than an hour of daylight remaining, Porter immediately wrote orders for Morell to send out a pair of regiments, with two more in support, to dislodge the artillery in his front and test that theory of a Rebel retreat. Lieutenant Francis Earle, Morell's new chief of staff, carried that order the two miles from Bethlehem Church to Morell, at Dawkin's Branch. Earle, or one of Porter's aides, also delivered an order to Colonel Warren, marked 5:45 P.M., to move up and support Morell as he started after the enemy. When Earle handed Morell his order, the sun was touching the tops of the trees — making the time somewhere near 6:15. About then Marshall came in to report movement around his left, and on learning of Porter's order to advance he disputed any notion of an enemy retreat. Morell thought the same, and he added that it was too late anyway. His troops could not cross more than half a mile of open ground to those guns before it was dark, he said: it was "out of the question." Observing how low the sun had dropped, Earle mumbled his agreement.[57]

Porter, still feeling weak, had lain back down on the ground near Bethlehem Church. Douglass Pope rode up with the 4:30 attack order just as the sun started going down — around 6:30 local time — and Porter rose only after he read it. He sent Locke racing ahead to deliver it to Morell, who misunderstood it as a reiteration of Porter's last order to send out a brigade. Morell remonstrated with Locke as he had with Earle, protesting that it was almost dark, and then Porter himself arrived. Colonel Marshall, who had been in the woods with the enemy all afternoon, told Porter of the strength he had seen out there. Porter questioned him closely about it. Finally, in a decision that would allow others to destroy his career, he called off the attack on his own responsibility, telling Morell to draw his skirmishers closer in and strengthen his line of battle for the night. He sent another aide to bring Captain Pope back, probably to inform him of Porter's decision for General Pope's benefit, and by the time young Pope reached his uncle's headquarters night had long since fallen.[58]

The battle around Groveton had petered out by then. One final clash had erupted in the gloaming, with Hatch getting his nose badly bloodied when he obeyed more of Pope's misguided orders to pursue the "retreating" enemy. That blunder served as McDowell's main contribution to the day's fighting, much to the disgust of Franz Sigel, whose little corps had been battered all day on Pope's promise that McDowell and Porter would capitalize on his sacrifice.[59]

Captain Pope insisted that he delivered his uncle's 4:30 order within half an hour, but even his courier allowed that their ride might have taken a full hour. Everyone else who witnessed their arrival contradicted both of them, and most concurred that they brought the message near sunset, nearly two hours after they left headquarters with it. Two officers serving with Captain Pope in the postwar army testified under oath long afterward that, in private iterations of that story, he often admitted that he lost his way and that it was dark before he reached Porter.[60] Returning to headquarters consumed an hour or more, too, and only then did his uncle learn that Porter would not make the desired attack—which he should have known long before by the dispatch Weld delivered about 5:45 P.M. Pope had apparently paid no attention to that, so only on his nephew's news did he talk of arresting Porter. On McDowell's advice, it seems, he settled for dictating ominously stern instructions for Porter's next movements.[61]

That order was headed at 8:50 P.M. "Immediately upon receipt of this order," Pope began, "the precise hour of receiving which you will acknowledge, you will march your command to the field of battle of to-day, and report to me in person for orders. You are to understand that you are expected to comply strictly with this order, and to be present on the field within three hours after its reception, or after day-break to-morrow morning."[62]

Pope had clearly decided to hold the field, rather than retire across Bull Run for the rations and reinforcements his army needed so badly. "Our troops were tired to death," observed an officer with McDowell—"and very hungry"—but they would go another day without food. Choosing to fight on August 30 would be the worst of all the bad decisions Pope made in his brief command of a field army.[63]

It was six and a half hours before Pope's peremptory order reached Porter. The aide who carried it went first to Manassas Junction, whither he had been sent to deliver it—which showed that Pope did think Porter had retreated there. Instead, after positioning Morell's troops for a long night with no food and little water, Porter returned to bivouac at Bethlehem Church, where the courier found him.[64]

The delivery of Pope's attack order had finally disabused Porter of the idea that McDowell still exercised direct command over him. Had he sent a final report on his situation that evening it might have eased Pope's anger, but he probably believed the information he gave Pope's nephew had accomplished that purpose. Between the nephew finding Porter at Bethlehem Church and the uncle's abysmal inferential skills, the myth took firm root in Pope's mind that when Porter was ordered to attack he had done just the opposite.

12

SULLEN HYMNS OF DEFEAT

The first hint of daylight had not glimmered on Saturday, August 30, when Porter awakened to a hand shaking his shoulder and offering an envelope with Pope's directive of the night before. Lacking anything to eat for breakfast, his men needed no time for cooking. Sykes immediately roused his troops and put them on the road south, back toward Manassas, turning them sharply north on the Sudley Road after they passed the church. Porter personally awakened Lieutenant Monteith and gave him an order for Morell to pull in his pickets, withdraw from Dawkin's Branch, and follow Sykes. The steel gray of dawn fringed the horizon when the order reached Morell, and he disengaged more gingerly than he might have in the dark. Butterfield's brigade and what had been Martindale's slipped away under cover of the ridge and trailed close on Sykes's heels. Griffin's pickets crept so carefully through the brush that his brigade fell behind everyone else. The same instructions went to Sam Sturgis, with Piatt's brigade — to follow Sykes. Porter revealed his uncertainty about what troops he controlled when he asked Sturgis to notify any others that were supposed to move with him, "if you know of any."[1]

The threatening tone of Pope's order may have moved Porter to undue haste, and he overlooked two details in directing his troops: he neglected to post a guide at the sharp, critical turn on the Sudley Road, past Bethlehem Church, and he failed to designate a destination, probably because he wasn't certain where Pope would be. Sturgis missed the turn, and with no idea where he was supposed to go he continued on to Manassas. Griffin lagged even farther behind, and Morell had stayed with him to oversee the withdrawal, so they, too, followed the road to Manassas. Griffin supposed that Morell knew where he was going, ignoring a man in shirtsleeves who pointed up the Sudley Road, telling him the rest of Porter's men had turned that way. At Manassas they met Sturgis, and eventually they all marched the long way to Centreville, coming to a halt six miles east of the intended destination.[2]

Porter hurried the rest of his corps down Henry Hill to the stone house at the intersection of the Warrenton Turnpike. Leaving them there, he spurred his horse up the slope to Pope's headquarters, beneath a towering pine on Buck Hill, where he presented himself around seven o'clock.[3] He tried in vain to convince Pope that Longstreet's corps was on the field, extending much farther than supposed, and that it was threatening to fall on their left flank, but Pope would listen to nothing about it.[4]

Captain Paine observed that "Pope was bragging and over confident." He had been sending out exuberant reports of his imagined success since early morning, including pure gasconade about having driven the enemy from the field (which jubilant Confederates would soon hear of, and laugh about). Pope had already heard from General Patrick that the Confederates were pulling back toward Gainesville, and that was what he wished to believe; he seemed obsessed with catching the enemy in midretreat. He was also chafing under a message from McClellan, through Franklin, that seemed to reveal reluctance even to send him provisions, let alone reinforcements. That apparent disinclination to cooperate put him in no mood to trust so notorious a McClellan associate as Fitz John Porter.[5]

Porter joined Pope for at least a portion of a war council with McDowell, Heintzelman, and Sigel. They tentatively concluded to throw the weight of every corps except Sigel's against Jackson's left flank, which clung to Sudley Ford over Bull Run. In preparation for that assault, Porter rode back down to the intersection and guided his column westward on the turnpike half a mile before turning up a steep slope to the heights of Dogan Ridge, north of the pike. From Dogan's orchard, on the hilltop, Porter's troops could see over treetops on the upper forks of Dogan's Branch to an open field on an even taller ridge almost parallel to their own, three-quarters of a mile to the northwest. There lay the deepest part of the railroad cut, where Jackson's corps awaited the next assault. Rebel artillery near the cut threw occasional shells their way, wounding a man or horse now and then.[6]

Porter's skirmishers worked toward the intersection on the turnpike that marked the hamlet known as Groveton, where lay the ruins of a plantation house called Peach Grove. A few little houses stood on one corner, and a schoolhouse occupied the same side of the road half a mile north, just before that road bisected the unfinished railroad. That was the entire neighborhood. Some dead and wounded men and artillery wreckage littered the turnpike junction, where Hatch had brawled with Longstreet the night before. Longstreet's last division had come up during the night, and in the darkness had overshot the intersection and almost run into Union lines. Alerted to his mistake right before dawn, the commander of that division withdrew just in time for General Patrick to mistake it for the retreat he reported to Pope. The Rebels kept up that pretense of retreat, hoping to catch Pope's Yankees off guard. Skirmishers from Porter's Regulars chased the last Confederates out of the houses at the crossroads, collecting some Union wounded and at least one prisoner who insisted that the enemy was trying to get away to Thoroughfare Gap. Porter discounted that, as well as the word of a wounded Union soldier, but he sent the wounded man with the story to Pope's headquarters "for what it is worth."[7]

The rest of the morning passed in relative quiet for most of Pope's army. In preparation for their part in the three-corps attack, McDowell and Heintzelman undertook a personal reconnaissance of the Confederate left, leaving their horses and prowling behind bushes. They found Jackson's line lightly defended there, perhaps because they came upon it while several brigades had gone to the rear, to fill their stomachs and cartridge boxes. Some of those Confederates were filing away for that purpose just then, and one of McDowell's amateur aides scribbled in his diary that "there is no doubt but what the Enemy is retiring fast." Taking that optimistic discovery back to Pope, they arrived after he had seen the wounded man with the story of the Rebel retreat. Their apparent confirmation convinced Pope to resort to something more sweeping than a mere flank attack.[8]

"Every indication during the night of the 29th and up to 10 o'clock on the morning of the 30th pointed to the retreat of the enemy from our front," he insisted, five months later. His denial of all the contradictory warnings he had ignored illustrated the propensity for falsehood Pope was known for in the old army.[9]

One more time, the illusion of a fleeing foe so mesmerized Pope that he acted precisely as his enemy wished. He choreographed a pursuit in lieu of the flank attack. General Ricketts had passed the night near Henry Hill with his four brigades, and Pope had sent a couple of them farther up the Sudley Road to relieve troops that had been engaged the day before. One of those brigades, under Abram Duryée, swept out toward the railroad cut that McDowell and Heintzelman had found so thinly defended. Duryée's skirmishers no sooner spilled across that soft spot in the cut before Southern infantry returned on the run, and a battery opened on the interlopers with canister, one spent ball of which knocked Duryée himself down. One of the six brigades in A. P. Hill's Light Division drove Duryée's men back into the woods from which they had come, and as the Rebels ebbed back to the railroad cut they rifled the cartridge boxes of the dead Yankees.[10]

The repulse convinced Duryée and Ricketts that Stonewall Jackson had no intention of retreating, and they conveyed that impression to Captain Strother, who relayed it to Pope. Strother's news left Pope pacing and puffing on his cigar, perplexed by information inconsistent with his image of Jackson in full flight. "McDowell came in," Strother noted, in his eternally wry style, "and they spent the morning under a tree, waiting for the enemy to retreat."[11]

For an hour or two yet, Pope still indulged his vision of a Rebel retreat. At

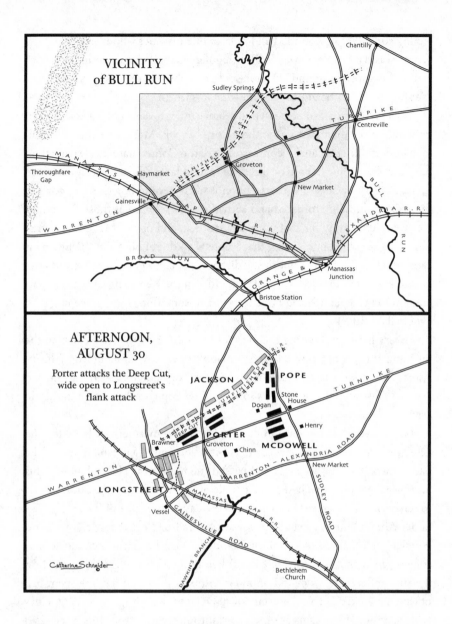

VICINITY
of BULL RUN

Chantilly

Sudley Springs

Centreville

TURNPIKE

Thoroughfare
Gap

MANASSAS

Haymarket

Gainesville

UNFINISHED R.R.

GAP

Groveton

New Market

WARRENTON

R.R.

BROAD RUN

ORANGE & R.R.

Bristoe Station

Manassas
Junction

BULL RUN

ALEXANDRIA R.R.

AFTERNOON,
AUGUST 30

Porter attacks the Deep Cut,
wide open to Longstreet's
flank attack

JACKSON

POPE

Stone
House

Dogan

Henry

UNFINISHED R.R.

DEEP CUT

PORTER

Brawner

Groveton

Chinn

MCDOWELL

TURNPIKE

WARRENTON

WARRENTON – ALEXANDRIA ROAD

New Market

SUDLEY ROAD

LONGSTREET

Vessel

MANASSAS
GAINESVILLE ROAD

GAP R.R.

DAWKIN'S BRANCH

Bethlehem
Church

Catherine Schneider

noon he named McDowell commander of the pursuit, directing Porter down
the Warrenton Turnpike with Reynolds's and Hatch's divisions. Heintzelman
and Ricketts were to chase Jackson on a parallel route, north of the railroad cut.[12]

Porter had already advanced his skirmishers. The 1st U.S. Sharpshooters
edged down into the Groveton woods. As the rest of the corps followed them
into the woods, the sharpshooters spilled across the road near the little schoolhouse, climbing a tall post-and-rail fence and trotting down an easy slope into
an as-yet-unnamed intermittent stream, under the shallow edge of which they
took cover. Morell's division, led this day by Dan Butterfield, took the front in

the woods, with Sykes behind him. Only Gouverneur Warren's two-regiment brigade remained near the turnpike below the ridge, where most of the Fifth Corps artillery stood parked.[13]

Confederate artillery on the heights to the northwest started pounding Butterfield's men as soon as they came into view. Intent on his earlier orders to attack Jackson's line, Porter had devised a plan to seize the offending guns or chase them away, and he was involved in that maneuver when the orders arrived to launch the presumed pursuit. He arranged with McDowell to break through Jackson's lines at the cut and then swing back toward the turnpike, taking the battery from the flank before joining the chase. No signal launched that pursuit, and it ended before it had fully begun, with most of the Union line not having stirred. On Porter's right, Ricketts found Confederate resistance redoubled, and McDowell ordered him to stand fast; on Porter's left, Reynolds sent men into woods south of the turnpike who ran into a skirmish line extending far beyond his left flank. Behind the skirmishers stood Rebel cavalry, and Reynolds suspected that it screened massed infantry, waiting out of sight for him to plunge deeper into the trap.[14]

Spinning about, Reynolds whipped his mount to a dead gallop as a flurry of small arms fire knocked one of his orderlies out of the saddle. He veered across the turnpike to warn Porter, and after dropping word there he raced for Buck Hill. McDowell was still with Pope when Reynolds reined up, his horse's side bleeding from spurring, and told them the enemy was curling around their left flank. Pope's chief of staff, Ruggles, heard Pope scoff, "I guess not." Reynolds indignantly replied that he had considered the news crucial enough to leave his command with it, and bolt through enemy fire, at which Pope told John Buford to take some cavalry and have a look. Buford, who suspected as much already, jabbed Ruggles in the waist and winked at him as he went for his horse. McDowell responded more collegially, riding back with Reynolds and withdrawing him from Groveton to the ridge that traversed the Chinn farm, halfway back to the Sudley Road. That would give him a better chance of confronting an assault on the flank, but it completely uncovered Porter's own flank. On his own initiative, Colonel Warren spread his two Zouave regiments out over the vacant ground Reynolds had held with three brigades.[15]

General Sigel sent a couple of regiments scouting south of the turnpike. When they reported the same threat Reynolds had seen, Pope grudgingly allowed Sigel to move one brigade to the knob at the eastern end of Chinn Ridge. Despite mounting evidence of Confederate strength below the turnpike, Pope stubbornly refused to cancel the attack above it.[16]

Coming in contradictory squalls, the orders from Pope and McDowell served mainly to confuse Porter. Failing as usual to communicate effectively, McDowell had not informed Porter that the pursuit had been suspended, and a couple of his messages strongly implied that the order was still in effect. When McDowell's chief of staff alluded to making "the movement suggested in your note," and "the service you are to perform," Porter supposed he referred to that preliminary assault on the railroad cut. Butterfield and one of his brigade commanders complained of a lack of support on their right, where they endured a raking fire whenever they tried to advance, and McDowell authorized Porter to use Hatch's division to support the attack. If that were not enough, he offered to order up Sigel's entire corps.[17]

It was already past two o'clock by then. Butterfield's two brigades were in position, with the Regulars under Sykes formed behind them. The better part of another hour expired before the last of Hatch's men were guided into position on Porter's right. Hatch's four brigades piled up seven ranks deep under cover of the Groveton woods, which were already swarming with stragglers from the morning action and the previous day's fighting.[18]

In retrospect, Porter's orders seemed ridiculously simple: "take possession" of the railroad cut and sweep to the left to overwhelm the battery. Around three o'clock, Butterfield called on those thousands of men to let the woods ring with three cheers before marching them across the road into the open. The front rank trotted past the schoolhouse and down to the intermittent stream at the rapid, shuffling gait of the quickstep. Beyond the stream the corresponding slope led upward to the railroad bed, climbing steeply to a narrow plateau at the crest, behind which ran what soon became notorious as the Deep Cut. At the base of that last precipitous incline regimental commanders resorted to speed to reduce the attrition of the Rebel musketry, bellowing, "Double-quick, charge," over the din. Mustering enough breath for what a New York major called "a mad yell," Butterfield's line swarmed up the slope toward those blazing rifles, shielded momentarily by the brow of the hillside until they surged over the crest.[19]

The momentum carried some of Butterfield's men across a weak point in Jackson's front, but Confederates from farther down the line rushed to drive them back. Union and Confederate flags fluttered as little as ten yards apart for nearly half an hour, falling only to be lifted again as men fired into each other's faces. Five successive color bearers went down with the flag of the 18th Massachusetts, and thirty-seven bullets ripped through the banner or grazed the staff, while more than half the regiment was shot down. Four days later thick rows of dead Yankees would still lie there, marking the Union battle line.[20]

Following in the wake of Hatch's leading brigade, General Patrick watched the guns to their left front pour shot and shell into the blue ranks "with great fury," tearing gaping holes in the formations. From the protection of their railroad embankment Jackson's infantrymen fired as fast as they could ram bullets home. The length of the cut and the diagonal approach of the Federals allowed Rebels at one end to level volleys into the Yankees' front while those at the other end fired into their flank, creating what Patrick called a "galling cross-fire." In a personal memo that night, Theodore Gates of the 20th New York State Militia described his regiment as "cut to pieces," with half the officers killed or wounded—including the colonel, whose death elevated Gates to the command.[21]

Butterfield's assault inclined toward the punishing artillery fire from his left front until Confederate infantry in the railroad cut began enfilading his regiments from the right. George Lockley, then a sergeant in Martindale's former brigade, faulted his temporary division commander for flinging troops at the Rebels one regiment at a time and leaving each "to its fate." Lockley, who would command his regiment by war's end, conceded that Butterfield called up another brigade to help, but complained that those supports fell flat on the ground a hundred feet out of the woods, coming no farther. "I never saw such mismanagement in conducting a Battle," wrote Lockley.[22]

Confederate reinforcements jogged up to plug holes in Jackson's line. That, and the fusillade from the field batteries to the northwest, wore down the determination of Porter's men, who were running low on ammunition. With no help in sight, regimental commanders began passing the word to fall back. Porter sent his own order up to bring everyone in, but the retreating troops had to navigate a hail of bullets and artillery fire spattering the ground thickly enough to remind one officer of a rain shower on a millpond. Regiments that had already suffered staggering casualties, especially among their officers, shed all order in the retreat. The 1st Michigan lost two-thirds of its men and three-quarters of its officers. The adjutant of the 18th Massachusetts admitted that "we got back the best way we could," leaving 140 of an estimated 250 men behind them—dead, wounded, or waiting to surrender. The 17th New York was almost entirely dispersed: 575 rank and file had gone into the fight, but only 80 could be found in line at the end of the day. Walking wounded had been stumbling back toward the road for some time, and comrades anxious for an excuse to leave the fight carried out a few with leg wounds. These were "the usual procession of limpers and crawlers," remarked a captain of Regulars, but next came the uninjured—at first singly or in squads, and then in thick clusters, often at a sprint. Skirting the Regulars who fanned out to cover the retreat, the panicked survivors flooded past Hatch's other two brigades. Porter, waiting with Butterfield near the schoolhouse, sent Lieutenant Weld after cavalry to brook that tide of stragglers, remaining near the schoolhouse himself to rally the remnants of regiments that came in clustered around their colors.[23]

From high ground on Chinn Ridge, near Reynolds, McDowell caught a glimpse of Porter's more frantic fugitives bolting back toward Dogan Ridge, and the sight threw him into a panic of his own. Forgetting the Confederate legions he had been warned of on the left, he ordered Reynolds to abandon his position and form a line across the turnpike to halt the stampede of Porter's men. Sigel had moved up to the top of Dogan Ridge when Porter advanced, and by the time the tide reached his line it had begun to slow: he did not find the retreat so alarming, noting that the men came out of the woods "in pretty good order." There was no use for Reynolds north of the turnpike, but he was badly needed south of it. With General Lee at his side, anxious to close the jaws of the trap, Longstreet had already decided to strike when he saw Porter's troops streaming back to safety. In sending Reynolds away, McDowell helped give Longstreet the most decisive victory of his career.[24]

The day had already grown later than was ideal for so ambitious a movement as Longstreet undertook, but four divisions surged ahead below the Warrenton Turnpike. They rolled unimpeded over Warren's thousand Zouaves, shooting nearly half of them. The 5th New York, wearing baggy scarlet pants and caught in the open, lost 298 out of 490 men in a matter of minutes, and to no real purpose; their sacrifice slowed the assault by a minute or two.[25]

Longstreet's juggernaut next struck a brigade of Pennsylvania Reserves that had not yet followed Reynolds. That brigade lined up behind a Pennsylvania battery, but the colonel in command was wounded early and the strength of the Rebels intimidated his successor, who withdrew with relatively light casualties. The artillerymen abandoned their guns to the enemy. That left only Nathaniel McLean's Ohio brigade and its battery, sent over earlier by Sigel, to stand between Longstreet's broad battle line and Henry Hill, commanding Pope's line of retreat.[26]

While those savage struggles played out, Porter concentrated on saving what was left of his corps. Butterfield's command had been whittled down by more than a third at the Deep Cut, and during the retreat the entire remnant of one regiment was swept away with Hatch's division. The two brigades of Regulars in Sykes's division had endured some casualties supporting the attack, and had lost three companies cut off with Warren, but those ten regiments formed the solid core of Porter's command. They provided the shield behind which Butterfield's dazed and dejected troops tried to regain their cohesion and courage. As Jackson's advancing artillery punished the Regulars, Sykes withdrew them in columns of regiments, retreating a few paces at a time and turning to fire again and again. Guns at the crest of Dogan Ridge slowed the Confederate pursuit, and covered the retreat.[27]

Sykes pointed to the plateau on top of Henry Hill, nearly a mile away, and asked Porter if he shouldn't get his men up there to defend that vital point. Porter agreed, and the Regulars shouldered their way through crowds of stragglers, confused and disorganized units, ambulances, wounded men afoot, and artillery caissons. On the way they picked up a gravely sober Colonel Warren and a few dozen of his conspicuously garbed survivors, whom Warren had collected on the bank of Young's Branch. A staff officer near the Sudley Road saw the ravine cut by Young's Branch filled with fugitives, and thought Pope's left wing beyond saving. Half the army seemed to be running from the enemy.[28]

Once out of range of the Rebel infantry, the Regular regiments marched by the flank toward the junction of the Sudley Road. William Chapman's brigade turned up the slope toward Henry Hill, where they would be of better use and hoped to find their first food of the day. John Pope happened to be flailing around there when they began to arrive, but the major commanding the 17th U.S. Infantry did not recognize him. In a demanding tone Pope asked what troops the major was leading, and where they were going; when the major mentioned looking for rations, Pope "soundly berated" him, ordering him to stay put. Later another general — McDowell, as the major later learned — came along and gave him "peremptory orders" to move into the woods west of the Sudley Road.[29]

Out beyond those woods, to the west, raged the last swirling fight of the evening. McLean's brigade stood just long enough before Longstreet for two brigades of Ricketts's division to reach the shoulder of Chinn Ridge, followed by two more from Sigel. Those troops were soon driven back with heavy losses, leaving their wounded and several guns behind, but they bought time for a stronger battle line to form along the Sudley Road on Henry Hill. At the behest of Captain Strother, of Pope's staff, the two surviving brigades under Reynolds took position on the lower part of Henry Hill, near the turnpike. Chapman filed his men into line uphill from Reynolds, moving into the woods toward Chinn Ridge, and Robert Buchanan's brigade of Regulars climbed the hill and lined up behind Chapman. The regiment on Buchanan's right formed near the charred remnants of the Henry home. The Regulars presented "a compact, firm, determined column," noticed Captain Paine, who heard some cheers at the sight of them, and he thought that "everybody's heart beat a little lighter" with their arrival. General Porter rode onto the field with them.[30]

As a blazing sun dipped low enough to turn the clouds scarlet over the Bull Run Mountains, Chapman's brigade faced the Confederate tide that had swept the last resistance from Chinn Ridge. Robert Milroy, one of Sigel's brigadiers, led his four regiments from Ohio and western Virginia into position beside Chapman, but long ranks of Rebel infantry reached into the distance beyond their left. A battery fired over their heads into the advancing Confederates, and Chapman exchanged volleys at a disadvantage for a time before retiring into the woods as the irresistible numbers of the enemy lapped around his flank. That put all the more pressure on the volunteers under the excitable Milroy, who galloped off looking for help.[31]

Hatless and waving his sword like a Cossack, the white-haired Milroy found McDowell, raving at him to lend assistance "for God's sake." McDowell had no spare troops except the Pennsylvania Reserves, who were already engaged and had nearly used up their ammunition. Besides Butterfield's two shattered brigades, the only uncommitted troops on Henry Hill were Buchanan's Regulars, but McDowell hesitated to give them orders with Porter and Pope both nearby. According to Milroy, McDowell said Porter "was a good fellow" and would help him; when Porter appeared a moment later, McDowell spoke with him, apparently asking if he would order the Regulars in to assist Milroy, and within a few minutes Buchanan was leading two of his battalions into the front line. In reporting the incident a couple of months later, McDowell failed to mention that it was Porter who sent the aid to Milroy, and took credit himself for making what proved to be a prudent decision.[32]

As the light faded, that end of the line began to weaken. The brigades of Buchanan, Chapman, and Milroy bent backward, buckled, and finally gave way, the Regulars again falling back firing. One of those small brigades from Burnside's corps, consisting of only three regiments, raced up to face the onslaught of Rebels, who in the growing darkness shouted that they were friends. Their ensuing volley proved otherwise, and the Yankees delivered one in return, standing their ground until the musket flashes began flickering from beyond their right and left. As they backed slowly down the hill, firing at will, Reynolds put his two brigades across the turnpike to cover the retreat of the army, while some of Heintzelman's corps staved off Jackson's troops, who were swarming down on the Union right.[33]

The rest of Pope's army stumbled and shuffled along the turnpike, bound for the safety of old Confederate fortifications at Centreville. A couple of miles beyond the bridge over Bull Run appeared the first sign of reinforcements from Franklin's Sixth Corps, in a line of infantry posted across the turnpike to arrest stragglers. They had to stand at "charge Bayonets" to hold back the panicked mob that led the flight.[34]

Lee, who had other plans, did not push the pursuit that evening, and the fugitive army reached Centreville safely, if famished and exhausted. The Regulars, forming the tail of Porter's corps, arrived there at midnight. For most of those men still with their commands, the adrenaline that had carried them across fifteen miles of ground and through four hours of fighting had probably subsided enough to let them sleep. Porter, Sykes, and some of their staff officers bivouacked together on the bare ground in the corner of a snake fence, warmed by a fire of rails that night and dampened by drizzle in the morning. Little sleep and prolonged crisis had taken a toll, and when Porter awoke in the morning he did not realize it was his fortieth birthday.[35]

If the sarcastically hypercritical Captain Strother wrote truthfully (and the skeptical reader wonders), John Pope preceded all his troops in escaping to Centreville that night. Five years later, Strother described Pope declaring that he would remain if he could be of any further use, but since he could not he would ride on to Centreville.[36]

So discreditable a tale about Pope would have seemed perfectly plausible to thousands in that army, and they would not have doubted it about McDowell, either. In the days and weeks to follow, believers would have been especially numerous among those who had come from the Army of the Potomac. In a journal entry written the next day or soon afterward, General Heintzelman observed that "neither officers nor men had any confidence in Pope, nor much in McDowell, who is his principal advisor." Gouverneur Warren, still furious over the slaughter visited on his command by the bumbling of McDowell and Pope, assured his brother that the world had never seen a general "more utterly unfit" than Pope. Captain John Ames of the 11th U.S. Infantry found it "so dispiriting to be under him, that we were almost demoralized." In the 4th Infantry Captain Avery Cain swore that he would resign before he would ever serve under "such a block head" as McDowell, and he doubted there were fifty men in the army with any confidence in him. George Meade, commanding a brigade in the Pennsylvania Reserves, felt the same. A captain in the 79th New York, of Burnside's Ninth Corps, characterized Pope as a "lying braggart," and explained that men simply would not fight for him, or McDowell, or *that ilk.*" From within the moribund Army of Virginia, a field officer in one of Gibbon's regiments agreed that Pope was "outgeneraled entirely." And then there was General Alpheus Williams, the division commander under Banks, who confessed to his daughter, "I dare not trust myself to speak of this commander as I feel and believe."[37]

Fitz John Porter may not have dared speak about Pope as he felt, either, except in confidence. Porter's subordinates, including his closest staff officers, all denied having ever heard disparaging comments from him about the man who was then their commanding officer. In person, Porter afforded Pope as much courtesy as he did any superior, although he evinced none of the personal regard he demonstrated for McClellan, Patterson, or Sidney Johnston. As little faith as he had in Pope, that discretion befit a general who valued discipline as much as Porter did. Correspondence that he considered private was another matter, as it was for most of Pope's detractors, but Porter would also have worried about further demoralizing the troops by openly disparaging the army commander. His staff sensed his want of confidence in Pope, and shared it, so it took no overt commentary to wring a dejected letter from Lieutenant Weld at Centreville on August 31. "If we ever reach Washington in safety, it will be more than I expect," Weld warned his father. "Pope knows he is dead if he retreats to Washington and so he keeps us here, where the enemy may cut off our supplies." In a letter to McClellan carried by Lieutenant Monteith that same day, Porter credited Halleck with the decision to stay in Centreville, although he thought it "a general disappointment" to everyone but Pope.[38]

Porter had attended a council with the corps commanders that drizzly Sunday in which Pope said that Halleck had ordered him to hold Centreville. That order had only been implied, however, and Halleck had offered it merely because Pope disguised the extent of his defeat. With telegraphic communication restored, Pope had sent Halleck a perfectly dishonest dispatch the night before, flagrantly underrepresenting how far he had been driven and denying his heavy losses in men and materiel. Halleck had sent an encouraging reply, bidding Pope not to yield any more ground, which Pope portrayed as an order to remain in Centreville. In Pope's more realistic next message, he revealed the pessimistic uncertainty behind his bravado, promising to put up as brave a fight "as I can force our men to stand up to," and asking darkly if Halleck had considered what to do "should this army be destroyed." Meanwhile, as Porter fully expected, Lee had sent Jackson on another roundabout flank march, hoping to cut Pope off from Alexandria and the food and ammunition his army needed so badly.[39]

Before August 31 ended, even Pope understood that the enemy was up to another flanking movement, and to secure his line of retreat to Alexandria he sent out infantry to guard the most vulnerable intersections. He supposed that once his army reached the forts around the capital it would pass into the hands of McClellan, and the impending humiliation heightened his anger over the disdain he felt from his army. He comforted himself with the belief that it was only the newcomers from the Army of the Potomac who despised him—not because of his own incompetence, but because they resented the abandonment of McClellan's grand campaign. The next morning, in a message advising Halleck to bring the army back into the defenses of Washington, Pope charged Porter in particular with undermining him and deliberately hanging back from the battle. Identifying Porter in all but name, he falsely accused him of retreating to Manassas when ordered to attack, while the Army of Virginia fought the greatest battle of the war. Griffin, he insinuated, had manufactured an excuse to keep his brigade out of the fight on August 30. Based on Porter's derisive letter to Kennedy and reports of open criticism from the habitually gruff Griffin, Pope lodged a complaint of "constant talk" against him from those two generals, "indulged in publicly and in promiscuous company."[40]

Those suspicions did not deter Pope from seeking Porter out a few hours later for his opinion on their situation. With a duplicity that came easily to him, Pope attributed their vulnerable predicament to the orders from Halleck, and asked what he should do. Answering Pope with as much candor as he believed Pope showed him, Porter counseled retreat, but advised consulting with the other generals first. As dark storm clouds began to roll in, a squad of generals convened at Franklin's headquarters, since he was the only one with a tent, and Franklin thought that Pope relied more on Porter than on the others. According

224 : *Sullen Hymns of Defeat*

to Porter, the other corps commanders all agreed with his assessment. Porter himself tended to recall events with an interpretation favorable to him, but he published his account of the council when everyone was still alive to confirm it, and Franklin corroborated him.[41]

While those generals met, two Union divisions ran into Jackson's corps four miles north of Centreville. A vicious little battle and a torrential downpour erupted at the same time near a plantation called Chantilly. The commanders of both divisions died needlessly, since Jackson had already learned of the infantry Pope had posted in his way, but news of the fighting may have lengthened the stride of the troops as Pope resumed his retreat.

While Pope's divisions trudged toward Washington, his portrayal of clandestine subversion by senior subordinates alarmed those in the government who knew of it. McClellan's hesitation in sending reinforcements had already started Lincoln wondering if he wanted Pope to fail. Believing so suited Stanton's hope of deposing McClellan, and he had already started collecting evidence that might achieve that goal, given the right prosecutor and a select military court. At the very moment Porter was forming his troops in the Groveton woods to assault the Deep Cut, Stanton had invited Lincoln to his house for lunch, where he spoke excitedly of having at least one court-martial. Stanton exuded faith in Pope's ability, and the president appeared to share it, which lent an air of logic to Stanton's insistence that only "foul play" could lose that battle, and he predicted it would come from McClellan "and his friends." As a contingent alternative to a court-martial, Stanton had begun lobbying cabinet members on August 29 to sign a petition asking for McClellan's dismissal from command, if not from the army.[42]

Stanton's efforts failed, at least for the moment. Halleck sent officers out to assess the state of Pope's troops, and they returned with reports of abject demoralization, with an almost universal preference for the reinstatement of McClellan. White House fear of an effort to sabotage Pope brought executive pressure on McClellan to use his own influence against it. At Lincoln's personal request, McClellan sent Porter an odd dispatch asking him and all their friends "for my sake, that of the country, and of the old Army of the Potomac" to give Pope the same support they would give him. Any implication that they would do otherwise raised the specter of heinous offenses, and Porter's enemies later invoked that telegram to imply as much. When Porter received that troubling message at Fairfax Court House on the morning of September 2 he tried to respond with immediate assurances. The telegraph operator would not send his reply because Pope was requiring official authorization on all outgoing telegrams, so Porter went straight to Pope's headquarters, in the home of Edward Ford.[43]

Reasoning that only a complaint from Pope could have initiated so insinuating a communication, Porter guessed that Pope was trying to blame the Army of the Potomac for his own failure. Handing Pope both McClellan's telegram and the reply he had wished to send, he asked what complaint had prompted McClellan to imply any lack of support. Pope deceptively denied making any complaint, and denied having any — except about Griffin going off to Centreville and staying there throughout the battle, and the derogatory remarks Griffin had made in front of Pope's own staff. Also, there was Porter's letter to Kennedy from Harrison's Landing, which the president had seen, that was so critical of both Pope and his plan for the campaign; yet Porter could not have known what the plan of campaign even was, Pope added, or that it had been imposed on him from Washington.[44]

Pope's knowledge of the letter took Porter aback. He said he remembered only the gist of it, and none of the details, and he expressed regret at Kennedy's breach of confidence, without which the letter would have done Pope no harm. Years later Porter recalled that he offered to make amends if he had been unjust, but pointed out that Pope's performance had demonstrated the accuracy of the criticism. Perhaps he did not rub salt as deeply into that wound as his account of the scene implies, for Colonel Ruggles sat nearby copying orders, and he heard Pope reply that Porter's explanations were "satisfactory," except about Griffin. Porter said Griffin would have to be responsible for his own statements, and that losing his way on the march could be "easily explained." Pope rose courteously when Porter did, and if they did not shake hands they parted in apparent harmony. Later Pope would deny being satisfied, or even having said that he was, conceding only that he might have said he would take no action against Porter.[45]

Unless Porter and Ruggles both misunderstood him or misrepresented him, Pope soon underwent a distinct change of heart, and began hunting for a proxy to take the action against Porter. His path to that decision began the same afternoon, while he and McDowell rode toward Washington on the last march of the Army of Virginia. One corps after another dropped off to its assigned campground as they neared the forts, until only McDowell's corps and Porter's remained, with Couch's division tagging along. McDowell's corps led, with John Gibbon's brigade in the van.

The day had turned hot and the roads had dried, so everyone in the column wore a frosting of dust, including the generals. The unfinished dome of the Capitol lay in sight from the crests of the hills they climbed, and atop Upton's Hill a cluster of horsemen waited alongside the road, their horses' tails swishing in the heat. Chief among them was McClellan, who had chosen a dramatic stage for receiving his command. Jacob Cox, an Ohio brigadier whom Porter would come to know all too well, waited with him. When Pope and McDowell recognized him and rode over, McClellan announced that the president had just put him in command of the defenses of Washington. Gibbon, who disliked Pope as much as anyone, picked up that news and rode off to the side, bellowing down the line that McClellan was back in command and calling for three cheers.[46]

Those cheers came spontaneously and endlessly, and McClellan was drawn to the sound of them as other men are drawn to perfume. The disconsolate Pope tipped his hat in farewell, unnoticed, as his triumphant rival cantered down the line to the din of an ovation that echoed after he was out of sight. "Such cheers I never heard before," wrote Lieutenant Weld, and nothing like it had ever stirred Pope's army.[47]

Pope must have realized it, too. He may already have begun conjuring a narrative to explain it, with Fitz John Porter as a central character.

McClellan's assignment to even so limited a command as the defenses of Washington bred consternation in Lincoln's cabinet, where Stanton and Chase had been conspiring to persuade the president to shelve him altogether. With Attorney General Edward Bates and Interior Secretary Caleb Smith, they had prepared a letter expressing their mistrust of Little Mac, but by the time they presented it, on September 2, the president had already appointed him. As distressed as Lincoln was by their opposition, he told them he could think of no one else who could raise the spirits of the demoralized army and put it back in fighting trim on such short notice. Chase suggested Hooker, Sumner, or Burnside, remarking that giving McClellan charge of the city's defenses seemed tantamount to handing it to the Rebels.[48]

Stanton said no more, but sought to engineer McClellan's downfall in other ways. Five days previously, he had prodded Halleck for evidence to convene a court-martial, asking whether McClellan had obeyed his orders to evacuate the Peninsula and reinforce Pope as promptly as "the national safety required." Halleck had obligingly replied that McClellan had been more dilatory than expected, blaming that delay for Jackson having caught Pope's army in vulnerable, advanced positions. McClellan had cited impediments to those movements that could make it difficult to prove willful disobedience even if the timorous Halleck were convinced to file the charges, but a good prosecutor might make them stick.[49]

Stanton's opportunity for strategic courts-martial improved further on September 3, the day after the cabinet meeting, when Pope stopped at the White House to give the president his account of what went wrong. In casting about for the cause of his failure he doubtless complained of how slow Franklin's corps had been in coming to his aid, for which Stanton (and the president, apparently) already held McClellan responsible. In further deflecting culpability to the McClellan clique, Pope may also have mentioned Porter's failure to attack on August 29. Lincoln had no criticism to offer Pope, and he implied that another army awaited his command: that very day he had ordered Halleck to prepare a field army, distinct from the forces defending the capital. Either in sympathetic understanding or to provoke him against a comrade who may have undermined his campaign, the president also told Pope of Porter's disparaging comments in those dispatches to Burnside. If the president did not show them to him, Stanton would gladly have let him read them at the War Department — where Pope probably stopped later that day, after dropping in on Chase at the Treasury Department. When he returned to his headquarters in General Lee's former home at Arlington, Pope wrote his report of the battle that evening with particular emphasis on Porter's real and imagined digressions from his orders.[50]

That same day, as Pope began piecing together his image of the McClellan clique's conspiracy to orchestrate his failure, Stanton secured the appointment of Joseph Holt as the U.S. Army's first judge advocate general. Holt, whom Stanton had come to know in the Buchanan cabinet, was the sort he could work with. Holt needed little more than a wink to understand a point that should remain unspoken, and like Stanton he showed a knack for turning with the direction of the political wind. The post had been created as a long-overdue promotion for Brevet Major John Lee, a loyal cousin of General Lee who had served as judge advocate of the army since 1849. Lee was too nonpartisan and conservative to suit Stanton, who lobbied Lincoln for the politically savvy Holt and had his way about it. Stanton presented Holt with his commission on September 3, and the offended Lee resigned the next day, after more than twenty-eight years as an army officer. Boorish as ever to those he had defeated, Stanton scribbled "Accepted" on Lee's resignation the moment it was handed to him.[51]

Pope returned to Lincoln's office the morning of September 4 with the rough draft of his report in hand. Welles, who was present when Pope read the document aloud, described it as more of a "manifesto" than a report. Pope complained that Porter had failed to meet his impossible schedule on August 28, neglecting to mention then what he would later admit — that the need for Porter's presence had "passed away" long before he arrived. Ignoring how late Porter would have received his 4:30 attack order, or how early the bulk of Longstreet's corps had reached the field, he swore that Jackson would have been "crushed" had Porter obeyed the order. "Why he did not do so I cannot understand," said Pope, who withheld the ameliorating facts Porter had reported to him. Alluding to Porter's note tentatively suggesting that he would fall back on Manassas, Pope misrepresented it as a reply to his attack order, and with Piatt's little brigade in mind he reported that some of Porter's corps did fall back. For good measure, he insinuated that Griffin had gone astray through deliberate design.[52]

This was just the sort of material Stanton was looking for, especially in conjunction with Porter's potentially incriminating telegrams to Burnside. Welles assumed that both Stanton and Chase had seen the report before Pope brought it to the president. Chase heard a similar story from McDowell, who came into the city that night and stayed over at Chase's home. McDowell probably told Chase the same tale he narrated for his wife, of the soldiers from McClellan's army coming to Pope "with a grudge and without any heart for the work." He, too, thought that McClellan's officers, at least, had wanted the army to fall back to Washington for the comfort of McClellan's leadership. Like Pope, McDowell theorized that Porter had willfully undermined any chance of victory. He also misunderstood that Porter had withdrawn from Dawkin's Branch on August 29, and that Griffin's errant brigade had gone to Centreville that night, instead of the next morning. Chase evidently inferred from McDowell's narration that Porter's precipitous repulse on August 30 was the result of still more perfidious behavior.[53]

McDowell seemed to believe his own accusations, as did Pope, who showed a pronounced habit of digesting information in the manner that best suited his desires. There was truth, too, in McDowell's claim that some of McClellan's men had come to the Army of Virginia "without any heart for the work." Their low opinion of Pope raised the fear that any sacrifices they made might be in vain, and they soon saw reason for that apprehension in Pope's utter confusion over Jackson's whereabouts. Yet, conversely, Porter's attack on the Deep Cut had illustrated that many of his troops had maintained an unduly optimistic spirit: it would have been difficult, for instance, to ascribe a lack of heart to Major Andrew Barney of the 30th New York, who rode his horse to certain death at the crest of the cut to encourage his men over the top. Nor had the crippling lack of confidence in Pope been confined to troops from the Army of the Potomac: it was an officer of Pope's army — Colonel Thornton Brodhead, mortally wounded in the final clash on August 30 — whose last letter appeared in newspapers across the country with his declaration that he "died a victim of Pope's imbecility and the treachery of McDowell."[54]

It was probably on September 5, three days after his humiliating encounter with McClellan at Upton's Hill, that Pope left his headquarters at Arlington House and started into Washington with his chief of staff, Colonel Ruggles. During their ride, Pope revealed that he planned to press charges against Porter for failing to obey orders, and he wanted Ruggles to serve as his "chief witness" in the case. Ruggles, still smarting over rude treatment by Pope, first reminded the general that he had told Porter he was satisfied with his explanations, which Ruggles had overheard. Next, he argued that he was not familiar with the case — that Pope had used him as little more than an aide-de-camp during the last week of the campaign, and had issued many orders through others, often leaving Ruggles in the dark. Pope remonstrated with him for a time, in the course of which he would have been very likely to mention the Burnside dispatches that he considered solid evidence of Porter's personal disloyalty.[55]

Ruggles had admired Porter since his days as a cadet under him. Ruggles was also a close friend of "Andy" Webb, of Porter's staff. His dismay at Pope's request, his personal dislike of Pope, and his friendship with Webb made Ruggles the likeliest conduit for Porter learning of Pope's prospective case against him, which was founded on the Burnside correspondence. Porter knew the sudden importance of those dispatches by early the next morning, when he wrote to McClellan's assistant adjutant general, asking him to forward Burnside a request for copies of them, to remind himself exactly what he had written.[56]

Robert E. Lee forced Pope's eager War Department collaborators to set this pet project aside, at least temporarily. Signalmen on the upper Potomac spotted Confederates crossing into Maryland opposite Leesburg on the afternoon of September 4, and that information was soon available in Washington. General Burnside appeared in the capital early on the morning of September 5, having evacuated his last troops from Aquia Creek, and he reported immediately. With Chase's recent suggestion in mind the president asked Burnside for the second time to take command of the army that Halleck was preparing for the field. Again he refused, recommending McClellan as the only person capable of wielding so large a force. With that, Lincoln collected Halleck and started for McClellan's residence on Jackson Square. They knocked on the door about nine o'clock in the morning. When they left, McClellan scrawled a jubilant note to his wife and started firing off orders to all the major generals, including Pope and Porter, to prepare their men for a march with three days' rations and extra ammunition. As word filtered through the army of McClellan's complete restoration, spirits soared.[57]

13

MY MARYLAND

Lincoln knew that reinstating McClellan as commander of the nation's principal army would ignite a furor in his cabinet. He had determined that Pope should not have that army because he lacked the confidence of the men, and that McDowell could lead no troops unless he was cleared by a court of inquiry. All this would throw Stanton and Chase into high dudgeon. To mollify them and Pope, Lincoln also ordered a court of inquiry to investigate Porter's conduct on August 29, as well as Griffin's departure from the battlefield on August 30. These were details he could only have learned from Pope, and he wrote the order himself. Pope had already written the president that day, asking to have his accusative report published for the sake of "the slaughtered victims of this conspiracy," but most cabinet members thought that imprudent, and the rest acquiesced.[1]

After the cabinet meeting, Chase invited McDowell back to his house. That evening he advised the general to request a court of inquiry himself, to hasten his return to a field command, and he suggested using Colonel Brodhead's deathbed accusation as an excuse. Such an investigation might implicate Porter, if not McClellan. Before retiring to Chase's guest room, McDowell agreed to do so.[2]

Stanton, too, went straight to work once the meeting ended, arranging the court of inquiry for Porter, Griffin, and Franklin, whose tardiness had also aroused the president's ire. Halleck, who would technically name the members of that court, wrote John Pope that day to tell him the ill will between generals had to stop if the government was to be saved. He may have supposed that such a court would stop it, but Halleck did not harbor malice enough to pack a court with hostile officers. Stanton, however, was sufficiently underhanded to choose members inclined toward an adverse finding: in his War Department, it became common practice in selected cases. Knowing that an inquiry into such matters as Franklin's delay might incriminate McClellan, Stanton would not have hesitated to compile a list of reliable judges, and Halleck lacked the will to resist so tyrannical a superior.[3]

The members assigned to the court therefore betrayed subtle prejudices of both a general and specific nature. George Cadwalader, who was to preside, was a friend of McDowell's. Silas Casey harbored a bitter grudge against both McClellan and Porter for removing him from command of the Pennsylvania Reserves. Joseph Mansfield had cultivated favor among Radicals by denouncing the return of runaway slaves to their owners, and he burned with jealousy of the younger generals who outranked him, such as McClellan and Porter. For judge advocate Stanton chose no mere assistant, instead assigning his dependable new judge advocate general, Holt. On September 5 Stanton relieved Porter, Franklin, and Griffin from duty "until the charges against them can be investigated by a court of inquiry." The court met the next day, but because Mansfield was absent, it promptly adjourned.[4]

The creation of that court was not officially known beyond its members, the president, Stanton, and Halleck, who nominally approved the judges. Information leaked out, but those who heard of it may have mistaken it for a rumor. Porter was only notified that he was relieved of duty pending a court, and more than sixteen years would pass before he learned that a court had actually been created.

Within hours, McClellan asked Stanton to restore Porter and Franklin for the immediate crisis, claiming that they were indispensable. The habitually two-faced secretary of war said he would "cheerfully agree" if Halleck did not object. In light of Stanton's conditional approval Halleck did not object, so McClellan's two favorite subordinates enjoyed temporary reprieves that carried a prospect of ultimate redemption. Such prompt accommodation should have aroused McClellan's suspicion: it was his direct experience with Stanton, after all, that had formed the basis of Porter's opinion that the secretary was "a scoundrel of the blackest dye."[5]

Restored to duty almost as soon as he was relieved, Porter stopped in at army headquarters a few days later. Halleck made a comment to him that Porter remembered as, "We shall have to cut off the heads of some of you general officers of the Army of the Potomac, to teach you that you must obey orders of all placed over you." Porter recollected replying that no one needed to teach him his duty, and he asked specifically what Halleck referred to. Halleck cited the charges made against him by General Pope, and when Porter returned to his headquarters at Arlington he applied to the adjutant general for a copy of those charges. Unaware of the court of inquiry, he requested a court to investigate any allegations, but despite the reference to "charges" in the order relieving him from duty, none had been preferred. His request went unanswered.[6]

Porter spent those turbulent days at his old Arlington haunts, first at Hall's Hill and later at Fort Corcoran, acting effectively as McClellan's monitor of affairs below the Potomac. With a reliable friend back at the head of the army,

Porter resumed his old habit of "respectfully" remarking censoriously on the lapses of others—and particularly, now, on the lapses of those who might have an interest in seeing him prosecuted. He accused McDowell of neglecting his picket line, and instead of bringing it up with McDowell directly he took pains to make it known at McClellan's headquarters.[7]

When McClellan asked for troop returns from his corps commanders, Porter replied that casualties, sickness, and absence among regimental commanders, adjutants, and brigade staff officers made that task extremely difficult. By working late into the night he tallied almost exactly ten thousand men under Butterfield, Sykes, and General Piatt, who was still with him. He characterized Piatt's brigade as "unfit to take anywhere," and with so many green officers he doubted it would improve on its own, so he proposed breaking it up and distributing the men through the two divisions. "Piatt I do not want," he added. The extent of Porter's command remained somewhat nebulous: he had to ask more than once what troops were included in his corps, and what the geographical limits of his responsibility were. On the day McClellan prepared to lead the field army into Maryland, Porter spent ten hours inspecting all the forts from the Aqueduct Bridge down to Alexandria.[8]

Until he was sure that most of Lee's army had gone into Maryland, McClellan kept Porter in charge of the southside approaches to the capital. Near midnight on the day of his inspection tour, Porter supplied some intelligence on the Maryland invasion himself. Two slaves belonging to officers in Jackson's army had escaped into Porter's lines, reporting that when they left the Rebel army it had been massed between Dranesville and Leesburg, preparing to swarm into Maryland. Two days later Porter telegraphed McClellan, who was directing the movements of the field army from Rockville, Maryland, to assure him that all was well below the river: his troops were nearly all in place, and Mac need not worry. The next morning Griffin, who was also back on duty, reported that only two Confederate videttes lingered at Dranesville, and not one at Fairfax Court House.[9]

By September 11, Lee's whole army had crossed into Maryland and moved up the Potomac beyond the confluence of the Monocacy, where some of his divisions were wading back to the Virginia side to encircle Harper's Ferry. McClellan, still at Rockville, had spread his army out in three wings between the Potomac River and the Baltimore & Ohio Railroad, to block any dash toward Baltimore. He had assigned Burnside to command the right wing, consisting of his heavily reinforced Ninth Corps and McDowell's old First Corps, led by Hooker. Franklin hugged the river with the left wing of the army, including his Sixth Corps and Darius Couch's division from the soon-to-disappear Fourth Corps. Sumner covered the ground between Burnside and Franklin with his own Second Corps and the new Twelfth Corps—formerly Banks's; Joseph

Mansfield, the missing man on Porter's court of inquiry, was on his way to take charge of that corps. Those commands had all been augmented with several dozen big new regiments in bright blue uniforms, many of them nine-month state militia units raised under threat of conscription.

Similar levies of novices had reinforced Porter's Fifth Corps, which McClellan asked Halleck to send him, and he wanted those of Heintzelman and Sigel as well. That sounded like the manpower-hungry McClellan of half a year before, and when apprised of the request President Lincoln hesitated. Ever anxious to keep heavy concentrations of troops around Washington, he reminded McClellan that "if Porter, Heintzelman, and Sigel were sent you, it would strip everything from the other side of the river." Still, he partially complied, adding that Porter would be ordered his way that night, and he hoped others could follow.[10]

Sykes had already gone ahead, and that evening Porter telegraphed to McClellan that he would join him the next day with Morell's division. McClellan also authorized him to take charge of two brigades made up almost entirely of new nine-month men, who would compose a third division for him under McClellan's erstwhile engineer, Andrew Humphreys. Taking command of that division on short notice, Humphreys saw Porter only for a couple of minutes when they met on the street in Washington just after noon on Friday, September 12. Porter warned him that his new division would be marching through town in a couple of hours, and urged him to hurry it along on roads to the northwest. Porter left the city right after his chat with Humphreys, and by nightfall he had come within seven miles of McClellan's Rockville headquarters, bivouacking at a crossroads then known as Leesborough with two of Morell's brigades; the third brigade camped three miles behind that. Entering Rockville the next morning, he discovered that McClellan had moved on to Frederick, from which he sent orders to hurry toward that point. Porter pushed as far as his men could go that night, pressing on to Frederick on Sunday, September 14.[11]

As fatiguing as they found the constant marching, Porter's veterans of the Peninsula reveled in their reception by a predominately loyal populace. "Pretty villages are frequent," wrote a bugler in Porter's original division, "and pretty girls more so, and instead of gazing at passing soldiers with scorn and contempt, they were always ready with a pleasant word and a glass of water." A sergeant in the 44th New York appreciated the children and adults at Urbana who met them with cheers and waving flags. The farmers in the ranks admired the well-tended fields of Maryland, in such contrast to the neglected cropland in embattled Virginia.[12]

Saturday evening, September 13, had brought McClellan an incredible gift in the form of a lost copy of Lee's orders splitting his command into five vulnerable segments. To capture the twelve-thousand-man garrison at Harper's Ferry, Lee had sent Lafayette McLaws with two divisions to Maryland Heights, overlooking the town from across the Potomac. John G. Walker took another division back to the Virginia side to seize Loudoun Heights, from which he could fire over the Shenandoah River into Harper's Ferry. Stonewall Jackson, meanwhile, marched far up the Potomac before crossing back into Virginia to attack the garrison from Bolivar Heights. According to the lost order, most of Longstreet's wing was guarding the passes over South Mountain from near Boonsboro, but in fact only D. H. Hill's division remained there; Lee had sent Longstreet and the rest ahead to Hagerstown.

Three gaps creased the long, steep ridge known as South Mountain. The historic National Road, leading from Frederick to Hagerstown and far beyond, passed over Turner's Gap, on the main road from Middletown to Boonsboro. A mile south of Turner's Gap, the Old Sharpsburg Road climbed over Fox's Gap. Five miles farther to the south, one more road traversed the ridge through Crampton's Gap. Burnside led the drive toward the two northern passes on Sunday, the fourteenth, turning the Ninth Corps to the left toward Fox's Gap while Hooker assailed Turner's Gap with the First Corps. D. H. Hill's outnumbered defenders put up a stiff fight on both fronts, with reinforcements from Longstreet late in the day. A skirmish erupted at dusk in which Jesse Reno was killed, but that night the last Confederates drew back toward Sharpsburg, closer to the Potomac and their scattered comrades.[13]

Porter had ridden ahead of Morell's division, catching up with McClellan at Middletown late on the morning of the battle. There he assumed command of Sykes's Regulars and the reserve artillery, and all those troops bedded down that night within sight of the towering steeple of Middletown's new Lutheran church. McClellan heard that the Rebels were retreating "in a panic," and he seemed eager to run down the weakened core of Lee's army. He issued orders that night for Sykes to depart Middletown at daybreak, but those instructions may have been relaxed to let Burnside's men clear the road over Fox's Gap and lead the way to Sharpsburg. The Regulars only started from town somewhere between nine and ten o'clock that morning. They marched the three miles to Bolivar, turned off on the road to Fox's Gap, and about halfway up the ridge they found their way blocked by wagons, artillery, and meandering sightseers from the Ninth Corps. Burnside's men, who had been ordered to take after Lee with the "utmost vigor" at 9:00 A.M., had not even broken camp near noon. Porter must have spoken with McClellan as he passed through Bolivar, for he knew Burnside's troops were supposed to be long gone by then, and he sent a note back to headquarters asking that Burnside be ordered to get out of the way. McClellan did issue such an order, along with an uncharacteristically formal requirement that Burnside explain the disappointing delay.[14]

Porter's officious demand seemed needless, given his long intimacy with Burnside, and it occasioned much speculation then and afterward about his and McClellan's change in sentiment toward their old friend. A malicious interpretation gained greater currency because McClellan had also relieved Burnside of wing command that morning, directing Hooker and the First Corps to Boonsboro while Burnside was to lead the Ninth Corps toward Sharpsburg. Taken together, those two actions hinted that Burnside's stock was suddenly plummeting in the McClellan-Porter orbit. Yet logic and logistics may have dictated the dissolution of Burnside's wing: McClellan eventually took the Twelfth Corps away from Sumner, too, and Reno's death left only a volunteer brigadier to command the Ninth Corps. Still, Porter's ostentatious fault-finding betrayed annoyance and more than a touch of defensiveness on his part.[15]

The encounter on the mountainside was Porter's first contact with Burnside since learning that he had passed those incriminating dispatches on to the president, and Burnside had had no opportunity to explain. Porter knew by then that those messages could lend his exercise of battlefield discretion the appearance of willful disobedience, if a court were to be convened. He had authorized Burnside to use his telegrams, presumably to emphasize Pope's blundering and encourage McClellan's assignment to overall command, but he had evidently expected some judicious editing if they were shared—and especially if shared with the president. Before sending them on to Washington, Burnside had discussed editing them with his chief of staff, so he had recognized that they might do Porter some damage. Sending them unabridged hardly resembled the act of a friend, so it was not unreasonable for Porter to suppose that Burnside had surreptitiously turned against him—and against McClellan, to clear a path for himself to army command. Burnside's dispatches, and the possibility of his treachery, would have been early topics during Porter's rendezvous with McClellan at the foot of South Mountain.[16]

The courier who carried Burnside's 9:00 A.M. order may have gone astray. McClellan later mentioned that Burnside "could not be found," and the order failed to reach Fox's Gap until near noon, but Porter saw an opportunity in pointing out Burnside's apparent lapse. By complaining, he illustrated that delays in complying with orders (such as he might be accused of) were a common occurrence, and he simultaneously demonstrated his own impatience to be after the enemy. Porter's direct appeal to McClellan, along with the reprimand it elicited and the suspension from wing command, all combined to hurt Burnside's feelings and germinate his own suspicions about McClellan, which the Ninth Corps staff shared. As the army moved toward Sharpsburg, fractures were developing in the once-convivial triumvirate of Burnside, McClellan, and Porter, and in the end the rupture would bring varying degrees of harm to them all. Mutual trust and camaraderie such as they had always previously shared might have bred a spirit aggressive enough to win enduring laurels in place of the clouds that settled over each of them before two more seasons had passed.[17]

Israel Richardson's division of the Second Corps led the way from Turner's Gap to Boonsboro, where Richardson turned south toward Sharpsburg. Porter pushed past Burnside with Sykes's Regulars, but the traffic jam at Fox's Gap had put Richardson ahead of him, and early on the afternoon of September 15 Richardson's leading brigade descended into the ravine that led to a stone-arch bridge over Antietam Creek. Three divisions of Confederate infantry, flanked by cavalry, stood in line of battle on the ridge between the creek and the outskirts of Sharpsburg. Rebel artillery opened as the Yankees came into sight, and while Richardson deployed his leading brigade he called on a Regular battery that accompanied the cavalry.[18]

Porter rode in Richardson's wake with Sykes, reaching the scene about 3:00 P.M. Sykes spread some of Buchanan's brigade out as skirmishers along the left bank of the creek, at the base of the precipitous hillside that towered two hundred feet above it. Porter rode to the top of that hill, climbing the steep farm road past John Ecker's new brick house to the crest of the bluff. McClellan joined him ere long, followed by his huge staff, and as that throng gazed off toward the opposing ridge Rebel guns threw a couple of shells at the assemblage. At McClellan's behest the staff pulled back out of sight while he and Porter continued to assess the enemy line and the terrain around them. The Ninth Corps had fallen in behind Sykes around 1:00 P.M. but had taken another road, and toward dusk it came in on Sykes's left, bivouacking about a mile away from another stone bridge spanning the creek farther downstream. The rest of Sumner's corps, Hooker's corps, and Mansfield's Twelfth Corps all piled up behind Sykes and Richardson. Franklin remained near Crampton's Gap with his Sixth Corps and that stray division of the Fourth, but the reserve artillery reported to Porter after dark, having been cut off by Burnside's march. McClellan's demeanor and commentary left those around him supposing that a battle would commence in the morning.[19]

Tuesday dawned with dense fog along the creek. Batteries from the reserve artillery flew about, looking for good visibility, and several of them galloped up the hill past the Ecker house, unlimbering on higher ground behind it. Porter located his headquarters on the crest there, where a panorama of the ridge east of Sharpsburg would unfold once the fog burned off. McClellan established tentative headquarters at the Samuel Pry house, three-quarters of a mile away upstream, where another hill rose to the same height, but he preferred the view from Porter's batteries. At 7:45 A.M. he declared that he would attack the Rebels if they had not retreated, but the fog hung too thick to determine whether they were still there.[20]

When the mist finally receded, the red Rebel battle flags were still fluttering along the ridgeline. McClellan reacted as though disappointed, dithering for hours as Lee gradually reunited his army and reduced the overwhelming odds against him. Morell's division arrived about noon, with the cheers of Keedys-ville villagers still ringing in their ears. Porter posted those three brigades under cover behind the bluff, alongside Sykes and near a hamlet called Porterstown. Humphreys and his footsore nine-month recruits stopped twenty miles behind at Frederick, in obedience to orders that Porter later attributed to Stanton's paranoia about Lee sneaking around McClellan to get at Washington. The pre-cious afternoon of September 16 slipped into the irretrievable past with most of the Army of the Potomac drawing rations and ammunition, catching up on lost sleep, or finding somewhere to hide from the long-distance fire of Rebel guns.[21]

When Morell arrived, McClellan was surveying his lines downstream, find-ing fault with Burnside's position. In an order carried by his new chief engineer, Captain James Duane, McClellan instructed Burnside to move the Ninth Corps nearer to the lower bridge, known locally as the Rohrbach Bridge, and to the reputed fords downstream from there. Duane took three of Burnside's aides to show them where each division should camp—McClellan having already de-cided not to launch an attack that day. The aides did not return from their jaunt with Duane until three o'clock; they were about to post the troops when a staff officer of McClellan's showed up, informing Burnside that McClellan was "not sure that the proper position had been indicated." He advised holding off, at which Burnside climbed into the saddle and spurred off to McClellan's head-quarters. McClellan was away with Hooker at the right of the line, so the frus-trated Burnside returned to his command. His troops did not begin shuffling off to screened bivouacs along the creek until nearly four, and some of them did not get under way until five.[22]

That evening, when McClellan learned how late the Ninth Corps had moved, he sent Burnside a more severe reprimand than he ever issued anyone. He phrased it in a way that exaggerated the delay involved, as though blaming Burnside for confounding plans for an afternoon assault when McClellan's own procrastination had precluded offensive action that day.[23] The afternoon had dwindled so far away before he ordered his other troops into position for an at-tack that most of the remaining daylight was consumed in marching them into place on the far side of the creek. The advance elements of Hooker's corps, then waiting back at Keedysville, did not start moving until at least 2:00 P.M., march-ing over a third stone bridge upstream or wading the creek at a nearby ford. Once the leading brigades had crossed, they waited for the rest of the corps, and some units never budged until three o'clock or later; one of Hooker's brigadiers reported fording the creek "near evening." By the time the corps had negotiated the intervening farmland and begun approaching the left of Lee's battle line, the day was nearly gone. Confederate skirmishers hiding in tall corn fired their warning shots and retired, and a fierce skirmish erupted just at dusk, but that flurry represented the only offensive action of the day. At Hooker's request, Mc-Clellan gave him Mansfield's corps as well, taking it from Sumner's control, but night had come before those men even stirred, and one division commander had already gone to bed.[24]

McClellan's strangely harsh rebuke smacked of a complaint contrived as a contingent excuse for his own lethargy, but the source from whom he learned of that delay is lacking from the record. The right of Burnside's skirmish line connected with Sykes's left, and from the bluff behind Ecker's house Porter had a good view of the progress of Burnside's divisions. McClellan's informant was therefore probably the same man who had turned so critical of Burnside the day before. Porter's intimacy with McClellan had always afforded him a receptive ear for his carping appraisals of others, and he felt more than one motive for criticizing Burnside.[25]

Drizzling rain disturbed the sleep of those without tents or blankets — and most of the veterans of Pope's campaign had lost theirs. Dawn of September 17 had not yet come when Hooker started rolling toward Sharpsburg from a league north of town, aiming for an elevation conspicuous for the white stone church belonging to Sharpsburg's Dunker congregation. Lee had prepared for him as well as he could, with two of Jackson's divisions and two brigades of Hood's division. Union artillery sent the Rebels reeling backward at first, and Hooker advanced about a mile with his three divisions abreast, but flank attacks on both sides stopped him. The opposing lines wavered back and forth for nearly two hours, until a determined counterattack drove the Yankees back over half the ground they had gained.[26]

Rather than coming in alongside the First Corps and overwhelming Jackson, Mansfield only brought the Twelfth Corps to the field as Hooker retired. One bullet caught Hooker in the foot, and another dropped Mansfield as he approached the front, but his fresh divisions renewed the pressure on Confederates who had already suffered heavy casualties. George Greene's two brigades drove the remnants of Jackson's resistance beyond the church, claiming the high ground there. Lafayette McLaws had recently arrived from Harper's Ferry with his division of Longstreet's corps, and he brought it racing to contest that claim.[27]

At midmorning John Sedgwick's division, of Sumner's Second Corps, marched into this maelstrom from the east in a battle formation three brigades deep. Sumner rode with it over the ridge near the church, across the Hagerstown Pike, and down into a broad grove that would be known as the West Woods to those who lived to come out of it. McLaws struck Sedgwick broadside, raking his lines lengthwise with withering volleys and crumbling his three brigades one after the other. Sedgwick came out wounded and dazed, and even

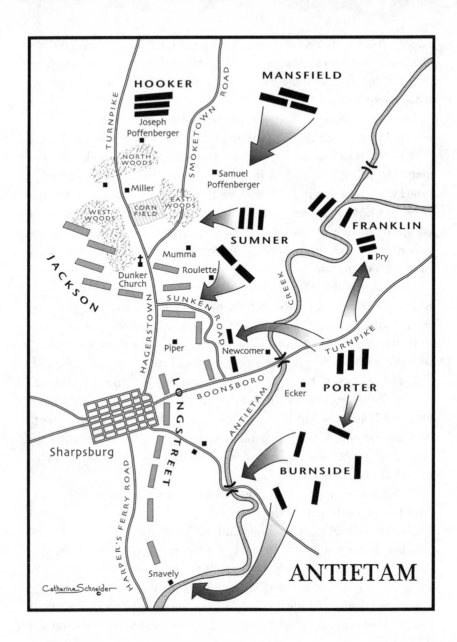

ANTIETAM

the fiercely combative Sumner betrayed signs of shock. Once Sedgwick's men had been chased from the West Wood, the Rebels who poured into it turned Greene's flank, forcing him to give up the Dunker church.[28]

Sumner's next division, under William French, stopped short at Sedgwick's repulse, wheeled ninety degrees to the south, and faced a sunken farm road filled with Rebel riflemen. Sumner's last division, under Richardson, joined that fight as soon as Morell's division replaced it in support of the batteries guarding the upstream side of the Middle Bridge. For two more hours the fighting concentrated on the Confederate center, where Richardson hurled his men against the Sunken Road. Late in the morning attrition among the defenders of that makeshift breastwork allowed Union infantry to break through, but desperate resistance by scattered Confederates plugged the gap. Richardson fell with a mortal wound, which seemed to sap the Federals' attack of its vitality, and the fighting there stalled.[29]

McClellan had watched the early stages of the fighting from the hill behind the Pry house, but around ten o'clock he mounted up and rode over to Porter's headquarters on the bluff. From there, officers in the Regulars had been able to see the assaults by Hooker and Mansfield, as well as the retreat of Jackson's men. The West Woods sank just below their line of sight, obscuring all but the smoke of that fight, and they missed the worst repulse of Union forces that morning.[30]

Before leaving his own headquarters, McClellan sent orders for Burnside to cross the creek and strike Lee's right, promising support once he was over: he hinted that the help would come from Franklin, whose corps was drawing near. The geographical impediments posed by the creek and the steep terrain on the opposite bank allowed the Confederates to hold the Ninth Corps off for several hours, freeing troops to fight the Twelfth and Second Corps. The Rohrbach Bridge sat directly beneath a precipitous hillside topped by a quarry, from which Georgia riflemen could aim down the throats of any Yankees who came that way. The creek ran deep enough in most places to discourage infantry from crossing, while precipitous bluffs lined the right bank, downstream from the bridge, and Confederate artillery swept the ground upstream.[31]

From about ten o'clock until one in the afternoon, Burnside assailed the Georgians defending the crossing, beginning with a direct assault on the bridge. Next he tried concentrated fire from several angles, but nothing budged the few hundred defenders until Burnside sent a division downstream to cross the creek at a farm ford and come up behind the Rebels' right flank. Confederates began backing away at that threat, diminishing the firepower at the bridge until two Union regiments were able to rush across and swarm up the embankment. The rest of the corps followed, and by the middle of the afternoon all four divisions were aligning in the fields south of Sharpsburg for the final drive toward Lee's escape route. Four Rebel brigades backed up near the outskirts of town to meet them.[32]

Well before noon the harbingers of Franklin's Sixth Corps had begun to show up, but Burnside was still trying to cross the creek so McClellan sent Franklin to Sumner's aid. Franklin wished to make an attack, but Sumner, who was usually the most pugnacious of corps commanders, advised against it. Citing the scattered and demoralized condition of all the Union forces on that part of the field, and fearing that a repulse might lead to wholesale rout, Sumner finally ordered him not to make the attempt. Franklin called on McClellan to come see for himself. After Burnside was across the creek and forming for what promised to be a decisive assault, McClellan rode over to the center to see what Franklin was talking about. Sumner presented such a dismal picture of the situation that McClellan called on Porter for reinforcements, ordering two of Morell's brigades over from the Middle Bridge. Those brigades were well on their way to the right of the line when McClellan countermanded the order, instead directing all commanders to hold their present positions until Burnside attacked. Morell's two brigades were nonetheless lost to Porter until after dark.[33]

As the day progressed, Porter sent increasingly urgent messages to Humphreys, back at Frederick, to hurry on with his division. "Give your men twenty additional rounds to carry in the pockets," he ordered shortly after noon, but he expected speed from them despite the additional burden. "Bring up your men so as to be as fresh as possible, but get here soon." Two hours later he again urged Humphreys to make "all haste." Remembering how his line had been broken at Gaines's Mill for lack of any reserves, Porter glanced with mounting anxiety at his shrinking command.[34]

Warren's few hundred survivors of Bull Run had already moved to the left, downstream, to back up Burnside, and they provided the only connection between the Fifth and Ninth Corps. Cavalryman Alfred Pleasonton, who had been unfriendly to Porter at Fort Leavenworth five years before, was using some of Sykes's Regulars as infantry support for his horse artillery atop Newcomer's Ridge, beyond the Middle Bridge. His guns ran out of ammunition in the afternoon, and he asked Sykes to replace them with his own batteries. Sykes reluctantly complied, and even sent the better part of Buchanan's brigade when Pleasonton asked for more infantry. That left Porter with one brigade of Morell's division and the equivalent of one brigade of Regulars, amounting to somewhere between three and four thousand men: he had distributed all but one battery of the artillery reserve to other parts of the field. With those two brigades Porter guarded all the army's supplies and its principal line of retreat, if that became necessary. As usual, McClellan believed himself outnumbered, and Porter again accepted his estimates, while the ferocity of the enemy resistance disguised the relative weakness of the Rebel legions. It did not seem improbable that Lee might be trying to wear their army out before landing a hammer blow of his own with a concealed phalanx. His audacity and the ferocity of the resistance implied a much greater force than he actually had.[35]

The infantry Sykes had sent to Pleasonton joined the artillery on the crest of Newcomer Ridge, half a mile from the eastern extremity of Sharpsburg. From there the Boonsboro Pike climbed one last ridge to the edge of town before dropping out of sight down the steep main street. Halfway to the crest of that ridge, Confederate marksmen were sniping at the gunners from behind haystacks south of the pike. Captain Hiram Dryer, commanding that brigade-strength collection of mixed Regular battalions, started edging them toward those sharpshooters and the village; in one dash at a post-and-rail fence some of Dryer's Regulars exchanged a few point-blank shots and parried bayonets with the most stubborn of the Rebels. The Virginia brigadier who held the turnpike there saw them coming, and off to his right he spotted the flags of Burnside's corps advancing to close off his retreat; with barely two hundred of his men in sight he decided it was time to leave. Pleasonton asked for still more infantry, but General Marcy replied for McClellan that there was none to spare, suggesting that he ask Porter. Porter told Pleasonton he dared send in no more, advising him to use Dryer's contingent, which he noted was pushing independently toward Sharpsburg, past a cornfield on his left that Porter said was "full of Rebel infantry."[36]

Captain Dryer was, in fact, trying to coordinate an assault on Sharpsburg with the Regulars he had on hand. Buchanan's assistant adjutant general, Lieutenant William Powell, realized what Dryer was up to, and knew it conflicted with Sykes's and Porter's intentions — not to mention McClellan's recent instructions for everyone to await Burnside's assault. Dryer had gone far ahead of any support and would fall under the guns of several Rebel batteries: when Powell informed Buchanan and Sykes of it, Sykes told him to ride out and order Dryer back to the bridge, immediately.[37]

Powell sped off to reel Dryer back in. He may have passed a courier going the other way with a message from Captain Matthew Blunt to Buchanan, describing light resistance and Dryer's wish to attack. Captain Thomas Anderson, who commanded Buchanan's last battalion on Ecker's Ridge, claimed he was talking with Buchanan at the crest when that message arrived, and that Buchanan relayed it to Sykes. Sykes was sitting on horseback nearby with Porter and McClellan, too far away for Anderson or Buchanan to hear any of their discussion, but long afterward Anderson wrote of having asked Sykes what happened. Sykes, who had been dead half a dozen years by the time Anderson's story appeared, supposedly replied that McClellan seemed inclined to throw the Fifth Corps in until Porter dissuaded him. "Remember, General," Porter allegedly said, "I command the last reserve of the last Army of the Republic."[38]

That tale echoed the prejudicial view of Porter cultivated by the court-martial of the following winter and propounded thereafter by Radicals in and out of the army, who waved the verdict like a battle flag, but Anderson's recollection defied fact and logic. Porter denied ever having seen such a message, or having ever had such a discussion with McClellan. Sykes was, besides, too friendly with Porter, and too respectful of him, to have retailed so unflattering an anecdote. Furthermore, Sykes's alleged statement that McClellan was considering sending in the Fifth Corps would have foundered on the fact that there was then no Fifth Corps to send in: of the eight brigades and fifteen batteries in Porter's three divisions and the artillery reserve, only two brigades and one battery still stood on the field, uncommitted. Finally, as Lieutenant Powell later emphasized in response to Anderson's accusative account, Buchanan already knew that Dryer had been recalled, which had decided the question asked by Blunt, so there would have been no reason to forward Blunt's message to any superior officer. Besides, McClellan had informed Pleasonton more than an hour before that he could afford to send no more infantry. Powell also contradicted an assertion by Anderson that Dryer had ridden inside Confederate lines to assess the situation for himself. Powell knew personally that this was not true, because when he went to recall Dryer the captain had not yet come within four hundred yards of the enemy.[39]

Porter seemed aggressive enough only minutes afterward. He noticed Burnside's corps finally lurching forward, aiming for the sun as it dropped toward the steeple of Sharpsburg's Lutheran church. Heavily outnumbered, the Confederate defenders fell back slowly but inexorably, and to them the end of Lee's briefly famous army must have seemed nigh. Advancing on Burnside's extreme right, the brand-new soldiers of the 17th Michigan came up abreast of the Regulars by the pike, enduring what they considered a severe fire, just as Dryer heeded Sykes's order to turn back for the bridge. Dryer must have been on his way back when Porter scrawled a note to Sykes, apprising him that Burnside was finally driving the enemy and asking him to urge the same of the men he had lent to Pleasonton.[40]

There was no time even to deliver that message, nor would it have done any good for Dryer to charge those retreating Virginians when he wanted to. A. P. Hill's division, the last of Lee's detachments from Harper's Ferry, was then almost sprinting toward Burnside's left flank. Hill's leading brigade shuffled hastily into a line of battle and slammed into Burnside, killing one of his division commanders and scattering a days-old Connecticut regiment to the winds. Those fugitives sparked similar panic among other new troops and threw even veterans into confusion. Burnside's assault promptly degenerated from a tardy but promising drive into a grudging retreat. The new regiments shed scores of runaways: Warren spread his two regiments out along the left bank of the Antietam to catch them, but many slipped through—some to spend days hiding in the woods before returning. A few never came back.[41]

So surprising an onslaught from an unexpected quarter resembled the overwhelming counterattack McClellan had feared all along. As the sun began to set, Burnside sent a desperate message for the reinforcements he had been promised, but in the face of the anticipated disaster McClellan reverted entirely to the defensive. At his dictation, Marcy told Burnside that he must guard the bridge with enough infantry and artillery to prevent the enemy from crossing it, "whatever the result of your affair tonight may be."[42]

In his sole performance as a war correspondent for the *New York Tribune*, George Smalley dramatized that exchange as an oral communication. Implying that he had been an eyewitness, Smalley portrayed McClellan "looking down into the valley where 15,000 troops are lying," and he assumed that those men were "fresh and only impatient to share in this fight." Then, according to Smalley, McClellan turned "a half-questioning look on Fitz John Porter, who stands by his side, gravely scanning the field," at which Porter ostensibly shook his head. By dint of sheer speculation, the reporter concluded that the reciprocal glances revealed that both generals were thinking the same thing: "They are the only reserves of the army; they cannot be spared." Smalley then quoted the commanding general telling Burnside's messenger, "I will send him Miller's battery. I can do nothing more. I have no infantry." Finally, Smalley depicted McClellan shouting after the courier as he rode away that if Burnside could not hold his ground then he must hold the bridge — "to the last man! Always the bridge! If the bridge is lost, all is lost!"[43]

George McClellan was certainly prone to such melodrama and exaggeration, but so was George Smalley, who saw four men for every one lying "fresh and only impatient" in the valley behind Ecker's Ridge. Even if Smalley actually was present to record the story, his factual misinformation was aggravated by subtly incriminating guesswork that long distorted the history of the battle and hounded Fitz John Porter the rest of his life. Smalley's thrilling prose provided source material for malicious postwar yarns that apparently included the one Captain Anderson told in 1886, but in September of 1862 such tales proved especially popular in the company Smalley kept. His *Tribune* story found a receptive readership among Radical Republicans who considered McClellan and Porter the chief agents in a conservative plot to thwart military victory.[44]

Burnside did hold the bridge, along with quite a bit of ground on the other side. Later that night, while the two battered armies lay down to sleep, he rode over to McClellan's headquarters to ask again about reinforcements, but found the commanding general too tired and ill to discuss it. McClellan told his wife he was sick with his "old disease" for most of three days after the battle, referring probably to the malarial symptoms of fever, headache, and diarrhea. He and Porter discussed renewing the fight in the morning, claimed a Twelfth Corps colonel who made the battle his life's study, but McClellan's physical condition and his preternatural caution combined to dissuade him from it. Lee's brazen decision to hold his position throughout that day only suggested further evidence of Confederate strength, and any breakfast-time thoughts McClellan entertained of renewing the battle withered under his desire for reinforcements. Some thirteen thousand fresh troops marched within reach at an early hour under Humphreys and Couch, but the day passed in peace. During a truce, parties from the opposing armies buried the dead and did what they could for their own and each other's wounded.[45]

An evening rainstorm soaked the combatants, giving them a chilly night. Before midnight on September 18 Sumner reported suspicious noises within Rebel lines, and thought they were withdrawing artillery. It was 4:00 A.M. before McClellan saw that message, but over the next half-hour he ordered everyone to push their pickets ahead and see if the enemy was retreating. Porter's pickets stopped a citizen venturing forth with a makeshift white flag who said that the Rebels had all left during the night. An officer and six men from Porter's command strode into Sharpsburg and some distance beyond without seeing an armed Confederate.

"The enemy have gone," Porter informed his ailing commander in a private note, "but where? Are you in telegraphic communication with Washington to know of any enemy there?" Sharing McClellan's apprehension about overwhelming Confederate forces, he seemed to suspect that Antietam might have been a diversion while the rest of Lee's army assailed the capital. Morell could head down the Antietam toward the Potomac at McClellan's call, he wrote, with Sykes and Humphreys ready to follow. In a postscript he hoped McClellan was well, "or at all events much better," and mentioned that Pleasonton was not up yet, although ordered out quite some time before.[46]

Porter's and other Union troops held firm possession of the empty streets by 6:00 A.M. McClellan wanted to form a wide battle line below Sharpsburg to sweep toward the Potomac, and Porter said he would try, but he warned that the broken country on the left would make it difficult. At twenty minutes after ten he was still in the town, abreast of the Harper's Ferry Road, where every house was "shot up" by bullet or shell and filled with Confederate wounded. He offered again to turn Morell toward Harper's Ferry if McClellan preferred not to send Burnside. Eventually McClellan gave up the idea of forming the whole army into a line and told Porter to march south straight out of Sharpsburg, toward neighboring Shepherdstown, Virginia. Pleasonton's cavalry had finally ridden ahead, and Porter would be needed to back them up.[47]

That cavalry detachment scooped up 167 straggling Rebels on the way to the Potomac, along with an abandoned fieldpiece and a flag, but the rest of the Army of Northern Virginia was already back in its namesake territory. The deserters and the flotsam of the Rebels' flight suggested demoralization and starvation to Porter. Arriving near the river early in the afternoon, he turned down the road to Boteler's Ford, where Lee had left some infantry and a few dozen guns on the Virginia side to hold back any pursuit. Porter decided to dash across the river, drive that rear guard away, and try capturing some of their guns, but first he lined the Chesapeake & Ohio Canal towpath with sharpshooters and directed all his batteries to find advantageous positions.[48]

While the artillerymen posted their guns, Porter scrawled a fraternal but decidedly hurried letter of encouragement and advice for his ailing friend, as though in his illness McClellan needed reminding of strategy and logistics. "I would urge you to get Harpers Ferry and the roads which converge from there," he coaxed, as he had hinted earlier. "That must be occupied and I believe you must take that as your main base — and I would urge you to put your command in motion with reference to that, with this idea. Fill mens bellies and the bellies of horses & guns [sic] & we will be all you want & can desire." With that sidelong allusion to the hunger of his men and much of the rest of the army, whose supply train had lagged in the rear for days, Porter promised McClellan that his artillery would open in a few minutes.[49]

The Virginia shore offered a shelf of land barely wide enough to accommodate some mill buildings before rising abruptly to a bluff carved by a single ravine at the middle of the contested reach of the river. The Confederate guns sat on the bluff and the infantry occupied the shelf below. Porter's guns easily matched those left behind by Lee, and through the afternoon they hammered at the right bank of the Potomac. The Confederates were running low on ammunition as the daylight started to fade, and their batteries began to limber up and pull away. The infantry on the toe of the bank had had enough by then, and when Porter sent a storming party across the river the Rebel riflemen scrambled up the bluff wherever it could be scaled, scurrying for the rear. Led by General Griffin, several hundred volunteers from his and another brigade plunged into the river and waded across, clambering up to the crest, where the Rebels had left behind several guns, a couple of caissons, and four hundred discarded rifles. Griffin discovered that one of the guns came from the battery he had lost to Stonewall Jackson at First Bull Run.[50]

Porter made arrangements to cross again the next day, in what he intended as either a reconnaissance in force or the beginning of a pursuit. McClellan was still under the weather, but his father-in-law promised that Pleasonton would have cavalry on hand by daylight to help Porter feel his way on the Virginia shore. Pleasonton, who was already blaming Porter for refusing him reinforcements on Wednesday, grumbled about him again that night for sending the cavalry back to camp, complaining that it cost those men a chance to get their rations.[51]

The sun had just risen at 6:00 A.M. on September 20 when Porter notified Marcy that no cavalry had reported to him yet. Major Charles Lovell's little brigade of Regulars forded the river about seven o'clock, as scheduled, and James Barnes's brigade of Morell's division followed them. Some of the enlisted men shed their shoes and socks and rolled up their trousers before crossing.[52]

McClellan felt better that morning, and Porter sent him regular reports heavily flavored with reservations about going very deep into Virginia without cavalry. He sent his own escort of two dozen mounted men to scout the road to Martinsburg, but he worried about having none to guard the flanks of his infantry advance. He assured McClellan that he would do whatever the commanding general deemed prudent, but he needed to know his wishes. Clearly he was nervous about the absence of any mounted troops: two regiments would do, he said. In case he stirred up a sizable force, he also reminded McClellan that Sykes had only about three thousand men and Morell six thousand — while the six thousand green troops under Humphreys were footsore and hungry.[53]

No cavalry had appeared by 9:15 that morning, when Lovell sent a warning back to the bluffs that he had run into Confederates at least a brigade strong, three-quarters of a mile out on a narrow, rocky road into the interior. As the ranking man on that side, Sykes had already ordered Barnes's brigade up the bluffs by way of the ravine, to be ready to help if Lovell called on him, and he urged Warren to hurry his two battle-thinned regiments across. To Porter he suggested that a lot more troops ought to be sent over, preferably under "some one in authority."[54]

Sykes's instincts proved as reliable as Porter's. A. P. Hill's entire division was coming, and while it was sharply reduced by Wednesday afternoon's fighting it still outnumbered Lovell better than five to one. Lovell retired by the book in line of battle, falling back and periodically facing about to fire a volley. At 10:30 A.M. Porter alerted McClellan that the enemy had appeared. Twenty minutes later he asked for last-minute orders, noting that he was going over to take command personally, although he had still not seen any sign of Pleasonton's cavalry. Before Porter crossed the river, a courier delivered McClellan's order to bring everyone back to the Maryland shore. That ended Porter's last opportunity to reaffirm his zeal to beat the enemy.[55]

Those who had carefully removed their shoes to wade over bounded into the water fully clothed on the way back. The 118th Pennsylvania of Barnes's brigade, a brand-new regiment, ran into trouble. That single regiment outnumbered most veteran brigades, but concentrated musketry brought down more than a third of its men before they reached the water's edge. Porter's sharpshooters and artillery on the Virginia shore covered their retreat, but some of the shells fell short and added to the slaughter of the Pennsylvanians. One of the company commanders had survived a similar stampede into the Potomac at Ball's Bluff, eleven months before, and he shuddered at the similarities. Numerous men were shot as they splashed across the ford. The bright new regimental flag had to be fished out of the water as it floated downstream. With bullets spraying all around, a captain in the Regulars admitted that even he "paddled through regardless of the wetting."[56]

That repulse, and a feint back into Maryland by Rebel cavalry at Williamsport, well upstream, brought the pursuit to an abrupt halt. Lee had escaped with the heart of his army, which would survive as the principal symbol of Confederate resistance two and a half years longer. Even amid the belief that Lee had been much stronger than he was, some observers recognized that McClellan had missed—or "thrown away"—a chance to effectively end the war at a stroke.[57]

McClellan ensconced his army in a broad arc behind the river crossings, from above Sharpsburg to Harper's Ferry, and set about restoring it to his high standards of equipage and training. Franklin's divisions camped between the battlefield and Williamsport, while Sumner, Burnside, and the Twelfth Corps occupied either side of the Potomac near Harper's Ferry. Porter took charge of the Shepherdstown sector of the river, camping between the left bank and Sharpsburg. The First Corps lay nearby, commanded by Meade while Hooker recuperated.

Equipment requisitions by the thousands fluttered from regimental and brigade headquarters to quartermaster depots at Frederick and Harper's Ferry and on to Washington. Every morning the camps rang with the barking of sergeants drilling their companies, and each afternoon officers taught (and learned) the finer points of battalion and brigade maneuvers. In moments of leisure the men boiled their clothing, to rid them of the lice that infested them after weeks without a change. Once the last of the Confederate dead had been buried and the putrefying carcasses of the horses had been burned, the pastoral landscape provided an especially sweet respite in the bright days of early autumn.[58]

For all the lost opportunities, Lee's retreat had made Antietam enough of a Union triumph that Lincoln dared announce a tentative proclamation abolishing slavery in any state that persisted in rebellion after the end of the year. Because he had at least technically beaten Lee, McClellan began to feel more secure in his position, despite what he perceived as a lack of appreciation from Washington. The same was true of Porter, whose threatened court of inquiry seemed forgotten: he still had no idea that a court had ever been appointed, or that Halleck had ordered it to adjourn indefinitely. John Pope still contended that McClellan and his favorites had engaged in a conspiracy to sabotage his campaign; he believed Lincoln knew it, too, but feared to press the case because McClellan enjoyed the loyalty of the army. Pope hoped to push that accusation by way of a congressional inquiry if his proxies could not instigate a military court, but even he knew the chances of prosecuting Porter or McClellan had waned with Lee's retreat into Virginia.

"I shall force the investigation if possible," Pope told the governor of Illinois four days after Antietam, "but under the present circumstances I doubt whether it will ever be made."[59]

14

THE SCAPEGOAT

September of 1862 ended in three warm, clear days that provoked muttering about McClellan's failure to wield his army. On the last of those three days Fitz John Porter spent an hour or more on a letter defending the long Maryland séjour to Manton Marble, at the *World*. He began by apprising Marble that Lee's defeat at Antietam could be attributed to how far he had ventured beyond his base of supplies. "Starvation had accomplished half the victory," he declared, relying on the admission of a well-informed Confederate during a truce, and he predicted that McClellan would err similarly if he chased Lee as impetuously as Lee had invaded Maryland. The wagon roads from Hagerstown and Frederick could not sustain an adequate flow of supplies, and the railroad bridge at Harper's Ferry had to be rebuilt first, to provide sufficient provisions at depots farther into Virginia.[1]

McClellan justified lingering above the Potomac on quartermaster deficits, blaming an inability to have horses and clothing distributed in a timely fashion, and some commanders were already recording those shortages. Porter's troops, and many others, had not yet even recovered the knapsacks that went missing from Harrison's Landing in August.[2] Additionally, Porter pointed to the condition of the men. The army had lost as heavily by straggling as in casualties, he claimed, implying that the inexperience of the new levies had contributed to the straggling. Fuming that state governors raised dozens of new regiments rather than sending recruits to replenish the old ones, he held that skeleton ranks in the veteran regiments depressed morale because it made death seem so much more likely. "Every battle reduces numbers," he explained, "and the men think the next one will be their last. They would not feel so if the regiments were full."

The new regiments, meanwhile, had shown themselves unreliable in battle and had been "very cautious, and *slow*, in some cases culpably slow." Perhaps that comment was aimed at the footsore recruits in the division Humphreys brought in on September 18, for McClellan had exaggerated how late they arrived in justifying his decision not to attack that day. Most of the new troops still desperately needed discipline and drill, and a score of other new regiments promised by the government had not arrived, causing a delay that Porter assumed would be blamed on McClellan. Yet Porter's own complaints implied that when those twenty new regiments did arrive they, too, would need training, and he argued that delay was actually necessary for other reasons, including a general reorganization.

"One week will do much," he contended, in the part of the letter he wrote on September 30, but he doubled his estimate of the desirable postponement in an addendum written three days later. His corps had been reviewed on October 3 for the first time since the battle, and after the review he reported seeing "gross deficiencies" in the performance. "I should be very loth to go into action with such troops," he wrote that evening, "but if advance now is the order, go I will and we will do our best. I feel we will be victorious but it will be at great loss. But two weeks will make a wonderful difference."

With that postscript the letter ultimately stretched to fourteen pages, moving Porter to apologize with his habitual irony for its "brevity and consiseness [*sic*]." He spent more than half of those fourteen pages lamenting and lambasting the Emancipation Proclamation. Certain that the threat of abolition would crush any sentiment for peace and reunion among citizens in the Confederacy, he belittled Lincoln's decree as "the absurd proclamation of a political coward." Better military management would eradicate slavery more effectively, he insisted, "for where the army goes slavery disappears." That required a more competent general-in-chief — presumably McClellan — and the replacement of the Radicals' mole, Stanton.[3]

Those were dangerous opinions for a soldier to hold. Major John Key, brother of one of McClellan's staff officers, had just been dismissed from the army merely for theorizing that hostility to emancipation explained McClellan's failure to pursue Lee's army. McClellan had just learned of Key's dismissal, and Porter may have written to Marble because of it, to defend McClellan's deliberation in preparing to meet an enemy whose resolve had been augmented by the unfortunate proclamation.[4]

Porter finished the letter a few hours after speaking to Lincoln, who came to see the army and talk to McClellan. Having heard that the president was still "very sore" over the Kennedy letter and the scornful dispatches to Burnside, Porter took the opportunity to sound him out. After the corps reviews of October 3, in which the troops snickered at the chief magistrate's ungainly form and drab haberdashery, the executive entourage dined at Porter's headquarters on Stephen Grove's farm, just below Sharpsburg. Alexander Gardner came along to photograph the dignitaries, arranging several group images, including one in which celebrity-seeking Joseph Kennedy stood immediately behind Porter. The census superintendent's presence may have allowed Porter an excuse to broach the subject during a moment alone with Lincoln, who denied that he was angry over Porter's indiscreet communications. The dispatches had been his only news from Pope's front for several days, he said, remarking that he was "satisfied" with them.[5]

If Porter recalled their exchange accurately, Lincoln was not being candid. Four weeks before, the president had personally composed an order for an investigation into Porter's performance at Bull Run. Three days after that, he had made remarks to Gideon Welles showing that he fully credited Pope's self-interested accusations. Eight weeks after talking to Porter, Lincoln admitted that he still thought Porter had deliberately disobeyed Pope—for whom those dispatches showed such contempt.[6]

Soon after the president returned to Washington, newspapers in the Radical camp began spreading inaccurate but disturbing gossip about Porter. Revising his account of Antietam to comport with George Smalley's innuendo, a correspondent for the Radical *Chicago Tribune* had already accused Porter of refusing to help Burnside, but now came talk of formal charges. The content implicated Stanton as a contributor to the canard, and Chase's network may have helped with distribution. Out in Ohio's Western Reserve, the *Ashtabula Weekly Telegraph* ran a story on October 4 headlined "Fresh Charges against Fitz John Porter," falsely crediting the *New York Times* as the source, but no such article ran in the *Times*. The *Telegraph* championed the congressional candidacy of Chase's protégé, James Garfield, who was then a guest at Chase's home, where Irvin McDowell repeatedly regaled him with a self-serving yarn of Porter's treachery at Bull Run. According to the *Telegraph*, Burnside and Pleasonton had both accused Porter "of refusing or neglecting to send reinforcements when they were needed." With a suspiciously vague reference to the original source of that story, too, the editor hypothesized that the charges "will be investigated on an early occasion," along with those of Pope.[7]

Two days later the *Chicago Tribune* reiterated that tale in different comments made by its correspondents in Washington and in the Illinois capital, Springfield. Offering information that must have been leaked near the top of the War Department, the *Tribune*'s Washington observer mentioned McClellan's strange telegram asking Porter to give Pope his full support. Further betraying his reliance on a cabinet-level informant, the correspondent speculated hopefully on Porter's case being taken up by a military commission presided over by Major General David Hunter. The president had recently relieved Hunter of command in South Carolina for proclaiming local emancipation, and he was the most prominent of relatively few Radical officers from the Regular Army: a prosecutor would covet that idle general as a judge of Porter's conduct, and Hunter headed the War Department's list of potential court-martial presidents. It was almost certainly no coincidence that Hunter was also stopping at Chase's house about that time, taking a chair at the dinner table along with Garfield.[8]

Those alarming newspaper stories surprised Porter, whose annoyance with Burnside had dissipated as the apparent threat of a court-martial receded. His report of the Maryland campaign, dated October 1, had taken a generous tone toward Burnside, whom he described as "gallantly and effectually" clearing Fox's Gap. Porter's complaints of Burnside blocking the road there and cutting off the march of the artillery reserve on September 15 survived in official records, but in his report he obscured the first incident and attributed the latter to accident.[9]

George Smalley's Antietam story, with its wild overestimate of Porter's available force and speculation on his thoughts, had resurrected the suspicion that he sought to engineer defeat. The *Chicago Tribune* article in particular revealed that powerful government officials were striving to further that impression by sharing official communications held by Stanton's department. In light of the embarrassing dispatches Burnside had passed on to Lincoln, it seemed perfectly plausible to Porter that his erstwhile friend had filed formal charges against him. He wrote first to headquarters to see if such charges had been presented, and then to Burnside, asking if he had filed any. Burnside assured him he had not, noting that McClellan had been the one to refuse the reinforcements.[10]

In truth, Burnside's staff remained livid over the failure to send those reinforcements, and Burnside struggled with his own disappointment and anger over McClellan's part in it.[11] Marcy later relayed Burnside's admission that once, when he was a little too much in liquor, he actually had groused to other officers about Porter refusing him aid. Porter nevertheless accepted the denial on its face. On the day Porter received Burnside's reply, Lieutenant Weld described the two of them as "great friends," and disclaimed rumors of them falling out. Twelve days later, General Marcy also assured McClellan's friend Barlow of Burnside's fidelity.[12]

Early in October, the *Alexandria Gazette* announced War Department plans for a topographical survey of the Antietam battlefield, and supposed it would "exculpate" Porter from Burnside's charges. That was the last journalistic reference to any accusation from Burnside, but the notion of Porter subverting victory at Antietam had been fixed in the memory of the partisan public. If the assurances from Lincoln and Burnside relieved Porter momentarily, optimism was not justified. Smalley's *Tribune* piece may have helped to poison even the president's mind against both Porter and McClellan: if a reminiscence recorded half a century later can be trusted, when Lincoln returned from visiting the army he was still muttering about Porter's "large reserve corps" sitting idle at Antietam.[13]

Many officers brought their wives down to their headquarters camps that autumn. Burnside's came early in October. Sykes raced to Baltimore to visit his own wife, after denying repeated requests from the commander of one of his regiments for leave to see his. McClellan slipped away to collect Ellen a few days later, leaving on the day after a thoroughly frustrated Halleck relayed the president's orders to "cross the Potomac and give battle to the enemy or drive him south." Lincoln had offered him tentative permission to visit his family, implying a preference for Mrs. McClellan coming to Washington, but McClellan went to Philadelphia to fetch her, sneaking off in a special rail car, wearing civilian clothes.[14]

Porter also sent for Hattie, who came down by rail as far as Hagerstown. He rode up there in an ambulance on October 7 with Lieutenant Weld, passing the pockmarked Dunker church, the wreckage of fences and trees, and endless mounded graves along the turnpike. Hattie was waiting for them in Hagerstown when they arrived, at half past five that afternoon. She had brought their four-year-old boy, Holbrook, but had left the toddler, Lucia, with someone in New York. Porter's mother came in from St. James College to meet them, and the next day they all drove out to the college, where they spent the balance of their reunion.[15]

An embarrassing security breach marred the generals' domestic diversion. At daylight on October 10, J. E. B. Stuart crossed the Potomac in low water up-river from Williamsport with a couple of thousand cavalry and horse artillery, scattering Union videttes there and reaching Mercersburg, Pennsylvania, by noon. He cast a covetous glance down the road to Hagerstown, where vast military stores had been stockpiled for McClellan's army. The Yankee videttes would already have carried the news of his presence to that depot, so Stuart turned the column toward Chambersburg, riding into that town and bivouacking there in the rain, after dark. Early in the morning his men burned the railroad station, machine shops, and storage sheds containing at least five thousand new firearms and great quantities of clothing. From there they reined back toward the Potomac, dodging one way and another to confuse pursuit and finally aiming for Leesburg, twenty miles downstream from the McClellans' hideaway.[16]

Sequestered with his family in a house at Knoxville, on the Maryland side below Harper's Ferry, McClellan knew nothing of the raid until very late in the afternoon of the tenth. Burnside's personal secretary assumed that the commanding general was still in Philadelphia, which would have given Burnside command of the army as senior officer, but General Marcy fielded the first reports from headquarters after the middle of the afternoon. Halleck knew about the incursion before McClellan could report it to him: McClellan's 10:00 P.M. reply to Halleck's telegram was the first communication that day to bear his signature. Marcy ordered both Pleasonton and Averell to go after Stuart that night, but distance delayed the messages and neither of those cavalry forces started until early the next morning. Just after noon on October 11 McClellan ordered Burnside to send a couple of brigades from Harper's Ferry to defend supply depots at Frederick and on the Monocacy River, but the Rebel cavalry pushed its way across well beyond there before evening.[17]

With his troops and headquarters located between Sharpsburg and Shepherdstown, at the center of the army, Porter took no part in the efforts to check or pursue Stuart. From his lodging with his wife and mother at the college, ten miles away, he sent McClellan the reports and rumors that came his way. He wondered whether the raid was meant to interrupt McClellan's advance, remarking how badly McClellan's soldiers needed that destroyed clothing before taking the field. Soldiers throughout the army were still short of shoes, blankets, and apparel — especially overcoats — as McClellan had been pointing out since Halleck ordered him to go after Lee. Quartermaster General Meigs threw the responsibility on McClellan and his distribution system, insisting that sufficient shoes must already have reached the army or its nearest rail depots. McClellan's chief quartermaster in turn blamed subordinate quartermasters within the army for tardiness in calling for what they needed.[18]

Porter suspected that the enemy was benefiting from information conveyed by the Confederate surgeons and nurses tending their own wounded within Union lines, and he advised their removal to a more secure location. Three days after Stuart disappeared back into Virginia, those Rebel doctors and hospital stewards started crowing about Lee's army fording the Potomac again, upriver. It seemed impossible for a large body of Rebels to have passed the line of pickets unreported, but low water made the boast more credible. Halleck also feared a raid farther down the river. Twice in two days he blamed such forays on the torpor of McClellan's army, once passing on Lincoln's wry observation that "if the enemy had more occupation south of the river, his cavalry would not be so likely to make raids north of it."[19]

While McClellan haggled with Washington over how many horses, tents, and shoes his army needed, and had received, he instructed Porter to reconnoiter the Confederate presence across the river. Porter was ailing again, but from his sickroom at the college he selected the troops for the expedition, relying on Andrew Humphreys to lead a division-sized force from the Fifth Corps into Virginia to feel around for Lee's army.[20]

This was a preliminary to the grand advance, Porter surely knew, and all those conjugal visits did hint at the coming of another campaign, for which Washington had been clamoring. Harriet Porter must have felt some relief at the army getting under way, for she sensed official impatience and had urged her husband that it was time to "get a move on, ready or not."[21] Porter was arranging for her return to New York when a summons to Washington arrived for him. Probably at the urging of Seward and Stanton, John Martindale had belatedly requested a court of inquiry about Porter's accusations concerning Malvern Hill, and that court finally wanted to hear from Porter.[22]

As the source of the charges, Porter should have been the first witness, but the inquiry had been proceeding for over a week when the notice reached him on the night of October 15. This court harbored at least as much antagonism toward Porter as the one Halleck had adjourned in Porter's case: the three members included the intensely hostile Silas Casey as well as David Birney, a confirmed abolitionist and McClellan antagonist. Presiding was General William Harney, who nursed a grudge over Porter's interference in Harney's St. Louis command in 1861. Porter, who was still quite sick on the afternoon of October 16, wished to testify because he felt the case reflected on his reputation. He would not yet have read the report on the early proceedings in the *New York Herald* of October 14, in which a reporter ventured the opinion that the charges against Martindale seemed "absurd." Porter asked Marcy if there was a possibility he could go to Washington on Saturday, the eighteenth.[23]

Humphreys had found the Confederate army still lingering in its camps near Winchester, so no enemy offensive lay in the offing. McClellan gave Porter leave to go, but he wired Halleck that Porter and several of his senior officers had all been subpoenaed, and he hoped their testimony could be taken promptly so they could return to duty. In company with Lieutenant Weld, Porter reached Willard's Hotel late Saturday evening and was allowed to testify on Monday. He told of seeing Martindale in the retreat without his command early on July 2, and explained that he only learned of the surrender proposal afterward. Nothing he said could have been considered a defense of his own reputation, and he added little to the prosecution's evidence except as yet another witness to Martindale abandoning his troops.[24]

Porter loitered in Washington through Tuesday as well, while Morell and Fred Locke took the stand. Like Porter, Locke, and later Griffin, Morell confirmed that Martindale rode on to Harrison's Landing alone, leaving his brigade to find its own way. Morell also corroborated that Martindale had suggested surrender, but while he thought it "improper" he did not consider it "misbehavior before the enemy" — which was the specific charge selected by the judge advocate of the court, based on the nature of Porter's complaint. Morell also rated Martindale's conduct at all the other Peninsula battles as "perfectly good." Numerous field officers in Martindale's former brigade contradicted that comment a few weeks later, alleging several instances of incompetence and cowardice.[25]

Some of those contradictory observations included admissions that Martindale's troops no longer wanted to serve under him, which would have heightened Porter's desire to be rid of him. Had Porter not put his complaints on paper, and asked to have Martindale informed of them, he might have succeeded in removing him without the court of inquiry. Whether he had wanted Martindale to know from a sense of fairness, or as a challenge to him to ask for an inquiry, the case ended in Porter's embarrassment. Martindale's main defense consisted of attacking his former corps commander for trying to remove him from command of his brigade with no chance of a trial—although Porter had deliberately presented him with the opportunity to request one. He insinuated that Porter himself had something to hide, asking whether such injustice was the mark of "a good man, conscious of his own integrity and impartiality and invulnerability." Assailing Porter's competence as well, Martindale implied that he would overlook Porter's treatment of him "if he will win one victory, by his talents or by accident."

Martindale leveled so searing an indictment of his accuser that it might have come from the lips of Edwin Stanton. "In this hour of peril," he concluded, "the country demands the services of brave Generals, who will not misbehave before the enemy, and of those also who are capable of achieving results by their gains—not those whom the obligations of juvenile friendship have exalted to positions for which they have neither proportionate experience, ability or patriotism."[26]

The court ultimately agreed that advocating surrender was "reprehensible," and "blameworthy," and conceded that an officer's place was "undoubtedly in most cases with his troops," but refused to find Martindale guilty. Harney, Casey, and Birney instead accepted Martindale's implied excuse that McClellan had demoralized him, citing "mitigating circumstances . . . which would involve the subject of the conduct of the operations of the Army in its retreat to James River." By dint of convoluted syntax, the New York Tribune granted Martindale front-page exoneration, asserting that "the Court of Inquiry . . . fully acquits that officer."[27]

Porter knew none of this for another week. Returning to Harper's Ferry on the morning train of October 22, he rode by McClellan's lodging on his way back to camp, where they had a chance to discuss his impressions of the trial over a meal that afternoon. He reached his own headquarters a little after sunset. The next day he resumed preparations for the movement Halleck had ordered October 6, inspecting the readiness of the various regiments and finding a disturbing proportion of his troops still lacking basic field equipment.[28]

Porter, Franklin, and John Reynolds had submitted lists of needed items on October 7. Some of that requisition did not reach Hagerstown until October 18, and distribution from there proceeded so slowly that new needs had already developed by the time the first shipments were delivered. On October 16 Porter had sent every wagon he had to Hagerstown for the rumored arrival of the requested clothing, but a week later the Fifth Corps still badly needed blankets, shoes, and overcoats. In Washington Porter had appealed to General Meigs, who claimed that twenty thousand more uniforms had been sent to the army than were requisitioned, again blaming inefficient distribution. That did seem to be part of the problem, but Porter put the onus for it on the quarter-master department, outside McClellan's authority. He complained that all his trains had to travel to the Hagerstown or Harper's Ferry depots and wait two or three days at a time in thousand-wagon lines when they were also needed to bring food and forage into camp. That consumed inordinate time and labor, he pointed out, suggesting that it would be faster and not keep all the army's transportation standing idle if the quartermaster department delivered supplies directly to each corps.[29]

Newspapers were sounding the alarm about autumn rains, nightly freezes, and daily thaws that would soften the roads and immobilize the army, but they flavored their warnings with partisan explanations for the army's inactivity. Democratic editors blamed sluggish supplies from Stanton's War Department; their Republican counterparts accused McClellan of deliberately and treacherously procrastinating, so as to exhaust the nation's resources and will to fight.[30]

To the dismay of McClellan's followers in the army, late in October Republican papers critical of him giddily credited gossip that he had been removed from command in favor of Joe Hooker. An ominous outburst from the president seemed to lend substance to it: McClellan mentioned his fatigued horses in a telegram, and in his reply Lincoln wondered what the army's horses had done since Antietam that fatigued "anything." Executive patience was clearly wearing thin, especially since Stuart's raid, and the army felt that mounting frustration. Officers began expressing their dread at losing McClellan, partly from personal regard and partly because he had "a certain hold upon the men individually, which no one else has or can get."[31]

Under imminent orders to move, Porter spent the evening of October 28 frantically telegraphing every department head in the army about the legions of sick men who would be left hungry and uncared for when he left Sharpsburg. Quite a few soldiers in his corps remained without serviceable shoes the next day, but on the morning of October 30 they dismantled their camp of the past six weeks. Sykes and Humphreys started their troops down the road toward Harper's Ferry, leaving Morell's division to follow later under its new commander, Dan Butterfield; Morell remained behind, assigned to troops guarding the Potomac.[32]

Porter and his staff avoided the dust by taking a byway parallel to the road traveled by the troops. As they ambled along through that Indian summer afternoon, Porter treated Lieutenant Weld to a disquisition on the war situation similar to the one he had provided to Marble at the *World*. He dwelt mainly on President Lincoln, whose management of the army he cast as inept interference, and whose political policies he deemed inadvisable and counterproductive. Porter did not have to remind his aide about the withholding of McDowell's corps, or the appointment of Pope. In light of such blunders, Weld thought his father would agree that they had "had enough of civilians like the President undertaking to manage a campaign."

What may have surprised the lieutenant was Porter's opposition to the proclamation the president had issued in the wake of Antietam, threatening to abolish slavery in all states that failed to forsake rebellion by January 1. The best and quickest way to defeat rebellion, Porter maintained, was essentially to follow Winfield Scott's underrated Anaconda Plan of 1861: seize all seaports, seal off the Ohio and Mississippi Rivers, divide the interior by incursions from that perimeter, and "starve and freeze the people" to turn them against the "wicked men" who had seduced them into secession. Threatening to free the slaves, Porter lamented, would only subvert that strategy by convincing all Southerners to resist, and to sustain their leaders instead of abandoning them. From the purely military perspective, Weld found his general's argument perfectly logical.[33]

McClellan, of course, shared Porter's view of the proclamation, as his letter to Lincoln at Harrison's Landing had foretold. Lincoln evidently spoke with McClellan about his proclamation during his October visit, for McClellan touched on it a few days later in a general order issued to the Army of the Potomac. As Porter had told Marble, and as a *New York Herald* chief in Washington had learned from myriad officers, the proclamation had angered and discouraged many soldiers who would have to fight a more determined enemy because of it. McClellan made only a sidelong reference to the proclamation in his order, devoting the bulk of it to the principle of civilian control over the military. Besides providing a cryptic explanation for his silence on the decree, which nearly everyone knew he opposed, McClellan's affirmation of a soldier's duty to sustain civil policy included an implied defense of the soldier's right to dissent. Discussions in the army about government policies tended to erode discipline and hamper efficiency, he cautioned, if they were "carried at all beyond temperate and respectful expressions of opinion." The order offered no hint of support for the proclamation, which Lincoln must have desired but probably did not expect; McClellan merely defined the limits within which those in uniform could criticize such a decree.[34]

Neither Porter nor Weld betrayed any sense that their private conversation on the subject exceeded the bounds of "temperate and respectful expressions of opinion." Despite disagreeing with administration policy, and opposing it in private, both gave the "firm, steady, and earnest support of the authority of the Government" that McClellan's order identified as "the highest duty of the American soldier."[35] Over the next thirty months Weld would repeatedly demonstrate his own devotion to his country's cause even as he fulminated over the president's military interference and "suicidal policy."[36] He never entertained a moment's doubt that his corps commander cherished a similar ambition to defeat the enemy, but Porter would not have another opportunity to prove it.

McClellan and most of the army rumbled across the Potomac on a pontoon bridge seven miles downriver from Harper's Ferry. On November 1 the Fifth Corps followed Darius Couch and the Second Corps over another span of pontoons into Harper's Ferry, where Porter shod the last of his troops with a supply of brogans that had been reserved for him. Marching over the Blue Ridge and then south, down the eastern slope of that range, Couch and Porter guarded the mountain gaps against any surprises from the Shenandoah Valley. Traveling in the vanguard of the corps with Sykes, Porter had not made six miles when he heard the echo of artillery fire ahead of him. He supposed it came from Couch's forces, trying to seize Snicker's Gap, but the sound probably heralded Pleasonton sparring with Stuart's cavalry.[37]

Stonewall Jackson remained on the far side of the Blue Ridge to delay, harass, and discourage McClellan's movements, but Longstreet was making tracks south with the right wing of Lee's army, to put himself in front of McClellan. On October 28, Longstreet left the vicinity of Winchester, sending his corps toward Culpeper in fragments over the next couple of days. Shielded by the Blue Ridge from the nearest Yankee cavalry, his columns were able to move quickly without fear of attacks from the flank or front, and one brigade covered more than sixty-five miles in four days. The first of Longstreet's men fell out near Culpeper at least by November 3, and most of the rest arrived the next day, while Porter was still guarding the gaps near Snickersville, no more than twenty miles from Harper's Ferry.[38]

Having just suffered the humiliation of another circumnavigation of his army by Rebel cavalry, McClellan dared not relax his customary caution. Apprehensive about Rebels whom Porter could see from the mountain passes, McClellan himself had ventured only as far as Upperville that day, thirty miles from his own crossing of the Potomac. Pleasonton had learned of Longstreet moving to Front Royal as early as the evening of November 2, on the first leg of his march to Culpeper, and the next day Sykes captured a prisoner at Snicker's Gap who confirmed it. From atop the Blue Ridge, one of Sykes's staff officers put a spyglass on a sprawling enemy camp beyond Berryville, over ten miles away, but from the same vantage point Confederate wagon trains could be seen moving south. Then Couch reported that local residents said Jackson was headed that way with his corps, too.[39]

Those reports convinced McClellan that Lee had abandoned the Shenandoah Valley and was racing to block his path to Richmond. At midafternoon of November 4, McClellan asked Porter to pull his troops out of Snicker's Gap and put them on the road to Upperville the next day "if there is no enemy in front of you." Porter sent back word that he faced at least an oversized brigade, and quite possibly more, with a couple of batteries. That evening McClellan reiterated his opinion that no sizable enemy force remained in the Shenandoah Valley, but he allowed Porter to postpone his departure until November 6; he also cautioned him not to send any more empty supply wagons to Harper's Ferry, and to hurry on those coming back with provisions. In fact, half the Rebel army remained in the Shenandoah, for Couch's informants had mistaken Longstreet's column for Jackson's. The error elicited unaccustomed haste from McClellan, whose belief that Lee's whole army had gone ahead of him overcame his usual fear of threats to his flank. Burnside, Franklin, and John Reynolds—now commanding Hooker's First Corps—each shifted fifteen to twenty miles south on November 5. Porter followed the next day, pulling the Regulars off the gap in the morning and camping twenty-two miles away that night; he positioned his cavalry at the rear of the column, to drive his infantry ahead and bring in stragglers. Lee himself noticed the accelerated pace, remarking nervously that McClellan's army was showing "more activity than usual."[40]

This was the vigor Lincoln had been hoping for from McClellan since Antietam, but it came too late. On November 5 the president gave Halleck an order relieving McClellan from command of the Army of the Potomac and appointing Burnside to his place. Among other details in the same order, he removed Porter from the Fifth Corps.[41]

Later the president told a story of having secretly devised a "test" to determine whether McClellan would keep his command. As his secretary John Hay recorded it from a personal interview nearly two years later, Lincoln saw that McClellan had the shorter road to Richmond and could "intercept" Lee as he hurried back to defend his capital. The test was whether he allowed the Confederate army to slip past him. "If he let them get away," Hay remembered Lincoln telling him, "I would remove him. He did so & I relieved him."[42]

The problem with this story is that when Lincoln wrote the order he did not yet know of any Confederate force ahead of McClellan beyond the usual cavalry. Most of Longstreet's infantry had already camped near Culpeper for a full day, and much of it for two, but as late as the final hour of November 5 McClellan knew nothing of that. In order to reach Washington by the time Lincoln authorized the change in command, word of Longstreet's arrival would have had to leak through or around McClellan's lines without anyone in his army knowing about it. Washington's *Evening Star* of November 4 published a rumor of thousands of Confederates at Warrenton, and the editor somehow interpreted this to mean that Longstreet was "in full retreat" for Culpeper. Equally inaccurate reports elsewhere placed Longstreet's entire force at either Snicker's Gap or Petersburg, a hundred and fifty miles away, and one paper confidently offered both contradictory reports on different pages of the same edition. No one in Washington appears to have been sure where Longstreet was on November 4 or, for that matter, on November 5; neither did anyone know that any significant enemy contingent had outdistanced McClellan. The city's first news of a large Confederate force at Culpeper, ahead of McClellan, came in the *Evening Star* of November 7.[43]

Lincoln simply could not have had the information on which he was later said to have based his decision. He was also accused of having waited to fire McClellan only until after the New York state elections of November 4, after which no blow at the Democrat McClellan could do further electoral harm to Republican candidates. For so attentive a politician as Lincoln, that finale to the annual cycle of state elections more likely dictated the timing, but he had probably been waiting several weeks for an advantageous opportunity to dismiss his dilatory general. The little fable Hay attributed to the president merely attempted to allay the stench of premeditation and political calculation that emanated from the order.

The tale may also have been designed to shield others who contributed to McClellan's removal—or thought they had. There had been a cabinet meeting on November 4 in which the increasingly hostile Stanton had complained of McClellan once again, sputtering that Halleck had given up trying to manage him. Lincoln revealed that he had offered to remove McClellan whenever Halleck wished, and to take the responsibility for doing so.[44] It would have been unusual if, once armed with such information, the scheming and domineering Stanton did not immediately start badgering Halleck to ask for McClellan's dismissal. It would also have been characteristic for the timid Halleck to comply, and for the president to abide by his promise to assume full blame for making the decision. The added touch of relieving Porter hinted further at the involvement of Stanton, who had stalked Porter as McClellan's surrogate since early September. Yet Stanton was not the only man in the administration ill-disposed toward Porter. It had been Lincoln, after all, who had rekindled John Pope's wrath by alerting him to the insulting dispatches to Burnside, without which Pope would have had less impulse to destroy Porter, and no ammunition with which to do it.

Stanton revealed the depth of his paranoia in the precautions he took for the delivery of the order. So fearful was he that McClellan might resist removal, and use the army to seize control of the government, that he arranged a complicated choreography designed to avoid a military coup. Separating the details of the order, he included only the relief of McClellan and ignored the sentence pertaining to Porter, who could easily be eliminated once McClellan was deposed. He entrusted the dispatch to Catharinus P. Buckingham, a former professor from Stanton's alma mater whom he had brought into the War Department for "special service" such as he was about to undertake. A special train was arranged to carry General Buckingham as close to the army as possible, after which he was to obtain a horse and find Burnside's headquarters. If Burnside refused the command, as he had already done twice before, Buckingham was to return to Washington without delivering the order. If Burnside accepted it, he and Buckingham were to go to McClellan together and inform him.

Buckingham arrived at Burnside's camp in the vortex of a heavy snowstorm, late on November 7. Burnside did remonstrate with him for a time, but with Buckingham's advice and that of his own staff he finally accepted, and the two of them proceeded through the blizzard to McClellan's tent. McClellan read the order and acquiesced without hesitation.[45]

Having fought four pitched battles under McClellan's orders and witnessed a fifth, all within sixteen weeks, Porter instinctively rejected the complaint that Little Mac would not fight. Venting his fury at the removal in another letter to Manton Marble, he wondered what possible justification there could have been for replacing a general "in the midst of a campaign, on the eve of, perhaps, an important and general battle." He predicted that the change might forestall aggressive activity for the rest of November and perhaps through the winter. Recognizing that Burnside had been promoted to reduce any impulse to rebellion among the troops, who saw him as McClellan's friend, Porter feared that Burnside merely stood as a placeholder for Hooker—or worse yet, Frémont.

"You may soon expect to hear that my head is lopped," Porter added presciently, expecting to face charges vaguely related to the accusations of Martindale, who had defended himself with aspersions on Porter and McClellan. Then there was the false newspaper report of Burnside levying charges against him, and the embers of trouble over Pope, which could be fanned back to life by one of his enemies in the army or administration. His disparaging telegrams to Burnside were "in their possession," he told Marble, "and brought up against me as proof of intention to cause disaster."[46]

Instead of leading the revolt Stanton had feared, McClellan stayed on for a couple of days to help Burnside with the transition. Burnside arranged one last grand review in honor of McClellan, who bid farewell to his army on November 10 in a display remarkable for the emotions recorded by those who saw it. The assorted corps lined up facing each other on either side of the Warrenton Turnpike, and as the echo of a sixteen-gun salute faded into the crisp air McClellan trotted between the ranked flags and men, just ahead of his staff. The cheers came louder than ever, wrote a young captain who would be killed a month later: "Everything showed that the army was still his."[47]

Officers described their men as outraged, disheartened, and depressed over the government taking their general away—"in a perfect uproar about it," admitted a Regular Army captain. "Every body has on a scowl," wrote the adjutant of a Maryland battery. "Soldiers swear they will fight no longer," he added, while the officers sputtered about resigning. "Very many of the men wept like children," noticed a field officer in the First Corps, most of which had served under McClellan for only two months; he watched men turn to gaze after the passing general "in mute grief, one may almost say despair." A captain in the Pennsylvania Reserves remarked on the depth of the gloom cast over the army, and a colonel in the Second Corps wrote that when McClellan left he took "the heart of the Army with him." Startled by the smoldering anger of their men, company and field grade officers believed the president had made an enormous mistake.[48]

The most poignant displays of affection arose in the Fifth Corps, where endless cheers greeted McClellan as the cannon saluted him. "The army is in tears," observed a Pennsylvania captain, and on returning to camp a Michigan sergeant wrote home that "the Army of the Potomac has just returned from its own funeral." Another sergeant who watched officers of the Fifth Corps offering their personal good-byes to McClellan had never seen them so disheartened.[49]

No sooner had McClellan's last review broken up than the Fifth Corps learned that Porter had also been ordered to leave them and report to Washington, as he had expected. The absurdity of Stanton's neurotic precautions must have become apparent even to the secretary himself, for he sent this order by telegraph, in the clear, on November 10. The Fifth Corps turned out again the next day, to bid adieu to the man for whom it had been organized.[50]

The sun rose bright in a blue sky that November 11, burning off the frost of the previous night, but a biting chill lingered. Eight brigades of infantry, nine batteries, and four regiments of cavalry assembled for Porter, representing nearly twenty thousand men, and he rode before them slowly, cap in hand and head bowed. As he passed in front of the Regulars in Sykes's division the band struck up "Auld Lang Syne," and he said good-bye to each of the officers, many of whom he had known since their cadet days. Floating crisply through the bittersweet autumn air, the notes wrought the intended nostalgia, and a captain in the front rank of the 11th Infantry detected the sadness glistening in Porter's eyes. "Don't think the tears theatrical," he cautioned his mother; "our lives have been in his hands so long, so many of us have gone to bloody graves, we have been together under fire so often, relying upon him always, that it is no wonder his feelings were somewhat excited at leaving us." Fifth Corps veterans remembering that adieu to their general a quarter of a century later agreed that "it was enough to move a heart of stone."[51]

Already desolate over the loss of McClellan, men who had known no other corps commander turned downright melancholy at the departure of Porter. A Massachusetts captain who had sensed the atmosphere of a funeral at McClellan's farewell review turned visibly angry after Porter's, damning "sneaking Politicians" for depriving the army of one of its best officers. George Millens, who had served under him from the day he arrived in the Army of the Potomac, characterized the corps as "pretty down about their taking Porter away." A lieutenant in the same company as Millens corroborated his observation, noting in his diary as Porter left for Washington that "the gloom thickens."[52]

The news of Porter's removal exhilarated Pope and his friends, whose whispered fantasies of Porter's treachery built momentum for a criminal case against him. William Butler—the state treasurer of Illinois, a friend of President Lincoln, and the father of one of John Pope's staff officers—had been commiserating with Pope since at least August about the treachery of the McClellan circle. During the course of their communication Pope had made some uncomplimentary remarks about his own superiors: for reinstating McClellan, Lincoln had been guilty of "feeble cowardly & shameful conduct," Pope wrote, adding that his commander in chief had "sold or given himself away to the Devil." Echoing his communications with Pope, Butler told Senator Orville Hickman Browning on November 12 that the government now had the goods on Porter. Passing on the sort of prevarication by which Pope hoped to vindicate himself, Butler told Browning that a message from Porter had been intercepted advising McClellan to withhold reinforcements because "we have Pope where we can ruin him."[53]

Leaving his horse at the railhead, Porter boarded a car of the Orange & Alexandria and arrived in Washington on November 13, accompanied by Lieutenant Weld. After reporting to the adjutant general's office in the War Department, as ordered, he repaired to his customary quarters at Willard's to await the administrative blow he anticipated. War Department leaks corroborated his suspicions through Washington newspapers, which reported that he would be investigated "for failing to support Gen. Pope" as soon as Pope could be brought back to the capital. From such sources and driblets of capital hearsay, Weld deduced that "every effort will be made to crush General Porter." When Dan Butterfield offered the lieutenant a place on his staff, the youth declined, opting to "hang on to General Porter through thick and thin."

"He is a brave, generous and good man," Weld explained to his father, "and he has a pack of cunning, wicked and lying men who are trying to hunt him down."[54]

Weld also alerted his father that he did not consider the mail a safe means of communication just then. Porter and McClellan both believed that postmasters had been instructed to set aside any letters they saw addressed to either of them, so that War Department snoops could open them for inspection. This seemed less preposterous a suspicion with an enemy such as Stanton targeting both of them, and messages that later went undelivered, or came opened, gave substance to their apprehension. Porter may have been doubly vulnerable: even if his mail reached the front desk of Willard's, one of McDowell's aides was half-owner of the hotel.[55]

Two days after he reached the city, Porter tried to end the uncertainty and bring things to a head, asking again for an investigation into the alleged charges Pope had made. That elicited a prompt response from Halleck, and a few evenings later Porter picked up an order establishing a military commission "to examine and report upon" Pope's charges. The commission was ordered to meet on November 20, and on the evening of the eighteenth Porter asked both Halleck and Joseph Holt for a copy of the portion of Pope's report that included his accusations. Both professed not to have the report, claiming it was in the hands of the secretary of war. The next morning Porter made the same request to the adjutant general's office, without response.[56]

The men appointed to the commission more ominously reflected the hand of Edwin Stanton than even Porter may have supposed. The dutifully antagonistic Washington correspondent of the *Chicago Tribune* recognized as much, crediting "the energy and persistence of Secretary Stanton, who was determined that the trial should proceed." Describing Porter as "the malignant spirit" of a conspiracy "to retard the suppression of the rebellion," the *Tribune*'s man assured his readers that all this would be revealed by a thorough investigation of "all the charges" — none of which were then known to anyone.[57]

Named to preside over the inquiry was David Hunter, the Radical general whom the same *Tribune* correspondent had previously admitted he would have selected to judge Porter; Hunter had already acted with noticeable coolness toward Porter in a casual encounter at Willard's. James Garfield, then living with Secretary Chase, had spent weeks aghast at Chase's and Irvin McDowell's prejudicial stories about McClellan and Porter, and Garfield's failure to recuse himself strongly implied a determination to put his bias to work. Benjamin Prentiss, a brigadier just released from captivity, was already making politically telltale speeches praising the president's proclamation on slavery. Napoleon Buford, the older half-brother of cavalryman John Buford, had returned to military service after a quarter-century hiatus, and he had attracted the attention of Edwin Stanton for reasons no one could fathom: Stanton had once impulsively considered him as a potential successor to McClellan. Brevet Brigadier General William W. Morris, a brevet brigadier with over forty years of service, completed the commission.[58]

At its inaugural meeting on November 20, the commission quickly adjourned until November 25. Porter paid $300 to retain a pair of lawyers, choosing the highly regarded Charles Eames, who lived three blocks from Willard's, and Eames's associate Reverdy Johnson, of Baltimore. Then he asked permission to go to New York for the weekend to see his family, probably so he could ask Harriet's aunt, Mrs. Holbrook, if she would lend him the balance of his attorneys' thousand-dollar fee. He did not mention that he hoped to speak to Johnson, who was also in New York just then, and he probably wished to consult with McClellan, too. In a demonstration of arbitrary antagonism more typical of the secretary of war than the general-in-chief, Halleck's office flatly denied that request.[59]

After a week of paying his own way at the hotel, Porter asked whether he would be provided with quarters and fuel, or with the customary compensation for those costs. His question was indirectly answered on November 25, when the military commission was abruptly dissolved without a finding. Stanton and Holt had apparently decided to forego a fact-finding commission and move directly to a court-martial. Porter was ordered in arrest until he could be tried on "the charges preferred by Major General John Pope," and he could hardly be expected to pay for his own incarceration. Once again, he asked for a copy of the charges, and to have the limits of his arrest defined. He specifically asked for the freedom to move about Washington and Georgetown, where one of his lawyers and several of his witnesses then lodged. That, too, was refused. Like most officers under arrest, he was trusted to keep within prescribed bounds without guards — but, in what could easily be interpreted as an effort to inhibit his ability to mount an effective defense, he was ordered not to leave the hotel.[60]

"From all I hear," he forewarned Harriet, "I am confident of the determination to break me down — on political grounds." He had numerous friends in the adjutant general's office, and at least one in the War Department, who kept him abreast of what they knew. It was probably Assistant Secretary of War John Tucker, who had provided steamers to hasten Porter 's corps to Pope's aid, who told of plans to devise charges that were technically true, and difficult to refute or mitigate.[61]

As Tucker also noticed — and as had been the case in the military commission — the selection of officers for the court betrayed an effort to orchestrate a conviction. The members of the dissolved commission were simply reappointed, including Prentiss, Buford, Morris, and the thoroughly prejudiced Garfield, with the hostile Hunter again presiding. In his eagerness to influence the outcome, Stanton invited Buford and his wife to his home for Thanksgiving dinner on November 27, only hours after the first meeting of the court. Also present at Stanton's table was Ethan Allen Hitchcock, another aging officer Stanton had pulled out of retirement for "special" services — and those services now included sitting on Porter's court. The next day Halleck showed Hitchcock correspondence from the president that put McClellan in a bad light, and Chase may have worked on Buford himself: Porter later asserted that John Buford, another friend of his, warned him that Chase had lobbied his half-brother for conviction.[62]

Three members of the court should never have been appointed, or should have recused themselves over glaring conflicts of interest. Two of them — Rufus King and James Ricketts — could avoid their share of blame for the disaster at Bull Run by finding Porter primarily responsible. Silas Casey obviously resented Porter for asking McClellan to remove him from command of the Pennsylvania Reserves.

Thus, four members of the court had been curried in the dining rooms of

Porter's two worst enemies in the cabinet, and three others had good reasons for wishing to see him found guilty. That left only General Prentiss and General Morris. Prentiss espoused politics antithetical to McClellan and Porter, but that was the extent of his potential antagonism. Morris, the junior member of the court in rank but the oldest in years, had been an officer in the 4th U.S. Artillery throughout Porter's time in that regiment. He was twenty-one years Porter's senior, and had graduated from West Point a quarter of a century before him, but they had both held the rank of brevet major for many years. Undoubtedly they knew each other, and perhaps well, because a generation later Porter still referred to him as "Major Morris." Morris raised a question about the legality of the court and was promptly removed, to be replaced by Brigadier General John P. Slough, whose Ohio schoolmate described him as "a warm personal friend of Secretary Stanton." With the possible exception of Prentiss, that tainted every member of the court with some measure of bias, all of it leaning against Porter.[63]

Nor did that mark the limit of official prejudice against the defendant, for any guilty verdict or sentence would have to be reviewed and approved, first by Judge Advocate General Holt and then by the president. The conniving Holt posed no concern to those hoping for conviction, but Lincoln might, because he had shown softheartedness toward some men undone by courts-martial.

The afternoon following Slough's assignment, and before the official charges had even been put to paper, Senator Browning dropped in to see Lincoln at the White House, and their conversation turned to the trial. Without mentioning the Kennedy letter or the Burnside dispatches on which his belief was founded, the president admitted that he strongly suspected Porter of bad faith toward Pope. He told Browning he "very much hoped" the investigation would relieve him of that suspicion, but "at present" he believed that Porter had cost the country a decisive victory by disobeying Pope and refusing to go to his aid.[64]

Even if Porter's conviction had not promised the political benefits to Lincoln that it did, the president's admitted prejudgment would have made it difficult for him to review the case favorably without an abundance of exculpatory evidence. Joseph Holt would make certain the president saw none of that.

15

THE TRIAL

Joseph Holt did not complete the charges and specifications until Monday, December 1. As the court opened that morning Holt handed Porter a copy of that carefully crafted document, suggesting an adjournment to give him time to examine it. General Hunter, anxious to proceed, asked Porter if he did want time, and Porter asked for three days to review the charges and compile a list of witnesses. Without answering, Hunter ejected everyone else from the room — purportedly to discuss the absence of Rufus King. Half an hour later the doors reopened, but the court promptly adjourned until the next morning without giving Porter a reply.[1]

The question of King's attendance was not an issue that seemed to require secret discussion, and that may have been an excuse for Holt to convey privately his real reason for proposing a delay. His primary witness, General Pope, had arrived in Washington only that morning, and Holt would have wished to consult with him about his testimony before putting him on the stand. When Pope finally did take the stand, it became evident that he had been the beneficiary of serious coaching.

Porter's request for three days of preparation remained unanswered on Tuesday, when the court again met briefly, and in the end he was given only as much time as it took General King to reach the capital. King was sitting at the table on Wednesday morning, December 3, and General Hunter showed great impatience to begin. He called Porter to the table and asked for any objections he might have to anyone named to the court detail.

The only members with obvious conflicts of interest were King and Ricketts, who bore some responsibility for the defeat at Bull Run. Raising the issue of Casey's grudge might have worked against Porter, because it would require admitting that he had refused to accept Casey in his corps. Hunter's unfriendly social demeanor might have seemed a petty complaint. Porter was not yet aware of the largely successful efforts by Stanton and Chase to proselytize Hunter, Garfield, Hitchcock, and Buford, and he probably knew nothing of Slough's friendship with Stanton.

By the end of the trial, Porter's attorneys had deduced that most of the court members were determined to find their client guilty no matter how much evidence weighed against it. Every single objection was decided in favor of the prosecution, often through blatant hypocrisy, and Reverdy Johnson remarked that the rulings on evidence "were so superlatively absurd as to almost destroy every hope of justice."[2] Before such displays of bias, and without specific evidence of it, Porter's lawyers may have advised against any challenges, which probably would have been rejected anyway. The order creating the court had been designed to discourage any objection to the carefully chosen panel, ending with the assertion that "no other officers than those named can be assembled without manifest injury to the service."[3]

Instead, Porter put his faith in the power of the press, asking the court to open the courtroom not only to the public but to newspaper reporters, as well. Noting that General Halleck's recent report on the Bull Run campaign had recently been published, complete with prejudicial remarks about Porter, he asked essentially for equal time. Hunter again cleared the room so they could deliberate on that request, after which Holt announced that the trial would be held in the open "in accordance with the custom of the service," which should have made the deliberation unnecessary. Nearly every question in the case would be decided in similar secrecy, despite the pretense of transparency.[4]

Immediately thereafter, Holt began reading the two main charges, with their assorted specifications. First came the charge of violating the Ninth Article of War by disobeying a lawful order in the presence of the enemy, for which he provided five different specifications. The first charged that Porter had not heeded the order to march for Bristoe Station at 1:00 A.M. on August 27, which was technically true. Next came "disobedience" of the rambling joint order from the morning of August 29, for McDowell and Porter to proceed to Gainesville, which had been nearly as difficult to understand as it would have been to satisfy. The third specification cited Porter's failure to obey Pope's 4:30 order to attack the enemy's "flank."

The fourth and fifth specifications divided a single strained allegation into two parts: for each of the two brigades that went astray to Centreville on August 30, Holt charged a separate offense of disobeying Pope's 8:50 P.M. order for Porter to report to him with "your command."[5] He clearly aimed to list enough specifications that at least one might stick, but it would have been only slightly more illogical to create a different specification for each regiment as it was to establish one for each brigade. For that matter, if the failure to bring up every man in his command had constituted disobedience of the order, he could have been prosecuted for losing stragglers on the way, or detailing guards or hospital attendants to remain behind. Specification four, and especially specification five, bespoke a determination to find Porter guilty of something, however ridiculous.

The second overall charge cited misbehavior in the face of the enemy, which violated the Fifty-Second Article of War. This was a particularly obnoxious allegation for Porter, or for any officer who cherished his reputation, because it was the one levied against those guilty of cowardice. It was the accusation another judge advocate had chosen to test, unsuccessfully, against Martindale. By varying the syntax of a single inaccurate accusation, Holt concocted three separate violations involving Porter's failure to launch an attack in the dusk of August 29. First, he had violated the 4:30 order by not making the attack. Second, while under the belief that Pope was being defeated, Porter had "shamefully retreated" instead of going to his aid. The third specification was essentially the same as the second, except for the additional misinformation that Porter's "retreat" took him all the way to Manassas Junction, but it offered Holt a chance to use "shamefully" twice more.

A fourth specification related to Porter's attack of August 30, alleging that he had taken so long preparing for it that the enemy was ready for him, and insinuating that he had intended as much. Then, Holt claimed, Porter had struck Jackson's line with too little force to break it, and had fallen back, making insufficient effort to rally his troops. This lacked a shred of evidence, but Holt read it for the newspapers to publish before telling the court he would offer no proof for it — as though he had any to offer. That preposterous accusation nonetheless remained in the record, and in the papers.[6]

A guilty finding for any of those specifications would have put Porter's life in peril, because both charges carried a penalty of death, or whatever other punishment the court decided. Had there been any truth in the specifications of the second charge, a firing squad would not have been considered inappropriate.

Before entering pleas, Porter and his attorneys raised an objection that the prosecution appeared to have anticipated. The complainant whose name appeared on the charges was that of John Pope's inspector general, known to his more contemptuous old-army acquaintances as Benny Roberts. The order for the military commission, issued two weeks previously, had called for an investigation of charges preferred against Porter by Pope himself. The Articles of War decreed that "whenever a general officer commanding an army, or a colonel commanding a separate department, shall be the accuser or prosecutor of any officer in the army of the United States, under his command, the general court martial for the trial of such officer shall be appointed by the President of the United States." Giving Abraham Lincoln the choice of court members would have risked the danger of impartiality through either the accident of random selection or a conscious effort by Lincoln to avoid prejudice. As Stanton and Holt demonstrated repeatedly over the next five years, they collaborated through tacit understandings, rather than explicit conspiratorial conversations. One of them must have become aware of this obscure regulation, and realized that it would deprive them of the ability to install the desired court members through the malleable Halleck. That may have accounted for the sudden dissolution of the military commission, and it certainly explained the substitution of Roberts as the accuser.[7]

That change blunted the force of Porter's objection, but he asked if the court did not consider the complaint of a senior member of Pope's staff tantamount to an act by Pope himself. Ignoring Porter's point and simply noting that Pope's name was not on the charges, Holt vociferously and disingenuously denied Roberts's obvious service as Pope's proxy, although Pope himself privately admitted that he made the charges himself. Roberts and Thomas C. H. Smith had spent weeks preparing allegations against Porter while nominally on official duty under Pope, who badgered Halleck to promote both of them for their indispensable services. In the middle of November Pope had sent them to Washington in the same role Ruggles had refused to play—as his agents in prosecuting Porter.[8]

Hunter again cleared the room so Holt and his colleagues could discuss the question in secret, coming back into public session to overrule the objection and declare the court perfectly legal. In light of future actions, that decision was predictable, but Porter and his lawyers lacked the benefit of hindsight. With this ruling, however, the defense must have begun to suspect that even the most overwhelmingly favorable testimony and evidence might not yield an acquittal.[9]

The next day Pope appeared, and for the better part of December 4 Holt allowed him to tell the story of Second Bull Run as he wished to remember it. He depicted himself magnanimously overlooking Porter's late arrival on August 28; he indicated that both Porter and McDowell failed to comply with his joint order, but he characterized it as disobedience only in the case of Porter. Evidence of Holt's coaching emerged from such minor embellishments as Pope's description of his order for Porter to report in person on the morning of August 30: the order had directed Porter to march his "command" to the battlefield, but in his testimony Pope claimed that he told him to bring his "whole" command. This subtle and erroneous addition sustained the pretext behind specifications four and five of the first charge, which transformed a wrong turn by any part of Porter's corps into criminal disobedience of orders.[10]

Pope fared worse under questioning by Reverdy Johnson. General Garfield thought Johnson "fierce as a tiger" in cross-examination, and within a few questions Pope began contradicting himself.[11] First he could not positively deny having said that he was satisfied with Porter's explanation for his tardiness at Bristoe Station, yet he added that "it is quite impossible that I could have been satisfied." He initially dismissed his conversation with Porter at Fairfax Court House as not having lasted more than two or three minutes at the outside, but in the next answer he expanded that to a maximum of five minutes, and then allowed that it "might, perhaps, have been more." He admitted that there had been a few other people in the room, but claimed he could not remember who they were — although in response to the next question he named Hooker and McDowell, and speculated on Heintzelman; when reminded, he conceded the presence of Colonel Ruggles. Ruggles, who later estimated the conversation at twenty minutes long, would remember Pope concluding it by saying that he would take no action against Porter for his failure to comply with all his orders. Twenty-one questions into his cross-examination, Pope admitted as much himself, to his immediate regret.[12]

If he was so certain Porter's disobedience had caused his army defeat and put the nation's capital in jeopardy, asked Johnson, why would he at any moment thereafter have considered not taking action against him? By failing to prefer charges against Porter, Pope had demonstrated either gross negligence or satisfaction that Porter was not guilty. Pope saw the trap, and refused to answer. Hunter closed the courtroom again to "deliberate." When the public and principals returned, Holt simply announced that the question had been deemed irrelevant, and Pope would not have to answer. Porter immediately submitted a formal protest that his attorneys had written during the closed session, in anticipation of just such a response. How (wondered counsel for the accused) could an apparent contradiction so damaging to the reliability of the chief witness for the prosecution be anything but relevant? At that everyone was ejected from the room again while Holt, Hunter, and the rest of the court considered their dilemma, for even the correspondents of Radical newspapers saw Pope's credibility crumbling. Finally the doors swung open for the last time that day. After Holt promised to resume debate on the question in the morning, the court adjourned.[13]

Like Porter, Pope lodged at Willard's during the trial, which was held in the "old courtroom" above Ferdinand Butler's restaurant, across Pennsylvania Avenue near the corner of Fourteenth Street. Returning to his room that afternoon, Pope wrote a hasty note to Holt. Despite the pretense that he had nothing to do with the prosecution, he suggested that Benny Roberts be called to testify in the morning, so he could sit at Holt's elbow during the rest of the trial. As the nominal complainant, Roberts had every right under the Articles of War to join the prosecution, and Roberts could remind the judge advocate general of all the details of the campaign. Pope evidently hoped that his own ordeal was over, but the end was not yet. Sometime that evening or the next morning, Holt convened with him and hammered out a solution.[14]

When the trial resumed at 11:00 on the snowy morning of December 5, Holt asked the court's permission to answer the controversial question. Porter's corner made no objection, but Hunter called another closed-door parley. Having declared the question irrelevant, the court might have seemed hypocritical if it allowed Pope to answer it, and some of the more prejudiced members may have worried that the reply would only worsen Pope's evident inconsistency. No newspaperman recorded how long the court remained sequestered, but the trial record indicated that it was for "some time," during which Holt may have conveyed the gist of what Pope intended to say. The reply promised not only to give Pope some cover, but to throw Porter in a bad light. That appeared to be the primary criterion for court approval in every decision made during the trial, which resumed with Pope taking his seat again and hearing the question reread.[15]

He said he could "now remember" having been apprised by friends in Washington of disparaging letters Porter had written to Burnside before joining him above the Rappahannock. Sometimes he referred to the correspondence as a single letter, and testified that he confronted Porter about it during the stop at Fairfax Court House. Porter expressed regret for having written "such a letter" even privately, Pope added, implying that he had accepted the apology as genuine. He told Porter he would take no action against him because he did not then believe Porter had deliberately failed him on the battlefield. Not until the president showed him more recent dispatches from Burnside with a similarly censorious flavor, and admitted that he had feared Porter would "fail" him, did Pope come to realize that he had probably been betrayed. The dispatches "opened my eyes," he said.

The single letter he spoke of was not one of the Burnside dispatches, but the letter to Joseph Kennedy. Revealing the actual recipient might have exposed Secretary Seward, who had brought Kennedy's letter to the White House, as well as Stanton, who had probably shown it to Pope. The question remained why he did not prefer formal charges as soon as Lincoln showed him the dispatches and voiced his concerns, but he contended that his critical portrayal of Porter in his report gave the government all the facts it needed to pursue the case.

"I have not preferred charges against him," he added gratuitously at one point, as though anxious to defend the court's legitimacy. He would abandon that sham after the trial ended, but for the present Pope persisted in the outright lie that he had had nothing to do with the charges.[16]

It had been a little messy, but with the help of Holt he had salvaged sufficient credibility to satisfy any member friendly to the prosecution. Pope then brought his allies Roberts and Smith into the story, also remembering that before the battle both those men had warned him Porter would "fail" him, and that he had rejected the notion. Johnson continued to question Pope the remainder of that day, all day December 6, and about half of Monday, December 8. The most productive questions revealed how little Pope knew about the exact location of Porter's corps on August 29, the position of which he could not locate on a map. Then Johnson presented him with the situation Porter had faced—unable to find the enemy's flank or to make contact with Reynolds: would failing to attack under those circumstances have constituted disobedience? A member of the court objected that Johnson was asking for an opinion, and Johnson responded that the judge advocate had been allowed to ask opinions of witnesses. Pope himself, despite his ignorance of Porter's position, had been permitted to express his "firm conviction" that had Porter attacked on the evening of August 29, "we should have destroyed the army of Jackson." The objecting court member nevertheless insisted that opinions had no bearing, and after another closed-door conference Holt said the witness would not be allowed to answer.[17]

As though to confirm their unmitigated bias, the court members made precisely the opposite ruling the next day in regard to an opinion the prosecution wanted from Benny Roberts. This was a man who knew military courts well, having been tried by a few himself, including two at West Point when he was a cadet. He ducked one in 1839, resigning to avoid prosecution for misappropriating government funds, and he was reinstated in 1846. The next year he survived a third court, but a fourth one convened late in 1850 and dismissed him for disobedience, gross and habitual neglect of duty, filing a false return, selling or misapplying government property, and conduct unbecoming an officer—for falsifying his pay accounts and lying to his superior officers. He was saved by political influence alone, and had still been a captain when the war began, but he had recently been promoted to brigadier general of volunteers. In the old army, Roberts had a reputation for mendacity eclipsing that of Pope: a colleague of Reverdy Johnson who knew both of them warned Johnson that "their *oaths*, *words*, and *bonds* are alike worthless." Several of Porter's Regular Army comrades expressed their willingness to testify how untrustworthy Roberts was.[18]

This was the man now called on to supply nothing but the truth about Fitz John Porter. In a brief and efficient series of responses, Roberts portrayed himself as a witness to the orders Porter was charged with disobeying, and he offered testimony that seemed to undermine some of Porter's reasons for diverging from them. Then, less than twenty-four hours after the court had ruled personal opinions irrelevant, Holt asked what Roberts supposed would have happened had Porter attacked as ordered on August 29. That naturally elicited an immediate objection from the defense. The room was emptied once more, and this time the court decided that opinions so likely to favor the prosecution were perfectly admissible. Asked again what would have happened had Porter attacked, Roberts replied, "I do not doubt at all that it would have resulted in the defeat, if not in the capture, of the main army of the Confederates that were on the field at the time." Neglecting their role as the eyes and ears of the public, even conservative newspapers published only the question and the response, failing to mention the objection of the defense — or to notice the blatant inconsistency of the court's ruling.[19]

Charles Eames handled the cross-examination of Roberts, who had not been anywhere near Porter's sector that day, in spite of his firm opinions about the tactical situation there. Eames drew him into faulting Porter for not making an attack even before he received Pope's 4:30 order, when he was still operating under McDowell's modifications of the joint order. As Eames reminded him, that order had mentioned no attack but simply ordered him to halt, and be ready to withdraw across Bull Run. Roberts countered with the latitude the order gave Porter to digress from it, which would have authorized him to pitch into the enemy if he could do so "to advantage." He also opined that Porter's force "was sufficient to have defeated Longstreet's, and to have attacked the right of Jackson's forces, and to have turned their rear." That belief reflected a deep misunderstanding of how many troops Longstreet had on the field, and how few men Porter had left after McDowell took King's division away, but Eames could not prove Longstreet's force without Confederate records. Instead, he focused on Roberts's ignorance of the combatants' tactical positions.[20]

Calculating the arrival of Longstreet's troops more conservatively than was possible even with the information already available, Roberts would only concede that a part of that corps had reached the field "about dark." He said he was referring to the Confederate division John Buford had spotted going through Gainesville at 8:45 that morning. Dark came at around 7:00 P.M. on that day, so Roberts assumed they had wasted more than ten hours marching the intervening three miles. Conversely, he estimated that Porter received the 4:30 attack order at the earliest possible time, putting it "before 5 o'clock." Thus did he create an imaginary two-hour window in which Porter might have made his way beyond Jackson's right flank without interference, and swept him from the field.[21]

When those two hours passed without Porter's attack, said Roberts, he recalled that Porter had also neglected to march at 1:00 A.M. on August 28, as Pope ordered. Those two factors convinced him Porter would continue to "fail" Pope, he claimed. He testified that he told Pope as much, and he tantalized everyone in the room by adding that "a major-general, whose name it is not necessary for me to mention," assured him that Porter "would fail General Pope." Of course Eames immediately demanded the source of that hearsay, since it had already been uttered, and Roberts named the conveniently dead Phil Kearny. The exchange purportedly transpired at Pope's headquarters, where numerous staff officers would have been present, and Eames asked who they were. Initially Roberts couldn't remember, but then he named a few, adding that they probably did not hear the comment; he and Kearny were drawn off to one side, and he doubted Kearny meant it to be heard.[22]

Kearny — an envious and censorious soldier who despised McClellan — had once described Porter as "weak as water," but he also considered him "good in nature," which seemed incompatible with deliberate treachery. Kearny was dead, but the court allowed Roberts to testify for him.[23]

Lesser staff officers periodically came before the court to document the timing or other details associated with the orders they carried. General Pope's nephew, Captain Douglass Pope, appeared on December 10, the day after Roberts, and corroborated him on the delivery of his uncle's 4:30 attack order. Although he described stopping to show it to General McDowell while delivering it, he swore that he put it in Porter's hands "by 5 o'clock." He judged the time by his recollection of how long it took him and by the hour in the heading of the order — which he seemed to assume had been dated after the order had been transcribed, just as it was given to him. He and Roberts alone alleged so early a delivery. Other than that nugget for the prosecution, young Pope offered nothing of value.[24]

Writing to Harriet the night after Captain Pope appeared, Porter told her, "My blood ran cold with his falsehoods." Careful comparison of prosecution testimony with the realities on the battlefield known at the time reveals only a handful of witnesses who appeared to resort to outright invention. The most damaging direct testimony against Porter came from Pope himself and the officers closest to him, whose foremost character trait was a notorious disregard for the truth. Any expectation of a fair trial seemed to be fading fast as Porter confided to his wife that "the members of the court are against me in almost every case." She clung to hope all the stronger, buoyed by the confidence of her husband's friends, who misapprehended that the case would be decided on the facts.[25]

The most palpably false testimony came from Thomas C. H. Smith, Pope's other principal collaborator, whose alleged observations required him to be both telepathic and omniscient. This was the officer who had stopped at Porter's tent on the afternoon of August 28 to discuss a supply of ammunition, and Holt made the most of him. Smith claimed that in their first brief conversation he deduced from Porter's "sneering manner" that the man was a traitor, and told Pope not to rely on him. Smith depicted Pope vehemently disagreeing (as Pope had also testified), arguing that Porter would "fight where I put him." Smith told the court that in reciprocal excitement he assured Pope, "I was so certain that Fitz John Porter was a traitor, that I would shoot him that night, so far as any crime before God was concerned, if the law would allow me to do it." The press jumped on the inflammatory word "traitor," without noting Smith's hyperbole or his ludicrous pretense to infallible intuition.[26]

Holt, confident that the court would sustain his own requests for opinions, asked Smith what the effect would have been had Porter attacked the enemy between five and six o'clock on the evening of August 29. A reflexive objection from the defense cleared the courtroom again but was ultimately overruled, as everyone must have anticipated by then. Smith began by professing inadequate knowledge of the numbers and position of the troops, and that aroused another defense objection on the grounds of his admitted incompetence. That, too, was rejected, so Smith started to describe the disposition of the Union and Confederate forces—locating Longstreet on the far side of Thoroughfare Gap, miles away, instead of right in front of Porter. In so doing, Smith (like Roberts) bolstered Pope's self-serving prediction that the attack Porter was ordered to make would have cut off Jackson's retreat.[27]

Some of Holt's earlier witnesses, including Pope, had run into trouble under cross-examination when forced to reveal that they had no idea what position Porter occupied on August 29. To avoid that problem with Smith, and allow him to reduce the damage of the revelation, Holt prompted him to admit that he did not know exactly where Porter was. Smith did so, and in a reply that was evidently rehearsed he approximated Porter's position by dust clouds he saw hovering over the road from Manassas. He grew confused when Holt inquired what time he saw the dust, rambling on about where it was rising, and finally he seemed to confess that it hadn't really meant anything. This last exchange between them failed to achieve the intent Holt obviously intended, and he gave it up.[28]

The first defense questions established Smith's relative innocence of military science. He had never had any military education, training, or service, and had mainly practiced law in Cincinnati until obtaining a direct commission as lieutenant colonel in the 1st Ohio Cavalry. During his ten months with that regiment he had seen no action save on the periphery of Halleck's Corinth campaign, after which he had come east on Pope's staff.

Having shown the limitations of Smith's general expertise, the defense then demonstrated the flaws in his understanding of Porter's tactical position. He denied the presence of Longstreet, who outnumbered Porter by two to one; he overlooked the gaping mile between Porter and his nearest support, yet still maintained that he could have outflanked the enemy and won the day. Unfortunately for Porter, the degree to which Smith misrepresented the situation at Dawkin's Branch would be more obvious to historians than to the court. The prosecution's case depended on Pope's stubborn contention that most of Longstreet's corps had not yet reached the battlefield, and the court had already accepted that. The incriminating testimony of men who knew virtually nothing of affairs on the Union left carried more weight for that panel than anything said by officers who had commanded troops there.[29]

Smith unblushingly defended his ability to deduce Porter's intentions toward Pope from their conversation about ammunition. Although Porter had specifically requested that ammunition, Smith described him as "indifferent" to it, and he awkwardly equated that indifference to disloyalty to Pope. "I do not know that I understood indifference in regard to the ammunition so much as his general indifference in regard to the success of General Pope in that campaign," Smith said. Yet they did not discuss the campaign, and mentioned Pope only in discussing retrieval of the wounded from Bristoe Station. Smith could not explain how he perceived a "sneering attitude" from Porter, and admitted that his manner was gentlemanly and courteous throughout. He could quote nothing Porter said to support such a characterization. Neither could he cite any facial expression, inflection, gesture, or posture to denote "sneering." At every request for evidence to support his assertion, he could only hark back to that "sneering, indifferent manner and tone," but he even backed away from that. "As for the sneering," he finally volunteered, "it was somewhat suppressed."[30]

One of Porter's lawyers asked how Smith could distinguish Porter's manner that day from his usual demeanor, since they had never met before. Smith said it was because he only resorted to "sneering" in speaking of the ammunition and the wounded. Nothing could shake him from his claim that "I had one of those clear convictions that a man has a few times, perhaps, in his life, as to the character and purposes of a person whom he sees for the first time." Such seditious language as Porter's plea that he had no officers to send for the ammunition firmly convinced Smith that Fitz John Porter was "a man with a crime on his mind."[31]

This was testimony reminiscent of the Salem witch trials. Except for a few congressmen who might find it useful to credit Smith's more absurd statements, the public had no chance to read them for nearly a quarter of a century. Until then, truncated newspaper renditions of his accusations of treason and criminal intent would disguise the implausibility of his psychic deductions. Only those who sat in the courtroom, and the congressmen who were favored with a private transcript, could have understood how seriously Smith expected his mindreading to be received. Many who lacked antipathy for Porter must have laughed it off, expecting the verdict to depend on more credible evidence. Porter's antagonists, including those who packed the court, may also have sensed the fantasy behind Smith's assertions, but they could overlook it and rely instead on the disdain Porter revealed for Pope in the dispatches to Burnside.

Those dispatches, after all, were the reason for all the emphasis on Roberts and Smith predicting that Porter would fail Pope. Given the reputations for casual prevarication that Pope and Roberts already bore, and Smith's deceptive display under oath, the obvious conclusion is that they all designed their testimony around Burnside's dispatches. Holt probably did not merely accept what they told him, either: as judge advocate general he would be credibly accused more than once of suborning perjury, nor did he seem troubled by hearing unmistakable examples of it in Porter's trial.

General Heintzelman took the stand the next day. He was one of those who had somewhat resented McClellan's favoritism toward Porter, but if Holt expected him to aid the prosecution he was disappointed. Heintzelman had been called to document the dire need for Porter to reinforce Hooker at Bristoe Station the night of August 27, but the best he could do was point out that a part of Hooker's division was nearly out of ammunition. He was quickly turned over to the defense, and started to make Porter's case about the crowding of the road from Warrenton Junction, and the darkness of the night. Holt jumped back in to reverse the damage, but only made it worse, asking if the train had not moved out of the way by the early hours of August 28; Heintzelman thought not. Holt finally supposed that it could not have been so dark that it was impossible for troops to move, and Heintzelman admitted that it was not, but he said "there would have been a great many stragglers." A member of the court tried to help, asking if there was only one road, but the witness thought there was, so the unnamed general on the court reminded Heintzelman of the railroad. That, said the grizzled Heintzelman, was very difficult to march on at night, with many of the ties and rails torn up and piled on the track, and with culverts and bridges destroyed. He was soon allowed to go.[32]

Waiting in the wings was Irvin McDowell. He was then in the middle of his own court of inquiry, which was investigating whether his conduct at Bull Run warranted the filing of any charges, and his interests necessarily conflicted with Porter's. If Porter were acquitted, the responsibility for that defeat would have to fall elsewhere, and political considerations seemed to demand atonement by someone besides Pope. Porter later maintained that he had expected McDowell to clear him, presumably by testifying to their conversation on the Gainesville Road, but he claimed McDowell testified so falsely that he feared not only conviction, but execution.[33]

Like other witnesses for the government, McDowell needed little prompting to relate at length the narrative the prosecutor expected him to tell. The court convened at eleven o'clock each morning, and adjourned by three in the afternoon, so Holt always had time for interviews on the next day's testimony, with whatever rehearsal or coaching might be needed.

In his narrative of August 29, McDowell diverged occasionally from the story Porter would have told, and whenever he did so he took a serious toll on Porter's case. He admitted that Porter had found the enemy right in front, and evidently in force, but he said it was his impression that Porter seemed hesitant to fight them. Porter's narrative was predicated on McDowell telling him to stay where he was, presumably until King's division came in between him and Reynolds. McDowell instead testified that he explicitly told Porter to "put your force in here," which he characterized as a direct order, or at least license, for Porter to make an attack on the enemy before him. Since he had effectively denied agreeing to bring King's division in on Porter's right, the defense could not ask him why he never did so, or why he expected Porter to attack without that anticipated cooperation.[34]

Even Reverdy Johnson recognized by this stage of the trial the futility of objecting to Holt's appeals for retroactive prognostication from his witnesses. Any opinions sought by the prosecution were clearly acceptable to David Hunter's court, but those desired by the defense were forbidden. When Holt asked McDowell what effect it would have had if Porter had thrown his two divisions at the Rebel right late in the afternoon, neither defense attorney breathed a word, and McDowell performed as desired. "I think it would have been decisive in our favor," he said.[35]

McDowell's memory grew suspiciously faint under cross-examination, as the questioning turned to the version of events remembered by officers in the Fifth Corps. He did not deny telling Porter that his command was "too far out" at Dawkin's Branch to make an attack, but he did not "recollect" having made such a statement. He did not "recollect" telling Porter, through Fred Locke, that he was going to take King's division, and that Porter should stay where he was or, if necessary, fall back on McDowell's left. The strongest denial he would offer was his "impression" that he did not say that. He did not "recollect" what time Douglass Pope showed him Pope's 4:30 attack order—which might have helped substantiate how late that order was delivered. He did not "recollect" telling Porter that Ricketts had already been driven out of Thoroughfare Gap, or whether he knew then that Longstreet had forced him out. He did not even "recollect" whether the contending forces at Groveton were fully engaged at midday of August 29.[36]

McDowell may have suffered from a genuine inability to remember some of what he was asked to recall. He had also been unable to judge the hour of certain events Holt had asked him to remember, although he managed to approximate his meeting with Porter near Dawkin's Branch at just before noon. He did not "recollect" that it was Douglass Pope who had shown him the 4:30 attack order, although he was acquainted with young Pope and it would not have hurt the case against Porter to remember who it was; he thought it had not been Pope, although he could not be "confident" of it. He did remember meeting an officer carrying the order, and remembered asking to see it, reading it, and handing it back. Yet he also recalled some details and statements that were very damaging to Porter, and retained them with remarkable clarity for someone with so relatively poor a memory.[37]

The next morning McDowell came back, and one or more unidentified members of the court began to ply him with questions that reflected a distinct wish for incriminating responses. Did Porter "put his troops in action" where McDowell indicated? It was already known that he had not. Could Porter have made such an attack, and still fallen back to Bull Run, as the joint order required? McDowell thought so, unequivocally. When McDowell departed with King's division up the Sudley Road, did he expect Porter to attack as soon as he could reach the enemy, and did McDowell consider it Porter's duty to do so? McDowell had already implied as much. If Porter had attacked at any time until the close of the fighting that day, would the decisive, favorable result McDowell predicted have followed? McDowell believed so, of course.[38]

As these questions were being asked in Washington, fighting had erupted below Fredericksburg, fifty miles away. The Army of the Potomac would suffer a costly, devastating defeat that day under the man with whom President Lincoln had most recently supplanted McClellan. With that disaster, public confidence in the administration's competence at managing military affairs would begin a monthlong descent toward its nadir. Cagey cabinet officials surely understood that this pejorative image might be alleviated if blame for the last stunning defeat were shifted from the shoulders of Pope—the other general regarded as Lincoln's substitute for McClellan. That logic may have occurred to the president himself.

The somber effects of Fredericksburg had not yet settled over Washington on that afternoon of December 13. The court had nevertheless already shown full cognizance of how desperately the administration—or at least the War Department—wanted Porter convicted, and another signal of that understanding came late in that day's proceedings. One of Porter's lawyers expected to argue that Porter could not have carried Pope's 4:30 order out fully, and McDowell had been commenting on the portions of orders that had to be obeyed, so he seemed competent on that topic. Defense witnesses were ready to testify that the terrain on Porter's right was too difficult for his artillery to navigate, and that there were no roads there, while Pope's 4:30 order instructed Porter to "use his batteries" in the attack. One of Porter's attorneys therefore asked McDowell if Porter would have been in disobedience of Pope's order if he had had to send his infantry in without his batteries.

That threatened much of the government case. One member of the court— perhaps Garfield, whom Porter described as playing prosecutor—objected that opinions could be offered only if they related to facts derived from information the witness knew, and not to points of law. By that reasoning, McDowell's opinion that an attack by Porter would have resulted in a decisive triumph was a "fact," but McDowell was incompetent to say whether incomplete obedience amounted to disobedience. Holt had been allowed to ask numerous witnesses similar questions, but after the requisite clearing of the court this objection—like every single objection made in Porter's court-martial—was decided for the prosecution. The question would not be answered, Holt said, when proceedings resumed.

To counter any doubts that might have arisen about the mobility of artillery in that quarter, another unidentified court member (or the same one) closed the day's session by asking McDowell if he carried his artillery with him on that day. McDowell obligingly replied that he had. He refrained from volunteering that the very reason he had chosen to join Reynolds via the Sudley Road was to avoid the difficult terrain on Porter's right, where artillery could not go.[39]

During McDowell's testimony, his fellow Ohioan Garfield could hardly restrain his admiration, gushing to his wife that "no amount of cross-examination can render him opaque or confused in the least degree." Despite McDowell's repeated claims of lapsed memory, Garfield thought his testimony "crushing."[40]

McDowell departed December 15, and Holt turned promptly to the Burnside dispatches. He first introduced a copy of the one Porter wrote at Warrenton Junction on the afternoon of August 27, in which he remarked sarcastically on the raids that had cut Pope's supply line. An exculpatory paragraph at the end of that dispatch had been deleted, so the defense submitted a complete copy of the dispatch and tried to grill the telegrapher who had sent it, but Hunter interrupted at that moment. He wished to preclude Porter's attorneys from questioning witnesses directly, and have Porter submit written questions for the judge advocate to read. Hunter obviously wanted to protect prosecution witnesses from incisive, professional interrogation, but he claimed he wished to save time. His proposal promised to consume still more time, however, and even his colleagues disagreed, allowing oral questions to continue, but they used that discussion to stipulate that Porter's attorneys could "address no argument to the court but by express permission."[41]

Holt then introduced the telegram Porter had written at breakfast on August 29, in the presence of Captain Strother. The defense objected that the dispatches were irrelevant without context, but Holt replied that they showed "the *animus* of the accused toward his commanding general" at the time of the "acts of disobedience." With that he entered another dispatch, beginning with "All that talk of bagging Jackson, &c., was bosh," and wryly describing the palpable confusion about where the enemy had gone. The first witness called by the defense, a few days later, came to verify dispatches Porter had sent to Burnside a few days on either side of those submitted by Holt. Those telegrams invited a more benign interpretation, showing that Porter's lack of confidence in Pope had not impaired his sense of duty, and that he thought the best way to draw Lee off was to attack his own line of communications. The court deemed those dispatches irrelevant, although (or more likely because) they tended to refute the impression of unbridled contempt Holt wanted to make. Porter did manage to prove that the portion of the August 27 telegram that would have been most helpful to him had been removed from the copy Holt submitted to the court. That broad hint of prosecutorial manipulation of evidence aroused no judicial curiosity from Hunter's court.[42]

Toward the end of the prosecution's presentation, the court developed a noticeable propensity for procrastination. On the excuse of a lack of witnesses, no court was held December 16 or 17. Only two witnesses appeared on December 18. With no witnesses for the government on Friday, December 19, the court merely heard the minutes read and adjourned until Monday—despite its habit of meeting on Saturdays. Three more men were heard on December 22, and that closed the government's case. Porter had encountered great trouble in corresponding with potential witnesses by mail: many of his letters and some of their replies went undelivered until long after the trial, when he received some of them in New York, already opened. Holt admitted that he had delayed sending for some of Porter's witnesses until they were needed, and the first of them could not be expected until Christmas Eve, so court was not held on December 23.[43]

Porter's defense began with the fruitless attempt to introduce telegrams that would have tempered any impression of disloyalty, disaffection, or insufficient zeal. They were not allowed. He followed that with a few staff officers who corroborated the intense darkness in the first hours of August 28 and the tardy arrival of the 4:30 attack order. Porter put great hope in his chief of staff, Colonel Fred Locke, who testified on the day after Christmas that McDowell had given him verbal instructions for Porter to stay where he was at Dawkin's Branch. Locke told of riding back toward Bethlehem Church to ask King to have his division stand ready, and finding him by a fence along the roadside, with McDowell. When he delivered the message to King, Locke said McDowell informed him that he was taking King's division with him. He told Locke that as for Porter, "I think he better remain where he is; but if it is necessary for him to fall back, he can do so upon my left."[44]

With his proximity to Porter and their distance from Pope at that hour of August 29, McDowell held command over Porter as the senior in rank on that part of the field. That made such a comment to Locke a direct order for Porter, whom it would have absolved of any disobedience for failing to attack until Pope's 4:30 order arrived. For ten days, Porter had reason to hope that Locke's testimony would save him from conviction on the worse specifications of the first charge, but it was not to be. After holding out until the defense had closed

its case, on January 5, Holt called King to step down from the court and testify that he had never seen McDowell or Locke on August 29. King admitted
being near Bethlehem Church about the time Locke specified, but he said he
did not recognize Locke and had received no such message. On the last day of
testimony, McDowell also came back to swear that he "did not recollect" that
exchange, either.

"Are you, or are you not," asked a court member, "confident that you did not
send a message on the 29th of August to General Porter that he better remain
where he was?" McDowell went only so far as to reply, "I do not think I did."
That seemed good enough for the court as a whole, but it fell short of the positive denial he might have been expected to offer if he never thought of giving
Porter such instructions.[45]

McDowell was at least mistaken. Lieutenant Washington Roebling, Mc-
Dowell's assigned bridge builder, later remembered the staff stopping early
that afternoon at a farm short of Bethlehem Church, where they gathered some
apples. It was there that Locke met McDowell, Roebling presumed, adding that
toward 2:00 P.M. they started away, passing General Warren's brigade at the
tail of Porter's column. At that point, he said, McDowell sent an aide to Porter
with a "message." That aide, Major Joseph Willard (of Willard's Hotel), had also
brought Porter's copy of the joint order earlier in the day, at McDowell's behest,
but in his diary he failed to mention carrying the afternoon dispatch. Willard
testified before McDowell's court on December 31, and his absence from Holt's
witness list in Porter's trial may have implied discomfort with the testimony he
might give.[46]

Porter himself did not remember receiving a written message, and none
that has survived matches the circumstances. Without such a dispatch, the
testimony of King and McDowell appeared to demolish Locke's, and Locke's
courier was not then available to corroborate his testimony, as he later would.
Shortly after McDowell tried to discredit the story, Locke returned to tell it
again in greater detail. He knew McDowell quite well from the months on Hall's
Hill, but said he had never met King before August 29. Yet when he asked if the
man standing by the fence was King, that officer responded affirmatively, and
when Locke came into the courtroom on December 26 he recognized King as
the man he had seen at Bethlehem Church. One of the lawyers asked Locke if
he was "entirely certain of it," and the witness replied unequivocally "I am positively certain of it."[47]

King admitted he was seriously ill all day August 29, suffering from a series of
epileptic seizures—which probably accounts for one of his brigade commanders accusing him of being drunk. During such an episode King may well not
have remembered the encounter, notwithstanding his assurance that his illness
did not affect his recollection. The contradictory testimony might also be ex-

plained if the man with McDowell had merely been someone who resembled King, who misunderstood when Locke asked if he were King; if he thought Locke was asking whether the surrounding troops belonged to King's division, he might have confirmed by word or nod that they did. Either scenario would also have had to involve another contributory lapse of memory by McDowell.

It is also possible that King or McDowell, or both, engaged in active deceit, while for Locke to have done so defies all logic. It would have been worse than useless for him to fabricate the incident, with King sitting right in front of him and McDowell available in the same building. Both generals would inevitably have refuted a fiction, to the detriment of any hope Porter entertained for acquittal. Telling the tale made sense only if Locke expected King and McDowell to remember their meeting—or at least not deny it. Porter sought supportive testimony from Gouverneur Warren, whom Locke had told of McDowell's instructions soon afterward, but the court did not summon Warren. Only years later did Warren's brother-in-law, Lieutenant Roebling, confirm that McDowell was located about where Locke said he found him, and Roebling did not recall whether King was there.[48]

King had two motives for lying. Foremost was the conflict of interest that should have kept him off the court: his own performance at Second Bull Run had involved an unauthorized retreat for which he, too, could be court-martialed—and McDowell's court of inquiry severely chastised him for it. Like McDowell, King stood to benefit from deflected attention if Porter became the scapegoat. King was also a fervent Republican, with a political interest in anathematizing Porter as an example of perfidious Democratic sentiment in the army. In light of King's role in this judicial travesty, which stained the integrity of every man on the court, outright duplicity on his part seems less implausible than it otherwise might.[49]

Artful deception would have been even more tempting for McDowell, whose own reputation now depended on the destruction of Porter's. His protestations about the meeting with Locke fell conspicuously short of a complete denial, and typified the selective memory that carried him unscathed through his own and Porter's court. Veiling his deception behind the faint possibility of forgetfulness avoided the unpleasant consequences of any epiphany in memory or morals by King, or from the discrediting testimony of any surprise witnesses, such as Locke's courier.

Despite the word of two witnesses against one, Locke's story rings truer, and McDowell's halfhearted, inadvertent order to stay put explained Porter's relative inactivity. Holt waited ten days to rebut Locke's testimony, partly to assess and coordinate the testimony of King and McDowell, but he may have harbored a strategic motive. Delaying that rebuttal until the final moments of the trial closed the proceedings — for both the court and the press — with a crippling blow to the credibility of the most important defense witness.

In the twenty-nine days since the creation of the court, it had met twenty-one times, spending fifteen days examining prosecution witnesses and six days on other business. Between December 24 and January 5, the defense was allowed only nine days to present its own witnesses before Edwin Stanton took the unusual step of ordering the proceedings cut short. On the excuse that the officers on the court were needed for other duty, he ordered Hunter to begin earlier in the day and ignore the usual closing time of 3:00 P.M. Yet Stanton felt no such urgency about McDowell's court of inquiry, which had then consumed forty-six days and continued for another forty days, without prodding.[50]

That extraordinary decree was probably not designed entirely to hobble Porter's defense and limit the time he could take to prepare his final argument. More than a dozen of the witnesses he had asked for were never summoned, partly because of the haste, but for the minister of war that was merely a collateral benefit.[51] Stanton, like Lincoln, was most anxious for news to counteract the rising tide of discouraging publicity over Burnside's humiliating defeat at Fredericksburg. That latest bloody failure appeared to confirm what Bull Run had first implied: that Lincoln, Stanton, and Halleck had blundered by replacing McClellan with inept substitutes. Stanton had recently badgered Burnside to relieve the administration of responsibility for the Fredericksburg disaster with a public letter taking the blame upon himself; Porter's prompt conviction would also absolve the administration for Pope's catastrophe.[52]

The cacophony of editorial criticism had only been amplified since Christmas by embarrassing press coverage of Porter's defense. Unreasonable refusals to admit exculpatory evidence, combined with the published testimony of defense witnesses, had already begun to betray the bias of the court and the falsity of the government's case. As an overture toward more favorable publicity, the court recalled and interviewed several prosecution witnesses after the defense had rested, including McDowell and Pope.[53]

All testimony came to an end on January 6, and the defense argument was scheduled for Saturday, January 10. Days before, Porter had already prepared himself for the worst. He warned Sam Barlow that he and McClellan both had so many personal enemies sitting on the court that "their conclusion is a foregone one." He suspected that promises of promotion or other professional advantages had been trolled before those on the court who lacked sufficient incentive for a guilty verdict, and he would soon find confirmation for that suspicion.[54]

With only three days to examine twenty-four days of testimony transcribed by hand on upward of a thousand pages, Eames managed to compile an argument more than twenty-five thousand words long. He demonstrated that an earlier departure for Bristoe Station would have brought the Fifth Corps there little sooner, and in a more exhausted condition, even if the need for an early arrival had not "passed away." Using McDowell's own testimony, he showed that Porter had obeyed the joint order, which did not require an attack. Thereafter his actions were guided by McDowell's order: whether McDowell or King remembered giving Locke that order, Locke had said he delivered it to Porter. As for the 4:30 order, it incorrectly assumed Porter's position to be on the enemy flank, and by the preponderance of testimony it arrived too late in the day for compliance.[55]

Relying on the testimony of officers who carried out the reconnaissance to Porter's front, Eames gave enough evidence that the enemy there was much stronger and covered a wider front than Pope supposed. He contended that the misdirection of Griffin's and Piatt's brigades had been inadvertent, rather than the result of some disloyal conspiracy. By virtue of including all the exculpatory telegrams with a protest against their exclusion, he managed to enter them into the record, diminishing any impression that Porter's poor opinion of Pope exerted any impact on his ardor against the enemy. The argument ended with an indictment of McDowell's ability to recall only what flattered him. If McDowell had actually ordered Porter to attack, as he claimed, Porter could not have done so without immediately asking him for reinforcements and support: that Porter did not make the request offered evidence that no such order ever reached him. Eames's summation introduced reasonable doubt against every specification, and more than reasonable doubt against most of them.[56]

When the court met again to hear the argument, Johnson and Eames read it aloud. Members of the court were evidently not required to pay attention while the closing argument was being read, nor were they even expected to pretend that they were listening. For most of the generals at the table, the detailed response of the defendant amounted to a tiresome formality. James Garfield, who had so obviously formed an immutable opinion about the case before the trial even opened, whiled away some of the time writing a letter to his mother.[57]

When the reading was done, Holt surprised some of those in attendance by announcing that he would not prepare a response for the court—to save the time it would take, he professed. Between the testimony that had been presented and Holt's apparent forfeiture of the contest, many who had sat through the trial assumed that Porter was bound to be found innocent. The *New York Times* concluded that neither the McDowell inquiry nor Porter's trial had revealed "any startling and terrible crimes." That suspicion of impending acquittal grew even stronger when the courtroom was cleared "for a few moments," whereupon the court came to a decision. The doors were opened one last time, the court reconvened only to adjourn, and Holt returned to the War Department with the verdict and the record.[58]

Holt needed no closing prosecution argument for the members of the court, whose intentions he read very well. With little time to deliberate on individual specifications, they hastily found Porter guilty of everything but sending the two brigades to Centreville. His punishment was to be cashiered — dismissed in disgrace — and "forever disqualified from holding any office of trust or profit under the Government of the United States."[59]

The verdict would remain secret until it went through the motions of formal review by the judge advocate general and the president. Halleck officially turned the trial record over to Stanton on Tuesday, January 13, but Holt had already taken news of it to the president, who had instructed him to "revise" the proceedings and "report fully." The definition of "revise," then as now, involved reviewing with an eye to amendments and corrections, but Lincoln would not have asked Holt to amend or correct the trial transcript. He wanted a summary of the case.[60]

Holt instead produced the closing prosecution argument he had not needed for the court, condensing adverse testimony and argument into the most inimical form possible. He mentioned defense testimony or arguments only in order to rebut them — often with deft falsehood. He credited McDowell with having corroborated how early the 4:30 order was delivered, although McDowell had specifically testified that he did not know what hour of the day it was when he saw it. Holt maintained that Porter had retreated from Dawkin's Branch, citing Douglass Pope's irrelevant testimony that the tail end of Porter's corps was still resting at Bethlehem Church when he delivered the 4:30 order. In fact Porter's line of battle had never budged from its advanced position, and plenty of evidence had proven as much, but Holt's misrepresentation wrought a profound effect when he delivered it on January 19.[61]

That was a busy time for the president. Holt's jaundiced summary sat in the White House no longer than sixty hours before Lincoln finished with it, but he does appear to have examined it. Robert Lincoln, who was still enjoying a Christmas break at the time, later testified that his father showed him a copy of Porter's message warning King and McDowell of his intention to withdraw to Manassas: he remembered his father saying that Porter would have deserved "a sentence of death" for it — which indicated that the president thought Porter actually had retreated, when ordered to attack. Whether that belief was based on Holt's review of the case or on the trial record, Robert could not say; nor did he know if his father ever saw the complete record, which ran to more than nine hundred pages.[62]

Had Lincoln been poring over the complete trial record, he should eventually have been able to deduce that Porter never fell back until ordered. He could think that Porter had withdrawn—or "retreated," as Holt characterized it—only by relying on Holt's summary, which incorporated the note to King and McDowell. The court had also found Porter guilty of retreating, and could only have justified such a finding by isolating Douglass Pope's testimony from pages of contradictory evidence. That coincidence suggests that the court's unseemly haste in its final deliberations was also accomplished by simply taking direction from Holt.[63]

Abraham Lincoln essentially did the same. The sixteenth president, who is usually described in superlative terms, is sometimes credited with an unusual talent for judging men, but his nearest associates knew better. Joshua Speed, an early and close friend, considered Lincoln rather gullible: Speed told none other than Joseph Holt that Lincoln was "so honest himself that he is slow to believe that others are not equally so." Indeed, Lincoln frequently proved easy game for manipulative opportunists. Even old friends imposed on his credulity to benefit themselves or their friends and relatives at government expense.[64]

It is therefore inviting to attribute Lincoln's approval of so patently unfair a tribunal to the prodigiously prejudicial review contrived by Holt—the very man whom Joshua Speed had assured of Lincoln's overly trusting nature. Lincoln was a lawyer, however, and could readily distinguish a prosecutorial screed from a case summary. Had his curiosity been aroused by the venomous one-sidedness of Holt's review, he might have called for the record, which he probably never saw. Detecting how badly Holt had distorted the evidence would have taken days of concentrated research, and Lincoln's desire to find such distortion would have been as limited as his leisure. On January 21 the Army of the Potomac was struggling in the mud of a torrential storm above the Rappahannock River, and many of Burnside's top generals had lost all faith in him. It must already have occurred to Lincoln that Burnside would also have to go, and soon—which would surely arouse another chorus of criticism for his administration and excite further opposition to the war.

Lincoln demonstrated his own wrath toward Porter in the order for the original court of inquiry, which he wrote in detail with his own hand, and as the trial began he admitted his bias in the case. Accumulated circumstances suggest that Lincoln was not merely the dupe of the unprincipled Holt. He ignored signals his professional legal experience should have attuned him to notice. In light of the political relief it might afford him, Lincoln can hardly be blamed for hoping for a conviction. His ability to see anything suspicious in Holt's relentless vilification would have been sorely hampered by an understandable impulse to leave his own opinion of Porter's guilt undisturbed. With the morale of the Army of the Potomac crumbling under an epidemic of mistrust in Burnside, the opportunity to criminalize a lack of confidence in military commanders may also have seemed irresistible. In one of his most unflattering moments, Lincoln affixed his signature to the document that ruined Fitz John Porter's life, and in so doing he became the last accessory to the most conspicuous miscarriage of military justice during his presidency. He was later said to have expressed a willingness, shortly before his assassination, to have Porter's case reexamined. If that was true, there may have been a touch of remorse in the sentiment.[65]

16

THE ABYSS

Porter spent the middle of January worrying about money, as well as his future. On the day of the verdict he gave Eames $700 for the balance of his thousand-dollar fee, having borrowed the money from Harriet's aunt, but five days later he received a bill from Johnson for another thousand. From his early conversations with Eames he had supposed that the first thousand covered both lawyers, since they were associates, but he was mistaken. Confessing outright mortification, he asked Harriet to see if Mrs. Holbrook would advance him that money, too. Two thousand dollars represented four and a half months' pay for a major general, and Porter had spent so much supporting his mother and invalid nephew that he had saved nothing. Still, he thought the lawyers had earned their fee. He told Harriet they had "been to me like parents."[1]

On January 20, Porter returned to the brick building across from Willard's where his court had met, having been called to McDowell's inquiry. Identifying himself for the last time as a general of the U.S. Army, he recounted his interactions with McDowell on August 29, including the reconnaissance across the railroad that culminated in McDowell suddenly galloping away from him; unbeknown to Porter, McDowell's own former chief of staff had described that scene to the court only the day before. Porter remained on the stand through the rest of the day, and came back the next morning. He testified that he checked his advance on Gainesville and stopped trying to connect with Reynolds as soon as Colonel Locke brought him what Locke and he both regarded as a direct verbal order to that effect from McDowell.[2]

His testimony ended when McDowell asked him to explain how his account of their exchanges differed from McDowell's testimony at Porter's trial, which Porter had characterized as doing him "great wrong and great harm." This court seemed nearly as determined to exonerate McDowell as Porter's had been to convict him, and one of the members—perhaps John Martindale, the lawyer and Porter nemesis—objected to giving Porter that forum for his own defense. The court refused to hear his reply, and no further testimony was taken from him.[3]

During the first day of Porter's testimony, the president had Holt's review of Porter's trial in his office, along with some other cases. That same day, Lincoln pondered two other convictions that aroused some of his renowned compassion. The young colonel of a Kentucky regiment had been dismissed for ordering runaway slaves returned to loyal owners, which the Fugitive Slave Act required until Congress prohibited the practice, in 1862: Lincoln thought about giving him "another chance" because of his stellar record on the battlefield, but evidently Stanton dissuaded him from restoring the man, which would have outraged Radicals. The second case was purely criminal, involving a man sentenced to prison for stealing from the U.S. Mail, but he was related to people with whom Lincoln was close, and that relationship afforded him an immediate executive pardon.[4]

On the afternoon of January 21, about the time Porter was being denied an opportunity to expound on the flaws in McDowell's testimony, the president was poring over Holt's polemic on Porter's court-martial. By 4:00 P.M. he approved the verdict, and within minutes that news was in the hands of a representative from Stanton's favorite New York paper, the New York Tribune. That reporter ran down Porter and asked if he had heard the results. Of course he had not, and he had even begun to anticipate exoneration. Porter's supposition that he had been acquitted had already evoked jubilation in Lieutenant Weld, on furlough back in Boston. Porter had even applied for leave the day before, having been home only twice, for a day or two apiece, since April of 1861. The Tribune man apprised him that he had been found guilty, and dismissed in disgrace. For the benefit of the next day's readers, he described Porter as "powerfully affected as well as astounded." The news came too late for the Evening Star to publish that day, but it made all the major newspapers the next morning.[5]

Even before Holt took his review to the president, a fat pamphlet had been circulating in the capital entitled Proceedings of a General Court Martial, for the Trial of Maj. Gen. Fitz John Porter, U.S. Vols. Bearing a publication date of 1862, but with no indication of the publisher, it consisted of the record of the trial up to the closing of the government's case, containing only the evidence and testimony for the prosecution. It therefore left the same impression of incontrovertible guilt as Holt's review. The pamphlet appeared in the mail of some Republican congressmen on news of Porter's dismissal, and bundles were apparently given to the more reliable of them for mailing to constituents under congressional franking privileges. Quite a few surfaced in Boston. This second distorted abridgment could not have been produced without the collusion of Stanton—or Holt, who was later implicated in the production of a similar pamphlet defending the court's decision. Those two had control of the court record, and it must have been through one of them that Benny Roberts and Colonel Smith had it printed. Holt, who knew of the project all along, had asked Roberts on January 6 for enough copies to distribute to the court when it went into deliberation, leaving anyone interested in examining the defense testimony to struggle with the manuscript. Porter heard about it only after his dismissal, and tried to counteract it by having the defense portion of the record published in the *National Intelligencer*, which fulminated for days over such official under-handedness.[6]

So tight a case did this collection of uncontested government testimony make that even those of Porter's friends who saw the pamphlet had assumed he would have to be found guilty. Holt's one-sided distillation of the prose-cution's case only confirmed that expectation. Down on the Rappahannock, George Meade discredited any notion of Porter's disloyalty, but believed all Holt's assertions: that Porter could have attacked on August 29, that he was or-dered to do so, and that he admitted retreating instead; Meade grumbled all the more because he had been with the Pennsylvania Reserves that day, waiting for the attack Pope kept promising Porter would make.[7] Charles Russell Lowell, a former McClellan aide and an admirer of Porter, must have received a copy of the *Proceedings* at his headquarters outside Boston, where he was raising a new regiment. Before Porter's conviction was even known, Lowell wrote to a friend that "the evidence leaves little doubt that Porter got 'demoralized'" and that "his frame of mind was un-officer-like and dangerous."

"This sort of feeling was growing in the army," Lowell continued, in an opin-ion that could have been based solely on the distorted pamphlet, "and the Gov-ernment and the Country felt that it must be stopped." As though the verdict was already public knowledge, Lowell concluded that "Porter was made the ex-ample," and while he admitted feeling very sorry for Porter he added, "I accept the lesson."[8]

Lowell's letters do not suggest that he ever studied the testimony of defense witnesses. His Harvard classmate Charles Francis Adams Jr. took precisely the opposite view, apparently without having seen anything about the Porter case that wasn't in the newspapers. To his father, Lincoln's minister to Great Britain, Adams denounced the stupidity of those at the head of the government, reveal-ing all the "demoralization" Lowell lamented. "Unable to run the army them-selves," Adams complained of the administration, "they take away McClellan, and when that leads to terrible disaster, they cashier Fitz John Porter, one of the best generals we have."[9]

As Porter's lawyers had anticipated, the men who had found him guilty real-ized immediate rewards. Stanton had already taken care of Slough, submitting his appointment as brigadier general for Senate confirmation the moment the prosecution closed its case. Once the verdict had been rendered, he also sent in Holt's commission as judge advocate general, and those of major general for Prentiss, Napoleon Buford, and Casey, along with a brevet as brigadier in the

Regulars for Casey. Promotions, and especially brevets, were usually given for distinction in battle, and Casey's was dated from May 31, 1862 — the day his division was surprised and fled the field of Seven Pines. As soon as the court closed, Stanton restored David Hunter to command of the Department of the South, from which he had been abruptly removed the previous August. Hitchcock, after testifying for his old friend McDowell at the court of inquiry, resumed his War Department duties with more congenial attention from Stanton, whose surliness had earlier inclined the old general toward resignation. Garfield went straight home for a week's visit that left his wife pregnant with their second child, reporting a few days later as chief of staff for William Rosecrans, commanding the Army of the Cumberland.[10]

Smith and Roberts were taken care of, as well. Smith earned a promotion to brigadier general in the volunteers, dated from the beginning of the trial, and Pope had Roberts brevetted a major general from Bull Run. Roberts had expected a full promotion to major general, and complained bitterly when Pope failed to come through with that ultimate prize.[11]

Rufus King and James Ricketts received no overt rewards, but neither was court-martialed for the "grave error" McDowell's court of inquiry attributed to them at Second Bull Run. The court particularly criticized King for his retreat on August 28, and Ricketts to a lesser extent for his. McDowell escaped blame on the curious ground that he had lost touch with his entire corps by going off to look for Pope and getting lost — yet the court found his errand unnecessary, and implicitly imprudent at such a "critical time." King went back to command of a division, and a few months later the president appointed him U.S. minister to Rome. Ricketts languished for more than a year on boards and commissions, but eventually he earned another field command, accumulating brevets as major general in both the volunteers and Regulars before the war ended.[12]

The margin of the vote for Porter's conviction was never determined. The Articles of War prohibited an officer who served on a court from revealing how any member voted, but some Radical newspapers declared that the court decision had been unanimous. Those friendlier to Porter countered with rumors that a single vote had tipped the scale to guilty, but unanimity would have been more likely. Hunter, Casey, Garfield, and Hitchcock surely voted for conviction, and Hitchcock opined privately that Porter should have been shot. Garfield showed such antagonism that Porter thought he "played the part of Judge Advocate." Slough and King had political and personal reasons to find him guilty, and although Reverdy Johnson thought Prentiss "did not concur in the sentence" he certainly voted for conviction: Prentiss later asserted that he never doubted the justice of the decision, and he deplored Porter's subsequent attempts at restoration. The timing of Stanton's recommendation that Slough, Buford, and Prentiss be promoted from the beginning of the court-martial signaled his satisfaction with their votes, which Holt could have intimated more easily if the decision was unanimous.[13]

Ricketts was slightly less vulnerable to prosecution for his performance at Bull Run than King was, and he was long ignored in the distribution of favors, but even he probably voted for conviction. If he did think Porter innocent, he never hinted at it to Porter or to anyone else during all the years that remained to him. The rumor of a unanimous verdict was probably accurate, leaking out through the Radical outlets with which Holt and Stanton maintained close contact.

Through either malicious design or simple indifference, nearly a week passed before Porter was officially notified of his dismissal, so he remained in Washington under the provisions of his original arrest. While he waited, he attempted to have Congress print the complete record of his trial. Senator Milton Latham of California entered a resolution to that effect on January 26, but when it came up for a vote William Pitt Fessenden of Maine said it had already been printed. Waving a copy of the *Proceedings* that had been sent to him anonymously, Fessenden said he would "be glad if every man in the country could read this record," and he saw no need to duplicate it. Latham, a Democrat, had not received a copy, so he knew nothing of the pamphlet's existence, or of its blatant bias, and his resolution failed by a small majority. Porter wrote to Fessenden the same day to explain the one-sidedness of the pamphlet, without response. By its very existence, that prejudiced précis foiled publication of the portion of the court record that demonstrated Porter's probable innocence, while also exaggerating the appearance of his guilt.[14]

Porter lingered in the city for a few days. Just before noon on January 24, he telegraphed George Sykes at Falmouth, alerting him that his child had scarlet fever and urging him to come up for his wife's sake. Once officially notified of his dismissal, he went straight home to 66 Union Place, where he, Hattie, and the children lived with Harriet's "Aunty." He spent part of most days writing letters — first to Reynolds and Butterfield, looking for a staff position for Lieutenant Weld, and then to officers who had served under him, to thank them for their expressions of continued regard. Webb and Butterfield both predicted he would eventually be cleared. Francis Parker, the former colonel of a Massachusetts regiment that served under him, assured Porter that he had been acquitted in the court of public opinion, which Parker said "now condemns the court." One of Porter's staff officers, who resigned from the army once the verdict was announced, wrote to say, "The whole country is astonished." From the army's camp above the Rappahannock, a captain in the 4th Michigan consoled him with the sentiment that the Fifth Corps still knew only one commander, adding, "Your name can be heard from one end to the other."[15]

Late in February the aldermen of New York City attempted to emphasize the political nature of Porter's conviction, condemning the government action and inviting Porter to a public reception at City Hall. Porter knew nothing about it, and the gesture caused him more grief than gratification. The Republican mayor, George Opdyke, rejected the council's resolution in a column-long veto borrowing heavily from what he called Holt's "able report" of Porter's trial to denounce Porter's "cowardice, insubordination, and disloyalty."[16]

Citizens generally adopted the opinions of their respective party organs, with most Democrats sharing the *New York Herald*'s suspicion that Porter had been sacrificed solely as a political blow at McClellan.[17] Even the more thoughtful Republicans assumed he had been guilty, as though doubting that a government dominated by their party would have allowed—let alone orchestrated—so concerted an act of injustice. George Templeton Strong, who had often invited Porter to dine at his home, accepted the verdict although he admitted the outcome "took my breath away."

"It seems incredible," Strong admitted. "The court was composed of good men, so far as I know them. Porter has been a favorite with the army; Pope, his virtual accuser, is disliked and despised. This finding is therefore entitled to every presumption in its favor, though so astounding to all who know the accused, as I have known him for twelve years at least." Porter's fate bothered Strong for days. In his ignorance of the animosities and political motivations of the generals on Porter's court, he persistently reminded himself that it must have been a fair trial, consigning his old friend to infamy with Benedict Arnold. For years thereafter Strong referred to his former acquaintance as "Poor Fitz-John Porter," but still blamed him for failing to march to the sound of the guns on August 29, 1862. Half-informed though he was, Strong probably knew more about the case than most, and his view of the verdict predominated on the street and in the ranks, at least outside the Fifth Corps.[18]

It was a dark time for Porter, who had to wonder whether friends believed the charges against him. To add a measure of paranoia, his mail often arrived opened, or letters he knew to be on the way were never delivered. He distracted himself by helping McClellan prepare a final report of his tenure in command of the Army of the Potomac, and McClellan may have asked him for the assistance in order to offer that distraction. He took up the operations before Yorktown in particular, having been director of the siege operations there, but he was not allowed to retire into the obscurity of his study. His War Department enemies found his humiliation too useful a political tool to let it fade, especially now that he was more firmly identified with the Democratic Party to which his only defenders belonged.[19]

Copies of Holt's review started filtering into the Army of the Potomac through official channels early in April. The commander of a New York regiment recorded that "almost every colonel in the army is being supplied with several copies," and supposed the War Department felt a need to justify itself. He also learned that copies of the *National Intelligencer*, with the defense testimony from Porter's trial, had been pulled from army mail. The *Report of the Joint Committee on the Conduct of the War*, freshly printed and highly critical of McClellan, appeared in camp at the same time, in an intense propaganda campaign to sever the army's attachment to that general and his circle.[20]

Holt's review reached into the western armies, too, where it wrought incalculable personal damage that Porter was never able to repair. James Garfield had no sooner arrived at headquarters of the Army of the Cumberland as chief of staff to William Rosecrans than a freshly minted brigadier there obtained a copy. "If the review presents the facts fairly," John Beatty noted, in what he later published as his diary entry of March 30, 1863, "Porter should have been not only dismissed, but hung." As Holt had intended, Beatty imagined Porter deliberately holding back "thirteen thousand men" while his comrades were being overwhelmed. That manufactured prejudice would pursue Porter to the grave.[21]

George Smalley's exaggerated estimate of Porter's available reserves at the critical moment of Antietam had also done much to besmirch the general. Prizing Smalley's praise, Joe Hooker reportedly offered him a staff position when he replaced Burnside as commander of the Army of the Potomac, but Smalley must have declined.[22] Certainly Hooker would have valued a skilled publicist at his elbow, but Smalley preferred to wage war with a pen. As the next state election season began in the spring of 1863, Smalley was writing editorials for the *New York Tribune*—which promptly started vilifying Porter again, and using him to malign McClellan, who was becoming politically popular in military limbo. Using Smalley's own story, the *Tribune* questioned why Porter and "all the reserves of the army, were left wholly out of the fight" at Antietam. With help from someone well versed in army regulations, the *Tribune's* purveyor of opinion suggested that McClellan should be punished for associating with a cashiered comrade. That slight followed Porter's appearance on the balcony of the Fifth Avenue Hotel with McClellan early in June, to receive the survivors of the 37th and 38th New York Volunteers at the conclusion of their two-year enlistments. Those men had belonged to Kearny's division, but they cheered McClellan lustily, with Porter standing right beside him.[23]

As each state election approached through the rest of 1863, Republican newspapers in those states started using Porter's Democratic affiliation to associate the party itself with treason. Some Democratic editors inadvertently abetted that campaign by reporting the praise and sympathy accorded him at party gatherings.[24]

Porter endured all this opprobrium in addition to severe economic straits. When Lee's army marched back through Maryland that summer, so many students fled the College of St. James that the school closed, forcing Porter's mother and his tubercular nephew to leave. With only her tiny pension for income, they had to rely on Porter, who had spent so much of his army pay supporting them that his own resources were depleted, and he could not provide her with a home. The generous Mrs. Holbrook solved his dilemma by offering hers. It may have been partly to relieve the pressure on 66 Union Place that Porter accepted an invitation to Oyster Bay, on Long Island, for the month of July. He probably took some or all of his family with him, for he seemed unaffected by the draft riot that engulfed New York in the middle of the month, raging on all sides of Union Square. Most New York militia had been called up for Lee's invasion of Pennsylvania before the riots erupted, and Governor Horatio Seymour proposed organizing new militia units to protect the city, considering Porter for the command of them. Rather than see a Democratic governor raising his own little army, and give Porter an opportunity to reclaim some prestige, Stanton rendered Seymour's supplementary legion unnecessary by sending federal troops.[25]

Command of even state troops would indeed have bestowed a little official dignity on a proud man who was now treated as a pariah by so many, and it would have bolstered his pride by providing at least a temporary income. By the end of July, unemployed and indebted to Mrs. Holbrook, Porter was growing desperate to earn some money. Even if he collected his army pay up to January 21, that could not have exceeded a few hundred dollars, which should have been nearly exhausted just in feeding his family. He had hoped to last until "a change of administration," which was to say until a Democrat replaced Lincoln in the White House, but on the last day of July he admitted to at least two correspondents that he was "brought to a stand." One of those correspondents was McClellan, who wrote privately to iron and railroad magnate Erastus Corning, asking if he could do anything for Porter.[26]

Even as he looked for gainful employment, Porter tried to collect evidence that might lead to reinstatement, or at least to a new trial. The conflict between Fred Locke's testimony and that of McDowell and King struck him as critical, for even so biased a court might have hesitated to convict him had McDowell admitted instructing him to remain where he was. Just after the battle of Gettysburg, Locke sent him an affidavit from the courier who had ridden with him to Bethlehem Church, corroborating his meeting with McDowell and the man he believed to be King. Whether or not the other man had been King, he now had two witnesses who positively identified McDowell in a spot he could not "recollect" standing.[27]

Because of the immediate effect it might have on public opinion, Porter may have felt more interest that month in Reverdy Johnson's preparation of a lengthy dissection of Holt's review of the case. Johnson was representing Maryland in the U.S. Senate, but during the congressional recess he applied himself to a pamphlet with the cumbersome title *Reply of Hon. Reverdy Johnson to the Papers Which Judge-Advocate Holt Furnished to the President, Urging General Porter's Condemnation*. He described the malicious, mendacious nature of the principle government witnesses — Pope, Roberts, and Smith — and the publication during the trial of their testimony, fraudulently presented as a complete record of the proceedings. He emphasized the invariably unfavorable and contradictory rulings on evidence that emerged from each secret deliberation, signaling the hostility of at least a majority of the members on the court. He recounted how the defense request for a five-day adjournment to prepare a closing statement was cut to three, and snidely noted the speed with which the verdict was rendered after the reading of that statement. So quickly did the nine officers digest over nine hundred manuscript pages and make their ruling, Johnson said, that "even charity can not but believe, that it was determined upon before a word of the defense was heard."[28]

Then Johnson questioned President Lincoln's failure to examine the record, which he should have noticed contained no summary by the prosecution. Johnson seemed fairly certain by then that all Lincoln had seen on the trial was Holt's review, without the amelioration of defense rebuttal, and he more than insinuated that as a lawyer Lincoln should have recognized the impropriety of it. He may have been thinking of exciting the president to executive clemency when he promised that Lincoln would have been amazed at the judgment and sentence if he had merely glanced at the defense testimony.[29]

After remarking sarcastically on the military merits of the court members who won promotion for no obvious reason but their service on the court, Johnson turned to Pope, Roberts, and Smith. He puzzled over the trust placed in Pope in the wake of his failure. He wryly complimented the convicted liar and cheat, Roberts, on his "well-known and universally acknowledged character for perfect veracity, almost chronic love of truth[,] and spotless reputation among his brother officers."[30]

Smith he mocked mercilessly for portraying Porter as a man with "a crime on his mind" with no evidence save fantastic intuition. To illustrate Smith's "conceited flummery," Johnson noted his alleged warning to Pope that he was so certain Pope was a traitor that he would have shot him, but for the law against it. He lampooned both Smith's clairvoyance and Holt's defense of such testimony as an honest effort to articulate the only evidence Smith could offer of Porter's state of mind. Johnson challenged Holt's judgment for that, and impugned his honesty for characterizing Smith as "a man of fine intelligence" in his review for the president, in which Holt had paraphrased Smith's testimony to make it seem less preposterous. In a question still worthy of examination today, Johnson also seemed to wonder whether Lincoln was actually credulous enough to trust Smith's mind reading and Holt's sophistry.[31]

With more searing irony, Johnson complimented Holt's talents, citing his selective use of Burnside's telegrams to sustain Smith's "ravings and wild fantasies." Johnson demonstrated that Burnside had specifically requested Porter's dispatches, so he could act in accordance with events on Pope's front: they contained much important intelligence and sound advice, and while they did occasionally express great frustration with the obvious confusion in Pope's army, every fact they conveyed was true. Moreover, General Burnside had testified that the "great lack of confidence" he saw in Porter's dispatches was voiced by "a large portion" of the officers in that theater.[32]

If Porter had been a traitor from August 27 through 29, Johnson wondered, why did he fight so desperately on August 30? Holt had reflexively charged him with perfidy on that day, too, without a shred of evidence, yet Porter had lost more than two thousand of the seven thousand men who were on the field with him. Johnson derisively lauded Holt's "generous clemency" in withdrawing the specification charging Porter with treachery on August 30, the absolute groundlessness of which was proven by Holt's own evidence.[33]

One argument Johnson did not present, except indirectly, was that the Articles of War stipulated that accusations should be made at the time of a perceived transgression, rather than being saved for later. Article 35, paragraph 8, generally prohibited the accumulation of offenses in order to "form collectively, a crime of sufficient magnitude to justify a prosecution." Charges should be filed on the spot, if the evidence warranted, and not be "subsequently revived" except in extraordinary cases. The case against Porter had been pressed a full three months after the fact, and it included elements such as the decision to march late on August 28, which should certainly have been prosecuted at the time if at all. Johnson made only a backhanded reference to that prohibition when he pointed out that Pope did not press charges at the time and denied having done so later.[34]

Once he had persuasively discredited the prosecutor and his witnesses, Johnson launched into a point-by-point rebuttal of all the specifications leveled against Porter. Even more effectively than in Eames's summation, he dismantled the government's entire case, but when the carefully proofread pamphlet appeared at midsummer it aroused predictable reactions. In Eliza Porter's old community of Alexandria, Virginia, the local paper recommended it as an "able reply," and quickly concluded that it was changing people's minds about Porter's conviction. A former Holt admirer in Baltimore admitted as much to Johnson.[35] The *Reply* was published just in time for the autumn elections, and did good service as a campaign document for the Democratic Party, exemplifying the injustice Radicals would exercise against conservatives. The booklet retailed for fifty cents, but party organizers bought hundreds of copies at ten cents each. Johnson earned good marks from editors of his political persuasion for his "conclusive refutation" of the slanders heaped on Porter, and for exposing Lincoln's partisan sacrifice of a loyal officer.[36]

Republican sheets mostly dissented, disparaging the *Reply* as long and tedious, perhaps in hopes of discouraging readership. The *Washington Chronicle*, the Lincoln administration's primary mouthpiece in the capital, published an indignant response to Johnson's *Reply*—anonymous, but readily identifiable as the work of Holt because it took such umbrage at the allegations against Holt. Holt asked Pope for a copy of the *Proceedings of a General Court Martial*, to facilitate an expanded retort, and Pope referred him to Smith, who had copies remaining.[37]

Holt's unsigned *Chronicle* piece claimed that shortly before Porter's conviction was announced, Johnson had declared before "several high officers of the Government" that the trial had been "perfectly fair." Johnson sent Porter a clipping of that article on the day it ran, calling the statement "entirely false."[38]

The most gratifying response Porter saw to Johnson's *Reply* may have come from the *Boston Daily Advertiser*, a Republican paper deep in the Lincoln camp. After comparing Johnson's *Reply* against Holt's review, which had been available for seven months, the editor concluded that the evidence did not justify Porter's sentence—and he seemed to mean that it failed to justify the verdict. "The evidence upon the essential points is weak," he noticed, "and whatever bears against him is contradicted." Attributing the conviction to "one of those unfortunate mistakes . . . which have characterized the management of the War Department," he reasoned that the Union cause was "too strong to need to be propped up by any such miserable expedient as the unjust attempt to sacrifice the character of any body, least of all that of a soldier so brave and so capable as Gen. Porter."[39]

Through the summer of 1863 Porter visited a succession of friends who had invited him to their rural retreats. After the relative isolation of Oyster Bay he spent a few weeks with General Patterson on his country estate in southern New Jersey. Next, he visited Theodore Randolph, a state senator living in Morristown, New Jersey. Randolph may have been introduced to Porter through McClellan's effort to find him employment, for he was interested in mining and railroads, which were both fields Porter was looking into.[40]

He returned to 66 Union Place in the latter half of September. Publication of Johnson's *Reply* spawned a new flurry of supportive letters, including two from gossipy census supervisor Joseph Kennedy, whose eagerness to share Porter's letter with Seward had first sparked Pope's annoyance. Over the next few months Porter wrote to friends who were still in the army, especially in the Fifth Corps, sending copies of Johnson's pamphlet in hopes of allaying any doubts about his innocence. Replies full of good wishes, and even hoping that he would return to the army, trickled back to him into the following winter, but by then

Porter had lost faith in an early restoration. He needed a job, and thanks to Randolph and Sam Barlow he found one.[41]

Late in January, Porter boarded a westbound train on a mission for sponsors in and around New York. In 1864 the railroad lines still ended on the Missouri River opposite Atchison, Kansas, and on the third of February he found overnight lodging in that town. The hotel clerk recognized his name and alerted the editor of the *Atchison Champion*, who duly noted the passage through his fair city of "Fitz John Porter, Esq.," formerly connected with the Army of the Potomac. Before he left, the next morning, the celebrated guest revealed that he was on his way to Colorado.[42]

For more than four hundred miles the stagecoaches bounded over the same route he had ridden to Utah seven autumns before, following the Platte River before veering southwest toward the new territory. By late February he was surveying the mining prospects around Black Hawk, a hard day's ride into the foothills of the Rockies west of Denver. He found the terrain promising, as did many, for he had arrived just as the region became the focus of wild speculation. In recognition of the demand for the land he hastened back East with an encouraging report to his sponsors — arriving in New York late in March, just as his nephew died of consumption.[43]

In talking to the potential investors, Porter emphasized what was called the Gunnell Lode, and on the last day in March the Gunnell Gold Company advertised its stock for sale in New York City. Porter's name served as the primary attraction in the advertisement as the author of a report "showing the enormous value of the property." Most Republicans might have demurred, but Democrats thought him as capable as ever, and enough subscribers came forward to buy four hundred feet of the Gunnell Lode for $300,000 and fund more speculation. The company named Porter general manager at $15,000 a year, sending him back to hire men, engineer the mine, and supervise construction of a mill. At the same time, he served as superintendent of the New York Gold Mining Company, with most of the same trustees and officers.[44]

Earning nearly three times as much as he had as a major general, Porter could rest easy about finances for a time. Curving like a centipede along a single dirt street gouged into Gregory Gulch, Black Hawk offered the disappointing amenities and exorbitant prices of any boomtown: during the following winter, board ran between ten and twenty dollars a week, and firewood the same per cord. Still, on half of his first year's salary he could support himself and his family and retire all his debts. The opportunity did not come too soon, for Harriet was pregnant again by the time he left New York.[45]

The newly flush mining engineer wrote to McClellan more than once to tell him how things stood, but none of those letters reached their destination. McClellan was running for president that fall, and he suspected his mail was being intercepted. Republican newspapers had intensified their campaign to vilify him for his association with Porter, and the War Department strove to taint him vicariously through theatrical treason investigations. When Stanton sent Ben Butler to New York with troops to "monitor" the presidential election, Butler claimed to have reports that Porter was in the city, and up to no good. Porter and a few other disaffected officers were organizing secret paramilitary legions, Butler claimed, with the intention of installing McClellan as president by force of arms if the election results came close enough. Porter, who was wholly occupied with affairs in Colorado, did not learn of that fabrication until years later.[46]

The Gunnell Lode ultimately did yield a great deal of gold, but such ventures require much capital and great risk, as Porter and the shareholders quickly learned. Six months into his tenure as superintendent, the mine's balance sheet ran heavily on the side of expenses. The cost of building what he called the Enterprise Mill far outran expectations, but Porter remained doggedly optimistic. Once he had installed the wheel and flume to power the stamping machines, he promised that the company would "soon realize the value of the outlay, in the great savings of wages and fuel." On November 18 his miners struck what he called the "paying vein," consisting of a fourteen-inch-wide stratum of "excellent pyritic ore." He planned to dig from forty to sixty feet lower, he informed the company secretary, and then start sloping upward. "The moment I commence sloping, the Company will have a constantly paying mine," he promised — as confidently as he had assured Manton Marble of the imminent capture of Richmond.[47]

Eastern investors stood a good chance of buying a claim with nothing in it, or that someone had jumped, for the law regarding titles remained rather fluid in the sixth summer of prospecting in Gilpin County. After listing a number of worthless or shallow lodes for one of his New York clients, Porter added eight that had been preempted by claim jumpers who were working them under other names. "I learned that the laws of Nevada District authorize the jumping of claims if abandoned or not worked for a certain length of time," he told the customer, indicating that "laws" differed from one gulch to another. The speculative fever of 1864 inspired such rampant fraud that deed offices instituted burdensome filing requirements, and Porter spent much of his time waiting for court orders and powers of attorney.[48]

Then came trouble with the Cheyenne and Arapaho on the plains of eastern Colorado. The very number of miners and speculators flooding into the region assured more encounters, and the friction inevitably bred hostility. The territorial governor reported the killing of settlers east of Denver in June, and asked for authority to raise a regiment of hundred-day troops. Two months later Stanton authorized it, and the recruiting siphoned so much labor out of the mining country that wages had to soar to attract anyone. Once the troops took to the field, hostile incidents accelerated, and the cavalry chased after wandering bands rather than focusing on Denver's communications with the East. That made any trip to the mining country so dangerous that transportation costs doubled the price of everything necessary to work a mine. Delivering the machinery for Porter's stone stamping mill at Black Hawk cost a small fortune, and with so little labor available it could not be put to use at once—nor did it ever go into operation. Then, as the enlistment of the hundred-day men was about to expire, Colonel John Chivington attacked a friendly Cheyenne village at Sand Creek, near the Kansas border, slaughtering mostly women and children and mutilating their bodies. Damning Chivington's "rascality and cowardice" in murdering friendly Indians and avoiding warriors, Porter anticipated a more widespread war that would seal them off from the East altogether.[49]

On top of all that came unexpectedly heavy snows and temperatures as low as twenty-eight degrees below zero. Work progressed slowly on the Gunnell Lode through the winter, much of which Porter spent surveying existing and prospective mines. He examined potential investments for shareholders in the company, and when time permitted he acted as an agent for others, including Barlow. He ranged as far as the headwaters of the South Platte, and considered making a trip into Utah for one New York City client, but that venture never materialized. He bought a few claims of his own, including one he called the Fitz John Porter Lode, where the ore assayed at $72.58 per ton for gold and $2.34 for silver. These holdings would be of great value if they could be worked, or sold, but lawlessness, war, and weather brought the speculative boom to a screeching halt. A year into his tenure as general manager he told a friend in New York that his fortunes had been "up and down," like those of the mining companies, but for him there had been more down than up. "Everything I seemed to touch came to misfortune," he confessed.[50]

The cutthroat culture of the gold fields shone brightly that spring. The superintendent of the rival Smith & Parmelee Gold Company had been trying to wrest the Gunnell Lode from Porter's company, and had sent thugs to drive the miners from that shaft. Porter confronted his nemesis personally and sued him for trespass, expecting that his suit would prevail if he remained on the scene to testify. When word reached Black Hawk of President Lincoln's assassination, partisan tempers flared, and one critic of the martyred president injudiciously revealed his glee at the news. A mob gathered, threatening violence to him, but Porter and the more conservative citizens collected the man and sent him off to Denver under what amounted to protective custody. Encouraged by the Smith & Parmelee superintendent, the mob held a formal meeting and passed a resolution demanding the expulsion of all "Democrats, Copperheads, Traitors etc." from the territory. Porter guessed that he was the main target of the resolution, and that it amounted to a patriotic pretense to prevent him from testifying.[51]

As a precaution, Porter apprised the commander of the military district of his opponents' motives, characterizing them as the same men who were siding with Chivington, whose popularity bore a partisan flavor. The Denver and Black Hawk newspapers had been dueling over Chivington for weeks, with the *Rocky Mountain News* chastising the *Black Hawk Journal* for abusing Denver's Indian-hunting hero. Similar animosities led to the assassination of Denver's provost marshal, who had recently testified against Chivington before the congressional committee investigating the massacre he unleashed at Sand Creek.[52]

Porter recovered possession of the mine, but with all the converging complications he produced only $109,000 worth of bullion for the company in his first full year as business manager and mining superintendent. Late in June he rode deeper into the mountains to examine rumored silver veins, anticipating disappointing results, but he came away favorably impressed. Nonetheless he had already decided to resign and go home, leaving a successor to reap better profits from the company's investment in quieter times. In August he rode to Denver, sold his horse, and boarded an eastbound stage. The transcontinental railroad had started reaching westward from Council Bluffs, Iowa, by the time he left the mines, and a stage line led to that railhead. Porter stopped in Des Moines for what Iowans were calling the Soldiers' State Convention, which the Radical papers characterized as the Copperhead convention. Porter had evidently been involved in an advisory role with Iowa Democrats living in Black Hawk, and was corresponding with state party officials, suggesting men for various offices from afar. He stayed in Des Moines long enough to see his candidates nominated, then continued homeward.[53]

There was a new baby at 66 Union Place when he arrived. Evelina Sanford Porter, who would become her father's last surviving defender, had been born there on January 20. Porter remained at home three months, but in his anxiety to restore his fortunes he applied for a passport early in December and sailed for England, where he hoped to sell some of his mining claims and those of some of his clients. He was gone three and a half months, returning to New York from Liverpool late in March of 1866, little wealthier than when he left.[54]

No sooner had Porter come home again than he found himself accused in a New Jersey newspaper of having left his company accounts in Black Hawk with a shortfall of $75,000. He complained about it to his friend William C. Prime, of the *Journal of Commerce*, in order to have it corrected. The secretary of the company provided him with a letter documenting that his accounts had closed with a shortfall of $108.12, which Porter paid at once in cash, and that it had been offset by a small surplus that he "declined to receive." The same malicious squib nevertheless turned up in newspapers across the country into the summer.[55]

At nearly the same time, early in May, a history of the Army of the Potomac appeared from the pen of William Swinton, a former correspondent for the *New*

York Times. The maps in Swinton's book had been drawn by Captain William H. Paine, formerly an aide to John Pope, and Paine's contempt for Pope may have shown through, for Swinton paid particular attention to Second Bull Run. He obtained Confederate reports from Longstreet and his corps, and with them he documented his conclusion that Confederates had "covered Porter's whole front" at Dawkin's Branch. In a footnote nearly two pages long he disproved the very foundation of the narrative of seditious inactivity the government had spent so many weeks and so much money composing. Swinton's book had not been available for a week before this detail of it started attracting newspaper notice, sometimes on the front page, and often with special recognition that this constituted vindication for Porter. Radical papers confirmed the significance of this new evidence by the very scorn they heaped on it. Both the *New York Tribune* and the *Chicago Tribune* attacked Swinton as well as Porter, with the Chicago paper reviewing the book under the heading of "A Copperhead Historian."[56]

Swinton's history caught Porter's attention right away, awakening a determination to restore his good name. John Pope also noticed the book, and recognized immediately that it undermined his primary excuse for the disaster at Second Bull Run. Sending excerpts of the relevant chapter to Smith, who had returned to civilian life, Pope accused Swinton of having "distorted or misstated the truth in the interest of the McClellan & Porter clique." The erstwhile *Times* man had misrepresented the battle through "suppressions & misstatements of the most ingenious character," Pope complained, and for the next two decades he would press Smith to write a more flattering book on his campaign.[57]

Family and employment distracted Porter from resuming his quest to restore his reputation. For the sake of either his children or Harriet's aunt, or both, he decided to move out of New York City shortly after his visit to England. Mrs. Holbrook had originally taken her niece in to fill a void in a home with plenty of room, but the children ranged in age from one to eight, and likely Porter thought of raising them in a less crowded environment. His association with Theodore Randolph had some influence on the decision, as well, for he rented a house in Randolph's home town of Morristown, New Jersey. He had to haggle with the previous tenant over replacing wallpaper and glass, and cleaning the cesspool, but he moved Hattie and the children into the new home early in the summer of 1866.[58]

Randolph had become interested in another enterprise known as the Spring Mountain Coal Company, which was mining eight hundred acres of slope below Hazelton, Pennsylvania. He was also involved in the Morris & Essex Railroad, and was soon installed as president; that line ran to Hoboken, New Jersey, and carried a great deal of Lehigh coal to New York from other mines in eastern Pennsylvania. Randolph and his brother, who owned the company together, authorized the contracts and put Porter to work in the firm's New York office. The company had a manager at the mine, but the coming of peace left great stockpiles of coal, and the decreased demand depressed wages, which spawned organized resistance from the miners. Strikes erupted that autumn all across the anthracite fields, where numerous absentee owners had divided the country-side into company towns, and while most of those actions had ended by winter they had to be resolved individually. The Spring Mountain mines faced a series of local strikes that lasted through the spring of 1866, but when they ended Por-ter began recruiting industrial customers among his corporate connections and old army friends. What compensation Porter received is not on record, but by September Randolph gave him $6,000 to invest in the Morris & Essex line on behalf of Harriet.[59]

A couple of months after Swinton's book raised the first doubts about the claims against Porter, editor Alfred Guernsey of *Harper's Weekly* wrote an equally pointed defense of him in an article on Bull Run for the *World*. That publicity stirred a former aide of Porter's — George Batchelder, who identified himself as a Radical Republican — to suggest that it was time for the general to seek official vindication. Since it was Republicans who had treated Porter so unjustly, Batchelder argued, Republicans ought to have the opportunity to rec-tify the wrong. Porter replied gratefully but doubtfully from the company office at 28 Trinity Place on Monday morning, August 20. New York's newspapers boiled over with political vitriol that day: the *New York Tribune* blasted Andrew Johnson as a traitor to the Radical cause for declaring the rebellion over and ending martial law; the *Herald* lauded Johnson for restoring the Union, and the *Sun* reported on the speeches of both Reverdy Johnson and President John-son, praising the resolutions of a conservative convention. Porter asked Batch-elder how he could possibly expect justice from ruling Republicans when they were the very people who had refused to publish the full proceedings of his trial. Wouldn't it be better to wait until "partisan passions became calmed," he asked — by which he again probably meant after Democrats had regained con-trol of the government.[60]

Batchelder had nonetheless kindled a fire. Porter had no sooner finished his reply to that encouraging missive than he dipped his pen in the inkwell again. Writing first to Marsena Patrick and then to John P. Hatch, he asked those two former brigadiers in Rufus King's division if they knew whether King had been with their command after it marched from Manassas on August 29, 1862. En-closing both notes in a letter to Colonel Chauncey McKeever, a trustworthy old friend at the Adjutant General's office, Porter asked him to forward them to the addresses on file for the pair at the War Department. With that day's correspon-dence, his twenty-year crusade for reinstatement had begun.[61]

17

THE QUEST

Marsena Patrick had Porter's note within four days and replied as soon as he read it. He thought the man with McDowell could not have been King, who (Patrick believed) had left his bivouac near Manassas on the morning of August 29 to go to Centreville, but he offered to come to New York and talk over the points Porter wished to prove. From his post at San Antonio, Hatch likewise answered immediately, and with the same opinion, although he attributed King's illness to "drinking hard," which left him "very much shattered." Hatch, too, invited Porter to ask for any help he could give, volunteering that any officer from the old Mounted Rifles would have testified that Benny Roberts could not be believed even under oath. "I certainly would have done so," he added.[1]

Confederate reports from the Second Bull Run campaign appeared serialized in the *Rebellion Record* early that summer of 1866, and Longstreet's report confirmed all Swinton had claimed. On September 7 Porter wrote to that ex-Confederate, asking a few questions about his part in the battle. Longstreet answered in a letter from northern Mississippi, showing remarkably good penmanship for a man who had only recently learned to write with his left hand: he asked only that his letter not be published, because of his vulnerable position as a prominent former Rebel. His corps was ready to receive an attack by 11:00 A.M. August 29, he wrote, and he remembered the ground on his right, south of the turnpike, being inhospitable for artillery or an infantry attack. "If you had attacked any time after 12 M.," he concluded, "it seems to me that we surely would have destroyed your army. That is, if you had attacked with less than twenty-five thousand men."[2]

Cadmus Wilcox, one of Longstreet's division commanders, was living in New York himself at the time. He recounted trailing the rest of Longstreet's corps from the Gainesville side of Thoroughfare Gap by 9:30 on the morning of August 29, with about fifty-five hundred men, and he attested to the vigor of Porter's attack the next day. Wilcox, who had spent three years at West Point with Porter, also confirmed the accuracy of Guernsey's article defending Porter in the *World*, insofar as his assertions about Confederate dispositions.

So did Robert E. Lee. Longstreet suggested that Porter write to Lee as the best possible witness, and he did, promising to keep his reply confidential. Lee confirmed that Confederate forces would have been prepared for any attack from the Gainesville Road on August 29. Porter never used the information during Lee's lifetime, but the erstwhile Rebel chieftain repeated that opinion within his own family: he told a cousin that he had seen Porter's troops himself, and that he outflanked them, rather than Porter outflanking him. Lee also speculated that the court-martial may have been less interested in finding the truth than in relieving Pope and Lincoln of responsibility for a campaign that reflected badly on both.[3]

Through the winter, friends encouraged Porter to petition President Johnson for a reconsideration of his case. Robert Eddy, his cousin in Boston, thought he had a good chance of success with such war heroes behind him as their other cousin, Admiral David Dixon Porter. Eddy said he knew that General Grant was in favor of him, too. George Batchelder approached Radicals of his acquaintance in and around Boston, including Senator Henry Wilson, the chairman of the Committee on Military Affairs. Porter had had some trouble with Wilson when he was the colonel of the 22nd Massachusetts, but the senator supplied a letter heartily recommending the examination of new evidence in his case. Batchelder also managed to pique the interest of John Andrew, the Radical war governor of Massachusetts, and abolitionist congressman George Boutwell. Down in Pennsylvania, relatives of General Patterson were at work for Porter, and in Washington he had the support of Lincoln's former postmaster general, Montgomery Blair. Ex-president Franklin Pierce and his predecessor, Millard Fillmore, both supplied letters deploring the injustice done Porter.[4]

In the middle of January Porter took the train to Washington, where he consulted with Reverdy Johnson about the petition to President Johnson. Once home, he prepared a letter outlining how the paranoia of 1862 had excited prejudice against him, and reminding Johnson that Confederate records cut the legs from under the government's case. His plea was endorsed by four of the most prominent U.S. Senators—including Henry Wilson—as well as Governor Andrew Curtin of Pennsylvania, Congressman Nathaniel Banks, and Horace Greeley of the *New York Tribune*—Republicans all. Folding in relevant excerpts from Swinton's book and Guernsey's article, Porter mailed it from New York on January 28.[5]

Other recommendations went directly to the president. Admiral Porter, then commandant of the U.S. Naval Academy, urged Johnson to intercede for "an officer who has gallantly served his country and met with calumny as his reward." He had known General Porter since childhood, wrote the admiral, "and when he was brought to trial for causes that never existed," and always knew him to be loyal. John Tucker, still assistant secretary of war and still indignant about

Porter's treatment, approached Stanton and secured what he thought was a promise not to oppose a reopening of the case. Patrick corroborated the intense darkness around Warrenton Junction the night Porter was ordered to march. Pope's former chief quartermaster sent a similar statement, relating how he lost sight of a guide who was mounted on a white horse, and could keep his party together only by continually having them answer to their names. Chauncey McKeever, who had been chief of staff to Heintzelman, reinforced that depiction and ridiculed Pope's suggestion that the troops could have marched on the railroad, littered as it was with torn-up rails and burning ties.[6]

The appeal languished without reply for more than seven months. While he waited, Porter moved into the first home he ever owned, buying it from Randolph. In April of 1867 he paid $20,000 for a house on six acres right beside Randolph's home on the north side of Madison Avenue, a mile and a half below Morristown. He covered most of the price with a mortgage, but recorded the purchase in Harriet's name. Behind the two houses lay only open fields and forests as far as the tracks of the Morris & Essex Railroad. That line carried him to the coal company office in New York while Harriet and the children enjoyed the fresh air and serenity of a town with fewer than six thousand residents.[7]

On May 3, Porter traveled to Philadelphia to meet John Tucker, who gave him an inside view of administration affairs.[8] Congress was engaged in open warfare with Andrew Johnson over Reconstruction policy by then, overriding Johnson's vetoes so routinely that he might not be able to do much for Porter beyond issuing a pardon. The battle for dominance between the legislative and executive branches concentrated finally on Edwin Stanton, who was serving as the Radicals' agent within the cabinet, and it came to a head at midsummer.

Early in August, Johnson learned inadvertently that the military commission trying the Lincoln conspirators had advised commutation of Mary Surratt's death sentence. He had not seen that recommendation when Holt brought the sentences for him to approve, at which time Johnson was confined to his bed. Holt effectively admitted that he had not specifically apprised the ailing president of it, insisting that Johnson's "eye necessarily fell on the petition"—but the papers were so arranged that his eye may have fallen on the meaningless reverse side of it. Holt had evidently cleared the way for Surratt's execution just as he had helped assure that Lincoln would approve Porter's conviction, but he would deny it with histrionic indignation. Stanton worked so closely with Holt that it was difficult to detect which of them lay behind such tricks, and Johnson dismissed Stanton as secretary of war, defying recent congressional legislation requiring him to seek Senate approval. He named General Grant as interim secretary of war, and Grant reluctantly accepted.[9]

The appointment of Grant inspired Porter to prod the bureaucracy once again. Stanton was out of the way, and in his place stood a man Robert Eddy thought was on Porter's side. Porter went to Washington again and called on Grant at the War Department on September 10. They met the next day, and Porter later said that Grant told him to expect a reopening of the case by September 17 — advising him to take all the documentation in his appeal packet home. Porter went to see the president the morning of September 12, anticipating that Grant would approve the request at the cabinet meeting on Friday, September 13. With that he returned to the company office in New York.[10]

Porter saw that some of his papers had been leaked to the press after his first interview with Grant. He did not suspect Grant, but Holt was involved, and such leaks were a common ploy of his. It was unquestionably through Holt that John Pope, commanding occupation forces in Atlanta, learned immediately of Porter's mission in Washington. Pope first wrote Grant about it on September 13, initially arguing against reopening the case and then begging that any review board be composed of "officers above partiality and prejudice." To chair that impartial board, Pope suggested his and Grant's good friend General Sherman. He followed up with a long letter echoing with desperation, in which he discounted the relevance of Porter's new evidence (which he had not yet seen), and he telegraphed Grant that the letter was coming, asking him to take no action until he had it.[11]

Instead of advising the president on September 13 to empanel a board to review the case, as Porter expected, Grant recommended that no action be taken until Porter produced evidence to refute the testimony that had convicted him. No such evidence accompanied the appeal, he said. Perhaps Grant misunderstood the crux of the complicated case against Porter, and failed to realize how exculpatory Longstreet's claims were. Porter explained in a long and detailed letter how the correspondence from various prospective witnesses dismantled the claims of the prosecution, charge by charge, but Holt obstinately maintained that they disproved nothing.[12]

Holt worked steadily on Grant to scuttle the appeal from inside. Grant asked him on September 15, as the War Department's presumed legal expert, if an officer dismissed by court-martial could have a new trial. Holt responded the next day with what he characterized as informal suggestions nearly two thousand words in length, mustering abundant case law and detail to support his predictable opinion that a new trial would be "improper." Grant was not familiar with the more telling details of Holt's malicious manipulation of the case, and those who did know his role never saw his letter. They did see a hostile article on Porter's appeal in the *Chronicle* the same day he gave Grant his opinion, and it, too, smelled strongly of Holt.[13]

Porter returned to Washington immediately to hand-deliver his response, bringing along the documentation and endorsements Grant had advised him to take home. He saw Grant on the morning of September 18, and Holt's influence emerged in Grant's preference to put the case before the attorney general, to determine whether the president could even grant a reexamination. Porter replied that cases such as his had previously been reopened, reconsidered, and reversed by the War Department, but he did not care whether he was afforded a court-martial, a court of inquiry, or some kind of board with only advisory capacity. His only goals, he said, were exoneration and remittal of his sentence.[14]

Porter complained of his troubles to Grant's West Point classmate William Franklin, and Franklin wrote to Grant, corroborating the improprieties of the court and Holt, and noting the mendacity of Pope and Roberts. An erstwhile army officer from Philadelphia supplied Porter with the records of three men who were dismissed and reinstated in 1848 alone. Porter also had court-martial records for Benny Roberts, who escaped dismissal in 1839 by resigning, was reappointed, and then dismissed in 1850 for falsifying his pay accounts and other frauds, only to have the secretary of war remit the sentence.[15]

Acting Adjutant General Edward Townsend, Porter's old friend, nevertheless told him that tradition and law precluded giving an officer a new trial, and without one the president could not reappoint him. Discounting Porter's belief that Holt was interfering, Townsend said it wasn't that at all: Grant simply wanted the attorney general to confirm that it was legal. With a supportive legal opinion perhaps Grant would have acted, but Pope had been alerted to Porter's progress with information known only to a few, so someone high in the War Department was working to foil him. Townsend himself may no longer have been perfectly reliable, having become a favorite of Stanton, who had named Townsend executor of his will.[16]

Holt's machinations, Pope's self-interested intercession, and Grant's equivocation posed only the first of the hurdles Porter would face. Senator Charles Sumner, who had been central to the undoing of Charles Stone, called for the papers in Porter's case, and when they appeared in the Senate he asked to have them all printed. They were, and that brought Franklin's derogatory letter about Pope and Roberts into the newspapers soon thereafter, causing Franklin some trouble with Roberts. Less than a week after Porter's file was ordered printed, his court-martial antagonist James Garfield, serving as a congressman from Ohio, entered a bill that backhandedly required Senate approval for any dismissed officer who was reappointed. Some in the chamber criticized that as a personal blow at Porter, but Garfield disingenuously denied it, noting that the bill was "general in its terms." Besides, he argued, it specifically allowed the president to reappoint an officer who had been dismissed or cashiered, so long as he had not also been barred from holding a position with the government — as Porter had been.[17]

Garfield's bill passed the House handily and went to the Senate, where it became an excuse to malign Porter anew. Reverdy Johnson tried to defend him, but he was outnumbered by opponents and opportunists. Ever venomous, Zachariah Chandler attacked with sarcasm and falsehood, denying Porter's part at Malvern Hill and resurrecting the old lie that he had marched his troops off the field at Second Bull Run when ordered to attack. Conflating George Smalley's speculative reporting with testimony before the Committee on the Conduct of the War, Chandler accused Porter of lying five miles away from the battle of Antietam—"and when McClellan suggested to him that he go in he shook his head."[18]

Simon Cameron, who as secretary of war in 1861 had prevented Porter from subduing rebellious Baltimore, showed the influence of the Radical view of Porter and aggravated it with a fantasy of his own. He told the Senate that early in the war he had admired Porter's talents and energy, but that he had later been disappointed in him. Accusing Porter of having dominated Robert Patterson's council of war in the standoff before Winchester, Cameron blamed him for having dissuaded Patterson from attacking Joe Johnston, thereby allowing him to aid Beauregard at Bull Run. Cameron said Patterson himself had confided how he refrained from attacking mostly on Porter's advice, but that could not have been true: Patterson was always a warm champion of his former chief of staff, and the minutes of the council in question attested that Porter was not even present.[19]

Henry Wilson calmed the rhetoric with the observation that Porter was not looking for reinstatement, but for vindication of his reputation, as Porter implied in a letter to Cameron that Cameron read into the record. Garfield's demonstrated bias as a member of Porter's court had not abated, and his bill was allowed to move through to eventual passage, posing another difficult impediment for Porter.

Any hope of executive relief under Andrew Johnson died in the struggle between him and Stanton. In January the Senate returned Stanton to office, and when Johnson tried to fire him again the House passed articles of impeachment, leading to a trial that left Johnson with only a shell of a presidency. "Any effort to stur [sic] the matter now will only grind me to pieces in the Radical mill," Porter lamented. Grant was elected president in November, and in the last days of the Johnson administration Porter wrote to ask for the return of his appeal packet, intending to file it anew following Grant's inauguration. After a search, Johnson's secretary had to report that none of his original papers could be found.[20]

An infuriated and understandably paranoid Porter described the file as "stolen." Over the course of nearly a year and a half, the papers had passed within range of Stanton, Holt, and a host of hostile clerks and congressmen. Eventually they were all found in Johnson's private papers, but not in time for Porter to use them, and probably they had been returned to the White House rather than to the attorney general after the Senate had them printed. The attorney general did not have the file to rule on, while the president thought it was with the attorney general, but both were probably content to let the question lie dormant.[21]

George Batchelder would not let it lie. He sent Senator Chandler a poignant reply to his innuendo and accusations, noting that Porter commanded the best division in the army, and he knew no one in it who did not "speak of him in warm terms of affection and admiration"—which, he added, was rare for any commander. Batchelder told Chandler that as a special messenger from Porter to Burnside he knew personally how anxious Porter was to aid Pope's army. He named a dozen generals who went unpunished for worse transgressions than Porter was accused of. "Fitz John Porter was as true a gentleman, as loyal and brave a man, and an abler soldier than any of the court that tried him," Batchelder concluded, urging Chandler to help right the wrong. "Do it now while the alleged offence is of a comparatively recent date and not wait till he is an old man worn out with struggling against disappointment and misfortune." Chandler ignored that stirring plea.[22]

Similar tribute from other high-ranking officers, including many staunch Republicans, failed to budge President Grant, who began to suppose that Porter must have been culpable somehow.[23] That assumption, the press of time, and the potential political consequences combined to dissuade Grant (as they had Lincoln) from making the close examination that would eventually convince him that Porter had been perfectly innocent.

Grant had not held the presidency four months when, in June of 1869, Porter published a pamphlet containing copies of all the documentation that had been lost in his last appeal. He prefaced it with a letter to General Sherman, whose brigade he had taken over in 1861 and who then commanded the armies of the United States, asking him to pass it on to the president. Repeating that he had proof he was unjustly convicted, Porter requested that Grant remit the part of his sentence banning him from any government position, and then nominate him to his old rank under the provisions of Garfield's 1868 bill. Sherman waited almost five months before he recommended removing the prohibition. He ignored the claim of exculpatory evidence, and advised against restoring Porter to his old Regular Army rank because there were already twenty colonels for whom there were no regiments; he considered it "impossible" to have another.[24]

Grant did nothing with the petition, but word of its receipt did travel to John Pope, who again dismissed Porter's new evidence and objected to any relief for the man who served as his scapegoat. It would constitute an insult to the whole army to mitigate Porter's sentence, he assured the secretary of war. Calling it justice to all "honorable officers" of the army, Pope pleaded with Grant to accept his own recently printed "Brief Statement of the Case of Fitz John Porter," which was founded entirely on carefully arranged misinformation. That five-page argument began with Thomas C. H. Smith's adroitly inaccurate map of the situation at Bull Run on August 29; then Pope inserted an excerpt of Stonewall Jackson's report that McDowell had sent him, in which Jackson described his desperate situation on August 30, but Pope's heading to that excerpt identified it as referring to August 29. That made it appear that Porter's inaction at Dawkin's Branch had saved Jackson from inevitable rout, when in fact the crisis Jackson mentioned had been caused by Porter's own attack the next day. Pope also included Porter's August 29 dispatch to McDowell and King, editing it to sustain the myth that Porter had retreated to Manassas. By such serial, active deception he accused Porter of "desertion from the field of battle with the strongest & best corps of the Army, without firing a gun & in positive disobedience of orders to attack the enemy, abandoning his comrades to defeat & disaster."[25]

Pope's "Brief Statement" nearly led him to a court-martial of his own. He tried to confine its circulation to the president, the secretary of war, and General Sherman, but he gave a copy to James Garfield, who sent it to the *Cincinnati Commercial*. Its publication in that paper eventually brought it to the attention of Porter, who asked Sherman whether the extract from Jackson's report had been certified by the Archive Office. Later he requested certified copies of Jackson's report and his dispatch to McDowell and King, to see if they had been accurately quoted, and Holt himself responded that they had been, but the copies he forwarded demonstrated otherwise. Pope insisted for years that the adjutant general had certified the extracts, but General Townsend finally deduced that Pope's captions and notes had introduced new, inaccurate information. General John Gibbon, whose brigade had been battered at Bull Run, hounded Pope about the discrepancy, and learned that Smith had helped Pope produce the "Brief Statement." When Smith publicly claimed that he had warned Pope about the inaccuracy before it was published, Gibbon accused Pope of forgery, filing formal charges against him for conduct unbecoming an officer. Pope read about the charges in the newspapers, but he appealed to Sherman as general of the army, and Gibbon's charges were never prosecuted.[26]

It was probably also Pope, then in Detroit, who put Senator Chandler back on Porter's scent. On February 21, 1870, Chandler praised Pope and attacked Porter again in a long speech delivered on the Senate floor. He belittled Porter's new evidence, and said that he had some of his own, producing J. E. B. Stuart's report of Bull Run, with its boast of having held Porter off by having his cavalry drag brush to raise clouds of dust. Chandler garnished it with a new accusation that he said came from a congressional employee he would not identify. According to Chandler's nameless source, Porter had essentially confessed his betrayal of Pope in a private moment during his court-martial. Chandler frequently bolstered his statements with vociferous but perfectly false assertions, and this was no exception: he told the Senate that the revelation was "sworn testimony, taken down within two minutes after the utterance was made." In fact, it had never been sworn to, and the assertion that it had been taken down at all was doubtful.[27]

Porter quickly published a pamphlet declaring the accusation "false in every particular," and chastising the senator for refusing him an opportunity to face his accuser. More than eight more years would pass before the mysterious witness was identified and subjected to a cross-examination, under which his story disintegrated. He was William Blair Lord, an official reporter for the House of Representatives. Lord appears to have been a creature cultivated by Holt, who occasionally groomed witnesses of doubtful credibility in cases of conspicuous political import. In an inquiry that seems to have been falsely dated in order to document an obvious fraud, Holt reminded Lord of the remarks he had ostensibly reported Porter making in 1862, suggestively hoping that Lord had some written record of it; he also wanted to know if Lord could produce another witness. Lord obliged him on all counts, claiming a *New York Times* reporter as his witness and mentioning that he had described the incident in a letter to his wife three days afterward. He didn't have the original letter (or the postmarked envelope), but he did have a copy of it in a letterbook — strange as it was for a man to keep verbatim copies of letters to his wife. Lord informed Holt that, by the purest coincidence, he had also just received a letter corroborating the tale from the reporter, although the letter turned out to be antedated by a year.[28]

Lord had been the stenographer Holt hired to record Porter's court-martial, and he alleged that on December 15, 1862, he and Porter left the courtroom to go to the general's quarters for some telegrams. He said they were accompanied by Waterman Ormsby, the *Times* reporter. According to Lord, while they were there Porter absentmindedly admitted that he had not served Pope faithfully. In the letter purportedly written to his wife, Lord quoted Porter talking like a backwoodsman, saying, "I warn't loyal to Pope; there is no denying that." In the misdated letter in which Ormsby purportedly remembered the same incident nearly a decade later, he used exactly the same words: "I warn't loyal to Pope," and in 1878 he would testify that this was precisely the pronunciation. He couldn't remember another word of the conversation, but he was positive about that. By 1878, however, Lord decided that Porter had said, "I was not loyal to Pope," despite his use of "I warn't" in the letter he said he wrote his wife three days after the fact.[29]

As one of Porter's lawyers later noted, their client did not use such crude speech, and it was absurd to suppose he would mumble a confession in front of a newspaper reporter and an employee of Holt's. Neither was it probable that two different people would recall precisely the same wording of an offhand comment eight years later, only to differ on it eight years after that. They also disagreed on who Porter was addressing, his tone of voice, where he was looking, and where the incident took place: Ormsby remembered them being in Porter's bedroom in "a very comfortable dwelling-house," rather than at Willard's Hotel, and Lord had no idea where Porter was lodging. One of Porter's attorneys later characterized the story somewhat generously as "improbable," lumping it with numerous instances of perjured testimony used either to convict Porter or to subvert his exoneration.[30]

The stench of collusion was overpowering, and Holt hardly seemed the innocent dupe he had claimed to be a few years earlier, in another case where he was suspected of falsifying evidence and suborning perjury. Holt and Lord could not even keep their stories straight about when Lord told him of Porter's supposed confession. Lord testified that he kept it to himself until the trial ended, but in his letter "reminding" Lord of the episode Holt purported that it had come in time to use in testimony, although he decided it was not needed. If it had not been necessary to secure a conviction in 1862, it was curious why Holt needed it so badly almost a decade later merely to prevent a rehearing. Yet that was what he wanted it for: in the letter he ostensibly wrote in 1871—a copy of which he had fortuitously retained—Holt implied that Lord's testimony would counteract a petition for reopening Porter's case submitted by a group of Fifth Corps veterans. Chandler's 1870 revelation of the claim, along with Ormsby's misdated letter, instead reveal that the scheme was spawned to subvert Porter's 1869 petition.[31]

Holt had not been entirely out of touch with Lord since Porter's trial. Late in 1864 Lord had written him to suggest that Holt's recent report on a mythical treasonous conspiracy in the West might lead to McClellan being court-martialed—"as Porter was." Implying political concurrence with Holt, whom he supposed would be judge advocate for such a case, Lord asked to be kept in mind to "assist" him again in taking testimony.[32]

Those who sought to block Porter from clearing his name waged their war against him mostly at public expense, while his serial appeals cost him dearly in printing, postage, travel, cartographers, and attorney fees. A modest income from the coal business fed his family, but the campaign to overturn his conviction limited his ability to save money. Randolph and some of his wealthy business associates in New York sought a more remunerative position for him as engineer in charge of the city's docks, but political impediments scuttled that effort, and Porter finally had to liquidate an asset. He owned 160 acres of bounty land near Nebraska City, Nebraska, from his Mexican War service, but had always kept it in his mother's name in case she needed it to support herself. By the time she reached her late sixties it was clear she would live the rest of her life with him, so he resumed ownership of that land and offered it for sale in the autumn of 1869. It may have been excess proceeds from this sale that allowed him to invest in another house on the other side of Madison Avenue from his home.[33]

After Senator Chandler's latest attack, one of New Jersey's elder statesmen wrote Randolph (who was by then the governor) to apprise him that Lincoln had once expressed a willingness to revisit Porter's case. William Newell, who had known Lincoln since they were in Congress together, said he asked the president about Porter late in 1864 — at Randolph's request, as he recalled. Lincoln told him he had had no time to study the case beyond Holt's review, but said he would happily reexamine it if new evidence were found. Newell's Republican credentials precluded any partisan purpose behind the claim, and he was indeed an old friend of Lincoln's, which lent his account authenticity. The detail that Lincoln relied entirely on Holt's jaundiced review also suggested that justice required a reexamination.[34]

The first appeal to President Grant nonetheless languished without an answer of any kind. Guessing that political pressures discouraged the new president from aiding him during his first term, Porter evidently decided to wait to submit another request until Grant was either reelected or replaced by a Democrat. While waiting, he corresponded steadily with friends and former enemies about Rebel troop strengths and positions at Dawkin's Branch, compiling a resounding rebuttal to the Pope faction's insistence that he had faced only light resistance.[35]

At the same time, he kept the War Department conscious of his case. Early in 1871 he submitted maps of the Bull Run battlefield showing the positions of enemy forces as described in Confederate reports. Statements made at his trial and in Union battle reports misrepresented the movements and strength of the enemy, he contended, and the existing maps reflected those errors. If his maps and letter were ever placed on file in the department, they were soon discarded.[36]

The spring of 1871 nevertheless brought Porter some gratification when the Society of the Fifth Army Corps met in Boston and resolved to appoint a committee to prepare a petition asking Grant to reopen the case. The resolution reportedly passed with only a single dissenting vote.[37] That resolution was carried to the president personally by Joshua Chamberlain, whom Grant had promoted to brigadier general in 1864, while the wounded Chamberlain lay on what everyone thought was his deathbed. The president told Chamberlain that Porter had better let the matter drop, because after looking into the case himself he thought another hearing would yield no advantage, and he would not advise reopening it.[38]

Gibbon assured Porter that Grant was "preeminently a just man," and that he would not let his friendship with Pope sway him "if he could only see his way clear in the matter of a rehearing," but Gibbon misinterpreted the impediment. Grant had evidently been persuaded of Porter's guilt by the perjury of key witnesses and the biased publications of Holt and Pope, and while he sat as

president he lacked the time for a close examination of the increasingly voluminous record. The foremost trait of Grant's character was his obstinacy: it often
served as his greatest virtue, but sometimes emerged as a glaring vice. He would
come to see Porter's side only in retirement, when he found the leisure to read
the entire trial transcript and study the record of the review that his successor
finally authorized.[39]

Meanwhile, Porter immersed himself in work. In Theodore Randolph's final
year as governor of New Jersey, he approved a new insane asylum to relieve the
overcrowded facility at Trenton. Just before his term ended, the state assembly
appropriated the funds and authorized a commission to select a site and oversee the project. Randolph appointed his neighbor, Judge Francis Lathrop, to
chair the commission, which chose a four-hundred-acre site on Morris Plains,
five miles north of Morristown. Both Randolph and Lathrop held Porter's engineering abilities in high regard, and a few days after Randolph left office the
commissioners announced that Porter would superintend the construction.[40]

Through this endeavor, the institution known as the lunatic asylum strove to
rebrand itself as the New Jersey State Asylum for the Insane. When completed,
it boasted the largest unbroken footprint of any building in the United States,
requiring a mile-long stroll to circle the complex. It was a classic piece of Second Empire artistry in granite, veneered in brick, with a five-story administration building facing east at its core, fronted with gigantic columns and topped
with a great dome. Three-and-a-half-story wings stretched away to the north
and south under a continuous mansard roof in a succession of right angles that
left every room in the building with a clear view of the surrounding countryside.
Ornate towers crowned each outer angle. Behind the facility sat an immense engine house, with boilers that heated the buildings through underground pipes
and a laundry to serve the staff and hundreds of patients. It was its own community, with a gasworks to the north, near the dammed brook called Asylum Pond,
which filled the icehouse in winter. West of the main building and the engine
house sat the barns, hogpens, and a farmhouse for the manager who oversaw the
patients' agricultural activities. Water came from two reservoirs created by Puff
Brook, south of the farm buildings. Railroad branches ran to the facility from
the nearby Morris & Essex line.[41]

Porter devoted the construction season of 1872 to excavating for the quarter-
mile-long foundation, using clay from the grounds to bake the first of five million bricks. He concentrated on the footings and foundation, so when work
stopped at the end of the year it seemed he had accomplished little, but progress
accelerated above ground level. Workmen returned early in the spring of 1873,
and by winter the northern wing that was to be the men's wards had been raised
and roofed. Between March and November of 1874 the shells of the women's
wing and the extensive central buildings were all completed, as were the bakery,

laundry, and boiler building. Underground connections fed steam to the radiators and hot and cold water to the kitchen and many bathrooms. When Porter filed his third annual report on November 1, he expected the entire complex to be enclosed by the first of the year. With heat installed via temporary boilers in the kitchen, work could continue through the winter, and Porter predicted that the masons, carpenters, and plasterers could finish the floors, walls, and interior trim by the spring of 1875.[42]

That tremendous preoccupation did not completely distract Porter from his principal ambition. Grant had won reelection in November of 1872, and Porter had kept in touch with him socially: they both attended the annual meeting of the Aztec Club at Robert Patterson's Philadelphia home in 1873, sitting barely five feet apart in a group portrait. The following autumn, four days before Porter submitted his 1874 report on the progress of the asylum, Porter again asked Grant to have his case reviewed. Once more he fattened the earlier file with new endorsements and the opinions of illustrious lawyers and judges who highlighted glaring improprieties in the court-martial. He included a new petition from the Society of the Fifth Army Corps, signed by hundreds of former officers, along with resolutions from the legislatures of New Hampshire and Pennsylvania calling for a new hearing or reinstatement.[43]

He was gambling that Grant was content with two terms as president, for if not he faced a political risk in approving the request. Unredeemed from the taint of treason, Porter remained a powerful bludgeon for Republicans to wield each election cycle, and the remaining Radicals would resent losing that weapon.

Grant told him once that if his new evidence exonerated him, every officer on the court-martial ought to demand that his case be reopened, and Porter made that suggestion to James Garfield. Garfield saw that Porter's persistence was starting to make the members of his court-martial look bad, but he would not take the bait. He denied that Porter had been wronged, and defended his recent legislation on the reexamination of old cases as a means of making sure new evidence was evaluated fairly. Garfield's own subsequent intrigues against Porter betrayed his insincerity on that point. With higher office in mind, he hoped to appear fair and impartial while working zealously to prevent any rehabilitation of Porter's reputation.[44]

Montgomery Blair, Lincoln's postmaster general, sympathized with Porter and tried the same tack with John Pope. Their families were old friends, and Blair chastised Pope for his opposition to Porter's efforts to prove his innocence. Pope replied that while Porter might well be pardoned, it seemed "incompatible with the facts" to suggest that he had done no wrong. Blair told Pope he was an incompetent judge, having accused Porter to relieve himself of responsibility, and he reminded Pope, "You still think your reputation concerned in his condemnation." Supporting a new trial for Porter would do Pope more credit, Blair concluded, than if he had won a victory at Bull Run. Pope rejected that sound advice, instead consulting with Holt and Smith about how to counter Porter's new plea.[45]

In spite of such resistance, Porter's cause gained momentum. The New Jersey legislature unanimously joined the official chorus for a review of his case. Then Mayor William H. Wickham, who was trying to clean up corruption in New York City, appointed Porter commissioner of public works. Wickham had helped rid the city of the syndicate run by "Boss" William M. Tweed, who had made most of his money and derived much of his power from his ability to deliver jobs and contracts in the city's public works projects. Tweed, himself a former commissioner of public works, was then in jail: when the sitting commissioner resigned early in 1875, Wickham offered the job to Porter—whose work on the well-known asylum project had demonstrated his ability, while his associates certified his honesty.[46]

With the building at Morris Plains nearing completion, Porter would soon need employment, and the commissioner's position offered both a professional challenge and a more conspicuous symbol of restored public trust. He accepted, submitting his resignation as superintendent of the asylum early in March. Lathrop and the commissioners replied in a joint letter of thanks for Porter's efficiency and good management over more than three years on the project. The quality of his oversight was reflected in the structural integrity that the enormous building retained over the next fourteen decades, despite many years of complete neglect.[47]

The envious hostility of the surviving Tammany Hall gang, in combination with the political antagonism of New York's Republican press, soon squelched any chance of the high-profile position restoring Porter's reputation. At the news of his appointment, the New York Times tried to stir up trouble by noting that Porter's New Jersey residence violated Tammany Hall's "home rule." There were good enough Tammany men who could have had that job, a Times reader pointed out.[48]

The conflict between the Tammany interests and Wickham illustrated an intraparty power struggle between corrupt Democrats and more honest ones, but the Times appeared to harbor a partisan grudge left over from the war. Despite sharing Wickham's opposition to the Tweed Ring, the Times grew disgruntled with the mayor for hiring Jefferson Davis's former private secretary for his own. That paper sneered at Porter's conservatism and Democratic connections in 1875 just as it had used him to smear McClellan's candidacy in 1864. The Times described the commission that hired Porter to build the "Lunatic Asylum" as a Democratic syndicate friendly to Governor Randolph, who was "willing to do almost anything for the cashiered General." Four days after Porter started work in City Hall the Times ran a long, malevolent piece reminding the public of his court-martial under the headline "Fitz John Porter's Case: The History of His Treachery." That editorial malice typified *Times* coverage of Porter's entire tenure, with later commentary likening him to Benedict Arnold and belittling his every effort to reduce waste, increase revenue, and improve services. The *Tribune* reacted only somewhat less pejoratively, while the *New York Herald* reported more sympathetically. Attempting to rehabilitate a department still permeated with graft and incompetence would have posed a daunting task even with the support of the public press.[49]

The negative publicity arising from his appointment did nothing to improve the odds of success for Porter's appeal, but it was probably doomed to failure in any case. He had not been on the job as commissioner for a full month when newspapers reported that Grant had asked his secretary of war, William Belknap, to examine Porter's new evidence and evaluate it for him. The secretary passed that task on to the judge advocate general of the army—who, in 1875, was still Joseph Holt. Pope sent Thomas C. H. Smith to Washington to guide the examination of records, and a predictably discouraging opinion filtered back to Belknap through Holt's assistant, William McKee Dunn, who was also a crony of Pope's. Belknap, who would resign in disgrace less than a year later over taking kickbacks, brought the unfavorable report on Porter's appeal to the cabinet meeting of May 28. He read it aloud, and with the concurrence of most of his cabinet Grant concluded to take "no action of any kind."[50]

Once again, Porter soothed this latest disappointment through employment, focusing on city projects. The Croton reservoir faced numerous problems, including theft of water, mains too small to carry water to upper stories, and faulty pumps that left some sections of the city dry. Enlarging the mains would require massive reconstruction, but he instituted triplicate billing to assure the collection of revenue, and by late summer user fees were paying for nearly 90 percent of the cost of supplying water. He proposed an ordinance to curb the unauthorized sprinkling of streets, but the aldermen declined to approve it. He cut wages that had been inflated to allow employees chosen by "a deeply rooted and vicious system of selection" to pay kickbacks to the superintendent who hired them. With the money saved from that corrupt extravagance he hired hundreds more men and expedited several neglected projects at no extra cost. Aldermen of the old Tammany school who were chosen in the November elections demanded that he restore the former pay scale. Porter refused, arguing that it was in the economic interests of both laboring men and the public to meet the demand for jobs by "unemployed men in this city, willing and begging to work at fair wages."[51]

In November, City Comptroller Andrew Green publicly accused Porter of incompetence and waste, hoping to derail his impending reappointment. Porter responded within two weeks by publishing the documentation of a twenty-eight-million-dollar boondoggle in the parks commission that Green had abetted during the Tweed era. That finished Green, but Republicans and Tammany Democrats on the new council balked when the mayor wanted the aldermen to approve Porter as commissioner for six years. Rumors surfaced that the police commissioner would resign and Wickham would replace him with Porter, giving Baldy Smith the public works department. Others suspected that a placeholder would be appointed and promptly resign, allowing Wickham to reappoint Porter for the balance of the term, but Wickham submitted Porter's name in a straightforward nomination. Unfriendly Democrats objected that the law only allowed a four-year appointment, asking the mayor to withdraw the nomination and submit another, but Republicans insisted that the Democrats put themselves on record for or against Porter.[52]

On January 13, 1876, the nominee saved the mayor from further contention. Porter thanked Wickham for the trust he had placed in him, but asked that his name be withdrawn from consideration because of the irreconcilable differences between him and the council. Requesting that someone relieve him of his duties immediately, he returned to Morristown. One of his immediate subordinates regretted losing so highly satisfactory a superior to "demaguogism," but assured Porter that the opposition of the city council amounted to a compliment to his integrity.[53]

He had not been home long when he started collecting information for yet another appeal. The gains Democrats made in the House of Representatives in the 1874 elections had encouraged him, and there seemed good prospects for that party taking the White House. Montgomery Blair had an idea that the overwhelming new Democratic House majority might subject Holt to a congressional investigation early in 1876. Holt seemed to think so, too, and retired on December 1, 1875. Porter must have rejoiced at the removal of the greatest obstacle to his vindication, but Colonel Dunn, Holt's successor, was already in Pope's camp.[54]

Porter's connection to the Randolphs' coal business would have been the only income he could depend on during 1876, but his family may have benefited from a recent windfall. His mother had died in 1873, leaving nothing, but the death of the childless Mrs. Holbrook early in the summer of 1875 probably yielded a bequest for her favorite niece. Harriet's widowed mother had been living with Mrs. Holbrook, and the Porters took her into the big house on Madison Avenue when 66 Union Place was sold. Porter's oldest son, Holbrook, spent the academic year at St. Paul's, a private school in Concord, New Hampshire, while Lucia attended a boarding school; Evelina and seven-year-old Robert Henry Eddy Porter went to school in town. Porter was renting out the house on the other side of Madison Avenue, and his own home was too big to heat in the winter, so every autumn he closed it up and moved into a comfortable suite in a boardinghouse. The costs of Porter's appeals abated while he waited for the next election, but a family with such living expenses would quickly consume any savings.[55]

Once again his reputation among the businessmen of Morris County rescued him from unemployment. In September of 1876 the New Jersey Central Railroad succumbed to swindling managers, and corporation stockholders sued for a receiver to take control. Francis Lathrop's committee had completed the insane asylum, and when Lathrop was appointed receiver he selected Porter as his chief assistant.[56]

That autumn brought a contested presidential election. President Grant's administration had seen so much corruption that his party nominated Rutherford B. Hayes. Democrats chose one of the reformers who took down Boss Tweed: Samuel Tilden, whose reputation for honesty shone brightly against recent Republican scandals. Porter attended a Tilden reception just before the election, and must have been delighted when initial returns brought his candidate within one electoral vote of victory. The results in four states remained in dispute, and through the winter a commission of congressmen and Supreme Court justices handled the issue in as partisan a fashion as any bipartisan body could. The fifteen-member commission tilted Republican by one member, and that eight-to-seven split decided every question for the Republicans. Tilden received 51 percent of the popular vote to less than 48 percent for Hayes, but the commission declared Hayes the winner. Porter, who very much wanted Tilden to win, thought it better to acquiesce to the fraud than to risk "riot & rebellion," and Tilden felt the same. The question was finally decided on March 2, 1877. Hayes took office two days later.[57]

Porter presumed that Hayes would be prejudiced against him for political reasons, and he was indeed biased, but not over party affiliation. Hayes had been colonel of the 23rd Ohio during the war, which had joined the Army of the Potomac just in time for the fight at South Mountain. Hayes had been wounded there, and while recovering from that wound he had commented favorably on Porter being court-martialed. In 1870 Hayes had also congratulated John Pope on vindicating himself and quashing Porter's first attempt at a rehearing. Hayes had been with his regiment at Upton's Hill when Pope led his defeated army there, and he told Pope, "I saw and heard things which settle my own opinions against Porter and his confederates in the most decided way." Nothing since then had changed his mind.[58]

18

THE RETRIAL

The beginning of another Republican presidency may have momentarily discouraged Porter, who was nearing fifty-five in the spring of 1877. His thinning hair and the continuous, Burnside-style moustache and muttonchops he wore from middle age onward had turned mostly gray. He still felt vigorous himself, but essential witnesses were growing old and going under the sod, including his Radical Republican admirer George Batchelder, who died at forty-five. George Morell was not well, and his memory seemed to be failing. Eventually, though, such losses only flavored Porter's pursuit of justice with greater urgency. Batchelder had argued that Republicans deserved a chance to correct a wrong their party had committed, and Porter saw that an acquittal under Republicans would carry greater moral weight. That summer he began gathering information for another attempt, corresponding with friends who might testify on his behalf, and numerous offers of help came his way, including one from John Pope's former chief of staff, George Ruggles.[1]

Hiring an attorney this time to help with his preparation, Porter sought witnesses as obscure as the three Confederate soldiers Morell's division had captured on the way to Dawkin's Branch, and for a time he thought they had been found. In September, after the annual Aztec Club dinner, he traveled down to Manassas and visited the battlefield to reacquaint himself with the topography. Time had wrought troubling changes there, too: all the timber between the Gainesville Road and Groveton had been cut, leaving a tangle of new growth. The ground between the Warrenton Turnpike and the Deep Cut was "hardly recognizable," and he had difficulty locating the positions his troops had held.[2]

Barely a week after Hayes took office, Boston attorney John Codman Ropes produced an unflattering analysis of Pope's campaign, accusing Pope of poor judgment and blaming McDowell for interfering with Porter's attack on August 29. Ropes, a friend of Porter's former aide Stephen Weld, was a diligent student of the campaign, and he delivered an address on the subject to the Military Historical Society of Massachusetts. His lecture was followed a month later by an equally supportive paper that Weld presented. This seemed a good portent for Porter's quest.[3]

Theodore Randolph, by then New Jersey's senior senator, dropped in to see President Hayes a few days after Christmas, 1877. He handed the president Porter's personal appeal and one of the pamphlets of unequivocal legal opinions, assuring him that Porter could show that his court was illegal, his judges were incompetent, and the witnesses against him were false. Hayes promised to read it without delay, and was as good as his word, calling Randolph back for a two-hour conference the next evening. He confessed that he was prejudiced in the case, having personally witnessed the contempt that officers in the Army of the Potomac harbored for Pope. Hayes had served in Jacob Cox's Kanawha Division, and he remembered some of McClellan's officers commenting that Pope "deserved" to be beaten; when Porter was court-martialed, Hayes had welcomed it as good news. To illustrate his feelings at the time, he read Randolph the entries from his 1862 diary. Nevertheless, he promised to consider Porter's request.[4]

Two weeks later Randolph advised an anxious Porter that only "gentle force" would move Hayes. A sympathizing friend from Boston sent Porter a letter he had received from Senator George Hoar, a Massachusetts Republican, who had spoken about Porter's case with Secretary of War George McCrary. General Burnside, then a senator from Rhode Island, had been present for the conversation, and Hoar found both Burnside and McCrary "strongly impressed with Porter's innocence."[5]

Evidence of such support from strong Republicans may have impelled Porter to pester Hayes in March by renewing his request "most respectfully but most urgently." On the afternoon of April 12, 1878, the War Department issued an order creating a board of officers to reexamine the case. Major General John M. Schofield chaired the detail as the ranking officer, assisted by Brigadier General Alfred H. Terry and Colonel George W. Getty. They were to meet late in June at West Point, where Schofield was serving as superintendent.[6]

Porter passed much of the next two months at his escritoire. The first person he wrote to was Gouverneur Warren, still on duty as a major in the engineers. He and Warren shared the ignominious distinction of having been stripped of command of the Fifth Corps under false pretenses—Warren having been relieved at the very end of the war by an opportunistic and vindictive superior. Warren went to Washington in May and found maps of the Second Bull Run battlefield at the War Department, but they were so inaccurate that he was forced to survey the field again and draw new ones. McCrary decided to authorize those maps as a War Department project, and Warren spent early June on the battlefield with an assistant, taking precise measurements and interviewing longtime residents.[7]

When the review board convened later in June, Porter ensconced himself at the West Point Hotel. By then he had retained two additional attorneys at great personal expense, and all three of them joined him there. To serve as recorder of the proceedings the War Department had assigned a judge advocate appointed under Holt, Major Asa Bird Gardner, whose immediate superior was Holt's protégé and Pope's friend, William Dunn. Gardner, a shady character with Tammany Hall connections, had served several short enlistments during the war, mostly in the New York militia, but he somehow finagled a Medal of Honor that was later revoked. His character seemed compatible with the type of justice dispensed during the Holt era: Governor Theodore Roosevelt would later remove Gardner as district attorney of New York City, citing "malfeasance, misfeasance, and misconduct" for the acquittals won by the vast majority of the accused criminals he prosecuted. Early in the West Point proceedings Gardner insisted on acting essentially as a prosecutor—although Schofield's review board had no judicial authority.[8]

Of the three board members, George Getty may have been the only one with no reason for bias against Porter. He and Porter had each commanded different companies of the 4th Artillery in the campaign to Mexico City, and Getty had served in Porter's artillery reserve on the Peninsula, where Porter commended his conduct. Terry, who had entered the army in 1861 as a volunteer officer with no military training, had evinced a decided prejudice against McClellan by the fall of 1862 that must have flavored his reaction to Porter's conviction. He admitted to Porter's friend George Ruggles that he had originally adopted Pope's view of the matter, but he had since read articles on the case that had raised some doubts. Ruggles said Terry was a "good" man who looked on the assignment as an unsolicited duty, and Ruggles thought he would be fair.[9]

Schofield had served for a time as secretary of war after Edwin Stanton resigned, during which he had called for the fat jumble of court-martial cases that included the record of his own trial for neglect of duty in his final cadet year. In it he found, or thought he found, the petition to remit his sentence of dismissal, from which he remembered Porter and George Thomas as the only two of the thirteen court members whose names were missing. He may have confused his petition with that of another cadet, but Schofield believed Porter had judged him harshly. Porter may not have even recalled the case, and evidently they never spoke of it.[10]

Proceedings began on June 25, one week after Porter attended his son Holbrook's graduation from Lehigh University. That afternoon the youngest of Porter's attorneys, Anson Maltby, started reading his opening statement. For nearly three hours he explained the points of the case, breaking off at the dinner hour and resuming the next morning at 10:00. Not until the middle of the afternoon on June 26 did he finally sit down, after which the board decided the procedural issues. Gardner, although identified as the recorder rather than the judge advocate, indicated that he intended to cross-examine witnesses and introduced a stenographer to take down testimony. That was acceptable to Porter, said counsel Joseph Choate, because as the petitioner his client wanted "the very fullest and most searching examination" of the case. He also wanted the witnesses to testify under oath, even in the absence of judicial authority, and Gardner agreed.[11]

Porter's lawyers nonetheless concurred that their client would not take the witness stand himself, "at least without careful drilling." He was too forthcoming, and as indiscreet in speech as he was in correspondence. In reviewing Porter's testimony to McDowell's court, Maltby found him unintentionally implying that Longstreet and Jackson had not yet joined forces at midday on August 29, thereby affirming the contention of Pope and Holt.[12]

The record of the original trial came to West Point from Washington by express. Because Congress had refused Porter's request to publish it, the judge advocate general had the only printed copies. For two days Porter's lawyers offered corrections to those transcripts—including the biased editing of original documents quoted in the record—after which the board took a nine-day recess to read it. Pope's cronies had worked to prevent congressional publication of the entire record precisely because the defense testimony so badly undermined the government's case, as must have become apparent while the board reviewed it. Porter had understood that he bore the burden of proving his innocence, and would not be given the benefit of any doubt a defendant should enjoy in an original trial, yet after the three officers finished reading the record he seemed to win a measure of their sympathy.[13]

Warren served as Porter's first witness, testifying for two days about his new map of the battlefield, scaled at four hundred feet to the inch and bigger than most dining room tables.[14] He claimed that his survey of the field corrected innumerable mistakes in the "Pope" map, which placed Porter far beyond his actual position and entirely misrepresented the Confederate deployment. Speaking of the battle itself, Warren said that Porter's corps had been pressing ahead to Dawkin's Branch and preparing to make an attack when McDowell rode up, whereupon all forward movement stopped. He challenged a myth that persisted, in spite of Pope's own report to the contrary, that Porter stood idly by as a heavy battle raged all that day within sight and sound of his position: most of the day there had been nothing but artillery dueling, Warren said. He also denied that Porter ever retreated on August 29, as Pope still maintained: Porter's battle line could not have fallen back without Warren knowing it, and Warren's brigade never retired more than a hundred yards. Over Gardner's objections, which the board usually overruled, Warren was also allowed to describe Porter's attack on the Deep Cut of August 30; his depiction of that valiant and bloody struggle acted as a counterweight to Porter's disdainful dispatches to Burnside, as an indication of whether his heart was in the fight. Warren even produced a dispatch dated 5:45 P.M., August 29, ordering him up to support Morell in the drive Porter had wanted Morell to make against the allegedly retreating Rebels, just before Pope's 4:30 attack order arrived.[15]

Robert Leipold, Fred Locke's courier, corroborated Locke's story of meeting McDowell at Bethlehem Church. General Longstreet came all the way from Georgia to confirm that most of his wing of Lee's army, at least twenty-five-thousand strong, was waiting for Porter when he reached Dawkin's Branch. Colonel Elisha Marshall of the 13th New York, who had testified from a hotel bed in 1863 while he thought he was dying from wounds, expanded on his assertion that Confederates outflanked Porter's left late in the afternoon of August 29; he added that Porter came up late in the day, determined to make an attack, and questioned Marshall sharply about his advice against it. Several officers from both armies agreed that there was no general battle on August 29, and the only serious infantry clash perceptible from the Gainesville Road action that day consisted of Hatch's dusk encounter with Hood. A colonel whose troops took a beating in Hatch's fight explained with dry irony that the enemy was not retreating quite as rapidly as Pope and McDowell had supposed. So many former Fifth Corps officers were asked to confirm that their men never retreated that Gardner questioned the relevance, despite the prejudice Joseph Holt had engendered with his false assertions about such a retreat.[16]

George Ruggles spent two days before the board. He began by attesting to Pope's arrogant introductory address to the Army of Virginia. Gardner challenged the relevancy of that, too, and Choate replied that the emphasis Holt had made of Porter's sarcastic telegrams to Burnside made it relevant. Pope's address illustrated his near-fatal indifference to basic military precautions, Choate intimated, which put Porter's sarcasm in a much less pejorative light. Schofield overruled Gardner's objection, and Ruggles went on to portray Pope as a general whose management fully warranted the doubts that Porter's snide remarks betrayed.[17]

John Pope seemed desperate to avoid being cross-examined by Porter's attorneys. He lobbied for the participation of his surrogate, Thomas C. H. Smith, for whom he had secured a new commission as army paymaster. Gardner, who was friendly with both Pope and Smith, passed the request on to the review board, and Smith joined him as an assistant, on the government payroll. His appearance eventually served Porter's legal team well, for Choate's incisive questioning shredded Smith's imaginative testimony. He swore to tell the truth on July 19, and began by telling a completely new tale about having been asked by Pope to conduct a scouting mission at one o'clock in the morning of August 28. The alleged reconnaissance had no apparent purpose except to allow him to testify that it was not too dark to move at the hour Pope ordered Porter to start for Bristoe. Smith claimed that he had no trouble navigating the roads, although he had never traveled them before and could not even say what route he took. It was "a medium night in the way of light," he recalled, with "a thin haze" over the moon — "if there was a moon." Choate tripped him up a few times over such details as how light it was, and at one point Smith implied that the smoldering wreckage at Manassas Junction helped illuminate the buildings at Bristoe Station, five miles away.[18]

Early in his testimony Smith had to be asked to stop making prosecutorial soliloquies, and simply answer the questions that were put to him. He admitted publishing the prosecution testimony during Porter's court-martial, and said he wrote Pope's report of the campaign immediately following the trial. He confessed that he had drawn Pope's faulty maps of Bull Run, although he had no training or experience in cartography. Choate had also learned that Smith was writing a history of Pope's campaign, and when asked about it Smith conceded that in his manuscript he "strongly" blamed Porter for the defeat.[19]

Having thus established Smith's bias, Choate assailed his credibility by dredging up Smith's account of the interview with Porter in which he allegedly "saw treason lurking in his eye." He asked Smith to name some of the other people whose characters he had been able to deduce on first encountering them, and Smith replied that he had never claimed any other instances. Choate then read Smith's 1862 remark on that point: "I had one of those clear convictions that a man has a few times, perhaps, in his life as to the character and purposes of a person whom he sees for the first time." Holt had used that statement as "a very material lever" to obtain Porter's conviction and persuade President Lincoln of his guilt, said Choate, so it was reasonable to examine the depth of his expertise in such telepathy. If he had never had another experience like it, Choate explained — and if he could name no one else who had — then perhaps his observation was worthless.[20]

Gardner objected to that line of questioning, and Schofield asked Choate if he regarded it as important. Choate replied that he did. Smith's presumed clairvoyance had apparently influenced the nine generals who sat in judgment on Porter, he said, and Holt had also emphasized it to great effect with Lincoln. Choate said he did not know whether Smith's claim meant anything to the three officers on the review board, but he was obliged to assume that it did. Schofield indicated somewhat cryptically that he and his colleagues were not so gullible. "We have no hesitation in saying that we do not regard the examination as necessary," he told Choate, hinting that they did not credit Smith's fantastic assertion.[21]

That day ended the board's first round of interviews. Not until September would the trio meet again, and over the summer Porter visited the battlefield again. He tramped the terrain on both sides of Dawkin's Branch and spoke with John Leachman, a local farmer Warren had met the previous spring while mapping the ground. Leachman and Alexander Payne, a former cavalry officer who had grown up nearby, had studied the court-martial testimony of Douglass Pope and his orderly, Charles Duffee, to determine the route they had ridden with the 4:30 attack order. Payne rode the two most likely variations of their path, taking a fresh horse in each instance. He timed himself at ninety-four minutes on the longer route and eighty-six minutes on the shorter. Young Pope had insisted that they covered the distance in half an hour, and Duffee had allowed "about an hour."[22]

Captain Pope's narrative became a topic of early attention when the review board reconvened. Payne testified on the first day, September 10. Then came evidence that Douglass Pope had told a different story a few years after the court-martial. Two officers who had served with him on western posts after the war were called to repeat what he had told them of his ride to Porter's headquarters. He had been nearly two hours ducking Confederates and getting lost, he had said more than once, and it was nearly dark when he delivered the order. The two men claimed to be friends of Pope, who was called back to the stand and devised an awkward explanation of how the phrase "two hours" might have crept into his story.[23]

Smith, who in another age might have been called John Pope's "fixer," set out to reinforce the damaged portion of the nephew's testimony. Duffee had been in Smith's regiment, and Smith took him back to the battlefield with young Pope, where they followed a faster route by carriage: a few days later, Pope and Duffee told the review board they had gone that way. Eventually one of Duffee's neighbors, a farmer named Archelaus Dyer, offered support by claiming that he, too, had accompanied them. With each rendition their ride changed slightly, and in one version Captain Pope had taken half a dozen orderlies or more — all from Smith's regiment. These strained efforts to corroborate the much-contradicted claim of timely delivery of the attack order collapsed under revealing flaws in the witnesses' details. Duffee, who claimed to know George Ruggles, said he had never seen him with the glasses that Ruggles always wore. When asked about his arrival at Porter's headquarters, Dyer described it as a tent standing near Bethlehem Church, and he identified it as a church because of its steeple. Yet Porter had had no tent that day or the next, and Bethlehem Church never had a steeple, or even a belfry; furthermore, it was a crumbling ruin in the summer of 1862, and unrecognizable as a church.[24]

At least ten of the witnesses for the government betrayed such mendacity that Porter's lawyers called their testimony "ridiculous," and even the review board characterized it as "worthless." Lord and Ormsby, who had ostensibly overheard Porter's absentminded confession, finally appeared through the assistance of the now-retired Holt, putting their names to that lie. A wartime spy contacted General Pope directly to offer his account of being detained at Porter's headquarters at Centreville, where he overheard Porter utter hostile remarks about Pope through the walls of that nonexistent tent. A Maryland cavalry sergeant told of meeting Porter way back at Manassas Junction on the afternoon of August 29, where he had supposedly retreated, but he described Porter without a beard and wearing a slouch hat—which he never did. To prove Porter's disdain for the order to march to Bristoe, a former surgeon swore he heard the general say, "I don't care a damn if we don't get there," but at a time hours after Porter had already arrived there.[25]

In an effort to show that Longstreet did not block Porter's way on August 29, Gardner called Captain George Dobson, from Banks's corps. Dobson said he took part in a reconnaissance that day from Bristoe Station toward Gainesville, into territory Longstreet should have occupied: he remembered being fed dinner there at the home of a Judge Baker that evening, and fleeing from Rebel cavalry as it swept in ahead of their main body. No other comrade or documentation sustained Dobson; no Judge Baker inhabited that vicinity, and Banks's corps had gone nowhere near Gainesville on August 29. Dobson could not easily have been confusing the events of August 29 with those of another day, and Maltby was probably justified in suggesting that the captain was "the only man of sufficiently lively imagination to remember this occurrence." It finally emerged that Dobson, too, had been recruited as a witness by Colonel Smith.[26]

A Confederate chaplain came forward on the same mission as Dobson, and failed as miserably. The Reverend John Landstreet, of the 1st Virginia Cavalry, also wished to support the tale that members of his regiment stopped Porter's progress by dragging brush to raise dust, simulating the arrival of infantry. He said that as Porter's men approached Dawkin's Branch he watched from a house that Warren's map identified as Hampton Cole's, and that Longstreet's men had not yet arrived. Landstreet offered a detailed explanation of how he remembered Cole's name, but no one named Cole lived in that neighborhood until Hampton Cole moved there, after the war. A lifelong resident debunked the chaplain's story by revealing that during the war the house belonged to "an old colored woman by the name of Lucas."

"Landstreet means to tell the truth," Maltby smirked, "but his bad memory won't let him." The unanimous testimony of several Confederate generals and the officers from Morell's skirmish line ought to outweigh that fable, he suggested.[27]

Nearly as difficult to believe was the parade of witnesses who vividly recalled that there had been sufficient visibility to march on the night of August 27, 1862, but remembered nothing of any other night that month. Most could not account for their special memories of that particular night—as Colonel Locke did by a painful leg injury he incurred, stumbling over a stump in the darkness, which left him hobbling for days afterward. Gardner called a procession of witnesses who provided little or nothing to bolster his argument, and their testimony sometimes helped Porter. A few Ohio veterans who had marched south from Bristoe in broad daylight on August 28 said their little party had no particular trouble, but they inadvertently confirmed that the road was clogged with trains and Porter's troops; they also showed that Porter's vanguard must have reached the vicinity of Bristoe Station fairly early that morning. Soldiers who had taken part in fierce infantry encounters on August 29 only demonstrated that their uncoordinated, brigade-sized attacks on Jackson's line had not produced the prolonged, rolling roar of musketry indicating a general engagement. That, along with Porter's distance from those disconnected clashes, effectively retired the argument that Porter should have known from the din that Pope needed his help in a major struggle.[28]

The appearance of President Lincoln's only surviving son aroused great interest. Robert Lincoln said that while his father was considering approval of the court-martial verdict he mentioned that Porter had retreated to Manassas when ordered to attack, adding that he thought it had warranted a death sentence. This story was meant to counterbalance William Newell's account of Lincoln saying he would consider new evidence in Porter's case, but it occurred two years before Newell's interview, allowing Lincoln time to learn more about the case and soften his opinion. To Porter's advantage, the son's testimony implied how powerfully the details of Holt's review of the case had guided the father's decision.[29]

Except for conflict over John Pope's refusal to appear, which elicited sharp exchanges between Schofield and Gardner, the most exciting moments of the review came in mid-October, when Irvin McDowell arrived from San Francisco. At the request of the board, McDowell and his wartime chief of staff had undertaken a "thorough overhauling" of his papers for relevant dispatches that had turned up three items, and he had forwarded them before beginning his journey. During his two days before the board, he may have wished that he had simply burned them.[30]

Unlike Pope, whose allegiance to the truth more clearly varied in conscious relation to his personal interests, McDowell's attachment to his version of Bull Run seemed fortified by an inability to recognize evidence of his own culpability. His convenient memory lapses implied a measure of deceit, but visceral aversion to the topic of his two lost battles below Bull Run may also have induced an involuntary blindness. The campaign culminating in Second Bull Run had been a "nightmare" for him ever since, he admitted.[31]

The newly discovered dispatches that McDowell forwarded to the review board illustrated how easily he missed glaring contradictions of his own exculpatory chronicle. They were all messages from Porter on August 29, 1862, that McDowell never answered, and while they did show Porter pondering a retreat to Manassas they also revealed his anxiety over the uncertain situation on the field, and the plans for that evening. Porter could not move to the right to meet the battle line he had expected McDowell to advance, and the enemy was too strong for him to push ahead in his isolated position, so he intended falling back on Manassas for water and food. One of the dispatches was dated "Aug 29 — 6 p.m.," and it indicated that Porter had not yet received Pope's 4:30 order to attack, undermining all the chicanery mobilized to sustain an earlier delivery of that directive. Yet all McDowell could see in that dispatch and the two others was strained support for his own interpretation of that day's events: Porter mentioned being unable to extend Morell's line of battle toward Groveton, and McDowell stretched that into an acknowledgment by Porter that McDowell had told him to engage his troops on the Dawkin's Branch front.[32]

If Joseph Choate suspected that McDowell was more psychologically impaired than wittingly untruthful, he gave no hint of it, and he made the unlucky general his particular victim. First he pounced on the excerpts McDowell had collected and printed from Stonewall Jackson's report and later provided to Pope, in which he had mistaken Jackson's desperate plea for help at 4:00 p.m. on August 30 for the afternoon of August 29. McDowell said he supposed that passage applied to the twenty-ninth, when he had it printed, and when this was later questioned he looked it over and concluded that Jackson had "mixed up" the two days' actions. He still thought the content at issue referred to the twenty-ninth until Choate pointed out Jackson's transitional introduction to a new day's action — "On the following day (thirtieth)" — which came six sentences before he described the crisis. In McDowell's defense, he had taken the text from the *Rebellion Record*, which broke the report up badly and buried that sentence in the paragraph before the one it should have introduced. Only when Choate emphasized that sentence did McDowell read through it again, and concede his point. He had just admitted that confusing the two days would have been "a great mistake," and then he acknowledged that he had, in fact, confused them. "It was a mistake that I made," he said, taking responsibility for it.[33]

That wasn't good enough for Choate, who plainly suspected McDowell of subterfuge, rather than self-interested sloppiness. Noting that the discrepancy had been found years before, he asked why McDowell had continued to pass around Pope's "Brief Statement" with the erroneous assertion. McDowell fell back on the certification he had obtained from Washington, which he assumed had applied to the date as well as the text. Choate pointed out that Jackson had mentioned Longstreet coming up to the rescue: hadn't McDowell denied Longstreet's presence on August 29, and shouldn't that have suggested August 30? Did McDowell know of any general Union attack at 4:00 p.m. on the twenty-ninth, Choate asked—and McDowell didn't—so how could he mistake that part of the report for the twenty-ninth? McDowell could not say when he had learned what time Longstreet arrived on the field, but Choate next pointed out that he knew by noon of the twenty-ninth that King and Ricketts had abandoned their positions, leaving Longstreet's road open.[34]

Sixteen years after the fact, McDowell continued to insist that Porter outnumbered Longstreet that afternoon. Choate asked whether he thought Porter still should have attacked if Longstreet had heavily outnumbered him, and McDowell called the question irrelevant, since it required him to render an opinion. Choate reminded him that neither he nor Pope had hesitated to offer an opinion during the court-martial, and their opinions had helped elicit a conviction.[35]

McDowell saw, finally, that this brought his own judgment into question, since he had taken away half of Porter's troops, and he replied that Porter himself had suggested that he take King to the right by the Sudley Road. McDowell thought he would have King ready on Porter's right within an hour, and admitted that he expected Porter to begin an attack of his own by then. Since King was not in position within an hour (or within five hours, for that matter), Choate asked if McDowell expected Porter to attack with no assistance from anyone. After dodging the question for a few minutes, aided by Gardner's objections, McDowell said it was not up to him whether Porter advanced with a line of battle or merely sent skirmishers ahead. It was already well established that Porter had thrown out a heavy skirmish line, Choate emphasized, before asking McDowell why it had taken him so long to bring King into position. McDowell said that King's men were fatigued from their march of the previous day and night, echoing the explanation Porter had offered for delaying his march to Bristoe—which the court-martial had deemed insufficient.[36]

While he still claimed not to remember any meeting with Colonel Locke at Bethlehem Church, McDowell did think he had sent Porter a verbal message as he took King's division away. In his mind, that message involved taking the offensive from Dawkin's Branch, rather than to hold fast where he was, despite the cavalcade of officers who remembered him saying Porter was "too far out." He criticized Porter mainly as it was necessary to defend himself, showing little interest in finding Porter at fault outside of that. When asked about the dispatch in which Porter mentioned falling back on Manassas, McDowell said it came at the end of the day, and exerted no adverse effect on Union dispositions. Nor did he accommodate Gardner's appeal for testimony about a loud, concerted, sustained attack on August 29 at Groveton, which Gardner insisted should have moved Porter to action.[37]

When he took his departure from the board's new hearing room on Governor's Island, McDowell was more to be pitied than despised. He was perhaps the only person in the room who failed to understand that he, rather than Porter, had squandered the best chance for overcoming Pope's misperceptions and turning the tables on Lee at Bull Run.

Within days of McDowell's testimony, newspapers began paying attention to John Gibbon's charges against Pope over the misrepresentations in his "Brief Statement." A California paper made much of Pope's reluctance to testify, speculating that he feared questions regarding his conflicting statements about pressing the charges against Porter. Under oath, he had denied any connection to the prosecution at the court-martial in 1862, but in 1865 he took full credit for it, telling the Committee on the Conduct of the War, "I considered it a duty I owed to the country to bring Fitz-John Porter to justice." Pope refused to appear at the review without a subpoena, and Gardner obligingly declined to issue one. That pitted the recorder against Schofield, who wanted Pope ordered to testify. Porter's team would not ask for the subpoena, either, because if Pope came as their witness they would not be allowed to subject him to the cross-examination that would expose his irreconcilable assertions. In the end Pope escaped, avoiding admissions that could well have ended his own career in disgrace, and Porter was deprived of the enormous satisfaction such an outcome would inevitably have conveyed.[38]

The board adjourned again for over a month, and Schofield spent the autumn considering the evidence, which he compared in fat sheaves of segregated notes. By early December he had come to a conclusion so positive that he doubted it could be changed, and began drafting an opinion. He apprised Terry and Getty that he had made a decision without revealing what it was, and suggested that if they felt the same there might be no need of hearing arguments from Gardner and the defense. Appearances more than uncertainty may have dictated that the two sides be heard, and in the first days of 1879 the attorneys delivered dayslong summations in the West Point library before a dense audience of officers and cadets.[39]

The board's evidentiary decisions and the attempt to force Pope's attendance suggested impartiality at least, if not outright sympathy, but Porter's recollection of his 1863 conviction left him apprehensive of unpleasant surprises. News coverage of the hearings still divided along partisan lines, as had reporting on the court-martial. Hostile papers fully credited the testimony of such frauds as Lord, Ormsby, and Dyer, while friendlier ones included the discrediting cross-examinations and editorialized on the more preposterous testimony. Not until late March did the board submit its report to the secretary of war, who forwarded it to President Hayes. Journalistic partisanship prevailed until the last moment, with antagonistic editors predicting only partial vindication or initiating rumors that the findings were "on the whole unfavorable" as late as April 2. The full report was released that day, giving Porter everything he could have hoped for.[40]

Point by point and unanimously, the board rejected the verdict of the court-martial. Porter's delay in marching from Warrenton Junction was justified by the conditions, and lay wholly within his discretion as a corps commander, besides which his troops would likely have arrived at Bristoe Station no earlier had he started in the darkness. His failure to attack on August 29 was largely due to McDowell, who arrested his advance and deprived him of nearly half the force he needed for an assault. Contradictory testimony from Douglass Pope and his couriers indicated that the 4:30 order could not have reached Porter in the time they claimed, and after initially trying to mount that attack Porter wisely called it off. Far from being guilty of the charges based on his conduct August 29, the board judged that he had been "obedient, subordinate, faithful, and judicious," and that his inactivity "saved the Union army from disaster on the 29th of August." By commending him for results that were more inadvertent than intentional, the board telegraphed an excess of sympathy for the petitioner, and those waiting to disagree would pounce on that to discredit the conclusions.[41]

The board commented on the court-martial with remarkable restraint, attributing Porter's conviction to "greatly erroneous perceptions" while overlooking the blatant bias of the proceedings. With equal discretion did the panel describe the distortion of Jackson's report by McDowell and Pope. Those two were neither named nor blamed for having "misconstrued" that report to confuse Confederate desperation on August 30 with the previous day, creating the illusion that Porter had lost a great opportunity on August 29. "The fierce and gallant struggle of his own troops on the 30th has thus been used to sustain the original error under which he was condemned," contended the three officers. "General Porter was, in effect, condemned for not having taken any part in his own battle. Such was the error upon which he was pronounced guilty of the most shameful crime known among soldiers. We believe not one among all the gallant soldiers on that field was less deserving of such condemnation than he."[42]

The board criticized only the "indiscreet and unkind terms" in which Porter had written about Pope. That could not be defended, the members said — although Choate had defended it very well, and pointed out that Pope had admitted disparaging McClellan more directly to the president. In its disapproval of the Burnside telegrams, the board recognized that such deprecatory correspondence had done less harm to Pope than to Porter, for it had led to "the misinterpretation of both his motives and his conduct." Porter could not deny that.[43]

In conclusion, the board recommended exactly what Porter had been hoping for since 1863. First, justice required whatever action might be necessary to annul the findings of the court-martial. Then Porter should be restored to the position he had been deprived of by his sentence, from the date of his dismissal.[44]

Porter conveyed effusive thanks to the board members individually. The report exhilarated his friends and silenced some of his longtime foes, the more open-minded of whom acknowledged their mistake. Editors at the *Nation* had never been friendly to Porter, but they instantly perceived that he had been vindicated by breaking down the perjury of government witnesses and the misrepresentations of John Pope. The initial reaction of that Radical-leaning journal was to characterize Porter's prosecution as "a most astonishing piece of deception practiced on the public." The next week the *Nation* mercilessly satirized Joseph Holt's credence in such poppycock as Colonel Smith's telepathy, which Holt had emphasized to Lincoln as proof of Porter's treachery. Reverence for the martyred president precluded any question of how Lincoln could have been gulled by such fabrication, or whether he had simply found the outcome too convenient to question.[45]

Porter went to Washington anticipating imminent action, convinced that a president who had shown enough open-mindedness to create the board would respond promptly to its advice. Many expected his immediate restoration, unaware of the pressure the Pope faction had applied to Hayes all during the review.[46]

Through the president's good friend, Judge Manning Force of Cincinnati, Pope had fed Hayes a stream of misinformation about Porter and the original court-martial. One of the favorite themes in the Pope legend was that some members of the court harbored great friendliness for the man they convicted. Among other inventions, Pope claimed that General Hitchcock had served as best man to Porter's father—at a time when Hitchcock was a cadet at West Point, just turned seventeen. He also said that Hitchcock had been Porter's godfather, and had enjoyed "relations of extreme intimacy with him." On Pope's authority, Force depicted David Hunter violating the secrecy of courts-martial enough to say that Porter's entire court had secretly favored the death penalty. In unbridled advocacy for Pope, Force regurgitated all the reckless falsehoods that Pope fed him, along with nearly verbatim repetitions of Pope's arguments impugning the legitimacy and credibility of Schofield's review. In a newspaper article he published under an alias, Force proved as loose with the truth as Pope, arguing that the Schofield board's report had to be a forgery.[47]

In Washington, Porter's exoneration drew congratulations on every hand, but no approval of the report came from the White House, nor a whisper about pardon or reinstatement. After a few days, Porter returned home.[48]

Hayes had not been swayed by Pope's vicarious importuning through Judge

Force, whose feelings he acknowledged while refusing to discuss it. He hesitated mainly because of sudden political weakness. With the Senate and House in the hands of Democrats, he had been forced to call a special session of the new Congress because its predecessor had failed to pass appropriations for government functions, including federal courts and the army. The House minority leader Hayes needed for pushing his agenda in that hostile forum was James Garfield, who took a personal interest in the case, since rehabilitating Porter constituted a rebuke of Garfield; it would also reflect badly on Irvin McDowell, whom Garfield so favored that he named a son after him. At first Hayes quibbled with Randolph over the details of reinstating Porter, arguing that if it included all the back pay Porter was due the Senate might reject the nomination. Then he pondered forwarding the report to Holt's successor, William Dunn, hinting that he would do nothing "until the case had been thoroughly reviewed" — as though a nine-month review had been too cursory. General Terry did not want the report going to Dunn, whom he considered "not a good lawyer" and "no soldier at all," but Hayes finally abdicated all responsibility. Pleading a lack of authority, he dumped the 1,720-page transcript of the board's proceedings on Congress with no recommendation, request, or instruction.[49]

Anxious to regain the respect of any old comrades who had thought badly of him, Porter had the review board's report printed. As he waited for congressional redress, he sent that report to men with whom he had served, along with summarized defense arguments and materials from his previous appeals. Out on the West Coast, former brigadier William Burns found the documentation superfluous. Burns, a classmate of Burnside's at West Point, assured Porter, "I did not need *any* of this to convince me of the crime committed *against you.*"[50]

With Democrats in control of both houses, it appeared the partisanship surrounding Porter's persecution might finally work in his favor, especially since some Republicans also seemed friendly. Burnside may have been the Republican from whom he expected the most. Burnside's memory had failed him about characters and events when Porter was seeking witnesses, but he was still urging support for Porter's cause through 1879.[51]

Randolph entered a Senate bill for Porter's restoration in December. As the review board had recommended, he included a provision for back pay from the day Porter was cashiered. The *New York Times* exaggerated the amount at $115,000, as though trying to turn the magnitude of Porter's undeserved loss into a reason to deny him justice, and that played well among Porter's political enemies. The figure did approach $60,000, but Porter had probably already spent much of that sum trying to clear his name, especially after paying three lawyers for the better part of a year.[52]

Randolph's bill was recommended by a majority of the Committee on Military Affairs, but out of the blue Burnside embraced the minority report and submitted an amendment for printing. He did not introduce the amendment just then, but it called for an entirely new court-martial. Burnside may have sincerely disliked the idea of "legislating a man into office," as he characterized the intent of the bill. He may also have felt that an acquittal by an actual court-martial would convey greater legitimacy, but as a civilian Porter could not be court-martialed again, so the amendment only attempted to impose another obstruction. Porter heard from a source he trusted that Garfield and Burnside's friend, Senator Henry Anthony, had converted Burnside in a long, confidential talk just before Burnside announced that he had prepared a speech on his amendment. Porter understood that the speech would do great harm to his appeal, and after seventeen years the strain of his ordeal had calcified the distinctions he made between friends and foes. For the second time he suspected Burnside of turning on him, and this time he was right. When the two old friends with the similar whiskers next brushed shoulders in the Senate hall, they did not even acknowledge each other.[53]

Porter knew that "Garfield was the principal devil at work" in the campaign against him. For all his pretended objectivity about the case, Garfield's own notes on the Schofield review dismissed the testimony of Porter's witnesses as "trash," and the exculpatory documentation as "his lying dispatches."[54]

Garfield had enlisted Jacob Cox to help win Burnside over. Cox served under Burnside in Maryland, and may still have harbored a grudge over George Smalley's insinuation that Porter advised against reinforcing the Ninth Corps—which Cox had commanded at Antietam. Cox had studied the report from Schofield's board, devouring much of the testimony and embracing useful portions of it. Ignoring the board's conclusion that McDowell had stopped Porter from making an attack at noon on August 29, Cox maintained that Porter had missed a golden opportunity there. Summarizing his impressions of the board's findings, Cox sent them to his recent congressional colleague, Garfield. Citing testimony that had been heavily contradicted by witnesses—and even by Union intelligence available as Porter deployed along Dawkin's Branch—Cox argued that Longstreet did not reach the field until late that afternoon. Garfield had Cox's letter when he and Anthony met with Burnside. Burnside asked to see it, and his next public comments on Porter's case reflected all the basic points of Cox's argument.[55]

Late in February, Garfield sent General Sherman a letter marked "personal," asking the general to officially assign Gardner to help prepare his case against the bill. Sherman attended Senate debate on it the afternoon of March 2, helping Garfield hold up a large map for Senator John A. Logan, a war hero and Radical Republican, as he distorted the circumstances with details fed to him by Gardner. Porter spoke of Sherman and Garfield "bobbing their heads" to confirm Logan's serial perversions.[56]

Sherman wrote to John Schofield about his reaction to the speeches for and against the bill, including that of General Logan—who, like Schofield, had served under Sherman during the war. Logan had evidently convinced the general-in-chief about Porter, but Schofield replied immediately and repeatedly, pointing out some of the worse flaws in Logan's reasoning. Recalling the day he and Sherman had fought before Atlanta, on July 22, 1864, Schofield used his own performance that day as a parallel to Porter's conduct at Bull Run, reminding Sherman that he had entirely approved of it. After reading Logan's tirade, Schofield wrote Sherman again, remarking that the most charitable thing he could say about Logan was that he "has failed to read the evidence and knows nothing of the merits of the case."

"Logan appears to have taken on trust such testimony as has been culled for him from the voluminous record, ignoring all the rest," wrote Schofield. He stopped short of accusing Logan of deliberately falsifying the evidence, but he did wrap quotation marks around Logan's presentation of "facts."[57]

For four consecutive days Logan held the floor, spewing a torrent of political venom, sarcastic innuendo, and self-congratulatory comparisons, feigning humility as he implicitly praised his own courage and energy by impugning Porter's. He repeated every slur that had ever been uttered or written about Porter, and invented some new ones. For a week the country's newspapers disgorged greater volumes of slander than Porter had endured in 1863, and all of it from the lips of Logan. The new veterans' monthly that served as Logan's mouthpiece, the *National Tribune*, offered all forty-six pages of his speech for a dime a copy.[58]

Logan's screed precipitated a flood of letters from men who claimed special knowledge of Porter's perfidy, most of it more ludicrous than the worst perjury offered to the review board. A New York man captured at Bull Run ostensibly overheard three Confederate generals discussing how fortunate they had been that Porter had not moved against them; others, regurgitating incriminating dialogue presented in the court-martial or review, claimed they had heard those same remarks themselves. One who confused an old story about McDowell ascribed it to Porter, alleging that he saw Porter ride close to the Confederate lines without harm, wearing a straw hat that identified him as a friend to the enemy. Another told of Porter riding in a train about the time of his arrest, loudly damning President Lincoln and his abolitionist friends. Still another, the editor of an obscure Wyoming newspaper, claimed that he was "quite well acquainted" with Lincoln, who personally assured him of Porter's treachery. Numerous soldiers swore that Porter's men were "crazy" with desire to be thrown into the battle of August 29.[59]

Toward the end of his philippic, when Logan had exhausted falsehood and insinuation, he resorted to technicality. Congress could not reinstate Porter, he contended, because he was not pardoned, and there was no mechanism for setting aside the verdict of a court-martial. As a last-minute concession Randolph proposed an amendment limiting Porter's appointment to the grade of colonel, with the hint that he would go on the retired list, but after Logan's diatribe it was no use. A few days later the Senate tabled the bill altogether.[60]

Still undaunted, Porter resumed his relentless personal lobbying almost immediately. A friend from Philadelphia who had received a copy of Cox's fifteen-page letter to Garfield read it to Porter, and Porter wrote to Cox to ask for a copy. After some hesitation Cox forwarded him one, and Porter spent several weeks with it before returning a thirty-nine-page rejoinder, politely pointing out the errors in the testimony on which Cox had based his conclusions.[61]

As George McClellan had noticed during the war, it seemed that no accumulation of defeats and discouragement could divert Porter from his purpose. He still continued to collect evidence that discredited the prosecution witnesses, in case Burnside's suggestion for a new trial gained traction. An Ohio lawyer who had been doing detective work for Porter found some veterans of Colonel Smith's regiment—comrades of Duffee and Dyer—who indicated that they had also been solicited to say they had accompanied Captain Pope. Dyer had not ridden with Pope, it seemed, and one of those potential new witnesses thought that even Duffee had not gone with him. The lawyer, Francis Collins of Columbus, had interviewed Duffee before he testified to the Schofield board, and when Duffee did testify he admitted lying to Collins about some details. If there were a new trial, the prompt delivery of the 4:30 order that was so crucial to Porter's conviction might finally be exposed as an elaborate, collaborative fabrication.[62]

James Garfield stood as his party's nominee for president that summer of 1880. Porter's name again became an epithet among Republicans on the hustings, tossed out in connection with ex-Confederates and Democrats, who were still taunted as Copperheads; Porter and his cause drew actual hisses from the more fervid crowds. In December, Garfield entered the last session of the Forty-Sixth Congress as the president-elect, determined that his inauguration would not be marred by the embarrassment of Porter's exoneration.[63]

One week into the session, the Senate resumed debate on Porter's resolution, which had been stripped of the provision for back pay. The bill would have ended the prohibition against him holding a government position, but it merely authorized the president to reappoint him if he chose to do so, rather than requiring it. The next day, December 14, Senator Henry Dawes of Massachusetts further hobbled the bill by establishing an eighteen-month window in which it had to be offered. With Garfield about to enter the White House for four years, that restriction effectively closed the door to reinstatement. The amendment passed handily.[64]

Ambrose Burnside then rose to offer his own amendment, which would have completely changed the bill again to authorize a new court-martial. If he had composed that motion the previous February with equal devotion to the maintenance of army discipline and his friendship for Porter, the evidence of that friendship had since disappeared. The points he made closely followed Cox's analysis of the Schofield review, but he garnished it with a heavy sprinkling of bitterness that Cox had not imparted.

The Schofield board had taken Porter's side in every instance, Burnside said. That was not exactly true, but Burnside insisted that it was—as had Cox. Like Cox, he also failed to note that the original court-martial had done precisely the opposite, ruling against Porter on every single question of evidence, to the point of flagrant hypocrisy. In fact, Burnside failed even to mention the court-martial, the record of which neither he nor Cox ever commented upon: his ludicrous praise for the fairness of that court argued powerfully that he had never read the record.

Burnside went on to complain about the board discrediting the testimony of "young Captain Pope (now deceased)," although that testimony had been sustained only with perjury that grew more obvious with each new witness. Cox, too, had believed the lamented Captain Pope. Burnside also imitated Cox by admitting that Porter may have been handled too harshly because of the public hysteria, but he objected (as Cox had) to restoring Porter to a position of honor for inactivity, even if that inactivity proved to have been justified.

When Burnside finally did depart from Cox's argument, he took a direction no one had expected. In a peroration charging that Porter had been guilty of negligence at Bull Run, he essentially prejudiced the very new trial he proposed. A soldier, Burnside said, "is bound at all times to show alacrity, to show co-operation, and to smother any feeling of mistrust which he may have of his superior officers." On December 31, 1862, Burnside had defended Porter's ironic dispatches about Pope, denying that they indicated Porter would fail to do his full duty; he had testified that Porter's comments merely revealed doubts about Pope that were rife in that army. On December 14, 1880, he took the opposite view. With his final melodramatic sentence he implied that Porter's remarks had betrayed a criminal lack of faith in his commander, accusing him of having felt more concern in the career of George McClellan than in victory on the battlefield.[65]

Senator Burnside had given way to General Burnside, whose command of the Army of the Potomac collapsed under the mistrust of his subordinate generals soon after he appeared at Porter's court-martial. Burnside's friendliness since the war showed that he had not yet drawn a parallel between Porter's lack of faith in Pope and the similar source of his own humiliation, but his speech betrayed a belated recognition of the similarities. The architect of his epiphany was James Garfield, president-elect.[66]

Burnside's amendment was not adopted, and eventually the Senate passed the resolution as Dawes had crippled it. That would inevitably have led to ultimate disappointment even if the House had concurred, but it never came to a vote. Representative Edward Bragg, commander of a regiment in King's division at Second Bull Run, tried several times to bring it up for discussion, but the Republican leadership parried it. On February 18, 1881, as the House was about to take the bill off the table for discussion, sly parliamentarians swept it from the calendar by a margin of only four votes. That killed the bill in the House, and left its Senate counterpart to die a natural death in March, when the Forty-Sixth Congress adjourned.[67]

The same partisan political motives that had destroyed Porter's career and reputation again denied him even the restoration of his good name. His perennial champion, Senator Randolph, left the Senate the day James Garfield entered the White House, and Garfield's antipathy clouded any hope for the foreseeable future. Porter could have been forgiven for succumbing to despair, but it seemed not to be in his nature. A few days into the new administration he joined George McClellan for a dinner at the Manhattan Club in honor of Winfield Hancock, the Democratic candidate Garfield had just defeated. If Porter's cause was to be reduced to a political contest, his only chance lay in the ascendancy of the Democratic Party.[68]

19

TWILIGHT

In her mid-eighties, Fitz John Porter's last surviving child told a visitor, "I never once heard my father laugh." His mind "worked along serious lines," she said, and when he played with the children his cheerfulness seemed superficial. Unjust dismissal had "broken something within him," she surmised. He always remained quiet, even at the dinner table, and early each evening he would retire to his room to write letters and study. The volume and content of the material he left behind confirms that he devoted most of those nights to his struggle for vindication.[1]

The cost of that crusade was beginning to embarrass him financially by the spring of 1881. The barriers of a Garfield presidency and a Republican House, along with a period of physical exhaustion, induced his first lapse in correspondence on the case in fifteen years. Meanwhile, he sought some means of increasing his income and reducing his expenses. He decided to rent both of his Madison Avenue houses, asking $300 a month for each during the summer, or $3,000 per year. After haggling with difficult tenants who demanded costly renovations, he dropped his price to $1,800 a year—or $1,500, if the agent could not find a tenant at the higher rate. He, Harriet, and Lucia—who had just turned twenty—had rented more modest lodgings while the two younger children attended boarding schools; Holbrook was working in New York. As the summer waned, the disappointing rental income and mounting costs of four lawyers moved him to confide to a house-hunting naval officer that both houses were for sale. For the big house on the six-acre lot beside Senator Randolph's he wanted $50,000, and for the smaller one across the street, $40,000.[2]

Amid all that, President Garfield died. He had been shot on July 3 by an office seeker "half-crazed" with disappointment. The wound would not have been lethal, but infection set in and he died on September 19. He was the second of Porter's judges to be murdered: John Slough had been shot to death in New Mexico in 1867.[3]

News of the shooting bestirred Porter, and a week later he wrote the first of many letters he would send to his firmest opponents. A vague but severe illness struck him almost as soon as that letter went in the mail, stilling his pen for weeks, but once back on his feet he resumed those direct appeals to avowed enemies. To many he offered copies of supportive letters he had received from their common friends, or from people he knew the recipient respected. Sometimes he asked for a meeting in which he could explore the misconceptions he thought underlay their differences. Such requests implied that politics did not motivate their antagonism, but it nearly always did. John Logan, whom Porter had called "a dirty dog" while that senator was turning his relief bill into political capital, replied that he would be glad to meet Porter, but he essentially promised that he would never change his mind. Opposing Porter was, after all, Logan's most productive political strategy.[4]

Since at least 1869, Ulysses Grant had felt certain that Porter had done something worthy of punishment at Bull Run. Grant maintained that he had studied the case closely, but Holt's prejudice had heavily influenced every examination he attempted. The frailties in the prosecution argument lay too many pages away from the contradictory defense testimony for ready comprehension, and untrustworthy testimony was more difficult to detect without complicated comparisons. Only someone as familiar with the reams of testimony as Porter or one of his lawyers could have detected the blatant bias in Holt's review, which was the only extant synopsis of the case. As Grant finally showed Porter, Pope's "Brief Statement" had also led him astray: he had assumed that Porter stood by doing nothing during decisive fighting on August 29, when in fact the fiercest part of the battle was fought August 30, and mainly by Porter's own troops.[5]

Two days before Garfield died, Porter wrote Grant to say that he wished to have the good opinion of so eminent a soldier, asking if the ex-president would meet him. When he received a promising answer, he sent Grant a copy of a letter Alfred Terry had written him after the Schofield board finished its review. In 1862 Terry had thought Porter guilty, and only after diving into the record and examining the more accurate maps did he see he had been mistaken. That letter had the desired effect, and Porter met Grant in New York on December 12. In that initial encounter Porter explained some of the finer points, but in two more interviews over the next couple of weeks Grant did all the talking, enumerating discrepancies he had found.[6]

To Porter's surprise and delight, after several days of concentrated study of the court record and the Schofield review, Grant replied that he was convinced of Porter's innocence. As a good friend of Logan, Grant wrote to him, too, to express his newfound conviction. There was no budging that politician once he had taken so public a stand, but Grant's opinion swayed many who, like Simon Cameron, had assumed that Porter deserved his fate without glancing at the voluminous record.[7]

With his responsibilities as assistant receiver of the New Jersey Central

Railroad winding down, Porter would soon have to seek other employment. The limitations imposed by the sentence of his court-martial may have moved him finally to seek executive clemency, which he had previously resisted on the grounds that he had committed no crime for which he should ask pardon. Rather than appeal to President Chester Arthur for a pardon, he sought remission of the penalty against holding any position in the federal government. Arthur honored his request without hesitation on May 4, 1882, citing the grave doubts about Porter's guilt. With that, Porter was at last relieved of restrictions more stringent than those that had been lifted from former Confederates fifteen years before. He immediately submitted a new petition for reinstatement in the army through Senator William J. Sewell, of New Jersey, and Congressman Bragg, both of whom had fought at Second Bull Run. The bill again survived committee review, and was scheduled for later debate.[8]

For years, the War Department had been collecting the official reports and correspondence of Union and Confederate armies and government authorities, and publication began in 1880. By the end of 1881 the series had progressed through five volumes, to the eve of the Peninsula campaign. Porter corresponded occasionally with the keeper of the records, assuring that his own reports were not overlooked and monitoring the project enough to guard against the insertion of erroneous material by Pope or his allies. When the volume on Pope's campaign included the entire transcript of McDowell's court of inquiry but nothing on Porter's trial, Porter noted the omission, and the next year his court-martial record appeared as a supplemental volume.[9]

John Ropes had expanded his study of the Second Bull Run campaign into a book that appeared in 1881, but Jacob Cox assailed Ropes's interpretation of the battle. Ignoring the patent unfairness in the conduct of Joseph Holt and the court-martial, Cox focused on discounting the relevance of the testimony of former Confederates who confirmed Longstreet's presence during the battle. Pope had validated Porter's mistrust of his ability to collect and process intelligence — but, like Holt, Cox twisted that justifiable lack of confidence into evidence that Porter actively hoped for Pope's defeat.[10]

More understandably, Cox mistook Porter's 5:45 P.M. order to Warren as evidence that Pope's 4:30 attack order had arrived in good season. Less forgivable was his insistence that John Buford's personal observation of a Confederate division passing through Gainesville before 9:00 A.M. amounted to "mistaken information." To contradict Buford, Cox quoted Cadmus Wilcox's timing of his march as though his division had been the first of Longstreet's corps through Gainesville — instead of the last, as Wilcox specifically testified. Cox's book no sooner appeared than James B. Fry, an old friend of Porter's, cited that particular blunder and others in a scathing book review that challenged Cox's accuracy, judgment, and understanding of military principles. He censured Cox for intimating that Porter owed Pope "blind obedience," and for his generally hostile, antagonistic, and unfair treatment of the entire episode. Grant, Schofield, Terry, and Getty were among the few who had thoroughly and objectively studied the Porter case, wrote Fry, and he accorded their diametrically opposite conclusions far greater moral weight.[11]

General Grant effectively repudiated Cox's interpretation with an article of his own in the *North American Review* for December of 1882. He characterized Porter's conduct at Bull Run as judicious at every turn. With schematic maps comparing what Pope thought the tactical situation was on August 29 to what it actually was, Grant illuminated the misconception by which Pope had deluded him and much of the rest of the public for twenty years. Yet he blamed no one, including the members of the court-martial, although with Garfield still widely mourned that charity may have been more politic than heartfelt.[12]

That plea from the country's best-known living soldier appeared just before the Senate took up discussion of Porter's latest bill for reinstatement, for which he traveled to Washington again to make personal appeals. General Terry thanked Grant for supporting the legislation. Logan, angered by the disagreement of his famous friend, made an even more furious attack on the bill than he had before, but his colleagues again sided with Porter, and with Grant. In the House of Representatives, where more frequent elections breed more timid officeholders, the bill again died untouched at the end of the session, on March 4, 1883.[13]

With dogged persistence, Porter resubmitted his petition in December. It was introduced in the House by Henry Slocum of New York, who as a division commander had criticized Porter over Gaines's Mill. Slocum had since learned his mistake in that matter, and had become one of Porter's foremost champions in the lower chamber. When antagonists argued that there was no appeal from the decision of a court-martial, Slocum protested that a fifty-dollar civil dispute could be appealed all the way to the Supreme Court, and if Congress alone could grant Porter justice, it should. The House passed the bill, finally, by more than a two-to-one margin in February.[14]

Ever anxious to arouse the veterans in his political base, Logan launched another offensive in the Senate, reiterating his former assertions, although they had all been contradicted. This election year he made a special effort, adding long lists of dismissed volunteer officers who might appeal for similar reinstatement, although few had a Regular Army commission to reclaim. Another senator read a new letter from Lincoln's manipulative friend Leonard Swett — who, inspired by Robert Lincoln's 1878 testimony, now claimed that he, too, had seen Lincoln point to the court-martial record and say Porter should have been shot. Those politicians were merely pandering to the partisan prejudices of their own constituencies, and the outcome was already decided. The measure passed, 36 to 25.[15]

Once the two houses concurred on the language of the bill, it went to the president. At least three men in Arthur's cabinet remained inimical to Porter. Robert Lincoln was Arthur's secretary of war, and his Interior secretary was also said to be "violently opposed." Arthur's attorney general gave him an opinion that the decision of Porter's court-martial was irrevocable, and that suited the president. On July 2 he vetoed the bill on the excuse that it would overturn a court-martial verdict that Abraham Lincoln had approved. He had implied much the reverse when he remitted Porter's sentence, and General Grant called the veto message "the merest sophistry." The House immediately overrode the veto by a two-thirds majority, but the Senate killed the bill with a tie vote. Some Republican newspapers heralded the news just below the banner endorsements of their presidential candidate, James G. Blaine, and his running mate—John Logan. "This probably ends the Fitz John Porter business," crowed one paper, right beneath the Blaine-Logan banner.[16]

That editor clearly did not know Porter, who would have entered the bill in each new Congress as long as he lived. An overwhelming proportion of the House stood behind him, and had nine senators changed their vote his victory would have been complete. His lawyers from the review board supplied him with briefs dismantling the opinion of the attorney general, and Porter plied Arthur with that, to no avail. His only recourse, once again, was to await the next Congress.[17]

After the Central New Jersey Railroad went out of receivership, Porter became superintendent of the Excelsior Life Safety Car-Coupling Company, with offices on Broadway. The company was new, and precarious, and enough time passed between his two positions that he was once again beset with worry about money. He had to renegotiate premium payments on his life insurance policy, and the rent from his two houses had become his principal source of income, with occasional dividends from Harriet's railroad stock. Then, in the autumn of 1884, a member of New York City's police commission died, and the mayor offered Porter the unexpired term, with a salary of $5,000 a year. Recalling how opponents had used his New Jersey residence against him, he took lodgings in a city hotel and later a boardinghouse, at least during the week. His family remained in Morristown, but his connection to that town had weakened with the death of Theodore Randolph the previous November. In the spring of 1885 Porter sold the big house beside Randolph's for $20,000 less than he originally asked, but he shed the mortgage, half of which was still outstanding.[18]

A week after Porter took his oath as a police commissioner, Democrat Grover Cleveland was sworn in as president. A solid majority of Democrats

350 ⋮ Twilight

dominated the House, and while Republicans would hold a slim margin in the Senate many of them had sided with Porter before. Congress would meet next in December.

In 1883 *Century Magazine* had published Charles P. Stone's memoir of affairs in Washington between secession and Fort Sumter. That inspired the editors to publish a series on the war, which they began running the next year with P. G. T. Beauregard's account of First Bull Run. They secured a promise from Porter to write a pair of articles. Starting with "The Battle of Gaines's Mill, and Its Preliminaries," he recounted his first victory at Hanover Court House and his first defeat. That appeared in the June issue of 1885, and in August he supplied his recollections of Malvern Hill. The second piece required some awkward ambiguity to avoid embarrassing McClellan with too glaring a description of Confederate demoralization the evening of July 1, when Porter had thought the enemy could be driven. McClellan died a couple of months after the second article appeared, but Porter remained as loyal to him as ever. Eventually *Century* collected the war articles in a special serialized edition, and finally they were bound under different titles in a four-volume set.[19]

Porter had evidently taken a liking to writing. That October his opinions on "How to Quell Mobs" appeared in the *North American Review*. His advice on that topic consisted of training police departments in riot control and schooling employers in exercising "true Christian philanthropy" toward their workers, to ease the labor unrest then causing most riots.[20]

Century Magazine evidently did not ask Porter to cover Second Bull Run. The edition for January of 1886 carried John Pope's twenty-six-page treatise on that campaign, and he devoted a third of it to explaining how Porter lost the battle for him. He (or his ghost writer) ridiculed Porter's reasons for the delayed march of August 28, and clung to his nephew's tale of promptly delivering the 4:30 order, insisting that Porter "should have" attacked by 5:30 on August 29. He quoted Porter's dispatch warning that he intended to retire to Manassas, but craftily avoided admitting that he never retreated. Of Porter's epic fight on August 30, Pope recounted passively that "Porter's corps was repulsed after some severe fighting," and he still implied that Longstreet's troops were just arriving on the battlefield that afternoon. He pointed out that Porter had been court-martialed and cashiered for his performance at Bull Run, but never mentioned the contradictory results of the review board. So completely did he rely on innuendo and ambiguity that he seemed perfectly cognizant that the foundation of his narrative had crumbled.[21]

The editors inserted a footnote moderating one of Pope's comments, and another promising that a different perspective on Porter's case would follow, but it never did, either in the magazine or in the book. The only defense of Porter in the articles on Bull Run came from Longstreet, whose account of the campaign was published in the next issue of *Century* and in the same volume of the set. Longstreet corroborated that much of his corps was waiting for Porter at Dawkin's Branch, with a force two or three times the size of his.[22]

The war lay two decades behind, and Porter's former comrades were beginning to fade away. Burnside died only nine months after his speech against Porter's reinstatement. Porter had written him an angry letter, accusing him of hypocrisy and personal treachery, but at Burnside's death he asked Senator Anthony to find that letter in Burnside's papers and destroy it. Warren succumbed to diabetes within a year after that: a commission similar to Schofield's had already exonerated Warren from the accusations that had led to his own removal from command of the Fifth Corps, but he did not live to see it. Then Grant fell ill, and when a bill entered Congress to award him retirement pay as a general, Porter beseeched a Democratic foe of Grant's in Congress to push it through his committee. That also came too late. Grant died at the height of summer in 1885, and Porter attended his funeral with the other police commissioners, all attired in the black Prince Albert coats and tall white hats peculiar to their office.[23]

Next came McClellan, felled by a heart attack on October 29. Porter may have been responsible for the hundreds of police who appeared at his funeral on November 2, lining both sides of the street from William C. Prime's house to Madison Square Presbyterian Church. Half a dozen officers guarded each entrance to the church. Porter joined William Franklin, Winfield Hancock, and their old foe Joe Johnston among the pallbearers, along with Prime and Sam Barlow.[24]

Joseph Wheeler, once a Confederate general, entered Porter's latest bill in the House at the end of December. It came out of committee in January, and thanks to the written opinions of Porter's three review lawyers the committee concluded that President Arthur's reason for vetoing the last bill was completely unfounded.[25]

Discussion in the House began on February 11. Martin Haynes, a Republican from Porter's native New Hampshire, was the first member to speak.[26] Haynes, whose brigade had made one of those uncoordinated attacks on the railroad cut on August 29, had barely escaped capture there. The claim that a great general battle raged near Groveton on August 29 was false, Haynes said: his own brigade had been sent in alone and unsupported, like others, and had failed as a result.

"How often have we been appealed to by the memory of those who fell at Groveton," Haynes asked—"a worse than useless sacrifice, and all ascribed to Porter's treachery!" Claiming a better right to address that appeal than most men had, Haynes said that in his opinion it was time to finally give Porter justice.[27]

Over the next week there followed a host of such soliloquies, most of them demonstrating what one observer regarded as a desire to indulge in "personal displays of military autobiography." As Haynes had noted in his opening lines, there was nothing new to say about the bill, and on February 19 it passed by another comfortable majority, 171 to 113. After the anticipated opposition of Logan, the Senate concurred by a vote of 30 to 17 on June 25, 1886. President Cleveland signed the bill on July 1 — the twenty-fourth anniversary of Malvern Hill. In a grateful letter to Joe Wheeler, Porter described himself as "overcome with joy."[28]

That left only the matter of his nomination as colonel, which was sent to the Senate July 26 and reported favorably the next day. He was confirmed on August 3, with the commission backdated to August 5, 1861. He immediately asked to be retired, and his name went on the retired list August 7. Philip St. George Cooke, still bitter over Porter's effort to blame him for losing the guns at Gaines's Mill, tried and failed to press some vague charges between Porter's confirmation and retirement.[29]

The end of his long ordeal brought no financial relief, for he had waived tens of thousands of dollars in back pay to satisfy the politicians who held control over his restoration. As a colonel he would have received only thirty dollars a month had he applied for the disability pension most veterans sought, but he never did. Technically he had been in the army for forty years, making him eligible for retirement at three-quarter pay under a new system, but that particular retirement list was limited to four hundred officers, and it was always full. Had he drawn such a salary, he would not likely have worked as long as he did, especially after his health began to fail. Eventually he sought a service pension as a veteran of the Mexican War, which yielded only eight dollars per month. His salary as a police commissioner remained vital.[30]

Porter's reputation as a disciplinarian carried into his duties on the police commission, and eventually collided with the internal politics of the department and city government. Three years into his term he launched his own investigation of demoralization, poor discipline, and perhaps corruption in the Thirty-Fourth Precinct, and on December 2, 1887, he brought complaints against Captain John M. Robbins, a sergeant, and some roundsmen. Robbins, who was within two months of the mandatory retirement age of sixty, immediately submitted a request to retire, admitting that he didn't want to risk his thousand-dollar-a-year pension. The other commissioners seemed amenable, but Porter insisted that Robbins should first stand the investigation. The president of the commission said he hoped Porter would withdraw his opposition, but Robbins had to retire on a four-to-one vote.[31]

Early the next year Porter looked into multiple fights that city police had engaged in with each other. He seemed to be the commissioner most inter-

ested in good conduct among officers, and that may have hastened his departure. He raised the hackles of John Watts de Peyster, a wealthy cousin of Phil
Kearny, over the routine reassignment of a patrolman, inspiring de Peyster to
some absurd and unflattering remarks about Bull Run. Porter laughed it off, but
while he was well regarded at police headquarters his reappointment became
a betting matter when his term neared its end in early May of 1888. Instead of
giving him the standard five-year term as police commissioner, a new mayor appointed Porter to a one-year term on the fire commission, which evidently also
needed his discipline. At his first meeting, two firemen were hailed before the
commission for drunkenness, another for failing to answer calls, and a fourth for
not coming to work at all.[32]

In May of 1889 Porter apparently declined reappointment. That summer he
sold his other Madison Avenue house, moving Hattie and the girls into a row
house on West Sixty-Eighth Street, less than a block from Central Park. Robert
stayed in Morristown: he had become enchanted with Edith Nast—the daughter of their neighbor, the celebrated political cartoonist Thomas Nast—and
within two years they would be married.[33]

The Madison Avenue house brought $40,000, and it was the last sizable
sum of cash Porter ever realized. Some of the securities he acquired to support
Harriet after his death would have come from that windfall.[34]

At the end of the decade, *Century Magazine* began serializing what would become a ten-volume biography of Lincoln by two of his former secretaries, John
Hay and John G. Nicolay. The chapter that included Second Bull Run appeared
in January of 1889, and to Porter it must have seemed that the authors did their
best to make a case against him on behalf of Pope and McDowell. In fact they
had done precisely that, albeit as subtly as possible. Hay had written it more
than three years previously, and when he sent Nicolay the manuscript Nicolay had chided him dryly for what he called "the extreme fairness—gentleness,
almost, accorded to Porter and McClellan."[35] Hay explained that he had done
them what damage he could while trying not to show his hand. Of McClellan,
he said, "It is of the utmost importance that we should *seem* fair to him, while
we are destroying him." It was the same with Porter, he added. "Porter was the
most magnificent soldier in the Army of the Potomac, ruined by his devotion
to McClellan." He and Nicolay were in the minority thinking him guilty, Hay
argued, and showing too much antagonism would do their work more harm
than it would Porter. "It would be taken to show that we were still in the gall and
bitterness of twenty years ago," he concluded.[36]

Nicolay and Hay wrote at the pleasure of Robert Lincoln, who owned his
father's papers, and they had to satisfy him. The two leaned to the hagiographic
side in any case, for they had dearly loved Lincoln, whose mistake in elevating
Pope would glare more brightly if Porter were cleared. Hay wrought the damage

he wished to inflict by adopting the script that Pope and McDowell had separately developed, and by selectively enumerating the subsequent events. He depicted McDowell telling Porter to "put your force in" at Dawkin's Branch, rather than suggesting that Porter wait for him to move King into position. He minimized the time it took for Douglass Pope to deliver the 4:30 order. He trotted out the disproven lie about Porter's retreat, writing that he "waited in position till it grew dark and then retired in the direction of Manassas Junction." Noting that Porter was court-martialed and cashiered for that day's performance, Hay betrayed his own dishonest intentions by ignoring the review board's findings, as Pope had. Revealing that he did still wallow in the gall and bitterness of twenty years before, Hay concluded with an opinion of Porter's thinking that required clairvoyance worthy of Pope's press agent, Colonel Smith. "What he gallantly and gladly did for the glory and honor of a commander he loved and admired, he was incapable of doing when the glory and honor was to inure to the benefit of a commander whom he hated and despised."[37]

Once Porter learned of the magazine article, he wrote to the pair and objected to "the persistence with which you have, to say the least, presented only one side of the question involved in my case." Their presumption of his motives, their aspersions on his loyalty, and Hay's malicious political commentary about him while campaigning for Garfield in 1880 highlighted the political animosity Hay had hoped to conceal, he told them. "I have been forced to the conclusion, either that there was so great a prejudice existing in your minds that evidence could not overcome it; or else that you had not examined the case with that care which ought to be given by impartial historians." For nineteen typed legal pages he regaled them with corrections and complaints, sensing that their sophistry would go into book form and permanently distort the interpretation of Bull Run.[38]

Within ten days he received a reply that promised "fair and careful consideration to the arguments and suggestions which you present." Two months later he supplied them with several pages of suggested sources about Pope's campaign and Patterson's 1861 Shenandoah Valley campaign, in which he said they had also misstated facts. Given their friendliness toward McDowell, he suggested that they consult a summary of his own case written by Theodore Lord, an employee at McDowell's headquarters in California, with information gathered from McDowell and his staff. That eighty-page brief had taken Pope, Holt, and Hunter's court to task for mistakes and misfeasance, sparing only Lincoln from the charge of deliberately sacrificing Porter for personal and political reasons.[39]

The "fair and careful consideration" Porter received at their hands consisted of a slight reshuffling of words, without the correction of inaccurate facts or the amelioration of obvious hostility. In the bound volume covering Bull Run, Hay deleted the words "in the direction of Manassas Junction" from the sentence in which he still implied that Porter had retreated when ordered to attack. A full decade after Schofield's board had demolished that myth, Hay wrote that when Porter received the order to attack he "waited in position till it grew dark and then retired." He cited the court-martial as confirmation that Porter had disobeyed orders. This time he did mention the subsequent exoneration and restoration, but portrayed it as a partisan political triumph. In a footnote, Hay quoted President Grant's early opinion that Porter did not appear to have been wronged, but omitted Grant's better-known later conclusion that Porter had, in fact, been treated unjustly. To garnish the whole, Hay excerpted the most sarcastic of Porter's comments to Burnside to lend an air of insidious motive to the exaggerated semblance of disobedience, much as Holt did in the review he wrote for Lincoln.[40] *John Logan*

The court-martial had stained Porter's name forever, notwithstanding the contrary findings of the Schofield board. John Logan—the last, loudest, and best example of a political opportunist exploiting Porter's vulnerability—may have prejudiced a majority of the war's surviving soldiers against Porter in the effort to rally voting veterans to his own standard. Logan was vigorously abetted in that effort by the *National Tribune*—the country's most influential publication among veterans in the Grand Army of the Republic. Veteran loyalty to Porter ran high among those who had served in the Fifth Corps, but the rest of the Army of the Potomac was no better than evenly divided, while veterans from the West had no reason to favor Porter at all. Unfortunately for Porter, reviling an alleged traitor is an effective traditional means of signaling patriotism for those who have no other evidence of their own.

Treachery is also a convenient excuse for failure, for private soldiers as well as commanding generals. Veterans high and low, stirred by the partisan feud of the 1880s, cached false evidence of Porter's perfidy in manuscripts they stored away for posterity. Nathan Webb, a private with the 1st Maine Cavalry, claimed some competence as a judge of Second Bull Run because he participated in it, and he kept a diary. During Porter's long struggle with Congress, while Senator Logan occasionally vilified him for the pages of the *Congressional Record* and the *National Tribune*, Webb began transcribing his diary. At the conclusion of the Bull Run campaign his brief daily comments gave way to a two-page polemic on Porter, whom Webb suddenly blamed for having deliberately engineered the enemy victory. He claimed that he had just learned of it—this in the entry of September 3, 1862—but he included details that only emerged in the court-martial, and he anticipated some accusations that were not cast until years afterward. Contaminated with similar anachronistic acrimony, such manuscripts lay in attics and libraries for generations, waiting to taint the opinions of the artless with the undeserved authority of primary sources. The ruthless politicization of Porter's struggle for vindication may have poisoned more hearts against him than the original court-martial had.[41]

No sooner did Porter win nominal restoration to the army than his health began to deteriorate. Three weeks after his bill was signed, he declined an invitation from Weld to come see the officers of the Fifth Corps, fearing the fatigue and excitement. Through the spring of 1887 he remained in bed whenever he did not have to appear for police commission meetings, and he suffered a noticeable relapse in August, recovering slowly through the early autumn. The fatigue he described, in such contrast to the extraordinary energy he showed during his first six decades, probably signaled the onset of the diabetes that eventually killed him.[42]

Poor physical condition kept Porter from many of the Union veterans' gatherings he finally felt inclined to attend. Until he was exonerated, he had indulged himself in the Aztec Club, mingling with men who had fought in Mexico and gone on to wear blue or gray, but death had made serious inroads in that cohort. Porter had joined a handful of former Union and Confederate generals in presenting Robert Patterson with a complimentary dinner at Delmonico's in 1880, but the annual Aztec Club banquets at Patterson's mansion had ended with his death in 1881. For a couple of years the survivors met in New York around the anniversary of the battle for Mexico City, but by the time Porter was restored to the rolls of the army those celebrations were petering out. The club continued with less ostentatious gatherings, and in 1893 the members elected Porter president.[43]

Funerals occasioned his more frequent interactions with old comrades, when he and they were chosen as pallbearers to bid farewell to common friends. Early in 1887, while Harriet, Lucia, and Evelina were enjoying a vacation amid Washington society, Porter joined Sherman, Schofield, John P. Hatch, Stewart Van Vliet, and a handful of other West Point alumni to carry Charles P. Stone to his grave.[44]

After 1886, Porter traveled to the summer reunions of the Army of the Potomac when he felt well enough, and he was always elected president of the Society of the Fifth Army Corps—present or not. In the summer of 1887 he felt too fragile to attend, and he missed the 1888 gathering at Gettysburg as well. The next year the reunion was held in nearby Orange, New Jersey, and when he showed up Dan Butterfield presented him with a solid-gold Fifth Corps badge, with a major general's stars on a pendant bar set with diamonds. Watching that presentation with a touch of partisan acrimony, the correspondent of a Maine newspaper of Republican proclivities commented that "things have changed with Porter since Logan died." In 1890 the affair was held at Mechanics' Hall in Portland, Maine, where Porter sat at the head table with General Sherman, Hannibal Hamlin, Joshua Chamberlain, and his old friend and chief of staff,

Fred Locke. Remarking from a towering stage that his listeners looked much as they had from the basket of a balloon, he gave them a typically short speech, and to the surprise of no one Chamberlain followed him with a longer one.[45]

The necessity of earning a living as long as he was able drove Porter into increasingly mundane occupations for which his primary qualification may have been his reputation for honesty. For about two years he presided over a company that specialized in asphalt roofing and paving that his daughter later said was "not too prosperous." When Grover Cleveland was reelected president, he appointed Democrat Charles W. Dayton postmaster of New York, and Dayton installed Porter as treasurer of that vast institution on August 31, 1893. It was Porter's seventy-first birthday.[46]

The duties were more than nominal, but without the cost and labor of the fight to restore his good name his salary proved sufficient and he mustered enough vigor to meet his obligations. He devoted his limited leisure to rest or to history, corresponding with friends and foes seeking to sort out the details of their battles. He exchanged letters with George McClellan's cousin, Colonel Carswell McClellan, who was writing a history of the Fifth Corps. When Colonel McClellan died, Porter cast about for a substitute, and an officer from the Regulars finished the book. Porter approached Theodore Lord, who had written a summary of his case while working in McDowell's office, about writing his biography, and Lord began the attempt, but he made little headway. The volume of material seemed to overwhelm him.[47]

John Ropes frequently asked Porter questions as he strove to compile a multivolume history he called *The Story of the Civil War*. Porter tried to give him McClellan's perspective, leavened by the sympathy of a colleague. Ropes still found much to criticize about Little Mac, drawing some of the evidence for it out of Porter, in whose letters the lawyer's eye detected efforts to protect an old friend through ambiguity. In that way did Ropes conclude, for example, that Porter—like Franklin and Baldy Smith—had urged McClellan to lunge for Richmond while Porter held Lee back at Gaines's Mill, and Ropes blamed McClellan for wasting the chance.[48]

A somewhat frail Porter boarded a train in mid-June of 1895 for the Army of the Potomac reunion at New London, Connecticut. He took one of the girls along as his attendant—probably Evelina, rather than the sickly Lucia. After growing up in a world where her father was often snubbed or scorned, she now had a chance to see him greeted with fraternity and even reverence. John Gibbon lauded him in a speech, and in his reply Porter lapsed momentarily into the rivalries of 1862, inadvertently slighting Pope's soldiers by complimenting the Army of the Potomac for having saved the capital and the government that fateful summer.[49]

That was his last reunion. The next year he complained that he was growing feeble, and his memory was slipping. As he contemplated the assembly he wrote to some of his old friends, among them Chamberlain, who had worked hard to help restore his reputation. Chamberlain replied that Porter's letter served as a reminder that nothing was so precious as "the communion of a true heart." He credited Porter with having offered him a lesson in character by the way he bore "trials and injustice of the sorest kind" with "a divine patience and forgiveness."[50]

Early in 1897 Porter gave up his latest New York residence, at 119 West Forty-Seventh Street. Taking Hattie and the girls back to Morristown, he secured a three-year lease on a big new house at 1 Farragut Place. Politics likely dictated the change, for a Republican would assume the presidency on March 4, and that would inevitably lead to new postmasters, especially in New York. Porter soft-pedaled the political pressure, complaining that the travel from Morristown was wearing him out and telling a friend that he had decided to retire when Dayton did. By June he had gone home for good to fresh air and remarkable quiet, but even noises in the house bothered him. His health was deteriorating rapidly, and he spent the middle of June in bed or on his lounge, sleeping all night as well as much of the day. He had hoped to attend one more reunion, but that year it was to be held in Troy, and by August he knew he would not be able to bear the journey.[51]

Porter's house grew a little quieter after the spring of 1898. On June 9, at the age of thirty-three, Evelina married Walton Doggett, a divinity student. He was ordained the next year, and his first assignment took them to central Nebraska.[52]

In the first week of 1899, Porter reported that diabetes-induced weakness had prevented him from venturing more than two miles from his house. Visitors came frequently, however, bringing colds, with his two grandsons among them. Holbrook, who was living in Pennsylvania, sometimes brought his nine-year-old son, Fitz John Porter. Robert and Edith often came down from the city to see both pairs of grandparents: their first child, a girl, had died in infancy, but their boy, Thomas Nast Porter, was then about four years old.[53]

Robert sold steam engines and pumps from a shop in New York City. In the summer of 1899 he treated Edith to a seaside cottage at Point Pleasant, New Jersey, riding down by train on Friday nights and returning each Monday. One Wednesday evening in September he came down unannounced, finding a family friend named Robert Adams at the cottage. The two men engaged in a heated argument and scuffle in which Adams slashed Robert's hand with a knife before stepping back, pulling a capsule from his pocket, and swallowing it. Adams soon collapsed, and died of strychnine poisoning that night.[54]

Only a day or two after he would have learned of this tragedy, Porter wrote to the secretary of the Society of the Army of the Potomac to say he could not bear the trip to Pittsburgh in October for the annual meeting. He pleaded constant pain, and said he could not stand the least cold or exertion. Hinting at the scandal, he admitted, "I have to be on my lounge all day, trying to sleep to forget my troubles." When the society did meet, the Fifth Corps association suspended its rules and elected Porter "president for life."[55]

Robert Henry Eddy, the wealthy older cousin for whom Porter had named a son, had died shortly after Porter's reinstatement. Eddy left $30,000 to his cousin Fitz's native Portsmouth for a statue to honor him, stipulating that it be raised in a prominent spot and dedicated on July 1 of the year it was completed, to commemorate Porter's victory at Malvern Hill.[56] A committee of Portsmouth citizens apprised Porter of the fund and its purpose, and asked him to select a sculptor. Porter showed some reluctance, but in his days at the post office he had met James Kelly, who was on the committee's list of sculptors, and after some delay he recommended Kelly to the committee.[57]

Kelly arrived at Farragut Place for the first sitting in that troublous summer of 1899. Porter, who had come from the dentist's not long before, descended the stairs looking "quite feeble." He was wearing a skullcap, dark clothing including a frock coat, and thick slippers. At each session they chatted while Kelly worked, and the artist later wrote down their conversations. Porter sometimes lapsed from the patience and forgiveness Chamberlain had praised him for, speaking harshly of Alfred Pleasonton, and faulting Burnside for harboring undue ambition.[58]

When Kelly next came to the house, on June 17, 1900, he thought Porter looked stronger. On that visit they were interrupted by Hattie, just returning from church with Robert, who was visiting alone, and later that day General Oliver Otis Howard dropped in to see Porter. At Thanksgiving, Kelly returned to a houseful of Porters — including Holbrook, with his wife and son, and Robert, without his. The one Porter he did not see was the general himself, who was confined to his bed, but he had come only to show them sketches of the statue that was taking shape in his studio. Just after Christmas he returned to sketch Porter as he would have held his reins, and the old man grasped a piece of string, perching on the edge of the sofa and hunching a little. Hattie barked at him — "Sit up, Fitz!" — and he snapped upright.

"I hope you will put more hair on him than he has now," Harriet giggled, but under the veneer of good humor it pained her to watch her husband in decline. After one session she and Kelly walked the neighborhood while Porter rested, and she lamented his deterioration.

"I can hardly realize that he is the same man," she said. "He used to be so handsome." It was horrible for her "to look on that wreck," she told the sculptor.[59]

Kelly last came to Porter's home on March 4, 1901, to show him the model of the statue. It was the day of William McKinley's second inauguration, but that would not have been noticed in Porter's house. General McClellan's widow, Nell, was visiting when Kelly arrived. Porter could not come down, and Kelly carried the model upstairs, finding the general seated, wearing a dressing gown. Placing the statuette on the table beside his armchair, Kelly pulled off the covering and Porter fixed his eyes on it. He was still staring at it when Harriet came up and stood beside him with her hand on his shoulder. She asked if it wasn't nice to see himself "young and handsome—as you used to be?" He nodded pensively, and continued looking at the miniature of his younger self as they left him. Harriet and Lucia fed Kelly lunch, and Porter came down in the afternoon, remaining with the family for dinner. The artist slept that night in the room beside Porter's, leaving in the morning to return to his studio and finish the statue.[60]

Porter died exactly eleven weeks later, breathing his last early on May 21, after a terrible night. So imminent had the outcome seemed for several days that all the children were present at his bedside but Evelina, out on the Great Plains. The members of the Society of the Army of the Potomac were then packing their valises to go to Chicago for their thirty-second reunion. An Indiana newspaper remarked that Porter's passing "recalls one of the greatest personal injustices of the war of the rebellion." Some of the veterans learned the news only as they arrived in Chicago, and so many years away from their war even the younger of them must have heard the echo of bells that tolled for them. The first order of business was a resolution of sympathy.[61]

Three days later the casket was carried out of Trinity Church, where Fitz John Porter and Harriet Cook had been married forty-four years before; the same man who had officiated at their wedding also preached the funeral sermon. A full military escort attended, along with nearly a score of official pallbearers, including Alexander Webb, William Franklin, Baldy Smith, Joshua Chamberlain, John Schofield, and David Farragut's son, Loyall. From there it was a short journey to sprawling Green-Wood Cemetery, across the river in Brooklyn, where Mrs. Holbrook and her husband had bought a plot.[62]

Porter had outlived them all. Joseph Holt and every member of the courtmartial died before him, along with Roberts, Smith, Pope, and McDowell.

Porter's statue would be several more years in the making, enduring a local version of the politically motivated opposition that had dogged Porter's search for official absolution. Plans to have it dominate Portsmouth's central intersection were finally abandoned, partly in anticipation of complaints from veterans attuned to the ranting of John Logan. In the search for a less conspicuous site, the committee charged with the project decided on Porter's actual birthplace, in a little park that had been created by jacking up the house and moving it to a side street a few rods away. The marble pedestal was not finished until the spring of 1904, and the statue appeared atop it that June. Kelly was still affixing bronze bas-relief panels on the base as late as August of 1905, which delayed the official dedication until July 1, 1906, but that brought the event to an even more appropriate date. Eddy had meant to commemorate Porter's victory at Malvern Hill, but the ceremony also took place on the twentieth anniversary of his restoration to the army.[63]

Marines from the navy yard and the navy band joined the police and national guardsmen who paraded through Portsmouth that Sunday afternoon. Dignitaries included the commander of New Hampshire's department of the Grand Army of the Republic, Osmon B. Warren, who as a teenager had crossed Burnside's Bridge at Antietam within range of Porter's binoculars. Holbrook Fitz John Porter appeared on behalf of his father. Joshua Chamberlain, suffering from his old wound, sent his regrets. Alexander Webb delivered the dedication address for his old commander and friend, telling the crowd that everyone who served under or near Porter felt certain that one day his service would be remembered in bronze. Webb promised he would not reproach those who had made Porter suffer, but indignation overcame him before he finished, and he denounced Porter's prosecution as "indecent and indefensible." Those who initiated it meant to profit politically from the war, he told the crowd, and they had demanded a sacrifice "to save the administration," but their malice had been undone and Porter's last years had been "gladdened by vindication." Because Porter's reputation had eventually been restored, Webb reasoned, his statue not only honored a good soldier and true patriot, but stood as "a symbol of national justice."[64]

Perhaps none of those listening that day questioned Webb's logic, but even someone as determined as Fitz John Porter could not extricate himself from so dense a web of fabrications. The second half of his life was shadowed by the casual contempt harbored by many of his contemporaries, despite overwhelming evidence that it was undeserved. Porter's conviction clouded his name even among serious historians, if only for his ideological concurrence with a large proportion of generals who were never subjected to show trials for their opinions. In trying to commemorate his old friend's character, General Webb went too far in celebrating his exoneration. The ceremony was neither elaborate nor especially well attended, and uncertainty about Porter's innocence would persist for the lifetime of all who heard Webb speak. The last of the little crowd departed by late afternoon, leaving Porter's statue standing in an obscure location dictated by lingering political prejudices, where it still represents the triumph of justice less than it does the tenacity of injustice.

EPILOGUE

THE DUTIFUL DAUGHTER

The death of the moral figurehead brought woe to the Porter family. News of the fatal scuffle between Robert and Edith's visitor somehow failed to excite the community at the time, but the adulterous implications ultimately destroyed the marriage, and in 1903 Robert abandoned the family. Gossip may have rippled through the neighborhood when he disappeared, but no open scandal broke until Edith filed for divorce, in 1906. By then Robert's whereabouts were unknown.[1]

After his father's demise, Holbrook took control of the securities that provided his mother's principal income, but he pledged the stocks as collateral in a complicated arrangement that prevented him from paying her the interest. In 1907 she applied for her husband's Mexican War pension, which still paid only $8 a month, and in 1913 she appealed to Congress for an increase. It was denied because she still technically owned the securities, with an apparent income of $1,500 a year, and before reapplying she filed suit against Holbrook for $26,000. Considering that her husband had never been granted back pay, that Lucia was "an invalid," and that Harriet's income had been reduced to $250 a year, Congress finally raised her pension to $50 a month.[2]

Harriet and Lucia remained in Morristown until at least 1911, but as their resources dwindled they retreated to an apartment in New York City, where Lucia died early in 1917. In her last years Harriet moved in with Evelina and her husband. They lived in Massachusetts in 1924, and on September 2 of that year Evelina admitted her mother to Medfield State Hospital, where Harriet died five hours before midnight on November 30, aged ninety. Because she had not lived out the month, the pension department denied her estate the November payment, but sympathetic bureaucrats guided Evelina through an appeal.[3]

Evelina became her father's champion. In 1947, at eighty-two, she toured the Manassas battlefield with the superintendent of the national park, walking the still-unpaved road over Dawkin's Branch and standing on the spot where her father had watched the assault on the Deep Cut. She convinced Otto Eisenschiml, an amateur historian with a reputation for tackling controversies, to undertake a book about the court-martial and its aftermath. Eisenschiml betrayed the indignation that often besets the closest students of Porter's court-martial, and he seasoned that indignation with his own infusion of irony. For three-quarters of a century his book served as the nearest thing to a biography of Porter that existed.[4]

Another amateur historian, Kenneth P. Williams, had just published a book on the war in the Eastern Theater when Eisenschiml's appeared, and in covering the Bull Run campaign Williams revisited Porter's performance. In his second volume he implied that Porter had done nothing wrong at Dawkin's Branch, but backhandedly argued that Porter deserved to be cashiered for the obvious disdain for Pope in his dispatches to Burnside. Even Joseph Holt had known that the dispatches were irrelevant in the absence of alleged malfeasance — hence his strained accusations of disobedience, to portray the dispatches as evidence of malicious motivation — but Williams saw crime in the dispatches themselves. Missing all the evidence to the contrary, Williams also fell for the old canard that Porter retreated to Manassas on the night of August 29. He showed surprising credulity in Thomas C. H. Smith, and faulted Porter's lawyers for discrediting Douglass Pope, whose testimony conflicted with that of everyone but the perjurers solicited by Smith. Finally, Williams adopted George Smalley's old Antietam myth of Porter refusing aid from a fifteen-thousand-man reserve with a "fatal shake of the head."[5]

Evelina Porter Doggett took exception to this slipshod assessment, as did Eisenschiml, who contrived a review board of his own in Chicago essentially to try Williams. A state judge, an attorney, a law professor, two professors of history, an army general, and a member of the Chicago Civil War Round Table submitted a "fact-finding" report about Williams's book on June 15, 1951. Williams declined to contribute a defense. The panel's assessment was billed as Porter's third trial, but it amounted only to a devastating book review. The relative accuracy of its criticisms was marred by a condescending tone and a tendency to impute deception, such as interpreting Williams's cursory research as the deliberate suppression of evidence. Evelina found the results gratifying nonetheless, and mailed copies of the report to manuscript repositories, much as her father had distributed the pamphlets and reports illuminating various aspects of his case.[6]

Evelina was the last survivor of Fitz John Porter's children. She died on January 19, 1952, the day before her eighty-seventh birthday, leaving one son who survived her by two decades. Robert's only son had taken his stepfather's last name by 1910, and carried it to his grave. The only other grandchild, whom Holbrook had christened in honor of his father, left no sons when he died, in 1946.[7] One century after Brevet Lieutenant Fitz John Porter first landed on the coast of Texas, determined to earn a name that his children could be proud of, that name had disappeared among his descendants.

ACKNOWLEDGMENTS

One thing I have learned over the past thirty-five years is that no one writes a book alone, and an author's best assets are the friends willing to read a manuscript and offer an honest evaluation. For this project I had the benefit of detailed and insightful commentary from Will Greene, whose encyclopedic knowledge of Civil War characters, events, and battlefields has brought him a national reputation and saved me from many a blunder. I am constantly humbled by the breadth and depth of his scholarship. John Hennessy, the sage of Second Bull Run, probably should have written this book, having clarified the confusing campaign that led Fitz John Porter to his choreographed downfall. John's trove of materials on the subject hinted that he was on the way to such a project, and his willingness to share them and comment on the manuscript reflected the sort of collegiality that makes Civil War history such an inviting field. Stephen Sears, who knew Porter of old through his long association with George McClellan, favored me with numerous lengthy exchanges about their characters, goals, and motivations. George Rable passed on sheaves of Porter tidbits during his own research into McClellan and his war, and I hope the intersection of our research parameters proved half as helpful to him as it was to me.

Just as the manuscript was about to go to press, Kevin Donovan, an attorney from West Windsor, New Jersey, mailed me a copy of his 1999 article on Porter's court-martial. It was gratifying to read that a legal professional also found that court as astoundingly corrupt as I did. Our views of history would change dramatically if historians treated all their sources with the evidentiary rigor required in civil courtrooms.

In chasing down Fitz John Porter's story I have been cordially abetted by a small army of librarians, manuscript specialists, and public historians. Chief among them were Jeff Flannery, Bruce Kirby, Patrick Kerwin, and Lewis Wyman, at the Library of Congress; Jim Burgess and Hank Elliott, at Manassas National Battlefield Park; Steve Bye and Rich Baker, at the Army Heritage and Education Center; Janet Bloom, in the Clements Library at the University of Michigan; Nan Card, of the Rutherford B. Hayes Presidential Library; Thomas A. Wharton, at Phillips Exeter Academy Archives; Nicole Cloutier, of the Portsmouth, New Hampshire, Public Library; Johanna Russ, Senior Archival Specialist, Chicago Public Library; Suzanne Christoff, Susan Lintelmann, and Alicia Mauldin, at the U.S. Military Academy; Bill Massa and Michael Frost, at Yale's Sterling Memorial Library; Adrienne Leigh Sharpe, Access Services Assistant at the Beinecke Library, Yale; Tammy Kiter and Erin Weinman, in the Manuscripts Department at the New-York Historical Society; John Haas, at the Ohio Historical Society (now the Ohio Historical Connection, if I can ever get used to saying that); Andy Corrigan and Sean C. Benjamin, of the Louisiana Research Collection, Tulane University; Kaitlyn Pettengill and Andrew Williams at the Historical Society of Pennsylvania; Gregory M. Walz, in the Research Center of the Utah State Archives & Utah State History; Olga Tsapina, at the Huntington Library in San Marino, California; and special thanks to Megan Klintworth, iconographer at the Abraham Lincoln Presidential Library and Museum.

I also owe a nod to Steve Phan, Historian of the National Park Service's Civil War Defenses of Washington, whom I first encountered at Stone's River National Battlefield in 2015 and recognized in a Gettysburg bar three years later. His particular expertise allowed me to take confidence in my opinion of where Porter's first division headquarters stood.

And then, of course, there's my gratitude to Ellen Schwindt for weathering my obsession. During long marathons of research or writing, it's always very comforting to hear the sound of her piano drifting up through the heat registers, assuring me that she hasn't left yet.

NOTES

ABBREVIATIONS

AAS	American Antiquarian Society
AHEC	Army Heritage and Education Center
ALP	Abraham Lincoln Papers, Library of Congress
BL	University of Michigan, Bentley Historical Library
BU	Boston University
BV	Bound Volume
CG	U.S. Congress, *Congressional Globe*
CR	U.S. Congress, *Congressional Record*
CHS	Connecticut Historical Society
CL	University of Michigan, William L. Clements Library
CWL	Basler, *The Collected Works of Abraham Lincoln*
CWP	Sears, *The Civil War Papers of George B. McClellan*
FJP	Fitz John Porter
FJPP	Fitz John Porter Papers, Library of Congress
FSNMP	Fredericksburg and Spotsylvania National Military Park
GBM	George B. McClellan
GBMP	George Brinton McClellan Papers, Library of Congress
HD	Diary, Reel 2, Samuel P. Heintzelman Papers, Library of Congress
HJ	Journal, Reel 7, Samuel P. Heintzelman Papers, Library of Congress
HSP	Historical Society of Pennsylvania
HL	Huntington Library
LC	Library of Congress
MHS	Massachusetts Historical Society
MOS	McClellan, *McClellan's Own Story*
NHHS	New Hampshire Historical Society
NYHS	New-York Historical Society
NYSL	New York State Library
OHC	Ohio History Connection
OR	*War of the Rebellion: Official Records of the Union and Confederate Armies.* All citations from Series 1 unless otherwise stated

PEA Phillips Exeter Academy
PUSG Simon, *The Papers of Ulysses S. Grant*
RBHPL Rutherford B. Hayes Presidential Library
Supplement Hewett, Trudeau, and Suderow, *Supplement to
the Official Records of the Union and Confederate
Armies*. All citations from part 1.
USMA United States Military Academy
WHS Wisconsin Historical Society

PREFACE

1. Pease and Randall, *Diary of Orville Hickman Browning*, 1:589. The quotation is Browning's paraphrasing of Lincoln's admission.

2. Nevins, *War for the Union*, 2:400; Nevins, *Diary of Battle*, 91; Sears, *Controversies and Commanders*, 71; Emerson, *Life and Letters of Charles Russell Lowell*, 231–32.

3. Ford, *Cycle of Adams Letters*, 1:250.

CHAPTER 1

1. *Boston Gazette*, August 27, 1781, cited in Allen, *Massachusetts Privateers of the Revolution*, 76–77; Maclay, *History of American Privateers*, 90. The surrendered privateer was the *Aurora*.

2. George Washington to Alexander Hamilton, August 5, 1792, Washington Papers, LC; George Gale to Washington, September 4, 1792, and Tobias Lear to Thomas Jefferson, October 26, 1792, both Miscellaneous Letters, Entry 113, RG59, NA; Syrett, *Papers of Alexander Hamilton*, 12:199.

3. "Officers and Enlisted Men Who Died in the Active Service of the U.S. Navy, 1776–1885," 16, Navy Department Library, Washington Navy Yard; Callahan, *List of Officers*, 189, 441; Long, *Nothing Too Daring*, 41, 305, 307. "Captain" David Porter's remains rest in Westminster Burying Ground, North Greene Street, Baltimore, in the same enclosure as Edgar Allan Poe. His wife, Rebecca, died August 31, 1801, and lies in Baltimore's Green Mount Cemetery.

4. Callahan, *List of Officers*, 189, 441; *Register of the Officers and Agents, . . . 1825*, 100; Long, *Nothing Too Daring*, 262; FJP's autobiographical notes, Reel 25, FJPP; *Story of a Portsmouth Born Soldier*, 1; Mooney, *Dictionary of American Naval Fighting Ships*, 1:147; *New-Hampshire Gazette* (Portsmouth), December 28, 1813; *Register of the Officers and Agents, . . . 1817*, 66; Samuel Evans to Benjamin Crowninshield, January 24, February 27, 1816, Reel 48, Letters Received (M125), RG45, NA. Charles Brewster, who corresponded with Eliza Porter toward the end of her life, reported that she and John Porter were married in 1815 (*Rambles about Portsmouth*, 284), but a genealogical chart prepared by Fitz John Porter (Reel 25, FJPP) gave the year as 1816. According to her baptismal record of November 4, 1820, Lucia Chauncey Porter was born in April of 1816 (Records of St. John's Church, 1795–1884, Portsmouth Public Library), so she was probably conceived in July of 1815, about the time Lieutenant Porter left for the Mediterranean; if he and Eliza were not married when he left, they did so in haste when he returned. Census and other information implies that Eliza was born late in 1799.

5. Logbook of the *Boxer*, March 13–July 18, 1816, New York Public Library; John Porter to Daniel T. Patteson, [October] "29th," 1816, and Patteson to Benjamin Crowninshield, November 7, 1816, both on Reel 51, Letters Received (M125), RG45, NA; *Message from the*

President, 25–26, 35–36; *Acadian Recorder* (Halifax, N.S.), January 3, 1818; *Daily Exchange* (Baltimore), August 9, 1859; *New York Herald*, September 21, 1859.

6. *Register of the Officers and Agents, . . . 1819*, 79; *Register of the Commissioned and Warrant Officers of the Navy of the United States* (1821, 1822), 4; Brewster, *Rambles about Portsmouth*, 147; Baptisms, 1824, Records of St. John's Church, 1795–1884, Portsmouth Public Library; FJP's autobiographical notes, Reel 25, FJPP.

7. David Porter to the secretary of the navy, March 14, 1823, Letters Received (M125), RG45, NA; Mooney, *Dictionary of American Naval Fighting Ships*, 3:158.

8. David Farragut memoir, quoted in Loyall Farragut, *Life of David Farragut*, 91–92.

9. Lord, *Nothing Too Daring*, 209; Farragut, *Life of David Farragut*, 92.

10. John Porter to David Porter, March 6, 1823, Reel 80, Letters Received (M125), RG45, NA; David Porter to his daughter Evalina, quoted in Long, *Nothing Too Daring*, 209; David Porter to the secretary of the navy, August 12, 1823, Reel 83, Letters Received (M125), RG45, NA.

11. *Register of the Officers and Agents, . . . 1823*, 92; Records of St. John's Church, 1795–1884, Portsmouth Public Library.

12. FJP's autobiographical notes, Reel 25, FJPP; *Register of the Officers and Agents, . . . 1825*, 101, also 1828 (113) and 1829 (116); *Register of the Commissioned and Warrant Officers of the Navy of the United States*, 1827 (4), 1829 (6–7).

13. Charles Morris to John Porter and to Samuel Southard, both February 2, 1829, Reel 135, Letters Received (M125), RG45, NA; "Officers and Enlisted Men Who Died in the Active Service of the U.S. Navy, 1776–1885," 16, Navy Department Library, Washington Navy Yard.

14. FJP's autobiographical notes, Reel 25, FJPP.

15. FJP's autobiographical notes, Reel 25, FJPP; Fifth Census (M19), Reel 14, 258, RG29, NA.

16. FJP's autobiographical notes, genealogical chart, and draft biographical sketch, Reel 25, FJPP; Callahan, *List of Officers*, 189, 441; *Fayetteville (N.C.) Weekly Observer*, September 8, 1835; *Military and Naval Magazine of the United States*, 156.

17. Register of Students, 1830–1854, PEA. Early in 1861 Porter applied for a passport, declaring that he was thirty-six years old when he was really thirty-eight, and in 1865 he gave his birthdate as August 31, 1825, rather than 1822: Reels 94, 135, U.S. Passport Applications, 1795–1925 (M1372), RG59, NA.

18. *Catalogue of the Officers and Students of Phillips Exeter Academy, New-Hampshire, for the Academic Year 1835–6*, 6, 9–11.

19. Register of Grades, PEA.

20. Register of Students, 1830–1854, PEA; *Catalogue of the Officers and Students of Phillips Exeter Academy, New-Hampshire, for the Academic Year 1837–38*, 7, 11–12.

21. Register of Students, 1789–1840, PEA; FJP to Robert Henry Eddy, September 21, 1838, File 158-207, Reel 117, and Recommendations from Louisiana, Vol. 10, 1838–39, Reel 1, both USMA Cadet Applications (M688), RG94, NA; Heitman, *Historical Register*, 1:800.

22. Peabody, *Harvard Graduates I Have Known*, 220–21; At Large USMA Cadet Applications (M688), Vol. 11, 1839–40, Reel 2, RG94, NA.

23. At Large USMA Cadet Applications (M688), Vol. 12, 1840–41, Reel 2, RG94, NA.

24. Schofield, *Forty-Six Years in the Army*, 10; Scott, *Forgotten Valor*, 51–52, 67–68; Morrison, "Getting through West Point," 312–13; Keyes, *Fifty Years' Observation*, 196; Cadets Admitted to the U.S.M.A., 1800–1845, USMA Archives.

25. Scott, *Forgotten Valor*, 52; Morrison, *Best School*, 118–19; Schaff, *Spirit of Old West Point*, 53.

26. *Official Register* (1842), 18; Register of Delinquencies, 3:82, USMA Archives.

27. Orders No. 35, July 6, 1841, Post Orders, USMA Archives; *Regulations*, 66; Morrison, "Getting through West Point," 307–9; Strong, *Cadet Life at West Point*, 181–85; Scott, *Forgotten Valor*, 67; Register of Delinquencies, 3:82, USMA Archives.

28. Grant, *Memoirs*, 1:42; Orders No. 41, August 24, 1841, Post Orders, USMA Archives; Heitman, *Historical Register*, 1:895; Morrison, *Best School*, 163.

29. *Official Register* (1842), 23; Morrison, *Best School*, 160; Heitman, *Historical Register*, 1:301. Mensuration encompasses the means of measuring areas and volumes.

30. *Official Register* (1842), 23; Morrison, "Getting through West Point," 317; Scott, *Forgotten Valor*, 59.

31. *Official Register* (1842), 13, 15, 19.

32. *Official Register* (1843), 12; Scott, *Forgotten Valor*, 55.

33. Morrison, "Getting through West Point," 315–16; F. J. Porter Passport Application No. 594, 1861, Reel 94, U.S. Passport Applications, 1795–1925 (M1372), RG59, NA.

34. Morrison, *Best School*, 160–63; Schaff, *Spirit of Old West Point*, 274.

35. *Official Register* (1843), 10, 12.

36. *Official Register* (1843), 16–17.

37. Register of Delinquencies, 3:82, USMA Archives.

38. Sixth Census (M704), Reel 35, 212, and Seventh Census (M432), Reel 233, 20, RG29, NA.

39. Morrison, *Best School*, 161–62; *Official Register* (1844), 8, 17, 21; Register of Delinquencies, 3:82, USMA Archives.

40. Scott, *Forgotten Valor*, 53, 55; Register of Delinquencies, 1843–1847, USMA Archives; *Official Register* (1844), 19; GBM to Ellen Marcy, [1859], Reel 5, GBMP; FJP to Ambrose Burnside, December 23, 1880, Porter Papers, USMA Library.

41. *Official Register* (1845), 3, 20; Scott, *Forgotten Valor*, 58; Schaff, *Spirit of Old West Point*, 104, 337. James Morrison reassesses Mahan's impact on Civil War strategy (*Best School*, 94, 153), noting that cadets sat through only nine hours of Mahan's section on the science of war. Jon Scott Logel evaluates Mahan's influence on West Point graduates as civil engineers in *Designing Gotham*, 44–53.

42. *Official Register* (1845), 21.

43. *Official Register* (1845), 3, 20; Scott, *Forgotten Valor*, 52; Edward Porter Alexander to Theodore Lord, February 11, 1902, Caleb Huse to Lord, July 2, 1902, and John P. Hawkins to Lord, September 30, 1902, all on Reel 30, FJPP. George McClellan's own 1861 cavalry manual (*Regulations and Instructions for the Field Service of the U.S. Cavalry*) fails to explain the exercise called "cutting Turk's head." Presumably it involves the mounted sabreur riding a series of tight, looping, interwoven turns suggestive of the pattern in a Turk's head knot.

44. Morrison, *Best School*, 114–15; *Official Register* (1845), 2, 7, 17; Register of Delinquencies, 3:82, USMA Archives.

45. Staff Records, 4:88, USMA Archives; Joseph Totten to Secretary of War William Marcy, July 3, 1845, Reel 305, Letters Received (M567), RG94, NA.

46. FJP to Roger Jones, July 23, September 4, 1845, Reel 302, Letters Received (M567), RG94, NA; *Official Register* (1846), 13–14. Porter's future acquaintances in the class of 1849 included John G. Parke, who ranked first in his plebe year, and Elisha G. Marshall, who ranked so low that he was turned back to the class of 1850.

CHAPTER 2

1. U.S. House, *Messages of the President*, Ex. Doc. 60, 30th Cong., 1st sess., 81, 97–99; Nevins and Thomas, *Diary of George Templeton Strong*, 1:264; Croffut, *Fifty Years in Camp and Field*, 193–95.

2. FJP to Roger Jones, July 23, September 4, 1845, Reel 302, Letters Received (M567), RG94, NA.

3. "The Mexican War," 1, Reel 30, FJPP.

4. "The Mexican War," 1, Reel 30, FJPP; FJP to Roger Jones, June 8, 1846, Reel 323, Letters Received (M567), RG94, NA. A number of cadets who had been dismissed from the military academy had been commissioned in the mounted rifles regiment by the time Porter declined, including two from his class: Washington L. Elliott and Robert M. Morris. Benjamin Roberts, who would become Porter's particular nemesis (and had resigned from the army in disgrace several years previously), had also reentered the service with a commission in that regiment, from which he was later dismissed by court-martial. Heitman, *Historical Register*, 1:402, 728, 835.

5. "The Mexican War," 1, Reel 30, FJPP; U.S. House, *Messages of the President*, Ex. Doc. 60, 30th Cong., 1st sess., 5–6.

6. U.S. House, *Messages of the President*, Ex. Doc. 60, 30th Cong., 1st sess., 138–39, 142–44; Longstreet, *Lee and Longstreet at High Tide*, 144–45; Meade, *Life and Letters*, 1:66–67; Heitman, *Historical Register*, 1:193, 652. Theodoric Porter was also a close friend of Second Lieutenant Ulysses Grant.

7. U.S. House, *Messages of the President*, Ex. Doc. 60, 30th Cong., 1st sess., 4–9, 140–42, 295–98; Meade, *Life and Letters*, 1:79–82. These early battles are the focus of Douglas Murphy's *Two Armies on the Rio Grande*. For the two major campaigns south of that river, John D. Eisenhower's geographically organized *So Far from God* and K. Jack Bauer's heavily researched, chronologically presented *Mexican War* still provide reliable general histories.

8. FJP to Robert Henry Eddy, August 31, 1846, quoted in "The Mexican War," 3–4, Reel 30, FJPP; *Correspondence of John Sedgwick*, 1:4, 5; Cutrer, *Mexican War Diary*, 36–37, 44; Isaac Bowen to Katie Bowen, May 20, 1846, Box 3, Bowen Papers, AHEC.

9. U.S. House, *Messages of the President*, Ex. Doc. 60, 30th Cong., 1st sess., 345–50, 379–82; Cutrer, *Mexican War Diary*, 34, 38–39; "The Mexican War," 4–5, Reel 30, FJPP; Nathaniel Lyon to "Dear Brother," November 4, 1846, Lyon Papers, AAS; Livingston-Little, *Mexican War Diary of Thomas D. Tennery*, 32–36; Isaac Bowen to Katie Bowen, October 18, 1846, Bowen Papers, AHEC (on Mexican women).

10. Heitman, *Historical Register*, 1:799, 928.

11. U.S. House, *Messages of the President*, Ex. Doc. 60, 30th Cong., 1st sess., 839–40, 861–63; "The Mexican War," Reel 30, FJPP; Nathaniel Lyon to John B. Hasler, February 23, 1847, Lyon Papers, AAS.

12. U.S. Senate, *Message from the President*, Ex. Doc. 1, 30th Cong., 1st sess., 245–55.

13. U.S. Senate, *Message from the President*, Ex. Doc. 1, 30th Cong., 1st sess., 216–30; "Journal of Francis Collins," 47–48; Cutrer, *Mexican War Diary*, 82–83; *Correspondence of John Sedgwick*, 1:68–74; Meade, *Life and Letters*, 1:191, 193.

14. U.S. House, *Messages of the President*, Ex. Doc. 60, 30th Cong., 1st sess., 928–29; *Correspondence of John Sedgwick*, 1:79–81.

15. U.S. Senate, *Message from the President*, Ex. Doc. 1, 30th Cong., 1st sess., 274–75; Ramsey, *Other Side*, 147–48, 200–202, 205; William T. H. Brooks to his father, May 22, 1847, Brooks Papers, AHEC.

16. U.S. Senate, *Message from the President*, Ex. Doc. 1, 30th Cong., 1st sess., 261, 291; Croffut, *Fifty Years in Camp and Field*, 250–51. Some veterans of the battle (for example, Furber, *Twelve Months Volunteer*, 583) misunderstood which of the two hills was El Telegrafo.

17. U.S. Senate, *Message from the President*, Ex. Doc. 1, 30th Cong., 1st sess., 280, 287–88; Croffut, *Fifty Years in Camp and Field*, 251.

18. Ramsey, *Other Side*, 206; U.S. Senate, *Message from the President*, Ex. Doc. 1, 30th Cong., 1st sess., 290–91; Livingston-Little, *Mexican War Diary of Thomas D. Tennery*, 80–81.

19. Croffut, *Fifty Years in Camp and Field*, 251; Cutrer, *Mexican War Diary*, 117–19.

20. U.S. Senate, *Message from the President*, Ex. Doc. 1, 30th Cong., 1st sess., 275–76, 280–81, 288–90, 298–99; "Journal of Francis Collins," 63; Livingston-Little, *Mexican War Diary of Thomas D. Tennery*, 82.

21. Croffut, *Fifty Years in Camp and Field*, 251, 253; *Correspondence of John Sedgwick*, 1:87–88; Anderson, *Artillery Officer in the Mexican War*, 137; U.S. Senate, *Message from the President*, Ex. Doc. 1, 30th Cong., 1st sess., 257–58; Cutrer, *Mexican War Diary*, 121; Sargent, *Gathering Laurels in Mexico*, 9, 54–55.

22. Livingston-Little, *Mexican War Diary of Thomas D. Tennery*, 84; Cutrer, *Mexican War Diary*, 122, 124; Semmes, *Service Afloat and Ashore*, 186–87; Sargent, *Gathering Laurels in Mexico*, 10.

23. U.S. House, *Messages of the President*, Ex. Doc. 60, 30th Cong., 1st sess., 993; Anderson, *Artillery Officer in the Mexican War*, 190; Croffut, *Fifty Years in Camp and Field*, 258; Heitman, *Historical Register*, 1:799; Register of Enlistments (M233), Reel 79, 158, RG94, NA.

24. *Correspondence of John Sedgwick*, 1:96–99; U.S. House, *Messages of the President*, Ex. Doc. 60, 30th Cong., 1st sess., 993; Semmes, *Service Afloat and Ashore*, 238; Croffut, *Fifty Years in Camp and Field*, 257–59.

25. "Journal of Francis Collins," 74–75.

26. Hughes and Johnson, *Fighter from Way Back*, 150; FJP to "My Dear Friend," January 2, 1900, David St. Leon Porter file, Box 21, Aztec Club Archives, AHEC. David St. Leon Porter was commissioned on May 22, 1847, only thirty-nine days before his death, from the state of Louisiana, where he may have been living with John Waddell, the widower of his sister, Lucia (Heitman, *Historical Register*, 1:799).

27. *Correspondence of John Sedgwick*, 1:107–8; Sargent, *Gathering Laurels in Mexico*, 15; Hughes and Johnson, *Fighter from Way Back*, 105–6.

28. U.S. Senate, *Message from the President*, Ex. Doc. 1, 30th Cong., 1st sess., 303; "Journal of Francis Collins," 77.

29. U.S. Senate, *Message from the President*, Ex. Doc. 1, 30th Cong., 1st sess., 303–4.

30. Hughes and Johnson, *Fighter from Way Back*, 109; "Journal of Francis Collins," 78–79; U.S. Senate, *Message from the President*, Ex. Doc. 1, 30th Cong., 1st sess., 304.

31. Hughes and Johnson, *Fighter from Way Back*, 110; Sargent, *Gathering Laurels in Mexico*, 16; *Correspondence of John Sedgwick*, 1:109–10; U.S. Senate, *Message from the President*, Ex. Doc. 1, 30th Cong., 1st sess., 304.

32. U.S. Senate, *Message from the President*, Ex. Doc. 1, 30th Cong., 1st sess., 304–5, 322–23; Hughes and Johnson, *Fighter from Way Back*, 111; Ballentine, *Autobiography of an English Soldier*, 250–52.

33. U.S. Senate, *Message from the President*, Ex. Doc. 1, 30th Cong., 1st sess., appendix, 91; "Journal of Francis Collins," 80; Hughes and Johnson, *A Fighter from Way Back*, 111–12; Register of Enlistments (M233), Reel 79, 158, RG94, NA.

34. U.S. Senate, *Message from the President*, Ex. Doc. 1, 30th Cong., 1st sess., 305–6, 327–28, appendix, 91–92; Croffut, *Fifty Years in Camp and Field*, 277.

35. U.S. Senate, *Message from the President*, Ex. Doc. 1, 30th Cong., 1st sess., 307, 328–29, appendix, 92–93; "Journal of Francis Collins," 81; Hughes and Johnson, *Fighter from Way Back*, 112–13; Croffut, *Fifty Years in Camp and Field*, 278.

36. U.S. Senate, *Message from the President*, Ex. Doc. 1, 30th Cong., 1st sess., 308, 329, appendix, 93, 95, 100; Hughes and Johnson, *Fighter from Way Back*, 113; "The Mexican War," 39–40, Reel 30, FJPP. In his report of the battle, Scott mistook Padierna for the village of Contreras, some distance to the south; Mexicans referred to the battle as Padierna. U.S. Senate, *Message from the President*, Ex. Doc. 1, 30th Cong., 1st sess., 307–9; Ramsey, *Other Side*, 268.

37. U.S. Senate, *Message from the President*, Ex. Doc. 1, 30th Cong., 1st sess., 308–14, 333; Hughes and Johnson, *Fighter from Way Back*, 113–14; *Correspondence of John Sedgwick*, 1:111–12; Croffut, *Fifty Years in Camp and Field*, 280; Semmes, *Service Afloat and Ashore*, 428.

38. U.S. Senate, *Message from the President*, Ex. Doc. 1, 30th Cong., 1st sess., 355; Ramsey, *Other Side*, 325–30.

39. Blackwood, *To Mexico with Scott*, 216–17.

40. Ramsey, *Other Side*, 333–34; *Correspondence of John Sedgwick*, 1:118.

41. U.S. Senate, *Message from the President*, Ex. Doc. 1, 30th Cong., 1st sess., 361–62, appendix, 135–37, 154.

42. U.S. Senate, *Message from the President*, Ex. Doc. 1, 30th Cong., 1st sess., 363–64, appendix, 145, 150–51; Croffut, *Fifty Years in Camp and Field*, 297; *Correspondence of John Sedgwick*, 1:123–24; Hughes and Johnson, *Fighter from Way Back*, 122.

43. U.S. Senate, *Message from the President*, Ex. Doc. 1, 30th Cong., 1st sess., appendix, 137–38, 154–56; Anderson, *Artillery Officer in the Mexican War*, 311–12; Hughes and Johnson, *Fighter from Way Back*, 122.

44. Croffut, *Fifty Years in Camp and Field*, 296–98; U.S. Senate, *Message from the President*, Ex. Doc. 1, 30th Cong., 1st sess., 371; Hughes and Johnson, *Fighter from Way Back*, 123; *Correspondence of John Sedgwick*, 1:124, 138; "Journal of Francis Collins," 84; Ramsey, *Other Side*, 242–43; Anderson, *Artillery Officer in the Mexican War*, 310; William T. H. Brooks to De Lorma Brooks, September 20, 1847, Brooks Papers, AHEC.

45. Croffut, *Fifty Years in Camp and Field*, 300–301; U.S. Senate, *Message from the President*, Ex. Doc. 1, 30th Cong., 1st sess., 376.

46. U.S. Senate, *Message from the President*, Ex. Doc. 1, 30th Cong., 1st sess., 377, appendix, 230; Wilcox, *History of the Mexican War*, 453; Sargent, *Gathering Laurels in Mexico*, 17.

47. U.S. Senate, *Message from the President*, Ex. Doc. 1, 30th Cong., 1st sess., 377–78, appendix, 230; Croffut, *Fifty Years in Camp and Field*, 301–2.

48. U.S. Senate, *Message from the President*, Ex. Doc. 1, 30th Cong., 1st sess., 377–78, appendix, 210, 230.

49. Hughes and Johnson, *Fighter from Way Back*, 125–26; U.S. Senate, *Message from the President*, Ex. Doc. 1, 30th Cong., 1st sess., 378–80, 401, 404, appendix, 230.

50. *Correspondence of John Sedgwick*, 1:127–28.

51. U.S. Senate, *Message from the President*, Ex. Doc. 1, 30th Cong., 1st sess., 382, appendix, 223, 227, 230.

52. U.S. Senate, *Message from the President*, Ex. Doc. 1, 30th Cong., 1st sess., 381–82, appendix, 223, 227, 230; Hughes and Johnson, *Fighter from Way Back*, 127; "The Mexican War," 69–70, Reel 30, FJPP.

53. U.S. Senate, *Message from the President*, Ex. Doc. 1, 30th Cong., 1st sess., appendix, 231; Hughes and Johnson, *Fighter from Way Back*, 127, 136. The spot where Drum and Benjamin were killed, just inside the Garita de Belén, is now the busy intersection where Avenida Cuauhtémoc and Avenida Bucareli meet Avenida Chapultepec; the site of the Ciudadela, one block beyond, is now Mexico City's public library.

54. U.S. Senate, *Message from the President*, Ex. Doc. 1, 30th Cong., 1st sess., 383.

55. U.S. Senate, *Message from the President*, Ex. Doc. 1, 30th Cong., 1st sess., 383–84; Hughes and Johnson, *Fighter from Way Back*, 127–28; Ballentine, *Autobiography of an English Soldier*, 272–73; Semmes, *Service Afloat and Ashore*, 465–67; *Correspondence of John Sedgwick*, 1:129–30; "Journal of Francis Collins," 86; William T. H. Brooks to De Lorma Brooks, September 20, 1847, Brooks Papers, AHEC.

CHAPTER 3

1. Hughes and Johnson, *Fighter from Way Back*, 128–31, 141; *Correspondence of John Sedgwick*, 1:135–37, 145; Nathaniel Lyon to "Dear Hasler," October 24, 1847, Lyon Papers, AAS; "Journal of Francis Collins," 88–89.

2. Hughes and Johnson, *Fighter from Way Back*, 132, 135.

3. Cutrer, *Mexican War Diary*, 131; *Constitution of the Aztec Club*, 3–6; Fitz John Porter file, Box 21, Aztec Club Archives, AHEC. On Regular Army officers' preference for conciliatory policies, see Hsieh, *West Pointers and the Civil War*, 72–73.

4. Hughes and Johnson, *Fighter from Way Back*, 143, 163; "Journal of Francis Collins," 90.

5. Hughes and Johnson, *Fighter from Way Back*, 139; "Journal of Francis Collins," 89; FJP to Roger Jones, November 14, 1847, Reel 355, Letters Received (M567), RG94, NA; Sargent, *Gathering Laurels in Mexico*, 18.

6. *Correspondence of John Sedgwick*, 1:152; Sargent, *Gathering Laurels in Mexico*, 18; Hughes and Johnson, *Fighter from Way Back*, 147, 150; Robert Patterson and Fitz John Porter files, Box 21, Aztec Club Archives, AHEC. Patterson was inducted into the club as Original Member No. 109, and Porter as No. 114.

7. Register of Enlistments (M233), Reel 79, 159, RG94, NA; Hughes and Johnson, *Fighter from Way Back*, 170.

8. "Journal of Francis Collins," 100–105; Register of Enlistments (M233), Reel 79, 159, RG94, NA. Four months later Lovell took convalescent leave to recover from the effects of his recent bout of yellow fever (Mansfield Lovell to Roger Jones, November 12, 1848, Reel 382, Letters Received [M567], RG94, NA).

9. "The Mexican War," 80, Reel 30, FJPP; "Journal of Francis Collins," 106–8; Register of Enlistments (M233), Reel 79, 159, RG94, NA.

10. Register of Enlistments (M233), Reel 79, 160, RG94, NA; FJP to Roger Jones, September 13, October 28, 1848, Reels 388, 389, and Mansfield Lovell to Jones, November 12, 1848, Reel 382, all in Letters Received (M567), RG94, NA; *Daily Union* (Washington, D.C.), August 31, 1848.

11. *Daily National Whig* (Washington, D.C.), March 27, 1849; *Boston Daily Atlas*, March 31, 1849; *Correspondence of John Sedgwick*, 1:159–60; Caleb Huse to Theodore Lord, June 26, 1902, Reel 30, FJPP.

12. A. D. Bache to James J. Andrews, June 29, 1849, enclosed with William Meredith to George W. Crawford, July 6, 1849, Reel 411, and FJP to Jefferson Davis, November 12, 1855, Reel 524, all in Letters Received (M567), RG94, NA; *Report of the Superintendent of the U.S. Coast Survey*, 246.

13. *Official Register*, 1849, 3–4, 7–8, 23; Returns from U.S. Military Posts (M617), Reel

857, RG94, NA. Among the cadets Porter faced later was Charles Field, whose brigade attacked Porter at Mechanicsville, Gaines's Mill, and Malvern Hill, and Porter's men returned the favor at Second Bull Run; Alfred Cumming was wounded leading a Georgia regiment against Porter's lines at Malvern Hill, and Beverly Robertson commanded a brigade of cavalry that confronted Porter on the road from Manassas Junction to Gainesville, Virginia, on the most controversial day of Porter's entire career.

14. *Official Register*, 1849, 3–4, and 1850, 5–6, 9–16, 19–21.

15. Andrew Evans to Theodore Lord, June 5, 1902, David M. Gregg to Lord, June 19, 1902, and Mrs. James McMillan to Lord, June 23, 1902, all on Reel 30, FJPP.

16. Caleb Huse to Theodore Lord, July 2, 1902, Reel 30, FJPP.

17. Edward Porter Alexander to Theodore Lord, February 11, 1902, and Caleb Huse to Lord, July 2, 1902, both on Reel 30, FJPP.

18. Caleb Huse to Theodore Lord, June 26, 1902, and George Ruggles to Lord, June 30, 1902, both on Reel 30, FJPP; Sumner, *Diary of Cyrus B. Comstock*, 184, 186.

19. Andrew Evans to Theodore Lord, June 5, 1902, Reel 30, FJPP.

20. Sumner, *Diary of Cyrus B. Comstock*, 87, 90, 157, 167, 177, 183, 184.

21. *New York Tribune*, June 11, 1850; *New York Herald*, June 30, 1851, June 20, 1853, June 18, October 30, 1854; Nevins and Thomas, *Diary of George Templeton Strong*, 2:37, 55.

22. Seventh Census (M432), Cornwall, N.Y., Dwelling 538, Reel 573, 181A, RG29, NA; GBM to "My dear Maria," January, 1849, Reel 1, GBMP.

23. Thomas Jonathan Jackson to Laura Arnold, September 3, 1850, Jackson Papers, LC; FJP to Stephen M. Weld Jr., August 10, 1877, Porter Papers, MHS.

24. Maury, *Recollections*, 53, 55–56; "Editor's Easy Chair," 705.

25. Bailey, *My Boyhood at West Point*, 11; *Republic* (Washington, D.C.), November 26, 28, 1850; *Register of the Commissioned and Warrant Officers of the Navy of the United States* (1852), 44; New York Census of 1855, Cornwall, Orange County, E.D. 2, Sheet 23, Family No. 24, New York State Archives; application dated February 18, 1851, Bounty Land Warrant File 1850-160-12110, RG15, NA.

26. FJP to Rufus Jones, December 13, 1850, and January 22, 1851, Reels 433 and 451, Letters Received (M567), RG94, NA.

27. George Ruggles to Theodore Lord, June 30, 1902, Andrew Evans to Lord, June 5, 1902, Samuel Breck to Lord, November 14, 1902, and Edward Porter Alexander to Lord, February 11, 1902, all on Reel 30, FJPP; *Official Register*, 1853, 3.

28. Testimony of Rodman P. Lewis, Lunsford L. Lomax (frog problem), Joseph Stevens (ladder quotation), John C. Frary ("inverted woman"), Dabney Herndon, and numerous others, Case File HH-214, and Special Orders 141, September 9, 1852, Case File HH-215, both in Court Martial Case Files, RG153, NA. Herndon, a distant cousin of Dabney Herndon Maury, left West Point after being found deficient in mathematics, turning instead to medical school; he later served as a Confederate surgeon.

29. James W. Schaumburg to FJP, September 20, 1867 (swindler quotation), William B. Franklin to FJP, September 20, 1867, and July 22, 1868, and John P. Hatch to FJP, September 6, 1866, all on Reel 3, FJPP; Montgomery Blair to FJP, July 18, 1878, Reel 7, FJPP; published proceedings of Roberts's 1849 court-martial at Fort Laramie, Reel 1, FJPP.

30. *Official Register* (1852), 9; Testimony of Alfred Church, William Bartlett, Joseph Reynolds, William H. Boggs, and James McPherson, with court finding and sentence of September 28, 1852, Case File HH-215, both in Court Martial Case Files, RG153, NA.

31. Testimony of John M. Jones and Bradford Alden, Case File HH-214, and proceedings of September 29, 1852, with recommendation for clemency, Case File HH-215, all in Court Martial Case Files, RG153, NA.

32. Proceedings of September 29, 1852, and petitions for clemency for John M. Schofield, Nelson B. Sweitzer, and Samuel Kinsey, Case File HH-215, Court Martial Case Files, RG153, NA; Schofield, *Forty-Six Years in the Army*, 241–42. Case File HH-215 contains the records of numerous courts-martial—the unnumbered, handwritten, and heavily water-stained pages of which are badly intermixed, making it difficult to determine which defendant is the subject of each clemency petition. The only names on what appears to be Schofield's petition are those of Benjamin S. Roberts, court president Joseph Plympton, Lucien Webster, E. R. S. Canby, and Thomas Duncan.

33. Eckert and Amato, *Ten Years in the Saddle*, 43.

34. *Official Register*, 1852, 4; *New York Herald*, June 20, 1853 (reporting Sacket's weight at 245); Edward Porter Alexander to Theodore Lord, February 11, 1902, and John P. Hawkins to Lord, September 30, 1902, both on Reel 30, FJPP; Sumner, *Diary of Cyrus B. Comstock*, 93, 97, 99, 148, 157, 167, 184, 186, 193–94, 196.

35. *Official Register*, 1852, 4; George W. Cullum to FJP, July 18, 1854, Reel 503, Letters Received (M567), RG94, NA.

36. *New York Herald*, October 30, 1854; Bailey, *My Boyhood at West Point*, 8. In a letter to Secretary of War Jefferson Davis a year later, Porter explained that he had not served with troops armed as infantry since before Molino del Rey and that he had forgotten much of the drill. FJP to Davis, November 12, 1855, Reel 524, Letters Received (M567), RG94, NA.

37. *Doggett's New-York Directory*, 177, and Street Directory appendix, 13; Perris, *Maps of the City of New York*, 4:47; Nevins and Thomas, *Diary of George Templeton Strong*, 2:232.

38. Letters to Adjutant General Samuel Cooper from Delos Sacket (March 23, 1855, Reel 526), Edmund Kirby Smith (August 10, 1855, Reel 527), George H. Thomas (July 18, 1855, Reel 529), and Robert E. Lee (September 6, 1855, Reel 567), all in Letters Received (M567), RG94, NA.

39. FJP to Samuel Cooper, March 23, 1855, and to Jefferson Davis, November 12, 1855, and Davis to FJP, November 29, 1855, Reel 524, and Cooper to Davis, November 7, 1855, Reel 516, all in Letters Received (M567), RG94, NA.

40. FJP to Samuel Cooper, September 19, 1855, Reel 524, August 3, 4 (two letters), 1856, Reel 545, and George Gibson to Cooper, April 18, 1856, Reel 544, all in Letters Received (M567), RG94, NA; *Ballou's Pictorial* (Boston), May 9, 1857, 296. Porter officially vacated his commission in the 4th Artillery on October 31, 1856. *New York Herald*, June 10, 1857.

41. FJP to Samuel Cooper, August 31, 1856, Reel 545, Letters Received (M567), RG94, NA; quotation from extracts of FJP's letters to Harriet, September 10, 1857, Reel 25, FJPP; *Transactions of the Kansas State Historical Society*, 497–98; *Squatter Sovereign* (Atchison, Kans.), August 26, 1856; *Kansas Weekly Herald* (Leavenworth), August 16, 23, September 6, 1856; *Kansas City (Mo.) Enterprise*, August 30, September 13, 1856.

42. *Transactions of the Kansas State Historical Society*, 508.

43. *Transactions of the Kansas State Historical Society*, 499–501.

44. Higginson, *Letters and Journals*, 140–41; *Transactions of the Kansas State Historical Society*, 514–16. Owen Brown's 1888 account of fleeing Kansas with his father comports with Colonel Cooke's reports to FJP, Reel 2, Stutler Collection, Kansas State Historical Society.

45. *Transactions of the Kansas State Historical Society*, 517–18; Joseph E. Johnston to FJP, October 18, 1856, Beinecke Library, Yale; Johnston to GBM, November 18, 1856, Reel 3, GBMP; FJP to Samuel Cooper, November 30, 1856, Reel 545, Letters Received (M567), RG94, NA.

46. FJP to Samuel Cooper, December 31, 1856, Reel 545, and January 20, 27, March 3, 12,

1857, Reel 565, all in Letters Received (M567), RG94, NA; Seth Williams to GBM, January 16, 1857, Reel 5, GBMP.

47. Affidavit of Morgan Dix, Harriet Porter Dependent Certificate 14819, Mexican War Pension Files, RG15, NA. In 1900 Harriet Porter reported that she was born in May of 1833 (Twelfth Census [T623], ED68, Sheet 16B, Morristown, N.J., Family 332): the last number is nearly obscured by an inkblot and is incorrectly transcribed on the digitized version, but her age is calculated at sixty-seven. Her entry on the U.S. Census of 1850 (Seventh Census [M432], 18th Ward, New York City, Reel 557, p. 105B, Family 1605) comports with that, but in other census records she grew progressively younger. She is listed as twenty on the New York census of 1855 (New York State Census, 1855, Election District 1, 18th Ward, New York City, Family 425, New York State Archives), and federal census marshals recorded her as thirty-six in July of 1870 (Ninth Census [M593], Reel 877, Morris Township, p. 270A, Family 816), as only forty-two in June of 1880 (Tenth Census [T9], Morristown, N.J., Reel 793, p. 253A, Family 107), and as seventy in 1910 (Thirteenth Census [T624], Manhattan, N.Y., Ward 19, Reel 1042, ED 1156, Sheet 1A, Family 5); her gravestone in Brooklyn's Green-Wood Cemetery gives her year of birth as 1835.

48. FJP to Samuel Cooper, March 31, April 30, 1857, Reel 566, Letters Received (M567), RG94, NA.

49. *Evening Star* (Washington, D.C.), May 2, 1857; *New Orleans Picayune*, May 1, 1857; *New York Tribune*, May 14, 1857; *Daily Union* (Washington, D.C.), May 15, 1857; FJP to Samuel Cooper, May 31, 1857, Reel 566, Letters Received (M567), RG94, NA.

50. Winfield Scott to John B. Floyd, September 7, 1857, Reel 574, and Alfred Pleasonton to Samuel Cooper, June 15, 1857, Reel 566, and to James Buchanan, July 11, 1857, Reel 560, all in Letters Received (M567), RG94, NA; U.S. House, *Utah Expedition*, Ex. Doc. 71, 35th Cong., 1st sess., 5–9, 11.

51. Hammond, *Utah Expedition*, 7, 15–17; James Uhler Journal, 6, 8–9, AHEC; U.S. House, *Utah Expedition*, Ex. Doc. 71, 35th Cong., 1st sess., 17–18; U.S. House, *Covode Investigation*, 36th Cong., 1st sess., H. Rept. 648, 118–19 (for Kansas governor Robert Walker's desire to retain Harney there); William Harney to Samuel Cooper, June 12, July 29, 1857, Reel 560, and Winfield Scott to Albert Sidney Johnston, August 28, 1857, Reel 561, and to John B. Floyd, September 7, 1857, Reel 574, all in Letters Received (M567), RG94, NA.

52. FJP to Samuel Cooper, September 1, 1857, Reel 566, Letters Received (M567), NA; extracts from FJP's letters to Harriet, September 1–2, 1857, Reel 25, FJPP.

53. Extracts from FJP's letters to Harriet, September 2–14, 1857, Reel 25, FJPP; U.S. House, *Utah Expedition*, Ex. Doc. 71, 35th Cong., 1st sess., 202–3. Johnston's son recorded his father's height and weight in *Life of Gen. Albert Sidney Johnston*, 72.

54. Robert E. Lee to Albert Sidney Johnston, October 25, 1857, Johnston Papers, Tulane.

CHAPTER 4

1. U.S. House, *Utah Expedition*, Ex. Doc. 71, 35th Cong., 1st sess., 21–22; William Harney to Samuel Cooper, September 16, 1857, Reel 560, and Alfred Pleasonton to Cooper, October 1, 1857, Reel 566, both in Letters Received (M567), RG94, NA.

2. "The Utah Expedition," 13, Reel 30, FJPP.

3. Extracts from FJP's letters to Harriet, September 14, 1857, Reel 25, FJPP. Porter's revelations about Harney were enclosed in Winfield Scott's letter of October 30, 1858, to John B. Floyd, and Scott's paraphrasing of Porter's information is quoted in MacKinnon,

Sword's Point, 161. Porter acknowledged that he knew McDowell had showed his letters to Scott and implied that they were intended for that purpose: FJP to Stephen M. Weld Jr., June 17, 1879, Porter Papers, MHS.

4. U.S. House, *Utah Expedition*, Ex. Doc. 71, 35th Cong., 1st sess., 21–22; extracts from FJP's letters to Harriet, September 17–22, 1857, Reel 25, FJPP; James Uhler Journal, 9–10, AHEC.

5. Extracts from FJP's letters to Harriet, September 19, 22, 1857, Reel 25, FJPP.

6. Extracts from FJP's letters to Harriet, September 24, 1857, Reel 25, FJPP; *Daily Union* (Washington, D.C.), January 24, 1858.

7. Extracts from FJP's letters to Harriet, September 24, 1857, Reel 25, FJPP; FJP to Samuel Cooper, December 31, 1857, Reel 566, Letters Received (M567), RG94, NA; Randolph Marcy to Ellen Marcy, August 10, 1857, quoted in MacKinnon, *Sword's Point*, 205; James Uhler Journal, 11–12, AHEC.

8. "The Utah Expedition," 18–20, Reel 30, FJPP; extracts from FJP's letters to Harriet, September 25–October 1, 1857, Reel 25, FJPP; U.S. House, *Utah Expedition*, Ex. Doc. 71, 35th Cong., 1st sess., 23–26.

9. U.S. House, *Utah Expedition*, Ex. Doc. 71, 35th Cong., 1st sess., 21–22, 27–28; extracts from FJP's letters to Harriet, October 5, 1857, Reel 25, FJPP.

10. U.S. House, *Utah Expedition*, Ex. Doc. 71, 35th Cong., 1st sess., 29, 63, 80–81; Hammond, *Utah Expedition*, 74.

11. U.S. House, *Utah Expedition*, Ex. Doc. 71, 35th Cong., 1st sess., 29–30, 41–44, 64–65, 81–82; extracts from FJP's letters to Harriet, October 10–15, 1857, Reel 25, FJPP.

12. U.S. House, *Utah Expedition*, Ex. Doc. 71, 35th Cong., 1st sess., 64–65; extracts from FJP's letters to Harriet, October 17–18, 1857, Reel 25, FJPP.

13. U.S. House, *Utah Expedition*, Ex. Doc. 71, 35th Cong., 1st sess., 14, 29–30, 38–39; *Daily Pioneer* (St. Paul, Minn.), November 17, 1857; *Burlington (Iowa) Hawk-Eye*, November 18, 1857.

14. Extracts from FJP's letters to Harriet, October 18, 1857, Reel 25, FJPP.

15. Extracts from FJP's letters to Harriet, October 25, 26, 30, 1857, Reel 25, FJPP; U.S. House, *Utah Expedition*, Ex. Doc. 71, 35th Cong., 1st sess., 46, 62–63; FJP to Samuel Cooper, October 31, 1857, Reel 566, Letters Received (M567), RG94, NA; Hammond, *Utah Expedition*, 89; diary of Captain John W. Phelps, quoted in MacKinnon, *Sword's Point*, 393–97.

16. U.S. House, *Utah Expedition*, Ex. Doc. 71, 35th Cong., 1st sess., 46–47, 62–63.

17. Hammond, *Utah Expedition*, 90–92.

18. Extracts from FJP's letters to Harriet, November 7, 15, 1857, Reel 25, FJPP; FJP to GBM, February 28, 1858, Reel 5, GBMP.

19. Hammond, *Utah Expedition*, 92–94; FJP to Samuel Cooper, December 31, 1857, Reel 566, Letters Received (M567), RG94, NA; *Daily Union* (Washington, D.C.), January 24, 1857. Page 2 of the *Daily Union* carried an account of the march dated November 29, 1857, that William MacKinnon ("Letter," ix) concluded was written by Porter to Irvin McDowell. MacKinnon's reasoning is confirmed by Porter's transcribed extract from his letter to Harriet of November 30 (Reel 25, FJPP), in which he describes spending the entire morning "writing a semi official letter to Genl McDowell." The inadvertent, anachronistic reference to "Genl" McDowell betrayed how much later Porter transcribed the diary; presumably he had begun the letter the evening previously or misdated the heading by a day.

20. U.S. House, *Utah Expedition*, Ex. Doc. 71, 35th Cong., 1st sess., 96–99.

21. Philip St. George Cooke to William T. Sherman, May 7, 1889, Reel 40, William T. Sherman Papers, LC.

22. FJP Diary, November 17, 1857, Reel 25, FJPP; *Daily Union* (Washington, D.C.), January 24, 1858; FJP to Samuel Cooper, December 31, 1857, Reel 566, Letters Received (M567), RG94, NA; Hammond, *Utah Expedition*, 123–24, 183, 273.

23. FJP Diary, "October" [November] 28, 1857, and extracts from FJP's letters to Harriet, November 26, 30, 1857, Reel 25, FJPP. Randolph Marcy described the ordeal of his New Mexico mission in *Thirty Years of Army Life*, 225–43.

24. Extracts from FJP's letters to Harriet, December 13, 1857, Reel 25, FJPP; *Daily Union* (Washington, D.C.), January 24, 1858; *New York Tribune*, May 17, 1858; FJP to "J. Monroe" [John Munroe], May 11, 1859, Porter Letters, NYHS. Porter mentioned the Washakie interview in a letter quoted in Johnston's *Life of Gen. Albert Sidney Johnston*, 235.

25. FJP to Samuel Cooper, December 31, 1857, Reel 566, Letters Received (M567), RG94, NA; *Daily Union* (Washington, D.C.), January 24, 1858.

26. Extracts from FJP's letters to Harriet, January 19, 1858, Reel 25, FJPP.

27. Hammond, *Utah Expedition*, 99–100, 106, 109, 129–32, 135–37; extracts from FJP's letters to Harriet, January 19, February 13, 1858, Reel 25, FJPP.

28. FJP Diary, March 13, April 2–6, 1858, Reel 25, FJPP; Brigham Young to Thomas L. Kane, March 9, 1858, and Albert Sidney Johnston to Kane, March 15, 1858, both on Reel 1, FJPP.

29. Hammond, *Utah Expedition*, 128, 137, 273; *New York Tribune*, March 1, 1858; FJP Diary, April 2, 1858, Reel 25, FJPP.

30. Henry Jackson Hunt Diary, June 7, 1858, Hunt Papers, LC; Hammond, *Utah Expedition*, 128, 136, 155, 157; FJP Diary, April 10, 13, 1858, Reel 25, FJPP. Holbrook Fitz John Porter's birthdate is listed as February 28, 1858, in *Herringshaw's American Blue Book of Biography*, 948.

31. FJP Diary, April 2–6, 1858, Reel 25, FJPP; *Compilation of the Messages and Papers of the Presidents*, 4:3024–26; "Utah War," 14, 15; Hammond, *Utah Expedition*, 170.

32. Hammond, *Utah Expedition*, 172, 174–75; "Utah War," 16–17.

33. "Utah War," 20–27; Hammond, *Utah Expedition*, 176–77.

34. "Utah War," 26–28; Hammond, *Utah Expedition*, 177; Canning and Beeton, *Genteel Gentile*, 75–76; extracts from FJP's letters to Harriet, July 2, 1857, Reel 25, FJPP. In *The Mormon Conflict* (202), Norman Furniss ascribes the request for "One-Eyed Riley" to Fitz John Porter, citing Captain Albert Tracy's diary reference to "the adjutant" having directed the band to play it ("Utah War," 27). As appealing as that anecdote would be to ameliorate Porter's customary prudishness, Tracy almost certainly alluded instead to Henry Maynadier, the regimental adjutant of the 10th Infantry; Porter was the assistant adjutant general of the Utah army, not simply "the adjutant," and when Tracy mentioned Porter he used either Porter's full name or his full title.

35. Hammond, *The Utah Expedition*, 176–83; "The Utah War," 28–32; extracts from Porter's letters to Harriet, July 2, 9, 1857, Reel 25, FJPP; FJP to Samuel Cooper, August 1, 1858, Reel 586, Letters Received (M567), RG94, NA.

36. Extracts from Porter's letters to Harriet, September 16, October 16, 1858, Reel 25, FJPP; "The Utah War," 34–35.

37. Johnston, *The Life of Gen. Albert Sidney Johnston*, 229–30; extracts from FJP's letters to Harriet, July 9, August 13, September 16, 1858, Reel 25, FJPP. On April 3, 1860, as Captain Albert Tracy arrived in Washington from Camp Floyd, he looked forward to his first glimpse of his son, who was nearly three years old ("Utah War," 117).

38. Extracts from FJP's letters to Harriet, September 16, 1858, Reel 25, FJPP.

39. Copy (in FJP's hand) of Scott's endorsement on FJP to Lorenzo Thomas, April 21, 1859, Reel 1, FJPP.

40. Extracts from FJP's letters to Harriet, April 16, July 9, August 13, 1858, Reel 25, FJPP; Hammond, *Utah Expedition*, 188–89.

41. Extracts from FJP's letters to Harriet, August 13, 1858, Reel 25, FJPP; "Utah War," 32–33, 84–86; Hammond, *Utah Expedition*, 187–88.

42. Hammond, *Utah Expedition*, 185; extracts from FJP's letters to Harriet, November 24, December 23, 1858, Reel 25, FJPP; "Utah War," 53–54.

43. John Cradlebaugh to Peter K. Dotson, April 2, 1859, Dotson to Henry Heth, April 3, 1859, FJP to Cradlebaugh, June 8, 1859, Dotson to Alex Wilson, June 20, 1859, FJP to Dotson June 27, 1859, Dotson to Albert Sidney Johnston, June 30, 1859, and Johnston to Samuel Cooper, July 6, 1859, all on Reel 593, Letters Received (M567), RG94, NA; Johnston, *Life of Gen. Albert Sidney Johnston*, 236–37; extracts from FJP's letters to Harriet, March 31, 1859, Reel 25, FJPP; U.S. Senate, *Massacre at Mountain Meadows*, 36th Cong., 1st sess., Ex. Doc. 42, 9, 19–20.

44. Extracts from FJP's letters to Harriet, May 11, August 16, 1859, Reel 25, FJPP.

45. "Utah War," 72; Alexander Wilson to Charles F. Smith, August 6, 1859, Reel 1, FJPP; *New York Tribune*, September 17, 1859. The *Tribune* account relied on a letter Sergeant Pike wrote to his brother soon after the incident.

46. FJP to Albert Sidney Johnston, August 11, 1859, Reel 1, FJPP; "Utah War," 72–74; *New York Tribune*, September 17, 1859; "An Incident of Army Life among the Mormons," 1–5, Reel 25, FJPP.

47. "Utah War," 73–74; Sadler, "Spencer-Pike Affair," 87, 90.

48. For counterfeiting incidents, see *Ottawa (Ill.) Free Trader*, January 10, 1845; *Niles' National Register* (Baltimore), January 3, 1846; *Warsaw (Ill.) Signal*, April 24, 1844, January 7, 1846; *Vermont Phoenix* (Brattleboro), June 11, 1851; *New York Herald*, June 27, 1851; and Bigler and Bagley, *Mormon Rebellion*, 345–46.

49. "A Characteristic (Mormon) Conspiracy," 1–3, Reel 25, FJPP.

50. "A Characteristic (Mormon) Conspiracy," 3–9, Reel 25, FJPP; *New York Tribune*, August 11, 1859; Eighth Census (M653), Reel 1313, 6, Salt Lake County, Utah, Penitentiary; *CG*, 37th Cong., 3rd sess., appendix, 124; extracts from FJP's letters to Harriet, August 25, 1859, Reel 25, FJPP; *Deseret News* (Salt Lake City), September 7, 1859, and George H. Crosman to W. A. Gordon, October 5, 1859, both quoted in Bigler and Bagley, *Mormon Rebellion*, 347–48. Porter's narrative about the incident differs from contemporary accounts in regard to Brewer, and a gentile named John M. Wallace was portrayed at the trial as the person who tipped Porter off to the counterfeiting.

51. Extracts from FJP's letters to Harriet, February 29, March 29, 1860, Reel 25, FJPP; "Utah War," 81–82; "A Characteristic (Mormon) Conspiracy," 9–16, Reel 25, FJPP; FJP to Samuel Cooper, February 29, Reel 630, Letters Received (M567), RG94, NA. Quoting the *Deseret News* of May 23, 1860, Bigler and Bagley date Brewer's murder May 17, 1860, in Salt Lake City (*Mormon Rebellion*, 348), while Porter recounted finding a body in the desert that he thought was Brewer's.

CHAPTER 5

1. *New York Herald*, March 16, May 11, 1860; *Polynesian* (Honolulu), June 23, 1860; FJP to Samuel Cooper, April 28, May 1, 1860, Reel 630, Letters Received (M567), RG94, NA. The

log of the *Levant* vanished with the ship, so the date of its arrival in Panama is not known, but the *Herald* of May 11 reported that the captain's clerk died there on April 20.

2. FJP to Samuel Cooper, June 1, 7, July 1, August 1, September 1, October 1, 20, 31, November 4, 1860, and to Lorenzo Thomas, October 20, 1860, all on Reel 630, Letters Received (M567), RG94, NA; Cooper to FJP, November 1, 1860, Reel 22, FJPP.

3. *OR*, 1:70–71. On McClellan's Whiggish antecedents, see Rafuse, *McClellan's War*, 84–85, 122–24.

4. *Yorkville (S.C.) Enquirer*, November 1, 1860; *Newbern (N.C.) Weekly Progress*, November 6, 1860; *OR*, 1:70–71. In a penciled note on the front page of his original report, now in the Civil War Letters Collection, NYHS, Porter noted that he "arrived in Charleston the day after Lincoln's election."

5. *OR*, 1:69–71; Hughes and Johnson, *Fighter from Way Back*, 127, 163.

6. Theodore Talbot to "My dear Sister," November 20, 1860, Talbot Papers, LC; *OR*, 1:70.

7. *OR*, 1:70.

8. FJP to Samuel Cooper, December 1, 1860, Reel 620, Letters Received (M567), RG94, NA; *OR*, 1:69, 72–73; Theodore Talbot to "My dear Mother," November 16, 26, 1860, and to "My dear Sister," November 20, 1860, Talbot Papers, LC.

9. FJP to Johnston, December 1, 1860, Reel 1, FJPP; "A Cursory (but Thoughtful) Narrative," 2, Reel 25, FJPP.

10. FJP to Samuel Cooper, December 31, 1860, Reel 630, Letters Received (M567), RG94, NA; FJP to Cooper, January 31, March 1, 1861, Reel 45, Letters Received (M619), RG94, NA; S.O. 142, November 30, 1860, Reel 22, FJPP.

11. *Polynesian* (Honolulu), June 23, 1860, February 23, 1861 (with quotation from the *Intelligencer*); *Baltimore Exchange*, December 6, 1860; *Alexandria (Va.) Gazette*, February 5, 1861; *National Republican* (Washington, D.C.), March 1, 28, 1861; *New York Herald*, March 29, 1861.

12. *OR*, 1:579–84, 586.

13. *OR*, 1:585, 587–88, 52(1):128; FJP to Cooper, March 1, 1861, Reel 45, Letters Received (M619), RG94, NA.

14. FJP inspection report of *Daniel Webster* and "Texas Expedition," 3–5, Reel 25, FJPP.

15. *OR*, 1:503–4, 597. Joseph Holt also tried to foist responsibility on Major Anderson for his (and President Buchanan's) failure to resupply or reinforce Fort Sumter. See Marvel, *Mr. Lincoln Goes to War*, 14–15, and Marvel, *Lincoln's Autocrat*, 138.

16. *OR*, 52(1):128, 53:486; "Texas Expedition," 5–8, Reel 30, FJPP.

17. "Texas Expedition," 5–8, Reel 30, FJPP; *OR*, 52(1):128–29, 132–33, 53:487.

18. "Texas Expedition," 11–12, Reel 30, FJPP; *OR*, 52(1):128. The 1900 census records Lucia's birth in March of 1862, but she was nineteen on the 1880 census and Porter always recorded her birth year as 1861; his months at home in the middle of 1860 also coincided with the window of conception for a birth in March of 1861, while he was constantly on duty in the field between April of 1861 and the following autumn. In Porter's family, "Chauncey" was sometimes spelled "Chauncy."

19. *OR*, 1:248; FJP to H. L. Scott, April 8, 1861, Reel 45, Letters Received (M619), RG94, NA.

20. "A Cursory (but Thoughtful) Narrative," 2–3, Reel 25, FJPP; FJP to Albert Sidney Johnston, April 8, 1861, copies in Porter Papers, RBHPL, and Reel 1, FJPP; *OR*, 50(1):471–72, 496. Porter repeated the story of his correspondence with Johnston, and the general's

relief from command, in a letter to William Preston Johnston dated December 8, 1884, that the recipient included in "Albert Sidney Johnston at Shiloh," 541.

21. FJP to GBM, April 15, 1861, and GBM to Winfield Scott, April 23, 1861, both on Reel 5, GBMP; Sears, *Civil War Papers*, 4–5.

22. Eckert and Amato, *Ten Years in the Saddle*, 249; *OR*, 1:648.

23. *OR*, 51(1):345–46.

24. *OR*, 51(1):346, 352–53; Burlingame, *With Lincoln in the White House*, 35–37.

25. McClure, *Abraham Lincoln and Men of War-Times*, 372; *OR*, 51(1):346–47, 353–55.

26. *OR*, 51(1):350.

27. *OR*, 51(1):347–48, 353, 360–66; Simon Cameron to FJP, September 3, 1881, Reel 1, FJPP. Cameron's change of heart about defending the railroad, which he alluded to in the 1881 letter, is also evident in an April 27, 1861, letter to a Philadelphia correspondent. *OR*, 2:603–4.

28. FJP to Harriet Porter, presumably April 22, 1861, quoted in Eisenschiml, *Celebrated Case of Fitz John Porter*, 24; Nevins and Thomas, *Diary of George Templeton Strong*, 3:127. In the late 1940s Porter's last surviving child, Evelina Porter Doggett, allowed Eisenschiml access to her father's personal correspondence, including many of his surviving letters to and from Harriet, but those letters dropped from sight after her death.

29. *OR*, 51(1):349, 356–58, 367; *Reading (Pa.) Times*, January 13, 1883.

30. *OR*, 51(1):349–50.

31. *OR*, 51(1):350; manuscript memoir, Reel 1, FJPP; typescript chapter on the Harrisburg episode, 31, Reel 30, FJPP.

32. *OR*, 2:601, 607, 615, 619–20, 622, 626–28.

33. *OR*, 2:628–29, 631–32, 635.

34. George Brown to Isaac Trimble, May 6, 1861, Trimble Papers, Maryland Historical Society; *OR*, 2:29.

35. *OR*, 2:28, 645–48, 652.

36. *OR*, 2:880–81.

37. *OR*, 2:615, 51(1):391–92.

38. *OR*, 2:660–61, 684, 51(1):397, 400; FJP memorandum on river depth, June 7, 1861, Reel 1, FJPP.

39. *New York Herald*, June 20, 1861; *Evening Star* (Washington, D.C.), June 22, 1861. The *Star* misplaced Hagerstown Female Seminary at Williamsport.

40. FJP memorandum for Townsend, June 9, 1861, Reel 1, FJPP; *OR*, 51(1):397–98.

41. *OR*, 2:689, 692.

42. *OR*, 2:691, 692, 51(2):139, 143; *Report of the Joint Committee*, 1:235; Strother, "Personal Recollections: Patterson's Campaign," 143. Strother's postwar observations were drawn from his wartime daily journal, but in many passages he appears to have revised the entries to reflect subsequent events and developments.

43. *OR*, 2:691–92, 695–96, 51(2):143.

44. *OR*, 2:697–98, 701, 707.

45. *OR*, 2:702–3.

46. *OR*, 2:702.

47. *OR*, 51(1):389–90, 413–14.

48. FJP to "My dear Colonel," June 21, 1861, Reel 1, FJPP.

49. *OR*, 2:711.

50. *OR*, 2:725; *Report of the Joint Committee*, 1:153.

51. *OR*, 2:729–30; Strother, "Personal Recollections: Patterson's Campaign," 1:142.

52. *OR*, 2:729–30, 735.

53. *Supplement*, 1:193; *OR*, 2:179–81, 184–86; Kenton Harper's report of the 5th Virginia, Pendleton Papers, Duke; Trout, *With Pen and Saber*, 14.

54. *OR*, 2:157–58; *Report of the Joint Committee*, 1:195.

55. *OR*, 2:159; Strother, "Personal Recollections: Patterson's Campaign," 152. On July 20, a farmer who had recently visited Winchester gave Patterson an amateur estimate that Johnston had had 35,200 men there, including 5,000 militia, and Patterson seemed to credit it (*OR*, 2:172; *Report of the Joint Committee*, 1:96, 141). Charles Stone, who had no access to Patterson's intelligence reports, "imagined" that Johnston had "not far from 20,000 men, including his militia," although he heard unsubstantiated rumors that the Confederate force numbered anywhere from 15,000 to 30,000 (*Report of the Joint Committee*, 1:75). Strother insisted that he interrogated deserters on July 16 who performed the impressive feat of naming every unit in Johnston's army, and they put his forces at no more than 17,000, with 31 guns; Strother complained that when he presented that information to Patterson's staff officers they instead believed reports that Johnston had 42,000 men and 70 guns ("Personal Recollections: Patterson's Campaign," 155). Strother's rendition of these events deserves some skepticism because by the time he published those claims he had become antagonistic to Porter and to the entire conservative element he represented—including Newton and Patterson. Sometime between July and December, Porter told McDowell that Patterson had received reports giving Johnston "something like 40,000 men," but Porter did not appear to take those estimates seriously (*Report of the Joint Committee*, 1:40). Until any chance of fighting was over, neither Patterson nor anyone on his staff officially reported any estimate of Johnston's forces higher than the potential 26,000 mentioned on July 6.

56. *OR*, 2:158–59, 161, 967.

57. *OR*, 2:162–63. Patterson's July 9 letter as published in 1880 in *OR*, 2:163, reads, "I am very desirous to know when the General-in-Chief wishes me to approach Leesburg," which makes no sense. The version published in 1863 instead reads, "I am very desirous to know when the general-in-chief wishes me to approach Winchester," and in Patterson's testimony before the Committee on the Conduct of the War he read it as "Winchester" (*Report of the Joint Committee*, 1:102, 130). The original of the letter has never been found, as is noted in the draft chapter on "General Patterson's Campaign," 24, Reel 30, FJPP.

58. *Report of the Joint Committee*, 1:128, 130, 195; *OR*, 2:163–64; FJP to Joseph Kirkland, January 21, 1883, Reel 3, FJPP.

59. *OR*, 2:967; Johnston, *Narrative*, 31.

60. Major Abner Doubleday, of the Regular artillery, assumed the army had about 11,000 men on July 2 (*Supplement*, 1:198), but six months later he testified that he heard estimates of Patterson having had about 20,000 men (*Report of the Joint Committee*, 1:68). General Charles Sandford, who brought Patterson reinforcements, later claimed they increased his numbers to 22,000, and David Birney, the colonel of one of Sandford's regiments, supposed there were 20,000 to 25,000 at Martinsburg (*Report of the Joint Committee*, 1:56, 163). An aristocratic private in the 17th Pennsylvania, who later commanded a regiment, thought their army amounted to 26,000 after Stone's arrival, and 30,000 after Sandford's last men came in (James Biddle to Gertrude Biddle, July 9, 10, 1861, Biddle Letters, HSP). One of Patterson's aides swore he had no more than 19,000 altogether, of whom only 15,000 to 16,000 were "fighting men," and another aide set the maximum at 18,000 (*Report of the Joint Committee*, 1:185, 194). A topographical engineer reported from Patterson's headquarters on July 4 that "we are probably about 10,000 strong" (*OR*, 2:179), but much of the force was engaged in moving and guarding supplies, and that was before reinforcements arrived. Official returns from the end of June gave Patterson 14,344 and

Johnston 10,654 "present for duty," but that did not count some 2,200 Virginia militiamen Johnston had called up (*OR*, 2:187, 969).

61. *OR*, 2:163; *Report of the Joint Committee*, 1:137, 139.

62. *OR*, 2:164, 711; *Report of the Joint Committee*, 1:155.

63. *OR*, 2:165–66.

64. *OR*, 2:166; *Report of the Joint Committee*, 1:141, 157.

65. *OR*, 2:166–67, 473, 973–74, 982; *Report of the Joint Committee*, 1:163; Trout, *With Pen and Saber*, 18. John Casler, a new recruit in an incomplete regiment of Jackson's brigade who had reached the front only the day before, later described deploying and tearing down fences on July 16 to confront Patterson, and waiting for him into the next day (*Four Years in the Stonewall Brigade*, 29).

66. *Report of the Joint Committee*, 1:155–57; Locke, *Story of the Regiment*, 33.

67. *Report of the Joint Committee*, 1:156–57.

68. *Report of the Joint Committee*, 1:157–58, 196–97; *OR*, 2:169, 170; Locke, *Story of the Regiment*, 33–34.

69. *Report of the Joint Committee*, 1:165, 198; Abbott, *First Regiment New Hampshire Volunteers*, 142–43; Keyes, "1861—The First Wisconsin Infantry," 99. David Birney answered a leading question under oath early in 1862, denying that anyone in his brigade had shown any demoralization until they reached Charles Town, on July 17, after "they ascertained that they were not going to be led against the enemy" (*Report of the Joint Committee*, 1:165). That was not true, as Birney surely knew: written evidence for that demoralization came on July 13 from all ten captains of the 6th Pennsylvania—one of only three regiments in Birney's brigade—when they warned Patterson that their men fully expected to be home by the expiration of their enlistments (*Report of the Joint Committee*, 1:141).

70. *OR*, 2:167–68; *Report of the Joint Committee*, 1:158–59; *Supplement*, 1:199.

71. *OR*, 2:473, 982. According to Casler's memoir, *Four Years in the Stonewall Brigade*, 30, Johnston's camp was rife with measles.

72. *OR*, 2:159, 166–68.

73. *OR*, 2:171–73.

74. *OR*, 2:175–77; *National Republican* (Washington, D.C.), August 10, 1861 (for an example of partisan exaggeration of Patterson's situation); *Report of the Joint Committee*, 1:5, 39, 40–41.

75. *OR*, 2:719–20. McDowell took about 35,000 men to Bull Run, reasoning that Beauregard had 25,000 men in the ranks and about 10,000 more that might be called on from elsewhere (besides Johnston's force), and he expected to prevail against that many; most estimates credit Beauregard with about 22,000 and Johnston with about 11,000 during the battle.

76. *OR*, 2:178.

77. FJP to GBM, August 1, 1861, quoted in *MOS*, 74; *OR*, 2:174–75.

CHAPTER 6

1. Robert Patterson to John Sherman, June 29, 1861, Box 29, John Sherman Papers, LC; FJP to the adjutant general, August 7, 1861, Reel 46, Letters Received (M619), RG94, NA.

2. *National Republican* (Washington, D.C.), March 1, 28, July 15, August 15, 1861; *Polynesian* (Honolulu), June 15, 1861; *Daily Exchange* (Baltimore), August 6, 15, 1861; *Delaware State Journal and Statesman* (Wilmington), September 20, 1861; *Yarmouth (N.S.) Herald*, January 30, 1862; Hague, "Doubtful Island in the Pacific," 488–89; Lost and

Wrecked Ships, 1801–1941, Navy Casualty Reports, Navy Department Library; *CG*, 37th Cong., 1st sess., 224, 281.

3. FJP to Lorenzo Thomas, August 9, 1861, Reel 46, Letters Received (M619), RG94, NA.

4. *CWL*, supplement, 90; Beatie, *Army of the Potomac: Birth of Command*, 427, quotes McClellan's list of recommended promotions, July 29, 1861, Letters Received (M1064), RG94, NA. On the reasons for McClellan's appointment (and how those reasons contributed to his downfall), see Neely, *Union Divided*, 66–79.

5. Harvey Browne to Montgomery Meigs, July 26, 1861, ALP; *CWL*, 4:411. Although Browne signed his name with an "e," he is listed as Harvey Brown in army records.

6. FJP to GBM, August 16, 1861, ALP; FJP to GBM, 6:30 P.M., August 16, 1861, Reel 11, GBMP; *OR*, 51(1):455, 456, 461; Simpson and Berlin, *Sherman's Civil War*, 129. Lehigh University, from which Porter's eldest child graduated in 1878, has a cypher copy of the 6:30 P.M. telegram of August 16.

7. Orléans, *Voyage en Amérique*, 89–90; Norton, *Army Letters*, 24. Fort Corcoran stood on what is now Key Boulevard, opposite North Ode Street, on the site of a modern condominium complex called the Atrium.

8. Simpson and Berlin, *Sherman's Civil War*, 130, 132–34; *Rochester (N.Y.) Evening Express*, August 6, 8, 9, 1861; "Fifth Army Corps," 8–9, Reel 25, FJPP.

9. *Rochester (N.Y.) Democrat*, September 2, 1861; Samuel S. Partridge to "My dear Brother," August 23, 1861, BV 146:5, FSNMP; FJP to Randolph Marcy, October 9, 1861, Reel 12, GBMP.

10. FJP's September 13 endorsement on John M. Wilson to Headquarters, Army of the Potomac, September 2, 1861, Endorsements Sent, RG393, Part 2, NA; Heitman, *Historical Register*, 1:790; Woodward, *Our Campaigns*, 48; "Fifth Army Corps," 8–9, Reel 25, FJPP.

11. FJP to Seth Williams, September 16, 18, 20, 27, 1861, Reel 12, GBMP; General Orders 26, 28, 39 (paginated individually), *Index of General Orders*.

12. *OR*, 51(1):455, 464, 470; Heitman, *Historical Register*, 1:694, 724; Sumner, *Diary of Cyrus B. Comstock*, 213.

13. Randolph Marcy to GBM, September 6, 1861, and GBM to brigade and division commanders, September 7, 1861, both on Reel 12, GBMP; *CWP*, 100. In *West Pointers and the Civil War* (146, 229 n. 27), Wayne Hsieh documents Porter's bayonet drill with a host of general and special orders issued from Hall's Hill.

14. Edward B. McMurdy to Henry Halleck, September 26, 1862, Reel 121, Letters Received (M619), RG 94, NA: *Report of the Joint Committee*, 173; *OR*, 5:884–86.

15. *New York Times*, September 5, 1861; *Baltimore Exchange*, September 6, 1861. Judging from the date of the *Times* story, Stansbury Haydon assumed that Porter's first ascent was September 5 (*Military Ballooning*, 220), but Horatio Taft saw the balloon on September 4 and described September 5 as very rainy (Horatio Taft Diary, LC).

16. Frederick T. Locke to Thaddeus S. C. Lowe, September 6, 1861, Box 83, Institute of Aerospace Sciences Archives, LC; *OR*, Series 3, 3:261–62; FJP's endorsement on Lowe to FJP, September 16, 1861, Endorsements Sent, RG393, NA.

17. *OR*, 5:215–17, and Series 3, 3:263–64; Randolph Marcy to FJP, September 21, 1861, EG Box 40, Eldridge Collection, Huntington Library.

18. *OR*, Series 3, 3:263; *Report of the Joint Committee*, 1:115; Sears, *For Country, Cause, and Leader*, 97–99; Orléans, *Voyage en Amérique*, 109. Munson's Hill, the crest of which has been flattened to accommodate dense residential development, is largely covered with the commercial glut of what is known as Seven Corners.

19. Orléans, *Voyage en Amérique*, 109; George Monteith to "My dear Mother," September

30, 1861, UM; FJP to William B. Franklin, [September] 29, [1861], Franklin Papers, LC; *Report of the Joint Committee*, 1:118, 134.

20. Strother, "Personal Recollections: Patterson's Campaign," 152; FJP endorsement of January 23, 1862, on George E. Tyler's application for pay, Endorsements Sent, RG393, Part 2, NA.

21. Jonas D. Richardson to "Dear Parents and Brother," October 4, 1861, Richardson Letters, BL; Orléans, *Voyage en Amérique*, 109.

22. Walter J. Phelps Jr. to "Dear E[liza]," October 1, 1861, Phelps Papers, AHEC; Jonas D. Richardson to "Dear Parents and Brother," November 7, 1861, Richardson Letters, BL; Orléans, *Voyage en Amérique*, 109–10.

23. George Monteith to his parents, August 20, September 5, 1861, Monteith Letters, BL; FJP to Randolph Marcy, October 9, 1861, Reel 12, GBMP; Auchmuty, *Letters*, 4; *OR*, 51(1):490, 493; "Reminiscences of a Life in Peace and War," 3, Reel 25, FJPP. McClellan's chief of staff consulted Porter about the merits of George Gordon, who had been with Patterson as colonel of the 2nd Massachusetts, and Gordon was promptly assigned as an acting brigadier (Randolph Marcy to FJP, September 16, 1861, Reel 12, GBMP; *OR*, 5:16).

24. For example, see FJP's rejection of George C. Putnam's resignation, August 30, 1861, Letters Sent, and of Putnam's requests for leave, September 26, October 17, 1861, Endorsements Sent, and FJP on the resignations of Robert Sturgeon, October 22, 1861, and Mortimer F. Stillwell, January 23, 1862, Endorsements Sent, all in RG393 Part 2, NA, as well as FJP on revoking the resignation of John A. Bowman, December 16, 19, 1861, Register of Letters Received, Reel 9, Correspondence and Issuances (M2096), RG393, Part 1, NA.

25. FJP endorsement of October 31, 1861, on John Pickell's letter to him, Endorsements Sent, RG393, Part 2, NA; FJP to Army of the Potomac Headquarters, January 21, 1862, Register of Letters Received, Reel 9, Correspondence and Issuances (M2096), RG393, NA.

26. John Pickell to William Henry Seward, November 23, 1861, with FJP's endorsement of November 27, Reel 48, Letters Received (M619), RG94, NA; FJP to J. T. Sprague, January 15, 1862, Porter Letters, NYHS; FJP to E. D. Morgan, January 27, 1862, Civil War Letters Collection, NYHS; FJP to Seth Williams, February 16, 1862, and Frederick T. Locke to Thomas B. W. Stockton, February 19, 1862, both in Letters Sent, RG393, Part 2, NA; FJP endorsement of January 7, 1862, on John Martindale's report of the 13th New York, and his February 28, 1862, endorsement on Pickell's letter to GBM, both in Endorsements Sent, RG393, Part 2, NA; Jesse Gove Journal, February 20, 1862, LC; U.S. Congress, *Senate Executive Journal*, 37th Cong., 2nd sess., March 13, 1862, 163; FJP's rendition of the Pickell episode, Reel 3, FJPP.

27. George Monteith to Carl Stephan, February 14, 1862, Letters Sent, RG393, Part 2, NA.

28. Norton, *Army Letters*, 48; testimony of John Martindale, Case File II-680, Court Martial Case Files, RG153, NA; *New York Herald*, December 11, 1861, March 5, 1862.

29. FJP to Seth Williams, October 18, 19, 1861, Reel 13, December 30, 1861, Reel 14, January 21, 1862, Reel 15, all in GBMP; *New York Times*, December 10, 11, 1861.

30. John Martindale's endorsement on Captain Sturgeon's resignation of October 22, 1861, FJP endorsement on same, on Surgeon Fisk's resignation, November 27, 1861, and on Martindale's request to drop Quartermaster Cook and Lieutenant Fay, November 4, 1861, all in Endorsements Sent, RG393, Part 2, NA; FJP to Randolph Marcy, October 26, 1861, Reel 13, to Seth Williams, November 4, 21, 29, 1861, and to Albert V. Colburn, November 7, 1861, Reel 14, all in GBMP.

31. FJP to Randolph Marcy, October 26, 1861, Reel 13, GBMP; Orléans, *Voyage en Amérique*, 148; Cutler, *Letters from the Front*, 11; Norton, *Army Letters*, 29, 31; Horatio Taft Diary, October 26, 1861, LC.

32. Orléans, *Voyage en Amérique*, 148, 165.

33. GBM to Winfield Scott, August 8, 1861, and Scott to Simon Cameron, August 9, 1861, ALP; *OR*, 51(1):491–93.

34. Benjamin Wade to Caroline Wade, October 25, 1861, Reel 3, Wade Papers, LC; Zachariah Chandler to Letitia Chandler, October 27, 1861, Reel 1, Chandler Papers, LC; Burlingame and Ettlinger, *Inside Lincoln's White House*, 28; *CWP*, 113–18; James Biddle to Gertrude Biddle, November 6, 1861, Biddle Letters, HSP.

35. *CWP*, 114; Orléans, *Voyage en Amérique*, 153; *CWL*, 5:9–10.

36. FJP to Manton Marble, October 23, November 22, 1861, Marble Papers, LC.

37. *Evening Star* (Washington, D.C.), November 4, 1861; Horatio Taft Diary, November 4, 1861, LC. McClellan's "hometown" newspaper, the *Cincinnati Daily Press*, had dubbed him the Young Napoleon as early as October 7, but the *New York Herald* adopted the sobriquet independently on November 3, 1861.

38. Orléans, *Voyage en Amérique*, 92, 132.

39. Orléans, *Voyage en Amérique*, 165–66, 172.

40. *Evening Star* (Washington, D.C.), November 8, 9, 11, 19, 1861; Orléans, *Voyage en Amérique*, 171–72; Horatio Taft Diary, November 9, 1861, LC.

41. Jonas B. Richardson to "Dear Parents and Brother," November 23, 1861, Richardson Letters, BL; Burlingame, *With Lincoln in the White House*, 61–62; French, *Witness to the Young Republic*, 380–81; Orléans, *Voyage en Amérique*, 183–84; Jesse Gove Journal, November 20, 1861, LC; Horatio Taft Diary, November 20, 1861, LC.

42. Norton, *Army Letters*, 33; Isaac Bevier to "Dear Parents," November 20, 1861, Allen County Public Library; Jonas B. Richardson to "Dear Parents and Brother," November 23, 1861, Richardson Letters, BL; Burlingame, *With Lincoln in the White House*, 63; French, *Witness to the Young Republic*, 381; Orléans, *Voyage en Amérique*, 184; Jesse Gove Journal, November 20, 1861, LC; Horatio Taft Diary, November 20, 1861, LC.

43. Orléans, *Voyage en Amérique*, 186; Horatio Taft Diary, November 24–29, 1861, LC; Jesse Gove Journal, November 30, 1861, LC.

44. *CWL*, 5:34.

45. *CG*, 37th Cong., 2nd sess., 29–32, 40, 110, 153; Beale, *Diary of Gideon Welles*, 2:633, 3:362–63. Zachariah Chandler's drinking elicited frequent comment throughout his public life, even in an era when heavy drinking was common. Beale, *Diary of Edward Bates*, 260; *Pioneer and Democrat* (St. Paul, Minn.), December 26, 1862; *Cairo (Ill.) Bulletin*, April 19, 1874; *Marshall County Republican* (Plymouth, Ind.), July 16, 1874; *Chicago Tribune*, May 18, 1879.

46. William Doubleday to Zachariah Chandler, December 6, 1861, Reel 1, Chandler Papers, LC.

47. *CWL*, 5:34–35; *OR*, 5:1006–7; Orléans, *Voyage en Amérique*, 221, 236; Cutler, *Letters from the Front*, 13–14; *Evening Star* (Washington, D.C.), December 20, 1861; *National Republican* (Washington, D.C.), December 24, 1861. The *OR* index identifies Fitz John Porter as the general mentioned, but Provost Marshal Andrew Porter (who was also a general) was more often in the city.

48. Ellen McClellan to Elizabeth McClellan [December, 1861], Reel 61, GBMP; George Monteith to "my numerous relatives and friends," December 21, 1861, Monteith Letters, BL; Jesse Gove Journal, February 20, 1862, LC; George W. Morell to Seth Williams, December 23, 24, 1861, and to Randolph Marcy, December 25, 26, 27, 1861, all on Reel 14, GBMP.

49. *Report of the Joint Committee*, 1:68–70; Orléans, *Voyage en Amérique*, 236; Barnes, *Medical and Surgical History*, 5:365; *Evening Star* (Washington, D.C.), December 27, 28, 1861, January 14, 1862; *National Republican* (Washington, D.C.), December 27, 1861; *Boston Daily Advertiser, Boston Herald*, and *Chicago Tribune*, January 3, 1862; Beale, *Diary of Edward Bates*, 218–20.

50. *Report of the Joint Committee*, 1:170–73.

51. *Report of the Joint Committee*, 1:175–77, 179–82.

52. *Report of the Joint Committee*, 1:171, 174, 179; Cutler, *Letters from the Front*, 13, 15, 16; Jesse Gove Journal, November 15, 30, 1861, February 18, 1862, LC; William T. H. Brooks to "Dear Father," December 25, 1861, February 18, 1862, Brooks Papers, AHEC; J. Hartwell Keyes to "Friend Diantha," February 7, 1862, Liljenquist Family Collection, LC; Norton, *Army Letters*, 56.

53. Samuel S. Partridge to "My dear Ed," December 27, 1861, BV 146:5, Partridge Letters, FSNMP.

54. *Report of the Joint Committee*, 1:73; Julian, *Political Recollections*, 201–2.

55. *CWL*, 5:94; FJP to Seth Williams, January 8, 10, 1862, Reel 15, GBMP; *Report of the Joint Committee*, 2:152–59; George Monteith to "My dear Mother," January 2, 1862, Monteith Letters, BL.

56. Raymond, *Life and Public Services of Abraham Lincoln*, 772–76; Niven, *Salmon P. Chase Papers*, 1:324–25. The only detailed contemporary description of these meetings is Irvin McDowell's memorandum, which Raymond published verbatim.

57. Raymond, *Life and Public Services of Abraham Lincoln*, 776–78.

58. *MOS*, 153–54; Salmon P. Chase to William Pitt Fessenden, January "15" [14], 1862, Chase Papers, LC; Niven, *Salmon P. Chase Papers*, 1:326; *CWP*, 154; *Report of the Joint Committee*, 1:75–76.

59. *New York Herald*, January 21, 1861.

60. *National Intelligencer* (Washington, D.C.), September 10, 1861; FJP to Irvin McDowell and McDowell to FJP, both January 26, 1862, Reel 15, GBMP; FJP to Seth Williams, January 26, 1862, Reel 16, Correspondence and Issuances (M2096), RG393, NA; FJP to Williams, January 27, 1862, Reel 16, GBMP.

61. Unnumbered order, January 28, 1862, signed by Edwin Stanton, and "E. J. Allen" [Allen Pinkerton] to GBM, February 6, 1862, both on Reel 16, GBMP. The best summary of Charles Stone's case is Sears, *Controversies and Commanders*, 27–50. A new paragraph was approved to the Articles of War on March 13, 1862, prohibiting U.S. military officers from returning runaway slaves even to loyal owners (*OR*, Series 3, 1:937–38).

62. *War Diary and Letters of Stephen Minot Weld*, 60.

63. FJP to Seth Williams, January 28, 30, February 6, 1862, Reel 16, GBMP; *Evening Star* (Washington, D.C.), February 1, 1862; *War Diary and Letters of Stephen Minot Weld*, 47–53.

64. *CWP*, 162–70; *War Diary and Letters of Stephen Minot Weld*, 54. At a council of war on March 7, Porter indicated that he had known of the Urbanna plan for about six weeks (HJ, March 8, 1862).)

65. Meade, *Life and Letters*, 1:243, 247–48.

66. *New York Tribune*, February 20, 1862.

67. *War Diary and Letters of Stephen Minot Weld*, 61; *PUSG*, 1:34, 44.

68. Auchmuty, *Letters*, 25–28; *War Diary and Letters of Stephen Minot Weld*, 49, 56, 59, 61, 64, 67.

69. *New York Tribune*, February 22, 1862; *New York Times*, February 24, 25, 26, 1862; Sparks, *Inside Lincoln's Army*, 45; Orléans, *Voyage en Amérique*, 320; Edwin Stanton to Charles A. Dana, January 24, 1862, quoted in Dana, *Recollections of the Civil War*, 5.

CHAPTER 7

1. *OR*, 5:46, 48–49; Orléans, *Voyage en Amérique*, 298; Meade, *Life and Letters*, 1:249; *War Diary and Letters of Stephen Minot Weld*, 63–64; Auchmuty, *Letters*, 32.

2. Burlingame, *With Lincoln in the White House*, 72–73; Horace White to Joseph Medill, March 3, 1862, Ray Papers, Huntington Library; Palmer, *Selected Letters of Charles Sumner*, 2:103; *Letter of the Secretary of War*, 52–53; *CWP*, 193–95.

3. *War Diary and Letters of Stephen Minot Weld*, 64, 66–67; HJ, March 4, 1862.

4. *War Diary and Letters of Stephen Minot Weld*, 68; FJP to GBM, March 6, 1862, Reel 18, GBMP.

5. *War Diary and Letters of Stephen Minot Weld*, 70, 73; Orléans, *Voyage en Amérique*, 321; HJ, March 8, 1862; *New York Herald*, December 4, 1864.

6. Edwin Stanton's memo, Reel 2, and Erasmus Keyes to Stanton, March 14, 1862, Reel 4, both in Stanton Papers, LC; HJ, March 8, 1862; Franklin, "First Great Crime of the War," 79–80; Pease and Randall, *Diary of Orville Hickman Browning*, 1:552; Orléans, *Voyage en Amérique*, 324. The Comte de Paris thought the eight junior generals voted against corps organization while the four senior generals favored it (Orléans, *Voyage en Amérique*, 323), but Heintzelman and Franklin, who were present, contradicted him.

7. *OR*, 5:18, 50.

8. FJP to Seth Williams, March 8, 9, 1862, and to Randolph Marcy, March 8, 1862, and GBM to Marcy (three telegrams), March 9, 1862, all on Reel 18, GBMP; *OR*, 5:739–41, and Series 3, 3:271–72; Pease and Randall, *Diary of Orville Hickman Browning*, 1:532; Auchmuty, *Letters*, 33.

9. *OR*, 5:739–42; *War Diary and Letters of Stephen Minot Weld*, 69; Auchmuty, *Letters*, 34.

10. John W. Ames to "My dear Mother," March 12, 1862, Ames Papers, AHEC; Norton, *Army Letters*, 59; Orléans, *Voyage en Amérique*, 327–28; *War Diary and Letters of Stephen Minot Weld*, 69; George Morris letter, *Dansville (N.Y.) Advertiser*, March 27, 1862.

11. Orléans, *Voyage en Amérique*, 328; *War Diary and Letters of Stephen Minot Weld*, 69–70; Auchmuty, *Letters*, 34; FJP to Randolph Marcy, 2:15 P.M., 2:30 P.M., March 10, 1862, Reel 18, GBMP; FJP to Army Headquarters, March 11, 1862, Reel 10, Correspondence and Issuances (M2096), RG393, Part 1, NA.

12. Orléans, *Voyage en Amérique*, 330–33.

13. Orléans, *Voyage en Amérique*, 333–35; FJP to Randolph Marcy, March 12, 1862, Letters Sent, RG393, Part 2, NA; Jesse Gove Journal, March 12, 1862, LC; *War Diary and Letters of Stephen Minot Weld*, 73.

14. *OR*, 5:50, 54; *War Diary and Letters of Stephen Minot Weld*, 72; Orléans, *Voyage en Amérique*, 335; *New York Times*, March 14, 1862.

15. Jesse Gove Journal, March 16, 1862, LC; Cutler, *Letters from the Front*, 19; Henry Aplin to "Dear Brother," March 18, 1862, Aplin Family Papers, CL; Auchmuty, *Letters*, 35.

16. John D. Wilkins to "My Dearly beloved wife," March 16, 1862, Wilkins Papers, CL.

17. Stedman and Gould, *Life and Letters*, 1:271–73.

18. *OR*, 5:54; FJP to Manton Marble, October 23, November 22, 1861, March 17, 1862, Marble Papers, LC; Edwin Stanton to Charles Dana, February 1, 1862, and Benjamin Wade to Dana, February 3, 1862, Dana Papers, LC.

19. FJP to Manton Marble, March 17, 1862, Marble Papers, LC.

20. On the tension between politics and the military see, for example, Stowe, "Longest and Clearest Head," 145; Neely, *Union Divided*, 66–67, 175–76; and Hsieh, *West Pointers and the Civil War*, 145, 164–65. Hsieh criticizes Porter's disdain for some civilian and military superiors as "unmilitary and dangerously close to outright insubordination" (234 n.12),

but Porter was infallibly subordinate—no matter how poor his opinion of a superior, how much he expressed that opinion privately, or how justified he was in holding it.

21. U.S. Congress, *Senate Executive Journal*, 37th Cong., 2nd sess., March 7, 13, April 28, 1862, 157, 163, 270.

22. Irvin McDowell to GBM, March 13, 1862, Reel 18, GBMP; *OR*, 5:755; Auchmuty, *Letters*, 35, 37; HJ, March 17, 19, 20, 1862. See Charles S. Hamilton to Senator James Doolittle, January 30, February 11, 1863, Doolittle Papers, WHS, for Hamilton smearing officers who stood in the way of his advancement.

23. *OR*, 11(3):25, 28, 29; HJ, March 17, 1862; Samuel P. Heintzelman to GBM, March 21, 22, 1862, Reel 19, GBMP; Cutler, *Letters from the Front*, 20; George Monteith to "My dear Mother," March 24, 1862, Monteith Letters, BL; Norton, *Army Letters*, 61; Cutler, *Letters from the Front*, 20; Auchmuty, *Letters*, 38; Jesse Gove Journal, March 21, 22, 24, 1862, LC. The *Rochester (N.Y.) Democrat* of September 2, 1861, alluded to the plethora of discharges.

24. *War Diary and Letters of Stephen Minot Weld*, 89–90; itinerary of Porter's division, March 22, 1862, Reel 1, FJPP; HJ, March 22, 1862.

25. George Monteith to "My dear Mother," March 24, 1862, Monteith Letters, BL; Jesse Gove Journal, March 22, 1862, LC.

26. HJ, March 24, 1862; George Monteith to "My dear Mother," March 24, 1862, Monteith Letters, BL; Jesse Gove Journal, March 24, 1862, LC; Auchmuty, *Letters*, 39; Peet, *Civil War Letters*, 97; itinerary of FJP's division, March 23–24, 1862, Reel 1, FJPP.

27. HJ, March 24, 1862; Norton, *Army Letters*, 62; George Monteith to "My dear Mother," March 24, 1862, Monteith Letters, BL; *War Diary and Letters of Stephen Minot Weld*, 90.

28. *OR*, 11(1):405–6; *War Diary and Letters of Stephen Minot Weld*, 92.

29. Itinerary of FJP's division, March 25, 26, 1862, Reel 1, FJPP; *War Diary and Letters of Stephen Minot Weld*, 90–91; HJ, March 26, 1862.

30. Peet, *Civil War Letters*, 98–102; *OR*, 11(3):37; *War Diary and Letters of Stephen Minot Weld*, 92; HJ, March 27, 1862; William Ripley to Cornelia Ripley, March 19, 1862, Ripley Papers, Duke.

31. Norton, *Army Letters*, 63; *OR*, 11(1):405, 11(3):42, 47, 51(1):564–65. Howard's Bridge appears to have been known locally as "Harwoods."

32. Auchmuty, *Letters*, 40–41; *OR*, 11(3):37, 42; Jesse Gove Journal, March 27, 1862, LC; Frederick T. Locke to Dwight A. Woodbury, March 27, 1862, Letters Sent, RG393, Part 2, NA.

33. *OR*, 11(3):42, 47, 51(1):564–65; HJ, March 28, 1862. On March 12, when Magruder counted his "efficient" force at somewhere between 11,000 and 11,500, Wool had guessed that Magruder had "15,000 to 18,000 men," and Heintzelman revised that to as many as 20,000. Magruder's original force had been augmented by two Alabama regiments on March 28, and he was reinforced the next day by a division about 3,000 strong, so Porter's March 30 estimate of no more than 15,000 hit the mark almost exactly (*Official Records of the Union and Confederate Navies*, 7:100; *OR*, 11[1]:405, 11[3]:47, 412, 436, 481).

34. HJ, April 3, 1862; *CWP*, 225.

35. HJ, April 3, 1862; *OR*, 11(1):9. Heintzelman guessed that the three divisions in his column numbered about 33,000, and Keyes had recently reported nearly 35,000 in his three divisions, two of which were present (*OR*, 11[3]:53).

36. *OR*, 51(1):565–66; *War Diary and Letters of Stephen Minot Weld*, 93; Auchmuty, *Letters*, 42, 43; itinerary of FJP's division, April 4, 1862, Reel 1, FJPP; FJP to Samuel P. Heintzelman, April 4, 1862, Reel 20, GBMP.

37. *OR*, 11(1):10, 358–59.

38. Blight, *When This Cruel War Is Over*, 108–9; Jesse Gove Journal, April 11, 1862, LC; *OR*, 11(1):10, 405.

39. *OR*, 11(3):71; HJ, April 5, 1862; Keyes, *Fifty Years' Observations*, 442–45; William B. Franklin to GBM, April 7, 1862 (two copies), Reel 1, FJPP; *War Diary and Letters of Stephen Minot Weld*, 103.

40. *OR*, 11(3):76, 79. A visitor who left McClellan's headquarters the next day carried information that Magruder had 30,000 men when his army amounted to barely half that (*OR*, 11[3]:73). For the details of Stanton's effort to convince Lincoln to withhold a corps from McClellan, see Marvel, *Lincoln's Autocrat*, 183–85.

41. *OR*, Series 3, 2:2–3.

42. *OR*, 11(3):79.

43. *New York Tribune*, April 10, 1862; Jesse Gove Journal, April 12, 13, 1862, LC; *Boston Herald*, April 26, 1862; FJP's April 15, 1862, endorsement on Gove's letter of April 13, Endorsements Sent, RG393, Part 2, NA.

44. *OR*, 11(3):73–74, and Series 3, 3:273–74; Frederick T. Locke to Thaddeus S. C. Lowe, April 6, 1862 (two telegrams), Institute of Aerospace Sciences Archives, LC; FJP to Albert V. Colburn, April 7, 1862, Reel 20, GBMP. Lowe reported that it was the Comte de Paris who made the ascent with Porter on April 6, but the count maintained that it was his brother, the Duc de Chartres, and the duke's daily journal confirms it (*OR*, Series 3, 3:273; Orléans, *Voyage en Amérique*, 383).

45. George Monteith to "Commanding Officer, Balloon," April 10, 1862, and FJP to Thaddeus S. C. Lowe, April 11, 1862 (first of two telegrams), Institute of Aerospace Sciences Archives, LC; "Balloon Services," 5–6, Reel 25, FJPP; *OR*, Series 3, 3:274.

46. "Balloon Services," 6, Reel 25, FJPP.

47. HJ, and HD, April 11, 1862; "Balloon Services," 6–8, Reel 25, FJPP. Porter thought he smelled the hydrogen, which is odorless, but it may have absorbed a scent from the fabric of the balloon.

48. "Balloon Services," 8–9, Reel 25, FJPP; *OR*, Series 3, 3:274; Orléans, *Voyage en Amérique*, 390–91, 395; *CWP*, 235.

49. *OR*, Series 3, 3:274; HJ, April 11, 1862; "Balloon Services," 9, Reel 25, FJPP; FJP to Thaddeus S. C. Lowe, April 11, 1862, Institute of Aerospace Sciences Archives, LC.

50. *OR*, 11(3):91, 97–99; Cutler, *Letters from the Front*, 21; Chauncey McKeever to Seth Williams, April 14, 1862, Reel 20, FJP to McKeever, April 21, 23–29, 1862 (many telegrams), and Charles S. Hamilton to Williams, April 23, 24, 1862, all on Reel 21, GBMP; FJP to Hiram Berdan, April 8, 1862, Letters Sent, RG393, Part 2, NA; *War Diary and Letters of Stephen Minot Weld*, 92.

51. *OR*, 11(3):125.

52. FJP to Manton Marble, April 18, 26, 1862, Marble Papers, LC.

53. Joseph Hooker to Henry Wilson, April 4, 1862, Wilson Papers, LC; *OR*, 51(1):581, 582; HJ, April 23, 1862; Henry Naglee to GBM, April 30, 1862, Reel 22, GBMP.

54. HJ, April 29, 1862; *OR*, 11(3):129; FJP to John Martindale, April 2, 1862, and to Chauncey McKeever, April 26, 1862, Letters Sent, RG393, Part 2, NA.

55. *OR*, 11(3):130, 131; HJ, May 3, 1862; FJP to GBM, May 1, 3, 1862, to Henry Lansing, May 2, 1862, and to Albert V. Colburn, May 2, 3, 1862 (six telegrams), all on Reel 22, GBMP; Orléans, *Voyage en Amérique*, 428.

56. *OR*, Series 3, 3:275; Orléans, *Voyage en Amérique*, 434–35.

57. FJP to Albert V. Colburn, May 4, 1862 (four telegrams), Samuel P. Heintzelman to GBM, May 4, 1862, Reel 22, GBMP; HJ, May 4, 1862.

58. Orléans, *Voyage en Amérique*, 443–44; *OR*, 11(3):140–41; Hass, "A Volunteer Nurse

in the Civil War," 136; Samuel P. Heintzelman to Albert V. Colburn and to GBM, both May 4, 1862, Reel 22, GBMP.

59. Orléans, *Voyage en Amérique*, 444; *Report of the Joint Committee*, 570; William Sprague to Edwin Stanton, May 3, 1862, Reel 2, Stanton Papers, LC.

60. *OR*, 11(1):614–17, 629–33, 11(3):162, 503–4.

61. FJP to Albert V. Colburn, May 7, 1862, Reel 22, GBMP; *OR*, 11(3):149; Peet, *Civil War Letters*, 132; Jesse Gove Journal, May 8, 1862, LC; Hass, "Volunteer Nurse in the Civil War," 137.

62. *OR*, 11(3):153–55.

63. Charles C. Suydam Diary, May 13, 1862, Suydam Papers, LC; Auchmuty, *Letters*, 53.

64. *OR*, 11(3):184, 51(1):619, 624; Jesse Gove Journal, May 18, 19, 1862, LC.

CHAPTER 8

1. *War Diary and Letters of Stephen Minot Weld*, 106; Jesse Gove Journal, May 13–14, 1862, LC; Auchmuty, *Letters*, 55; John D. Wilkins to "My Dearly beloved wife," May 14, 1862, Wilkins Papers, CL; Orléans, *Voyage en Amérique*, 500–502.

2. Orléans, *Voyage en Amérique*, 506, 508; *OR*, 11(1):24; FJP to GBM, 3:40 P.M., 4:20 P.M., 4:25 P.M., 4:30 P.M., May [18], 1862, Reel 23, GBMP.

3. *OR*, 11(1):26–29.

4. FJP to Manton Marble, May 21, 1862, Marble Papers, LC.

5. Robert McCreight to "Dear Brother," June 7, 1862, McCreight Letters, AHEC; August V. Kautz Diary, May 23, 24, 1862, Kautz Papers, LC; *OR*, 11(1):651, 653–54; William T. H. Brooks to "Dear Father," May 24, 1862, Brooks Papers, AHEC.

6. *OR*, 11(1):668–69; HJ, May 23, 24, 1862; FJP to Zachariah Chandler, May 24, 1862, Reel 1, Chandler Papers, LC.

7. *OR*, 11(1):30, 667–68, 737–38; Robert O. Tyler to FJP, May 24, 1862 (two messages, 2:00 A.M. and "No. 3"), and FJP to "General" [Randolph Marcy], 3:50 A.M., May 24, 1862, all on Reel 23, GBMP; FJP to Manton Marble, May 21, 1862, with May 23 addendum, Marble Papers, LC; FJP to Gouverneur K. Warren, May 25, 1862 (two dispatches), Box 20, Warren Papers, NYSL; Wittenberg, *"We Have It Damn Hard Out Here,"* 34–35.

8. *CWL*, 5:232–33, 235–37. The same telegrams appear in *OR*, 11(1):30–32, but with spelling revised and without all the times of transmission.

9. *OR*, 12(3):220–21; Irvin McDowell to "My dear Nelly," June 15, 1862, FSNMP; McDowell to Charles A. Hechscher, June 17, 1862, Box 42, Barlow Papers, Huntington Library.

10. *OR*, 11(3):191, 544, 550–51, 12(3):243; Moore, *Rebellion Record*, 5:158; Johnston, *Narrative*, 130; Orléans, *Voyage en Amérique*, 520.

11. FJP to Gouverneur K. Warren, May 25, 1862, Box 20, Warren Papers, NYSL; *OR*, 11(1):677, 740–41.

12. *OR*, 11(1):681–82, 722; Jesse Gove Journal, May 27, 1862, LC; FJP to Gouverneur K. Warren, 6:20 P.M., May 26, 1862, Box 20, Warren Papers, NYSL.

13. Timothy Vedder to "Dear Sister Nellie," June 9, 1862, Vedder Correspondence, AHEC; FJP to Randolph Marcy, 11:00 A.M., "May 28?" [27], 1862, Reel 23, GBMP; Joseph Simonds to "Dear Sister Susie," May 28, 1862, Simonds Letters, AHEC; Bennett, *Musket and Sword*, 48; Jesse Gove Journal, May 27, 1862, LC; Patrick Guiney to "My dear Jennie," May 31, 1862, College of the Holy Cross; Norton, *Army Letters*, 82, 84; *OR*, 11(1):722–23.

14. Joseph Simonds to "Dear Sister Susie," May 28, 1862, Simonds Letters, AHEC; FJP

to Randolph Marcy, 11 A.M., "May 28?" [27], 1862, Reel 23, GBMP; *OR*, 11(1):685, 694, 699, 701, 702; Samuel S. Partridge to Edward Partridge, June 3, 1862, FSNMP.

15. *OR*, 11(1):699, 715, 743–44; Jesse Gove Journal, May 27, 1862, LC.

16. *OR*, 11(1):701, 702, 741, 744, 11(3):550–51; Norton, *Army Letters*, 83–84. According to the *Rochester (N.Y.) Evening Express* of June 3, 1862, the 13th New York had seen another spate of resignations in May, with at least seven company officers leaving the regiment.

17. *OR*, 11(1):682, 686, 723; Norton, *Army Letters*, 84.

18. Jesse Gove Journal, May 27, 1862, LC; *Bangor (Me.) Daily Whig and Courier*, June 5, 1862; *OR*, 11(1):702–4, 708–9, 713–14, 741.

19. *OR*, 11(1):703; Jesse Gove Journal, May 27, 1862, LC.

20. *OR*, 11(1):682, 703–4, 717–18; Timothy Vedder to "Dear Sister Nellie," June 9, 1862, Vedder Correspondence, AHEC.

21. *OR*, 11(1):704, 716, 718, 728, 730; *Bangor (Me.) Daily Whig and Courier*, June 5, 1862; Patrick Guiney to "My dear Jennie," May 31, 1862, College of the Holy Cross ("indescribable disorder"); Timothy Vedder to "Dear Sister Nellie," June 9, 1862, Vedder Correspondence, AHEC ("Kiteing").

22. Statement of E. G. Marshall, undated (but late 1862 or early 1863), Reel 2, FJPP; *Rochester (N.Y.) Evening Express*, June 7, 1862; *Rochester (N.Y.) Daily Union and Advertiser*, June 13, 1862. There is no other evidence that Martindale was wounded.

23. FJP to GBM, "May 28?" (two messages, both actually May 27), 28, 1862, FJP to Randolph Marcy, May 28, 1862 (two messages, one marked "11 A.M.") Reel 23, GBMP; *OR*, 11(1):683, 684, 742; Alexander S. Webb to "My Dear Father," June 9, 1862, Webb Papers, Sterling Library, Yale.

24. John W. Ames to "My dear Mother," June 2, 1864, Ames Papers, AHEC.

25. Gouverneur K. Warren Journal, May 28, 1862, Box 20, Warren Papers, NYSL; Norton, *Army Letters*, 85, 86; Samuel S. Partridge to "My dear Ed," June 10, 1862, FSNMP.

26. *OR*, 11(1):711–12; Jesse Gove Journal, May 28, 1862, LC; Lawrence Williams to William Emory, May 28, 1862 (on the May 31–June 5 page of a diary), Reel 23, GBMP; August V. Kautz Diary, May 28, 29, 1862, Kautz Papers, LC; *CWP*, 279, 280; Orléans, *Voyage en Amérique*, 525; *CWL*, 5:244. In his journal Gove wrote that he was ordered to take two cavalry regiments, but his report mentions only a company of the 6th Pennsylvania Cavalry.

27. FJP to GBM, "May 28?" [May 27], 28, 1862, and to Randolph Marcy, 8:00 A.M., 9:30 A.M., 11:00 A.M., and no specific time, May 28, 1862, all on Reel 23, GBMP.

28. *OR*, 11(3):199–200; Gouverneur K. Warren to FJP, 8:40 A.M., 10:20 A.M., May 29, 1862, Reel 23, GBMP; Gouverneur K. Warren Journal, May 29, 1862, Box 20, Warren Papers, NYSL; August V. Kautz Diary, May 29, 1862, Kautz Papers, LC; Wittenberg, *"We Have It Damn Hard Out Here,"* 36–38.

29. GBM to Ellen McClellan, May 27, 1862, Reel 64, GBMP; *CWL*, 244–45; *War Diary and Letters of Stephen Minot Weld*, 111; *New York Herald*, June 4, 1862.

30. *OR*, 12(3):253, 265–66, 267–68, 269.

31. Johnston, *Narrative*, 130–33; Blight, *When This Cruel War Is Over*, 141; Orléans, *Voyage en Amérique*, 532; Norton, *Army Letters*, 83; *OR*, 11(3):204, 530–31.

32. *OR*, 11(1):813–15, 838–42, 879–81, 914–15, 933–34; Orléans, *Voyage en Amérique*, 532; Blight, *When This Cruel War Is Over*, 142.

33. Thaddeus S. C. Lowe to FJP, 3:10 P.M., May 31, 1862, Reel 23, GBMP; Dyer, *Journal of a Civil War Surgeon*, 22–23; Hodge, *Civil War Letters of Perry Mayo*, 210; *OR*, 11(1):684, 762, 763, 935, Series 3, 3:280–81; August V. Kautz Diary, June 9, 1862, Kautz Papers, LC.

34. Orléans, *Voyage en Amérique*, 542, 547; *OR*, Series 3, 3:282–82; Thaddeus S. C. Lowe to Randolph Marcy, June 1, 1862 (numerous telegrams), Reel 24, GBMP.

35. *OR*, 11(1):749, 11(3):220, 248; GBM to Edwin Stanton, June 15, 1862, Reel 3, Stanton Papers, LC; *CWL*, 5:361, 446.

36. *CWL*, 5:264, 10:138; *OR*, 11(3):207, 220–21; *CWP*, 293; Orléans, *Voyage en Amérique*, 560.

37. *OR*, 11(3):225. In "The Peninsular Campaign," 176, McClellan mentioned his contemplated shift to a base on the James River, as did Porter in "Hanover Court House and Gaines's Mill," 325.

38. Joseph C. G. Kennedy to GBM, June 12, 1862, Reel 25, GBMP.

39. *CWL*, 5:272–73; Irvin McDowell to GBM, June 12, 1862, Reel 25, GBMP.

40. *OR*, 11(2):490, 11(3):232–33; FJP to Albert V. Colburn, June 17, 1862, Reel 26, GBMP. Porter's ensuing reports refer to "the time when the operations of the right wing of this army were confided to my care" (*OR*, 11[2]:221, 223–24).

41. *OR*, 11(1):590–91, 1020–22, 1036–37, 11(3):589–90; Trout, *With Pen and Saber*, 72, 74.

42. *OR*, 11(1):1008, 1023–24, 1029–30; August V. Kautz Diary, June 13, 14, 1862, Kautz Papers, LC; *War Diary and Letters of Stephen Minot Weld*, 113–15, 116–17; FJP to Randolph Marcy, June 14, 1862, Reel 25, GBMP.

43. HJ, June 9, 12, 1862; *CWP*, 297; Randolph Marcy to FJP, 4:40 P.M., June 13, 1862, FJP to Marcy, June 13 (twenty-five messages), June 14 (twenty-one messages), 1862, Reel 25, GBMP. Colonel Jesse Gove noted on June 20, 1862 (Journal, LC), that his regiment took over the campsite McClellan had abandoned at Curtis's, as did his lieutenant colonel (William S. Tilton Diary, June 27, 1862, MHS). Dr. Curtis, who died July 31, 1862, at the age of seventy, is buried in Forest Lawn Cemetery in Richmond.

44. *OR*, 11(1):1028–30, 1038–39; Nevins, *Diary of Battle*, 80; FJP to Randolph Marcy, 2:45 P.M., June 14, 1862, Reel 25, GBMP; *Herrick's Almanac for the Year of Our Lord, 1862*, 15.

45. Randolph Marcy to FJP, 12:30 P.M., June 15, 1862, Reel 25, GBMP; *OR*, 11(1):1007, 1030.

46. *OR*, 11(1):1006; FJP to Randolph Marcy, 6:30 A.M., June 15, 1862, Reel 25, and William P. Mason to Marcy, 11:45 P.M., June 17, 1862, FJP to Marcy, June 17, 1862, FJP to Seth Williams, 11:45 A.M., June 20, 1862, FJP to Marcy, 2:45 P.M., June 21[?], 1862, and FJP to Williams, 9:30 A.M., June 22, 1862, all on Reel 26, GBMP.

47. *OR*, 11(3):232–36; *CWL*, 5:272–73.

48. FJP to Manton Marble, June 20, 1862, Container 3, Marble Papers, LC.

49. Joseph Holt to Theodore S. Bell, June 21, 1862, Civil War Letters Collection, NYHS.

50. Auchmuty, *Letters*, 62; *OR*, 11(3):238; FJP to William B. Franklin, 9:00 A.M., June 21, 1862, Reel 26, GBMP; FJP to Manton Marble, June 20, 1862, Marble Papers, LC. The 180,000-man figure, dated June 26, was based on the belief that Lee's and Jackson's combined forces included 200 regiments of infantry and cavalry (*OR*, 11[1]:269), which was accurate: a compilation of individual Confederate reports (*OR*, 11[2]:483–89) identified exactly 200 regiments and battalions of infantry and cavalry (this includes the 4th Virginia Heavy Artillery, serving as infantry). The overestimate evidently resulted partly from the assumption that the ranks of each unit were nearly full. In a calculation based on available returns supplemented by reports, orders, and correspondence, Stephen Sears credited Lee with 92,400 men present for duty in *To the Gates of Richmond* (156, 416 n.11).

51. *War Diary and Letters of Stephen Minot Weld*, 109–10; Samuel S. Partridge to 'My dear Ed," June 10, 16, 1862, Partridge Letters, FSNMP; Jonas D. Richardson to "Dear Parents," June 8, 1862, Richardson Letters, BL. Hanover County's 1860 slave schedules credited Dr.

Gaines with forty-three slaves, all of them male, while his son and namesake owned nine more (Eighth Census [M653], Reel 1391, RG29, NA), but a photograph of ten of Gaines's slaves in the Library of Congress includes three women and as many as three little girls.

52. FJP to GBM, 9:45 A.M., June 23, and to Marcy, 2:20 P.M., June 23, and GBM to FJP, 9:00 A.M., June 24, 1862, with endorsed reply, all on Reel 27, GBMP.

53. FJP to Albert V. Colburn, 3:40 P.M., and to Randolph Marcy, 11:20 A.M., 2:20 P.M., 3:30 P.M., 5:20 P.M., 10:45 P.M., all June 23, 1862, and William F. Smith to Marcy, June 23, 1862 (three messages), all on Reel 27, GBMP. The Pennsylvania-born Ellerson owned only three slaves, all working-age males (Eighth Census Slave Schedules [M653], Reel 1391, RG29, NA).

54. CWP, 307; FJP to Randolph Marcy, 5:00 A.M., 6:00 A.M., 8:30 A.M., 8:45 A.M., 9:30 A.M., 10:00 A.M., 10:30 P.M., June 24, 1862, Reel 27, GBMP.

55. Niven, *Salmon P. Chase Papers*, 3:220–21; Winfield Scott Memorandum, June 24, 1862, ALP.

56. Pope, "Second Battle of Bull Run," 449–50; *OR*, 12(3):435.

57. FJP to Randolph Marcy, 3:00 P.M., June 21, 1862, Reel 26, 11:00 A.M., June 23, 1862, Reel 27, GBMP; *CWP*, 309–10; *OR*, 11(3):258, 259.

58. *OR*, 11(3):264–65.

CHAPTER 9

1. *CWP*, 307; Thomas B. Leaver to "My Dear Mother," June 24, 1862, Leaver Letterbook, NHHS; Orléans, *Voyage en Amérique*, 590–91; John O. Stevens to "Dear Brother and Sister," June 26, 1862, Stevens Letters, NHHS; Haynes, *Minor War History*, 58; Sears, *For Country, Cause and Leader*, 254–55; *OR*, 11(2):96.

2. Orléans, *Voyage en Amérique*, 591–92; *OR*, 11(2):898; FJP to Randolph Marcy, June 25, 1862 (four telegrams, one marked 4:15 P.M. and one tentatively dated "June 25?"), Reel 27, GBMP.

3. Orléans, *Voyage en Amérique*, 592–93; *CWP*, 313; William F. Smith to Randolph Marcy, June 25, 1862, Reel 27, GBMP.

4. Orléans, *Voyage en Amérique*, 592–93; FJP to Randolph Marcy, June 17, 1862, Reel 26, GBMP.

5. Albert V. Colburn to FJP, June 26, 1862, Reel 27, GBMP; *CWP*, 315; Jones, *Rebel War Clerk's Diary*, 1:138.

6. Dowdey and Manarin, *Wartime Papers of R. E. Lee*, 198–201.

7. The reasons for Jackson's previously misunderstood performance that day were finally deduced in 1992 by A. Wilson Greene, who detected the incorrect map and reconciled Jackson's actions with his written orders in *Whatever You Resolve to Be*, 42–48.

8. Porter, "Hanover Court House and Gaines's Mill," 328–29; FJP to Randolph Marcy 11:40 A.M., 1:45 P.M., 3:00 P.M., June 26, 1862, and Marcy to Samuel P. Heintzelman and J. Hartwell Keyes, 12:45 P.M., June 26, 1862, all on Reel 27, GBMP; *OR*, 11(2):289.

9. Randolph Marcy to FJP, 4:00 P.M., June 26, 1862, FJP to Marcy, 4:00 P.M., June 26, 1862, and Marcy to GBM, June 26, 1862, all on Reel 27, GBMP; John W. Ames to "My dear Father and Mother," July 5, 1862, Ames Papers, AHEC; *CWP*, 314–15; Meade, *Life and Letters*, 1:279.

10. FJP to Randolph Marcy, June 26, 1862 (two telegrams, one marked 4:40 P.M.), Reel 27, GBMP; Benjamin Roher to "My Dear Wife," July 6, 1862, Roher Letters, AHEC; *OR*, 11(2):385, 835; Edmund Hawley to "Dear Brother," July 14, 1862, Hawley Papers, AHEC; John C. McMichael to Elizabeth Rooke, July 5, 1862, McMichael Papers, LC.

11. FJP to Randolph Marcy, 1:45 P.M., 4:50 P.M., June 26, 1862, Reel 27, June 26 (no time), 1862, Reel 28, GBMP.

12. *OR*, 11(2):491; Orléans, *Voyage en Amérique*, 597; FJP to Randolph Marcy, 4:00 P.M., June 26, 1862, Albert V. Colburn to Marcy, June 26 (two telegrams, one marked 4:00 P.M.), George A. Custer to Marcy, June 26, and Marcy to GBM, June 26, all on Reel 27, GBMP; *OR*, 11(3):259, 260.

13. *CWP*, 317; FJP to Harriet, [June 26, 1862], Reel 27, GBMP.

14. Orléans, *Voyage en Amérique*, 598; *OR*, 11(1):117–18, 11(2):223; "Seven Days' Battles," 125, 127, Reel 25, FJPP. Although this last account is written in the third person, this portion of it is in Porter's hand.

15. Lyman, "Some Aspects of the Medical Service," 200. Surgeon Lyman did name a witness, Captain William Powell Mason, who was still alive when Lyman spoke.

16. FJP to John C. Ropes, February 11, 1895, BU.

17. *OR*, 11(1):55, 11(2):222; *MOS*, 412.

18. GBM to Randolph Marcy, 11:30 P.M., June 26, 1862, Reel 27, GBMP; Porter, "Hanover Court House and Gaines's Mill," 336.

19. Schiller, *Autobiography of Maj. Gen. William F. Smith*, 41; Orléans, *Voyage en Amérique*, 594. In *Extraordinary Circumstances* (431 n. 32), Brian Burton noticed that Smith described stopping McClellan as the commanding general was on his way "to" Porter's headquarters, "about midnight" on June 26, and Burton supposed that McClellan would instead have been coming *from* Porter's camp at that hour. The journal of the Comte de Paris, cited above, confirms Burton's interpretation.

20. Orléans, *Voyage en Amérique*, 593–94; *OR*, 11(2):222. Whether their conversation was in English or in French, Orléans did not specify, but he quoted McClellan as saying he would abandon the White House line "pour les chances d'une retraite, si elle devenait nécessaire." McClellan's most meticulous biographer imputes a measure of deception to the general's failure to apprise Porter of his readiness to retreat (Sears, *Lincoln's Lieutenants*, 245–46), and McClellan may not have been altogether honest with himself on that point.

21. FJP to Randolph Marcy, June 26, 1862 (two messages), and to Albert V. Colburn, "2:10," June 27, 1862, Reel 27, and June 27, 1862, Reel 28, GBMP; *OR*, 11(2):316.

22. Seventh Census (M432), Reel 949, 415B, and Eighth Census (M653), Reel 1350, 383–84, RG29, NA. Webb, *Peninsula*, 131, identifies the local name.

23. Map of Hanover County, Va., Hotchkiss Map Collection, LC; Auchmuty, *Letters*, 69; *OR*, 11(1):55, 56, 118, 11(2):224, 227, 316. Stephen Sears reminded me of Barnard's deafness, surmising that Barnard may not have heard Porter's requests. In the same account in which Porter said that Barnard promised to ask for reinforcements and send axes, he ultimately absolved the chief engineer of blame: Barnard thought Slocum's men were the desired reinforcements, Porter supposed, and Barnard did not expect to have to provide the axes himself ("Seven Days' Battles," 125, 127, Reel 25, FJPP).

24. *OR*, 11(2):38–39, 224, 386; Truman Seymour to Ira Harris, July 7, 1862, Civil War Letters Collection, NYHS; HJ, June 27, 1862.

25. *OR*, 11(2):224, 272, 348, 387, 756; Randolph Marcy to Edwin Stanton, 5:00 A.M., June 27, 1862, Reel 28, GBMP.

26. *OR*, 11(2):224, 313, 772, 836; "Sharpshooting with Berdan," 8; Porter, "Hanover Court House and Gaines's Mill," 336.

27. *OR*, 11(2):429; "Seven Days' Battles," 125, 127, Reel 25, FJPP; FJP to John C. Ropes, February 11, 1895, BU.

28. Norton, *Army Letters*, 90; *OR*, 11(2):227, 273, 296, 301, 432.

29. Dowdey and Manarin, *Wartime Papers of R. E. Lee*, 203; *OR*, 11(2):348, 359, 624. Davidson had begged for leave the previous winter, after two of his children died, leaving his wife heartbroken, but McClellan refused despite recommendations up the line. Davidson was arrested and charged, but was allowed to resign (Delozier Davidson to Lorenzo Thomas, January 11, 1862, and to E. D. Townsend, December 8, 1862, Letters Received [M619], Reels 88 and 94, RG94, NA; Heitman, *Register*, 1:355).

30. *OR*, 11(2):313, 348, 378; Gouverneur K. Warren to Emily Chase, July 8, 1862, Box 1, Warren Papers, NYSL.

31. *OR*, 11(2): 301, 307, 316–17, 757, 773, 897, 900; Cutrer, *Longstreet's Aide*, 92–93; FJP to Randolph Marcy, June "28" [27], 1862, postscript marked "2:15," Reel 28, GBMP. Sears, *To the Gates of Richmond*, 249, nearly matched William Fox's figures for Porter's casualties at Gaines's Mill when he calculated the killed and wounded that day at 4,008, including those of his reinforcements: most of them and his 2,829 prisoners were lost in the final minutes of the battle. Sears tallied Lee's losses at 7,993 all day, almost all of them killed or wounded, and the lightest of those casualties came in the last of the fighting. Fox, *Regimental Losses*, 543, 550, recorded 4,001 Union killed and wounded, with 2,836 captured, and calculated Confederate losses at about 8,751.

32. *OR*, 11(2): 290–91; FJP to John C. Ropes, February 11, 1895, BU.

33. *OR*, Series 3, 3:290–91, 11(2):30–35; Randolph Marcy to Charles Sumner, 8:45 A.M., June 27, 1862, Reel 28, GBMP; William B. Franklin to Albert V. Colburn, June 27, 1862, Reel 28, GBMP.

34. Edmund Hawley to "Dear Brother," July 14, 1862, Hawley Papers, AHEC; *OR*, 11(2):225, 432–33. Slocum later wrote to Secretary Stanton criticizing Porter's performance at Gaines's Mill, and gave Porter the courtesy of a copy, but he may never have sent the letter. Henry Slocum to Edwin Stanton, July 19, 1862, and FJP to GBM, July 20, 1862, both on Reel 1, FJPP.

35. *CWP*, 320; *OR*, 11(2):349; Curtis, *From Bull Run to Chancellorsville*, 114, 304; Cyrus Stone to "Dear Mother and Father," July 11, 1862, Stone Papers, Minnesota Historical Society.

36. *OR*, 11(2):227; "Seven Days' Battles," 127, Reel 25, FJPP.

37. GBM to William B. Franklin, 5:25 P.M., June 27, 1862, Randolph Marcy to Edwin V. Sumner, 5:30 P.M., June 27, 1862, and to J. Hartwell Keyes, 5:50 P.M., June 27, 1862, all on Reel 28, GBMP; *CWP*, 321.

38. *OR*, 11(2):273, 291, 297, 301–2, 304, 307, 309, 349, 401, 568; John W. Ames to "My dear Father and Mother," June 28, 1862, Ames Papers, AHEC; Orléans, *Voyage en Amérique*, 604–5; Auchmuty, *Letters*, 69; John Faller to Cecelia Faller, July 12, 1862, Faller Letters, AHEC; Robertson, *Civil War Letters of General Robert McAllister*, 185–87; David A. Bennett to Frederick T. Locke, November 28, 1862, and statements of Francis A. Schoeffel and Job C. Hedges, all on Reel 2, FJPP.

39. Auchmuty, *Letters*, 69–70; Cassedy, *Dear Friends at Home*, 112; John W. Ames to "My dear Father and Mother," July 5, 1862, Ames Papers, AHEC; William S. Tilton Diary, June 27, 1862, MHS; Orléans, *Voyage en Amérique*, 608; Edmund Hawley to "Dear Brother," July 14, 1862, Hawley Papers, AHEC; *OR*, 11(2):42, 226, 273, 313.

40. *OR*, 11(2), 30–35, 70–71, 75–76; Herberger, *Yankee at Arms*, 45; Benjamin Roher to "My Dear Wife," July 6, 1862, Roher Letters, AHEC; Jacob Heffelfinger Diary, June 27, 28, 1862, AHEC; John M. Bancroft Diary, June 27, 1862, BL; John C. McMichael to Elizabeth Rooke, July 5, 1862, McMichael Papers, LC.

41. Orléans, *Voyage en Amérique*, 612–13; HJ, June 27, 1862; Auchmuty, *Letters*, 70.

42. FJP to Seth Williams, June 28, 1862, Reel 28, GBMP.

43. *OR*, 11(2):223, 389; John W. Ames to "My dear Father and Mother," June 28, 1862, Ames Papers, AHEC; John G. Barnard to Randolph Marcy, June 28, 1862, Reel 28, GBMP; Benjamin F. Ashenfelter to "Father Churchman," July 7, 1862, Ashenfelter Letters, AHEC.

44. Auchmuty, *Letters*, 65, 70; FJP to Randolph Marcy, June 28, 1862, Reel 28, GBMP; Norton, *Army Letters*, 91.

45. *OR*, 11(2):30–32, 227, 231, 277.

46. FJP to Stephen M. Weld Sr., July 2, 7, 16, 1862, Porter Papers, MHS.

47. Robertson, *Civil War Letters of General Robert McAllister*, 187; "Sharpshooting with Berdan," 9.

48. *OR*, 11(2):192, 274, 350, 389; Orléans, *Voyage en Amérique*, 616–17; Auchmuty, *Letters*, 70; HJ, June 28, 1862.

49. Orléans, *Voyage en Amérique*, 617; Joshua W. Ripley Diary, June 28, 1862, Ripley Papers, LC.

50. Rusling, *Men and Things I Saw*, 265; *OR*, 11(2):193, 227–28, 274, 350; Matthew Marvin Diary, June 30, 1862, and Charles Goddard to Catherine Smith, July 6, 1862, Smith Family Papers, both at Minnesota Historical Society; Howe, *Touched with Fire*, 58–59; Bruen and Fitzgibbons, *Through Ordinary Eyes*, 150; HJ, June 30, 1862; Sears, *For Country, Cause and Leader*, 259–60; John Burrill to "Dear Parents," July 5, 1862, Burrill Letters, AHEC; Haynes, *Minor War History*, 59.

51. Meade, *Life and Letters*, 283–96; *OR*, 11(2): 228, 389–92; HJ, June 30, 1862; Sears, *For Country, Cause and Leader*, 260–61.

52. HJ, "June 30" [July 1], 1862; Auchmuty, *Letters*, 71; *OR*, 11(1):121, 51(1):712.

53. Coco, *From Ball's Bluff to Gettysburg*, 108; Sears, *For Country, Cause and Leader*, 261; HJ, "June 30" [July 1], July 3, 1862.

54. *OR*, 11(2):202–3, 229–30, 496, 675–77. A map prepared by McClellan's engineers notes the Crew house as the home of Dr. John H. Mellert (*Atlas to Accompany the Official Records of the Union and Confederate Armies*, 19:1), who is recorded there (as "Mettert") on the 1850 census but does not appear in 1860. The West house, inhabited by Thomas I. West Sr. in 1850, is credited to West's widow on the engineer map, but both houses seem to have been empty in 1860.

55. FJP to GBM, 9:30 P.M., July 1, 1862, Reel 29, GBMP.

56. "Sharpshooting with Berdan," 5, 45.

57. *OR*, 11(2):496.

58. "Sharpshooting with Berdan," 45–46; *OR*, 11(2):229, 818–19; John M. Bancroft Diary, July 1, 1862, BL.

59. "Sharpshooting with Berdan," 48; *OR*, 11(2):229, 670, 677–78, 794, 818–19.

60. *OR*, 11(2):238, 260; Benjamin Roher to "My Dear Wife," July 6, 1862, Roher Letters, AHEC; Cutrer, *Longstreet's Aide*, 96–97.

61. *OR*, 11(2):204, 628–29; Francis C. Barlow to "My dear mother," July 4, 1862, Barlow Papers, MHS.

62. *OR*, 11(2):204, 230; Benjamin Roher to "My Dear Wife," July 6, 1862, Roher Letters, AHEC; Porter, "Battle of Malvern Hill," 421.

63. Auchmuty, *Letters*, 72; *OR*, 11(2):230, 238.

64. *OR*, 11(2):74, 230, 239, 314, 692–93, 794–95, 819; HJ, "June 30" [July 1], 1862; Auchmuty, *Letters*, 72; Norton, *Army Letters*, 93–94.

65. FJP to GBM, 9:30 P.M., July 1, 1862, Reel 29, GBMP; *OR*, 51(1):712–13.

CHAPTER 10

1. Porter, "Battle of Malvern Hill," 423. This article, originally entitled "The Last of the Seven Days' Battles," appeared first in the *Century Magazine* 30, no. 4 (August, 1885): 615–32.

2. Schiller, *Autobiography of Major General William F. Smith*, 47–48; Hyde, *Following the Greek Cross*, 81; Styple, *Generals in Bronze*, 161; Eisenschiml, *Celebrated Case of Fitz John Porter*, 310–11.

3. Porter, "Battle of Malvern Hill," 423; Auchmuty, *Letters*, 72; Samuel P. Heintzelman Diary, July 1, 3, 1862, Heintzelman Papers, LC.

4. Schiller, *Autobiography of Major General William F. Smith*, 47–48; *Report of the Joint Committee*, 1:579–80. In 1877 Francis Palfrey, who believed that the army should have advanced from Malvern Hill, mentioned no anger over the order to withdraw ("Battle of Malvern Hill," 274). By the 1890s veterans were remembering that they had found the withdrawal repugnant (William F. Biddle to John C. Ropes, March 27, 1895, BU), but no serious historian credited those belated assertions until nearly a century after the battle (Nevins, *War for the Union*, 2:137). Revision is evident in the histories Evan M. Woodward wrote of his regiment. In *Our Campaigns*, published in 1865, he called the retreat "necessary" (152) and recorded no reluctance about it. In 1883, in his revised *History of the Third Pennsylvania Reserve*, he described Porter (124) denouncing the order "in deep indignation" and exclaiming, "We ought rather to pursue the defeated foe than to be shamefully fleeing from him." On the next page Woodward credited Phil Kearny with an insubordinate soliloquy of equally dubious origins, in which Kearny protests "as an old soldier" against the retreat—arguing that they should instead march victoriously into Richmond, and blaming McClellan's "cowardice or treason" for the order. So melodramatic a tirade from the ever-critical Kearny is credible, but the lack of any contemporary reference to so quotable a speech strongly suggests that it belongs to the mythology of a better-informed era.

5. Testimony of Daniel Butterfield, George Morell, Charles Roberts, and FJP, Martindale Court of Inquiry, Case File KK-298, RG153, NA.

6. Testimony of Frederick T. Locke, Martindale Court of Inquiry, Case File KK-298, RG153, NA; Coco, *From Ball's Bluff to Gettysburg*, 108; Sears, *For Country, Cause and Leader*, 262; Blight, *When This Cruel War Is Over*, 264; Darius Couch to Adjutant General Edward D. Townsend, August 23, 1873, Letters Received (M1395), Year 1874, Reel labeled "Cooke-Couch"; John D. Wilkins to "My Dearly beloved wife," July 9, 1862, Wilkins Papers, CL; Auchmuty, *Letters*, 72.

7. Testimony of Frederick T. Locke, Martindale Court of Inquiry, Case File KK-298, RG153, NA.

8. *OR* 11(2):519–20, 922; HJ, July 3, 1862; John W. Ames to "My dear Father and Mother," July 5, 1862, Ames Papers, AHEC; Auchmuty, *Letters*, 74.

9. Burlingame, *With Lincoln in the White House*, 85; Blight, *When This Cruel War Is Over*, 164; *CWL*, 5:309–12.

10. HJ, July 2, 1862; Dyer, *Journal of a Civil War Surgeon*, 32; *OR*, 11(3):302–3.

11. *CWP*, 341–42; *OR*, 11(3):298.

12. William Sprague to Edwin Stanton, May 3, 1862, Reel 2, Stanton Papers, LC; *OR*, 11(3):299, 304–5; HJ, July 22, 25, 26, August 15, 1862; Phil Kearny's letter to O. S. Halsted Jr., August 4, 1862, was widely published in newspapers after his death, including the *New York Herald*, October 15, 1862, and the *Daily Democrat and News* (Davenport, Iowa), October 23, 1862.

13. *OR*, 11(3):297–98, 359, 51(1):715, 751. Sears, *Lincoln's Lieutenants*, 283, is more emphatic about Porter's involvement in John Barnard's removal.

14. *OR*, 51(1):714, 715; FJP's handwritten memoir, Reel 3, FJPP; FJP to "My dear Mc," undated, Reel 29, GBMP; *CWL*, 5:361, 446.

15. *OR*, 11(3):352; John Martindale to Lorenzo Thomas, July 16, August 2, 1862, Reel 117, William Henry Seward to Edwin Stanton, August 19, 1862, Reel 118, Letters Received (M619), RG94, NA. Curiously, Martindale did not request a court of inquiry until October 9, and it was not approved until the next day; yet a court was ordered and three officers—all unfriendly to Porter—were assigned to it on October 6, as though the general in chief (or secretary of war) were pursuing the inquiry independently and sought Martindale's request as an afterthought. See Martindale to Thomas, October 9, 1862, Reel 119, Letters Received (M619), RG94, NA; *OR*, 11(3):352.

16. George G. Meade to Margaret Meade, September 5, October 29, 1862, Meade Papers, HSP; *OR*, 11(2):388, 392.

17. *OR*, 11(3):310, 352; Pease and Randall, *Diary of Orville Hickman Browning*, 1:559; *CWP*, 370. Many letters from officers attesting to Martindale's skulking and timidity can be found on Reel 2, FJPP.

18. Truxall, *Respects to All*, 26; Coco, *From Ball's Bluff to Gettysburg*, 104–10.

19. FJP to Stephen M. Weld Sr., July 29, 1862, Porter Papers, MHS; *War Diary and Letters of Stephen Minot Weld*, 124–25; FJP to G. H. Heap, July 19, 1862, Schoff Collection, CL. In his 1950 book on Porter, Otto Eisenschiml quoted from some letters to Harriet that appear now to be lost but were then owned by Porter's last surviving child, Evelina Porter Doggett.

20. "Kennedy Correspondence" (manuscript in the hand of FJP), Reel 1, FJPP; *OR*, 12(3):473–74; Cox, *Military Reminiscences*, 1:222; Niven, *Salmon P. Chase Papers*, 1:349–50. In 1878 Pope's chief of staff testified that he transcribed the introductory address for distribution as a general order "from his hands, written in his handwriting" (*Proceedings and Report*, 2:305).

21. *OR*, 12(3):573; *CWP*, 344–45; Sparks, *Inside Lincoln's Army*, 108–10.

22. FJP to Joseph Kennedy, July 17, 1862 (several copies), Reel 1, FJPP.

23. Joseph Kennedy to William Henry Seward, July 22, 1862, and "Kennedy Correspondence," both on Reel 1, FJPP. A few months later Pope testified that he had seen a certain letter from Porter critical of him before Porter knew anything about Pope's orders or the dispositions of the contending armies in northern Virginia; perhaps to avoid revealing who had shown him Kennedy's letter, Pope confused it with Porter's unflattering dispatches to Burnside, but his description of the timing of that letter indicates that it must have been Kennedy's, and Porter specifically remembered discussing that letter with him (*OR*, 12[2, supplement]:840). Pope would have to have seen it between July 23 and July 29, perhaps through the president or—at that juncture—more likely via Stanton.

24. Sam Ward to William Henry Seward, July 23, 1862, Reel 70, Seward Papers, University of Rochester; Beale, *Diary of Gideon Welles*, 1:105, 108–9; John Hay to Mary Jay, July 20, 1862, Gilder-Lehrman Collection.

25. *Report of the Joint Committee*, 638; *OR*, 11(3):305, 320; Daniel Read Larned to "My Dear Sister," July "21" [26], 1862, Larned Papers, LC. On August 6, 1862, after he directed McClellan to bring his army north, Halleck indicated that he had gone to see him at Harrison's Landing despite pressure from "high officers" to simply order him up (*OR*, 11[1]:82).

26. Pease and Hickman, *Diary of Orville Hickman Browning*, 1:563.

27. HJ, July 25, 26, 1862; *OR*, 11(3):337–38. A. Wilson Greene, the closest student of conditions and operations around Petersburg, judged in *Civil War Petersburg* (103, 110) that McClellan's plan for moving south of the James would have subjected the city to "certain capture," but that Lincoln dismissed it through lack of confidence in McClellan — which the president revealed to Halleck just before sending him to Harrison's Landing. Thirty-two months later the capture of Petersburg immediately doomed Richmond and precipitated the collapse of Confederate resistance.

28. "General M. C. Meigs on the Conduct of the Civil War," 293–94.

29. HJ, July 26, 1862; *Report of the Joint Committee*, 638; *OR*, 11(3):337.

30. *CWP*, 372, 376; *Report of the Joint Committee*, 639, 650; Marvel, *Burnside*, 99–100, 440 n. 6.

31. *CWP*, 374, 376, 378.

32. *OR*, 11(1):76–77, 11(3):342, 12(3):521.

33. *OR*, 11(1):76–81, 12(3):524.

34. *OR*, 11(1):79, 80, 86, 12(3):524.

35. FJP to Manton Marble, August 5, 1862, Container 3, Marble Papers, LC; *CWL*, 5:301, 304.

36. FJP to Mrs. FJP, August 7, 1862, Dolan Telegrams, NYHS; *OR*, 11(1):86; FJP to Manton Marble, August 10, 1862, Container 3, Marble Papers, LC.

37. HJ, August 11, 1862; Phil Kearny to O. S. Halsted Jr., August 4, 1862, in *New York Herald*, October 15, 1862.

38. *OR*, 11(1):89–90, 11(3):372–73; Ambrose Burnside to FJP, undated (probably August 15, 1862), EG Box 8, Eldridge Collection, Huntington Library; Daniel Read Larned to "My Dear Sister," August 18, 1862, Larned Papers, LC; *War Diary and Letters of Stephen Minot Weld*, 128.

39. FJP to GBM, August 16, 1862 (two messages), Reel 29, GBMP; *OR*, 12(3):579; John M. Bancroft Diary, August 16, 1862, BL; Cassedy, *Dear Friends at Home*, 143.

40. GBM to FJP, 11:00 A.M., 12:30 P.M., August 17, 1862, Reel 29, GBMP; *OR*, 12(3):594; Cassedy, *Dear Friends at Home*, 143; Isaac Bevier to "Dear Parents," August 26, 1862, Allen County Public Library; John W. Ames to "My dear Mother," August 25, 1862, Ames Papers, AHEC.

41. *OR*, 12(2, supplement):1020, 12(3):600, 615, and Series 2, 4:437; Isaac Bevier to "Dear Parents," August 26, 1862, Allen County Public Library; *Report of the Joint Committee*, 596–97.

42. *OR*, 12(3):600, 615, 621–22, 639–40, 12 (2, supplement):938, 1006; *Proceedings and Report*, 2:294; *War Diary and Letters of Stephen Minot Weld*, 129; FJP's handwritten memoir, Reel 3, FJPP.

43. Meade, *Life and Letters*, 1:305; *OR*, 12(2):730–32. John Hennessy's *Return to Bull Run* is essential to understanding the confusing movements of this entire campaign.

44. Meade, *Life and Letters*, 1:306; *OR*, 12(2, supplement):1004–6.

45. John P. Hatch to "Dear Father," August 2, 1862, Hatch Papers, LC; Jesse Reno to Ambrose Burnside, August 16, 1862, Stuart Collection, LC; Sparks, *Inside Lincoln's Army*, 108; Quaife, *From the Cannon's Mouth*, 111; *War Diary and Letters of Stephen Minot Weld*, 132.

46. James Gillette to "Dear Mother," July 31, 1862, Gillette Papers, LC; Thirza Finch to "My Dear Jane," August 25, 1862, Finch Diary and Letters, CL; Orlando M. Poe to "My Dear," August 25, 1862, Poe Papers, LC; Isaac Bevier to "Dear Parents," August 26, 1862, Allen County Public Library.

47. *Proceedings and Report*, 2:308; *War Diary and Letters of Stephen Minot Weld*, 133. Weld lost the first page of the letter describing this incident and could not date it, but Webb recalled it happening at Centreville on August 31 (*Proceedings and Report*, 3:971–73).

48. *Report of the Joint Committee*, 597; *OR*, 12(3):691–92.

49. *OR*, 12(2):553–54; Osborne, *Civil War Diaries of Col. Theodore B. Gates*, 29–32.

50. *OR*, 12(2):401–2, 405–6, 539–44, 643–44; Jedediah Hotchkiss Journal, August 26–27, 1862, LC.

51. William H. Paine Journal, August 22, 27, 1862, Reel 2, FJPP. Gouverneur K. Warren gave transcribed excerpts of this journal to Porter, identifying the officer only as a member of McDowell's staff. Warren's brother-in-law, Washington Roebling, served on McDowell's staff, but Roebling's papers include no daily journal. Paine, who served on both McDowell's and Pope's staffs at different times, later worked with Roebling on the Brooklyn Bridge and would have known Warren at least through that connection. Paine's papers at the New-York Historical Society contain continuous diaries from 1848 through 1869, but the volume for the summer of 1862 is missing, and may have been removed to make the transcriptions for Porter's use.

52. *OR*, 12(2):35, 412, 12(3):684; Dowdey and Manarin, *Wartime Papers of Robert E. Lee*, 265–66; *Supplement*, 2:741–42; Jedediah Hotchkiss Journal, August 27, 1862, LC.

53. *OR*, 12(3):699–700; *War Diary and Letters of Stephen Minot Weld*, 132.

54. William B. Franklin to F. C. Adams, October 11, 1879, Harvard.

55. FJP's notes on the campaign, Reel 3, FJPP; George Ruggles to FJP, October 14, 1877, Reel 5, FJPP; *Proceedings and Report*, 2:307–8.

56. *OR*, 12(3):713, 12(2, supplement):830, 861; Heitman, *Historical Register*, 1:365; *New York Herald*, May 6, 1857; Kime, *Pierre M. Irving*, 186–87; *New York Tribune*, November 21, 1877. DeKay also served on the staffs of Joseph Mansfield and Joseph Hooker, both of whom sought to curry favor with Radical Republicans. See Mansfield to Zachariah Chandler, January 21, 1862, Reel 1, Chandler Papers, LC; and Hooker to Henry Wilson, April 4, 1862, Wilson Papers, LC.

57. *OR*, 12(3):713, 12(2, supplement):861, 965–67, 998, 1007; Quaife, *From the Cannon's Mouth*, 108.

58. *OR*, 12(2, supplement):862–64, 901, 955, 998, 1007. The U.S. Naval Observatory calculates the new moon near Warrenton at 4:40 A.M., August 25, 1862, and moonrise at 10:15 P.M. on August 27. Porter's papers contain numerous letters from officers for whom the jammed wagons and extreme darkness on the night of August 27–28 caused considerable trouble, including the depot quartermaster at Warrenton Junction, who left there for Bristoe Station at midnight with a mounted party and did not arrive until 8:00 A.M.; he told Porter the night was so "excessively dark" that he kept losing sight of his guide, who rode a white horse, and kept his party together by repeatedly having each man call out from the front of the line to the rear (Hyatt C. Ransom to FJP, January 1, "1862" [1863], Reel 1, and June 11, 1867, Reel 3, FJPP).

59. *OR*, 12(2, supplement):830, 831, 862, 901, 998, 1007; John W. Ames to "Dear Mother," August 31, 1862, Ames Papers, AHEC. Ethan Rafuse comments on the discretion corps commanders needed in *Corps Commanders in Blue*, 5. Warrenton Junction occupied the approximate site of present-day Calverton, while Bristoe Station stood about where Virginia Route 28 crosses Broad Run — still fully eleven miles away today, over a more direct modern highway.

CHAPTER 11

1. *OR*, 12(2, supplement):863, 998–99.

2. *Proceedings and Report*, 2:290–91; *OR*, 12(2, supplement):887, 947, 967. Porter wrote to Burnside from Bristoe at 9:30 A.M., reporting that his command would soon reach that place (*OR*, 12[2]:717). Sixteen years later, Lieutenant Weld remembered them reaching Broad Run by eight o'clock, with the head of the column only five or ten minutes behind (*Proceedings and Report*, 3:969).

3. Strother, "Personal Recollections," 712; Stephen M. Weld Jr. to FJP, November 11, 1867, Reel 3, FJPP; George Monteith to FJP, January 31, 1878, Reel 5, FJPP; *OR*, 12(2, supplement):889. Strother's journal, in both the version published serially in *Harper's* in 1866–67 and the 1961 volume edited by Cecil Eby, contains internal inconsistencies suggestive of ex post facto revisions that seem to satisfy his bitter bias against Porter.

4. *Proceedings and Report*, 2:291.

5. *OR*, 12(2, supplement):888–89, 895; *Proceedings and Report*, 2:334.

6. William H. Paine Journal, August 28, 1862, Reel 2, FJPP.

7. *OR*, 12(3):732–33. Porter misidentified Thoroughfare Gap as "Manassas" Gap.

8. *OR*, 12(2):335–36, 360, 384, 564, 644, 656, 670, 679; William H. Paine Journal, August 28, 1862, Reel 2, FJPP.

9. *OR*, 12(1):196, 12(2):74, 337, 360; William H. Paine Journal, August 28, 1862, Reel 2, FJPP. Two identical orders from Pope appear in *OR* 12(1):196 and *OR* 12(2):74, except that the first is headed "1:20 P.M." on August 28 and the other "2:00 P.M."

10. *OR*, 12(1):191, 316–17; William H. Paine Journal, August 28, 1862, Reel 2, FJPP; Joseph C. Willard Diary, August 28, 1862, LC; Washington Roebling to "Dear Father," August 24 [with addenda through September 2], 1862, Roebling Family Papers, Rutgers.

11. *OR* 12(1):206, 213–14. Pope later explained this as a misunderstanding, and that the orders were sent to McDowell—who, not being with his command that night, did not receive them (King, "In Vindication of General Rufus King," 495).

12. *OR*, 12(2):37, 518. Pope still adhered to his inaccurate view of his troops' location during the night of August 28 when he wrote his final report, five months later.

13. *OR*, 12(1):216, 12(2):265, 384, 393; William H. Paine Journal, August 22, 28, 1862, Reel 2, FJPP; Sparks, *Inside Lincoln's Army*, 131.

14. Eby, *Virginia Yankee in the Civil War*, 91–92.

15. *OR*, 12(3):733.

16. Strother, "Personal Recollections," 714; Eby, *Virginia Yankee in the Civil War*, 92.

17. *OR*, 12(2):88, 12(2, supplement):1046, 1061, 12(3):730; *Proceedings and Report*, 3:1064. John Hennessy's *Historical Report on the Troop Movements for the Second Battle of Manassas* gathers and reconciles an impressive array of often confusing and contradictory accounts to plot the peregrinations of commanders and their units over the three days of battle, and the magnificent maps that accompany the publication (now digitized by the Library of Congress) are essential to any valid interpretation of the battle.

18. Cadmus Wilcox to FJP, October 11, 1866, Reel 3, FJPP.

19. *OR*, 12(2, supplement):968, 973, 979; John W. Ames to "Dear Mother," August 31, 1862, Ames Papers, AHEC; Matthew Calhoun McCrary to "My dear wife," September 3, 1862, McCrary Papers, South Caroliniana Library.

20. *OR*, 12(2, supplement):902–3, 968, 973; Joseph C. Willard Diary, August 29, 1862, LC; William H. Paine journal, August 22, 29, 1862, Reel 2, FJPP; Washington Roebling to FJP, June 8, 1878, Reel 5, FJPP; FJP's notes on the meeting and statement of Robert H. T. Leipold, February 12, 1863, Reel 3, FJPP; *Statement of Gen. Fitz John Porter*, 19–20, 22. In

an addendum to a letter to his father begun on August 24, Roebling implied that Ricketts himself had gone ahead of his division and reached Manassas by the time McDowell arrived there (Roebling Family Papers, Rutgers).

21. *Proceedings and Report*, 2:323, 339, 430, 3:1064; *OR*, 12(1):243, 12(2, supplement):883–84, 973; *Statement of the Services of the Fifth Army Corps*, 19–20.

22. *OR*, 12(1):243, 247, 12(2, supplement):847, 1035–36; *Proceedings and Report*, 2:430–31; statement of Robert H. T. Leipold, February 12, 1863, Reel 3, FJPP; *Statement of the Services of the Fifth Army Corps*, 20–21; Marsena Patrick to FJP, August 24, 1866, Reel 3, FJPP. At McDowell's court of inquiry, five months later, Porter testified that he saw McDowell only twice that day, at Manassas in the morning and at Dawkin's Branch at noon (*OR*, 12[1]:241), but he stopped at the Weir house on his way toward Bull Run and again on the way back. Receiving Pope's order from Piatt was one of innumerable events from August 29 that McDowell was afterward unable to remember (*Proceedings and Report*, 3:1064). Addressing a Boston audience in 1877, Lieutenant Weld said Porter told him of McDowell's expectation that Pope would form a new line behind Bull Run (Dwight, *Virginia Campaign of 1862*, 226).

23. One of McDowell's staff officers heard a rumor that King had been drunk the previous night, rather than suffering another seizure (William H. Paine Journal, August 29, 1862, Reel 2, FJPP), and General Hatch corroborated that King "had been drinking hard and was very much shattered" (John P. Hatch to FJP, September 6, 1866, Reel 3, FJPP). Had King merely been drunk he would probably not have relinquished command of his division the following day.

24. *Proceedings and Report*, 2:78, 431; John M. Bancroft Diary, August 29, 1862, BL; Erastus W. Everson Diary, August 29, 1862, Reel 31, FJPP.

25. *OR*, 12(2):736.

26. *Proceedings and Report*, 2:425; *OR*, 12(2, supplement): 968, 983; Lyman Holford Diary, August 29, 1862, LC; Sparks, *Inside Lincoln's Army*, 131–32. Porter had no cavalry with him, and the troopers on the Gainesville Road must have been videttes from Buford's brigade, left behind by King to watch the rear of his column as he retreated.

27. *OR*, 12(2):736, 12 (2, supplement):968, 974, 983; *Proceedings and Report*, 2:79, 189, 348, 431–32, 440.

28. *Proceedings and Report*, 2:292, 297, 326, 431, 439, 440; *OR*, 12(2):625; James Longstreet to FJP, September 23, 1866, and Charles Marshall to FJP, June 9, 1869, both on Reel 3, FJPP.

29. *Proceedings and Report*, 2:467–68.

30. *OR*, 12(2):76, 12(2, supplement):983.

31. *OR*, 12(2, supplement):956, 963; statement of Robert H. T. Leipold, February 12, 1863, Reel 3, FJPP; Augustus P. Martin to FJP, December 19, 1862, Reel 2, FJPP; *Proceedings and Report*, 2:427.

32. *OR*, 12(1):248, 12(2, supplement):904, 905, 908, 974, 994; William H. Paine Journal, August 29, 1862, Reel 2, FJPP.

33. *Proceedings and Report*, 2:468.

34. *Proceedings and Report*, 2:293, 399; *Statement of the Services of the Fifth Army Corps*, 23–24; *OR*, 12(1):237, 242.

35. *OR*, 12(1):237; *Proceedings and Report*, 2:795.

36. *OR*, 12(2, supplement):983, 1068, 12(1):246.

37. *OR*, 12(1):242, 248, 12(2, supplement):955, 959, 1047–48; statement of Robert H. T. Leipold, February 12, 1863, Reel 3, FJPP; Marsena Patrick to FJP, August 24, 1866, Reel 3, FJPP; Osborne, *Civil War Diaries of Col. Theodore B. Gates*, 33.

38. *OR*, 12(2, supplement):907, 1036, 1041. Marsena Patrick corroborated that King had departed for Centreville that morning, and he doubted that the officer Locke approached would have been Hatch, who had not yet come up from his own brigade (Patrick to FJP, August 24, 1866, Reel 3, FJPP). Porter also wrote to Hatch, but the mystery was never solved (John P. Hatch to FJP, September 6, 1866, Reel 3, FJPP). King said that his adjutant general, Robert Chandler, was with McDowell that day, but Chandler was much younger than King. Locke always insisted that King, whom he met later at the court-martial, was the man with McDowell (*OR*, 12[2, supplement]:1036, 1048).

39. *OR*, 12(1):246, 12(2, supplement):1047; Gouverneur K. Warren to William J. Warren, September 5, 1862, Box 3, Warren Papers, NYSL; Washington Roebling to "Dear Father," August 24 [with addenda through September 2], 1862, Roebling Family Papers, Rutgers.

40. Based on the prominence given to the clouds of dust in newspaper accounts of Porter's court-martial, Stuart assumed that his brush-dragging brought Porter up short, but Stuart's own report indicates that he must have resorted to that ruse in the morning, before Confederate infantry arrived; Longstreet posted three divisions between Porter and the turnpike by noon, and Porter did not halt before Confederate resistance until nearly noon. The commander of Porter's skirmishers testified to seeing great clouds of dust in the afternoon, and Porter's own allusion to "the advancing masses of dust" appears in a message he would have sent around the same time. See *OR*, 12(2):524, 565, 579, 625, 736, 12(2, supplement):1013, and James Longstreet to FJP, September 23, 1866, Reel 3, FJPP.

41. *OR*, 12(2):76, 338–39, 12(2, supplement):904, 907; *Proceedings and Report*, 2:777–80. In his early and insightful analysis of Second Bull Run, John Ropes severely criticized McDowell's failure to either give Porter specific orders or explain that he was relinquishing command over him (*Army under Pope*, 95–98).

42. *OR*, 12(2, supplement):968, 1011; *Proceedings and Report*, 2:349, 431, 439–40.

43. *OR*, 12(2):564–65, 625–26, 12(2, supplement):983, 996, 1011–12, 1068, 12(3):734; *Proceedings and Report*, 2:120, 431–33.

44. *Proceedings and Report*, 2:431, 432; *OR*, 12(2, supplement):968, 1012.

45. *Proceedings and Report*, 2:688–93, 3:980–82; *OR*, 12(1):244, 12(2):401. Sturgis testified that he arrived at the front no later than 1:00 P.M., but King's division had already marched away by the time he passed Bethlehem Church, so Sturgis probably arrived sometime thereafter.

46. *OR*, 12(2):39, 12(2, supplement):1012; *Proceedings and Report*, 2:433; *Statement of the Services of the Fifth Army Corps*, 76–77.

47. *OR*, 12(2):339, 384, 387; Abram Duryée to James D. Cameron, November 27, 1876, *Supplement*, 735.

48. *OR*, 12(2):338–39, 367, 12(2, supplement):1068; *Statement of the Services of the Fifth Army Corps*, 26–27, 76–77; *Proceedings and Report*, 1:337. In 1878 Gouverneur K. Warren measured the distance from Bethlehem Church to the crossing of Dawkin's Branch at "about twenty feet short of two miles" (*Proceedings and Report*, 2:78).

49. *OR*, 12(2):625–26, 12(2, supplement):1012, 12(3):734; *Proceedings and Report*, 2:432–33.

50. *Proceedings and Report*, 2:689–90.

51. *OR*, 12(2):565, 598, 12(3):734–35; *Proceedings and Report*, 2:244. Stuart's warning of "heavy columns" advancing against Longstreet's right has been interpreted as the first sighting of Porter's troops, around noon, but his reference to "a late hour in the day" is more compatible with Major George Hyland's testimony that the 22nd Massachusetts reinforced the skirmish line "toward evening."

52. *OR*, 12(2):565, 598, 12(2, supplement):1068, 12(3):734–35; Cadmus Wilcox to FJP, October 11, 1866, Reel 3, FJPP; *Statement of the Services of the Fifth Army Corps*, 27–28; *Proceedings and Report*, 2:689–90.

53. *OR*, 12(2):41, 12(2, supplement):850; Eby, *Virginia Yankee in the Civil War*, 94. In his manuscript for a history of Pope's campaign designed to sanitize that general's blunders and blame his defeat on Porter, former Pope aide Thomas C. H. Smith still implied years later that Pope's "joint order" anticipated Porter and McDowell falling on Jackson's right near Groveton. That order required no attack at all, however, and it directed Porter and McDowell to march on Gainesville, rather than Groveton; by the time Smith composed that passage, it was already clear that moving on Groveton would have forced Porter and McDowell either to attack and defeat Longstreet or to pass directly before his guns across his entire front. Smith, who claimed to have telepathically deduced Porter's perfidious intent on August 28, attributed Porter's inactivity on August 29 to "the work he had laid out for himself, to withhold his support and compel Pope's withdrawal to Alexandria." See Smith's manuscript on the campaign, 154, Box 3, Smith Papers, and Schutz, "Memoir and Review," 134–35, 143, both OHC.

54. *OR*, 12(2, supplement):826, 875.

55. *OR*, 12(2, supplement):949–50, 952, 1049; HD and HJ, August 29, 1862. By Heintzelman's watch, McDowell was at Pope's headquarters at 5:45 P.M., and soon afterward Heintzelman learned of Porter's intended withdrawal—evidently from someone who had heard Lieutenant Weld report it, since Pope still seemed oblivious to the information.

56. Thomas C. H. Smith, manuscript memoir of Pope's campaign, 166A–167, Smith Papers, OHC.

57. *OR*, 12(2, supplement):950–51; *Proceedings and Report*, 2:99, 422, 435, 437, 441; *Statement of the Services of the Fifth Army Corps*, 29, 76–77.

58. *OR*, 12(2, supplement):878–81, 947, 952, 957, 958, 960–61, 968, 972, 1020–21, 1049; *Proceedings and Report*, 2:422–23, 437. The U.S. Naval Observatory calculates sunset at that latitude on August 29, 1862, to have been at 6:45 P.M., in the absence of Daylight Saving Time.

59. *Proceedings and Report*, 2:156, 158; Abner Doubleday Journal, *Supplement*, 2:695–97; Franz Sigel to FJP, November 2, 1867, Reel 3, FJPP.

60. *OR*, 12(2, supplement):875, 1031; *Proceedings and Report*, 2:557–60, 561–74, 577–78, 609; statement of Robert H. T. Leipold, February 12, 1863, Reel 3, FJPP; George Monteith to FJP, January 31, 1878, Reel 5, FJPP. The route Captain Pope said he followed to reach Porter should have taken him within sight of King's division and directly past Ricketts's division, but he testified to encountering no organized troops. In 1878, a few days after retracing his purported path in a carriage, he conceded that his ride might have consumed three-quarters of an hour, but no longer (*Proceedings and Report*, 2:569).

61. *OR*, 12(2, supplement):826; George Ruggles to FJP, October 14, 1877, Reel 5, FJPP; Washington Roebling to "Dear Father," August 24 [with addenda through September 2], 1862, Roebling Family Papers, Rutgers. Douglass Pope claimed he reached his uncle at "about 8 o'clock." Benjamin Roberts was apparently confusing Douglass Pope's report that Porter had called off the attack when he testified that General Pope received Porter's warning of his impending withdrawal to Manassas "between 8 and 9 o'clock at night" on August 29; Pope had actually received the first message about Porter's impending withdrawal from Lieutenant Weld around 5:45 P.M., but he had not read it and evidently did not listen to Weld's recitation of it. See *OR*, 12(2, supplement):874, 879, 952.

62. *OR*, 12(2, supplement):826.

63. Ropes, *Army under Pope*, 110, suggested that Pope would have been wiser to retire across Bull Run, and Hennessy (*Return to Bull Run*, 307) recognized the decision to stay and fight as the most important of the entire campaign. Both credited the decision to Pope's peculiar aptitude for misinterpreting intelligence.

64. *OR*, 12(2, supplement):949, 951, 968, 975, 1099; *Proceedings and Report*, 2:135, 246.

CHAPTER 12

1. *OR*, 12(2):476, 12(2, supplement):948, 957, 970, 988, 1008, 12(3):735–36; *Proceedings and Report*, 2:135.

2. *OR*, 12(2, supplement):985.

3. Strother, "Personal Recollections of the War, . . . Groveton," 715. In an 1883 address, a Porter admirer who fought at Second Bull Run clocked Porter's arrival at Pope's headquarters at precisely 8:17 A.M., although it's not clear how a mere corporal could have known (see Robins, "Battles of Groveton and Second Bull Run," 94; Robins was commissioned retroactively to June 27, but was still carrying a rifle in August). Pope tried to push the time of Porter's arrival forward as far as 10:00 A.M. (*OR*, 12[2, supplement]:854). A lieutenant in Martindale's brigade testified that they arrived at 6:00 A.M., which was not likely, and a Porter aide reported their arrival "early that morning" (*Proceedings and Report*, 2:246, 295). If the head of the column started by 4:00 A.M. and did not go astray, it should have covered the five miles within three hours or less, and Sykes's earliest regiments did arrive at 7:00 A.M. (*OR*, 12[2]:490).

4. FJP to John C. Ropes, September 7, 1897, BU; *Proceedings and Report*, 2:52, 295.

5. William H. Paine Journal, August 30, 1862, Reel 2, FJPP; FJP to John C. Ropes, September 7, 1897, BU; *OR*, 12(2):83, 12(3):741, 963–64; William Coleman to "My Dear sister," August 31, 1862, Papers of the Kennedy, Evans, Woods, Hinton, Coleman, and Babcock Families, South Caroliniana Library; *Statement of the Services of the Fifth Army Corps*, 50; HJ, August 30, 1862; Sparks, *Inside Lincoln's Army*, 133–34.

6. HJ, August 30, 1862; Stephen M. Weld Jr. to FJP, November 11, 1867, Reel 3, FJPP; Sparks, *Inside Lincoln's Army*, 133–34; *OR*, 12(2):481; *Proceedings and Report*, 2:448. According to Heintzelman, Porter took part in the council.

7. *OR*, 12(2):490, 577; *Proceedings and Report*, 2:246; George Monteith to FJP, January 31, 1878, Reel 5, FJPP; Stephen M. Weld Jr. to FJP, November 11, 1867, Reel 3, FJPP; William H. Paine Journal, August 30, 1862, Reel 2, FJPP.

8. HJ, August 30, 1862; Joseph C. Willard Diary, August 30, 1862, LC.

9. *OR*, 12(2):40–41, 12(3):741. William Franklin later offered to testify that neither Pope nor his inspector general, Benjamin Roberts, could be believed even under oath, and named several antebellum army officers who would corroborate it, including John Reynolds and George Thomas (who nonetheless demurred). General Hatch offered that Edwin Sumner said the same about Roberts, adding that he concurred, and he believed that any former officer of Roberts's old Regular Army regiment would have agreed (Franklin to FJP, September 20, 1867, and Hatch to FJP, September 6, 1866, both on Reel 3, FJPP). In his official report the next January, Pope contradicted his remark about Jackson's retreat only four paragraphs later, revealing that even he knew by then that the Confederates were being reinforced — although he still denied that Porter had faced any large force (*OR*, 12[2]:41, 42).

10. *OR*, 12(2):384, 387, 701, 712–13; Hough. *History of Duryée's Brigade*, 96–97. To approximate the pronunciation implied by the accented French spelling of Duryée's name without using an accent, it was often anglicized to "Duryea."

11. Strother, "Personal Recollections of the War, . . . Groveton," 717–18.

12. *OR*, 12(3):741.

13. *New York Times*, September 13, 1862; *OR*, 12(2): 488, 490; *Proceedings and Report*, 2:85, 246, 349.

14. *OR*, 12(2):384, 394, 488, 490, 12(3):959–60; *Proceedings and Report*, 2:246; *Statement of the Services of the Fifth Army Corps*, 50–52.

15. *OR*, 12(2):394, 503, 12(3):963–64; *Statement of the Services of the Fifth Army Corps*, 50; *Proceedings and Report*, 2:311; George Ruggles to FJP, October 14, 1877, Reel 5, FJPP; William H. Paine Journal, August 30, 1862, Reel 2, FJPP.

16. *OR*, 12(2):268.

17. *Statement of the Services of the Fifth Army Corps*, 51–52; *OR*, 12(2):472, 12(3):756, 759–61, 960.

18. *OR*, 12(2):368, 376, 471; Lyman Holford Diary, August 30, 1862, LC.

19. *OR*, 12(2): 471–72, 478; George Lockley Diary, August 30, 1862, BL.

20. *OR*, 12(2):646, 666; Stephen Thomas memorandum, *Supplement*, 2:751; *Proceedings and Report*, 2:349; George Lockley Diary, August 30, 1862, BL.

21. Sparks, *Inside Lincoln's Army*, 134–35; Lyman Holford Diary, August 30, 1862, LC; John C. Whiteside to "Dear Mother Church," October 4, 1862, BL; Osborne, *Civil War Diaries of Col. Theodore B. Gates*, 34.

22. William Breakey to "My dear Father Stevens," September 5, 1862, Stevens Papers, BL; George Lockley Diary, August 30, 1862, BL.

23. *Proceedings and Report*, 2:166, 246–48; George Lockley Diary, August 30, 1862, BL; Sparks, *Inside Lincoln's Army*, 135–36; John C. Whiteside to "Dear Mother Church," October 4, 1862, BL; John W. Ames to "Dear Mother," August 31, 1862, Ames Papers, AHEC; *OR*, 12(2):91, 477, 479, 480–81, 488; Lyman Holford Diary, September 4, 1862, LC; George Fairfield Diary, August 30, 1862, WHS; Abner Doubleday Journal, August 30, 1862, *Supplement*, 2:699–700; *War Diary and Letters of Stephen Minot Weld*, 134–35.

24. *OR*, 12(2):269, 394; *Supplement*, 2:699–700.

25. *OR*, 12(2):502–4.

26. *OR*, 12(2):286, 394–95, 51(1):130.

27. *OR*, 12(2):259–60, 482, 485–86, 488, 810; *New York Herald*, September 8, 1862; John W. Ames to "Dear Mother," August 31, 1862, Ames Papers, AHEC.

28. *OR*, 12(2):482, 488, 496; William H. Paine Journal, August 30, 1862, Reel 2, FJPP.

29. *OR*, 12(2):482, 501.

30. Rosenberger, "Ohiowa Soldier," 117; Strother, "Personal Recollections of the War, . . . Groveton," 718–19; *OR*, 12(2):395, 488, 496–97; William H. Paine Journal, August 30, 1862, Reel 2, FJPP.

31. Strother, "Personal Recollections of the War, . . . Groveton," 720; John W. Ames to "Dear Mother," August 30, 1862, Ames Papers, AHEC; *OR*, 12(2):497–502.

32. *OR*, 12(1):268–75, 12(2):322, 342–43, 488; William H. Paine Journal, August 30, 1862, Reel 2, FJPP; Stephen M. Weld Jr. to FJP, September 28, 1867, and Frederick T. Locke to FJP, September 15, 1877, both on Reel 3, FJPP; *Proceedings and Report*, 2:449. In reporting this incident two weeks later, Milroy forgot Porter's name and inserted dashes in its place, but he could only have referred to Porter.

33. *OR*, 12(2):483; John W. Ames to "Dear Mother," August 31, 1862, Ames Papers, AHEC; Loving, *Civil War Letters*, 62–63; HJ, August 30, 1862; *Supplement*, 700–701; John V. Hadley to "Miss Pett Barbour," October 6, 1862, Barbour Papers, LC.

34. Henry Keiser Diary, August 30, 1862, AHEC; Edward E. Schweitzer Diary, August 30, 1862, AHEC.

35. *Proceedings and Report*, 2:449, 3:973. The next day, August 31, Porter misdated a letter to McClellan, heading it August 30 (*OR*, 12[3]:768–69).

36. Strother, "Personal Recollections of the War, . . . Groveton," 720.

37. HJ, August 30, 1862; Gouverneur K. Warren to William J. Warren, September 5, 1862, Box 3, Warren Papers, NYSL; John W. Ames to "Dear Mother," August 31, 1862, Ames Papers, AHEC; Avery B. Cain to "Dear Father," September 4, 1862, Cain Letters, Vermont Historical Society; George G. Meade to Margaret Meade, September 5, 1862, Meade Papers, HSP; *War Letters of William Thompson Lusk*, 181; Edward S. Bragg to "My Dear Wife," September 13, 1862, Bragg Papers, WHS; Quaife, *From the Cannon's Mouth*, 111.

38. *War Diary and Letters of Stephen Minot Weld*, 132; *OR*, 12(3):768; memorandum of August 31–September 2, 1862, in FJP's handwriting, Reel 38, GBMP.

39. *OR*, 12(2):81, 12(3):768–69.

40. Sparks, *Inside Lincoln's Army*, 136; *OR*, 12(2):83, 12(3):771; undated memo on FJP's September 2 interview with Pope, Reel 30, GBMP.

41. William B. Franklin to FJP, July 7, 1876, Reel 38, GBMP (copy in Porter Papers, MHS); *Statement of the Services of the Fifth Army Corps*, 83; undated memo on the September 1 council, Reel 30, GBMP.

42. Burlingame and Ettlinger, *Inside Lincoln's White House*, 37; Niven, *Salmon P. Chase Papers*, 1:366–67.

43. *OR*, 12(3):771–72, 787–88, 798, 19(1):37; undated memo on Porter's September 2 interview with John Pope, Reel 30, GBMP; Joseph C. Willard Diary, September 1–2, 1862, LC.

44. *OR*, 12(2, supplement):838; undated memo on FJP's September 2 interview with John Pope, Reel 30, GBMP.

45. Undated memo on FJP's September 2 interview with John Pope, Reel 30, GBMP; *OR*, 12(2, supplement):836–38, 840, 976–77. In the ensuing trial, Pope said nothing about Kennedy's letter, substituting Porter's dispatches to Burnside as the offending correspondence, but on September 2 he could not yet have seen those.

46. Joseph C. Willard Diary, September 2, 1862, LC; Strother, "Personal Recollections of the War, . . . Groveton," 725; Cox, *Reminiscences*, 1:244. In *Lincoln's Lieutenants* (804, n.12), Stephen Sears corrected Jacob Cox's long-standing misidentification of John P. Hatch as the general who called for cheering.

47. *War Diary and Letters of Stephen Minot Weld*, 136.

48. Beale, *Diary of Gideon Welles*, 1:94, 104–5; Edward Bates's remonstrance about McClellan, September 2, 1862, ALP; Niven, *Salmon P. Chase Papers*, 1:368–69.

49. *OR*, 12(3):706, 739–41.

50. Niven, *Salmon P. Chase Papers*, 1:370; John Pope to Richard Yates, September 21, 1862, Pope Papers, Chicago History Museum; *OR*, 12(2, supplement):840, 12(3):14–16, 19(2):169. Pope testified that Lincoln "informed" him of the Burnside dispatches "on the 4th or 5th of September," but he probably learned of them on September 3, for Chase's diary records Pope visiting Lincoln that day. Cozzens noted as much in *General John Pope*, 369, n.67.

51. Joseph Holt to E. D. Townsend, September 3, 1862, Reel 106, and John F. Lee to Abraham Lincoln, September 4, 1862, Reel 113, Letters Received (M619), RG94, NA; Laas, *Wartime Washington*, 166, 170; memorandum for September 3, 1862, and handwritten narrative "The Provocation," Reel 2, FJPP. The endorsement on Lee's resignation is in Stanton's hand, and is signed by him, although the letter is addressed to Lincoln.

52. Beale, *Diary of Gideon Welles*, 1:109–10; *OR*, 12(2):14–16, 12(2, supplement):836.

53. Beale, *Diary of Gideon Welles*, 1:110; Niven, *Salmon P. Chase Papers*, 1:370; Irvin McDowell to "My dear Nelly," September 4, 1862, MS 07379, FSNMP.

54. *Chicago Tribune*, September 10, 1862; *Daily Gate City* (Keokuk, Iowa), September 10, 1862.

55. *OR*, 12(2, supplement):976–78. In trying to show that Ruggles was biased toward Porter, Holt asked him during the trial (977) if he remembered Pope mentioning Porter's disparaging messages to Burnside. Ruggles said he did not, but the question itself indicated that Pope probably had mentioned them to Ruggles, and told Holt about it while being coached on his testimony. Without a source inside Pope's circle, Porter would not have been forewarned that the dispatches would be used against him, and Ruggles was Porter's only friend at Pope's headquarters.

56. FJP to Seth Williams, September 6, 1862, endorsed to Ambrose Burnside by Williams as received at 11:40 A.M., and further endorsed by FJP at a later date, Reel 2, FJPP.

57. Brinkerhoff Miner to Nathaniel Banks, 4:00 P.M., September 4, 1862, quoted in Fischel, *Secret War for the Union*, 211; *Report of the Joint Committee*, 453, 650; *CWP*, 435; *OR*, 51(1):788; Nevins, *Diary of Battle*, 91; Scott, *Fallen Leaves*, 140; John W. Ames to "Dear Mother," September 6, 1862, Ames Papers, AHEC; John C. Whiteside to "Dear Mother Church," October 4, 1862, BL.

CHAPTER 13

1. Niven, *Salmon P. Chase Papers*, 1:370; Beale, *Diary of Gideon Welles*, 1:110–11; Special Order 222, September 5, 1862, Court Martial Case File MM-51, RG153, NA; John Pope to Abraham Lincoln, September 5, 1862, ALP. Special Order 222 is a newly discovered document in Lincoln's hand, not included in any published collections of Lincoln's writings, and as of the spring of 2020 was awaiting chronological inclusion in the Papers of Abraham Lincoln project.

2. Niven, *Salmon P. Chase Papers*, 1:370–71.

3. Henry Halleck to John Pope, September 5, 1862, Eldridge Collection, Huntington Library, quoted in Doubleday & Co. Collection, LC.

4. Court Record, Case File MM-51, RG153, NA; "Court Martial Incidents," Reel 25, FJPP; Joseph Mansfield to Zachariah Chandler, January 21, 1862, Reel 1, Chandler Papers, LC; *OR*, 12(3):811, 19(2):182, 188.

5. *CWP*, 436–37; *OR*, 19(2):197; FJP to Harriet Porter, circa September 6, 1862, quoted in Eisenschiml, *Celebrated Case*, 67. Within hours after the court was appointed, Heintzelman spoke to a general who had just been to the War Department and learned who the members were (HJ, September 5, 1862).

6. "Court Martial Incidents," Reel 30, FJPP; FJP to Lorenzo Thomas, September 10, 1862, Reel 2, FJPP.

7. FJP to Randolph Marcy, 7:20 P.M., September 4, 1862, 10:20 P.M., 11:50 P.M., September 5, Reel 31, GBMP.

8. FJP to Randolph Marcy, 10:00 P.M., September 5, 1862, and to Seth Williams, 12:15 A.M., 3:30 P.M., 11:55 P.M., September 6, 10:10 A.M., 8:15 P.M., September 7, all on Reel 31, GBMP.

9. FJP to Seth Williams, 11:30 P.M., September 7, 1862, and FJP to GBM, 9:00 P.M., September 9, 9:00 A.M., September 10, all on Reel 31, GBMP.

10. *OR*, 19(2):197–98, 253–54.

11. *OR*, 19(1):370, 19(2):209, 211, 239, 258; FJP to Seth Williams, September 11, and noon, September 12, 1862, FJP to GBM, September 12, 1862, and FJP to Marcy, September 13, 1862, all on Reel 31, GBMP. The site of Leesborough was swallowed up by what is now Wheaton, Maryland.

12. Norton, *Army Letters*, 119; Frank Kelley to "My Dear Parents," September 22, 1862, AHEC; Lyman Holford Diary, September 9, 1862, LC.

13. *Report of the Joint Committee*, 640.

14. *OR*, 19(1):296, 297, 338, 350, 51(1):832, 835, 837; *CWP*, 463.

15. *OR*, 19(2):297. In "'Poor Burn?': The Antietam Conspiracy That Wasn't," Ethan Rafuse persuasively argued that McClellan did not remove Burnside from wing command to diminish his prominence, as numerous historians have contended (myself included). It is more difficult to discount personal motive in Porter's unkind response to Burnside's tardiness on September 15.

16. *OR*, 12(2, supplement):1003.

17. *MOS*, 586; Cox, *Reminiscences*, 1:297; Daniel Read Larned to "Dear Henry," October 16, 25, 1862, Larned Papers, LC. If Burnside supplied a written response to McClellan's demand for an explanation of his failure to move his troops, it has not been found. McClellan claimed that Burnside cited the fatigue and hunger of his men as an "excuse."

18. *OR*, 19(1):210–11, 293; Watson, *From Ashby to Andersonville*, 20; George A. Custer to McClellan, September 15, 1862, Reel 32, GBMP.

19. *OR*, 19(1):338, 350, 355, 359, 51(1):838; Alexander S. Webb to "Dear Mr. Remsen," September 28, 1862, Webb Papers, Sterling Library, Yale; John B. Bailey Journal, September 15, 1862, NHHS; John E. Wilcox Diary, "August" [September] 15, 1862, NHHS; Sparks, *Inside Lincoln's Army*, 146; *CWP*, 464–65. Jacob Cox twice described that cavalcade of officers drawing artillery fire, and in the second version he added that Porter was the only officer who remained on the bluff with McClellan after he asked the others to retire. Cox included himself, Burnside, and other generals in the group, but in his letter thirteen days after the incident Alexander Webb described the assemblage as consisting of McClellan's staff and, presumably, Porter's. Neither Webb nor McClellan mentioned any other general officers in that gathering (Cox, *Reminiscences*, 1:298–300; Cox, "Battle of Antietam," 631; *MOS*, 586).

20. Watson, *From Ashby to Andersonville*, 20–21; *OR*, 19(1):353, 19(2):307–8, 51(1):839; Strother, "Personal Recollections: Antietam," 282.

21. *OR*, 19(1):338, 372, 51(1):835; Frank Kelley to "My Dear Parents," September 22, 1862, AHEC; FJP to Joseph Choate, December 15, 1878, Reel 8, FJPP; John B. Bailey Journal, September 16, 1862, NHHS; Watson, *From Ashby to Andersonville*, 21; Sauers, *Civil War Journal of Colonel William J. Bolton*, 85; Priest, *From New Bern to Fredericksburg*, 69–70; Osborne, *Civil War Diaries of Col. Theodore B. Gates*, 40.

22. *OR*, 19(2):308, 314; Watson, *From Ashby to Andersonville*, 21; John B. Bailey Journal, September 16, 1862, NHHS; John E. Wilcox Diary, "August" [September] 16, 1862, NHHS.

23. *OR*, 19(2):314. In his memoirs, McClellan again exaggerated that delay, ignoring the explanation Burnside had long since given him (*MOS*, 588–89).

24. *OR*, 19(1):223, 235, 243, 263, 268, 51(1):839; Osborne, *Civil War Diaries of Col. Theodore B. Gates*, 40; Sparks, *Inside Lincoln's Army*, 146; Lyman Holford Diary, September 16, 1862, LC; Quaife, *From the Cannon's Mouth*, 124; *Diary of General S. M. Jackson*, 47.

25. *OR*, 19(1):351. Heavy tree growth now obscures the views from behind Ecker's.

26. *Report of the Joint Committee*, 581; *OR*, 19(1):218–19; Walter Phelps Jr. to "Dear E.," September 28, 1862, Phelps Papers, AHEC.

27. *Report of the Joint Committee*, 368, 581.

28. Coco, *From Ball's Bluff to Gettysburg*, 124, 127; *Report of the Joint Committee*, 368; Sparks, *Inside Lincoln's Army*, 148–50.

29. *OR*, 19(1):61–62, 277, 338; Lewis Masonheimer Diary, September 17, 1862, AHEC; Sears, *Mr. Dunn Browne's Experiences*, 9; Holden, Ross, and Slomba, *Stand Firm and Fire Low*, 47–49.

30. Lossing, *Pictorial History*, 2:476; John W. Ames to "My dear Mother," September 21, 1862, Ames Papers, AHEC. Benjamin Lossing's information about McClellan's movements that morning came from an interview with Mr. Pry and his wife.

31. *OR*, 51(1):844. On the difficulty posed by the creek, see Marvel, "More Than Water under Burnside's Bridge," and Clemens, "Why Did Burnside Cross the Bridge?"

32. *OR*, 19(1):419, 19(2):315; Priest, *From New Bern to Fredericksburg*, 71; Sauers, *Civil War Journal of Colonel William J. Bolton*, 86; Loving, *Civil War Letters of George Washington Whitman*, 67; Henry J. Spooner to "My Dear Father," September 20, 1862, Spooner Letters, Rhode Island Historical Society.

33. *Report of the Joint Committee*, 626–27; *OR* 19(1):62, 338–39.

34. *OR*, 51(1):843.

35. *OR*, 19(1):62, 339, 351, 342–43, 358, 359, 360, 367; FJP to Joseph Choate, December 15, 1878, Reel 8, FJPP; FJP to Thomas T. Gantt, October 8, 1886, Reel 25, FJPP; FJP to Lafayette McLaws, June 16, 1886, McLaws Papers, Duke. In March of 1863, McClellan testified that he had "fought pretty close upon 100,000 men" at Antietam (*Report of the Joint Committee*, 441).

36. *OR*, 19(1):357, 896–97, 51(1):845; Cassedy, *Dear Friends at Home*, 152–54; Joseph Kirkland to Pleasonton, 4:30 P.M., September 17, 1862, quoted (from a private collection of Alfred Pleasonton's papers) in E. B. Long notes, Doubleday & Co. Collection, LC.

37. Powell, "More Light on 'The Reserve at Antietam,'" 804.

38. Powell, "More Light on 'The Reserve at Antietam,'" 804; Anderson, "Reserve at Antietam," 783.

39. Powell, "More Light on 'The Reserve at Antietam,'" 804; Anderson, "Reserve at Antietam," 472; George Sykes to "My dear Porter," March 6, 1875, Reel 4, FJPP.

40. *OR*, 19(2):316; 366–67; Elon G. Mills to unidentified correspondent, September 18, 1862, Mills Diary and Letters, BL.

41. James Abraham to "Dear Friends," September 20, 1862, Abraham Letters, AHEC; Elizur Belden Diary, September 19, 1862, CHS; William H. Drake to "Dear Cousin," September 29, 1862, CHS; David A. Thompson to "Dear Electa," September 21, 1862, Thompson Collection, CHS; Edward E. Schweitzer Diary, September 17, 1862, AHEC; Charles M. Coit to unidentified recipients, September 18, October 4, 1862, Coit Papers, Sterling Library, Yale; John B. Stickney to "My dear Parents & Sister," September 28, 1862, Stickney Papers, CL; Albert Taft Diary, September 17–20, 1862, Nelson Town Archives; Loving, *Civil War Letters of George Washington Whitman*, 68; Priest, *From New Bern to Fredericksburg*, 73; Watson, *From Ashby to Andersonville*, 22–23; *OR*, 19(1):367.

42. *OR*, 51(1):844.

43. *New York Tribune*, September 20, 1862. Perhaps Smalley overheard the exchange, but any of Burnside's staff would also have gladly fed him or his colleagues the gist of McClellan's written message, and Smalley copied the misinformation prevalent at Ninth Corps headquarters: Burnside testified that he and his staff incorrectly supposed that Porter had "perhaps 15,000 to 20,000 men" standing idle in reserve (*Report of the Joint Committee*, 641). Smalley's depiction of Porter's implied refusal of reinforcements also

echoed critical comments in Pleasonton's initial report of the battle, which Pleasonton deleted when McClellan apprised him of his mistaken assumptions about Porter and his command. The original version of Pleasonton's report, with the missing paragraph, is on Reel 35, GBMP.

44. Smalley's repetition of that fourfold exaggeration of Porter's available troops helped to distort historical depictions of that moment for a century and a half after the war, despite such conspicuous corrections as Palfrey, *Antietam and Fredericksburg*, 123, and Sears, *Landscape Turned Red*, 292. See, for example, Catton, *Mr. Lincoln's Army*, 319, and Marvel, *Burnside*, 144.

45. *Report of the Joint Committee*, 641–42; *CWP*, 473; *OR*, 19(1):66, 372, 374, 19(2):322, 336; James Abraham to "Dear Friends," September 23, 1862, Abraham Letters, AHEC. Burnside testified months later that McClellan saw him that night, but he may have been confusing that with the next morning, for on the night of the battle his staff heard that McClellan was too tired to see him. Daniel Larned to "Dear Henry," October 4, 1862, Larned Papers, LC. Ezra Carman's observation that McClellan "consulted only with Porter" (*Maryland Campaign*, 2:502) seemed only to reflect the widespread belief that Porter was McClellan's principal confidant; Carman cited no other authority, and he would have had no personal knowledge of their interactions that night.

46. George Lockley Diary, September 19, 1862, BL; *Report of the Joint Committee*, 441; *OR*, 19(2):331, 51(1):848–49, 850, 852; Porter to "My dear Mc—," September 19, 1862 (speculatively dated September 20), Reel 32, GBMP.

47. George Lockley Diary, September 19, 1862, BL; FJP to GBM, 10:20 A.M., September 19, 1862, Reel 32, GBMP; *OR*, 19(1):339; memorandum of events, Ferrier Papers, BL; Cassedy, *Dear Friends at Home*, 154.

48. *OR*, 19(1):212, 339; FJP to "My dear Genl.," undated but September 19, 1862, Reel 32, GBMP.

49. FJP to "My dear Genl.," undated but September 19, 1862, Reel 32, GBMP.

50. *OR*, 19(1):339–40, 353, 831–33; John M. Bancroft Diary, September 19, 1862, BL; FJP to GBM, 8:00 P.M., September 19, 1862, Reel 32, GBMP; *War Diary and Letters of Stephen Minot Weld*, 139. The next morning Porter described the ford as very deep in places (FJP to Randolph Marcy, 6:00 A.M., September 20, 1862, Reel 32, GBMP).

51. *OR*, 19(2):331, 334.

52. FJP to Randolph Marcy, 6:00 A.M., September 20, 1862, Reel 32, GBMP; *OR*, 19(1):351; George Lockley Diary, September 20, 1862, BL.

53. FJP to Randolph Marcy, 6:00 A.M. and no specific time, September 20, 1862, Reel 32, GBMP; *CWP*, 473.

54. *OR*, 19(1):346, 351, 19(2):334–35; John W. Ames to "My dear Mother," September 21, 1862, Ames Papers, AHEC.

55. John W. Ames to "My dear Mother," September 21, 1862, Ames Papers, AHEC; FJP to GBM, 10:30 A.M., 10:50 A.M., September 20, 1862, Reel 32, GBMP; *OR*, 19(2):334.

56. George Lockley Diary, September 20, 1862, BL; *OR*, 19(1):346–49; Acken, *Inside the Army of the Potomac*, 133–6; Plumb, *Your Brother in Arms*, 25; John M. Bancroft Diary, September 20, 1862, BL; John W. Ames to "My dear Mother," September 21, 1862, Ames Papers, AHEC.

57. Albert D. Richardson to Sidney Gay, September 19, 1862, Gay Papers, Columbia University Library.

58. Cassedy, *Dear Friends at Home*, 157; Acken, *Inside the Army of the Potomac*, 142–45; Sparks, *Inside Lincoln's Army*, 156.

59. Court Record, Case File MM-51, RG153, NA; John Pope to Richard Yates, September 21, 1862, and to William Butler, September 26, 1862, Pope Papers, Chicago Historical Society.

CHAPTER 14

1. Nevins, *Diary of Battle*, 108; Nevins and Thomas, *Diary of George Templeton Strong*, 3:266; [FJP] to "My dear friend," September 30, 1862, Container 3, Marble Papers, LC; *War Diary and Letters of Stephen Minot Weld*, 139. General Lee's son, a Harvard classmate of Weld's, told him of the shortage of Confederate provisions.

2. *OR*, 19(2):489; Meade, *Life and Letters*, 1:319; Nevins, *Diary of Battle*, 108; William T. H. Brooks to "Father," October 2, 1862, Brooks Papers, AHEC; Alexander S. Webb to Delos B. Sacket, October, 1862, Webb Papers, Sterling Library, Yale.

3. [FJP] to "My dear friend," September 30, 1862, Container 3, Marble Papers, LC.

4. Montgomery Blair to GBM, September 27, 1862, Reel 32, GBMP; Beale, *Welles Diary*, 1:146.

5. *War Diary and Letters of Stephen Minot Weld*, 83; Thomas C. Cheney Diary, October 3, 1862, Cheney Papers, University of New Hampshire; Lewis F. Cleveland to "Dear Louise," October 5, 1862, Cleveland Letters, AHEC; Charles M. Coit to "Dear All," October 4, 1862, Coit Papers, Sterling Library, Yale; George Chandler to "dear Kate," October 3, 1862, Chandler Papers, NHHS; Longacre, *Antietam to Fort Fisher*, 48; FJP to Joseph Choate, December 15, 1878, Reel 8, FJPP.

6. Gienapp and Gienapp, *The Civil War Diary of Gideon Welles*, 33–34; Pease and Randall, *Diary of Orville Hickman Browning*, 1:589.

7. *Chicago Tribune*, September 28, 1862; *Ashtabula (Ohio) Weekly Telegraph*, October 4, 1862; Williams, *Wild Life of the Army*, 141, 148. The microfilm version of the *New York Times* carries no article about charges preferred against Porter between September 20 and October 4.

8. *Chicago Tribune*, October 6, 1862; Niven, *Salmon P. Chase Papers*, 1:418, 419, 420–21, 422.

9. *OR*, 19(1):338–39.

10. FJP to Seth Williams, October 6, 1862, Reel 20, Letters Received (M2096), RG393, Part 1, NA; Ambrose Burnside to FJP, October 9, 1862, Reel 2, FJPP (copy in BW Box 47, Barlow Papers, HL).

11. Albert D. Richardson to Sydney Gay, September 27, 1862, Gay Papers, Columbia University Library; Daniel Larned to "Dear Sister," October 3, 1862, Larned Papers, LC; Hammond, *Diary of a Union Lady*, 179.

12. FJP to Samuel L. M. Barlow, April 28 [1863], BW Box 47, Barlow Papers, HL; *War Diary and Letters of Stephen Minot Weld*, 143; "Your friend M" to Barlow, October 21, 1862, BW Box 42, Barlow Papers, HL.

13. *Alexandria (Va.) Gazette*, October 9, 1862; Endicott, *Reminiscences*, 20.

14. Daniel Larned to "Dear Henry," September 30, 1862, Larned Papers, LC; John D. Wilkins to "My Dearly beloved wife," October 6, 1862, Wilkins Papers, CL; *OR*, 19(1):72; Henry Halleck to "My dear Wife," October 7, 1862, Halleck Letters, CL; *CWL*, 5:452; John W. Garrett to GBM, October 8, 1862, Reel 33, GBMP; Larned to "My Dear Sister," October 12, 1862, Larned Papers, LC; Mary Ellen Marcy to Mary Shipman, October 15, 1862, CHS; *War Letters, 1862–1865*, 1.

15. *War Diary and Letters of Stephen Minot Weld*, 142–43.

16. *OR*, 19(2):52–53.

17. *OR*, 19(2):59–65, 51(1):878; Daniel Larned to "My Dear Sister," October 12, 1862, Larned Papers, LC; Randolph Marcy to Burnside, 1:00 P.M. October 11, 1862, Box 3, Burnside Papers, NA.

18. *OR*, 19(2):69, 430, 464–65; Quaife, *From the Cannon's Mouth*, 140; Rufus Ingalls to Randolph Marcy, October 17, 1862, Reel 33, GBMP.

19. *OR*, 19(2):40, 421, 422, 424–25, 429.

20. Alexander S. Webb to Randolph Marcy, October 15, 1862, and FJP to Marcy, no hour noted, 1:45 P.M. (two at that time), 5:40 P.M., 8:00 P.M., October 16, 1862, all on Reel 33, GBMP.

21. Harriet Porter to her sister, October, 1862, quoted in Eisenschiml, *Celebrated Case of Fitz John Porter*, 69.

22. FJP to Alexander S. Webb, October 14, 1862, Reel 2, FJPP; summons, dated October 8, 1862, Reel 2, FJPP. Martindale's petition for the court was dated three days after the court was created, as though the impetus originated with higher authority and his formal request was solicited as an afterthought. See John Martindale to Lorenzo Thomas, October 9, 1862, Reel 119, Letters Received (M619), RG94, NA; and Special Orders 80, October 6, 1862, Case File KK-298, RG 153, NA.

23. FJP to E. W. West, October 15, 1862, Dolan Telegrams, NYHS; Proceedings, October 8–17, 1862, Case File KK-298, RG 153, NA; FJP to Randolph Marcy, 1:45 P.M., 10:00 P.M., October 16, 1862, Reel 33, GBMP; *OR*, 19(2):82, 86–88; *New York Herald*, October 14, 1862.

24. FJP to Randolph Marcy, October 16, 1862 (five telegrams), Dolan Telegrams, NYHS; *OR*, 19(2):439, 440; *War Diary and Letters of Stephen Minot Weld*, 145; Proceedings, October 20, 1862, Case File KK-298, RG 153, NA; *New York Tribune*, October 28, 1862.

25. Proceedings, October 21–22, 1862, Case File KK-298, RG 153, NA. For statements alleging Martindale's misbehavior at Gaines's Mill and elsewhere, see the examples of D. A. Bennett to Frederick T. Locke, November 28, 1862, and the statements of F. W. Whittelsey, November 24, 1862, Thomas J. Hoyt, November 25, 1862, and F. A. Schoeffel, E. G. Marshall, and Job C. Hedges, all undated but November, 1862, all on Reel 2, FJPP.

26. *New York Tribune*, October 28, 1862; *Frank Leslie's Illustrated Newspaper (New York)*, November 22, 1862, 135.

27. Proceedings, October 21–24, 1862, Case File KK-298, RG 153, NA; *New York Tribune*, October 29, 1862.

28. FJP to GBM, 1:45 P.M., October 21, 1862, to Randolph Marcy, 7:40 P.M., October 22, 1862, and to Seth Williams, October 23, 1862, all on Reel 34, GBMP; *War Diary and Letters of Stephen Minot Weld*, 145–46.

29. FJP to Randolph Marcy, October 16, 1862, Reel 33, GBMP; *OR*, 19(2):465, 492; FJP to Seth Williams, October 23, 1862 (forwarding report of G. K. Warren's quartermaster), Reel 34, GBMP.

30. *New York Herald*, October 23, 1862; *Chicago Tribune*, October 21, 24, 1862.

31. *Chicago Tribune*, October 23, 24, 1862; *Portland (Me.) Daily Press*, October 23, 24, 1862; *OR*, 19(2):485; John D. Wilkins to "My Dearly beloved wife," October 26, 1862, Wilkins Papers, CL; John C. Whiteside to "Dear Mother Church," October 4, 1862, BL; Alexander S. Webb to "My Dear Father," October 29, 1862, Webb Papers, Sterling Library, Yale.

32. FJP to Seth Williams, Rufus Ingalls, Jonathan Letterman, and Henry F. Clarke, October 28, 1862, Dolan Telegrams, NYHS; *OR*, 19(2):505–6, 512, 514; FJP to Randolph Marcy, 11:15 A.M., 2:00 P.M., and two without time, October 30, 1862, Reel 34, GBMP.

33. *War Diary and Letters of Stephen Minot Weld*, 147.

34. *OR*, 19(2):395–96; FJP to Manton Marble, September 30, 1862, Marble Papers, LC; L. A. Whitely to James G. Bennett, September 24, 1862, Bennett Papers, LC.

35. *OR*, 19(2):396.

36. *War Diary and Letters of Stephen Minot Weld*, 217, 227.

37. FJP to Seth Williams, 11:00 A.M., November 1, 1862, and to Randolph Marcy, November 1 (two messages, one 8:00 P.M.), all on Reel 34, GBMP; *OR*, 19(2):112–13, 505–6, 51(1):906–10.

38. *OR*, 19(1):152, 19(2):686; Silver, *Life for the Confederacy*, 114–15.

39. *OR*, 19(2):113–14, 540, 544, 51(1):919–20; Acken, *Inside the Army of the Potomac*, 156–58; *War Diary and Letters of Stephen Minot Weld*, 148–49; FJP to Randolph Marcy, 1:30 P.M., November 2, 1862, 6:00 P.M. November 3, and FJP to GBM, 1:45 P.M., November 2, all on Reel 34, GBMP.

40. *OR*, 19(2):543, 697, 51(1):923; Dowdey and Manarin, *Wartime Papers of Robert E. Lee*, 330; FJP to George Ruggles, 7:00 P.M., November 4, 1862, 3:00 P.M., November 5, Reel 34, GBMP; Circular Order November 5, 1862, General Orders, Special Orders, and Circulars, 36, RG393, Part 2, NA; FJP to GBM, 12:00 P.M., November 7, 1862, Orders and Letters Received and Sent, RG393, Part 2, NA; Nevin, *Diary of Battle*, 121–22; Priest, *From New Bern to Fredericksburg*, 85; Cassedy, *Dear Friends at Home*, 185–86.

41. *OR*, 19(2):545.

42. Burlingame and Ettlinger, *Inside Lincoln's White House*, 232.

43. *Evening Star* (Washington, D.C.), November 4, 7, 1862; *National Republican* (Washington, D.C.), November 4, 1862; *Alexandria (Va.) Gazette*, November 3, 1862.

44. Beale, *Diary of Gideon Welles*, 1:179.

45. *OR*, 19(2):545, 548; Daniel Larned to Mary Burnside, November 9, 1862, Larned Papers, LC; *Chicago Tribune*, September 6, 1875 (the page with Buckingham's account is misdated September 5).

46. FJP to Manton Marble, November 9, 1862, Container 3, Marble Papers, LC.

47. William Adams Moore to "Father," November 18, 1862, Moore Correspondence, NHHS.

48. John D. Wilkins to "My Dearly beloved wife," November 11, 1862, Wilkins Papers, CL; John Bigelow to "Dear Judge," November 10, 1862, Bigelow Letters, NYHS; Nevins, *Diary of Battle*, 125; Benjamin F. Ashenfelter to "Dear Mother," November 12, 1862, Ashenfelter Letters, AHEC; Holden, Ross, and Slomba, *Stand Firm and Fire Low*, 53; Elijah Cavins to "Dear Ann," November 9, 1862, Cavins Papers, Indiana Historical Society; William Speed to "My Dear Sister," November 13, 1862, Speed Letters, CL.

49. Cassedy, *Dear Friends at Home*, 186; Acken, *Inside the Army of the Potomac*, 159; Edward H. C. Taylor to "My dear sister," November 11, 1862, Taylor Civil War Letters, Hobart and William Smith Colleges; John M. Bancroft Diary, November 11, 1862, BL.

50. *OR*, 19(2):569; Cassedy, *Dear Friends at Home*, 188.

51. Priest, *From New Bern to Fredericksburg*, 87; John W. Ames to "My dear Mother," November 16, 1862, Ames Papers, AHEC; Parker, *Henry Wilson's Regiment*, 214.

52. John D. Wilkins to "My Dearly beloved wife," November 13, 1862, Wilkins Papers, CL; L[ouis] N. T[ucker] to "Dear John" [Tucker], November 14, 1862, Reel 2, FJPP; George W. Millens Diary, November 13, 1862, and Irvin Miner Diary, November 12, 1862, quoted in Bertura and Crawford, *4th Michigan Infantry in the Civil War*, 111.

53. William Butler to John Pope, August 30, 1862, Butler Papers, and Pope to Butler, September 26, 1862, Pope Papers, both Chicago History Museum; Pease and Randall, *Diary of Orville Hickman Browning*, 1:584–85.

54. *War Diary and Letters of Stephen Minot Weld*, 150; *Evening Star* (Washington, D.C.),

November 12, 1862; *Daily National Republican* (Washington, D.C.), November 13, 1862 (the *National Republican* became the *Daily National Republican* on November 10, 1862).

55. *War Diary and Letters of Stephen Minot Weld*, 150; *CWP*, 532–33; FJP to Montgomery Blair, May 1, 1863, Reel 35, Blair Family Papers, LC.

56. FJP to J. C. Kelton, November 15, 1862, Reel 2, FJPP; FJP to E. D. Townsend, November 19, 1862, Reel 129, Letters Received (M619), RG94, NA.

57. *Chicago Tribune*, November 22, 1862.

58. Special Order No. 350, Reel 2, FJPP; typescript comments on the trial, Reel 25, FJPP; Williams, *Wild Life of the Army*, 141, 148, 155, 303–16; Pease and Randall, *Diary of Orville Hickman Browning*, 1:539; *New York Tribune*, October 20, 1862; *Buchanan County Guardian* (Independence, Iowa), October 28, 1862. Creating a military commission to investigate charges against an officer was an unusual digression from the customary court of inquiry. The Articles of War specified that a court of inquiry could only be appointed at the request of the officer himself or by the direction of the president, and the commission probably served as an artifice to distance the president from the prosecution.

59. FJP to E. D. Townsend, November 21, 1862, with endorsement of J. C. Kelton, Reel 22, FJPP; FJP to Charles Eames, January 15, 1863, Orders and Letters Received and Sent, RG393, Part 2, NA; FJP to David Hunter and to J. C. Kelton, both November 22, 1862, Reel 2, FJPP.

60. FJP to Edward D. Townsend, November 21, 25, 1862, Reel 129, Letters Received (M619), RG94, NA; *OR*, 12(2, supplement):821; "Court Martial Incidents," Reel 30, FJPP; FJP to Townsend, November 25, 1862, Reel 2, FJPP. Porter's confinement to the hotel was later relaxed.

61. FJP to Harriet, November, 1862, quoted in Eisenschiml, *Celebrated Case of Fitz John Porter*, 74. John Tucker and Adjutant General Edward D. Townsend were probably the two "intimate assistants" of Stanton whom Porter credited with keeping him informed of affairs in that department (see FJP to Adam Badeau, September 22, 1892, Porter Letters, Abraham Lincoln Presidential Library and Museum).

62. Ethan Allen Hitchcock Diary, November 26–28, 1862, Gilcrease Museum. FJP mentions Tucker's comment that the detail of the court "was made to convict" in typescript comments on the trial, Reel 25, FJPP; he reports John Buford's warning in his chronology on Reel 2 as well as in the typewritten comments on Reel 25.

63. Heitman, *Historical Register*, 1:728; typescript comments on the trial, Reel 25, FJPP; *OR*, 12(2, supplement):822; *Impeachment Investigation*, 665. Porter thought Morris questioned the court being appointed (at least nominally) by Halleck rather than by President Lincoln, as the Articles of War required. The *Evening Star* of November 28, 1862, instead supposed Morris had objected that as a Regular Army officer it was not legal for him to sit in judgment on a man who was being tried for conduct as a general of volunteers. He may simply have pointed out that Porter was due a court composed entirely of general officers, and that as a brigadier only by brevet he should not sit.

64. Pease and Randall, *Diary of Orville Hickman Browning*, 1:589.

CHAPTER 15

1. *OR*, 12(2, supplement):822–23; *Evening Star* (Washington, D.C.), December 1, 1862.

2. Reverdy Johnson to Henry Halleck, December 14, 1863, Reel 3, FJPP.

3. *OR*, 12(2, supplement):821, 823–24.

4. *OR*, 12(2, supplement):824; *Daily National Republican* (Washington, D.C.), December 1, 3, 1862; *Cleveland Morning Leader*, December 3, 1862.

5. *OR*, 12(2, supplement):824–26.

6. *OR*, 12(2, supplement):826–27.

7. *OR*, 12(2, supplement):828; *General Regulations for the Army of the United States*, 262.
In *Fitz-John Porter, Scapegoat of Second Manassas*, Donald Jermann contended (216–18)
that there was no conspiracy to convict Porter, but every point in Jermann's argument is
fraught with misunderstanding and misinformation. He discounted a conspiracy because
it would have required corruption on the part of Stanton and Halleck, which he doubted
because Abraham Lincoln trusted both of them and Lincoln "was an excellent judge of
character." In fact, Stanton never hesitated to pervert his authority for political purposes,
and his frequent chicanery illustrated how flawed Lincoln's judgment could be. Stanton's
overbearing nature and Halleck's weak will also lend credence to the inside report that
Stanton gave Halleck the list of officers and that Halleck acquiesced. Jermann also
assumed that the secrecy of the proceedings would have prevented Stanton from knowing
which of the court members to reward for finding Porter guilty, but Jermann failed to
consider that Stanton's crony Holt sat with the court during all its deliberations. Jermann
claimed that reporters covering Porter's original trial believed him guilty, when in fact
the guilty verdict surprised almost all of them. Finally, Jermann defended the absolute
honesty of the court because six members were West Point graduates and the others
later achieved high political office — as though either of those accomplishments were a
guarantee of probity. Many West Point graduates were sentenced to dismissal before and
during the Civil War for mendacity and corrupt practices — including Porter's nominal
accuser, Roberts, who once resigned in disgrace and once had his dismissal annulled by
political intervention. Jermann conducted such limited research on the trial that he was
unaware even of James Garfield's long-published admission that he was wholly prejudiced
against Porter.

8. *OR*, 12(2, supplement):828, 13:658, 668, 709; John Pope to Valentine B. Horton,
November 1, 1862, Civil War Letters Collection, NYHS; Pope to Henry Halleck,
November 13, 1862, Box 34, Banks Papers, LC; *Chicago Tribune*, November 19, 24, 1862
(on the passage of Roberts and Smith to Washington). Cozzens (*General John Pope*, 213–
14) leaves little doubt that Roberts and Smith were Pope's primary henchmen in his effort
to make Porter his scapegoat, and their assorted correspondence confirms it.

9. *OR*, 12(2, supplement):828; *New York Herald*, December 4, 1862.

10. *OR*, 12(2, supplement):829–36, 868.

11. Williams, *Wild Life of the Army*, 191.

12. *OR*, 12(2, supplement):836–38.

13. *OR*, 12(2, supplement):838–39; *Chicago Tribune*, December 5, 1862.

14. John Pope to Joseph Holt, December 4, 1862, Box 35, Holt Papers, LC. James
Garfield identified the location of the court in an interview with the *National Republican*
on April 16, 1878; the address of Butler's restaurant is variously given as 167 or 47
Fourteenth Street (*Evening Star* [Washington, D.C.], September 30, 1863, July 5, 1864,
December 19, 1864).

15. Williams, *Wild Life of the Army*, 188; *OR*, 12(2, supplement):839; *Evening Star*
(Washington, D.C.), December 5, 1862.

16. *OR*, 12(2, supplement):840–41; *Evening Star* (Washington, D.C.), December 5,
1862. One week after proclaiming under oath his disassociation with the prosecution,
Pope offered to go over the prosecution testimony with Holt to determine what other
points still had to be proved. Not quite three years later, Pope openly claimed credit for
prosecuting the case, congratulating himself in an official report that "I considered it a
duty I owed to the country to bring Fitz-John Porter to justice" (John Pope to Joseph

Holt, December 13, 1862, Box 36, Holt Papers, LC; *Supplemental Report of the Joint Committee*, 2:190). In his impressively thorough Ph.D. dissertation on the Porter case, Henry Gabler demonstrated that Pope's claimed distance from the prosecution reflected more of that general's prevarication, meant to preserve the legality of a court ostensibly appointed by Halleck. Their correspondence demonstrates that Holt colluded with Pope in that masquerade, in conjunction with or on behalf of Stanton.

17. *OR*, 12(2, supplement):834, 841–60.

18. James W. Schaumburg to FJP, September 23, 1867, and "S.H.P." [Samuel H. Porter] to Reverdy Johnson, February 24, 1864, both on Reel 3, FJPP; Case Files CC-78, BB-117, EE-506, and GG-210, RG153, NA; John P. Hatch to FJP, September 6, 1866, Chauncey McKeever to FJP, June 21, 1867, and William B. Franklin to FJP, September 20, 1867, all on Reel 3, FJPP. Samuel H. Porter was no apparent relation to FJP.

19. *OR*, 12(2, supplement):868; *Evening Star* (Washington, D.C.) and *New York Herald*, December 10, 1862.

20. *New York Herald*, December 10, 1862; *OR*, 12(2, supplement):868–71.

21. *OR*, 12(2, supplement):868–71.

22. *OR*, 12(2, supplement):872–73.

23. Phil Kearny to O. S. Halsted Jr., August 4, 1862, in *New York Herald*, October 15, 1862.

24. *OR*, 12(2, supplement):875–83.

25. FJP to Harriet, December 10, 1862, and Harriet to her sister, December 11, both quoted in Eisenschiml, *Celebrated Case of Fitz John Porter*, 175, 176.

26. *OR*, 12(2, supplement):888–89; *Evening Star* (Washington, D.C.), December 11, 1862; *Daily National Republican* (Washington, D.C.) and *Chicago Tribune*, December 12, 1862.

27. *OR*, 12(2, supplement):890–91.

28. *OR*, 12(2, supplement):892.

29. *OR*, 12(2, supplement):892, 897.

30. *OR*, 12(2, supplement):894–96. 898.

31. *OR*, 12(2, supplement):890, 894–95, 899.

32. *OR*, 12(2, supplement):900–902.

33. Incidents of the trial, Reel 25, FJPP.

34. *OR*, 12(2, supplement):902–4, 907, 909; *Statement of the Services of the Fifth Army Corps*, 24.

35. *OR*, 12(2, supplement):906; Reverdy Johnson to Henry Halleck, December 14, 1863, Reel 3, FJPP.

36. *OR*, 12(2, supplement):906–11.

37. *OR*, 12(2, supplement):904–5.

38. *OR*, 12(2, supplement):911–14.

39. *OR*, 12(2, supplement):215–17.

40. Williams, *Wild Life of the Army*, 195.

41. *OR*, 12(2, supplement):918–21, 12(3):699–700. The court had employed a stenographer who was able to record questions and answers in real time, which exposes Hunter's suggestion as a disingenuous effort to deprive Porter of effective cross-examination. Had it not threatened to impose a glacial pace on the trial, the rest of the court might well have accommodated Hunter. Other than the initial decision to open the trial to the public, this was the only instance of apparent conflict between members of the court.

42. *OR*, 12(2, supplement):923–25, 937–39.

43. *OR*, 12(2, supplement):926–36; trial chronology, Reel 2, FJPP.

44. *OR*, 12(2, supplement):940–55.

45. *OR*, 12(2, supplement):1035–36, 1043–45.

46. Washington Roebling to FJP, June 8, 1878, Reel 5, FJPP; Joseph C. Willard Diary and transcript version, August 29, 1862, LC; *OR*, Series 12(1):161–62.

47. *OR*, 12(2, supplement):1046–48.

48. *OR*, 12(2, supplement):1047; trial chronology, Reel 2, and incidents of the trial, Reel 25, FJPP; Washington Roebling to FJP, June 8, 1878, Reel 5, FJPP. Johnson, *Reply*, 21, mentions McDowell's court being held in the same building. Warren had intimated his knowledge of McDowell having told Porter to remain in place in a letter to his brother (Gouverneur K. Warren to William J. Warren, September 5, 1862, Box 3, Warren Papers, NYSL).

49. *OR*, 12(1):330. King owned a Republican newspaper in Milwaukee, and received one of Lincoln's earliest ambassadorial appointments (*National Republican* [Washington, D.C.], March 21, 1861; *Watertown [Wis.] Republican*, March 29, 1861; *Emporia [Kans.] News*, March 30, 1861).

50. *OR*, 12(2, supplement):1051, 1053, 12(1):36–323; David Hunter to "Dear Judge" [Joseph Holt], "Monday afternoon" [January 5, 1863], Box 36, Holt Papers, LC.

51. Trial chronology, Reel 2, and lists of witnesses dated December 4, 9, 1862, Reel 22, FJPP.

52. "Extracts from the Journal of Henry J. Raymond," 424.

53. *Evening Star* (Washington, D.C.), December 26, 27, 29, 1862, January 3, 5, 6, 1863; *New York Herald*, December 27, 28, 29, 30, 31, 1862, January 1, 3, 4, 6, 7, 1863; *OR*, 12(2, supplement):1031–46.

54. FJP to Samuel L. M. Barlow, December 29, 1862, Box 41, Barlow Papers, HL.

55. *OR*, 12(2, supplement):1075–85. Johnson, in his *Reply*, 3, credited Eames with preparing the entire defense statement.

56. *OR*, 12(2, supplement):1086–1109.

57. *OR*, 12(2, supplement):1050; Williams, *Wild Life of the Army*, 213.

58. *OR*, 12(2, supplement):1051; *New York Times*, January 12, 1863; *Daily National Republican* (Washington, D.C.), January 12, 1863; *Alexandria (Va.) Gazette*, January 14, 1863. In his *Reply*, 3–4, Reverdy Johnson indicated that the court deliberated for less than three and a half hours, retiring about 2:30 P.M. and rendering its verdict before 6:00 P.M.: that was certainly more than the "few moments" one reporter observed, but it was astonishing celerity in light of such voluminous testimony.

59. *OR*, 12(2, supplement):1051.

60. *OR*, 12(2, supplement):1052, 1134; Webster, *American Dictionary*, 951.

61. *OR*, 12(2, supplement):1112–33, esp. 1123, 1124.

62. *Proceedings and Report*, 2:853–56.

63. *OR*, 12(2, supplement):1051, 1112.

64. Joshua Speed to Joseph Holt, December 31, 1861, Box 31, Holt Papers, LC. For examples of Lincoln's close associates taking advantage of their friendship with him for their own gain or that of others, see Marvel, *Lincoln's Autocrat*, 295–96, 502, n. 37.

65. *OR*, 12(2, supplement):1052; *Proceedings and Report*, 2:320–21. William Newell, who entered Congress in March of 1865, testified in 1878 that Lincoln told him he would welcome the introduction of new evidence in Porter's case, if there was any. Newell was a Republican, which was not common among Porter advocates, but his remarks fit Porter's needs a little too perfectly to avoid at least a little skepticism—besides which, Porter had not yet begun his campaign for a new trial when Newell said he spoke to Lincoln about it.

CHAPTER 16

1. FJP to Harriet, ca. January 15, 1863, quoted in Eisenschiml, *Celebrated Case of Fitz John Porter*, 177, 330; FJP to Charles Eames, January 15, 1863, Orders and Letters Received and Sent, Part 2, RG393, NA; FJP to William C. Prime, July 31, 1863, Reel 3, FJPP. The pay of a major general in 1863 was $445 per month ("Pay of the Army and Navy," 328).

2. *OR*, 12(1):241–48.

3. *OR*, 12(1):249. Porter maintained that his answers would have shown that McDowell lacked the integrity to hold a command, "especially when his interests or his own reputation may come in conflict with the proper administration of justice to others" (FJP to George Cadwallader, January 22, 1863, Reel 22, FJPP).

4. *CWL*, 6:62–63, 65, 67.

5. *New York Tribune, Evening Star* (Washington, D.C.), *Daily National Republican* (Washington, D.C.), *New York Herald, Alexandria (Va.) Gazette*, January 22, 1863; *World* (New York), January 23, 1863; FJP to Stephen M. Weld (both Jr. and Sr.), January 16, 1863, Porter Papers, MHS; *War Letters*, 74. Gabler, "Fitz John Porter Case," 288, thought that a *New York Times* reporter apprised Porter of his conviction, but that newspaper did not mention how Porter learned the news, while the *Tribune* did know how he was told and described his reaction at length. Eisenschiml, who had access to Porter's now-lost correspondence, depicted a *Tribune* reporter informing him (*Celebrated Case of Fitz John Porter*, 171).

6. FJP to Stephen M. Weld Jr., January 16, 1863, Porter Papers, MHS; *Urbana (Ohio) Union*, July 29, 1863; Charles G. Kerr to FJP, June 5, 1867, Reel 3, FJPP; *National Intelligencer* (Washington, D.C.), January 31, 1863; *Weekly National Intelligencer* (Washington, D.C.), February 5, 1863; Joseph Holt to "Dr General," "Tuesday" [January 6, 1863], Box 36, Holt Papers, LC. Pope admitted Smith's involvement (and implied his own) in a letter to Holt dated September 24 [1863] currently misfiled with 1862 correspondence in Box 34, Holt Papers, LC.

7. George G. Meade to Margaret Meade, January 26, 1863, Meade Papers, HSP.

8. Emerson, *Life and Letters of Charles Russell Lowell*, 231–32.

9. Ford, *Cycle of Adams Letters*, 1:250.

10. U.S. Congress, *Senate Executive Journal*, 37th Cong., 3rd sess., January 19, 22, 1863, 33, 59, 89–90; *Alexandria (Va.) Gazette*, January 14, 1863; *OR*, 12(1):218–22, 14:376, 390–91, 23(2):92; Williams, *Wild Life of the Army*, 223–24. Garfield's sojourn with his wife ended on January 19, 1863, and Harry Augustus Garfield was born October 11.

11. Heitman, *Historical Register*, 1:835, 903; George Ruggles to FJP, October 14, 1877, Reel 5, FJPP.

12. *OR*, 12(1):330–31, 29(2):344, 33:732; Heitman, *Historical Register*, 1:830.

13. *General Regulations*, 255; Croffut, *Fifty Years in Camp and Field*, 445; FJP to Stephen M. Weld Sr., January 23, 1863, Porter Papers, MHS; *Daily National Republican* (Washington, D.C.), January 22, 1863; *Evening Star* (Washington, D.C.), January 23, 1863; *New York Herald*, January 24, 1863; *Alexandria (Va.) Gazette*, January 24, 1863; Johnson, *Reply*, 6; Benjamin Prentiss to John A. Logan, March 19, 1880, BV 753, Logan Papers, Abraham Lincoln Presidential Library and Museum. Johnson thought Prentiss did not agree with the sentence, but he may have objected to its lenience; Prentiss told Logan he wished secrecy could be waived so he could reveal who added the prohibition on holding federal office.

14. "The Provocation" (Porter's notes on the trial), Reel 2, FJPP; *CG*, 37th Cong., 3rd

sess., 505, 527; FJP to William Pitt Fessenden, January "21" [27], 1863, Reel 3, FJPP; FJP to Stephen M. Weld Jr., February 22, 1863, Porter Papers, MHS.

15. FJP to George Sykes, January 24, "1862" [1863], Porter Papers, FSNMP; FJP to Stephen M. Weld Sr., February 1, 1863, Porter Papers, MHS; FJP to Samuel L. M. Barlow, February 3, 1863, BW Box 47, Barlow Papers, HL; Alexander Webb to FJP, January 25, 1863, and Daniel Butterfield to FJP, January 26, 1863, both in Porter Papers, USMA Library; Francis J. Parker to FJP, January 23, 1863, Joseph Kirkland to FJP, January 24, 1863, and John A. Morgan to FJP, March 7, 1863, all on Reel 3, FJPP.

16. *New York Tribune*, March 3, 1863; *New York Times*, March 3, 10, 1863; FJP to Samuel L. M. Barlow, May 2, 1863, BW Box 47, Barlow Papers, HL.

17. *New York Herald*, January 22, 1863.

18. Nevins and Thomas, *Diary of George Templeton Strong*, 3:289, 291, 415, 454. A Sixth Corps soldier who was prone to repeating camp rumors assured his father after Porter's trial that "the Battle of Bull Run was lost only because one general would not help another" (Wilson, *Shouts and Whispers*, 117).

19. FJP to Montgomery Blair, May 1, 1863, Reel 24, Blair Family Papers, LC; *CWP*, 541; Charles Griffin to FJP, March 28, 1863, Reel 3, FJPP.

20. Nevins, *Diary of Battle*, 182; Jordan, *Civil War Journals of John Mead Gould*, 264.

21. Beatty, *Citizen-Soldier*, 240.

22. *Daily Evansville (Ind.) Journal*, February 9, 1863; *Gallipolis (Ohio) Journal*, April 2, 1863.

23. Smalley, *Anglo-American Memories*, 154; *New York Tribune*, April 4, June 13, 1863; *New York Herald* and *World* (New York), both June 9, 1863. The Eighty-Fifth Article of War implied that dismissed officers should be shunned by those still in the service (*General Regulations*, 257).

24. For example, see *Portage County Democrat* (Ravenna, Ohio), July 1, 1863; *Daily Gate City* (Keokuk, Iowa), July 2, 1863; *Cadiz (Ohio) Democratic Sentinel*, July 8, 1863; *Rutland (Vt.) Weekly Herald*, July 9, 1863; *White Cloud Kansas Chief*, July 9, 1863; *Western Reserve Chronicle* (Warren, Ohio), July 15, 1863; *Chicago Tribune*, July 18, August 25, September 3, 1863; *Independent* (Oskaloosa, Kans.), July 25, 1863; *Daily Intelligencer* (Wheeling, W.Va.), August 22, 1863; and *Portland (Me.) Daily Press*, September 14, 1863.

25. FJP to William C. Prime, July 31, 1863, Reel 3, FJPP; Helen McCalla Diary, July 17, 1863, LC; Nevins and Thomas, *Diary of George Templeton Strong*, 3:335–40; *Cleveland Morning Leader*, July 18, 1863; *Democrat and Sentinel* (Ebensburg, Pa.), July 22, 1863.

26. FJP to William C. Prime, July 31, 1863, Reel 3, FJPP; GBM to Erastus Corning, August 1, 1863, Gratz Collection, HSP.

27. Frederick T. Locke to FJP, July 12, 1863, and FJP to William C. Prime, July 5, 1863, both on Reel 3, FJPP.

28. Johnson, *Reply*, 3. Publishing condensed the trial record to 298 pages (Johnson, *Reply*, 4).

29. Johnson, *Reply*, 5–6.

30. Johnson, *Reply*, 8–10.

31. Johnson, *Reply*, 8–10; Holt, *Review*, 11–12.

32. Johnson, *Reply*, 10–13.

33. Johnson, *Reply*, 14.

34. *General Regulations*, 92; Johnson, *Reply*, 8.

35. *Alexandria (Va.) Gazette*, August 5, 7, 1863; William S. Murdoch to Reverdy Johnson, August 20, 1863, Reel 3, FJPP.

36. *Evening Star* (Washington, D.C.), August 19, 1863; *New York Tribune*, September

15, 1863; FJP to William C. Prime, September 4, 8, 1863, and Robert Patterson Jr. to FJP, September 26, 1863, both on Reel 3, FJPP; *Columbia Democrat* (Bloomsburg, Pa.), August 15, 1863; *Cadiz (Ohio) Democratic Sentinel*, August 26, 1863.

37. *Daily Intelligencer* (Wheeling, W.Va.), August 22, 1863; *Washington (D.C.) Chronicle*, September 19, 1863; John Pope to Joseph Holt, "September 24" [1863], Box 34, Holt Papers.

38. Reverdy Johnson to FJP, September 19, 1863, Reel 3, FJPP.

39. *Boston Daily Advertiser*, quoted in *Weekly National Intelligencer* (Washington, D.C.), September 3, 1863.

40. FJP to Samuel L. M. Barlow, August 5, 1863, BW Box 47, Barlow Papers, HL; FJP to William C. Prime, August 22, 1863, FJP to Hiram Ketchum, September 25, 1863 (draft), and Robert Patterson Jr. to FJP, September 26, 1863, all on Reel 3, FJPP; FJP to Ketchum, September 12, 1863, published in *Daily Ohio Statesman* (Columbus), September 24, 1863.

41. Joseph Kennedy to FJP, August 25, September 23, 1863, Henry Noble Strong to FJP, August 26, 1863, Stephen M. Weld Jr. to FJP, August 28, September 10, 1863, Joseph Hayes to FJP, January 21, 1864, all on Reel 3, FJPP.

42. *Atchison (Kans.) Champion*, quoted in the *Union (Junction City, Kans.)*, February 13, 1864; *Emporia (Kans.) News*, February 13, 1864.

43. Fossett, *Colorado*, 253; *New York Times*, March 28, 1864; Supplement to the *New York Herald*, March 31, 1864.

44. Fossett, *Colorado*, 253, 255, 256. Trustees and officers of the two companies are listed on advertisements (along with Porter's titles) in every issue of the *American Mining Gazette and Geological Magazine* for 1865.

45. *Rocky Mountain News* (Denver), January 19, 1865.

46. CWP, 626; *American Citizen* (Butler, Pa.), October 19, 1864; *Tiffin (Ohio) Weekly Tribune*, October 20, 1864; *Chicago Tribune*, October 30, 1864; *Xenia (Ohio) Sentinel*, November 4, 1864; *New York Times*, November 9, 1864; FJP to William C. Prime, November 8, 1864, Reel 3, FJPP; *Private and Official Correspondence of Gen. Benjamin F. Butler*, 5:305, 327. Decades later, Butler exaggerated this even further, claiming that Stanton warned him Porter meant to instigate a riot and declare the city's entire vote for McClellan, driving would-be Republican voters from the polls (Butler, *Butler's Book*, 753–54).

47. "Gunnell Gold Mining Company," 287–88; "New York Gold Mining Company, of Colorado," 30–31.

48. FJP to William H. Russell, August 26, 1864, to Edward P. Tesson, October 15, November 10, December 3, 13, 1864, and to Alfred E. Tilton, November 28, 1864, all on Reel 22, FJPP.

49. OR, Series 3, 4:432, 608;41(1):237–40, 969–71, 41(2):673; *Rocky Mountain News* (Denver), August 16, 1864; Fossett, *Colorado*, 256–57; FJP to William H. Russell, December 18, 1864, to "My dear Sir," December 20, 1864, and to Frederick Schuchardt, March 28, 1865, all on Reel 22, FJPP. The Sand Creek massacre put Porter on the same side as Senator Ben Wade, chairman of the Joint Committee on the Conduct of the War, who also abhorred the mass murder of innocent Cheyenne.

50. FJP to Joseph Thatcher, November 10, 1864, to Francis Lathrop, November 10, 1864, to Joseph Kenyon and Robert Willis, November 11, 1864, to Ben Holliday, November 26, 27, 1864, to W. L. Halsey, November 26, 1864, to Alfred E. Tilton, November 28, 1864, to James A. Harlan, November 28, 1864, to Samuel L. M. Barlow, November 29, December 18, 1864, January 11, 1865, to Gilbert C. Currie, November 30, 1864, to W. G. Williams, December 12, 1864, to Hugh Butler, December 24, 1865, to W. F. Roelofson, January 7, 1865, to William H. Russell, January 9, April 2, 1865, to Louis E. Johnson, January 12,

"1864" [1865], to John W. Reminey, February 1, 1865, to Roger Jones, February 12, 1865, to Theodore Randolph, February 13, 27, 1865, and to James Mills, April 7, 1865, all on Reel 22, FJPP; FJP to William C. Prime, July 1, 1865, Reel 3, FJPP; FJP to Barlow, January 11, 24, 30, February 14, 20, March 7, 11, 1865, BW Box 59, Barlow Papers, HL.

51. FJP to "General" [Brigadier General Patrick Edward Connor], April 16, 1865, Reel 22, FJPP.

52. FJP to "General" [Brigadier General Patrick Edward Connor], April 16, 1865, Reel 22, FJPP; *Rocky Mountain News (Denver)*, March 4, 1865; *Montana Post (Virginia City)*, May 20, 1865.

53. Fossett, *Colorado*, 257; FJP to William C. Prime, July 1, 1865, Reel 3, FJPP; tax schedule, Black Hawk, Colorado, June, 1865, and FJP to S. E. Brown, May 31, 1865, both on Reel 22, FJPP; *Daily Gate City* (Keokuk, Iowa), August 26, 1865; *Chicago Tribune*, August 24, 1865; *Baltimore County Union*, September 2, 1865.

54. FJP biographical notes, Reel 25, FJPP; Evelina Porter headstone, Indian Hill Cemetery, Middletown, Conn.; FJP passport application, December 6, 1865, Reel 135, U.S. Passport Applications, 1795–1925 (M1372), RG59, NA; *Raftsman's Journal* (Clearfield, Pa.), February 14, 1866; *Evening News* (Gold Hill, Nev. Terr.), April 3, 1866; FJP to William Traverse, July 27, 1866, May 5, 1867, and to James Mills, April 5, 1867, all on Reel 22, FJPP; *New York Times*, March 23, 1866. On this passport application Porter gave his birthdate as August 31, 1825, rather than 1822.

55. FJP to William C. Prime, June 2, 1866, and John A. Rolston to FJP, June 2, 1866, both on Reel 3, FJPP; *Portland (Me.) Daily Press*, May 24, 1866; *Montana Post* (Virginia City), July 28, 1866.

56. Swinton, *Campaigns of the Army of the Potomac*, 5, 186–87; *Evening Star* (Washington, D.C.), May 9, 1866; *Nashville Daily Union*, May 9, 1866; *Public Ledger* (Memphis, Tenn.), May 10, 1866; *Chicago Tribune*, May 11, 1866; *New York Tribune*, May 31, 1866; *Daily Evening Telegraph (Philadelphia)*, June 2, 1866; *Evening Argus* (Rock Island, Ill.), July 16, 1866.

57. Pope to Thomas C. H. Smith, May 9, 1866, February 12, 1869, March 17, 1874, June 10, 1885, Box 1, Smith Papers, OHC.

58. *West-Jersey Pioneer* (Bridgeton, N.J.), June 30, 1866; FJP to John Howe, July 31, 1866, Reel 22, FJPP.

59. *New York Times*, September 29, 30, October 15, 1865; FJP to William C. Prime, October 8, 1868 (on Spring Mountain Coal Company letterhead), Reel 3, FJPP; FJP to "My dear Cousin" [Robert H. Eddy], August 7, 1866, to Ambrose Burnside and Erastus Corning, both August 27, 1866, and to treasurer of M&ERR, September 10, 1867, all on Reel 22, FJPP. Porter's first civilian income dwarfed that of William B. Franklin, who took an executive position with the Colt Firearms Company that year at an annual salary of $6,000 (Franklin Diary, November 15, 1865, Connecticut State Library).

60. FJP to Alfred H. Guernsey, July 6, 1866, and to Manton Marble, July 8, 1866, Reel 22, FJPP; Nevins and Thomas, *Diary of George Templeton Strong*, 4:98; *New York Tribune, New York Herald*, and *Sun (New York)*, August 20, 1866; FJP to George Batchelder, August 20, 1866, and Batchelder to FJP, August 26, 1866, both on Reel 22, FJPP.

61. FJP to Marsena Patrick, John P. Hatch, and Chauncey McKeever, August 20, 1866, all on Reel 22, FJPP.

CHAPTER 17

1. Marsena Patrick to FJP, August 24, 1866, and John P. Hatch to FJP, September 6, 1866, both on Reel 3, FJPP.

2. *St. Cloud (Minn.) Democrat*, June 28, 1866; *Lewistown (Pa.) Gazette*, August 15, 1866; FJP to James Longstreet, September 7, 1866, Reel 22, FJPP; Longstreet to FJP, September 23, 1866, Reel 3, FJPP. In the bound version of Moore, *Rebellion Record*, the Confederate reports appear in 9:569–726.

3. James Longstreet to FJP, October 7, 1867, FJP to Robert E. Lee, October 25, 1867, both on Reel 3, FJPP; Lee to FJP, October 31, 1867, Reel 22, FJPP; FJP to Charles Marshall, January 22, 1870, Porter Papers, FSNMP; John F. Lee to FJP, July 24, 1870, handwritten transcript in Reel 37, GBMP.

4. Robert Eddy to FJP, January 2, 1867, George Batchelder to FJP, November 26, 1866, FJP to William C. Prime, January 10, 1867, W. C. Patterson to FJP, January 19, 1867, Franklin Pierce to FJP, September 18, 1866, and Millard Fillmore to FJP, September 19, 24, 1866, all on Reel 3, FJPP.

5. FJP to Andrew Johnson, January 14, 1867, with attached letters, Reel 22, FJPP; FJP to William C. Prime, January 29, 1867, Reel 3, FJPP.

6. David Dixon Porter to Andrew Johnson, February 21, 1867, W. C. Patterson to FJP, February 4, 1867, Marsena Patrick to FJP, February 23, 1867, Hyatt Ransom to FJP, June 11, 1867, and Chauncey McKeever to FJP, June 21, 1867, all on Reel 3, FJPP.

7. Deed Book D, 34–36, and Mortgages, Book N2, 189, Morris County Courthouse. Beers, *Atlas of Morris Co.*, 9, indicates that the site of Porter's home is now occupied by the front parking lot of the Morristown Medical Center.

8. FJP to Reverdy Johnson, May 4, 1867, Reel 22, FJPP.

9. *Evening Star* (Washington, D.C.), August 4, 1867; William Moore Diary, August 5, 6, 11, 12, 1867, Reel 50, Johnson Papers, LC; Holt, *Vindication*, 6; Beale, *Diary of Gideon Welles*, 3:167–69; Johnson to Edwin Stanton, August 12, 1867, Reel 12, Stanton Papers, LC. On Holt and the Mary Surratt petition, see Marvel, *Lincoln's Autocrat*, 382–86.

10. Ulysses Grant to "General" [FJP], September 10, 1867, FJP to "My dear friend" [Theodore Randolph], September 12, 1867, and FJP endorsement on copy of Grant to FJP, September 13, 1867, all on Reel 3, FJPP.

11. *PUSG*, 17:332–36.

12. William G. Moore to FJP, September 14, 1867, Ulysses Grant to FJP, September 13, 1867, with FJP endorsement, and FJP to Grant, September 16, 1867, all on Reel 3, FJPP.

13. *PUSG*, 17:329–32; FJP to Manton Marble, September 18, 1867, Box 15, Marble Papers, LC.

14. FJP to Ulysses Grant, September 18, 1867, Reel 3, FJPP.

15. William B. Franklin to FJP, September 20, 1867, and James W. Schaumburg to FJP, September 20, 23, 1867, both on Reel 3, FJPP; *PUSG*, 17:336–38; printed proceedings in the court martial of Benjamin S. Roberts, Reel 1, FJPP. The reputations of two of those dismissed in 1848, George Crittenden and Lucius Northrop, suffered again in Confederate service.

16. FJP to "My dear Friend" [Theodore Randolph], September 21, 1867, Reel 3, FJPP; *New York Times*, January 30, 1870, identifies Townsend as Stanton's executor.

17. *CG*, 40th Cong., 1st sess., 802; FJP to Manton Marble, December 3, 19, 26, 1867, Box 16, Marble Papers, LC; U.S. Congress, *Senate Journal*, 40th Cong., 2nd sess., 30, 48; *CG*, 40th Cong., 2nd sess., 132–34.

18. *CG*, 40th Cong., 2nd sess., 232, 1498–1500; *Western Reserve Chronicle* (Warren, Ohio), March 30, 1870.

19. *CG*, 40th Cong., 2nd sess., 1500–1501; *OR*, 2:163–64.

20. William G. Moore to FJP, February 27, 1869, Reel 3, FJPP.

21. FJP to Manton Marble, January 25, 1868, Box 16, Marble Papers, LC; Porter's furious note about the "stolen" documents is on Reel 3, FJPP.

22. George Batchelder to Zachariah Chandler, May 6, 1868, Reel 3, FJPP.

23. Horace Binney Sargent to Ulysses Grant, July 28, 1869, Joshua Chamberlain to FJP, August 14, 1869, Alexander McClure to FJP, September 14, 1869, William S. Tilton to FJP, September 23, 1869, and George H. Thomas to FJP, October 18, 1869, all on Reel 3, FJPP.

24. *Appeal to the President*, 1–6; *PUSG*, 19:524–25.

25. *PUSG*, 19:525–26; John Pope to William W. Belknap, December 6, 1869, Reel 3, FJPP; "Brief Statement of the Case of Fitz John Porter," File R574, Letters Received, 1867 (M619), Reel 581, RG94, NA. The pamphlet is also published in *Proceedings and Report*, 2:728–34. McDowell later admitted sending the excerpt to Pope (*Proceedings and Report*, 2:724).

26. Extensive documentation of the nine-year process of uncovering Pope's deception is filed with Porter's appeal (File R574) in Letters Received, 1867 (M619), Reel 581, RG94, NA: John Pope to Edmund Schriver, December 30, 1869, Schriver to Pope, January 7, 1870, Pope to E. D. Townsend, February 1, 1870, FJP to William T. Sherman, May 31, 1871, and to William W. Belknap, November 14, 1871, Joseph Holt to Belknap, December 13, 1871, Oscar Mack to Pope, December 15, 1871, Pope to Mack, December 19, 1871, John Gibbon to Townsend, September 25, November 15, 1874, September 30, 1878, Townsend to Gibbon, October 7, 1874, Charges and Specifications dated September 30, 1878 (Case File DD 4689), and Pope to Sherman, October 22, 23, 1878. See also Gibbon to Pope, July 24, August 24, September 17, November 5, 1874, Reel 4, and Gibbon to FJP, December 20, 1877, Reel 5, all in FJPP.

27. *CG*, 41st Cong., 2nd sess., 1444–48.

28. *Gen'l Fitz John Porter's Reply*; Waterman Ormsby to William Blair Lord, May 22, 1870, Container 63, Joseph Holt to Lord, May 27, 1871 (copy), and Lord to Holt, May 30, 1871, Container 64, all in Holt Papers, LC. The dates on the three letters are inconsistent with the order in which their content implies they were written.

29. Waterman Ormsby to William Blair Lord, May 22, 1870, Container 63, and Lord to Joseph Holt, May 30, 1871, Container 64, both in Holt Papers, LC; *Proceedings and Report*, 2:640, 910. Lord's 1878 version of Porter's alleged utterance implies that his inconsistent quotation from a letter to his wife was fabricated, perhaps from the dialogue suggested by Ormsby's misdated letter.

30. *Proceedings and Report*, 2:638–44, 909–19, 3:1269–70.

31. Joseph Holt to William Blair Lord, May 27, 1871, Container 64, Holt Papers, LC; *Proceedings and Report*, 2:912–13. For examples of Holt's efforts to suborn perjury, see Marvel, *Lincoln's Autocrat*, 378, 408, 425, and George, "Subornation of Perjury in the Lincoln Conspiracy Trial?"

32. William Blair Lord to Joseph Holt, November 13, 1864, Container 45, Holt Papers, LC.

33. FJP to H. W. Tilton, April 8, May 2, 1867, to Gardner Childers, May 2, 1867, to J. D. Test, May 27, 1867, to Messrs. Corliss, November 7, 1867, to Byron Reed, September 27, 1869, and to Stephenson & Pierson, December 9, 1870, all on Reel 22, FJPP; Wilson G. Hunt to Theodore Randolph, July 19, 1870, Reel 4, FJPP; Deed Book B8, 561–64, Morris County Courthouse. Porter located his bounty land "at Nebraska City" (FJP to Cassady & Test, May 5, 1867), but the Otoe County Deed Books from 1855 to 1900 record no property in Porter's name.

34. William Newell to Theodore Randolph, March 11, 1870, Porter Papers, MHS;

Proceedings and Report, 2:320–21. In 1861 Lincoln alluded to Newell as one of his old allies from Congress (*CWL*, 4:502).

35. John F. Lee to FJP, March 15, 1870, Charles Marshall to FJP, June 14, 16, 21, 25, 1870, James Longstreet to FJP, June 16, 1870, Cadmus Wilcox to FJP, April 25, October 26, November 11, 1871, Jubal Early to FJP, May 9, 1871, and Gouverneur K. Warren to FJP, May 9, 1871, all on Reel 4, FJPP; FJP to Marshall, June 11, 1869, Chicago Public Library.

36. FJP to William W. Belknap, January 9, 1871, with maps and notes, Theodore Randolph to George W. McCrary, May 30, 1878, and McCrary to Randolph, June 11, 1878, all in File R574, Letters Received (M619), Reel 581, RG94, NA.

37. *Alexandria (Va.) Gazette*, May 15, 1871; *Wheeling (W.Va.) Daily Register*, May 19, 1871.

38. Joshua Chamberlain to James McQuade, May 14, 1874, Reel 4, FJPP.

39. John Gibbon to FJP, February 24, 1874, Reel 4, FJPP.

40. *Annual Reports*, 7; *West-Jersey Pioneer* (Bridgeton, N.J.), January 12, 1872; *Chicago Tribune*, January 29, February 3, 1872.

41. *Annual Reports*, 7, 90–91; *West-Jersey Pioneer* (Bridgeton, N.J.), January 12, 1872; *Report of the Commissioners*, 11–13; *Robinson's Atlas of Morris County*, 13.

42. *Report of the Commissioners*, 11–13.

43. FJP to Ulysses Grant, October 28, 1874, B. R. Curtis to William T. Sherman, January 30, 1874, Reverdy Johnson to FJP, October 24, 1874, Charles O'Conor opinion, October 22, 1874, J. B. Schweitzer to Society of the Fifth Army Corps, May 1, 1874, James A. Watson to Grant, August 14, 1874, John Hartrtanft to Grant, September 2, 1874, all in File R574, Letters Received, 1867 (M619), Reel 581, RG94, NA; dozens of pages of petition signatures, Reel 4, FJPP; *Chicago Tribune*, May 13, 1874; *Indiana State Sentinel (Indianapolis)*, May 19, 1874; *Opinions and Memorials in the Case of Fitz John Porter*.

44. FJP to James A. Garfield, January 28, February 3, 1875, Reel 30, Garfield Papers, LC; U.S. Congress, *Journal of the House*, 43rd Cong., 2nd sess., January 18, 1875, 198; Garfield to FJP, February 19, 1875, Reel 4, FJPP.

45. John Pope to Montgomery Blair, February 12, 1874, and Blair to Pope, February 17, Reel 35, Blair Family Papers, LC; Pope to Thomas C. H. Smith, March 22, 1873, February 12, July 26, 1874, Smith Papers, OHC.

46. Joseph D. Bedle to Ulysses Grant, April 5, 1875, File R574, Letters Received, 1867 (M619), Reel 581, RG94, NA; *West-Jersey Pioneer* (Bridgeton, N.J.), March 4, 1875; *New York Herald*, December 31, 1871; *New York Times* and *World* (New York), March 2, 1875.

47. Francis Lathrop et al., to FJP, March 16, 1875, Reel 4, FJPP. The original buildings of the asylum survived intact and structurally sound amid a maze of later additions until 2015, when the last of the entire complex was finally demolished.

48. *New York Times*, March 2, 4, 1875.

49. Nevins and Thomas, *Diary of George Templeton Strong*, 4:553; *New York Times*, March 4, 6, 12, 15, 20, April 3, 6, September 23, November 17, 1875, January 16, 1876; *New York Tribune*, August 27, 1875; *New York Herald*, May 21, December 28, 1875.

50. *West-Jersey Pioneer* (Bridgeton, N.J.), April 1, 1875; John Pope to Thomas C. H. Smith, July 26, 1874, April 12, 1875, Smith Papers, OHC; FJP to the adjutant general, June 5, 1878 (asking for the judge advocate general's report of April 8, 1875), and Belknap's unsigned confidential memorandum of May 31, 1875, both in File R574, Letters Received (M619), Reel 581, RG94, NA.

51. *New York Herald*, May 21, 1875, January 14, 1876; *New York Tribune*, August 27, 1875.

52. *Fitz John Porter, Commissioner of Public Works, to Andrew H. Green, Comptroller of the City of New York*, December 2, 1875; *New York Times*, September 23, October 17, November

17, 1875, January 7, 11, 12, 13, 1876; *New York Herald*, January 7, 1876. Porter's travails as commissioner of public works are outlined in Logel, *Designing Gotham*, 159–61.

53. *New York Times* and *New York Herald*, January 14, 1876; Adolphus Wydler to FJP, January 19, 1876, Reel 4, FJPP.

54. William B. Franklin to FJP, July 1, 1876, FJP to Stephen M. Weld Jr., July 8, 1876, Comte de Paris to FJP, August 4, 1876, and Gouverneur K. Warren to FJP, November 7, 1876, all in Porter Papers, MHS; FJP to GBM, August 17, 1876, Reel 38, GBMP; Montgomery Blair to FJP, December 1, 1874, Blair Family Papers, LC; Heitman, *Historical Register*, 1:539.

55. *Alexandria Gazette and Virginia Advertiser*, May 17, 1873; FJP to Stephen M. Weld Jr., September 30, 1876, March 15, 1877, Porter Papers, MHS.

56. *New York Herald*, September 30, 1876, February 16, March 28, 1877.

57. *New York Herald*, October 31, 1876; FJP to Stephen M. Weld Jr., January 8, 1877, Porter Papers, MHS; FJP to John P. Nicholson, February 25, 1877, Nicholson Collection, HL.

58. Rutherford B. Hayes to "Dear Uncle," November 12, 1862, and to John Pope, April 6, 1870, Hayes Papers, RBHPL.

CHAPTER 18

1. FJP to Stephen M. Weld Jr., February 16, March 13, 15, May 17, June 9, August 13, September 15, 24, 1877, and George Morell to Porter, May 26, 1877 (two letters), all in Porter Papers, MHS; FJP to George Batchelder, August 20, 1866, and Batchelder to FJP, August 26, 1866, both on Reel 22, FJPP.

2. *Proceedings and Report*, 2:340–41; FJP to Stephen M. Weld Jr., September 24, 1877, Porter Papers, MHS.

3. FJP to Stephen M. Weld Jr., August 10, October 1, December 30, 1877, Porter Papers, MHS. The part of Ropes's address that criticized Pope and McDowell, and absolved Porter, was delivered in Boston on March 12, 1877, and was first published by the society in 1886 before being included finally in Dwight, *Virginia Campaign of 1862*, v, 73–97. Weld's address appears in pages 223–62 of the same volume.

4. FJP to Theodore Randolph, December 26, 27, 1877, and Randolph to FJP, December 29, 30, 1877, all on Reel 5, FJPP; Rutherford B. Hayes to Sardis Birchard, November 12, 1862, Hayes Papers, RBHPL.

5. Theodore Randolph to FJP, January 12, 1878, and George Hoar to Frank Parker, February 23, 1878, both on Reel 5, FJPP.

6. FJP to Rutherford B. Hayes, March 9, 1878, File R574, Letters Received, 1867 (M619), Reel 581, RG94, NA; *New York Times*, *New York Herald*, *Evening Star* (Washington, D.C.), and *National Republican* (Washington, D.C.), all April 13, 1878.

7. FJP to Gouverneur K. Warren, April 6, 10, 15, May 27, June 3, 8, 10, 13, 17, 1878, Warren to FJP, May 20, 29, 1878, and J. A. Judson to FJP, June 12, 1878, all in Warren Papers, NYSL.

8. FJP to Gouverneur K. Warren, June 27, 1878, Warren Papers, NYSL; Heitman, *Historical Register*, 1:445; *New York Tribune*, December 25, 1900, October 21, 1901.

9. U.S. Senate, *Message from the President of the United States*, Ex. Doc. 1, 30th Cong., 1st sess., 93; *OR*, 11(2):230; Alfred Terry to "Dear Sissy," November 16, 1862, Terry Family Papers, Sterling Library, Yale; George Ruggles to FJP, April 26, 1878, Reel 5, FJPP.

10. Proceedings in the trials of John M. Schofield, Nelson Bowman Sweitzer, Samuel Kinsey et al., Case File HH-215, RG153, NA; Schofield, *Forty-Six Years in the Army*, 241–42.

11. *Carbon Advocate* (Lehighton, Pa.), June 22, 1878; *Proceedings and Report*, 2:64–68; *New York Tribune*, June 26, 27, 1878.

12. Anson Maltby to John C. Bullitt, May 28, 1878, Reel 6, FJPP.

13. *Proceedings and Report*, 2:64, 67, 71–76; *New York Herald*, June 29, 1878.

14. Gouverneur K. Warren's big map, or a copy thereof, lies in his papers at NYSL.

15. *Proceedings and Report*, 2:77–88, 93–94, 98–99. In the report he submitted right after Porter was dismissed, Pope conceded that the fighting subsided to "very severe skirmishes" between noon and 4:00 P.M. on August 29; see *OR*, 12(2):39. Schofield or the board as a whole overruled most — but not all — of Gardner's objections. See, for examples, *Proceedings and Report*, 2:139, 320, 357, 377, 630, 644–45, 676–77, 691, 698–99, 717, 719, 723, 727–28, 736, 737, 746, 749, 750, 752, 768, 770, 784, 795, 813, 815–16, 853–54, 862, 882, 3:1093.

16. *Proceedings and Report*, 2:113–33, 140, 146–47, 152, 156–57, 161, 166–67, 196, 203–4, 239, 244–45, 252, 325, 337.

17. *Proceedings and Report*, 2:305–6.

18. *Proceedings and Report*, 2:68–69, 358, 364, 370, 371; Pope to Thomas C. H. Smith, December 16, 1874, April 12, 1875, and Asa Bird Gardner to Smith, December 25, 1878, Box 1, Smith Papers, OHC.

19. *Proceedings and Report*, 2:365–69, 377–80.

20. *Proceedings and Report*, 2:380–81.

21. *Proceedings and Report*, 2:381–82.

22. *Proceedings and Report*, 2:389, 393–95, 399, 922; *OR*, 12(2, supplement):875, 1031.

23. *Proceedings and Report*, 2:393–95, 559–60, 563–64, 566–79, 595–96.

24. *Proceedings and Report*, 2:576–78, 609–13, 616–19, 628, 3:1095–1106, 1107–16.

25. Thomas C. H. Smith to Joseph Holt, Container 72, Holt Papers, LC; *Proceedings and Report*, 2:837–41, 844–53, 897–907, 3:1251–52, 1267–71, 1707; Basil T. Bowers to the adjutant general, July 2, 1878, File R574, Letters Received, 1867 (M619), Reel 581, RG94, NA.

26. *Proceedings and Report*, 3:1057–63, 1260.

27. *Proceedings and Report*, 3:997–1107, 1119, 1197.

28. *Proceedings and Report*, 2:321, 324, 819–37, 863–81.

29. *Proceedings and Report*, 2:853–56; *Alexandria Gazette and Virginia Advertiser*, October 15, 1878.

30. *Proceedings and Report*, 2:776, 3:952–58, 1018, 1026–36; Irvin McDowell to the adjutant general, August 20, 1878, File R574, Letters Received, 1867 (M619), Reel 581, RG94, NA.

31. *Proceedings and Report*, 2:741.

32. *Proceedings and Report*, 2:771–74, 776, 794.

33. *Proceedings and Report*, 2:720–25, 735–37; Moore, *Rebellion Record*, 9:578. The paragraphs in Jackson's report are more logically divided in *OR*, 12(2):646–47, making the transition to August 30 much more obvious.

34. *Proceedings and Report*, 2:738–40, 753.

35. *Proceedings and Report*, 2:765–67.

36. *Proceedings and Report*, 2:779–82.

37. *Proceedings and Report*, 2:774–77, 786–87.

38. *Supplemental Report*, 2:190; *Daily Herald* (Los Angeles), October 20, 1878; *Portland (Me.) Daily Press* and *New North-West* (Deer Lodge, Mont. Terr.), October 25, 1878; *Cincinnati Star*, October 29, 1878; John M. Schofield to John Pope, October 18, 21, 1879, Box 82, Schofield Papers, LC.

39. John M. Schofield to "My dear Gen." [Alfred Terry], December 5, 1878, copy in

Box 2, Gibson-Getty McClure Families Papers, LC; John Millis to "Pa," January 11, 1879, Millis Correspondence, CL.

40. *Sun* (New York), October 21, 1878; *Alexandria Gazette and Virginia Advertiser*, October 15, 1878; *Boston Evening Transcript*, October 16, 1878; *New York Herald*, October 25, 1878, March 23, 1879; *Portland (Me.) Daily Press*, March 24, 1879; *Public Ledger* (Memphis, Tenn.), April 2, 1879; *Evening Star* (Washington, D.C.), April 2, 3, 1879.

41. *Proceedings and Report*, 3:1699–710.

42. *Proceedings and Report*, 3:1719.

43. *Proceedings and Report*, 3:1665, 1720.

44. *Proceedings and Report*, 3:1720.

45. FJP to John A. Schofield, March 31, April 7, 1879, Box 82, Schofield Papers, LC; FJP to George W. Getty, April 5, 1879, Box 2, Gibson-Getty-McClure Families Papers, LC; Montgomery Blair to FJP, April 3, 1879, Reel 23, and Joseph Twitchell to FJP, April 29, 1879, Reel 9, both in FJPP; *Nation* (New York), 28, no. 719 (April 10, 1879): 240, and no. 720 (April 17, 1879): 260–62.

46. *Chicago Tribune*, April 10, 1879; *Newtown (Conn.) Bee*, April 15, 1879.

47. Manning F. Force to Rutherford B. Hayes, April 21, October 23, 1878, April 22, 1879, Hayes Papers, RBHPL; John Pope to Force, January 15, November 12, 1878, March 31, April 11, 18, 1879, and FJP to Force, January 17, 1882, all on Reel 4, Force Papers, University of Washington; "The Fitz-John Porter Inquest," *Cincinnati Daily Gazette*, April 18, 1879.

48. Theodore Randolph to FJP, April 29, 1879, and to John C. Bullitt, May 3, 1879, both on Reel 9, FJPP; FJP to John A. Schofield, May 5, 1879, Box 82, Schofield Papers, LC.

49. Rutherford B. Hayes to Manning F. Force, April 26, 1879, Hayes Papers, RBHPL; *Evening Star* (Washington, D.C.), March 6, 19, May 26, June 5, 1879; *Daily Globe* (St. Paul, Minn.), May 29, 1879; Irvin McDowell to "My dear Mrs. Garfield," December 6, 1870, Lucretia Rudolph Garfield Papers, LC; Alfred Terry to John A. Schofield, May 28, 1879, Box 82, Schofield Papers, LC.

50. William W. Burns to FJP, October 13, 1879, Schoff Collection, CL.

51. Ambrose Burnside to FJP, July 17, 30, 1878, August 20, 1879, and FJP to Ben Perley Poore, August 30, 1883, all on Reel 2, FJPP.

52. *CR*, 46th Cong., 2nd sess., 112; *New York Times*, August 7, 1879.

53. *CR*, 46th Cong., 2nd sess., 492–500, 778, 803, 938, 1222–27, 1357; U.S. Senate, *Views of the Minority*, 46th Cong., 2nd sess., S. Rep. 158, 1; FJP to Benjamin Perley Poore, August 30, 1883, Reel 2, FJPP.

54. FJP to Stephen M. Weld Jr., March 22, 1880, Porter Papers, MHS; James A. Garfield's notes, Reel 50, Garfield Papers, LC.

55. Jacob Cox to James A. Garfield, February 14, 1880 (copy), Porter Papers, AAS; Ambrose Burnside to Garfield, March 2, 1880, Reel 51, Garfield Papers, LC. To prove Longstreet's later arrival, Cox relied on information implied by the testimony of Benjamin S. White, of J. E. B. Stuart's staff, but William W. Blackford, also of Stuart's staff, contradicted White on two key points (*Proceedings and Report*, 2:672–75, 3:984–85).

56. James A. Garfield to William T. Sherman, February 19, 1880, Reel 26, Sherman Papers, LC; *Princeton (Minn.) Union*, March 10, 1880; FJP to Stephen M. Weld Jr., March 22, 1880, Porter Papers, MHS.

57. Sherman to John M. Schofield, March 5, 1880, typescript of Schofield Board record, Orders, Proceedings, and Other Records, RG153, NA; John M. Schofield to William T. Sherman, March 8, 9, 10, 13, 29, 1880, Reel 27, Sherman Papers, LC.

58. *Evening Star* (Washington, D.C.), March 2, 4, 1880; *New York Tribune* (Washington, D.C.), March 3, 4, 5, 6, 1880; *New York Times*, March 3, 6, 1880; *Chicago Tribune*, March 3,

4, 5, 1880; *Sun* (New York), March 4, 5, 6, 1880; *CR*, 46th Cong., 2nd sess., appendix, 47–92; *National Tribune* (Washington, D.C.), April 1, 1880.

59. Letters from George Prentiss, January 2, 1883, Joseph C. Smith, December 29, 1882, L. L. Wilson, March 5, 1880, December 30, 1882, and A. Patze, January 3, 1883, all in BV 4680, Logan Papers, Abraham Lincoln Presidential Library and Museum. Over several years Logan collected enough such letters vilifying Porter to fill five bound volumes.

60. *CR*, 46th Cong., 2nd sess., 1357, 1480.

61. FJP to Jacob Cox, May 24, June 29, July 21, 1880, and to Wharton Barker, July 2, 1880, Reel 23, FJPP; FJP to Cox, November 22, 1880, and to James A. Garfield, December 20, 1880, both on Reel 10, FJPP.

62. FJP to William T. Sherman, April 7, 1880, Reel 10, FJPP; FJP to Peter Getz, July 7, 1880, and to Henry S. Limes, August 7, 1880, both on Reel 23, FJPP; *Proceedings and Report*, 2:618–20, 625–26.

63. *West-Jersey Pioneer* (Bridgeton, N.J.), August 26, 1880; *New York Tribune*, October 18, 1880; *Chicago Tribune*, October 24, 1880.

64. *CR*, 46th Cong., 3rd sess., 93–97, 124.

65. *CR*, 46th Cong., 3rd sess., 125, 127–29.

66. Readers of Marvel, *Burnside* (423–24) will note that the interpretation of this episode has changed subtly in the intervening thirty years as a result of correspondence in the Garfield Papers, LC, and the Porter collections at the AAS, MHS, and LC.

67. *CR*, 46th Cong., 3rd sess., 129, 1802–3; Theodore Randolph to FJP, February 18, 1881, Reel 11, FJPP.

68. *Chicago Tribune*, March 13, 1881; *Sacramento (Calif.) Daily Record-Union*, March 14, 1881; *Emporia (Kans.) News*, March 18, 1881.

CHAPTER 19

1. Eisenschiml, *Celebrated Case of Fitz John Porter*, 309, 314–15.

2. FJP to William H. Guion, July 15, 20, September 28, 1881, to H. M. Dalrymple, July 20, 1881, to Frank Turnbull, August 25, 1881, and to Theodore Ayres, September [one date illegible], 28, 1881, all on Reel 23, FJPP.

3. *Sun* (New York) and *New York Tribune*, both July 3, 1881; *Evening Star* (Washington, D.C.), September 20, 1881.

4. FJP to Thomas M. Browne, July 10, 1881, to Henry Anthony, November 18, 1881, and many others on Reel 23, FJPP; FJP to John A. Logan, October 4, 25, 1881, and Logan to FJP, October 14, December 12, 1881, all on Reel 12, FJPP; FJP to John C. Ropes, August 8, 1881, BU; FJP to Logan, December 4, 1881, Porter Papers, USMA; FJP to Joseph R. Hawley, November 11, 1882, Hawley Papers, CHS; FJP to Stephen M. Weld Jr., January 13, 1881, Porter Papers, MHS.

5. Ulysses Grant to FJP, November 3, 1883, Reel 23, FJPP.

6. FJP to Ulysses Grant, September 17, November 19, 1881, Grant to FJP, November 19, 1881, and FJP to Anson Maltby, December 13, 1881, all on Reel 23, FJPP; FJP to Thomas F. Bayard, January 5, 1882, Box 60, Bayard Papers, LC.

7. Ulysses Grant to John A. Logan, December 30, 1881, Reel 12, FJPP; FJP to Logan, December 28, 1881, Reel 23, FJPP; Simon Cameron to FJP, December 19, 1881, January 5, 1882, both on Reel 1, FJPP.

8. *CR*, 47th Cong., 1st sess., 3769, 3727.

9. FJP to James B. Fry, March 31, 1881, and to Robert N. Scott, August 12, 1881, March 6, 1883, all on Reel 23, FJPP.

10. Cox, *Second Battle of Bull Run*, 5–8, 15, 62.

11. Cox, *Second Battle of Bull Run*, 20, 62–63; *Proceedings*, 2:264; Fry, "Cox's Second Battle of Bull Run," 278.

12. Grant, "Undeserved Stigma," 536–46.

13. FJP to John Sherman, January 4, 1883, Box 289, John Sherman Papers, LC; Alfred Terry to Ulysses Grant, November 19, 1882, Reel 17, FJPP; *CR*, 47th Cong., 2nd sess., 671–86, 692–701, 752–86.

14. *CR*, 48th Cong., 1st sess., 98, 318, 482, 839–40; Henry Slocum to Edwin Stanton, July 19, 1862, and FJP to GBM, July 20, 1862, both on Reel 1, FJPP.

15. *CR*, 48th Cong., 1st sess., 587, 1825–65. Swett's character is illuminated by his effort to misrepresent a legal case to Lincoln in order to obtain executive authority to seize control of a quicksilver mine from the rightful owners on behalf of a syndicate that offered him a handsome fee. See Marvel, *Lincoln's Autocrat*, 295–96.

16. *National Tribune* (Washington, D.C.), September 18, 1884; *Compilation of the Messages and Papers of the Presidents*, 6:4808–10; Ulysses Grant to FJP, July 4, 1884, Reel 15, FJPP; *Morning Journal and Courier* (New Haven, Conn.), July 3, 1884; *Wood County Reporter* (Grand Rapids, Mich.), July 3, 1884; *Evening Star* (Washington, D.C.), July 3, 1884; *Bridgeton (N.J.) Pioneer*, July 10, 1884.

17. FJP to Chester Arthur, October 14, December 8, 1884, File R574, Letters Received, 1867 (M619), Reel 581, RG94, NA.

18. FJP to W. H. Corcoran, March 26, 1883 (on stationery of the Excelsior company), Porter Correspondence, NHHS; FJP to W. Huxton, February 6, 1884, and to F. C. Durand, March 4, April 18, 1884, all on Reel 23, FJPP; *Salt Lake Herald* (Salt Lake City, Utah Terr.), October 29, 1884; *Alexandria Gazette and Virginia Advertiser*, October 30, 1884; *Trow's New York City Directory for the Year Ending May 1, 1886*, 1530; Deed Book N-11, 88–91, Morris County Courthouse. Evelina Porter Doggett recalled the salary sixty-five years later (Eisenschiml, *Celebrated Case of Fitz John Porter*, 314).

19. Stone, "Washington on the Eve of War"; Beauregard, "Battle of Bull Run." Porter's article "Gaines's Mill, and Its Preliminaries," became "Hanover Court House and Gaines's Mill" in the bound set, while "The Last of the Seven Days' Battles" was renamed "The Battle of Malvern Hill."

20. Porter, "How to Quell Mobs," 351–60.

21. Pope, "Second Battle of Bull Run," 475, 481–82, 487.

22. Pope, "Second Battle of Bull Run," 466, 481; Longstreet, "Our March against Pope," 519–20, 523.

23. FJP to Ambrose Burnside, December 23, 1880, Porter Papers, USMA; FJP to Henry Anthony, November 18, 1881, and to William Rosecrans, December 17, 1884, both on Reel 23, FJPP; *Portland (Me.) Daily Press*, August 14, 1882; *Sun* (New York), August 9, 1885.

24. *Sun* (New York), November 3, 1885; *Somerset (Pa.) Herald*, November 4, 1885; *Morning Journal and Courier* (New Haven, Conn.), November 3, 1885.

25. *National Tribune* (Washington, D.C.), December 31, 1885; *Evening Star* (Washington, D.C.), January 19, 1886.

26. *Evening Star* (Washington, D.C.), February 11, 1886.

27. *Speech of Hon. Martin A. Haynes*, 5–6, 9–10, 12–14.

28. Walker, "Inefficiency of the Lower House of Congress," 806; *Evening Star* (Washington, D.C.), February 11–13, 15–19, July 2, 1886 (quoting FJP letter to Wheeler); *Alexandria Gazette and Virginia Advertiser*, July 26, 1886.

29. *Evening Star* (Washington, D.C.), July 27, August 3, 1886; *Alexandria Gazette and Virginia Advertiser*, August 2, 7, 1886.

30. Clark et al., *History of Public Sector Pensions*, 137; Porter's original claim was dated September 18, 1888, Mexican War Invalid Certificate 12861, RG15, NA.

31. *New York Times* and *World* (New York), December 3, 1887.

32. *World* (New York), January 18, February 18, May 4, 11, 24, 1888.

33. *World* (New York), May 2, 1889; *Sunday Herald (Washington, D.C.)*, October 11, 1891. Evelina Porter Doggett thought her father "resigned" from the fire commission (Eisenschiml, *Celebrated Case of Fitz John Porter*, 314), but he finished his term.

34. Deed Book V12, 232, Morris County Courthouse.

35. John G. Nicolay to John Hay, August 7, 1885, Brown.

36. Thayer, *Life and Letters of John Hay*, 2:30–31.

37. Nicolay and Hay, "Announcement of Emancipation," 429–31.

38. FJP to John G. Nicolay and John Hay, July 22, 1889, Porter Correspondence, NHHS.

39. FJP to John G. Nicolay and John Hay, October 10, 1889, Porter Correspondence, NHHS; Lord, *Summary of the Case of General Fitz-John Porter*.

40. Nicolay and Hay, *Abraham Lincoln*, 6:10–13.

41. Nathan B. Webb Journal, August 30–September 3, 1862, CL.

42. FJP to Stephen M. Weld Jr., July 22, 1886, April 15, May 4, 1887, Porter Papers, MHS; FJP to John Page Nicholson, October 4, 1887, Porter Papers, RBHPL.

43. Memorial booklet for Patterson's dinner, January 6, 1880, Aztec Club Archives, AHEC; *National Republican* (Washington, D.C.), September 16, 1881; *National Tribune* (Washington, D.C.), September 22, 1882; *New York Tribune*, September 15, 1883; *Constitution of the Aztec Club of 1847 and the List of Members, 1893*, 6, 8, 10.

44. *Evening Star* (Washington, D.C.), January 15, 1887; *Alexandria Gazette and Virginia Advertiser*, January 24, 1887; *Portland (Me.) Daily Press*, January 28, 1887.

45. FJP to John Page Nicholson, October 4, 1887, Porter Papers, RBHPL; *Iola (Kans.) Register*, June 21, 1889; *Portland (Me.) Daily Press*, June 18, 1889, July 4, 1890; Society of the Army of the Potomac, *Report of the Nineteenth Annual Reunion*, 43, 57, *Report of the Twentieth Annual Reunion*, 88, *Report of the Twenty-First Annual Reunion*, 39–41.

46. *Trow's Directory for the Year Ending May 1, 1891*, 986; FJP to Carswell McClellan, May 8, 1891 (on stationery of the Asphaltic Slag Pavement and Roofing Company), Reel 31, FJPP; Eisenschiml, *Celebrated Case of Fitz John Porter*, 314; Charles W. Dayton to FJP, August 31, 1893.

47. FJP to Lafayette McLaws, June 16, 1886, McLaws Papers, Duke; FJP to Henry Carey Baird, July 30, 1889, Gardiner Collection, HSP; FJP to William Biddle, May 18, 1894, Porter Papers, Duke; FJP to Carswell McClellan, May 8, 1891, Reel 31, FJPP; FJP to John Tidball, March 27, 1892, Porter Papers, FSNMP; FJP to Theodore Lord, October 28, 1889, June 12, 1897, June 19, 1900, Reel 30, FJPP.

48. FJP to John C. Ropes, November 26, 30, December 8, 28, 1893, March 19, 1894, February 11, 13, 17, March 19, 25, 29, 1895, January 12, 1897, BU; Ropes, *Story of the Civil War*, 2:172–74.

49. Society of the Army of the Potomac, *Report of the Twenty-Sixth Annual Reunion*, 8–29, 45, 61–62; *Indianapolis Journal*, June 19, 1895; *National Tribune* (Washington, D.C.), June 27, 1895. The *National Tribune*, always a venomous critic of Porter, ignored Gibbon's flattering speech about him in its coverage of the reunion.

50. FJP to Horatio King, August 6, 1896, King Papers, LC; Joshua Chamberlain to FJP, August 24, 1896, Schoff Collection, CL.

51. FJP to Alexander S. Webb, June 6, 1897, Webb Papers, Sterling Library, Yale; FJP to Theodore Lord, June 17, 1897, Reel 30, FJPP; FJP to Horatio King, August 17, 1897, King Papers, LC.

52. *Army and Navy Journal (New York)*, 35, no. 1 (June 11, 1898): 825; *Custer County Republican* (Broken Bow, Neb.), January 18, 1900.

53. FJP to John C. Ropes, January 2, 1899, Porter Papers, FSNMP; *New York Tribune* and *Washington (D.C.) Times*, January 17, 1906.

54. Robert H. E. Porter to Mark B. Hatch, November 6, 1897, David St. Leon Porter file, Aztec Club Archives, AHEC; *Sonntags-Correspondent (Baltimore)*, September 24, 1899. This implicitly scandalous incident seems not to have been widely reported, but the German-language *Sonntags-Correspondent* named all the members of Edith's family.

55. FJP to Horatio King, September 24, 1899, King Papers, LC; Society of the Army of the Potomac, *Report of the Thirtieth Annual Re-Union*, 14, 75.

56. "Deaths: Annie Goddard Eddy," 134.

57. Styple, *Generals in Bronze*, 195.

58. Styple, *Generals in Bronze*, 194–96.

59. Styple, *Generals in Bronze*, 196–203.

60. Styple, *Generals in Bronze*, 203–4.

61. *New York Tribune* and *New York Times*, May 22, 1901; *Indianapolis Journal*, May 23, 1901; *Washington (D.C.) Times*, May 24, 1901.

62. *New York Tribune* and *New York Times*, May 22, 1901; affidavit of Morgan Dix, Dependent Certificate 14819, Mexican War Pension Files, RG15, NA.

63. *Silver Messenger* (Challis, Idaho), January 20, 1903; *Ordway (Colo.) Era*, October 27, 1905; *States and Union* (Portsmouth, N.H.), July 5, 1906.

64. *National Tribune* (Washington, D.C.), July 5, 1906; *Portsmouth (N.H.) Daily Chronicle*, July 2, 1906; *States and Union* (Portsmouth, N.H.), July 5, 1906; fragmentary drafts of the Portsmouth speech, Box 6, Webb Papers, Sterling Library, Yale.

EPILOGUE

1. *New York Tribune* and *Washington (D.C.) Times*, January 17, 1906. Soon after the divorce Edith married a man named St. Hill. Robert H. E. Porter surfaced in Lake Worth, Florida, in 1940 as the owner of a grocery store (Sixteenth U.S. Census, Palm Beach County, Fla., E.D. 50–38, sheet 20B, household 114), and he died in Palm Beach late in 1948 (*Palm Beach [Fla.] Post*, December 24, 1948).

2. *Washington (D.C.) Times*, February 14, 1914; *Evening Star* (Washington, D.C.), March 4, 1914; *Norwich (Conn.) Bulletin*, February 4, 1913; *Evening Journal* (Wilmington, Del.), March 9, 1915; Widow's Briefs for Mexican War Pensions, November 12, 1907, September 14, 1914, Dependent Certificate 14819, Mexican War Pension Files, RG15, NA.

3. *Summer Social Register, July 1911*, 230; *New York Social Register, April, 1917*, 529; Evelina Porter Doggett to Pension Bureau, December 10, 1924, February 3, March 10, 1925, all in Dependent Certificate 14819, Mexican War Pension Files, RG15, NA.

4. Eisenschiml, *Celebrated Case of Fitz John Porter*.

5. Williams, *Lincoln Finds a General*, 1:312–24, 344, 346, 2:786, 788. In a letter to James D. Cameron, February 4, 1882, Grant conceded that such snide criticism among generals was common, and he deemed the Burnside dispatches rather innocuous (*Grant's Unpublished Correspondence*, 14). Complaint might have been made about Porter's letters to Manton Marble, but even those more seditious-sounding missives consisted only of hyperbole.

6. "The Third Trial of General Fitz John Porter," WHS.

7. Thomas Nast St. Hill grave marker, Greenwood Memorial Park, San Diego, Calif.; Fitz John Porter obituary, *New York Times*, April 3, 1946, 24.

BIBLIOGRAPHY

MANUSCRIPTS

Abraham Lincoln Presidential Library and Museum, Springfield, Ill.
    John A. Logan Memorial Collection
    Fitz John Porter Letters
Allen County Public Library, Fort Wayne, Ind.
    Lincoln Financial Foundation Collection
        Isaac Bevier Letters
American Antiquarian Society, Worcester, Mass.
    Nathaniel Lyon Papers
    Fitz John Porter Papers
Army Heritage and Education Center, Carlisle, Pa.
    James Abraham Letters
    John Worthington Ames Papers
    Benjamin F. Ashenfelter Letters
    Aztec Club Archives
    Isaac Bowen Papers
    William T. H. Brooks Papers
    John Burrill Letters
    Lewis Frederick Cleveland Letters
    John and Leo Faller Letters
    Edmund Hawley Papers
    Jacob Heffelfinger Diary
    Henry Keiser Diary
    Frank Kelley Letter
    Robert McCreight Letters
    Lewis Masonheimer Diary
    Walter Phelps Jr. Papers
    Benjamin Roher Letters
    Edward E. Schweitzer Diary
    Joseph Simonds Letters
    James Uhler Journal
    Timothy Vedder Correspondence
Boston University
    Military Historical Society of Massachusetts Collection
        John C. Ropes Papers

Brown University, Providence, R.I.
    John Hay Papers
Chicago History Museum
    William Butler Papers
    John Pope Papers
Chicago Public Library
    Fitz John Porter Papers
College of the Holy Cross, Worcester, Mass.
    Patrick R. Guiney Letters
Columbia University, New York
    Sydney Howard Gay Papers
Connecticut Historical Society, Hartford
    Elizur Belden Diary
    William H. Drake Letter
    Joseph Roswell Hawley Papers
    Letters to Mary Shipman
    David Austin Thompson Collection
Connecticut State Library, Hartford
    Records of the Colt Patent Fire Arms Manufacturing Company
        William B. Franklin Diary
Dartmouth College, Hanover, N.H.
    R[euben] D[elevan] Mussey Papers
Duke University, Durham, N.C.
    Lafayette McLaws Papers
    William Nelson Pendleton Papers
    Fitz John Porter Papers
    William Young Ripley Papers
Fredericksburg and Spotsylvania National Military Park, Fredericksburg, Va.
    Irvin McDowell Letters
    Samuel Selden Partridge Letters
    Fitz John Porter Papers
Gilcrease Museum, Tulsa, Okla.
    Ethan Allen Hitchcock Diaries
Gilder-Lehrman Collection, New York
    John Hay Letter
Harvard University, Cambridge, Mass.
    Houghton Library
        Frederick M. Dearborn Collection
            William B. Franklin Letter
Rutherford B. Hayes Presidential Library, Fremont, Ohio
    Rutherford B. Hayes Papers
    Miscellaneous Manuscripts
        Fitz John Porter Papers
Historical Society of Pennsylvania, Philadelphia
    James Cornell Biddle Letters
    Edward Carey Gardiner Collection
    Simon Gratz Autograph Collection
    George G. Meade Papers

Hobart and William Smith Colleges, Geneva, N.Y.
    Edward H. C. Taylor Civil War Letters
Huntington Library, San Marino, Calif.
    Samuel L. M. Barlow Papers
    James W. Eldridge Collection
    John P. Nicholson Collection
    Charles H. Ray Papers
Indiana Historical Society, Indianapolis
    Elijah H. C. Cavins Papers
Kansas State Historical Society, Topeka
    Boyd B. Stutler Collection of John Brown Papers
Lehigh University, Bethlehem, Pa.
    Fitz John Porter Telegram
Library of Congress, Washington, D.C.
    Nathaniel Prentiss Banks Papers
    Lucian Barbour Papers
    Thomas F. Bayard Papers
    James Gordon Bennett Papers
    Blair Family Papers
    Zachariah Chandler Papers
    Salmon P. Chase Papers
    Charles A. Dana Papers
    Doubleday & Co. Collection
    William B. Franklin Papers
    James A. Garfield Papers
    Lucretia Rudolph Garfield Papers
    Gibson-Getty-McClure Families Papers
    James J. Gillette Papers
    Gove Family Papers
        Jesse Gove Journal
    John P. Hatch Papers
    Samuel P. Heintzelman Papers
    Lyman Holford Diary
    Joseph Holt Papers
    Jedediah Hotchkiss Journal
    Jedediah Hotchkiss Map Collection
    Henry Jackson Hunt Papers
    Institute of Aerospace Sciences Archives
    Thomas Jonathan Jackson Papers
    Andrew Johnson Papers
    August V. Kautz Papers
    Philip Kearny Papers
    Daniel Read Larned Papers
    Liljenquist Family Collection of Civil War Photographs
    Abraham Lincoln Papers
    Manton Marble Papers
    Helen Varnum Hill McCalla Diary
    George B. McClellan Papers

John C. McMichael Letter
Orlando M. Poe Papers
Fitz John Porter Papers
Joshua W. Ripley Papers
John M. Schofield Papers
John Sherman Papers
William T. Sherman Papers
Edwin M. Stanton Papers
George Hay Stuart Collection
Charles Crooke Suydam Papers
Horatio Nelson Taft Diary
Theodore Talbot Papers
Benjamin Wade Papers
George Washington Papers
Willard Family Papers
    Joseph C. Willard Diary
Henry Wilson Papers
Maryland Historical Society, Baltimore
    Isaac Trimble Papers
Massachusetts Historical Society, Boston
    Francis Channing Barlow Papers
    Fitz John Porter Papers
    William S. Tilton Diaries
Minnesota Historical Society, St. Paul
    Matthew Marvin Diary
    Orrin F. Smith Family Papers
    Cyrus R. Stone Papers
Morris County Courthouse, Morristown, N.J.
    Deed Books
National Archives, Washington, D.C.
    Records of the Department of Veterans Affairs, RG15
        Index to Mexican War Pension Files (T317)
        Individual Pension Files
        Bounty Land Warrant Applications
    Records of the Bureau of the Census, RG29
        Fifth Census of the United States (M19)
        Seventh Census of the United States (M432)
        Eighth Census of the United States (M653)
        Ninth Census of the United States (M593)
        Tenth Census of the United States (T9)
        Twelfth Census of the United States (T623)
        Thirteenth Census of the United States (T624)
        Fourteenth Census of the United States (T627)
    Naval Records Collection, RG45
        Letters Received by the Secretary of the Navy (M125)
    General Records of the Department of State, RG59
        Miscellaneous Letters, Entry 113
        U.S. Passport Applications, 1795–1925 (M1372)

Records of the Adjutant General, RG94
    Generals' Papers and Generals' Reports and Books
    Ambrose E. Burnside Papers
    Letters Received by the Adjutant General, 1822–1860 (M567)
    Letters Received by the Adjutant General, 1861–1870 (M619)
    Letters Received, Commission Branch, 1863–1870 (M1064)
    Letters Received by the Appointment, Commission, and Personnel
        Branch of the Adjutant General's Office, 1874–1894 (M1395)
    Register of Enlistments in the U.S. Army, 1798–1914 (M233)
    Returns from U.S. Military Posts, 1800–1916 (M617)
    U.S. Military Academy Cadet Application Papers, 1805–1866 (M688)
Records of the Office of the Secretary of War, RG107
    Letters Received, 1849–1896, Entry 329
Records of the Office of the Judge Advocate General, RG153
    Court Martial Case Files
    Orders, Proceedings, and Other Records, 1864–1911, Entry UD 1001
Records of U.S. Army Continental Commands, RG393, Part 1
    Correspondence and Issuances, Headquarters, Army
        of the Potomac, 1861–1865 (M2096)
Records of U.S. Army Continental Commands, RG393, Part 2
    Endorsements Sent, 1861–1865, Entry 4262
    General Orders, Special Orders, and Circulars, 1861–1863, Entry 4267
    Letters Sent, Porter's Division, February, 1862–June, 1865, Entry 4261
    Orders and Letters Received and Sent by General Fitz John Porter, Entry 258
Navy Department Library, Washington Navy Yard, Washington, D.C.
    Navy Casualty Reports, 1776–1941: Lost and Wrecked Ships, 1801–1941
    "Officers and Enlisted Men Who Died in the Active
        Service of the U.S. Navy, 1776–1885"
Nelson Town Archives, Nelson, N.H.
    Albert H. Taft Papers
New Hampshire Historical Society, Concord
    John Batchelder Bailey Journal
    George H. Chandler Papers
    Thomas B. Leaver Letterbook
    William Adams Moore Correspondence
    Fitz John Porter Correspondence
    John O. Stevens Letters
    John E. Wilcox Diary
New-York Historical Society, New York
    John Bigelow Letters
    Civil War Letters Collection, 1862–1901
    Thomas Dolan Telegrams
    William H. Paine Papers
    Fitz John Porter Letters
New York Public Library, New York
    Logbook of the U.S.S. *Boxer*
New York State Library Manuscripts and Special Collections, Albany
    New York Census, 1855
    Gouverneur Kemble Warren Papers

Ohio History Connection, Columbus
    Schutz, Walter, ed., "Memoir and Review of Pope's Campaign
            in Virginia, July, August, September 1862"
    Thomas C. H. Smith Papers
Otoe County Courthouse, Nebraska City, Nebraska
    Deed Books
Phillips Academy, Exeter, N.H.
    Register of Students, 1789–1840
    Register of Students, 1830–1854
    Register of Grades, September, 1828–August, 1836
Portsmouth Public Library, Portsmouth, N.H.
    Records of St. John's Church, 1795–1884
Rhode Island Historical Society, Providence
    Henry J. Spooner Letters
Rutgers University, New Brunswick, N.J.
    Roebling Family Papers
South Caroliniana Library, Columbia, S.C.
    Papers of the Kennedy, Evans, Woods, Hinton, Coleman, and Babcock Families
    Matthew Calhoun McCrary Papers
Tulane University, New Orleans, La.
    Albert Sidney and William Preston Johnston Papers
United States Military Academy, West Point, N.Y.
    United States Military Academy Archives
        Cadets Admitted to the U.S.M.A., 1800–1845
        Post Orders No. 1, February 19, 1838 to June 3, 1842
        Registers of Delinquencies
        Staff Records, Volume 4
    United States Military Academy Library
        Fitz John Porter Papers
University of Michigan, Ann Arbor
    Bentley Historical Library
        John M. Bancroft Diary
        William Ferrier Papers
        George Lockley Diary
        Elon G. Mills Diary and Letters
        George Monteith Letters
        Jonas D. Richardson Letters
        William Collins Stevens Papers
        John C. Whiteside Letter
    William L. Clements Library
        John Millis Correspondence
        James S. Schoff Civil War Collection
            Aplin Family Papers
            Thirza Finch Diary and Letters
            Henry Halleck Letters
            Fitz John Porter Letters
            John Darragh Wilkins Papers
        William and Frederic Speed Letters

John B. Stickney Papers
Nathan B. Webb Journals
University of New Hampshire, Durham
Thomas Carleton Cheney Papers
University of Rochester, Rochester, N.Y.
William Henry Seward Papers
University of Washington Libraries Special Collections, Seattle
Manning F. Force Papers
Utah State History Research Center, Salt Lake City
1939 Federal Writers' Project Typescripts
Vermont Historical Society, Barre
Avery B. Cain Letters
Washington Navy Yard, Washington, D.C.
Navy Department Library
"Officers and Enlisted Men Who Died in the Active
Service of the U.S. Navy, 1776–1885"
Wisconsin Historical Society, Madison
Edward S. Bragg Papers
James R. Doolittle Papers
George Fairfield Diary
Yale University, New Haven, Conn.
Beinecke Library
Western Americana Collection
Albert Sidney Johnston Letter
Joseph E. Johnston Letter
Sterling Library
Charles M. Coit Papers
Terry Family Papers
Alexander S. Webb Papers

PUBLISHED SOURCES

Abbott, Stephen G. *The First Regiment New Hampshire Volunteers in the Great Rebellion.* Keene, N.H.: Sentinel, 1890.

Acken, J. Gregory, ed. *Inside the Army of the Potomac: The Civil War Experience of Captain Francis Adams Donaldson.* Mechanicsburg, Pa.: Stackpole Books, 1998.

Allen, Gardner Weld. *Massachusetts Privateers of the Revolution.* Boston: Massachusetts Historical Society, 1927.

Anders, Curt. *Injustice on Trial: Second Bull Run, Fitz John Porter's Court-Martial, and the Schofield Board Investigation That Restored His Good Name.* Zionsville, Ind.: Clerisy, 2002.

Anderson, Robert. *An Artillery Officer in The Mexican War, 1846–7: Letters of Robert Anderson, Captain 3rd Artillery, U.S.A.* Foreword by Eba Anderson Lawton. New York: G. P. Putnam's Sons, 1911.

Anderson, Thomas M. "The Reserve at Antietam." *Century Magazine* 32, no. 3 (September, 1886): 783.

Andrews, J. Cutler. *The North Reports the Civil War.* Pittsburgh, Pa.: University of Pittsburgh Press, 1955.

Annual Reports of the Managers and Officers of the State Asylum for the Insane for the Year Ending October 31st, 1891. Trenton, N.J.: John L. Murphy, 1891.

Appeal to the President of the United States for a Re-Examination of the Proceedings of the General Court Martial in His Case, by Maj. Gen'l Fitz John Porter, with Accompanying Documents. Morristown, N.J.: No pub., 1869.

Atlas to Accompany the Official Records of the Union and Confederate Armies. Washington, D.C.: Government Printing Office, 1891–1895.

Auchmuty, Richard Tylden. *Letters of* ——, *Fifth Corps, Army of the Potomac.* N.p.: privately printed, [1895].

Bailey, William W. *My Boyhood at West Point.* Providence: Rhode Island Soldiers and Sailors Historical Society, 1891.

[Ballentine, George.] *The Autobiography of an English Soldier in the United States Army.* New York: Stringer & Townsend, 1853.

Barnes, Joseph K. *The Medical and Surgical History of the War of the Rebellion (1861–65).* 15 vols. 1870. Reprint, Wilmington, N.C.: Broadfoot, 1990.

Basler, Roy P., ed. *The Collected Works of Abraham Lincoln.* 10 vols. New Brunswick, N.J.: Rutgers University Press, 1953–1955, 1974.

Bauer, K. Jack. *The Mexican War, 1846–1848.* New York: Macmillan, 1974.

Beale, Howard K., ed. *The Diary of Edward Bates, 1859–1866.* Washington, D.C.: Government Printing Office, 1933.

——, ed. *Diary of Gideon Welles.* 3 vols. New York: W. W. Norton, 1960.

Beatie, Russel H. *The Army of the Potomac.* 3 vols. 1: *Birth of Command, November 1860–September 1861,* and 2: *McClellan Takes Command, September 1861–February 1862,* Cambridge, Mass.: Da Capo Press, 2002, 2004; 3: *McClellan's First Campaign, March 1862–May 1862.* New York: Savas Beatie, 2007.

Beatty, John. *The Citizen-Soldier: Or, Memoirs of a Volunteer.* Cincinnati, Ohio: Wilstach, Baldwin, 1879.

Beauregard, [Pierre] G. T. "The Battle of Bull Run." *Century Magazine* 29, no. 1 (November, 1884): 80–106.

Beers, F. W. *Atlas of Morris Co., New Jersey.* New York: Beers, Ellis & Goule, 1868.

Bennett, Edwin C. *Musket and Sword, or the Camp, March, and Firing Line in the Army of the Potomac.* Boston: Coburn, 1900.

Bertura, Martin N., and Kim Crawford, eds. *The 4th Michigan Infantry in the Civil War.* East Lansing: Michigan State University Press, 2010.

Bigler, David L., and Will Bagley. *The Mormon Rebellion: America's First Civil War, 1857–1858.* Norman: University of Oklahoma Press, 2011.

Blackwood, Emma Jerome, ed. *To Mexico with Scott: Letters of Captain E. Kirby Smith to His Wife.* Cambridge, Mass.: Harvard University Press, 1917.

Blight, David W., ed. *When This Cruel War Is Over: The Civil War Letters of Charles Harvey Brewster.* Amherst: University of Massachusetts Press, 1992.

Brewster, Charles W. *Rambles about Portsmouth.* 1st ser. Somersworth, N.H.: New Hampshire Publishing, 1971.

Bruen, Ella Jane, and Brian M. Fitzgibbons, eds. *Through Ordinary Eyes: The Civil War Correspondence of Rufus Robbins, Private, 7th Regiment, Massachusetts Volunteers.* Lincoln: University of Nebraska Press, 2005.

Burlingame, Michael, ed. *With Lincoln in the White House: Letters, Memoranda, and Other Writings of John G. Nicolay, 1860–1865.* Carbondale: Southern Illinois University Press, 2000.

Burlingame, Michael, and John R. Turner Ettlinger, eds. *Inside Lincoln's White House: The Complete Civil War Diary of John Hay*. Carbondale: Southern Illinois University Press, 1997.

Burton, Brian K. *Extraordinary Circumstances: The Seven Days Battles*. Bloomington: Indiana University Press, 2001.

Butler, Benjamin F. *Butler's Book*. Boston: A. M. Thayer, 1892.

Callahan, Edward W., ed. *List of Officers of the Navy of the United States and of the Marine Corps from 1775 to 1900*. New York: L. R. Hamersly, 1901.

Canning, Ray R., and Beverly Beeton, eds. *The Genteel Gentile: Letters of Elizabeth Cumming, 1857–1858*. Salt Lake City: University of Utah Library, 1977.

Carman, Ezra A. *The Maryland Campaign of September 1862*. 3 vols. Edited by Thomas G. Clemens. El Dorado Hills, Calif.: Savas Beatie, 2010, 2012, 2017.

Casler, John O. *Four Years in the Stonewall Brigade*. Guthrie, Okla.: State Capital Printing, 1893.

Cassedy, Edward K., ed. *Dear Friends at Home: The Civil War Letters and Diaries of Sergeant Charles T. Bowen, Twelfth United States Infantry*. Baltimore: Butternut & Blue, 2001.

Catalogue of the Officers and Students of Phillips Exeter Academy, New-Hampshire for the Academic Year 1835–6. Exeter, N.H.: News-Letter Office, 1836.

Catalogue of the Officers and Students of Phillips Exeter Academy, New-Hampshire for the Academic Year 1837–8. Exeter, N.H.: John C. Gerrish, 1838.

Catton, Bruce. *Mr. Lincoln's Army*. Garden City, N.Y.: Doubleday, 1951.

Clark, Robert L., Lee A. Craig, and Jack W. Wilson. *A History of Public Sector Pensions in the United States*. Philadelphia: University of Pennsylvania, 2003.

Clemens, Thomas G. "Why Did Burnside Cross the Bridge?" *America's Civil War* 15, no. 4 (September, 2002): 64–71.

Coco, Gregory A., ed. *From Ball's Bluff to Gettysburg and Beyond: The Civil War Letters of Private Roland E. Bowen, 15th Massachusetts Infantry, 1861–1864*. Gettysburg, Pa.: Thomas, 1994.

A Compilation of the Messages and Papers of the Presidents. 11 vols. Washington, D.C.: Bureau of National Literature, 1913.

The Constitution of the Aztec Club of 1847 and the List of Members, 1893. Washington: Judd & Detweiller, 1893.

Correspondence of John Sedgwick, Major-General. 2 vols. New York: C. and E. B. Stoeckel, 1902–3.

Cox, Jacob Dolson. "The Battle of Antietam." In *Battles and Leaders of the Civil War*, edited by Robert U. Johnson and Clarence C. Buel, 2:630–662. New York: Century, 1884–88.

———. *Military Reminiscences of the Civil War*. 2 vols. New York: Charles Scribner's Sons, 1900.

———. *The Second Battle of Bull Run, as Connected with the Fitz-John Porter Case*. Cincinnati, Ohio: Peter G. Thomson, 1882.

Cozzens, Peter. *General John Pope: A Life for the Nation*. Urbana: University of Illinois Press, 2000.

Croffut, W. A., ed. *Fifty Years in Camp and Field: Diary of Major-General Ethan Allen Hitchcock, U.S.A.* New York: G. P. Putnam's Sons, 1909.

Curtis, Newton M. *From Bull Run to Chancellorsville: The Story of the Sixteenth New York Infantry Together with Personal Reminiscences*. New York: G. P. Putnam's Sons, 1906.

Cutler, Cyrus Morton. *Letters from the Front, October, 1861, to September, 1864*. [San Francisco, Calif.]: privately published, 1892.

Cutrer, Thomas W., ed. *Longstreet's Aide: The Civil War Letters of Major Thomas J. Goree.* Charlottesville: University Press of Virginia, 1995.

—, ed. *The Mexican War Diary and Correspondence of George B. McClellan.* Baton Rouge: Louisiana State University Press, 2009.

Dana, Charles A. *Recollections of the Civil War, with the Leaders at Washington and in the Field in the Sixties.* New York: D. Appleton, 1898.

"Deaths: Annie Goddard Eddy." *New England Historical and Genealogical Register* 55, no. 1 (January, 1901): 134.

Diary of General S. M. Jackson for the Year 1862. Apollo, Pa.: privately published, 1925.

Doggett's New-York City Directory for 1845 & 1846. New York: John Doggett Jr., 1845.

Donovan, Kevin C. "The Court-Martial of Fitz-John Porter." *Columbiad* 2, no. 4 (Winter, 1999): 73–97.

Dowdey, Clifford, and Louis H. Manarin, eds. *The Wartime Papers of R. E. Lee.* New York: Virginia Civil War Commission, 1961.

Dwight, Theodore F., ed. *The Virginia Campaign of 1862 under General Pope* (Vol. 2, *Papers of the Military Historical Society of Massachusetts*). 1895. Reprint, Wilmington, N.C.: Broadfoot, 1989.

Dyer, J. Franklin. *The Journal of a Civil War Surgeon.* Edited by Michael B. Chesson. Lincoln: University of Nebraska Press, 2003.

Eby, Cecil D. Jr., ed. *A Virginia Yankee in the Civil War: The Diaries of David Hunter Strother.* Chapel Hill: University of North Carolina Press, 1961.

Eckert, Edward K., and Nicholas J. Amato, eds. *Ten Years in the Saddle: The Memoirs of William Woods Averell.* San Rafael, Calif.: Presidio Press, 1978.

"Editor's Easy Chair." *Harper's New Monthly Magazine* 7, no. 41 (October, 1853): 700–707.

Eisenhower, John S. D. *So Far from God: The U.S. War with Mexico, 1846–1848.* New York: Random House, 1989.

Eisenschiml, Otto. *The Celebrated Case of Fitz John Porter: An American Dreyfuss Affair.* Indianapolis, Ind.: Bobbs-Merrill, 1950.

Emerson, Edward W. *Life and Letters of Charles Russell Lowell.* Boston: Houghton Mifflin, 1907.

Endicott, William. *Reminiscences of Seventy-Five Years.* Boston: privately printed, 1913.

"Extracts from the Journal of Henry J. Raymond." *Scribner's Monthly* 19, no. 9 (January, 1880): 419–24.

Farragut, Loyall. *The Life of David Glasgow Farragut, First Admiral of the United States Navy.* New York: D. Appleton, 1879.

Fischel, Edwin C. *The Secret War for the Union: The Untold Story of Military Intelligence in the Civil War.* Boston: Houghton Mifflin, 1996.

Fitz-John Porter: Speech of Hon. John A. Logan, of Illinois, in the Senate of the United States, Thursday, March 13, 1884. Washington, D.C.: No pub., 1884.

Fitz John Porter, Commissioner of Public Works, to Andrew H. Green, Comptroller of the City of New York, December 2, 1875. [New York]: privately printed, 1875.

Ford, Worthington Chauncey, ed. *A Cycle of Adams Letters, 1861–1865.* 2 vols. Boston: Houghton Mifflin, 1920.

Fossett, Frank. *Colorado: A Historical Descriptive and Statistical Work on the Rocky Mountain Gold and Silver Mining Region.* Denver: Daily Tribune, 1876.

Fox, William F. *Regimental Losses in The American Civil War, 1861–1865.* Albany, N.Y.: Albany Publishing, 1889.

Franklin, William B. "The First Great Crime of the War." In *The Annals of the War, Written by Leading Participants North and South*. Philadelphia: Philadelphia Weekly Times, 1878.

French, Benjamin Brown. *Witness to the Young Republic: A Yankee's Journals, 1828–1870*. Edited by Donald B. Cole and John J. McDonough. Hanover, N.H.: University Press of New England, 1989.

F[ry], J[ames] B. "Cox's Second Battle of Bull Run." *Journal of the Military Service Institution of the United States* 3, no. 10 (1882): 277–79.

Frye, Dennis. "Burnside Betrayed?" *America's Civil War* 28, no. 4 (September, 2015): 24–31.

Furber, George C. *The Twelve Months Volunteer; or, Journal of a Private in the Tennessee Regiment of Cavalry, in the Campaign, in Mexico, 1846–47*. Cincinnati, Ohio: J. A. and U. P. James, 1850.

Furniss, Norman F. *The Mormon Conflict, 1850–1859*. New Haven, Conn.: Yale University Press, 1960.

"General M. C. Meigs on the Conduct of the Civil War." *American Historical Review* 26, no. 2 (January, 1921): 285–303.

General Regulations for the Army of the United States; Also, the Rules and Articles of War, and Extracts from Laws Relating to Them. Washington, D.C.: War Department, 1835.

Gen'l Fitz John Porter's Reply to Hon. Z. Chandler's Speech in the U.S. Senate, Feb. 21, 1870. Morristown, N.J.: No pub., 1870.

George, Joseph Jr. "Subornation of Perjury in the Lincoln Conspiracy Trial? Joseph Holt, Robert Purdy, and the Lon Letter." *Civil War History* 38, no. 3 (September, 1992): 232–41.

Gienapp, William E., and Erica L. Gienapp, eds. *The Civil War Diary of Gideon Welles, Lincoln's Secretary of the Navy*. Urbana: University of Illinois Press, 2014.

Grant, Ulysses S. "An Undeserved Stigma." *North American Review* 135, no. 313 (December, 1882): 536–46.

———. *Personal Memoirs of* ———. 2 vols. New York: Charles Webster, 1885.

Greene, A. Wilson. *Civil War Petersburg: Confederate City in the Crucible of War*. Charlottesville: University of Virginia Press, 2006.

———. *Whatever You Resolve to Be: Essays on Stonewall Jackson*. Baltimore: Butternut and Blue, 1992.

"Gunnell Gold Mining Company." *American Mining Gazette and Geological Magazine* 2, no. 5 (May, 1865): 287–88.

Hague, James D. "A Doubtful Island in the Pacific." *National Geographic* 15, no. 12 (December, 1904): 476–89.

Hammond, Harold Earl, ed. *Diary of a Union Lady, 1861–1865*. New York: Funk & Wagnall's, 1962.

Hammond, Otis G., ed. *The Utah Expedition, 1857–1858: Letters of Capt. Jesse A. Gove, 10th Inf., U.S., of Concord, N.H., to Mrs. Gove, and Special Correspondence of the New York Herald*. Concord: New Hampshire Historical Society, 1928.

Hardy, Michael C. *The Battle of Hanover Court House: Turning Point of the Peninsula Campaign, May 27, 1862*. Jefferson, N.C.: McFarland, 2006.

Hass, Paul H. "A Volunteer Nurse in the Civil War: The Letters of Harriet Douglas Whetten." *Wisconsin Magazine of History* 48, no. 2 (Winter, 1964–65): 131–51.

Haydon, F. Stansbury. *Military Ballooning during the Early Civil War*. 1941. Reprint, with an Introduction by Tom D. Crouch. Baltimore: Johns Hopkins University Press, 2000.

Haynes, Martin A. *A Minor War History Compiled from a Soldier Boy's Letters to "The Girl I Left behind Me."* Lakeport, N.H.: privately published, 1916.

Heitman, Francis B., *Historical Register and Dictionary of the United States Army, 1789–1903*. 2 vols. Washington, D.C.: Government Printing Office, 1903.

Hennessy, John J. "Conservatism's Dying Ember: Fitz John Porter and the Union War, 1862." In *Corps Commanders in Blue: Union Major Generals in the Civil War*, edited by Ethan S. Rafuse, 14–60. Baton Rouge: Louisiana State University Press, 2014.

———. *Historical Report on the Troop Movements for the Second Battle of Manassas, August 28 through August 30, 1862*. Denver, Colo.: National Park Service, 1985.

———. *Return to Bull Run: The Campaign and Battle of Second Manassas*. New York: Simon and Schuster, 1993.

Herberger, Charles F., ed. *A Yankee at Arms: The Diary of Augustus D. Ayling, 29th Massachusetts Volunteers*. Knoxville: University of Tennessee Press, 1999.

Herrick's Almanac for the Year of Our Lord 1862. Albany, N.Y.: Dr. Herrick & Brother, [1861].

Herringshaw's American Blue Book of Biography. Chicago: American Publishing, 1915.

Hewett, Janet B., Noah Andre Trudeau, and Bryce A. Suderow, eds. *Supplement to the Official Records of the Union and Confederate Armies*. 100 vols. Wilmington, N.C.: Broadfoot, 1994–98.

Higginson, Mary Thacher, ed. *Letters and Journals of Thomas Wentworth Higginson, 1846–1906*. Boston: Houghton Mifflin, 1921.

Hodge, Robert W., ed. *The Civil War Letters of Perry Mayo*. East Lansing: Michigan State University Museum, 1967.

Holden, Walter, William E. Ross, and Elizabeth Slomba, eds. *Stand Firm and Fire Low: The Civil War Writings of Colonel Edward E. Cross*. Hanover, N.H.: University Press of New England, 2003.

[Holt, Joseph]. *Review by the Judge Advocate General of the Proceedings, Findings, and Sentence of a General Court Martial Held in the City of Washington, for the Trial of Major General Fitz John Porter, of the United States Volunteers*. Washington, D.C.: Daily Chronicle, 1863.

———. *Vindication of Hon. Joseph Holt, Judge Advocate General of the United States Army*. Washington, D.C.: Chronicle, 1873.

Hough, Franklin B. *History of Duryée's Brigade, during the Campaign in Virginia under Gen. Pope, and in Maryland in the Summer and Autumn of 1862*. Albany, N.Y.: J. Mussell, 1864.

Howe, Mark DeWolfe, ed. *Touched with Fire: Civil War Letters of Oliver Wendell Holmes Jr., 1861–1864*. Cambridge, Mass.: Harvard University Press, 1947.

Hsieh, Wayne Wei-siang. *West Pointers and the Civil War: The Old Army in War and Peace*. Chapel Hill: University of North Carolina Press, 2009.

Hughes, Nathaniel Cheairs Jr., and Timothy D. Johnson, eds. *A Fighter from Way Back: The Mexican War Diary of Lt. Daniel Harvey Hill, 4th Artillery, USA*. Kent, Ohio: Kent State University Press, 2002.

Hyde, Thomas W. *Following the Greek Cross; or, Memories of the Sixth Army Corps*. Boston: Houghton Mifflin, 1894.

Impeachment Investigation: Testimony Taken before the Judiciary Committee of the House of Representatives in the Investigation of the Charges against Andrew Johnson. Washington, D.C.: Government Printing Office, 1867.

Index of General Orders, Army of the Potomac, 1861. [Washington, D.C.]: Head-Quarters Printing Office, 1862.

Jermann, Donald R. *Fitz-John Porter, Scapegoat of Second Manassas: The Rise, Fall and Rise of the General Accused of Disobedience*. Jefferson, N.C.: McFarland, 2009.

Johnson, Reverdy. *Reply of Hon. Reverdy Johnson to the Papers Which Judge-Advocate Holt*

Furnished to the President, Urging General Porter's Condemnation. [New York]: privately printed, [1863].

Johnston, Joseph E. *Narrative of Military Operations Directed, during the Late War between the States, By* ——. New York: D. Appleton, 1874.

Johnston, William Preston. "Albert Sidney Johnston at Shiloh." In *Battles and Leaders of the Civil War*, edited by Robert U. Johnson and Clarence C. Buel, 1:540–64. New York: Century, 1884.

——. *The Life of Gen. Albert Sidney Johnston.* New York: D. Appleton & Co., 1878.

Jones, J[ohn] B[eauchamp]. *A Rebel War Clerk's Diary at the Confederate States Capital.* 2 vols. Philadelphia: J. B. Lippincott, 1866.

Jordan, William B., ed. *The Civil War Journals of John Mead Gould, 1861–1866.* Baltimore: Butternut and Blue, 1997.

"The Journal of Francis Collins, an Artillery Officer in the Mexican War." *Quarterly Publication of the Historical and Philosophical Society of Ohio* 10, no. 1 (January–March, 1915): 39–109.

Julian, George W. *Political Recollections, 1840 to 1872.* 1884. Reprint, New York: Negro Universities Press, 1970.

Kastenberg, Joshua E. *Law in War, War as Law: Brigadier General Joseph Holt and the Judge Advocate General's Department in the Civil War and Early Reconstruction.* Durham, N.C.: Carolina Academic Press, 2011.

Keyes, Dwight W. "1861 — The First Wisconsin Infantry, U.S.V., Its Organization and Move to the Front." In *War Papers: Being Papers Read before the Commandery of the State of Wisconsin, Military Order of the Loyal Legion of the United States*, 3:90–101. Milwaukee: Burkdick & Allen, 1903.

Keyes, E. D. *Fifty Years' Observation of Men and Events Civil and Military.* New York: Charles Scribner's, 1884.

Kime, Wayne. *Pierre M. Irving and Washington Irving: A Collaboration in Life and Letters.* Waterloo, Ont.: Wilfrid Laurier University Press, 1978.

King, Charles. "In Vindication of General Rufus King." In *Battles and Leaders of the Civil War*, edited by Robert U. Johnson and Clarence C. Buel, 2:495. New York: Century, 1888.

Laas, Virginia Jeans. *Wartime Washington: The Civil War Letters of Elizabeth Blair Lee.* Urbana: University of Illinois Press, 1991.

Lawton, Eba Anderson, ed. *An Artillery Officer in the Mexican War, 1846–7: Letters of Robert Anderson, Captain 3rd Artillery, U.S.A.* New York: G. P. Putnam's Sons, 1911.

Letter of the Secretary of War, Transmitting Report of the Organization of the Army of the Potomac, and of Its Campaigns in Virginia and Maryland, under the Command of Maj. Gen. George B. McClellan, from July 26, 1861, to November 7, 1862. Washington, D.C.: Government Printing Office, 1864.

Livermore, Thomas L. *Numbers and Losses in the Civil War in America, 1861–65.* Boston: Houghton Mifflin, 1900.

Livingston-Little, D. E., ed. *The Mexican War Diary of Thomas D. Tennery.* Norman: University of Oklahoma Press, 1970.

Locke, William Henry. *The Story of the Regiment.* Philadelphia: J. B. Lippincott, 1868.

Logel, Jon Scott. *Designing Gotham: West Point Engineers and the Rise of Modern New York, 1817–1898.* Baton Rouge: Louisiana State University Press, 2016.

Long, David F. *Nothing Too Daring: A Biography of Commodore David Porter, 1780–1843.* Annapolis, Md.: United States Naval Institute, 1970.

Longacre, Edward G., ed. *From Antietam to Fort Fisher: The Civil War Letters of Edward King Wightman, 1862–1865.* Rutherford, N.J.: Fairleigh Dickinson University Press, 1965.

Longstreet, Helen D. *Lee and Longstreet at High Tide: Gettysburg in Light of the Official Records.* Gainesville, Ga.: privately printed, 1904.

Longstreet, James. "Our March against Pope." In *Battles and Leaders of the Civil War,* edited by Robert U. Johnson and Clarence C. Buel, 2:512–26. New York: Century, 1888.

Lord, Theodore A. *A Summary of the Case of General Fitz-John Porter.* San Francisco, Calif.: H. S. Crocker, 1883.

Lossing, Benjamin J. *Pictorial History of the Civil War in the United States of America.* 3 vols. Philadelphia: G. W. Childs, 1866–68.

Loving, Jerome M., ed. *Civil War Letters of George Washington Whitman.* Durham, N.C.: Duke University Press, 1975.

Lyman, George H. "Some Aspects of the Medical Service in the Armies of the United States during the War of the Rebellion." In *Papers of the Military Historical Society of Massachusetts,* 13:175–228. 1913. Reprint, Wilmington, N.C.: Broadfoot, 1990.

MacKinnon, William P. *At Sword's Point, Part 1: A Documentary History of the Utah War to 1858.* Norman: University of Oklahoma Press, 2008.

———. "Letter." *Journal of Mormon History* 38, no. 3 (Summer, 2012): vii–x.

Maclay, Edgar Stanton. *A History of American Privateers.* New York: D. Appleton, 1899.

Marcy, Randolph B. *Thirty Years of Army Life on the Border.* New York: Harper & Brothers, 1866.

Marvel, William. *Burnside.* Chapel Hill: University of North Carolina Press, 1991.

———. *Lincoln's Autocrat: The Life of Edwin Stanton.* Chapel Hill: University of North Carolina Press, 2015.

———. *Mr. Lincoln Goes to War.* Boston: Houghton Mifflin, 2006.

———. "More Than Water under Burnside's Bridge." *America's Civil War* 18, no. 6 (January, 2006): 46–50, 52.

Maury, Dabney Herndon. *Recollections of a Virginian in the Mexican, Indian, and Civil Wars.* New York: Charles Scribner's Sons, 1894.

McClellan, George B. *McClellan's Own Story: The War for the Union, the Soldiers Who Fought It, the Civilians Who Directed It, and His Relations to It and to Them.* Edited by William C. Prime. New York: Charles L. Webster, 1887.

———. "The Peninsular Campaign." In *Battles and Leaders of the Civil War,* edited by Robert U. Johnson and Clarence C. Buel, 2:160–87. New York: Century, 1888.

———. *Regulations and Instructions for the Field Service of the U.S. Cavalry in Time of War.* Philadelphia: J. B. Lippincott, 1861.

McClure, A[lexander] K. *Abraham Lincoln and Men of War-Times: Some Personal Recollections of War and Politics during the Lincoln Administration.* Philadelphia: Times Publishing, 1892.

McDowell, Irvin. *Statement of Major Gen. Irvin McDowell, in Review of the Evidence before the Court of Inquiry.* Washington, D.C.: L. Towers, 1863.

Meade, George. *The Life and Letters of George Gordon Meade, Major-General United States Army.* 2 vols. New York: Charles Scribner's Sons, 1913.

Message from the President of the United States, Communicating Information of the Proceedings of Certain Persons Who Took Possession of Amelia Island and of Galveston, during the Summer of the Present Year. Washington, D.C.: E. DeKrafft, 1817.

The Military and Naval Magazine of the United States from Sept. 1835 to Feb. 1836. Washington, D.C.: Benjamin Homans, 1836.

Mooney, James L., ed. *Dictionary of American Naval Fighting Ships*. 8 vols. Washington,
   D.C.: Naval Historical Center, 1959–81.

Moore, Frank, ed. *The Rebellion Record, a Diary of Events with Documents, Narratives,
   Illustrative Incidents, Poetry, etc.* 12 vols. 1861–68. Reprint, New York: Arno Press,
   1977.

Morrison, James L. Jr. *The Best School: West Point, 1833–1866*. Kent, Ohio: Kent State
   University Press, 1998.

———. "Getting through West Point: The Cadet Memoirs of John C. Tidball, Class of
   1848." *Civil War History* 26, no. 4 (December, 1980): 304–25.

Murphy, Douglas A. *Two Armies on the Rio Grande: The First Campaign of the US-Mexican
   War*. College Station: Texas A&M University Press, 2014.

Nash, Eugene Arus. *A History of the Forty-fourth Regiment, New York Volunteer Infantry,
   in the Civil War, 1861–1865*. Chicago: R. R. Donnelley & Sons, 1911.

Neely, Mark E., Jr. *The Union Divided: Party Conflict in the Civil War North*. Cambridge,
   Mass.: Harvard University Press, 2002.

Nevins, Allan, ed. *A Diary of Battle: The Personal Journals of Colonel Charles S. Wainwright,
   1861–1865*. New York: Harcourt, Brace, & World, [1962].

———. *The War for the Union*. 4 vols. New York: Charles Scribner's Sons, 1959–71.

Nevins, Allan, and Milton Halsey Thomas, eds. *The Diary of George Templeton Strong*.
   4 vols. New York: Macmillan, 1952.

"The New York Gold Mining Company, of Colorado." *American Mining Gazette and
   Geological Magazine* 2, no. 1 (January, 1865): 30–31.

New York Social Register, April, 1917. New York: Social Register Association, 1917.

Nicolay, John G., and John Hay. *Abraham Lincoln: A History*. 10 vols. New York: Century,
   1890.

———. "The Announcement of Emancipation." *Century Magazine* 37, no. 3 (January,
   1889): 427–47.

Niven, John, ed. *The Salmon P. Chase Papers*. 5 vols. Kent, Ohio: Kent State University
   Press, 1993–98.

Norton, Oliver Willcox. *Army Letters, 1861–1865*. [Chicago: O. L. Deming], 1903.

Official Records of the Union and Confederate Navies in the War of the Rebellion. 31 vols.
   Washington, D.C.: Government Printing Office, 1894–1927.

Official Register of the Officers and Cadets of the U.S. Military Academy, West Point, New-York.
   N.p.: no pub., 1842–55.

Opinions and Memorials in the Case of Gen. Fitz John Porter. Morristown, N.J.: "Banner"
   Steam Book and Job Printing, 1874.

Orléans, Philippe d', Comte de Paris. *Voyage en Amérique, 1861–1862: Un prince français
   dans la guerre de Sécession*. Edited with an introduction by Farid Ameur. Paris: Perrin/
   Fondation Saint-Louis, 2011.

Osborne, Seward R., ed. *The Civil War Diaries of Col. Theodore B. Gates, 20th New York State
   Militia*. Hightstown, N.J.: Longstreet House, 1991.

Palfrey, Francis W. *The Antietam and Fredericksburg*. New York: Charles Scribner's Sons,
   1882.

———. "The Battle of Malvern Hill." *Papers of the Military Historical Society of
   Massachusetts* 1 (1876): 253–75.

Palmer, Beverly Wilson, ed. *The Selected Letters of Charles Sumner*. 2 vols. Boston:
   Northeastern University Press, 1990.

Parker, John L. *Henry Wilson's Regiment: History of the Twenty-Second Massachusetts*

Infantry, the Second Company Sharpshooters, and the Third Light Battery, in the War of the Rebellion. Boston: Regimental Association, 1887.

"The Pay of the Army and Navy." *United States Army and Navy Journal, and Gazette,* January 16, 1864, 328–29.

Peabody, Andrew Preston. *Harvard Graduates I Have Known.* Boston: Houghton Mifflin, 1890.

Pease, Theodore Calvin, and James G. Randall, eds. *The Diary of Orville Hickman Browning.* 2 vols. Springfield: Illinois State Historical Library, 1925, 1933.

Peet, Frederick Tomlinson. *Civil War Letters and Documents of* ——. Newport, R.I.: privately printed, 1917.

Perris, William. *Maps of the City of New York.* New York: Perris & Browne, 1859.

Plumb, Robert C., ed. *Your Brother in Arms: A Union Soldier's Odyssey.* Columbia: University of Missouri Press, 2011.

Poll, Richard D., and Ralph W. Hansen. "Buchanan's Blunder: The Utah War, 1857–1858." *Military Affairs* 25, no. 3 (Fall, 1961): 121–31.

Pope, John. "The Second Battle of Bull Run." In *Battles and Leaders of the Civil War,* edited by Robert U. Johnson and Clarence C. Buel, 2:449–94. New York: Century, 1888.

Porter, Fitz John. "The Battle of Malvern Hill." In *Battles and Leaders of the Civil War,* edited by Robert U. Johnson and Clarence C. Buel, 2:406–26. New York: Century, 1888.

——. "Hanover Court House and Gaines's Mill." In *Battles and Leaders of the Civil War,* edited by Robert U. Johnson and Clarence C. Buel, 2:319–43. New York: Century, 1888.

——. "How to Quell Mobs." *North American Review* 141, no. 347 (October, 1885): 351–60.

Powell, William H. "More Light on the Reserve at Antietam." *Century Magazine* 33, no. 3 (January, 1887): 804.

Priest, John Michael. *From New Bern to Fredericksburg: Captain James Wren's Diary.* Shippensburg, Pa.: White Mane, 1990.

Private and Official Correspondence of Gen. Benjamin F. Butler during the Period of the Civil War. 5 vols. Norwood, Mass.: Plimpton Press, 1917.

Proceedings and Report of the Board of Army Officers, Convened by Special Orders No. 78, Headquarters of the Army, Adjutant General's Office, Washington, April 12, 1878, in the Case of Fitz-John Porter. 3 vols. Washington, D.C.: Government Printing Office, 1879.

Proceedings of a General Court Martial, for the Trial of Maj. Gen. Fitz John Porter, U.S. Vols. Washington, D.C.: No pub., 1862.

Quaife, Milo M., ed. *From the Cannon's Mouth: The Civil War Letters of General Alpheus S. Williams.* Detroit, Mich.: Wayne State University Press, 1959.

Rafuse, Ethan S., ed. *Corps Commanders in Blue: Union Major Generals in the Civil War.* Baton Rouge: Louisiana State University Press, 2014.

——. *McClellan's War: The Failure of Moderation in the Struggle for the Union.* Bloomington: Indiana University Press, 2005.

——. "'Poor Burn?': The Antietam Conspiracy That Wasn't." *Civil War History* 54, no. 2 (June, 2008): 146–75.

Ramsey, Albert C., ed. *The Other Side; or, Notes for the History of the War between Mexico and the United States.* New York: John Wiley, 1850.

Raymond, Henry J. *The Life and Public Services of Abraham Lincoln, Sixteenth President of the United States.* New York: Derby and Miller, 1865.

Register of the Commissioned and Warrant Officers of the Navy of the United States, including Officers of the Marine Corps, &c. &c. Washington, D.C.: Various publishers, 1822–30, 1852.

Register of the Officers and Agents, Civil, Military, and Naval, in the Service of the United States on the 30th of September, 1817–1831. Washington, D.C.: Various publishers, 1818–32.

Regulations Established for the Organization and Government of the Military Academy at West Point, New-York. New York: Wiley & Putnam, 1839.

Report of the Commissioners Appointed to Select a Site and Build an Asylum for the Insane of the State of New Jersey. Trenton, N.J.: W. S. Sharp, 1874.

Report of the Joint Committee on the Conduct of the War. 3 vols. Washington, D.C.: Government Printing Office, 1863.

Report of the Superintendent of the U.S. Coast Survey, Showing the Progress of the Survey During the Year 1854. Washington: A. O. P. Nicholson, 1855.

Robertson, James I., Jr., ed. *The Civil War Letters of General Robert McAllister*. Baton Rouge: Louisiana University Press, 1965.

Robins, Richard. "The Battles of Groveton and Second Bull Run." In *Military Essays and Recollections: Papers Read before the Commandery of the State of Illinois, Military Order of the Loyal Legion of the United States*, 3:69–96. Chicago: Dial Press, 1899.

Robinson's Atlas of Morris County, New Jersey. New York: E. Robinson, 1887.

Ropes, John Codman. *The Army under Pope*. New York: Charles Scribner's Sons, 1881.

———. *The Story of the Civil War: A Concise Account of the War in the United States of America between 1861 and 1865*. 2 vols. New York: G. P. Putnam's Sons, 1894, 1898.

Rosenberger, E. H., ed. "Ohiowa Soldier." *Annals of Iowa* 36, no. 2 (Fall, 1961): 110–48.

Rusling, James F. *Men and Things I Saw in Civil War Times*. New York: Eaton & Mains, 1899.

Sadler, Richard W. "The Spencer-Pike Affair." *Utah Historical Quarterly* 76, no. 1 (Winter, 2008): 79–93.

Sanborn, Alvin F., ed. *Reminiscences of Richard Lathers: Sixty Years of a Busy Life in South Carolina, Massachusetts, and New York*. New York: Grafton Press, 1907.

Sargent, Chauncey Forward. *Gathering Laurels in Mexico: The Diary of an American Soldier in the Mexican American War*. Edited by Ann Brown Janes. Lincoln, Mass.: Cottage Press, 1990.

Sauers, Richard A., ed. *The Civil War Journal of Colonel William J. Bolton, 51st Pennsylvania*. Conshohocken, Pa.: Combined, 2000.

Schaff, Morris, *The Spirit of Old West Point*. Boston: Houghton Mifflin, 1907.

Schiller, Herbert M. *Autobiography of Major General William F. Smith, 1861–1864*. Dayton, Ohio: Morningside Press, 1990.

Schofield, John M. *Forty-Six Years in the Army*. New York: Century, 1897.

Scott, Robert Garth, ed. *Fallen Leaves: The Civil War Letters of Major Henry Livermore Abbott*. Kent, Ohio: Kent State University Press, 1991.

———, ed. *Forgotten Valor: The Memoirs, Journals, and Civil War Letters of Orlando B. Willcox*. Kent, Ohio: Kent State University Press, 1999.

Sears, Stephen W. *Controversies and Commanders: Dispatches from the Army of the Potomac*. Boston: Houghton Mifflin, 1999.

———, ed. *The Civil War Papers of George B. McClellan: Selected Correspondence, 1860–1865*. New York: Ticknor & Fields, 1989.

———, ed. *For Country, Cause and Leader: The Civil War Journal of Charles B. Haydon*. New York: Ticknor & Fields, 1993.

———. *George B. McClellan: The Young Napoleon*. New York: Ticknor & Fields, 1988.

———. *Lincoln's Lieutenants: The High Command of the Army of the Potomac*. Boston: Houghton Mifflin Harcourt, 2017.

————. *Mr. Dunn Browne's Experiences in the Army: The Civil War Letters of Samuel W. Fiske*. New York: Fordham University Press, 1998.

————. *To the Gates of Richmond: The Peninsula Campaign*. New York: Ticknor & Fields, 1992.

Semmes, Raphael. *Service Afloat and Ashore during the Mexican War*. Cincinnati, Ohio: Wm. H. Moore., 1851.

"Sharpshooting with Berdan: William C. Kent's Eyewitness Account of the Seven Days' Battles." *Civil War Times Illustrated* 15, no. 2 (May, 1976): 4–9, 42–48.

Silver, James W., ed. *A Life for the Confederacy: As Recorded in the Pocket Diaries of Pvt. Robert A. Moore*. Wilmington, N.C.: Broadfoot, 1987.

Simon, John Y., ed. *The Papers of Ulysses S. Grant*. 30 vols. Carbondale: Southern Illinois University Press, 1967–2008.

Simpson, Brooks D., and Jean V. Berlin, eds. *Sherman's Civil War: Selected Correspondence of William T. Sherman, 1860–1865*. Chapel Hill: University of North Carolina Press, 1999.

Smalley, George W. *Anglo-American Memories*. New York: G. P. Putnam's Sons, 1911.

Society of the Army of the Potomac. *Report of the Nineteenth Annual Re-Union at Gettysburg*. New York: Macgowan and Slipper, 1888.

————. *Report of the Twentieth Annual Re-Union at Orange, N.J.* New York: Macgowan and Slipper, 1889.

————. *Report of the Twenty-First Annual Re-Union at Portland, Me.* New York: Macgowan and Slipper, 1890.

————. *Report of the Twenty-Sixth Annual Re-Union at New London, Conn.* New York: Macgowan and Slipper, 1895.

————. *Report of the Thirtieth Annual Re-Union at Portland, Me.* New York: Macgowan and Slipper, 1899.

Soini, Wayne. *Porter's Secret: Fitz John Porter's Monument Decoded*. Portsmouth, N.H.: Peter Randall, 2011.

Sparks, David S., ed. *Inside Lincoln's Army: The Diary of Marsena Rudolph Patrick, Provost Marshal General, Army of the Potomac*. New York: Thomas Yoseloff, 1964.

Speech of Hon. Martin A. Haynes, of New Hampshire, in the House of Representatives, Thursday, February 11, 1886. Washington, D.C.: No pub., 1886.

Starr, Louis M. *Bohemian Brigade: Civil War Newsmen in Action*. New York: Knopf, 1954.

Statement of the Services of the Fifth Army Corps, in 1862, in Northern Virginia, by General Fitz-John Porter. Washington, D.C.: Government Printing Office, 1879.

Stedman, Laura, and George M. Gould. *Life and Letters of Edmund Clarence Stedman*. 2 vols. New York: Moffat, Yard, 1910.

Sterling, Pound [William P. Maxson]. *Camp Fires of the Twenty-Third*. New York: Davies & Kent, 1863.

Stone, Charles P. "Washington on the Eve of War." *Century Magazine* 26, no. 3 (July, 1883): 458–66.

The Story of a Portsmouth Born Soldier. Portsmouth, N.H.: Daily Chronicle, 1905.

Stowe, Christopher S. "The Longest and Clearest Head of Any General Officer: George Gordon Meade as Corps Commander, December 1862–June 1863." In *Corps Commanders in Blue: Union Major Generals in the Civil War*, edited by Ethan S. Rafuse, 112–55. Baton Rouge: Louisiana State University Press, 2014.

[Strong, George C.] *Cadet Life at West Point*. Boston: T. O. H. P. Burnham, 1862.

Strother, David H. "Personal Recollections of the War, by a Virginian: Antietam." *Harper's New Monthly Magazine* 36, no. 213 (February, 1868): 273–91.

———. "Personal Recollections of the War, by a Virginian: Groveton." *Harper's New Monthly Magazine* 35, no. 210 (November, 1867): 704–28.

———. "Personal Recollections of the War, by a Virginian: Patterson's Campaign." *Harper's New Monthly Magazine* 33, no. 194 (July, 1866): 137–60.

Styple, William B. *Generals in Bronze: Interviewing the Commanders of the Civil War.* Kearny, N.J.: Belle Grove, 2005.

———, ed. *Letters from the Peninsula: The Civil War Letters of General Philip Kearny.* Kearny, N.J.: Belle Grove, 1988.

Sumner, Merlin E., ed. *The Diary of Cyrus B. Comstock.* Dayton, Ohio: Morningside, 1987.

Summer Social Register, July 1911. New York: Social Register Association, 1911.

Supplemental Report of the Joint Committee on the Conduct of the War. 2 vols. Washington, D.C.: Government Printing Office, 1866.

Swinton, William. *Campaigns of the Army of the Potomac.* New York: Charles B. Richardson, 1866.

Syrett, Harold C., et al., eds. *The Papers of Alexander Hamilton.* 27 vols. New York: Columbia University Press, 1961–87.

Thayer, William Roscoe. *The Life and Letters of John Hay.* 2 vols. Boston: Houghton Mifflin, 1908.

Transactions of the Kansas State Historical Society, Embracing the Fifth and Sixth Annual Reports, 1866–1888. Topeka: Kansas Publishing House, 1890.

Trout, Robert J. *With Pen and Saber: The Letters and Diaries of J. E. B. Stuart's Staff Officers.* Mechanicsburg, Pa.: Stackpole Books, 1995.

Trow's New York City Directory for the Year Ending May 1, 1886. New York: Trow's, 1885.

Trow's New York City Directory for the Year Ending May 1, 1890. New York: Trow City Directory, 1889.

Trow's New York City Directory for the Year Ending May 1, 1891. New York: Trow City Directory, 1890.

Trow's New York City Directory for the Year Ending May 1, 1892. New York: Trow City Directory, 1891.

Trow's New York City Directory for the Year Ending May 1, 1894. New York: Trow City Directory, 1893.

Trow's New York City Directory for the Year Ending May 1, 1895. New York: Trow City Directory, 1894.

Truxall, Aida Craig, ed. *Respects to All: Letters of Two Pennsylvania Boys in the War of the Rebellion.* Pittsburgh, Pa.: University of Pittsburgh Press, 1962.

U.S. Congress. *Congressional Globe.* 37th Congress.

———. *Congressional Record.* 46th–49th Congresses.

———. *Journal of the House.* 43rd Congress.

———. *Senate Executive Journal.* 37th Congress.

———. *Senate Journal.* 40th Congress.

U.S. House. *The Covode Investigation.* 36th Cong., 1st sess., 1860. H. Rept. 648.

———. *Messages of the President of the United States with the Correspondence, Therewith Communicated, between the Secretary of War and Other Officers of the Government on the Subject of the Mexican War.* 30th Cong., 1st sess., 1848. Ex. Doc. 60.

———. *The Utah Expedition.* 35th Cong., 1st sess., 1858. Ex. Doc. 71.

U.S. Senate. *Message from the President of the United States, to the Two Houses of Congress at the Commencement of the Thirtieth Congress.* 30th Cong., 1st sess., 1847. Ex Doc. 1.

———. *Message of the President of the United States, Communicating, in Compliance with a Resolution of the Senate, Information in Relation to the Massacre at Mountain Meadows, and Other Massacres in Utah Territory.* 36th Cong., 1st sess., 1860. Ex. Doc. 42.

———. *Views of the Minority.* 46th Cong., 2nd sess., 1880. S. Rep. 158.

"The Utah War: Journal of Capt. Albert Tracy, 1858–1860." *Utah Historical Quarterly* 13, nos. 1–4 (January–October, 1945): 1–128.

Walker, Albert H. "The Inefficiency of the Lower House of Congress." *Century Magazine* 32, no. 5 (September, 1886): 805–7.

War Diary and Letters of Stephen Minot Weld, 1861–1865. Boston: Massachusetts Historical Society, 1979.

War Letters, 1862–1865, of John Chipman Gray and John Codman Ropes. Cambridge: Massachusetts Historical Society, 1927.

War Letters of William Thompson Lusk. New York: privately printed, 1911.

War of the Rebellion: A Compilation of the Official Records of the Union and Confederate Armies. 128 vols. Washington, D.C.: Government Printing Office, 1880–1901.

Watson, Ronald G., ed. *From Ashby to Andersonville: The Civil War Diary and Reminiscences of George A. Hitchcock.* Campbell, Calif.: Savas, 1997.

Webb, Alexander S. *The Peninsula: McClellan's Campaign of 1862.* New York: Charles Scribner's Sons, 1905.

Webster, Noah. *An American Dictionary of the English Language.* Springfield, Mass.: George and Charles Merriam, 1864.

Wilcox, Cadmus M. *History of the Mexican War.* Washington, D.C.: Church News, 1892.

Williams, Frederick D., ed. *The Wild Life of the Army: Civil War Letters of James A. Garfield.* East Lansing: Michigan State University Press, 1964.

Wilson, Nancy D., ed. *Shouts and Whispers: The Civil War Correspondence of D. D. Priest of Mount Holly, Vermont.* Manchester Center, Vt.: Shires Press, 2011.

Wittenberg, Eric J., ed. *"We Have It Damn Hard Out Here": The Civil War Letters of Sergeant Thomas W. Smith, 6th Pennsylvania Cavalry.* Kent, Ohio: Kent State University Press, 1999.

Woodward, E[van] M. *History of the Third Pennsylvania Reserve.* Trenton, N.J.: McCrellish & Quigley, 1883.

———. *Our Campaigns, or the Marches, Bivouacs, Battles, Incidents of Camp Life and History of Our Regiment during Its Three Years Term of Service.* Philadelphia: John E. Potter, 1865.

NEWSPAPERS

Acadian Recorder (Halifax, N.S.)
Alexandria (Va.) Gazette
Alexandria Gazette and Virginia Advertiser
American Citizen (Butler, Pa.)
American Mining Gazette and Geological Magazine (New York)
Army and Navy Journal (New York)
Ashtabula (Ohio) Weekly Telegraph
Atchison (Kans.) Champion
Ballou's Pictorial (Boston)
Baltimore County Union (Towsontown, Md.)
Baltimore Exchange
Bangor (Me.) Daily Whig and Courier
Boston Daily Advertiser

Boston Daily Atlas
Boston Evening Transcript
Boston Gazette
Boston Herald
Bridgeton (N.J.) Pioneer
Buchanan County Guardian
   (Independence, Iowa)
Burlington (Iowa) Hawk-Eye
Cadiz (Ohio) Democratic Sentinel
Cairo (Ill.) Bulletin
Carbon Advocate (Lehighton, Pa.)
Chicago Tribune
Cincinnati Daily Gazette
Cincinnati Daily Star
Cleveland Morning Leader
Columbia Democrat
   (Bloomsburg, Pa.)
Custer County Republican
   (Broken Bow, Neb.)
Daily Democrat and News
   (Davenport, Iowa)
Daily Evansville (Ind.) Journal
Daily Evening Telegraph
   (Philadelphia)
Daily Exchange (Baltimore)
Daily Gate City (Keokuk, Iowa)
Daily Globe (St. Paul, Minn.)
Daily Herald (Los Angeles)
Daily Intelligencer (Wheeling, W.Va.)
Daily National Whig
   (Washington, D.C.)
Daily National Republican
   (Washington, D.C.)
Daily Ohio Statesman (Columbus)
Daily Pioneer (St. Paul, Minn.)
Daily Union (Washington, D.C.)
Dansville (N.Y.) Advertiser
Delaware State Journal and Statesman
   (Wilmington)
Democrat and Sentinel
   (Ebensburg, Pa.)
Deseret News (Salt Lake City)
Emporia (Kans.) News
Evening Argus (Rock Island, Ill.)
Evening Journal (Wilmington, Del.)
Evening News (Gold Hill, Nev. Terr.)
Evening Star (Washington, D.C.)

Fayetteville (N.C.) Weekly Observer
Frank Leslie's Illustrated Newspaper
   (New York)
Gallipolis (Ohio) Journal
Independent (Oskaloosa, Kans.)
Indianapolis Journal
Indiana State Sentinel (Indianapolis)
Iola (Kans.) Register
Kansas City (Mo.) Enterprise
Kansas Weekly Herald (Leavenworth)
Lewistown (Pa.) Gazette
Marshall County Republican
   (Plymouth, Ind.)
Montana Post (Virginia City)
Morning Journal and Courier
   (New Haven, Conn.)
Nashville Daily Union
Nation (New York)
National Intelligencer
   (Washington, D.C.)
National Republican
   (Washington, D.C.)
National Tribune
   (Washington, D.C.)
Newbern (N.C.) Weekly Progress
New-Hampshire Gazette
   (Portsmouth)
New North-West
   (Deer Lodge, Mont. Terr.)
New Orleans Picayune
Newtown (Conn.) Bee
New York Herald
New York Times
New York Tribune
Niles' National Register (Baltimore)
Norwich (Conn.) Bulletin
Ordway (Colo.) Era
Ottawa (Ill.) Free Trader
Palm Beach (Fla.) Post
Pioneer and Democrat (St. Paul,
   Minn.)
Polynesian (Honolulu)
Portage County Democrat
   (Ravenna, Ohio)
Portland (Me.) Daily Press
Portsmouth (N.H.) Daily Chronicle
Princeton (Minn.) Union

Public Ledger (Memphis, Tenn.)
Raftsman's Journal (Clearfield, Pa.)
Reading (Pa.) Times
Republic (Washington, D.C.)
Rochester (N.Y.) Daily Union
and Advertiser
Rochester (N.Y.) Democrat
Rochester (N.Y.) Evening Express
Rocky Mountain News (Denver)
Rutland (Vt.) Weekly Herald
Sacramento (Calif.)
Daily Record-Union
St. Cloud (Minn.) Democrat
St. Louis (Mo.) Republican
Salt Lake Herald (Salt Lake City, Utah Terr.)
Silver Messenger (Challis, Idaho)
Somerset (Pa.) Herald
Sonntags-Correspondent (Baltimore)
Squatter Sovereign (Atchison, Kans.)
States and Union (Portsmouth, N.H.)
Sun (New York)

Sunday Herald (Washington, D.C.)
Tiffin (Ohio) Weekly Tribune
Union (Junction City, Kans.)
Urbana (Ohio) Union
Vermont Phoenix (Brattleboro)
Warsaw (Ill.) Signal
Washington (D.C.) Chronicle
Washington (D.C.) Times
Watertown (Wis.) Republican
Weekly National Intelligencer (Washington, D.C.)
Western Reserve Chronicle (Warren, Ohio)
West-Jersey Pioneer (Bridgeton, N.J.)
Wheeling (W.Va.) Daily Register
White Cloud Kansas Chief
Wood County Reporter (Grand Rapids, Mich.)
World (New York)
Xenia (Ohio) Sentinel
Yarmouth (N.S.) Herald
Yorkville (S.C.) Enquirer

MISCELLANEOUS

Evelina Porter Doggett headstone, Indian Hill Cemetery, Middletown, Conn.
Gabler, Henry. "The Fitz John Porter Case: Politics and Military Justice." Ph.D. diss., City University of New York, 1979.
Holland, William Warren. "A Breach of Conduct: James A. Garfield and the Court-Martial of Fitz John Porter." M.A. thesis, San Jose State University, 1991.
Plaque at the entrance to Westminster Burial Ground, Baltimore.
Rebecca Porter tombstone, Green Mount Cemetery, Baltimore.
Thomas Nast St. Hill grave marker, Greenwood Memorial Park, San Diego, Calif.

INDEX

Page numbers in italics refer to illustrations or their captions.

Gunnell Gold Mining Company, 303, 304, 305

Halleck, Henry W., 188, 191, 234; Scott's choice for general-in-chief, 92; appointed general-in-chief, 183; at Harrison's Landing, 184–85; orders McClellan away from Peninsula, 185, 186, 187; FJP on, 187; FJP warns of Pope's danger, 188; obsolete intelligence from, 191; and Pope's retreat, 223–24, 225; and Stanton's effort to court-martial McClellan, 227; prepares field army, 227–28; and McClellan's restoration to command, 230; nominally appoints members of FJP courts, 231, 232, 417n63, 419n16; cowed by Stanton, 231, 272, 418n7; on Pope as the source of charges against FJP, 232; adjourns court of inquiry, 249, 256; and Stuart's October raid, 254; prods McClellan, 254, 255, 257; and removal of McClellan, 261, 262; orders military commission to investigate Pope's charges against FJP, 265–66; converts commission to a court-martial, ordering FJP into arrest, 267; interest in seeing FJP convicted, 287; delivers court record, 289

Hallowell, Benjamin, 4

Hamilton, Charles S., 109, 110, 112, 113, 117, 118, 120

Hamlin, Hannibal, 357

Hancock, Winfield S., 345, 352

Hanover Court House, battle of, 125–31

Hardee, William, 39

Harney, William A., 18–19, 42–43, 45, 47, 66, 256, 257

Harris, Ira, 114

Harrison, William Henry, 6

Hatch, John P.: on Pope, 189; in Second Bull Run campaign, 201, 210, 211, 214, 216, 218, 219, 220, 330; and appeal of FJP, 308, 309; at Stone's funeral, 357

Hay, John, 261, 262, 281–82, 354–56

Hayes, Rutherford B., 325, 327, 339–40

Haynes, Martin A., 352, 353

Heintzelman, Samuel P., 159, 273; Brady photo, 93, 142; generals' conference,

105; corps command, 105, 109; before Yorktown, 111, 112, 114, 119; on FJP, 117, 119, 180, 187; before Richmond, 122, 123, 131, 132, 167, 169–70, 172, 173, 175–76; overestimates enemy forces, 164; Harrison's Landing conferences, 179, 185; withdrawal from Peninsula, 187, 188; on darkness of August 27, 194; in Second Bull Run campaign, 198, 199, 204, 208, 214, 215, 216, 222; on Pope and McDowell, 223; McClellan seeks troops of, 234; testimony of, 280

Herndon, Dabney, 36, 375n28

Hero, 110

Heth, Henry, 56, 57

Hill, Ambrose Powell: at Beaver Dam Creek, 156, 157, 159, 160, 164; at Gaines's Mill, 166, 167, 168; at Second Bull Run, 215; in Maryland campaign, 244, 248

Hill, Daniel Harvey, 60; in Mexico, 29, 30; at Fair Oaks, 131, 132; at Beaver Dam Creek, 157, 158, 160; at Gaines's Mill, 165, 168; at Malvern Hill, 174–75; and Maryland campaign, 235

Hitchcock, Ethan Allen, 267, 269, 295, 339

Hoar, George, 327

Holbrook, Nancy, 39, 42, 266, 292, 296, 299, 307, 324, 361

Holt, Joseph, 328, 340, 364; selected to prosecute the McClellan faction, xi, 228; as secretary of war, 62, 381n15; on McDowell, 137; appointed to FJP court of inquiry, 232; and FJP military commission, 266, 267; as prosecutor in FJP court-martial, 267–90 passim, 410n55; suborning perjury, 280, 318, 319, 332–33, 425n31; summary of FJP court-martial, 289–90, 293, 294, 297–98, 299, 300, 319, 329, 330, 331, 334, 339, 347, 348, 356; reward, 294; collaboration with Stanton, 296, 311, 418n7, 418–19n16; Johnson's reply to, 299–302; and Mary Surratt execution, 311; blocks appeals by FJP for rehearing, 312–13, 314, 316, 317–18, 322, 323, 324; retirement of, 324, 333; criticized in Lord summary, 355; death, 361

Hood, John B., 33, 168, 330

Hooker, Joseph, 273, 280; reputation as drinker, 109; resents FJP, 117; pursuit of Johnston, 119; at Oak Grove, 156; on Confederate morale, 178; at Bristoe Station, 191–92, 193; Chase proposes for army command, 227; Maryland campaign, 233, 235, 236, 237, 238–39, 241, 249; rumors about, 258, 263; Fredericksburg campaign, 261; and Smalley, 298

Howard, Oliver O., 360

Humphreys, Andrew A., 147, 234, 238, 242, 246, 248, 250, 255, 256, 258

Hunt, Henry J., 147, 173, 174, 176

Hunter, David, 149; as Radicals' preference to preside over FJP court-martial, 252; groomed by Chase, 252; assigned to preside over FJP military commission, 266; Radical sympathies of, 266; in FJP court-martial, 267, 269, 270, 272, 273, 274, 281, 283, 284, 287, 419n41; restored to department command, 295; speculation on his vote, 295; violation of court-martial secrecy, 339; criticized in Lord summary, 355

Huse, Caleb, 33

Hyde, Thomas W, 177

Intrepid, 89

Jackson, Thomas J. "Stonewall": duty at West Point, 35; opposing Patterson, 72, 73, 74, 75, 80; Shenandoah campaign of, 124, 125, 131, 134, 139; Seven Days campaign, 136, 157, 158–59, 160, 164, 165, 167, 168, 204; Cedar Mountain, 187; Second Bull Run, 191–92, 193, 200, 208, 210, 227, 228, 229; eludes Pope, 196–97, attacks King, 198–99; engages Sigel, 200; at Deep Cut, 217, 218, 219, 220, 222; and Chantilly, 224, 225; Maryland campaign, 235, 239, 241, 247; Fredericksburg campaign, 260, 261; discussion of, in court-martial, 271, 275, 276, 278, 283; report of Second Bull Run misrepresented, 316, 335, 338; discussion of, in board review, 329, 334

Johnson, Andrew, 308, 310, 311, 314

Johnson, Charles, 126

Johnson, Reverdy: as attorney for FJP, 266, 270, 272, 273, 274–75, 281, 288, 292, 295; reply to Holt, 299–302; Senate remarks of, 308, 313–14; FJP consults with, 310

Johnston, Albert Sidney: assigned to Utah expedition, 43, 44; march to Fort Bridger, 45, 46, 47–48, 49; relations with FJP, 46, 50, 51–52; and Brigham Young, 51; at Camp Floyd, 54, 55, 58; and Governor Cumming, 56; last visit with FJP, 61; sides with Confederacy, 64; forced from his Kentucky line, 101

Johnston, Joseph E., 43; friendship with FJP, 41; opposes Patterson, 69, 70, 72, 73, 75, 76, 77, 78, 82; defeats McDowell, 80, 81, 82; on overestimating enemy strength, 76; at Manassas, 99, 107; retreat from Yorktown, 119–20; before Richmond, 125, 131; wounded, 132, 134

Joint Committee on the Conduct of the War, 96, 97, 99, 100, 178, 298; Radical domination of, xi, 96, 97

joint order, 199–200, 204, 205, 206, 208, 406n53; as an impediment to attack by FJP, 207; testimony about, 270, 272, 276, 282, 285, 298

Joinville, Prince de (François d'Orléans), 88, 94

Jones, John M., 37

Kane, Thomas L., 52, 53

Kearny, Philip, 298, 354, 399n4; on the Peninsula, 131, 156; on FJP, 180, 187, 399n4; Second Bull Run campaign, 176–77, 191

Keim, William H., 70, 76

Kelly, James E., 360, 361–62

Kennedy, Joseph C. G., 147; letter to McClellan, 133; letter to FJP, 183, 190, 192, 224, 226, 251, 268, 274, 400n23, 409n45; supportive of FJP, 302

Kerrigan, James E, 90–91, 126

Key, John, 251

Keyes, Erasmus D., 120, 142, 159; at West Point, 12; corps command, 105, 109; before Yorktown, 113; defends McClellan, 114; before Richmond, 122,

visit, 184–85; on optimism of FJP, 185, 343; ordered to evacuate Peninsula, 185–86, 187; appeals decision, 186, 187; begins withdrawal, 187–88; troops of, reach Pope, 191; correspondence about Pope with FJP, 223, 225–26; greets returning army, 226–27; cabinet cabal against, 227, 231; resumes army command, 230; pursues Lee, 233–34, 246, 247, 248, 249, 260, 261; and South Mountain, 235; deprives Burnside and Sumner of wing command, 236; Antietam, 237–38, 239, 240, 242; declines to reinforce Burnside, 243, 244–45, 253; criticized for inactivity, 250–51, 254, 255, 258; and Emancipation Proclamation, 259; relieved of command, 261–63; discontent over removal of, 263–64, 294; report of, 297; criticized by Joint Committee, 298; seeks employment for FJP, 299, 302; presidential candidate, 303–4, 322; Burnside on, 344; at Democratic Party dinner, 345; FJP protects image of, 351, 358; death, 351, 352; Nicolay and Hay try to discredit, 354

McClellan, Mary Ellen (Marcy), 96, 97, 131, 160, 185, 254, 361

McClure, Alexander K., 66

McCrary, George, 327

McDowell, Irvin, xi, 84, *142*, 290, 358, 378n3, 378n19, 383n55; as West Point adjutant, 9; as Scott's adjutant general, 45, 48, 51, 65, 378n3, 378n19; army command, 73, 76, 77, 78, 80; and First Bull Run, 81, 106–7, 384n75; balloon observation, 89; Brady photo, 93; described, 94; at army review, 95; confers with Lincoln, 99–100, 388n56; generals' conference, 105; corps command, 105; as teetotaler, 109; troops of, withheld from McClellan, 113–14, 115, 122–23, 124, 132–33, 133–34, 136, 139–40, 258; argues for joining McClellan, 125, 133–34; War Department opinions on competence of, 137; assigned to Pope, 139, 140; and Sigel, 196, 200; and Longstreet's whereabouts, 197, 204–5; loses way, 197–98, 199; headgear of, 200, 342; confers with FJP, 200, 201, 204–5;

stops attack by FJP, 204, 329; leaves FJP uncertain of command situation, 205, 212, 284; ignores dispatches from FJP, 207, 208; meeting with Locke, 206, 281, 285–87, 299, 309, 330, 402n51, 420n48; keeps troops idle, 207, 208, 211–12, 336; Weld and, 209, 210, 211, 212; and "pursuit" of Jackson, 214, 215, 216, 217–18; and Longstreet's assault, 220, 221–22; lack of troops' confidence in, 223, 229; retreat to Washington, 226; friendship with Chase, 228–29, 231; friendship with Cadwalader, 232; prejudices Garfield against FJP, 252, 266; discussed at FJP court-martial, 270, 272, 273, 276, 277, 284, 288; testimony of, 280–83, 285, 287, 289, 293; court of inquiry, 280, 286, 287, 288, 292, 295, 348; responsibility for defeat, 288, 326, 337, 338; and Pope's "Brief Statement," 316, 334–35; "newly discovered" dispatches of, 334; testimony before review board, 335–37; Garfield's admiration for, 340; Hay and Nicolay favor, 354–55; death, 361

McKeever, Chauncey, 308, 311

McKenzie, David, 57

McKinley, William, 360

McLaws, Lafayette, 234–35, 239

McLean, Nathaniel C., 220, 221

McQuade, James, 128

Meade, George G., 86, 181, 189, 223, 249, 294

Meagher, Thomas F., 169, 175

Meigs, Montgomery C., 84, 184, 187, 255, 257

Mexico City, battle of, 26–29

Millens, George, 264

Milroy, Robert, 221–22, 408n32

Molino del Rey, battle of, 25–26, 32

Monitor, 110

Monteith, George, 195, 196, 213, 223

Morell, George W., 106, 107, 109, 118, 137, 147, 160, 186, 199, 216; brigade command, 86; testimony before Joint Committee, 98; dinner parties in camp of, 102; advance on Yorktown, 111, 113; division command, 120; at Hanover Court House, 125, 126, 127, 128; at Gaines's

Martindale, 181, 400n15; and Marcy, 182; accused of writing Pope's objectionable address, 182; efforts to court-martial McClellan, 225, 227, 231; determination to see FJP convicted, 228, 266; attempts to prejudice court members, 267, 269; and false report of charges against FJP, 252, 253; and Martindale court, 255, 257; and removal of McClellan and FJP from command, 262, 263, 264; and hostile composition of court of inquiry and court-martial, 266, 267, 268, 418n7; as crony of Holt, 271–72, 293, 296, 311, 418–19n16; interferes with court-martial proceedings, 287, 293; rewards court members, 294–96; orders troops to monitor elections, 299, 304; and Tucker, 311; as the excuse for Johnson's impeachment, 311, 314; and Townsend, 313; resigns, 328

Star of the West, 61, 64

Stephan, Carl, 90

St. Hill, Thomas, 359, 364

Stone, Charles P.: at West Point, 10, 11, 12, 13; promotion of, 16, 83, 84; in Mexico, 27; in Patterson's Shenandoah campaign, 75, 76, 383n55; and Ball's Bluff, 92; arrest and imprisonment of, 100–101, 109, 313, 388n61; article by, 351; funeral of, 357

Stoneman, George, 159, 160, 170

Strong, George Templeton, 34, 39, 297

Strother, David Hunter: and Patterson's campaign, 74, 75, 383n55; at Bristoe Station, 195, 199, 283; at Second Bull Run, 215, 221, 222–23; bias against FJP, 403n3

Stuart, James Ewell Brown, 192; opposes Patterson, 72, 75, 78; June raid, 134–36; joins Jackson, 159; bombards McClellan's camp, 179; Catlett Station raid, 189; Manassas raid, 191; at Second Bull Run, 202, 204, 207, 209, 405n40, 405n51; October raid, 254–55, 258; report of Second Bull Run, 316

Sturgis, Samuel D., 208, 213, 405n45

Sumner, Charles, 313

Sumner, Edwin V., 64, 113; generals' conference, 105; corps command, 105;

advance on Richmond, 122, 123; at Fair Oaks, 132; and Gaines's Mill, 167, 168, 169; council of war, 169; retreat to James, 170; at Glendale, 171; McClellan snubs, 172, 176; at Malvern Hill, 173, 174, 175; Harrison's Landing conferences, 179, 185; promotion, 180; Chase proposes for army command, 227; Antietam campaign, 233, 236, 237, 239, 240, 241–42, 246, 249

Swett, Leonard, 349–50, 432n15

Swinton, William, 306–7, 308, 309, 310

Sykes, George, 239; joins FJP, 120; at Hanover Court House, 129; and Stuart's June raid, 134; at Mechanicsville, 137; at Gaines's Mill, 164, 165–66, 167, 168, 169; retreat to James, 170, 171; at Malvern Hill, 173, 174; march to join Pope, 190, 193, 194, 195, 196; at Second Bull Run, 199, 200, 201, 202, 213, 217, 218, 222, 407n3; Maryland campaign, 234, 235, 237, 238, 242, 243–44, 246, 248; family of, 253, 296; Fredericksburg campaign, 258, 260; farewell review for FJP, 264

Talbot, Theodore, 60

Taylor, Zachary, 15, 16–18

Terry, Alfred H., 327, 328, 337, 340, 347, 349

Texas, 14, 62–63

Thomas, George H.: on West Point faculty, 36, 37, 38; Schofield court-martial, 36, 328; in 2nd Cavalry, 39; effort to pacify Baltimore, 66, 67; in Patterson's Shenandoah campaign, 74, 76, 79

Tilden, Samuel, 325

Tillinghast, Joseph, 6

Townsend, Edward D., 68, 70, 73, 76, 77, 84, 313, 316, 417n61

Townsend, Peter, 35

Tracy, Albert, 379n34, 379n37

Trent, Peterfield, 135, 138

Tucker, John, 188, 267, 310, 311, 417n61

Twiggs, David, xiv; in Mexico, 17, 18, 20, 21, 22, 24, 26, 30, 31; in Texas, 62–63

Tyler, Robert O., 124

U.S. Coast Survey, 32

Utah War, xiv, 42–54

1- JLC father

328- June 25, 1878 - trial begins
   West Point

334- News coverage of trial divided along
   partisan lines

338- Report of April 2, 1879
339- misinformation to deceive
   obstinate resistance from old
   Republican enemies denied him
   full restoration for 6 more years

340- a bill for restoration entered into Senate
   in December, 1879 but - 6 year

348- Grant against Porter, but changes mind
352-53- finally reinstated in June, 1886
356- John Logan - the loudest
   of opponents, even after reinstatement

361- 1901 death - JLC pallbearer
362- JLC sent regrets at unveiling of statue
   in Portsmouth